Political Science:
The State of the Discipline

Edited by Ada W. Finifter

1983

The American Political Science Association
1527 New Hampshire Avenue, N.W.
Washington, D.C. 20036

Library of Congress Cataloging in Publication Data

Main entry under title:

Political science.

   Includes bibliographies and index.
   1. Political science—Methodology—Addresses, essays, lectures. I. Finifter, Ada W., 1938-   . II. American Political Science Association.
JA73.P658 1983   320'.01'8   83-72628

ISBN 0-915654-57-1
ISBN 0-915654-58-X (pbk.)

Political Science:
The State of the Discipline

Edited by Ada W. Finifter

TABLE OF CONTENTS

Preface

When I was appointed Program Chairperson of the 1982 Annual Meeting of the American Political Science Association by APSA President-Elect Seymour Martin Lipset, I chose as a guiding theme for the meetings, "the state of the discipline." Nineteen eighty-two seemed a good year for some stock-taking. The heady days of the growth of the social sciences in the 1960s were only a faint memory for many of the current members of the profession. Some of the attempts at applying social science theory to public policy problems had produced unclear, and occasionally questionable, results. The social sciences were under great pressure to prove their worth in the more budget-conscious 1970s, and that pressure had increased under the current administration in Washington. It seemed a good time to review where we were and where we might be going. Nevertheless, despite my own conviction that a review of the intellectual developments in the field over the past twenty to twenty-five years was due, I had little inkling that many scholars were feeling a similar need.

The then newly appointed Executive Director of the American Political Science Association, Thomas E. Mann, responded enthusiastically to my choice of a theme and suggested that we capitalize on the attention the subject would be receiving at the convention by collecting a series of articles on the "state of the discipline" in an APSA publication. This idea was supported by the APSA Council, and I agreed to organize and guide the effort. If the volume is successful, a continuing series of this type may be authorized by the Council.

The overall goal for this volume is to begin to fill the continuing need for a frequently published overview of political science research. It is intended to be used in teaching and for research purposes, as well as by foundation and government officials who need regularly updated information on current research in the discipline. I hope that the book will be useful in introducing graduate students to the problems about which political scientists are currently concerned, and that it will help political scientists learn more about each other's work. The volume should also be useful to foundation and government officials, as they consider research opportunities in the discipline, and to people working in government and other applied fields, who wonder what political scientists can contribute to their daily concerns.

Since this book grew out of the theme of the 1982 Annual Meeting, it was designed in conjunction with the program for that convention. In each section of the program, a paper was commissioned to review the state of research and future directions of that subfield. Since most of the subfields include a variety of approaches to their subject matter, and cover enormous bodies of literature, the authors were given latitude to define their scope of coverage in a way that they felt was most meaningful to their own research interests. In some cases, an entire subfield (as defined by the program section title) is covered; in others, the author has defined a specific part of the subfield or some significant intellectual problem for more comprehensive coverage. Therefore, not every area of political science is included in this first review. If the series is continued over a period of years, any important omissions of particular subfields or within particular areas will certainly be addressed.

The authors were asked to define the area being reviewed; to analyze conceptual frameworks employed by scholars working in the area, including classical and older approaches if they were relevant for contrast with newer frameworks; to treat the cumulation of knowledge in the field by discussing the major research findings; to consider how important findings have been changed or modified as knowledge has developed; and to suggest the issues that need to be addressed in the future.

Each of the papers was presented at a "theme" panel at the 1982 Annual Meeting. A large number of colleagues throughout the discipline contributed by acting as discussants on these panels and commenting on the original versions of the papers. Most of the discussants also provided very helpful written comments on the papers. Following the meetings, the papers were reviewed by anonymous peer reviewers. Other colleagues provided informal consultation and advice. All of the papers benefited from this generous peer review.

The authors of the articles appearing in this volume are, of course, the primary sources of any insight and wisdom contained in it. Many of them also served as Section Chairs for the 1982 Annual Meeting of the APSA. In other cases, the Section Chairs contributed to the volume by suggesting colleagues especially well suited to prepare the "state of the discipline" papers, by establishing panels that focused on important issues in the discipline, and by their general encouragement and support.

The members of my own department at Michigan State University proved to be an uncommonly congenial and helpful group. David W. Rohde, the Chairman, was generous in his cooperation and support for this project. Marty Lipset, with his broad view of the development of the social sciences, supported the project from its inception and worked with me in its initial stages. Tom Mann deserves special recognition for his knowledge of the profession and his ever helpful advice and enthusiastic support. Members of the Association are forewarned should they receive a call from him: he's a man who can get almost anyone to say "Yes" to almost anything.

I am also very grateful to the following colleagues and scholars for their thoughtful and valuable contributions and would like to thank each of them for their assistance:

Joel D. Aberbach, University of Michigan
Paul R. Abramson, Michigan State University
John H. Aldrich, University of Minnesota
Eugene J. Alpert, Texas Christian University
Charles W. Anderson, University of Wisconsin, Madison
Thomas J. Anton, University of Michigan
W. Lance Bennett, University of Washington
Richard A. Brody, Stanford University
Bruce Bueno de Mesquita, University of Rochester
Naomi Caiden, California State College, San Bernadino
James A. Caporaso, University of Denver
Jonathan D. Casper, University of Illinois
Aage Clausen, Ohio State University

Richard Rosecrance, Cornell University
Virginia Sapiro, University of Wisconsin, Madison
Allen Schick, University of Maryland
Philip Schrodt, Northwestern University
Kenneth A. Shepsle, Washington University
John W. Sloan, University of Houston
Frank J. Sorauf, University of Minnesota
Harold J. Spaeth, Michigan State University
James Stimson, Florida State University
John L. Sullivan, University of Minnesota
Susette M. Talarico, University of Georgia
Norman C. Thomas, University of Cincinnati
Kathleen Toth, University of Texas, San Antonio
Sidney Verba, Harvard University
Jerry Weinberger, Michigan State University
Robert Weissberg, University of Illinois, Urbana
Aaron Wildavsky, University of California, Berkeley
Raymond E. Wolfinger, University of California, Berkeley
Deil S. Wright, University of North Carolina, Chapel Hill
Gerald C. Wright, Jr., Indiana University
Dina Zinnes, University of Illinois

The members of the profession indicated their interest in an intellectual review of the discipline by attending the 1982 "state of the discipline" theme panels in unusually large numbers. Many of the comments I received about the Denver convention related to the special attraction and the utility of having this kind of review take place in a forum that provided an opportunity for discussion and feedback from a diverse representation of political scientists. I hope that the publication of these papers will contribute to the continuation of this dynamic process.

Ada W. Finifter
East Lansing, Michigan
June 19, 1983

POLITICAL SCIENCE:
THE DISCIPLINE AND ITS
SCOPE AND THEORY

1
Political Theory:
The Evolution of a Sub-Field

John G. Gunnell

It is necessary to make a distinction between Political Theory as a sub-field of the discipline of political science (*PT*) and political theory as a more general interdisciplinary body of literature, activity, and intellectual community (*pt*). It is also necessary to distinguish between those aspects of *PT* that are closely tied to *pt* and those that are more directly related to various research programs in political science. This is not to suggest that there are not important relationships and points of overlap and intersection both between *PT* and *pt* and between the elements within *PT*, but locating the boundaries is important for an analysis of political theory as a whole and for an understanding of the controversies that have animated it. For example, according to some political scientists, one of the problems has been to make Theory relevant to the practice of the discipline of political science rather than an outpost of history, ethics, and other fields that contribute to the constitution of *pt*. On the other hand, some political theorists, while professionally and institutionally situated within political science, identify themselves intellectually much more closely with *pt*.

While there are recent works that attempt to characterize and survey the present condition of political theory and speculate about what it might or should be (e.g., Nelson, Ed., 1983), less detailed attention has been devoted to the "odyssey" of political theory in American political science (Toth, 1982). Most attempts at the latter have been quite general characterizations in the service of some critique or apology. My basic approach will be archaeological. I hesitate to say historical, since, in many respects, this is more an excavation, or the presentation of the results of such an endeavor, than what many might consider conventional history. I began at the surface and dug downward, even though I am presenting my report in standard chronological order. However much my personal concerns may be reflected in the course of sifting through this dense material, I am more concerned with uncovering previous sites of political theory than with evaluating their contents and achievements.

One characteristic of the subject matter is that the termini are poorly defined. Rather than reaching the "beginning" of Political Theory as a sub-field, I stopped when the traces seemed too amorphous to warrant further dredging. On the other end, the deposits build up so rapidly that any definite

3

conclusion is almost immediately obsolescent; I can do little more than in-dicate what an initial survey of the surface yielded and what prompted my particular angle of entry.

The state of both *PT* and *pt* in the 1980s is one of *dispersion*, and I will risk the claim that this will remain its dominant characteristic for some time. To some extent this is the result of developments within political science as a whole, but it is also a reflection and consequence of trends within the sub-field and its relationship to *pt*. *PT* has broken up and scattered in different directions and adopted various mediums of expression, but the spectrum that can be discerned is not the diffraction of any basic substantive issue or set of concerns. Dispersion is less a symptom than the very condition of the field. This condition grew out of the events of the 1960s, became clearly manifest in the 1970s, and defined the state of the field by the beginning of the 1980s.

Some might suggest that this diffusion is basically the result of increased specialization in political science as a whole as well as greater interdisciplinary involvement. Others would argue that what is happening is, in the still popular Kuhnian terminology, a paradigm breakdown or transformation. Each of these claims may be correct in some respects, or at least convey something about certain aspects of the situation, but rather than pursuing a particular causal explanation, I will attempt to reconstruct the basic contours of the evolution of the sub-field of Political Theory. But, first, it is appro-priate to be a bit more specific about the character of this putative dispersion.

In recent years, there has been a great deal of enthusiasm about the future of political theory. This is in sharp contrast to some of the attitudes that characterized the 1950s and 1960s when, in some quarters, political theory, at least in the form of political philosophy, was "thought to be on the verge of extinction" (Richter, 1980, p. 6). For a long time thereafter, it was considered to be an endangered species. While political theory, conceived as part of the scientific study of politics, was vigorously propagated, other modes of theory seemed to be on the decline. It now seems that, even among many of its former advocates and supporters, the commitment to "scientific" theory is somewhat muted, and many would argue that there is now, and should con-tinue to be, greater complementarity between empirical and normative theory. For example, the idea of political science as the study of public policy, which has provided a self-image for the discipline in recent years, might imply a closer relationship between *PT* and *pt* or between political science and political philosophy. But it has also been claimed that "the great vitality in the field of political theory during the last fifteen or twenty years" is the result of a divergence between *PT* and *pt* and the fact that much of political theory has "turned away from" and become "indifferent to much of academic political science." Both "may prosper, but not interdependently" (Kateb, 1977, pp. 135, 136).

It will be necessary to consider such positions more carefully, but, for the moment, it is enough to note that there is a continuing ambivalence about the relationship between political theory and political science that has persisted since the beginning of the Post-World War II period. There are sentiments for secession and exile as well as for unification and integration. Today, it is clear that at least in *pt*, and much of the literature of *PT* that is most closely allied with it, there is a sense of movement whose source is in some respects quite easy to identify but whose significance and direction are more nebulous.

There is a widespread belief that during the 1970s there was an "upswell of political and social theorizing" and that "political philosophy" now "obviously flourishes, all over the English-speaking world and outside it too" (Laslett & Fishkin, Eds., 1979, pp. 2, 5). This alleged upturn is usually linked with the publication of John Rawls's *A Theory of Justice* (1971) and related works of a similar genre such as Robert Nozick's *Anarchy, State and Utopia* (1974); the popularity of so-called Critical Theory and the work of individuals such as Jurgen Habermas; and the variety of critiques, summaries, and commentaries that grew up around this material and the pursuit of similar themes. Various explanations were advanced to account for this "upsurge in creative political theory" (Freeman & Robertson, 1980, p. 11) such as the release of moral philosophy from the grip of positivism and the shock of political events in the late 1960s, but it was generally acknowledged that political theory was born again. This sense of having overcome the past was quite evident by the end of the 1970s, but the present constitution and future form of *pt* is far from evident. The situation in *PT* is no clearer. Since most of the developments in *pt* are reflected there, its literature is equally diverse.

Dispersion does not mean that the universe of political theory cannot be charted, but it is difficult to discern some overall form. Collections purporting to represent the "frontiers" of political theory leave one in doubt both about the territory that these margins circumscribe and the nature of the terrain that is being penetrated. It is suggested that there is a "return to political theory in the grand manner" but that it is now "pluralist" to an unprecedented degree and can only be characterized by looking at "what political theorists do" (Freeman & Robertson, 1980, pp. 11, 1). An attempt by the journal *Political Theory* to project the "Prospects and Topics" of "political theory in the 1980s," seemed to reach the same conclusion, or nonconclusion. The editor decided simply to "invite a number of thoughtful senior colleagues . . . to get on with what they were thinking about," and claimed that the diverse contributions were "representative of both the scope of the field and the pushing forward of its concerns and frontiers" (Barber, 1980, p. 291).

THE EARLY YEARS: BEFORE 1899

The idea of political theory as a distinct kind of activity, vocation, and product is of relatively recent origin. The concept of political theory in its contemporary sense or senses has not only been largely a creation of the subfield of Political Theory in political science but a convention that can be attributed to the debates about the character and status of political theory that began in the 1940s and 1950s. Notions of theory that emerged at that time were read backward into the past and projected into the future. Even after the establishment of the American Political Science Association and the constitution of Political Theory as an official sub-field, political theory and/or political philosophy was basically a category that referred to certain types of claims and kinds of literature, various elements or functions in politics, and some reflections on the study of politics.

Why, exactly, the discipline of political science was officially born in 1903 with a sub-field called Political Theory and, precisely, how it came to receive this name is difficult to say. In part, it probably reflected the traditional theory/practice distinction in nineteenth century philosophy and the idea of social science as being concerned with the theory of the state. But to some extent, political science at the time of the creation of the APSA was less a distinct discipline than a holding company for a variety of endeavors that were in various ways related, but no longer easily resided in other disciplines. Political Theory was in part such a field.

Up through the late 1700s, the study of ethics and moral philosophy had included politics and political philosophy. When Francis Lieber, "the beginner in the United States of the systematic study of politics" (Haddow, 1939, p. 139), was appointed in 1857 as Professor of History and Political Economy at Columbia, he indicated his intention to teach and lecture on Political Philosophy which was concerned with the theory of the state and with political ethics. After political science became a distinct discipline in many universities after the Civil War, political theory began to find an even more definite place, and by the early 1890s, a "History of Political Theories" course appeared at Harvard (Haddow, 1939, p. 175). Political scientists, looking for their ancestors, would find them in the classics of moral philosophy that were concerned with politics, and thus began the idea that there was a tradition of political thought to which political scientists would understand themselves to belong.

In 1876, John Burgess succeeded Lieber at Columbia where he established the graduate school of political science which opened in 1880 and by 1891 consisted of three departments including the department of History and Political Philosophy. Courses dealing with the history of political theory and the philosophy of the state appeared here and at other major universities. The influence of Bluntschli's *Theory of the State* was evident as well as Yale's Theodore D. Woolsey's widely read text on *Political Science, or, the State Theoretically and Practically Considered* (1878). W. W. Willoughby, one of the most important figures in the early discipline of political science, particularly in Political Theory, was offering courses in both areas, first at Stanford in 1894 and then at Johns Hopkins in 1895; he published *An Examination of the Nature of the State; A Study in Political Philosophy* in 1896. With the establishment of the APSA, the general context for the development of *PT* took determinate form.

THE BEGINNINGS OF A DISCIPLINE: 1900-1919

During the early years of the discipline, political theory was still viewed more as a subject matter than a mode of analysis. Munroe Smith had stated in 1886, in the first issue of *Political Science Quarterly*, that the "domain of political science" was the historical and comparative study of the state, and this included what people had thought about it. To write the history of political theory was at once to write about the history of democratic institutions and about the development of political science which from the beginning was already traced through the canon of classic texts from the Greeks to modern political science. The influence of the evolutionary theories of Comte and Spencer as well as the Hegelian analysis of the state, with its subjective and objective division, was strong and provided the basic intellectual context in which both political science and the study of the history of political theories emerged.

The APSA was created for the purpose of "advancing the scientific study of politics in the United States," and six sub-fields, including Political Theory, were established with corresponding committees. The first Political Theory committee consisted of Willoughby, Charles Merriam, and William Dunning. In his presidential address to the APSA in 1904, Frank Goodnow said that political science was the study of the state and the "realization of the State will," and he viewed political theory as a special discipline concerned with the authorities that express that will. Furthermore, he suggested, "however contemptuous may be one's belief in the practical value of the study of political theory, it is none the less true that every governmental system is based on some more or less well-defined political theory" (1905, pp. 37-38). Political theory was understood in one way or another to be concerned with *ideas* in and about politics. Willoughby's 1904 article on the newly formed APSA claimed that the field consisted of three basic parts, and the first was the "province of political theory and philosophy" which aimed at "the analysis and exact definition of the concepts employed in political thinking" and a consideration of the "nature of the state" (p. 118). Most of the material published in Political Theory through 1920 was historical in the sense of Dunning's paradigmatic treatises on the "history of political theories" (1902, 1905, 1920). Although there was some precedent and parallel in European literature, the history of political theory was a distinctly American genre (Gunnell, 1979).

For Dunning, the study of political theory was the study of transformations in political consciousness and a way of scientifically grasping the dynamic character of politics that resulted from the interaction of institutions and ideas. Not only were science and history understood as integrally related, but the idea of political science as a practical science was a regulative assumption. This was true both in the older sense of providing political or citizen education and in the somewhat newer sense of a concern with participating in social reform and modes of social control that characterized most of the social sciences of this period. Between 1900-1920, the progressivist ideology consistently found expression in social science which was viewed by many as the link between knowledge and politics. Henry Jones Ford (1906) argued that political science must be universal in its scope, put on "an objective basis," and "experience the reconstruction which the general body of science has undergone at the hands of inductive philosophy," but the purpose was to "bring political science to a position of authority as regards practical politics" (pp. 203, 206).

After 1910, political theory as a specific subject was increasingly neglected as political scientists focused on practical issues in domestic and international politics, but the views of the formative period persisted. R. G.

Gettell, who wrote one of the most popular political science texts (1910) and one of the major works in the history of political theory (1924), offered an extended analysis of the nature and scope of political theory which reflected the dominant view in the discipline. Political theory in general was understood as reflection on the institutional state or the "objective" phase of the state which grew out of the need to cope with the environment. Thus political theory was not ultimately true but "relative in nature" and both cause and effect in that it simultaneously influenced and mirrored politics (1914, pp. 48, 50). At the same time, he noted that a fundamental and revolutionary change was taking place in political theory whereby it was being transformed from a deductive, normative, and idealist enterprise to an inductive and realistic one concerned with observation, classification, description, and generalization. Gettell distinguished three distinct but related elements of political theory: historical, analytical or descriptive, and applied (pp. 52, 54).

THE FIRST REVOLUTION IN POLITICAL THEORY: 1920-1929

In 1921, Merriam, in his presidential address to the APSA, announced that while he had intended to survey the field over the past four decades, he had decided, instead, to speak to the more pressing problem of the "reconstruction of the methods of political study" (p. 174). This would require that the "theory of politics" be transformed so as to reflect the substantive modern doctrine that "political ideas and systems . . . are the by-products of environment" and the methodological advances that had been made possible by "statistical observation" and the more accurate measurement of "facts and forces" (p. 174). Merriam's particular concern was with developing a theoretical "medium" (p. 175) for selecting and classifying the mass of facts that social science was accumulating and with releasing political theory from ideology or the "service of class and race and group" (p. 178). For Merriam, the basic aim was not pure science but rather the "cross fertilization of politics with science" and the more effective control and organization of practical matters in domestic and international politics. The goal of political science was to "interpret and explain and measurably control . . . the forces of human nature" (p. 183). But Merriam also believed that before the "processes of social and political control" could be grasped, it was necessary to have a "better organization of our political research." It would be impossible to contribute to "political prudence" if there were "anarchy in social science, or chaos in the theory of political order" (pp. 184-185).

Merriam's claims and concerns did not represent the disciplinary consensus. He was the major figure of that period in political science, and he influenced both his contemporaries and later phases of the discipline. But his ideas did not reflect the dominant research, publications, and curriculum of his own time. On the other hand, it is easy to mistake the degree to which Merriam's notions of theory and science diverged from his predecessors and contemporaries. What is striking, if compared with the later tension between the ideas of science and history, is that although Merriam attacked the historical-comparative approach in political science, this did not entail a confrontation with the history of political theory as conducted by individuals such as Dunning, Gettell, and C. H. McIllwain. All of these men agreed with regard to their assumptions about the relativity of ideas and institutions, the evolution of political thought toward science and democracy, and the practical mission of political science.

The APSA Committee on Political Research in 1923, under Merriam's leadership, identified social methodology as the "recent history of political thinking" (p. 275), and Merriam stressed the need in political inquiry to draw upon the methods of economics, statistics, history, anthropology, geography, and psychology as a basis for the "observation and description of actual processes of government" and for eschewing the older "a priori speculation" and the juristic and historical/comparative approaches (pp. 281-283). Here Merriam first offered his famous historical typology of the development of political inquiry that would appear in *New Aspects of Politics:* a priori deductive up to 1850; historical and comparative between 1850-1900; a tendency toward observation, survey, and measurement from 1900 to the present; and the future pointed in the direction of the "psychological treatment of politics" (a characteristic of the work of Graham Wallas and Walter Lippmann) (p. 286). Like later attempts to transform the discipline and distinguish what was conceived as innovation from the burden of the past, the image of the past was a somewhat contrived one, but the rhetorical point was clear.

In the "Report of the National Conference on the Science of Politics" in 1924 (previous conferences had been held in 1922 and 1923), it was maintained that "the great need of the hour is the development of a scientific technique and methodology for political science" (p. 119). But this was still understood as serving the practical concern of providing a scientific guide to legislation and administration which government had neither the time nor capacity to develop. What was required was intellectual authority if political science was to play a role and, therefore, a "fact-finding technique that will produce an adequate basis for sound generalization" and put "political research upon a scientific, objective basis" (pp. 120-121). Merriam argued that "the perfection of social science is indispensable to the very preservation of this same civilization" that created modern science.

THEORETICAL CONTINUITY: 1930-1939

Substantively, as well as methodologically, the 1930s were years of affirmation: affirmation of science, democracy, and their complementarity. Political theory was also still largely a functional or analytical category, and as a classification of literature, it referred to subjective matters, both cognitive and ideological. This tendency gained support, and maybe some new meaning, with the psychological concerns of Merriam and others in the 1920s, but long before and after, dissertations in Political Theory in the *APSR* were listed under "Political Theory and Psychology."

It was not until 1930 that Political Theory was offered as a distinct section in the annual meetings of the APSA, yet by the end of the 1930s, political theory as a category disappeared from the annual program as increasing pressures of domestic and international affairs drew attention away from issues about the scope and method in political science. Disciplinary concern in political theory was concentrated in two areas.

It was during the 1930s that the history of political theory fully crystallized as a genre of literature, and this literature largely embodied attempts to demonstrate and celebrate the development of liberalism and its divergence from fascism and communism. Many textbooks with similar versions of this history were published during the 1930s; the genre culminated in George Sabine's *A History of Political Theory* (1937) which, as David Easton (1953) has noted, "exercised deeper influence over the study of political theory in the United States . . . than any other single work" (p. 249). Writers of this period were untroubled about a simultaneous commitment to the study of the history of political theory and to the development of a scientific study of politics. For proponents of scientism, such as George Catlin (1939), the two endeavors were mutually confirming.

With respect to the trends initiated by Merriam, no one in the 1930s contributed more to their perpetuation than Harold Lasswell. The commitment to the idea of a science that could play a role in the reformation of society was not only sustained but in some respects radicalized. Lasswell (1939, 1941) put less emphasis on education than on the development of theories and testable hypotheses that would expose the reality behind politics and political ideology—largely a psychological reality—and provide the basis of a therapeutic policy science. Some of the work of Lasswell in the 1930s would recede as a matter of disciplinary concern, but his behavioral realism, as well as his emphasis on science and policy, would make a lasting impression on the aspirations of political science as a science.

Sabine (1939) suggested that political theories characteristically consisted of three logically distinct kinds of propositions: factual, causal, and valuational. He stressed the need to distinguish these aspects in both understanding the past and analyzing contemporary claims. The question of the status, relationship between, and priority of these aspects would occupy both *PT* and the discipline as a whole for some time, but even by the end of the 1930s, many political scientists were unhappy with what the discipline had achieved with regard to fulfilling the vision of science.

Some saw the problem as the failure of science, and others saw it as a failure to be adequately scientific. For the latter, who would eventually dominate the discussion, the problem seemed increasingly to be one centered around the issue of theory. What they perceived as a theoretical core in other disciplines seemed to be missing in political science. By the 1950s, many individuals would again be stressing that what was required in political science was a theoretical revolution, but the seeds of that second revolution were sowed in this much earlier period.

THE PRELUDE TO BEHAVIORALISM: 1940-1949

The claims about theory and science that are so familiar from the 1950s did not appear on the scene as suddenly as we are often led to assume. Benjamin Lippincott (1940) argued that, for the most part, political scientists still equated empiricism with fact collection and that this had been the case since the turn of the century. Political scientists still looked upon "theories or ideas about the facts [as] not only unnecessary but positively dangerous" (p. 130). Lippincott pointed out, however, that theories are always implicitly involved in the selection of facts and, consequently, the biases of the discipline are often concealed. But if theory was required, it was to be theory of a particular sort. William Foote Whyte (1943) represented an increasingly popular point of view when he claimed that political scientists should "leave ethics to the philosophers and concern themselves primarily with the description and analysis of political behavior" (p. 692).

In the 1940s there was manifested a new and focused concern with theory, but there was, from the start, a somewhat different emphasis on just what it was and how it should be related to political science. The pressures associated with the early years of the war had curtailed collegial discussion of political science and political theory, but by 1943 the Political Theory panel of the APSA Research Committee attempted to pick up and sort out the issues. Although no uniquely new idea of theory emerged from these discussions, there was an emerging sense of a "deep cleavage" on an "ultimate issue" which even the participants had difficulty articulating (Wilson, 1944, p. 726). This cleavage was variously understood in terms of "philosophical" reflection on the study of politics as opposed to "logical analysis"; the "theological approach" versus the "empirical" or increasingly popular " 'positivistic,' scientific, or *liberal* technique of social study"; the idea of a value-free science seeking laws of political behavior as opposed to a more evaluative set of concerns; and the conflict between the "philosophy of history" and an emphasis on "ends-means relationship" (Wilson, 1944, p. 727, emphasis added).

Although the behavioralist attack on the history of political theory in the 1950s is often characterized as an "offensive," there is reason to suggest that it was a preemptive strike or a conservative reaction in defense of the traditional "liberal technique of social study" that had dominated the discipline long before the war. With the influence of emigre scholars such as Eric Voegelin and Leo Strauss, new and somewhat "foreign" issues dealing with natural law, relativism, and positivism were being introduced. There is no doubt that at this time Political Theory did equal, in large measure, the history of political theory, but the tradition of which Sabine was a part was not hostile to the equally traditional commitment to science. Something new was happening in Political Theory which was not easily defined. One can point to very little in the way of concrete literature, but individuals such as Voegelin were becoming active in the profession. Marcuse's work would not become a strong influence in political theory until the late 1960s and early 1970s, but *Reason and Revolution* with its anti-scientific implications appeared in 1941. Although the great tradition of political theory was deeply embedded in American political science, the new generation of philosophical historians would soon give that tradition new meaning, and the study would take on a different significance that involved less the celebration of modern values and social science than a critique not only of modernity but even of the liberal vision of science and democracy.

There is little question but that the impending conflict between "scientific" and "traditional" theory was also a consequence of the increasing shift toward a vision of pure as opposed to applied science, and a perceived need, for several reasons, to place theory on an even firmer footing by demonstrating its "scientificness." However, the discourse about political theory through the 1940s increasingly revolved around questions of ethics, relativism, and positivism which tended to produce a redefinition and reconstruction of many issues in American political science (Hallowell, 1944; Brecht, 1948).

Historically, these issues had not been a matter of great concern to American political scientists. While in Europe fundamental value choices and the grounds for them were practical as well as philosophical problems, the American consensus and the belief in progress had made pragmatism and instrumentalism a reasonable position. The relativism of political values and beliefs had been constantly stressed by historians of political theory from Dunning to Sabine as well as by the more scientific school of individuals such as Merriam and his successors. Although the atmosphere preceding and during the war had raised questions about the ground of democratic values, relativism had been basically viewed as in some way essential to liberalism. For many of the Europeans and others touched by the transcendental urge, the issue was somewhat different. Their philosophical background lent great suspicion to the very enterprise of modern science which Americans had trusted so basically, and, particularly, to its impact on politics and society. Issues that concerned positivism, relativism, and historicism, were world-historical matters of political as well as philosophical urgency that manifested themselves in modern events.

The decade ended with the growing conviction of many political scientists that there was a definite need for more work in the "field of scientific method" that would yield "a body of testable propositions concerning political nature and activities of man that are applicable throughout the world" and "at all times" and that in the end would make possible a science of "human political behavior" (Anderson, 1949, pp. 309, 314-315). This summed up the governing motif of the forthcoming behavioral movement, but it was also a reaffirmation of a basic faith. The rekindling of the scientific mood was still tied to concerns about the realization of liberal values; this connection would become, if not more attenuated, at least more submerged. The growing sense that political science in the post-World War II period must be more than a science of American politics and that liberalism was more than an American mission moved the discipline further toward articulating a vision of a universal conception of political science.

THE BEHAVIORAL REVOLUTION: 1950-1959

The behavioral revolution was a theoretical revolution in several senses. First, it was a revolution in the theory of science. It introduced an unprecedented metatheoretical consciousness about scientific theory and scientific explanation. Second, much of the energy of behavioralists went into calling for, creating, and applying, what they took to be theories. Third, there was a distinct emphasis on pure or theoretical science and a turning away from the idea of liberal reform and social control as the rationale of social science. Finally, many of the individuals who were centrally involved in effecting the behavioral revolution were by training political theorists of the historical and normative kind; they were what they sought to replace. This group, who at least wrote dissertations in traditional political theory, included David Easton, Robert Dahl, Heinz Eulau, John Wahlke, Karl Deutsch, Herbert McClosky, Albert Somit, Ithiel de Sola Pool, Alfred and Sebastian de Grazia, and Austin Ranney, to name just a few.

The 1950s were the crucial decade in the development of both *PT* and *pt*. Although there were echoes of the move toward scientism in the 1920s, there were some important differences. First, the image of science embraced by behavioralism had a significantly greater impact on the research programs within the discipline. For the most part, historical, legal, and descriptive institutional analyses actually did dominate the field well into and beyond the 1940s; in the early 1950s, the belief that the practice of political science had not lived up to its scientific promise was vehemently expressed. Samuel Eldersveld (1951) noted that it was not necessary to change a syllable of Merriam's 1925 statement that there are "signs of hope that genuine advance may be made in the not distant future toward the discovery of scientific relations in the domain of political phenomena" (p. 87). Second, although some still linked the need for a "profound understanding of political behavior" to practical issues and the advance of democracy (White, 1950, p. 18), few explicitly held fast to the old alliance. Lasswell (1950, 1951) continued to remind the discipline that the basic purpose of political science was "to decrease the indeterminacy of important political judgments" and enhance the chances for a rational democratic society (1950, p. 425), but for most behavioralists the internal scientific conversion of the discipline was the first order of business. Third, the discussions focused in a much more specific way on the concept of theory and the place of theory in science. The view was that any change in the direction of scientific progress would require a change in the nature of theory in the discipline. Fourth, the claims of behavioralists about science and theory fractured both the discipline and the sub-field of Political Theory. Fifth, the arguments in defense of and opposition to behavioralism engaged political theorists in a wide range of philosophical and metatheoretical arguments. Finally, a distinct difference between *PT* and *pt*, and the problem of the relationship between them, became apparent.

Lippincott, in 1950, attempted a critical analysis of the field of Political Theory. He took it to be the "most scientific branch" of political science but an area in which political scientists had "produced little" if theory were defined, as he believed it should be, as "the systematic analysis of political relations" (p. 208). The methods in Political Theory had been basically historical, and the "emphasis placed upon the history of political ideas has meant very largely the abandonment of the aim of science" (p. 214). Some of the shortcomings of Political Theory could also be attributed to the "inadequacy of empiricism," or the crude inductivist misunderstanding of empiricism which eschewed both evaluation and generalization (p. 218). Political theorists had not contributed much to understanding the great political issues and events of the age.

The call for scientific theory was often accompanied by an attack on current practices in the discipline and particularly on Political Theory. Theory was characterized as teleological, moralistic, historical, ethical, and, in general, in about the same state that Aristotle left it. Herbert Simon (1950) was one of the first to suggest that much of the previous work in the field did not deserve the name of theory and that it was "time that we maintained a consistent distinction between political theory (i.e., scientific statements about the phenomena of politics) and the history of political thought (i.e., statements about what people have said about political theory and political ethics)" (p. 411). He emphasized the need for interdisciplinary model construction that would yield predictive generalizations and observably testable propositions.

Exactly what was involved in this commitment, or recommitment, to science and method was not very clearly defined. Most of the claims about science were in terms of very abstract demands about the need for observation and generalization and reflected versions of arguments about the logic and epistemology of science that came, in a secondary or tertiary manner, from the philosophy of science. The new scientific outlook was informed by—or perhaps, more accurately, justified by—"a thorough-going empiricist philosophy of the sciences" based on "logical positivism, operationalism, instrumentalism" (Lasswell & Kaplan, 1950, pp. xii, xiv). But no one was directly coming to grips with the question of exactly how these philosophical claims related to social scientific practice.

When viewed in historical perspective, Easton's now classic analysis of the "decline of political theory" (1951; 1953) does not seem to startling. His indictment of Political Theory for falling into historicism and failing to engage in either creative and relevant evaluative theorizing or developing causal scientific theory reflected, as well as gave impetus to, an increasingly concretely articulated sentiment. Easton's initial essay appeared as part of a symposium on the relationship of political theory to political research. All the essays advocated a sharp break with past modes of theorizing; "the integration of theory, methodology and research; interdisciplinary co-operation; and a treatment of theory as much more than utopian goodness" (de Grazia, 1951, p. 35). Although it is possible to recognize some attributes of the past literature in these critiques of the early 1950s, it is equally clear that these characterizations did not accurately represent either the motives or practice of most past political theorists. In part, the critique aimed at creating an image for justifying a different direction in concrete research programs in the discipline. But the problem also seems to have been what political theory was feared to be becoming; it was charged with moralism and antiquarianism more on this basis than on the basis of what it had been.

I have stressed this "conservative" aspect of the behavioral critique because it has been neglected, but it is necessary to recognize that actual research in political science had never corresponded to the scientific vision of the discipline, and the critics were determined to change the practice. To do this required an image of the past as well as the future. Although it would be a mistake to attempt an explanation exclusively in terms of the sociology of knowledge (response to funding sources, the need to clear political science of ideological bias, etc.), it is useful to note that it was a matter of concern to political scientists that "the National Roster of Scientific and Specialized Personnel, set up to find useful talent during World War II, classified Political

Theory on the advice of the APSA as concerned with political ethics and the history of political ideas" (Smithburg, 1951, pp. 61, 68). The notion that political theory was at the time basically the history of ideas was probably true in terms of the portion of the university curriculum that was designated as Political Theory, and, apart from some scope and methods courses, this would remain generally the case through the mid-1960s at most institutions.

Two developments in the 1950s are quite clear. First, there was the establishment of a basic dispute between "new" and "old" ways of theorizing—based on less than accurate images albeit accepted by protagonists on both sides. Second, *PT* was slowly but consistently differentiated from, but involved with, the wider realm of *pt* that was in the process of formulation.

This attention to the concept of theory during the 1950s began to have the effect of changing it from a category and a subject matter designation to a term that was assumed to refer to a definite element in both science and politics. Furthermore, the focus on theory created a whole realm of discourse and controversy about the "theory of theory" that became increasingly difficult to separate from theory itself and that had a considerable impact on theoretical practice. By the early 1950s, the debate about science and theory was already being transformed into a debate about philosophical positivism. In a symposium on "Recent American Political Theory," the comments by Simon on an essay by Dwight Waldo had less to do with the substantive issues than with Simon's perception of Waldo as a political theorist attached to a pre-scientific conception of that role. Simon charged that the essay was "characteristic of the writings of those who call themselves 'political theorists' and who are ever ready to raise the battle cry against positivism and empiricism" as a threat to democracy but continue to write in a "loose, literary, metaphysical style" (1952, pp. 494, 496).

One of the earliest attempts to specify the content of the behavioral vision of political inquiry was the 1952 report of the Social Science Research Council seminar on political behavior. Here the approach was "distinguished by its attempt to describe government as a process made up of the actions and interactions of men and groups of men" and to "discover the extent and nature of uniformities" (p. 1004). These goals were to be accomplished by the formulation of systematic concepts and hypotheses; the development of explanatory generalizations that would raise inquiry beyond mere factual empiricism; interdisciplinary borrowing; empirical methods of research; direct observation; and a distinct separation from concerns about "how men *ought* to act" (p. 1004). This would all be codified in the behavioral credo by the mid-1960s (Easton, 1965a, p. 9).

A significant factor in this behavioral affirmation was the problem posed by the emerging field of comparative politics that seemed more than any other aspect of the discipline to require a theoretical advance in order to deal with new and complex data. An SSRC report in 1952 stated that "the problem of comparative method revolves around the discovery of uniformities" and the "need for taking some kind of methodological position prior to or along with the collection and descriptive enumeration of facts" (1953, p. 643). This sense of being overwhelmed by facts was hardly novel in the history of the discipline. Although the answer to the problem that was given—political theory—was not novel either, the commitment to the answer in the form of developing a "scheme of inquiry" or "analytical scheme" that would give direction to inquiry and form to the data was unprecedented. The possession of a model or conceptual framework would be the badge of the empirical political scientists in the 1960s.

The poles of the argument within the discipline were increasingly represented in terms of normative concerns and the study of the history of political theory versus theory as part of an empirical science of politics (Easton, 1953; Hacker, 1954; Driscoll & Hyneman, 1955; Glaser, 1955). At the same time, "theoretical" controversies were fast becoming more metatheoretical debates. By the mid-1950s, political theory could be considered a subject of analysis with a whole range of types and categories that would have been difficult to conceive in the 1930s (e.g., Jenkin, 1955). For behavioral political scientists, the problem was to find out what theories were in science and what role they played and to build or construct them. Thus, methodology involved not only techniques of research but reading in the "fields of epistemology, logic, philosophy of science" (Driscoll & Hyneman, 1955, pp. 192-193). To turn to this literature, or more commonly to secondary accounts of it, was to turn to a field almost entirely dominated by logical positivism and logical empiricism; this then, was reflected in the discipline of political science and in the image of science accepted by both the advocates and opponents of behavioralism.

Even a conference on political theory in the study of politics that was by no means dominated by proponents of the behavioral persuasion was reported as reaching a consensus on the view that "all types of inquiry involve the construction of theory" and "that the title of 'political theory' has been unjustifiably appropriated by historians of political thought" (Eckstein, 1956, p. 476). The spirit of the conference seemed to be in favor of demonstrating that there was a "false distinction between 'behaviorists' and 'theorists,' " but the conferees seemed unable to end the distinction. There was a major split between the "behaviorists"—they were not quite united on the term—who wanted "to transform the field of political studies into a genuine scientific *discipline*" and "anti-behaviorists" (or political philosophers) who believed that "the end of the study of politics was something called political *wisdom*" (pp. 476-477).

By the late 1950s, it was generally agreed that political theory had "entered upon a time of troubles." On one side were those who saw theory as a "historical, reflective, and 'literary' discipline more akin to moral philosophy" than science (Smith, 1957, pp. 734, 743), and on the other side were those who saw it as a set of systematic generalizations for dealing with empirical data. For some, the theoretical enterprise was grounded in a search for political wisdom, and for others it was based on a "greater clarification of the epistemological foundations of science" and "training in theory construction" (Apter, 1957, p. 761). V. O. Key, Jr.'s analysis of the state of the discipline in 1958 focused on this dilemma. Key suggested that most of the "worries about the state of our discipline relate in one way or another to the place of political theory in our studies" (p. 967). While theory had been understood largely as the history of political thought and had possessed a relatively autonomous place within the discipline, the behavioral unification raised the question of "what relevance has political theory for other branches of political science." Many believed that a radical reconstruction of the sub-field was necessary. Key claimed that it was clear that there was an "odd relation" between "theoretical and empirical work" that tended to be "one of antagonism, if not hostility" and which had important implications for the future of the discipline (pp. 967-968). For some, such as Norman Jacobson, the situation by the late 1950s was such that the autonomy of political theory was threatened. There was a danger of its absorption into the poles of scientism and moralism as a consequence of the growing distance between "scientific" and "ethical political theory" (1958).

Another view of the fate of Political Theory was offered by Robert Dahl. In an extended review of Bertrand de Jouvenel's book on *Sovereignty,* Dahl treated it as a "serious" but, in many ways, vestigial "effort to do political theory in the grand style. In the English-speaking world, where so many of the interesting political problems have been solved (at least superficially) political theory is dead. In the Communist countries it is imprisoned. Elsewhere it is moribund" (1958, p. 89). Dahl believed that political theory had been reduced, in political science, to a kind of parasitic form of "textual criticism and historic analysis," and that although attempts to return to political theory in the grand manner in the modern age were to be applauded, they were faced with the inherent "impossibility of satisfying the scientific function of political theory" (p. 95).

Many of those individuals who worked within the traditional sub-field of Political Theory were, both through inclination and coercion, pushed further away from the mainstream of the discipline. In the late 1950s, however, political theorists who felt alienated were able to find little support in a wider literature of political theory. Today we are accustomed to the notion that political theory is a general field drawing from, and constituted by, work in a number of disciplines including political science, history, and philosophy; such a field simply did not exist or, at least, was seldom consciously perceived as existing in the 1950s. To the extent that it was perceived, it was seen as declining and it offered little support to political theorists in political science.

For individuals such as Strauss, the very notion of theory in modern social science, as exemplified in the behavioral movement, signified the "decline of political philosophy," while for Easton the identification of theory with the history of political theory was symptomatic of the "decline." But the argument about decline was also coming from other quarters. Arnold Brecht (1959) elaborated his earlier views about relativism and the crisis of political theory; Judith Shklar (1957) found decline to be part of the syndrome of post-enlightenment thought; Alfred Cobban (1953; 1959) believed it was manifest in the alienation of political theory from politics and its transformation into an academic discipline as well as the tendencies of historicism. Finally, the notion of the decline of political philosophy and/or theory was beginning to appear outside political science. It was a product of perceptions of the implications of positivist ethical theory for the status of moral reasoning and notions of rationality in normative discourse. Philosophers such as T.D. Weldon (1953; 1956) in effect suggested that much of traditional political philosophy rested on a mistaken belief that moral and political principles were, like empirical scientific claims, in some substantive sense demonstrable. In the early 1950s, philosophers did not really have much basis for questioning the positivist image of either science or ethics, and to the extent that the possibility of political philosophy was tied to the belief in grounded value judgments, Peter Laslett (1956) concluded that the "tradition has been broken" and "political philosophy is dead."

RECOUPING AND REGROUPING: 1960-1969

Although the tension between the images of traditional and scientific theory was a central motif in the literature of the 1960s, other things were happening in Political Theory. As a result, any general characterization of the state of the field is more difficult than it was in the 1950s.

The writings associated with the Straussian persuasion in political philosophy (e.g., Strauss, 1959; Jaffa, 1960; Storing, Ed., 1962; Strauss & Cropsey, Eds., 1963) and to a lesser extent the work of Voegelin (1952; 1956) and Hannah Arendt (1958; 1961) represented a distinct counterpoint to behavioralism both in that they dominated work in the history of political theory and in that they constituted an alternative to the behavioral approach and its philosophical assumptions. For some, this indicated a "revival" of political theory (Germino, 1963). Sheldon Wolin's *Politics and Vision,* published in 1960, was in many respects a significant departure from the type of historical analysis associated with Sabine and at the same time represented a position that was not altogether compatible with the direction of arguments such as those of Strauss (e.g., Schaar & Wolin, 1963). Wolin indicated that the great tradition was the basic object of the study of political theory and stressed its relevance for understanding and dealing with the present. He offered a general view about the decline or "sublimination" of political theory in the modern age that reinforced the general mood in political philosophy. More than any other work of the period, his book focused on the very idea of theory, the theorist, and the activity of theorizing in a manner that constituted, at least implicitly, a challenge to the behavioral notion of theory.

The presidential address to the APSA in 1961 suggested that behavioralism and "the move toward scientism has made it more essential to define the role of political philosophy in the study of political science" (Redford, p. 758). But there were growing indications that the tensions would not abate and that much of political theory would seek its reference point outside the discipline of political science. There were pleas for reintegration, or at least complementarity (e.g., Thorson, 1961; Bluhm, 1965), but these often pleased neither the behavioralists nor their opponents. It was, however, not the case, as it is sometimes believed or suggested, that political theory, as history and philosophy, was ostracized. The pages of professional journals during this period contained more political theory of the non-behavioral genre than ever. Although political scientists as a whole apparently did not believe that, as a field, Political Theory was producing very significant work, it was the only field between 1953 and 1961 that indicated any "startling" increase in interest (Somit & Tanenhaus, 1980). It is probably accurate to say that what was taking place was less the rejection of traditional political theory than its differentiation.

By the late 1960s, the profession had officially divided Political Theory into three parts—"Political Theory and Philosophy: historical, normative, and empirical" (APSA Biographical Directory, 1968). Dissertation listings in the *APSR* changed to "Political Philosophy, Theory, and Methodology" and the latter category (which included methods as well as metatheoretical material in the philosophy of science and philosophy of social science) was also part of the listing for Book Notes and Bibliography. Annual meetings of the APSA, by the late 1960s, began to make a definite distinction between empirical political theory and political philosophy (or "traditional political theory"). By this time, the Foundations of Political Theory, the Caucus for a New Political Science, and various other unaffiliated groups that represented the diverse concerns of political theory in both *PT* and *pt* had begun to offer panels at the annual meetings. But whether the basic distinctions within political theory were bipartite or tripartite or even more complex, they did not adequately capture the diversity that was becoming characteristic of the field. The problem is to disentangle some of these elements and reconstruct the relationship between them.

The 1960s were a decade of optimism about the advance of scientific theory and the achievement of the behavioral goal of "a science of politics modeled after the methodological assumptions of the natural sciences" (Easton, 1965a, p. 8). Although, today, some of the more extravagant claims about the development of predictive causal theory that would rival modern physics (advanced at that time) seem less than credible, these claims were not simply rhetorical. The vision was one of a "general theory" that would consist of "a deductive system of thought so that a limited number of postulates, as assumptions and axioms, a whole body of empirically valid generalizations might be deduced in descending order of specificity" and provide predictive causal explanations of political behavior (Easton, 1965a, p. 9). Behavioralists believed that theories were arising, or would arise, inductively from a wide variety of empirical studies and data gathering (e.g., Berelson & Steiner, 1964); but more than anywhere else, the heartland of political theory for political science in the 1960s was located in the development of "models," "orientations," "approaches," "strategies" of inquiry, and various conceptual and analytical frameworks. This was the product of theory "construction" and theory "building" in the discipline. These activities were seldom accepted as entirely fulfilling, in themselves, the scientific vision, but they were seen as definite steps in that path or as prototypes of fully scientific theory. Whether it was a form of systems theory, structural functionalism, decision theory, game theory, or some other such construct, these "varieties" (Easton, Ed., 1966; Pool, Ed., 1967) were directed toward the same general goal of empirical theory.

Paramount to all of these efforts was some notion of politics as a "system." Karl Deutsch's *Nerves of Government* was published in 1963, and Easton's *A Framework for Political Analysis* and *A Systems Analysis of Political Life* in 1965. Sociologists such as Talcott Parsons, Marion Levy, and Robert Merton had a significant impact on analytical theory in political science during this period. By 1965, David Truman, drawing upon Thomas Kuhn's model of paradigmatic scientific change, revised Merriam's history and cast the story of American political science in terms of a movement from an early period (1880s-1930s) of "non-theoretical empiricism" or "almost total neglect of theory in any meaningful sense of that term" to "a new disciplinary consensus" based on the "emergence of an explicit interest in the political system" as well as a "revival of interest in theory" and a "self-conscious and fruitful awareness of the necessary conjunction of theory and empirical investigation" (pp. 867, 870, 871).

Truman noted that "the theory chorus" was in some respects "less polyphonus than cacophonus" and that "in practice" it might not be possible in the "predictable future" to develop "general models" that would constitute "hypothetico-deductive theories," but it was clear that contemporary political science had made "a recommitment to the goal of science" and that this recommitment was manifest in its theoretical program (pp. 871, 872). Truman allowed that political scientists still had a certain obligation to address normative issues and that the new consensus would, "for an indefinite future," include "a less or non-scientific component" which could best be filled by a study of the "classics" of political thought which the earlier non-theoretical consensus had "thrust . . . out of the mainstream" but which could again constitute part of a fruitful dialogue within the field (p. 874).

A survey of the field of political theory in the mid-1960s argued that "theory" in general should be understood as a concern with "what 'is' or exists in politics" and specifically as a "search for a coherent image of the political system" (Deutsch & Rieselbach, 1965, p. 139). Concerns about "ought" questions should be considered as part of "political philosophy" or some such category. Political scientists were still concerned that in Political Theory the "preoccupation has been with history, exegesis, and methodological conservatism" in "contrast to other fields in both natural and social science, where theoretical physics and economic theory are clearly distinguished from the history of past theories." The authors argued that a systems analysis of the field of Political Theory itself in terms of structural-functional categories might be useful. They concluded that, from this perspective, "at present political theory is not a well-integrated field, nor does it seem well-oriented toward a prominent goal," but they did see a healthy tendency toward "adaption" which they defined as becoming more scientific and less concerned with "pattern maintenance" or traditional political theory (p. 162). In 1966, Gabriel Almond, once more drawing upon Kuhn's scheme as a basis for a revisionist history of the discipline, reaffirmed Truman's views and claimed that "in the last decade or two the elements of a new, more surely scientific paradigm seem to be manifesting themselves rapidly" and that it could be summed up by the concept of the "political system" (p. 869).

By the mid-1960s the "heterodoxy" of behavioralism had become the "new orthodoxy" (Pool, 1967), and it was attacked as both politically and methodologically conservative. Critics were concerned with the substantive political messages both in what political scientists said and did not say. Many believed that whether it was the commitment to pure science or an implicit ideological bias, political science seldom spoke to, or about, significant current political issues. Despite the problems in Vietnam, the crises of the American cities, the civil rights movement, international tensions, uprisings on college campuses and the like, political issues were largely absent from the literature of political science. In most instances, it was political theorists who took up this critique.

As late as 1965 and 1966, individuals such as Robert Lane were speaking about the "decline of politics in a knowledgeable society" and about how the "age of affluence," beginning in 1950, had produced "a growing state of confidence between men and government" that in many respects was making both ideology and conventional politics obsolete (1965, p. 895; 1966). The notion of the "end of ideology" advanced by Daniel Bell (1960) and similar themes in the work of individuals such as Seymour Martin Lipset (1960) and the revision of democratic theory in the voting studies to accommodate empirical findings (Campbell, *et al.*, 1960) were giving support, or otherwise linked, to various claims about the decline or death of political theory (see Partridge, 1961; Rousseas & Farganis, 1963; LaPalombara, 1966; Waxman, Ed., 1969). In 1968, the introduction to a symposium on the "advance of the discipline," noted that "the discontinuity between classic Political Theory and modern political theory is obvious." Political theory with a normative emphasis "has had much less appeal to the post-war generation of political scientists," and this was a consequence of the fact that the "official ideologies of the 1950s became increasingly unsupportable in empirical theory and untenable in normative philosophy" (Irish, 1968, pp. 298, 299).

During these years, the liberal-pluralist vision of political reality, which was embedded in much of American political science and reflected in both its methodology and substantive concerns, was criticized both as a descriptive and prescriptive claim. Although behavioralism, mainstream political science, and advocates of pluralist democracy were not entirely congruent categories, they often coincided in the work of individuals such as V.O. Key, Jr., David Easton, Robert Dahl, Gabriel Almond, and David Truman. Dwight Waldo (1956) had already noted, in the middle of the previous decade, that the basic structure and values of the American political order had been accepted and endorsed by political science and that the very idea of science in the discipline assumed a fundamental agreement on ends that allowed political theory to be transformed into methodology. This theme was more fully developed by Bernard Crick in 1959. Individuals such as C.W. Mills (1956; Horowitz, Ed., 1963) and Barrington Moore, Jr. (1958) had raised questions about both the conservative stance of social science and its account of the political world; arguments such as these became the property of dissident political theorists who attacked the theory and practice of American politics in both domestic and foreign affairs (e.g., Green & Levinson, Eds., 1970).

From the beginning to the end of the decade, the health of pluralist liberalism was questioned by individuals such as Henry Kariel (1961; 1969) and Theodore Lowi (1969). Its philosophical assumptions were criticized (Wolff, 1969), and the ideological biases of political science hidden behind claims to scientific objectivity were examined (Connolly, 1967; Connolly, Ed., 1969). There was, it was claimed, substantive political theory embedded in the disciplinary matrix of political science and in its various methodologies and conceptual frameworks, and political theorists turned to a critique of those assumptions. Arguments such as those of Dahl (1961) and Nelson Polsby (1963) about the character and structure of political power were countered by individuals such as Bachrach and Baratz (1962a; 1967) and Jack L. Walker (1966), and revisionist notions of democracy advanced by political sociologists and political scientists were attacked also (Duncan & Lukes, 1963; Davis, 1964). It was argued that there was a "behavioral syndrome" consisting of "*conservatism, fear of popular democracy,* and *avoidance of vital political issues*" (McCoy & Playford, Eds., 1967, p. 10); by the end of the decade the Caucus for a New Political Science claimed that there was, or should be, an "end to political science" as it was practiced (Wolfe & Surkin, Eds., 1970). For the most part, there was, however, little direct joining of issues. While some voices, such as that of Morgenthau, pointed to the "complacency" of Political Theory and the lack of social purpose in political science, the discipline continued to emphasize methodology and technique (Charlesworth, Ed., 1966).

Some of the material published in the late 1950s and 1960s that would significantly contribute to shaping the concerns of political theory in the 1970s was still invisible, or barely visible, in both the literature and the curriculum. This included such works as Marcuse's *One Dimensional Man* (1964) and Arendt's *Human Condition* (1958). A category such as Critical Theory was simply not part of the discourse of the 1960s. Although some of this material, as well as Continental literature reflecting neo-Marxist thought, existentialism, and phenomenology, was discussed by political theorists in courses and professional meetings, the discussions rarely surfaced in the professional publications. For example, not one article in either the *APSR* or *JOP* in the 1960s dealt in any direct way with such themes. The material that would constitute the substance of *pt* in the 1970s was appearing, but the form was not yet evident.

More prominent in the literature of the period was the influence of British analytic philosophy and linguistic analysis. By the early 1960s, the pessimism about the condition and future of ethics and political philosophy that had marked the 1950s had given way to a guarded optimism based on the appearance of a number of works in post-positivist philosophy and particularly in the area of moral reasoning (e.g., Toulmin, 1950; Hare, 1952; 1963). Certain thinkers were coming to the conclusion that social science and political theory were not mutually exclusive but rather complementary enterprises. All empirical work involved value assumptions, and empirical evidence was relevant in making and sustaining evaluative and prescriptive arguments (Runciman, 1963; Taylor, 1967). Political philosophy entailed both conceptual and substantive claims and, like normative reason in general, constituted a certain form of discourse that, while not scientific, was rationally autonomous. To the extent that political philosophy was a type of normative reasoning or involved producing knowledge in the form of conceptual clarification that guided action as well as understanding, it seemed to many that "political philosophy in the English-speaking world is alive again" and that it would "not wholly perish from the earth" (Laslett, 1967; Berlin, 1962).

The influence of this literature on *PT* was not very great in the 1960s, even though there were some important examples (e.g., Thorson, 1962; Flathman, 1966; Pitkin, 1967). What this approach promised was a way of actually "doing" political theory—rather than merely talking about its history and condition—and of doing it in a manner that was intellectually secure from the kinds of criticism leveled by positivists such as Simon in early years. It was rigorous yet normative.

Despite all the things that political theorists had said about science, few, if any, of these individuals had any concrete knowledge of, or association with, the practices of natural science. For the behavioralist as well as the anti-behavioralist, science was an image, and it was an image gained by and large from various philosophical sources. Both parties embraced basically the same image. As the issues revolving around the possibility and desirability of the scientific study of politics sharpened, the articulation of this image became a matter of great importance; increasingly it was inseparable from concrete theoretical claims and actual techniques of analysis. Before the 1960s, there were relatively few books available, outside technical literature in the philosophy of science, that spoke to the question of the nature of science and scientific method, let alone its application to social science (Cohen & Nagel, 1934; Kaufman, 1944). Arnold Brecht's *Political Theory* (1959) expanded the scope of the discussion about science, but few political theorists, let alone political scientists in general, were at that time interested in submerging themselves in the intricacies of European thought (positivism, natural law, phenomenology, etc.). Brecht was not happy with the implications of what he termed "scientific value relativism" for the future of normative political theory, but he was forced to confirm the positivist notion of scientific rationality and its impact on Political Theory as well as the positivist image of scientific explanation associated with the "hypothetico-deductive" model which nearly everyone equated with "science."

By the beginning of the 1960's, this genre of mediational literature standing between philosophy and social science began to bloom. One of the most influential works used in scope and methods courses of the period was Abraham Kaplan's *Conduct of Inquiry* (1964). Although Kaplan stressed the autonomy of inquiry, or the relativity of the logic of explanation with regard to the subject matter, and distinguished between philosophical idealizations of scientific explanation and the practice of science, he nevertheless presented a synthetic but in the end largely Americanized logical empiricist account of science that stressed the underlying unity of science and its philosophy. The book also suggested that it could provide a methodological foundation for the practice of inquiry in social science.

Much of the debate about science (e.g., Charlesworth, Ed., 1962), through the mid-1960s, had been about the possibility and desirability of applying scientific methods to the study of politics with both sides generally accepting the idea of the unity of scientific method and the account of natural science that had become standard in the literature of the philosophy of science, that is, logical positivism and the emendations of logical empiricism (Nagel, 1961; Hempel, 1965; Popper, 1961). However, by the late 1950s and early 1960s, both the approach and claims of this school were being challenged in the philosophy of science by authors such as Kuhn (1962) (see also, Hanson, 1958). The implications for the image and demands of science in the social sciences, as well as for the question of the relationship between science and the philosophy of science, were considerable, but Kaplan, for example, did not mention Kuhn.

Although Kuhn's impact on the literature of Political Theory was eventually of singular importance, there was a general growing awareness that more was involved than merely the question of accepting or rejecting the methods of the natural science. There were numerous instances of mediational works both in social science and the philosophy of social sciene (e.g., Gibson, 1960; Van Dyke, 1960; Brown, 1963; Taylor, 1964; Meehan, 1965; Braybrooke, 1965; Rudner, 1966; Frohock, 1967; Brodbeck, 1968; Greer, 1969; Isaak, 1969). Although much of it may have tended to confirm, and give aid to, the long standing assumption or claim of most behavioralists that there was a basic identity among the philosophical reconstructions of science produced in the literature of logical positivism and empiricism, the practice of natural science, and the demands of scientific inquiry in social and political science, the consciousness of political scientists regarding these matters was being raised to a significant degree.

Another closely related body of literature that appeared in the 1960s, which to some degree overlapped the material discussed above, was a series of works in the philosophy of social science that challenged philosophical and social scientific assumptions about the applicability of scientific methods to the study of social phenomena (Winch, 1958; Natanson, 1963; Schutz, 1967; Appel, 1967; Louch, 1966; MacIntyre, 1962). Much of this work was grounded in post-Wittgensteinian philosophy and in Continental phenomenology, with certain strong affinities with, or parallels to, notions of the explanation of social action in the work of Max Weber. There was, however, a fundamental ambiguity running through much of this material with regard to whether it was challenging the idea of the unity of science, and claiming that the subject matter of the social sciences demanded another or autonomous method of inquiry and notion of explanation, or whether it was claiming that scientific methods of explanation were inappropriate for understanding social phenomena. Although this literature in the philosophy of social science was beginning to enter the discourse of political theory, there were few specific attempts in the 1960s to apply these ideas to issues in *PT* or to relate them to challenges to positivism in the philosophy of science (Gunnell, 1968). By the early 1970s, however, the concern with these arguments and their application would constitute a relatively distinct body of literature in Political Theory.

In the 1968 symposium on the state ("advance") of the discipline, the analysis of Political Theory made a point of the fact that political theory as a field and political theory as an intellectual activity were far from coterminous. The authors claimed that while the activity of theorizing within the discipline had increased, dissatisfaction with the field was on the rise. In their judgment, the field was broad, diverse, fragmented, and replete with paradoxes and perplexities. Despite the fact that most major departments still treated Political Theory as a basic sub-field, it had little to do with the discipline as a whole. While most social scientists viewed theory as "a systematic and self-conscious attempt . . . to explain diverse phenomena that have been or can be observed," theory in political science had traditionally involved much more than this "explanatory" type (McDonald & Rosenau, pp. 317, 318). It had included, and continued to include, various dimensions of political philosophy, or normative theory and ideology, that were inconsistent with the concerns of the "behavioral revolution" and the conception of theory in contemporary political science as a whole. The result was "sustained and unrestrained argumentation" (pp. 320, 321).

In the authors' view, the future of this sub-field, with its current "ungainly structure," might proceed in three possible directions. First, empirical political theory and theorizing might spread throughout the discipline, while the "philosophical" component was retained as a separate sub-field. Second, the behavioral approach to theory might take over the sub-field while Political Philosophy became an additional sub-field. Third, political science as a whole might become an entirely empirical science while the normative and philosophical components would find a place as appendages or elements of other departments.

The authors were relatively optimistic about what they saw as the two principal directions of political theory as an intellectual activity. First, although the many conceptual frameworks and methodological strategies such as systems analysis that had appeared in recent years were, at best, pretheoretical and of doubtful durability, there were indications that "theory at all levels in all fields will soon experience previously unimaginable breakthroughs because of technological advances" (p. 334). Second, there was a "growing appreciation of the theoretical relevance of the great works of political thought" and, "perhaps as a reaction to the behavioral revolution, the inclination to treat them as historical artifacts, philosophical formulations, and ideological tracts has given way to a growing concern for probing their theoretical content" (p. 337). Although none of these predictions would prove to be precisely accurate and although the hopes for theory might not be realized, the tendency toward dispersion was perceived, and the differentiation between *PT* and *pt* was recognized.

Another development was subtle and incremental; it would be more obvious in discussions of political theory in the 1970s but less consciously recognized as a transformation. It has already been noted that in the beginning of the century, "political theory" was understood more as a functional category, a sub-field name, or a literature classification than a distinct entity or activity. This gradually changed through the 1950s, but it was primarily the debates about theory in the 1960s that gave rise to the contemporary notion that theory is actually an element in the practice of science, and more than an analytical specifiable element; that political theory is a concrete activity with a past and future; and that theorizing is a distinct endeavor. There is a definite sense in which the contemporary notion of political theory was invented in the context of the debates about behavioralism and the decline, and revival, of political theory. The concept became reified to a degree that would have been unintelligible to earlier generations, and the growth of *pt* lent credence to this idea. This can be concretely illustrated.

In the 1937 edition of the *International Encyclopedia of the Social Sciences,* not only was Political Theory not a separate heading, it was not even treated as a distinct sub-division in the discipline of political science. In the 1968 edition, Political Theory was not only given prominence and separate status in the section on Political Science, where it was treated as an activity, product, and sub-field, but it became a separate and equal topic where it was discussed almost as if it were an autonomous discipline with its various divisions, problems, dimensions, and history. Although the views of theory, as presented by Easton in a discussion of theory in "Political Science," and by Wolin and Brecht, in their analysis of "Political Theory," were in many respects quite antithetical, they both exemplified this reification of theory as well as the tension between notions of theory in *PT* and the growing distinction between *PT* and *pt*.

Easton argued that political science, by mid-century, was still "a discipline solving its "identity crisis" and emerging with a "systematic theoretical structure of its own" that was largely the consequence of "the reception and integration of the methods of science into the core of the discipline" (p. 282). The basic thrust of this "theoretical revolution" was a turn toward functional and systems analysis as opposed to a focus on institutions such as the state. According to Easton, the core of the behavioral movement was a "shift from an institutional and practical problem orientation" to pure science, and this shift was most "sharply revealed" in "the sub-field of political theory." The changes were distinctly reflected here, and at the same time the work in theory was crucial in moving the discipline in an analytical direction (p. 243). Easton claimed that behavioralism had dispensed with "the last remnants of the classical heritage in political science." It produced "a profound transformation in conceptions about the role that theory plays as a tool in political research" — a role that was distinguished by a separation of fact and value and an attempt "to drive political science away from a prescriptive problem-directed discipline to one in which research depends increasingly upon empirically oriented theoretical criteria" (p. 296).

Although Wolin took issue with Easton's notion of science and the role that theory played in science, he disagreed less with Easton's description of what theory had come to mean and to be in political science and with the basic "traditional"/"scientific" distinction than with the implications of this development. For Wolin, what was happening in political science was a serious deviation from the historical role of theory and theorizing and its relationship to politics. According to Wolin, "the quest for a scientific theory of politics has altered the character of theorizing in several significant ways" and what it has produced on the whole has been the "sterilization of political theory" (pp. 325, 328). In an important sense, theory for both sides was something even bigger than political science and politics but something that might be manifest or realized in either.

Those who valued the study of the history of political theory were seeking to articulate exactly what it was all about in order to defend it against the behavioral challenge. George Kateb (1968), for example, attempted to specify the principal characteristics of "traditional political theory" and to justify its uses in an age in which it had "fallen on hard times." For the behavioralist, the realization of theory was in the near future in political science, and for the historian the future of theory depended on the recovery of its past. Claims such as those of Easton and Wolin capture much of the flavor of the debates about theory that characterized the 1960s, but the last year of the decade indicated some new directions that would permeate discourse in and about political theory during the 1970s.

First of all, in 1969 Easton announced, or called for, "a new revolution in political science." This was to be a "post-behavioral revolution" which was not "theoretical" or a change in the methods of inquiry but a change in orientation that grew out of a "deep discontent with the direction of contemporary political research" and which advocated, at least in the short run, more attention to the public responsibilities of the discipline and to relevant research on contempoary political problems and issues (p. 1052). The shift in distribution of emphasis from Easton's stress on the priority of "pure science" and the separation of fact and value in the "behavioral credo" (1965, p. 17) as well as his statements about political science and political theory the previous year was, at least on its face, dramatic. This, in some ways, was the official birth announcement of the public policy enterprise which would become the basis of the self-image of orthodox political science in the 1970s, and in terms of which it would attempt to establish its identity. With this shift would come a distinct de-emphasis of the concern with general unified theory as the core of the discipline as well as a retreat from any pointed confrontation with the history of political theory.

In the same issue of *APSR* in which Easton announced the new revolution, Wolin presented his defense of "political theory as a vocation." This was in a very real sense the quintessential statement, as well as, in many respects, the effective terminus of the critique of behavioralism from the standpoint of the history of political theory. Although Wolin's position might not spring from the same intellectual and ideological source as that of Strauss and others, he spoke for a generation of political theorists when he defended the role of the historian of political theory as conservator and transmitter of "political wisdom" against the "methodism" of political science and its "historyless" posture that neglected the "tacit political knowledge" that should inform both scientific and political judgment. He spoke also for the preservation of that "vocation by which political theories are created" in the midst of a world that is governed by "giant, routinized structures" and which is "impervious to theory" and in which political science is marked by "complacency" in the face of political crisis and chaos (pp. 1070-1071; 1077; 1080-1081). Although Wolin's arguments articulated the sentiments of many political theorists, his statement was shouted in a desert, and it was clear that he as well as other political theorists would have to seek a forum outside political science. Behavioralism, which in the immediate sense at least, had begun the war with the history of political theory, was disengaging. On the other hand, there was a distinct sense in Wolin's essay that the history of political theory no longer had a home in political science.

Although it would be several years before developments had progressed sufficiently for a discussion of the "new history of political theory" as a positive enterprise, Quentin Skinner — who would be prominently associated with this position in the 1970s—offered a comprehensive and influential critique of past research in the history of Political Theory in 1969. It was an indication of the anomalous situation of much of this literature, caught between political science and *pt*, that Skinner's methodological critique, in terms of understanding in the history of ideas, tended to neglect the philosophical, political, and disciplinary contexts in which many of the arguments such as those of Strauss developed. But the arguments of individuals such as Skinner were not simply critical but legislative. In the 1970s much of the literature dealing with the history of political theory would revolve around matters of the advocacy and criticism of the "new history". The shift was decidedly outside the context of political science in both a methodological and substantive sense.

Finally, by the end of the 1960s, there were indications of a distinct transformation in the theoretical or philosophical critique of political science. It is easy to forget how little had been published in criticism of the behavioral image of science by the late 1960s that went beyond general concerns about treating politics scientifically and practicing science politically. Although there were growing concerns about the integrity and validity of the behavioral image of science, the critique of behavioralism had in many respects been an external one that was relatively easy to defuse by drawing lines between those who were committed to science and those committed to some other approach to the study of politics. In the same issue of the *APSR* in which Wolin and Easton's articles appeared, there was a critique of the philosophical assumptions of the basic model of scientific explanation that had been adopted by political scientists and of the relationship between philosophical claims about science and the practice of social scientific inquiry (Gunnell, 1969). This critique was published as part of a symposium that included two editorially solicited rebuttals.

There had been a great educational, financial, intellectual, and emotional investment in the behavioral image of science and theory, and despite all the talk about policy, that image was at the core of disciplinary practice. The battle over this issue was, in many respects, yet to come. The question of the philosophical status of this image of science and related ideas would occupy a central place in the literature of political theory (both *PT* and *pt*) during the next decade and would, as a matter of fact, contribute significantly to the dispersion of political theory.

THE DIASPORA OF POLITICAL THEORY: 1970-1979

In the 1970s, there was the disappearance of an issue center within *PT*, and the sub-field was progressively transformed into *pt* writ small as the autonomy of the latter became more firmly established. Journals such as *Philosophy and Public Affairs* (1971) and *Political Theory* (1973) had begun publication. Political theory was no longer centered in the discipline of political science, and political science no longer defined the issues in the literature of Political Theory. New influences, such as the translation of the work of Habermas, came onto the scene the same year as the publication of

Rawls' book; commentaries on, and tributaries of, this material occupied much of the space in Political Theory during the decade. Throughout the late 1960s, graduate education in Political Theory had continued to be traditional with an emphasis on the history of political theory. Although there was some increased attention given to scope and method courses, and although a few thinkers such as Camus, Sartre, Arendt or Marcuse were featured fairly prominently in some limited contexts, few graduate students were exposed, in any systematic or extensive manner, to much more than the traditional canon. This was true even at institutions where theory was prominent. But during the 1970s, graduate education changed significantly in response to developments in *pt*. Names such as Rawls, Nozick, Habermas, Heidegger, Foucault, Gadamer, Lukacs, Gramsci, Althusser, Kuch, and Popper, became common currency, and students were asked to come to grips with such exotic fields such as sociobiology, hermeneutics, and structuralism. It is easy to forget just how radical the transformation was that began in the 1970s in both education and the scholarly literature. Assessing its significance is a contentious matter.

Many would see the developments of the 1970s as growth in the independence of political theory, and as a break from its less than happy home in political science. But although *pt* became a recognizable body of literature, and even a partially institutionalized interdisciplinary field with journals and organizations that reflected its concerns, it was largely a collection of intellectual enclaves with limited communication between them. However one views the implications of the events of the 1970s, the result was the dispersion of political theory both between and within *PT* and *pt*. To disentangle the various themes and threads is not an easy task, but a natural starting point is an examination of the remnant of political theory that was distinctly attached to the discipline of political science.

It was clear from the beginning of the decade that, in practice at least, the discipline's emphasis on universal theory was waning. The disjoining of the debate between historians and scientists led to a more pluralistic view of theory; behavioralism was quite willing to be tolerant of diversity once it had captured the center; the "new revolution" also placed less emphasis on theory; diversity and tolerance were forced on the discipline by the critics in the late 1960s; and specialization in research was leading to more emphasis on intellectually localized research strategies. By the early 1970s, it was not easy to find coherence among the trends or to bring the discipline together into a common notion of theoretical endeavor.

In attempting to understand this situation, Karl Deutsch's 1970 presidential address to the APSA is instructive as an attempt to confront the problem (1971). Several things were quite clear in Deutsch's eclectic view of theory. First, it was a very sharp departure from the conscious attempt by himself and others in the mid-1960s to define theory in a narrow manner and to make a sharp distinction between empirical political theory and political philosophy. Second, there was a good deal of at least implicit reproof as well as conciliation directed toward both academic and political critics of the discipline. And third, there was a distinct call for political relevance which echoed the statement of Easton. Deutsch was determined to find a middle ground between scientism and political radicalism, between theory as an instrument for knowing reality and as ideology, and to present various analytically distinguishable aspects of theory as "an integrative process" involving "stages in a single production cycle of political knowledge and political action" (p. 17). All this required many different types of people and diversity in distribution of emphasis. In the end, Deutsch wanted to give all sides a place while to some degree maintaining the priority of the behavioral vision of theory, but as with most attempts at intellectual synthesis after the fact of differentiation, it did little to change the situation and involved such an amorphous notion of theory that the very thing that was to be identified became still more elusive.

The resonant note in Deutsch's essay was the idea of political science as a policy science; this would also be sounded in Heinz Eulau's analysis of the "Skill Revolution and the Consultative Commonwealth" (1973), Avery Leiserson's call (1975) for a synthesis of science and politics and a reaffirmation of the traditional American faith in the complementarity of "scientific truth and democratic decision making," and Austin Ranney's (1976) celebration of the vision of a "divine science" that had traditionally informed political science in the United States from the time of the Founders and that could provide a basis for the contemporary need to recognize the possibility of "political engineering in American culture." This was the tone of the textbooks and other less official statements about the purpose and direction of the discipline during the 1970s, and although "post-behavioralism" in political science was a concept that meant many things (Graham, Ed., 1972), it certainly included the policy turn in the mainstream of the discipline. But it also represented the ideological critique of the field as it was in the late 1960s and the philosophical critique of the behavioral image of science. "Post-behavioralism" was more a condition or a name for less than coherent congeries of interests than an intelligible intellectual movement or even mood.

The old controversy about political science as a science was, by the early 1970s, largely focused on the critique and defense of the behavioral image of science in terms of the philosophy of science and philosophy of social science. A second symposium in the *APSR*, in which a battery of political scientists and philosophers was enlisted by the editor to exorcize dissident philosophical claims about scientific inquiry, appeared in 1972. In this case, the article (Miller) at the center of the symposium was, ironically, far from fully supportive of, or concerned with, the new philosophy of science represented by individuals such as Kuhn. It was written from a Straussian perspective and focused on matters such as the historicism implied in Kuhn's work as well as the positivism of behavioralism. The critiques, which indicated where the primary sensitivities of the discipline resided at this point, fastened, however, on the alien images in the philosophy of science.

By the mid-1970s, there were philosophically sophisticated critiques of behavioral assumptions about political theory (Spragens, 1973); books defending the behavioral image of science in terms of both the basic logical empiricist philosophy of science and the responses of this school to criticisms mounted by individuals such as Kuhn and Feyerabend (Gregor, 1971); and books which aimed at demonstrating, in light of the contemporary work in philosophy, both the dubious character of logical positivism and logical empiricism and their impact on the conduct and understanding of inquiry in political science (Gunnell, 1975). This kind of controversy was inevitable, but it had the effect of drawing political theory into a realm of metatheoretical debates that in many respects had decreasing relevance to both politics and political inquiry. Somewhat the same problem is apparent in the literature that attempted to apply new ideas in the philosophy of social science (Dallmayr & McCarthy, Eds., 1977) to a critique of positivism in social and political science and to a reconstruction of social scientific inquiry. Such synthetic accounts drawn from linguistic analysis, phenomenology, and critical and interpretative theory (e.g., Bernstein, 1976) were largely summaries and restatements of material in philosophy, and, while useful and interesting in many respects, this material transformed political theory into a less than autonomous mode of discourse.

Compared to the 1960s, with the fixation on theory as conceptual frameworks, it is difficult to discern exactly what orthodox political scientists understood theory to be. The 1973 Supplement to the Biographical Directory for the APSA separated out Methodology (which included epistemology and the philosophy of science) and divided Political Theory into systems of ideas in history, ideology systems, political philosophy (general), and methodological and analytical systems. The (unofficial) *Handbook of Political Science* published in 1975, devoted Volume One to the *Scope and Theory of Political Science* which included chapters on: the history of the discipline; an analysis and synthesis of opposing philosophical views about the nature of social scientific explanation; an essay on the contemporary relevance of the classics; a neo-positivist philosophical analysis of the language of political inquiry and political concepts; and a philosophical discussion of the language of political evaluation. Volumes Two and Three were devoted respectively to what was designated as Micro- and Macro-political Theory, but these were largely categories for encompassing various subjects and research programs rather than specifications of particular theoretical formulations (Greenstein & Polsby, Eds.).

The official panels at the APSA meetings obviously had increasing difficulty deciding exactly what the structure of political theory was or should be. Constantly changing configurations attempted both to capture the diversity within the field and to reflect topical issues. "Formal" or "positive" theory emerged as a distinct category in 1970, and diverse remaining panels were listed under "Philosophical Analysis and Politics." In 1971, the panels were divided between Formal Theory, Ethical Theory, and the Philosophical Analysis of the Science of Politics. By 1972, the attempt to make any general divisions in the sub-field was abandoned in favor of a potpourri including various substantive, conceptual, and methodological issues. In 1973, there was an attempt—without much apparent success since it included panels as diverse as Statistical Problems and Research on Electoral College Reform—to carve out an area designated as Methodological and Analytical Theory. The 1974 panels were divided between Macro Theory and Micro Analysis on the one hand and Political Theory and Ideological Conflict on the other hand with a large number of issues (post-behavioralism, epistemological alternatives to behavioralism, etc.) relegated to the unaffiliated panels. An attempt was made in 1975 and 1976 to hold on to a basic division between Political Theory and Epistemology and Methodology, but it gave way in 1977 to Political Theory, Methods and Empirical Theory, and American Political Thought.

From 1978 through 1983 there has been some basic division between Analytical (and/or Empirical) Theory and Political Philosophy (and/or Political Theory or Thought) with the continued representation of many issues in a wide variety of unaffiliated panels. But the criteria of demarcation has not been very clear or consistent. By 1982, the APSA Directory and the Guide to Graduate Study in Political Science divided the field into Political Theory and Philosophy, Formal or Positive Theory, and Methodology, but these categories are not particularly descriptive of the field or the ten percent of the members of the APSA who designate themselves as primarily political theorists.

Although a general neo-positivist or logical empiricist view of science, scientific explanation, and theory continued to be quite pervasive in the discipline at large, it usually found expression, in pro forma terms, in textbook introductions and methodological prefaces. There were few criteria for connecting this persistent philosophical image of science with what political scientists actually did. The criticism and defense of this image did not peak until the mid-1970s; thereafter, even some of those who had done the most to propagate it began to disavow it. The irony was, however, that this image, in the face of heavy criticism, had only recently received its most thorough explication and defense. At the very point at which many dedicated younger centrist scholars in political science found and accepted it at the core of their education, the older generation began to deny it.

In 1977, Almond, for example, was ready to concede—or "discover," since he did not acknowledge or mention any of the criticism that had been mounted within the discipline during the past few years—most of the points that had been advanced against the philosophical foundations of behavioralism. He suggested that the commitment to these methodological doctrines had caused political science to lose touch with its "ontological base" and mistakenly attempt, with the encouragement of neo-positivist philosophers of science and their partisans, to treat political phenomena as natural events when they should instead have developed approaches "appropriate to human and social reality" (p. 522). He argued that such constructs as the deductive model advanced by logical empiricists as well as the general "explanatory strategy of hard science had only a limited application to the social sciences" and that the "search for regularities and lawful relationships" and the "enshrining of the notion of generalization" represented the wrong direction for the discipline to have taken (p. 493).

Few orthodox political scientists so openly rejected the essence of the behavioral faith, but few attempted to defend it. Some, such as William Riker, continued to describe and justify their work and define theory in terms of notions of the unity of science based on "positivist or objectivist philosophy," as set forth by individuals such as Hempel and Nagel, and to pass off the criticism that by this time had come close to a new orthodoxy in the philosophy of science as "idealist interpretations of science" (1977, p. 16). But such attempts to restrict the idea of theory in this manner were not common.

For both the critics and defenders of behavioralism, the deep but inevitable involvement of political theory in the issues of the philosophy of science and epistemology had become a problem. Theorists were being drawn off into a realm of metatheoretical concerns that alienated them from substantive political issues and a concern with political phenomenon in general (Kress, 1979). Heinz Eulau noted that the cycle of justification, criticism, and defense of behavioral claims in philosophical terms had produced an "exaggerated, almost pathological, concern" that culminated in "the curious notion that the philosophy of science is the high road to scientific knowledge, as if the business of the philosophy of science were science rather than philosophy" (1977, p. 6). This precise point had been made by critics of behavioralism over a decade earlier. Although one might not agree with the particular biopolitical concerns of John Wahlke, his critique of behavioralism (1979) also indicated a certain basic agreement with many of the critics who viewed behavioralism as an empty commitment to methodism. Wahlke argued that despite all the talk about theory and despite the technical methodological advances, political science was still characterized by a "paucity of theoretical concerns."

By the end of the 1970s what had happened to the history of political theory? It was alive and living at least a large portion of its life in *pt*. Although some reverberations from the active discussions in *pt* might surface in the literature of political science, most of the controversy that was generated was not felt in the discipline in general. There was no question that the history of political theory was accepted as part of the field of political science, but it was not at the center of concerns about theory in the discipline. Its new found autonomy guaranteed its existence, but it was increasingly divorced from the issues that had dominated the field and the claims of both its advocates and critics for so many years. Autonomy meant a new self-consciousness which issued in the call for a "new history" (e.g., Skinner, 1979; Pocock, 1971) that would reflect "truly" historical methods and recover the actual meaning of classic texts as well as trace "actual" historical traditions. In the view of the new historians, this required turning away from the philosophical concerns and assumptions which they believed had governed past scholarship. While a considerable body of literature voicing and reflecting this position emerged during this period and added significantly to the understanding of classic authors such as Locke (e.g., Ashcraft, 1980; Tarlton, 1979), the purpose of this activity, its relationship to political science, and a range of similar issues were not only unresolved but seldom directly discussed.

To adequately convey the structure of political theory, whether in *PT* or *pt*, during the 1970s and into the early 1980s would require listing many different and discrete enterprises. Different interests and concerns would yield different distributions of emphasis. The important point is that the field was becoming too dispersed for there to be any core set of issues that would be readily agreed upon as establishing its identity.

Significant work in conceptual analysis was apparent (e.g., Pitkin, 1972,

1978; Flathman, 1972, 1976), and analytical political philosophy was well represented in works such as the continuing series of *Philosophy, Politics and Society*. Although the Straussian project remained active after the death of Leo Strauss, it was dispersed within itself and increasingly insulated from the discipline of political science. There was a legacy of arguments about scientific method and the nature of explanation, but these reflected continually finer drawn points in the philosophy of science and philosophy of social science. The large body of literature that surrounded the work of Rawls continued to grow as well as other quasi-transcendental arguments in normative theory (e.g., Dworkin, 1977). One of the trends that characterized the 1970s was a growing concern with political economy and renewed attention to the "state" as an object of inquiry. Much of this material was not in political science proper (O'Connor, 1973; Wolfe, 1977; Skocpol, 1979), but it influenced the discipline (Lindblom, 1977). There were continuing attempts to bring the world of Continental philosophy closer to the concerns of American political theorists. The problem of summarizing Habermas and keeping up with his dicta was supplemented by problems of understanding individuals such as Foucault, Gadamer, and Althusser. The world seemed accessible only through what somebody else said about it, and authors more than their subjects became the object of analysis.

This somewhat impressionistic account could be expanded considerably and still not adequately encompass the varieties of political theory. The problem is less one of inclusiveness than of determining how to assess the state of the field. The proliferation signified for many that there was vital energy in political theory, but it was difficult to identify any basic coherence. One might, at a certain level of abstraction, find underlying connections or similarities in the literature, such as a concern with language and interpretation or the problem of achieving some transcendental ground for political values. But such characterizations tell us less about the field per se than about what someone might find interesting. Although one could say that the field was vital, it could just as easily be said that it was without definite direction or focus.

PROSPECTS: THE 1980s

Since it is only in retrospect that we can know exactly where we were, what I have termed the dispersion of political theory may, in future years, appear to be something quite different. But an external vantage point— temporal or spatial—often imposes a restricted perspective. Even now it is interesting to note how the situation in political theory is described by an outside observer. The results of one such investigation, while not intuitively counterfactual, would probably be unsatisfactory to most participants in the field. A report on the state of political theory by the American Association for the Advancement of the Humanities described it as a "discipline" that had "died and been reborn several times." The conclusion was that in its present "incarnation" it consisted principally of a debate between Straussians, analytical philosophers, and contextualist historians and that these debates, marked by "intellectual irreconcilability," structured both academic and professional life (Herbert, 1981, p. 8). A much more extensive study of political theory in the United States has been in progress in Germany by the late Peter Lutz and now by the executors of his academic estate, but the difficulty facing such anthropologists of political theory is in part a matter of where they happen to cut into the culture and the categories that they bring to their analysis. They also probably fail to grasp the complexity of the society with which they are dealing. One might not want to say that their results are wrong, but their conclusions are too partial and narrowly focused. The principal difficulty of all these analyses is that they are seeking the identity of political theory.

The dispersion of political theory that took place in the 1970s has resulted in a *loss* of identity (both in *PT* and *pt*). The idea of political theory advanced by behavioralists, the counter arguments of historians of political theory, and the controversy in which they were joined may all be rightfully interred. But these arguments gave a shape to the field that is lacking today. The loss may not be at all lamentable, and there is no obvious reason why a discussion of prospects should assume a need to reconstitute such a form. But it is necessary to ask questions about the elements of the dispersed residue of that form and the relationship between them as well as their relationship to politics.

Although there are some individuals in political theory who believe that the field would be best served by finalizing the divorce from mainstream political science, such views must assume that there is a space for the activity of political theory outside political science. Often, however, such ideas are based upon abstract world-historical views of political theory when in fact the very idea of political theory has been largely a product of the evolution of political science. Its future outside of the discipline may be something of an illusion. There is, for example, little reason to think that *pt* is likely to become anything more than the loose collection of endeavors that now comprise it. But the question of whether there is a life for political theory in political science cannot be avoided.

Political theorists are often not only alienated from the concerns of most research programs in political science, but not even engaged in a critical assessment of these programs. Their principal reference point is the world of *pt*. On the other hand, within political science, there are the views of those who seek to narrow the meaning of political theory not only to orthodox political science but to a particular position within the discipline. For example, William Riker (1983) claims that "the main line of development during the last generation" has been in the direction of social choice theory, and he defines theory in terms of the logical empiricist deductive nomological model which he in turn equates with the practice of natural science. These positions have the unfortunate effect of artificially limiting critical and interesting discussion in or about political theory.

It is probably too optimistic to believe, however, that contemporary trends reflect an end to the conflict between "humanists" and the "science establishment" and signal a "paradigm synthesis" (Bluhm, 1982, p. 3). Nor is it likely that an answer lies in a synthesis of philosophical perspectives about the nature of social scientific explanation (Moon, 1975; 1982). Although it would be nice to believe that the problem is basically one of "communication among all scholars committed to understanding and explaining political phenomena" (Graham, 1982, p. 206), the problems run deep, are substantive as well as methodological in nature, and have to do with the very idea of social science and the relationship between social science and politics.

It is probably true, as the advocates of synthesis believe, that there are "no *necessary* barriers that currently prevent discourse across the methodologies and paradigms of political science" (Graham, p. 222). We are not in the situation of the mid-1960s when there were severe obstacles to discussion both within political science and between political science and other disciplines such as economics and philosophy. Clearly there are, in both theory and practice, synthetic exercises that have brought together philosophy, economics, and political science in areas as diverse as public policy analysis and critical theory. And the general ability of political scientists to move between these areas is much more apparent than ever before. Furthermore, the general mood of the early 1980s is not along the lines of the focused intransigent confrontational discourse that marked the 1960s and 1970s. The problems may be more those of pure tolerance.

Brian Barry, whose own work is part of what many believe to be the renaissance in political philosophy, sees, in comparison with the lack of political philosophy in the early 1960s, a positive movement. But he also admits to an occasional "nightmarish feeling that 'the literature' has taken off on an independent life and now carries on like the broomstick bewitched by the sorcerer's apprentice" (1980, p. 283). The question is not whether there is a great deal of political theory and philosophy being written but whether we have a wealth or a "glut" (1980, p. 284) and whether there is any vital dialogue. Many believe that there is not only a need for more "organizational boundary crossing" between political science and political philosophy (Barry, 1977, p. 299) but "a need to improve the quantity and quality of discussion across the different schools that have gradually established enclaves in political theory" (Nelson, 1983, p. 24).

One prediction that seems totally safe is that *PT* and *pt* will never again be one, and it is unlikely that either will become a more concentrated field. The latter is an interdisciplinary body of literature that shows no signs of consolidation, and most of the sentiment seems clearly in favor of pluralism. Everybody on record is hoping for mutual interaction and cross fertilization, but few seem to care if it is actually effected. Since much of *PT* is now a reflection of the structure, or lack of structure, in *pt*, a more central focus there seems just as unlikely. If we look within *PT* for a core of theory directed toward the empirical study of politics in the mode of the behavioral vision, it seems to be very close to disappearing altogether. But there are some who still hold out hope for a unified center.

Most commentators recognize that in one way or another post-behavioralism also means post-positivism. The question is whether there is a life for scientific theory "beyond positivism." Elinor Ostrom suggests that "we are coming to the end of an era in political science, a slow, whimpering end" which indicates that "the hoped for cumulation of knowledge into a coherent body of theory has not occurred" (pp. 11, 13). Individuals such as Ostrom, however, continue to stress "the need for the development of theory as the basis of our discipline." This, however, would be a more eclectic notion of theory that would transcend both "the naive acceptance" of positivism and some of the narrow approaches to empirical analysis that it was used to justify and which are relevant to modern political issues. For Ostrom, as for a number of others who have celebrated the policy turn in contemporary political science, the demands of both science and relevance seem to be met best in the application of economic models involving rational choice and collective choice and the metatheoretical explication of such models. But, again, there is little clear evidence at this point that a unifying vision of political theory will or should emerge from this material (Moon, 1983).

Unity is still the message of most presidential addresses. Warren Miller predicts unification based on the research methods developed since World War II and claims that only problems of inadequate personnel and funding now stand in the way of bringing "political science into a new age of intellectual ferment and maturity as a discipline" which can at once "make a massive contribution to the welfare of the nation while evolving into a conceptually coherent scholarly enterprise" (1981, pp. 14, 15). A basic fact of intellectual continuity in the field is the belief that we belong to an unfinished discipline in which an imminent theoretical breakthrough will not only verify the discipline as a science but demonstrate its relevance to public policy. The question is *exactly* what is to be the form of interaction between public and academic discourse and the vehicle of that interaction. We can see what Merriam, Wilson, Beard, Bentley, Lasswell and others gave for answers to these questions, and we might well ask what, precisely, is the answer of the modern political scientist?

A survey of the presidential addresses to the APSA, as well as various other intellectual signals in the literature, seems to suggest a liaison between political scientists and policy elites that would take place through consultation, the movement of political scientists in and out of the actual policy process, and the influence of journals such as the *Public Interest*. Although the role is not perceived as necessarily uncritical, the principal thrust is more in the direction of service than reform, let alone anything resembling a more basic critique of political institutions. The mood, for the most part, is conservative.

There are, however, some other directions in public policy analysis and the relationship between political science and politics. First of all, it is not merely in Critical Theory that a vision of a critical social science is present (Connolly, 1981). There are even some obvious shifts within what might be taken as the political science establishment. Charles Lindblom, in his 1981 Presidential Address to the APSA, recognized and endorsed the claims of the dissenting academy. He claimed that the discipline as a whole and most of the major figures in the behavioral movement had largely accepted and reinforced the initial premises, research programs, and methods of "a complacent view of the liberal democratic process, government, and state" (1982, p. 9). Even many erstwhile critics, he suggested, are actually "committed to the conventional view and give little sustained analytical attention to the radical model" which is manifest in contemporary neo-Marxist thought and other elements of contemporary political theory such as "phenomenology, hermeneutics, interpretative theory, and critical theory" (pp. 12, 20).

If the history of political science provides any clue, the argument will be noted, but the direction of the discipline will not be fundamentally altered. Whatever the impact of critical notions of political theory and political science on the discipline, the very fact that they remain in the discipline will probably ensure that such discourse remains ultimately academic. Through the medium of education and osmosis, it may have some practical effect but not the form of engagement often implied. There are some things happening in the world of political theory that obviously suggest a more definite idea about how to make political theory political or at least make contact between political theory and politics. A venture such as that represented by Sheldon Wolin's involvement with the journal *Democracy* deserves consideration.

There is an assumption that political theory must, or should, reach a wider public audience and that there must be a mediating mode of discourse. Exactly what this means, or can mean, is more difficult to say. It does not seem that the basic purpose is to lead or support what might be termed movement politics. Neither is it principally an attempt to enter directly the activity of what might be termed conventional politics. It might be more accurately understood as an attempt to evoke in a wide range of educated individuals, in a variety of contexts, a sense of public consciousness and virtue that transcends the mundanely political but which is not confined to the academic world. Yet the project remains bound within the ambiguities of the relationship between political and academic discourse.

The extent to which practical concerns, and the attempt to make such concerns effective, will have an impact on the discipline of political science and the direction of political theory, and, in turn on politics, is a definite question for the 1980s. Archaeological analysis tends to produce skepticism, since it demonstrates the inevitability of mortality and the demise of the present. Digging into the past of American political science is no exception. Furthermore, the history of the sub-field of Political Theory does not demonstrate any great ability to transcend American political culture. As Norman Jacobson has noted, the idea of a social science as the embodiment of a provocative vision has not been indigenous to American political science. Today political theory is bringing many new ideas into the discipline, but a study of the past indicates "that the genius of American social and political science has been less the cultivation of novel ideas than their domesticator" (1982, p. 6). This has been the case in the sub-field of Political Theory.

REFERENCES

Almond, Gabriel. Political theory and political science. *American Political Science Review*, 1966, *60*, 869-879.

Almond, Gabriel. Clouds, clocks, and the study of politics. *World Politics*, 1977, *29*, 489-522.

Anderson, William. Political science north and south. *Journal of Politics*, 1949, *11*, 298-317.

Appel, K-O. *Analytic philosophy of language and the Geisteswissenschaften.* Dordrecht, Holland: D. Reidel, 1967.

Apter, David E. Theory and the study of politics. *American Political Review,* 1957, *51,* 747-62.

Arendt, Hannah. *The human condition.* New York: Doubleday, 1958.

Arendt, Hannah. *Between past and future.* New York: Viking, 1961.

Ashcraft, Richard. Revolutionary politics and Locke's two treatises of government. *Political Theory,* 1980, *8,* 429-86.

Bachrach, Peter. *The theory of democratic elitism.* New York: Lieber-Atherton, 1967.

Bachrach, Peter & Baratz, Morton S. Two faces of power. *American Political Science Review,* 1962, *58,* 947-52.

Barber, Benjamin (Ed.). Political theory in the 1980s: Prospects and topics. *Political Theory,* 1980, *9,* 291-424.

Barry, Brian. The strange death of political theory. *Government and Opposition,* 1980, *15,* 276-78.

Barry, Brian. Do neighbors make good fences? *Political Theory,* 1981, *9,* 293-301.

Bell, Daniel. *The end of ideology.* New York: Free Press, 1960.

Berelson, Bernard & Steiner, Gary. *Human behavior.* New York: Harcourt, Brace, 1964.

Berlin, Isaiah. Does political theory still exist? In Peter Laslett & W. G. Runciman (Eds.). *Philosophy, society and politics.* New York: Barnes and Noble, 1962.

Bernstein, Richard. *The restructuring of political and social theory.* New York: Harcourt, Brace, Jovanovich, 1976.

Bluhm, William T. *Theories of the political system.* Englewood Cliffs, N.J.: Prentice-Hall, 1965.

Bluhm, William T. Introduction: a call for paradigm synthesis. In Bluhm (Ed.). *The paradigm problem in political science.* Durham, N.C.: Carolina Academic Press, 1982.

Bluntschli, J. K. *The theory of the state.* Oxford: Clarendon Press, 1885.

Braybrooke, David (Ed.). *Philosophical problems of the social sciences.* New York: Macmillan, 1965.

Brecht, Arnold. Beyond relativism in political theory. *American Political Science Review,* 1947, *41,* 470-88.

Brecht, Arnold. *Political theory.* Princeton: Princeton University Press, 1959.

Brodbeck, May (Ed.). *Readings in the philosophy of the social sciences.* New York: Macmillan, 1968.

Brown, Robert. *Explanation in social science.* Chicago: Aldine, 1963.

Campbell, Angus *et al.* The American voter. New York: Wiley, 1960.

Catlin, George. *The story of the political philosophers.* New York: McGraw-Hill, 1939.

Charlesworth, James C. (Ed.). *The limits of behavioralism.* Philadelphia: American Academy of Political and Social Science, 1962.

Charlesworth, James C. *A design for political science: Scope, objectives, and methods.* Philadelphia: American Academy of Political and Social Science, 1966.

Cobban, Alfred. The decline of political theory. *Political Science Quarterly,* 1953, *68,* 321-37.

Cobban, Alfred. *In search of humanity.* New York: G. Braziller, 1959.

Cohen, Morris R. *Reason and nature.* New York: Harcourt, Brace, 1931.

Cohen, Morris & Nagel, Ernest. *An introduction to logic and scientific method.* New York: Harcourt, Brace, 1934.

Connolly, William. *Political science and ideology.* New York: Atherton, 1967.

Connolly, William (Ed.). *The bias of pluralism.* New York: Atherton, 1969.

Connolly, William. *Appearance and reality.* Cambridge: Cambridge University Press, 1981.

Crick, Bernard. *The American science of politics.* Berkeley: University of California Press, 1959.

Dahl, Robert. Political theory: truth and consequences. *World Politics*, 1958, *11*, 89-102.

Dahl, Robert. *Who governs?* New Haven: Yale University Press, 1961.

Dallmayr, Fred & McCarthy, Thomas (Eds.). *Understanding and social inquiry.* Notre Dame, IN: University of Notre Dame Press, 1977.

Davis, Lane. The cost of realism. *Western Political Quarterly*, 1964, *17*, 37-46.

de Grazia, Alfred. Preface to four essays on the relation of political theory to research. *Journal of Politics*, 1951, *13*, 35.

Deutsch, Karl. *The nerves of government.* New York: Free Press, 1963.

Deutsch, Karl. On political theory and political action. *American Political Science Review*, 1971, *65*, 11-27.

Deutsch, Karl & Rieselbach, Leroy. Recent trends in political theory and political philosophy. *Annals of the American Academy of Political and Social Science*, 1965, *360*, 139-62.

Driscoll, Jean M. & Hyneman, Charles S. Methods for political scientists. *American Political Science Review*, 1955, *49*, 192-217.

Duncan, Graeme & Lukes, Steven. The new democracy. *Political Studies*, 1963, *11*, 156-177.

Dunning, William A. *A history of political theories* (3 Vols.). New York: Macmillan, 1902, 1905, 1920.

Dworkin, Ronald. *Taking rights seriously.* Cambridge: Harvard University Press, 1977.

Easton, David. The decline of modern political theory. *Journal of Politics*, 1951, *13*, 36-58.

Easton, David. *The political system.* New York: Knopf, 1953.

Easton, David. *A framework for political analysis.* Englewood Cliffs, N.J.: Prentice-Hall, 1965(a).

Easton, David. *A systems analysis of political life.* New York: Wiley, 1965(b).

Easton, David (Ed.). *Varieties of political theory.* Englewood Cliffs, N.J.: Prentice-Hall, 1966.

Easton, David. Political science. In David L. Sills (Ed.). *International encyclopedia of the social sciences* (Vol. 12). New York: Macmillan, 1968.

Easton, David. The new revolution in political science. *American Political Science Review*, 1969, *63*, 1051-61.

Eckstein, Harry. Political theory and the study of politics. *American Political Science Review*, 1956, *50*, 475-87.

Eldersveld, Samuel. Theory and method in voting behavior. *Journal of Politics*, 1951, *13*, 70-87.

Eulau, Heinz. The skill revolution and consultative commonwealth. *American Political Science Review*, 1973, *67*, 169-91.

Eulau, Heinz. Drift of a discipline. *American Behavioral Scientist*, 1977, *21*, 3-10.

Flathman, Richard. *The public interest.* New York: Wiley, 1966.

Flathman, Richard. *Political obligation.* New York: Atheneum, 1972.

Flathman, Richard. *The practice of rights.* Cambridge: Cambridge University Press, 1977.

Ford, Henry Jones. The scope of political science. *Proceedings of the American Political Science Association*, 1906.

Freeman, Michael & Robertson, David (Eds.). *The frontiers of political theory.* New York: St. Martin's Press, 1980.

Frohock, Fred M. *The nature of political inquiry.* Englewood Cliffs, N.J.: Prentice-Hall, 1967.

Germino, Dante. The revival of political theory. *Journal of Politics*, 1963, *25*, 437-60.

Gettell, Raymond G. *Introduction to political science.* Boston: Ginn and Co., 1910.

Gettell, Raymond G. Nature and scope of present political theory. *Proceedings of the American Political Science Association,* 1914.

Gettell, Raymond G. *History of political thought.* New York: Century, 1924.

Gibson, Quentin. *The logic of social inquiry.* New York: Humanities, 1960.

Glaser, William A. The types and uses of political theory. *Social Research,* 1955, *22,* 275-96.

Goodnow, Frank J. The work of the APSA. *Proceedings of the American Political Science Association,* 1905.

Graham, George J. & Carey, George W. *The post-behavioral era.* New York: McKay, 1972.

Graham, George J. A critical overview: The present status of the synthesis question. In William T. Bluhm (Ed.). *The paradigm problem in political science.* Durham, N.C.: Carolina Academic Press, 1982.

Green, Philip & Levinson, Sanford (Eds.). *Power and community.* New York: Vintage Books, 1970.

Greenstein, F. & Polsby, N. (Eds.). *Handbook of political science.* Reading, MA: Addison-Wesley, 1975.

Greer, Scott. *The logic of social inquiry.* Chicago: Aldine, 1969.

Gregor, James A. *An introduction to metapolitics.* New York: Free Press, 1871.

Gunnell, John G. Social science and political reality: The problem of explanation. *Social Research,* 1968, *34,* 159-201.

Gunnell, John G. Deduction, explanation, and social scientific inquiry. *American Political Science Review,* 1969, *63,* 1233-46.

Gunnell, John G. *Philosophy, science, and political inquiry.* Morristown, N.J.: General Learning Press, 1975.

Gunnell, John G. *Political theory: tradition and interpretation.* Boston: Little-Brown, 1979.

Habermas, Jurgen. *Knowledge and human interests.* Boston: Beacon, 1971.

Hacker, Andrew. Capital and carbuncles: The great books reappraised. *American Political Science Review,* 1954, *48,* 775-86.

Haddow, Anna. *Political science in American colleges and universities, 1636-1900.* New York: Appleton Century, 1939.

Hallowell, John H. Politics and ethics. *American Political Science Review,* 1944, *38,* 639-55.

Hanson, N. R. *Patterns of discovery.* Cambridge: Cambridge University Press, 1958.

Hare, R. M. *The language of morals.* Oxford: Oxford University Press, 1952.

Hare, R. M. *Freedom and reason.* Oxford: Oxford University Press, 1963.

Hempel, Carl. *Aspects of scientific explanation.* New York: Free Press, 1965.

Herbert, Wray. Political theory. *Humanities Report,* 1981, *3,* 4-9.

Horowitz, Irving (Ed.). *Power, politics, and people: The collected essays of C. W. Mills.* New York: Ballantine Books, 1963.

Irish, Marian D. Advance of the discipline. *Journal of Politics,* 1968, *30,* 291-310.

Isaak, Alan. *Scope and methods of political science.* Homewood, Ill.: Dorsey Press, 1969.

Jacobson, Norman. The unity of political theory. In Roland Young (Ed.). *Approaches to the study of politics.* Evanston, Ill.: Northwestern University Press, 1958.

Jacobson, Norman. Remarks. Presented at APSA annual meeting, Denver, Colo., 1982.

Jaffa, Harry. The case against political theory. *Journal of Politics,* 1960, *22,* 259-75.

Jenkin, Thomas. *The study of political theory.* New York: Doubleday, 1955.

Kaplan, Abraham. *The conduct of inquiry.* San Francisco: Chandler, 1964.

Kariel, Henry. *The decline of American liberalism.* Stanford: Stanford University Press, 1961.

Kariel, Henry. *Open systems.* Itasca, Ill.: Peacock, 1969.

Kateb, George. *Political theory: Its nature and uses.* New York: St. Martin's Press, 1968.

Kateb, George. The condition of political theory. *American Behavioral Scientist,* 1977, *21,* 135-59.

Kaufman, Felix. *Methodology of the social sciences.* New York: Oxford University Press, 1944.

Key, V. O., Jr. The state of the discipline. *American Political Science Review,* 1958, *52,* 961-71.

Kress, Paul. Against epistemology. *Journal of Politics,* 1979, *41,* 526-42.

Kuhn, Thomas. *The structure of scientific revolutions.* Chicago: University of Chicago Press, 1962.

Lane, Robert. Politics of consensus in an age of affluence. *American Political Science Review,* 1965, *59,* 874-95.

Lane, Robert. The decline of politics and ideology in a knowledgeable society. *American Sociological Review,* 1966, *31,* 649-62.

LaPalombara, Joseph. Decline of ideology: A dissent and interpretation. *American Political Science Review,* 1966, *60,* 5-16.

Laslett, Peter (Ed.). *Philosophy, politics and society.* New York: Barnes and Noble, 1956.

Laslett, Peter. Introduction. In Peter Laslett & W. G. Runciman (Eds.). *Philosophy politics and society.* New York: Barnes and Noble, 1967.

Laslett, Peter & Fishkin, James (Eds.). *Philosophy, politics and society.* New Haven: Yale University Press, 1979.

Lasswell, Harold. Discussion. *American Political Science Review,* 1950, *44,* 422-25.

Lasswell, Harold. *Psychopathology and politics.* Chicago: Chicago University Press, 1930.

Lasswell, Harold. *Democracy through public opinion.* Menasha, Wis.: George Banta, 1941.

Lasswell, Harold & Kaplan, Abraham. *Power and society.* New Haven: Yale University Press, 1950.

Leiserson, Avery. Charles Merriam, Max Weber, and the search for synthesis in political science. *American Political Science Review,* 1975, *69,* 175-85.

Lindblom, Charles E. *Politics and markets.* New York: Basic Books, 1977.

Lindblom, Charles E. Another state of mind. *American Political Science Review,* 1982, *76,* 9-21.

Lippincott, Benjamin. The bias of American political science. *Journal of Politics,* 1940, *2,* 125-39.

Lippincott, Benjamin. Political theory in the United States. *Contemporary Political Science.* Paris: UNESCO, 1950.

Lipset, Seymour M. *Political man.* Garden City: Doubleday, 1960.

Louch, A. R. *Explanation and human action.* Berkeley: University of California Press, 1966.

Lowi, Theodore. *The end of liberalism.* New York: Norton, 1969.

MacIntyre, Alasdair. A mistake about causality in social science. In Peter Laslett & W. G. Runciman (Eds.). *Philosophy, politics and society.* Oxford: Basil Blackwell, 1962.

Marcuse, Herbert. *Reason and revolution.* New York: Oxford, 1941.

Marcuse, Herbert. *Reason and revolution.* New York: Oxford University Press, 1941.

McCoy, Charles & Playford, John (Eds.). *Apolitical politics.* New York: Thomas Y. Crowell, 1967.

McDonald, Neil A. & Rosenau, James N. Political theory as an academic field and intellectual activity. *Journal of Politics,* 1968, *30,* 311-44.

Meehan, Eugene. *The theory and method of political analysis.* Homewood, Ill.: Dorsey Press, 1965.

Merriam, Charles. The present state of the study of politics. *American Political Science Review,* 1921, *15,* 173-85.

Merriam, Charles. Progress report of the committee on political research. *American Political Science Review,* 1923, *17,* 274-312.

Merriam, Charles. Report of the national conference on the science of politics. *American Political Science Review,* 1924, *18,* 119-66.

Merriam, Charles. *New aspects of politics.* Chicago: Chicago University Press, 1925.

Miller, Eugene F. Positivism, historicism, and political inquiry. *American Political Science Review,* 1972, *66,* 796-817.

Miller, Warren E. The role of research in the unification of a discipline. *American Political Science Review,* 1981, *75,* 9-16.

Mills, C. Wright. *The power elite.* New York: Oxford University Press, 1956.

Moon, Donald J. The logic of political inquiry. In F. Greenstein & N. Polsby (Eds.). *Handbook of political science* (Vol. I). Reading, Mass.: Addison-Wesley, 1975.

Moon, Donald J. Interpretation, theory and human emancipation. In Elinor Ostrom (Ed.). *Strategies of political inquiry.* Beverly Hills: Sage, 1982.

Moore, Barrington, Jr. *Political power and social theory.* Cambridge: Harvard University Press, 1958.

Nagel, Ernest. *The structure of science.* New York: Harcourt, Brace and World, 1961.

Natanson, Maurice (Ed.). *Philosophy of the social sciences.* New York: Random House, 1963.

Nelson, John S. Natures and futures for political theory. In Nelson (Ed.). *What should political theory be now?* Albany: State University of New York Press, 1983.

Nozick, Robert. *Anarchy, state and utopia.* New York: Basic Books, 1974.

O'Connor, James. *The fiscal crisis of the state.* New York: St. Martin's Press, 1973.

Ostrom, Elinor. Beyond positivism. In Ostrom (Ed.). *Strategies of political inquiry.* Beverly Hills: Sage, 1982.

Partridge, P. H. Politics, philosophy, ideology. *Political Studies,* 1961, *9,* 217-35.

Pitkin, Hanna. *The concept of representation.* Berkeley: University of California Press, 1967.

Pitkin, Hanna. *Wittgenstein and justice.* Berkeley: University of California Press, 1972.

Pocock, J. G. A. *Politics, language, and time.* New York: Atheneum, 1971.

Polsby, Nelson. *Community power and political theory.* New Haven: Yale University Press, 1963.

Pool, Ithiel de Sola. Foreword. In Pool (Ed.), *Contemporary political science: Toward empirical theory.* New York: McGraw-Hill, 1967.

Popper, Karl. *The logic of scientific discovery.* New York: Science Editions, 1961.

Ranney, Austin, 1976. The divine science of politics: Political engineering in American culture. *American Political Science Review,* 1976, *70,* 140-48.

Rawls, John. *A theory of justice.* Cambridge: Harvard University Press, 1971.

Redford, Emmett S. Reflections on a discipline. *American Political Science Review,* 1961, *55,* 755-62.

Research in political behavior. *American Political Science Review,* 1952, *46,* 1003-45.

Research in comparative politics. *American Political Science Review,* 1953, *47,* 641-679.

Richter, Melvin. Introduction. In Richter (Ed.), *Political theory and political education.* Princeton: Princeton University Press, 1980.

Riker, William H. The future of a science of politics. *American Behavioral Scientist,* 1977, *21,* 11-38.

Riker, William H. Political theory and the art of heresthetics. (This volume), 1983.

Rousseas, Stephen & Farganis, James. American politics and the end of ideology. *British Journal of Sociology*, 1963, *14*, 347-62.

Rudner, Richard. *Philosophy of social science.* Englewood Cliffs, N.J.: Prentice-Hall, 1966.

Runciman, W. G. *Social science and political theory.* Cambridge: Cambridge University Press, 1963.

Sabine, George. *A history of political theory.* New York: Holt, Rinehart, and Winston, 1937.

Sabine, George. What is a political theory? *Journal of Politics*, 1939, *1*, 1-16.

Schaar, John H. & Wolin, Sheldon S. Essays on the scientific study of politics: A critique. *American Political Science Review*, 1963, *57*, 125-50.

Schutz, Alfred. *The phenomenology of the social world.* Evanston, Ill.: Northwestern University Press, 1967.

Shklar, Judith. *After utopia.* Princeton: Princeton University Press, 1957.

Simon, Herbert. Discussion. *American Political Science Review*, 1950, *44*, 407-11.

Simon, Herbert. Replies and comments. *American Political Science Review*, 1952, *46*, 494-96.

Skinner, Quentin. Meaning and understanding in the history of ideas. *History and Theory*, 1969, *8*, 3-53.

Skocpol, Theda. *States and social revolutions.* Cambridge: Cambridge University Press, 1979.

Smith, David G. Political science and political theory. *American Political Science Review*, 1957, *51*, 734-46.

Smith, Munroe. The domain of political science. *Political Science Quarterly*, 1886, *1*, 1-8.

Smithburg, Donald W. Political theory and public administration. *Journal of Politics*, 1951, *13*, 59-69.

Somit, Albert & Tanenhaus, Joseph. *The development of American political science.* New York: Irvington, 1982.

Spragens, Thomas A., Jr. *The dilemma of contemporary political theory.* New York: Dunellen, 1973.

Storing, Herbert J. (Ed.). *Essays on the scientific study of politics.* New York: Free Press, 1962.

Strauss, Leo. *Natural right and history.* Chicago: University of Chicago Press, 1953.

Strauss, Leo. *What is political philosophy?* Glencoe, Ill.: Free Press, 1959.

Strauss, Leo & Cropsey, Joseph (Eds.). *History of political theory.* Chicago: Rand McNally, 1963.

Tarlton, Charles D. A rope of sand: Interpreting Locke's first treatise of government. *The Historical Journal*, 1979, *21*, 43-74.

Taylor, Charles. *The explanation of behavior.* New York: Humanities, 1964.

Taylor, Charles. Neutrality in political science. In Peter Laslett & W. G. Runciman (Eds.). *Philosophy, politics and society.* New York: Barnes and Noble, 1967.

Thorson, Thomas L. Political values and analytic philosophy. *Journal of Politics*, 1961, *23*, 711-24.

Thorson, Thomas L. *The logic of democracy.* New York: Holt, Rinehart and Winston, 1962.

Toth, Kathleen. Method and value: Lessons from the odyssey of political theory. Presented at American Political Science Association annual meeting, Denver, Colo., 1982.

Toulmin, Stephen. *An examination of the place of reason in ethics.* Cambridge: Cambridge University Press, 1950.

Truman, David B. Disillusion and regeneration: The search for a discipline. *American Political Science Review*, 1965, *59*, 865-73.

Van Dyke, Vernon. *Political science: A philosophical analysis.* Stanford, Calif.: Stanford University Press, 1960.

Voegelin, Eric. *The new science of politics.* Chicago: University of Chicago Press, 1952.

Voegelin, Eric. *Order and history* (Vol. I). Baton Rouge: Louisiana State University Press, 1956.

Wahlke, John C. Pre-behavioralism in political science. *American Political Science Review,* 1979, *73,* 68-77.

Waldo, Dwight. *Political science in the United States: A trend report.* Paris: UNESCO, 1956.

Walker, Jack L. A critique of the elitist theory of democracy. *American Political Science Review,* 1966, *60,* 285-95.

Waxman, Chaim (Ed.) *The end-of-ideology debate.* New York: Simon and Schuster, 1969.

Weldon, T. D. *The vocabulary of politics.* London: Penguin, 1953.

Weldon, T. D. Political principles. In Peter Laslett (Ed.). *Philosophy, politics and society.* New York: Barnes and Noble, 1956.

White, Leonard D. Political science, mid-century. *Journal of Politics,* 1950, *12,* 13-19.

Whyte, William Foote. A challenge to political scientists. *American Political Science Review,* 1943, *37,* 692-97.

Willoughby, W. W. *An examination of the nature of the state; A study in political philosophy.* New York: Macmillan, 1896.

Willoughby, W. W. The political science association. *Political Science Quarterly,* 1904, *19,* 107-11.

Wilson, Francis G. The work of the political theory panel. *American Political Science Review,* 1944, *38,* 726-31.

Winch, Peter. *The idea of a social science.* London: Routledge and Kegan Paul, 1958.

Wolfe, Alan. *The limits of legitimacy.* New York: Free Press, 1977.

Wolfe, Alan & Surkin, Marvin (Eds.). *An end to political science.* New York: Basic Books, 1970.

Wolff, Robert Paul. *The poverty of liberalism.* Boston: Beacon, 1969.

Wolin, Sheldon S. *Politics and vision.* Boston: Little-Brown, 1960.

Wolin, Sheldon S. Political theory: Trends and goals. In David L. Sills (Ed.). *International encyclopedia of the social sciences* (Vol. 12). New York: Macmillan, 1968.

Wolin, Sheldon S. Political theory as a vocation. *American Political Science Review,* 1969, *63,* 1062-82.

Woolsey, Theodore D. *Political science; Or, the state theoretically and practically considered.* New York: Scribner, Armstrong, 1878.

2

Political Theory and the
Art of Heresthetics

William H. Riker

My assignment for this essay is to review the present state of the field of political theory. This I will do by examining, first, the main line of its development during the last generation. Then I will look to the future, not only at the continuation of this main line of scholarship, but also at some possibly fruitful new directions, as, for example, the art of heresthetics.

It is necessary in the beginning, because of a usage peculiar to political science, to specify exactly what political theory is. In most scientific disciplines, the word "theory" refers to a set of deductively related sentences that together describe the portion of the world studied with a particular discipline. Etymologically this is correct; "theory" weds observation and contemplation. In political science, however, the word "theory" has come to refer primarily to moral philosophy. While I recognize the necessity and importance of moral philosophy for political studies, in this paper I intend to use the word "theory" as it is used in other sciences. Given our tradition, this is rather difficult because, until recently, there has been no set of sentences about politics to which "theory" could be applied with etymological justification. Beginning, however, with the publication of Duncan Black's essay, "On the Rationale of Group Decision Making" (*Journal of Political Economy*, 1948, although the main ideas were, as noted in Coase, 1981, worked out six years earlier), there has existed a deductive and testable theory about political events. Political theory developed gradually through the next two decades, and during the 1970s it came of age. It was the subject of books, essays, conferences, and convention panels, and now even a summary essay in a book on the state of the art.

I

The content of political theory is the authoritative allocation of values, following Easton's (1954) definition of politics, in that it involves the amalgamation of individual preferences into a social choice and the subsequent enforcement of the result. At this quite general level, the goal of political theory is to identify the conditions for an equilibrium of preferences. Such an equilibrium is a social choice that the members of every sub-group in the society that are capable of bringing about a social decision prefer to any other alternative. This equilibrium is one the society will arrive at for certain, regardless of its particular institutions; and, if by reason of some obstruction the society is deflected from it or forced to abandon it, the society nevertheless will return to it if the obstruction is removed. Equilibrium of this sort is there-fore a generally accepted outcome which is, moreover, self-enforcing because of the desire of individuals to arrive at it.

The goal of identifying the conditions for equilibrium is closely parallel to the goals of other scientific disciplines, both social and physical, in which the specification of conditions for equilibria is a central theme. The history of political theory over the last forty years has consisted largely of increasingly precise specification and increasingly deeper analysis of equilibrium conditions.[1]

As previously noted, Duncan Black (1948, 1958) began the construction of theory by looking for an equilibrium of majority rule. He soon rediscovered the paradox of voting (initially discovered by Condorcet, 1785, and then subsequently overlooked), the significance of which is that, when it occurs in a set of individual preference orders, it guarantees that there will be no major-ity winner (i.e., disequilibrium) within that set. Looking for a way around the paradox, Black devised the condition of the single-peakedness of a set of in-dividual preference orders as a sufficient — but not necessary — condition for the avoidance of the paradox and thus for the guarantee of an equilibrium. This was an excellent beginning. Among its other virtues, the condition of single-peakedness is highly practical because it allows for ready specification of the substantive content of an equilibrium outcome as the median voter's most preferred alternative.[2] Since it is often easy to identify the median voter, it is also easy in many analyses of public policy and political conflict to spell out the concrete details of the equilibrium social choice. As might be expected, this is the feature of Black's work most widely used in practical political and economic studies.

For the development of political theory, however, a more significant vir-tue of the condition of single-peakedness is that it has an obvious political interpretation. It reveals that an equilibrium among disputing voters rests on an underlying agreement among them about the dimension of political con-flict. The fact that equilibrium rests, in this case, on some kind of partial agreement has led to the specification of a variety of other conditions of equilibrium, all based on some kind of similarity of preferences, for example, value restrictedness, extremal restriction, limited agreement, separability, etc. (See Fishburn, 1970, for a method of classifying and generating all possi-ble conditions for equilibrium.)

A third and, for theory-building, perhaps most valuable feature of the condition of single-peakedness is that, once constructed out of the arrange-ment of preferences on a dimension of judgment, it may appropriately be used to inquire into the fragility of the condition. This Black and Newing (1951) did by analyzing the effect of introducing a second standard of judg-ment into a committee of three voters. In this case, they managed to find some special equilibria by imposing particular agendas (e.g., sequential voting on first one dimension, then another, then back to the first, *et seq.*). But, in the general case, the similarity of tastes required for equilibrium almost entirely disappeared, even with as few as three voters. The net effect of Black's work was, therefore, to identify conditions for equilibria in special cases, such as single-peakedness, while at the same time generating considerable doubt about the possibility of discovering a general equilibrium.

Arrow (1951) confirmed these doubts by demonstrating the possibility of outcomes analogous to the paradox of voting in any (unspecified) method of amalgamating individual preference. He proved that any such method, satisfying — as does majority rule — some elementary conditions of fairness, suffers from the same kind of defect as majority rule, namely the admission of some cases in which individually transitive preference orders amalgamate into an intransitive social outcome. Many writers have modified or explicated Arrow's theorem in order to soften its impact — for a survey, see Riker (1982a, pp. 123-136) — but his main point remains valid: There is an inherent conflict between voter-dominated procedures and logically consistent outcomes. For political applications, where it is necessary to choose a unique winner, it may be that consistency does not greatly matter. But as Arrow (1963) himself recognized and as Plott (1973) emphasized, failures of consistency mean that the outcome is not independent of the procedure by which it is reached. Hence random variations in procedure imply random variations in outcomes, which is just exactly what is meant by a disequilibrium of tastes. Hence Arrow's theorem may be regarded as a generalization — to all methods of amalgamating tastes — of the fundamental disequilibrium that Black perceived in majority rule. The various elaborations, refinements, and modifications of Arrow's theorem serve to emphasize the ineradicability of the potential for disequilibrium; Gibbard's (1968) theorem — that all methods of voting to amalgamate tastes or values can be manipulated by sophisticated voting reveals one concrete way in which the disequilibrium may be effected.

The fact that the potential for disequilibrium is ineradicable implies nothing, however, about the frequency of disequilibrium. Though ineradicable, it might — or might not — be so rare as to be insignificant. One line of investigation on this theme is to calculate the expected frequency of non-equilibrium outcomes, given that voters pick preference orders at random and equiprobably (Niemi & Weisberg, 1968; Garman & Kamien, 1968; DeMeyer & Plott, 1970; Gehrlein & Fishburn, 1976). The conclusion is that, as the numbers of alternatives and participants increase, the expectation of disequilibrium very quickly approaches infinity, although just a bit of prior agreement on values lowers the expectation of disequilibrium remarkably (Niemi, 1969; Fishburn, 1973b). The usefulness of this kind of inquiry is severely limited, however, because the assumption of equiprobability or of any particular degree of agreement in picking preference orders is arbitrary and unrealistic, especially when it may be worthwhile for participants to manipulate the distribution of preference orders.

A more fruitful line of investigation about the frequency of disequilibrium is to establish the conditions for equilibrium under a variety of assumptions. In one sense this is an examination of the robustness of conditions like single-peakedness, which seem initially to guarantee a considerable amount of equilibrium in one dimension of choice. However, Kramer (1973) examined these conditions for cases of more than one dimension, when voters' tastes can be represented by quasi-concave differentiable utility functions, and showed that, with even a modest amount of heterogeneity of tastes, majority rule breaks down completely. Kramer's work in effect demolished various special guarantees of equilibrium.

Another possibility is to define what is required for equilibrium. This direction of inquiry has led to an even more dramatic conclusion: equilibrium is nearly impossible. Black and Newing (1951) began the inquiry, as already noted above, by studying the condition for majority rule when three voters used two standards of judgment. They showed that even in quite constrained circumstances a sufficient condition for equilibrium was difficult to satisfy. Plott (1967) elaborated on this result by defining a sufficient condition for an equilibrium of majority rule when $m(\geqslant 3)$ voters use $n(\geqslant 2)$ standards of judgment to select among continuous alternatives. Plott's condition (see also Cohen, 1979) turns out to be so restrictive that even as few as five voters and two standards render disequilibrium almost certain. Schofield (1978b), taking a superficially different tack, defined a condition for an alternative to be undefeatable by any other alternative in its neighborhood. This condition is also extraordinarily restrictive, revealing that equilibrium is highly unlikely, unless tastes are extremely similar, and, indeed, is impossible when $n \geqslant \dfrac{m+3}{2}$.

The coup de grace for the expectation of equilibrium was supplied by McKelvey (1976) when he looked into the possibility of a small set of alternatives which together might be in equilibrium. The motivation for this research was the idea that, in a case with no majority-preferred alternative (i.e., disequilibrium), a small set—call it T—of similar alternatives might, even though themselves in a cycle, each beat all alternatives not in T. If so, there would be a kind of equilibrium outcome, not unique, of course, but nevertheless stable and predictable in the sense that it would always be a member of the set T, the "top cycle." McKelvey showed, however, that, given continuous alternatives and at least two standards of judgment, the set T is either a Plott equilibrium (which is very rare) or *all* points in the space. This means that any possible outcome is a feasible outcome, which is complete disequilibrium.[3]

This is where the matter now stands. (See Fiorina & Shepsle, 1982; Aldrich & Rohde, 1982; and Schofield, 1982b.) In the abstract case, with no institution assumed and the fewest possible restrictions on individuals' tastes or values, there is no reason to expect equilibrium. The generality and significance of this conclusion is sometimes misunderstood because it is believed to apply only to situations in which outcomes are chosen by voting. But on the contrary, the application is universal. If there is a majority preferred social policy, then, however it may be prescribed, it is welcomed and supported by that majority. Suppose it is prescribed by a dictator. That fact in itself does not make the majority that wants it unwilling to accept it, although perhaps—and this is a matter of local custom—the members of that majority might be even happier to have prescribed it for themselves. Furthermore, this contented majority is willing to retain the preferred policy, perhaps even to defend it; this is precisely what is meant by equilibrium. Obviously equilibrium is based primarily on the actual distribution of tastes and only incidentally, if at all, on the process of amalgamation. On the other hand, if there is no majority preferred alternative, then *any* alternative chosen as the socially enforceable outcome is, by definition, disliked by a majority. The dislike has nothing to do with the way the outcome is chosen—though commonly the majority dissidents blame the process that has frustrated them. And this irrelevance is revealed by the fact that, were another outcome to be chosen by a "better" process, there would still be another dissident majority denouncing the outcome and probably blaming the process. Thus, even if there is no institution (such as voting) by which participants can discover that a majority is dissatisfied, there is still a motive for every one of the individual members of that majority to search for a "better" outcome. This is the essence of disequilibrium and it derives, not from particular methods of amalgamating tastes (e.g., monarchy, oligarchy, democracy) but rather from the distribution of tastes in society. Hence, the theory developed by Black, Arrow, Plott, Schofield, and McKelvey is portentously relevant to all politics, regardless of whether or not particular forms of government involve decision by voting under majority rule.

II

However general the disequilibrium of tastes may be in theory, it is obvious that in the real world there do exist many local or partial equilibria which take the form of recurrent and often reaffirmed outcomes of particular categories of events. It is the task of political theory to explain the sources of these local equilibria. I turn now to an assessment of how well theorists have performed this task.

Inasmuch as something of the same situation (i.e., a fragile or nonexistent general equilibrium, along with strong partial equilibria) prevails in the science of economics, it is possible to begin the assessment by establishing a standard of comparison for the accomplishments of political theory. Economic theorists have long sought to identify a general equilibrium, quite consciously ever since the speculations of Walras and Edgeworth and at least implicitly since the days of Adam Smith. Although the economists' specified general equilibrium is confined to one institutional setting (i.e., the competitive market) that, by its structure, contains restraints (e.g., concave indifference curves) not found in the majority rule setting for a political equilibrium, the goal of a fully identified general equilibrium, divorced from institutions, has eluded them. All the equilibria defined and elaborated have stipulated special institutions (such as *tâtonnement* or coalition-formation of any possible sort, etc.) which, because they involve stochastic variation in costs of organization and information, fail to admit unqualified prediction or description of equilibrium outcomes. Certain tentative equilibria can, however, be identified and theorists can infer certain features of markets from them. Unfortunately the equilibria identified are extremely fragile, and probably therefore meaningless, because of the presence of these stochastically variable elements of preference (Weintraub, 1979; Fiorina & Shepsle, 1982). Consequently, the main bulk of economic science deals with partial equilibria, especially equilibrium prices for particular commodities as determined by quantities demanded and supplied. This kind of analysis has been extremely enlightening because it has, for example, led to non-intuitive revelations about the counter-productive effects of such policies as tariffs, price controls, subsidies, and monopolies. In a sense, however, it has been an easy kind of analysis because it has been based on highly constrained preferences (e.g., negatively sloping demand curves). The moral is that economics, clearly the most scientifically successful of the social sciences, has benefitted from some powerful simplifications not readily available in other social scientific work.

Political scientists, lacking some principle as widely applicable as the law of demand, have not been as successful as economists in identifying partial equilibria. Nevertheless, they have identified some, even though it is necessary for them to overcome more obstacles to theorizing than it is for economists. To illustrate this success and to point out one extremely important common feature of successful theorizing, I shall list three instances of fairly well described partial equilibria, chosen because they have been the subject of recent work.

1. *Duverger's Law:* This is the proposition that plurality voting is associated with two-party systems, or, to phrase it in terms of partial equilibria, the equilibrium number of political parties is, given the use of the plurality rule for deciding on the winner, exactly two. This is a nineteenth century observation that was eventually provided with a theoretical base in the form of a rational choice theory of individual behavior, namely that voters and political supporters choose the candidate with the highest expected value. In the context of plurality voting, this kind of individual choice eliminates third parties and thus stabilizes the two-party system. A number of recent studies have offered convincing evidence of the existence of rational individual choice in precisely the kind of voting involved in Duverger's Law (Black, 1978; Cain, 1978; Lemieux, 1977; Benzel and Sanders, 1979). I have recently surveyed the history of this law to illustrate: (1) its reformulation into progressively more precise and defensible sentences; and (2) its support with increasingly persuasive evidence of the validity of the underlying theory of rational choice (Riker, 1982b).

2. *The initiation of war:* One main intention of students of politics since ancient times has been to identify the cause of war. To do so would be equivalent to specifying a partial equilibrium, because a partial equilibrium is simply the situation that occurs when a cause (i.e., a necessary and sufficient condition) is present. Until recently, no one had been able to state and support either a necessary or a sufficient condition and the study of the cause of war had been largely anecdotal. Bueno de Mesquita (1981), however, formulates a precise statement of a necessary condition for warfare as well as convincing evidence that this condition applies across cultures and through a fairly wide space of time. The condition is that rulers who initiate war have a positive expected value for the anticipated outcome. This condition goes far beyond the conventional notion that rulers of more powerful nations start wars against less powerful ones. Since it is expressed in terms of expected utility rather than power, it allows for the inclusion of ideology and thus admits

application to situations in which, for example, weaker nations attack stronger ones or a ruler attacks allies. The expected utility analysis of international politics is just beginning (Gilpin, 1981) and one can hope that Bueno de Mesquita's necessary condition may ultimately be elaborated into a necessary and sufficient one.

3. *The size of parliamentary coalitions for the formation of cabinets:* Some years ago I enunciated the size principle (Riker, 1963) that, in situations with a constant sum character, participants form minimally winning coalitions. Although my derivation of this principle from the characteristic function of an n-person game has been (mistakenly) disputed (Butterworth, 1971; Hardin, 1976), it has now also been derived from theories about the solution of n-person games (Shepsle, 1974; Schofield, 1978a). It can, therefore, be regarded as well established theoretically. Its empirical validity is somewhat less certain, although it has been subjected to a large amount of testing in analyses of coalition-formation in the real world and in the laboratory. Some of this testing has been irrelevant because the situations studied have been non-constant sum, but cabinet formation is one kind of situation that, at least in the long run, should be constant sum. (That is, what is won or lost by cabinet coalitions is the chance to run the country and this should have about the same value over a period of years.) The evidence has, however, turned out to be ambiguous. Many coalitions have been larger (or smaller) than minimal and so a number of writers have sought to modify the principle with considerations of ideological similarity (DeSwaan, 1973; Axelrod, 1970). Interestingly enough, these modifications have turned out to be unnecessary when cabinets have been analyzed on a long-run basis. While oversized and undersized coalitions are often formed, they have not lasted very long; minimal winning coalitions last (Dodd, 1976). Recently Schofield (1982a) has gone over a set of data similar to, but larger than, Dodd's in order to study the stability of cabinets. He has found that the size principle predicts the duration of governments quite well. (This suggests that cabinet formation and support is indeed a constant sum game, though there may be ideological variations of a non-constant sum nature in the initial formation of cabinets.) In any event, the work of Dodd and Schofield establishes a theory of equilibrium about cabinet formation, provides good evidence of its credibility, and tends to verify a broader political law, namely the size principle.

III

These three examples of partial equilibrium are not intended to be representative of all branches of political science, although it does happen that they come from different traditions of empirical work. Indeed, in order to collect a reasonable sample, it is necessary to look into several such traditions; to date no one tradition could, in itself, yield as many as three examples. This is, of course, quite different from economic science, where many sub-fields would yield several examples of theoretically justified and empirically validated partial equilibria.

One appropriate question from this survey is, then: Why are the examples so few? I will undertake to offer some answers, in part as a guide to the improvement of the productivity of political theorizing.

One answer is, as I have already indicated, the fact that political science lacks a widely applicable, fundamental, and well-verified law of political behavior comparable to the law of demand. As a result, we political scientists have had no compass to guide us through the thickets of facts and we have, therefore, been prone to build theories around regularities we have happened, more or less randomly, to observe.

But this situation need not continue. We still have no widely applicable empirical law, but we do have in rational choice theory a widely applicable method of analysis. The proposition that, in political affairs, people choose the action (from among several) that yields the largest expected utility is assumed in the justification of Duverger's law; it is the starting point for the statement of Bueno de Mesquita's necessary condition for war; and, in Schofield's formulation at least, it is the basis for an equilibrium in the size of cabinet coalitions. It is no accident, I believe, that these three more or less validated theories of equilibrium share the rational choice assumption. As Ordeshook and I have argued elsewhere (Riker & Ordeshook, 1973, ch. 2), this assumption assures that actors in the political model behave regularly. It plays, indeed, the same role in contemporary social science that the principle of no action at a distance played in eighteenth-century physics: It banishes witchery and other inexplicable variations from the model. If there are regularities to be observed in the world—as indeed there are—then a theory in which regularities are anticipated can conceivably describe them, while approaches postulating actions based on emotional vagaries and variable intentions have no place for regularities and cannot possibly be used to explain them.

Although there are good reasons to believe that rational choice analysis is the traditional paradigm for politics, just as it has been for economics, political scientists have on the whole never quite adopted the rational choice model as a generally accepted paradigm. Now that our understanding of the paradigm has become conscious and explicit, we have begun to exploit the technique of rational choice analysis and it seems reasonable to expect that, as we learn how to use it better, we will be more successful, perhaps even as successful as economists.

A tool is not enough, however. We also need some understanding of how we should use it. It is the absence of this understanding that serves as a second answer to the question of why examples of partial equilibria are so few in political science. As many philosophers of science have pointed out, the selection of facts to be gathered in a science is largely dictated by the scientists' conception of what they are doing. In the initial stages of any science the professionals accept lay and common sensical categories for inquiry. Thus, for example, in the beginnings of biology the main lines of endeavor were anatomy, medicine, and taxonomy. But as the questions for research came to be posed by biologists themselves, the main fields became genetics, evolution and biochemistry, subjects of which the laity knows little and to which common sense has nothing to contribute. Similarly, in political science until now, subjects of research have typically been determined by the interests of rulers or reformers who want to use scholars' discoveries to keep or get control of society. This resulted in a science that consisted of the categorization of institutions and the compilation of rules of thumb about techniques of political management.

One great contribution of political theory, with its emphasis on the amalgamation and manipulation of tastes, has been to redirect the questions of political science away from the interests of rulers and reformers into the description of what both kinds of manipulators do. The goal of a general equilibrium theory is the identification of the consequences of distributions of tastes. This leads to questions about the actions dictated by particular distributions of taste, to questions about the origin, manipulation, and modification of tastes, and to questions about the processes by which tastes are transformed into social decisions. Unfortunately, when political theorists pointed political science in these directions there was little data in the conventional categories on which to base political analysis. Hence, along with the tool of rational choice theory, political science needs the accumulation of data appropriate for the application of that theory.

We need, I believe, a tradition of what I call *heresthetics,* which should have been—but was not—invented by the Greeks as the counterpart in the study of politics to rhetoric in the study of literature. It is perhaps odd that in a survey of political theory one should advocate the accumulation of another categorization of events. But theorizing must begin somewhere and it must use appropriate data. It is to the initiation of that task that I dedicate the rest of this paper.

IV

Heresthetics, in my coinage of the word, has to do with the manipulation of the structure of tastes and alternatives within which decisions are made, both the objective structure and the structure as it appears to participants. It is a study of the *strategy* of decision. Its source is the Greek αἱρεῖσθετοι, which has to do with choosing and electing.[4] I describe it with a Greek-like word because it is a branch of knowledge that should have been, but was not, invented by Athenian philosophers and sophists. The modern impetus to heresthetics comes from game theory and social choice theory, both of which are methods of describing social decisions abstractly. The concrete decisions themselves take many forms, however, and heresthetics is the categorization of the circumstances of these decisions in a way that makes them more amenable to abstract theoretical description. Concrete grammars are necessary for the development of an abstract linguistics and heresthetics serves in an analogous role in the development of the theory of social decision.[5]

Two examples of what would have properly been called heresthetics, if the word had existed when they were written, are:

(1) Pliny the Younger's letter 14 of book 7, to Titus Aristo, as used by Robin Farquharson for his running example in the *Theory of Voting* (1958 and 1969). It is not clear whether Pliny intended this letter as a commentary on social decision or merely as a cry to Titus for help in defending the con-

stitutionality of Pliny's ruling from the chair of the Senate. About Farquhar-son's intent, however, there is no doubt for he offered the letter as an example of alternative methods of voting. Quite unbeknownst to him—for he had a bad translation—the letter also serves as a commentary on manipulation of the agenda (by Pliny) and on sophisticated voting (by Pliny's unnamed opponent) (Pliny, Ed. by Radice, 1969). In the incident described in the letter to Titus, Pliny ruled for plurality choice among three alternatives on a single division, while the customary procedure would have been a sequence of pair-wise decisions. His motive was to ensure the victory of his preferred alternative over the Condorcet winner, which he placed second. In the voting, however, one group of his opposition voted sophisticatedly so that the Condorcet win-ner actually won, doubtless to Pliny's chagrin.

(2) Schelling, *The Strategy of Conflict* (1960). Several chapters of this volume concern manipulative techniques. When originally published (in 1956 and 1957) as scientific papers, Schelling interpreted them as contributions to a theory of bargaining, but later (in 1960) he believed they were contributions to the theory of games. He was entirely justified in his uncertainty about the classification of these chapters which concern threats, promises, and commit-ments generally. They are not a theory of bargaining because they have nothing to say about the compromise of tastes (and thus are quite unlike the work of, say, Harsanyi, 1980). Nor are they about game theory because they are not concerned with the way the interaction of players' choices determine an outcome. Rather, they are about the strategems that participants use in selecting their own actions and in limiting the choices of others. They are about the strategies to create situations in which game theory and bargaining theory apply. As such, they are squarely in the field of heresthetics.

Both Schelling's and Farquharson's work are regarded as path-breaking, and properly so, because they deal with a kind of data no one had thought to collect before and furthermore with data that is highly relevant to theories of social decision. To think about the subject matter of these theories—which is what both writers wanted to do—it helps to be able to refer to concrete detail of the sort they collected. In that sense, the content of heresthetics can be said to come out of the demands of science, not out of lay language and observa-tion; it ought, therefore, to be regarded as a significant and new kind of data in the study of society.

It is hard to define heresthetics other than by examples because the pur-pose of the concept is to provide an open-ended set of categories for events that have not heretofore been systematically categorized.[6] One more example may be helpful, so I offer one that was brought to my attention by Richard A. Smith who used it as an introductory example of agenda-setting in his superb dissertation (1980) on agenda-setting by lobbyists. This example, as related in Redman (1973), concerns Senator Warren Magnuson, who was trying to stop the transport of nerve gas across his state of Washington, enroute from Okinawa to Colorado. Because relatively few other Senators shared his pro-vincial concern for impressing the voters of the state of Washington, he expected to lose. But he won, mainly, so Redman reports, because of clever heresthetical tactics. Redman tells the story well (p. 207):

. . . during the Senate debate on his [Magnuson's] amendment to block shipment, . . . I prepared another memorandum cataloguing the arguments he had marshaled against the shipment and took it to him at his desk on the Senate Floor. He surveyed the memo cursorily, then handed it back with an annoyed "No, no, no!" Bewildered, I retreated to the staff couch and waited to hear what argument he intended to use instead of the familiar ones of possible sabotage, dangerous sections of track along the proposed route, and populations that would have to be evacuated as a precaution against leakage. When the time came, he took a wholly novel and ingenious approach. The issue, he told his colleagues, was not one of the people versus the Pentagon, as the news media seemed to assume. Instead, it was another case of the President versus the Senate. The Senator from West Virginia (Robert C. Byrd) had recently offered a resolution, which the Senate had passed, stating that the Senate expected the President to keep it informed throughout the treaty negotiations with the Japanese government on the subject of Okinawa. The President's sudden decision to move the nerve gas off Okinawa must reflect some aspect of those treaty negotiations, Magnuson insisted — and the Senate had not yet been informed of, much less consented to, any such agreement. To allow the nerve-gas shipment under such circumstances, he asserted, would be to abandon the Byrd Resolution and to abdicate the Senate's rightful role in treaty-making generally. The President, Magnuson said, might get the idea that he could ignore the Senate and its Constitutional prerogatives whenever he wished. Jolted by this reasoning, the Senator from West Virginia and his Southern colleagues — friends of the Pentagon almost to a man, but vigilant guardians of the Senate's Constitutional responsibilities — voted down the line with Magnuson. The amendment, which had been doomed a few minutes earlier, passed overwhelmingly.

Even though the collection of heresthetic detail is recent, the human behavior involved is easy to observe in vastly different times and places. Heresthetics is in fact universal. One of the settings in which it is easy to observe the manipulation of tastes is the parliamentary assembly, where there are many groups, where individual loyalties are shifting, and where leaders win by assembling ad hoc winning coalitions. Not surprisingly, the Roman Senate is the locale for Farquharson's example (i.e., Pliny's letter) and the American Senate is the locale for Smith's example (i.e., Redman's story about Magnuson). One would expect, therefore, that examples for heresthetical categories could be found in the assemblies of classic Greece, the earliest historical assemblies. And so they can. W. Robert Connor (1971) describes the Athenian assembly as "kaleidoscopic" or "polycentric," composed of several relatively small groups of friends, almost clubs, which come together in support of particular motions and then regrouped on others. This is precisely the kind of setting in which the open manipulation of the agenda and of the salience of dimensions of judgment is likely to be most visible. And indeed, tiny as the historical record is (mostly Thucydides' *History* and in the next century Demosthenes' *Orations*), it contains quite a large number of descriptions of heresthetical devices. Connor discusses, for example, Thucydides' account of the development of the coalition against Alcibiades. That coalition, having failed to halt the disastrous Sicilian expedition, turned to an attack on Alcibiades, its main sponsor. The leaders of the coalition raised the issue of impiety against him — the charge was profaning the mysteries and defacing the statues of Hermes — and, although they failed initially, they ultimately

had Alcibiades recalled from his command, though the expedition itself was
not stopped, and he deserted to Sparta (Thucydides, VI, 28-29, 61). Connor
sees this as an example of the structuring of a coalition, but it is also an example of the introduction of a new issue (Alcibiades' impiety) to transform the
coalition against the expedition from a minority to a majority. An even better
example of the heresthetical tactic of introducing a new dimension is found a
bit earlier (Thucydides, VI, 8-24), in Nicias' argument against the expedition. Initially he opposed it on the ground that it was too large an undertaking and that it was intended only to gratify Alcibiades' tastes for the
magnificent. When Alcibiades carried the day by promising to make the
Athenians the rulers of all Hellas, Nicias responded in fine heresthetical
fashion by introducing a new dimension of judgment. Thucydides wrote (VI,
19-24):

> Nicias, seeing that his old argument would no longer deter them, but that he
> might possibly change their minds if he insisted on the magnitude of the force
> which would be required, came forward and spoke as follows: ". . . I say,
> therefore, that we must take with us as a large heavy armed force both of
> Athenians and of allies. . . . Our naval superiority must be overwhelming. . . ."
> These were the words of Nicias. He meant either to deter the Athenians by
> bringing home to them the vastness of the undertaking or to provide as far as he
> could for the safety of the expedition if he were compelled to proceed. The result
> disappointed him. Far from losing their enthusiasm, . . . they [i.e., the
> Athenians in assembly] were more determined than ever.

This reads just like an event in modern democratic politics: A politician who
loses on one platform or set of arguments tries another and, when he loses on
the second, his friends try still a third (i.e., the attack on Alcibiades' alleged
impiety) on which they finally win, at least in part. I find in Thucydides quite
a few other examples of heresthetics: false presentation of an issue (V, 45-47);
coalition building around a new issue (IV, 84-88); agenda control (II, 21-22);
and the addition of a dimension of judgment (I, 80ff.). Altogether, therefore,
it is clear that, given similar settings in different cultures, heresthetical
behavior is universal.

Furthermore, since it clearly concerns the dynamics of the approach to
important human decisions, one would expect that, even in classic Greek
times, men would have begun to collect and classify examples of heresthetic,
just as they did for rhetoric, which concerns another feature of the approach
to decision. And there was indeed a tiny start in that direction. Demosthenes
was a master of heresthetic as well as rhetoric and his orations have enough
detail for the modern reader to understand the full scope of his strategy. His
modern biographer, Werner Jaeger, commenting on Demosthenes' speech,
On the Symmories, in which he advocated a larger navy based on a wider
assessment of taxes, ostensibly in support of a proposed Persian War, but
actually—and successfully—to dampen enthusiasm for that war by emphasizing its cost, observed that this was the same heresthetical technique Nicias
had used against Alcibiades. In the *Art of Rhetoric* the pseudo Dionysius of
Halicarnassus classified Demosthenes' maneuver with a similar maneuver by

the Spartan king Archidamas (as reported by Thucydides, I, 80ff.) to introduce a fiscal dimension to defeat an outcome expected to win if determined only by a military dimension (Jaeger, 1938, pp. 226-227). The false Dionysius, putting the story of Archidamus and the text of Demosthenes together indeed started up a heresthetical tradition. Unfortunately, it never developed further.

I wonder, why not? One possible answer is that, while heresthetic and rhetoric were initially entwined in classical thought, as the democratic assembly—the one place where political strategy could be easily observed—disappeared from classical institutions, only rhetoric in the sense of persuasion was left to be observed and classified. In the classical tradition it was customary to categorize the settings for rhetoric into the deliberative (i.e., in assemblies), the forensic (i.e., in courts), and the epideictic (i.e., in ceremonies). Two historians of Greek rhetoric, Wilcox (1942) and Kennedy (1963), assert that the early rhetoricians were concerned mainly with deliberative persuasion. They argue in support, first, that rich young men of prominent families would hardly have paid the sophists large fees simply to be taught how to be lawyers, and second, that Plato's intense hostility (in *Gorgias* and *Protagoros*) to rhetoricians must have been based on a fear that they would teach people how to distort public policy in general (i.e., in the assembly) rather than in simply private disputes (i.e., in the courts). These arguments seem persuasive to me, especially since the rhetorical tradition from the beginning emphasized persuasion by eloquence rather than persuasion by argument. Jacqueline de Romilly (1974) has argued that rhetoric began in the association of poetry and magic (i.e., spells and charms) with public speech and argument and was developed by the sophists into an art to persuade about the correctness of any preferred alternative. "Plato resented," she wrote, "not the magic [in Gorgias' thought] but the offensive pretense of turning it into science" (de Romilly, 1974, p. 38). Aristotle tried to save rhetoric for philosophy by cleansing it of what Plato despised, by, in fact, turning it into a policy science in which persuasion consists of showing that sentences have a high probability of truth. In particular, he wished to banish eloquence from style so that it "be transparent, not magical" (de Romilly, 1974, p. 73). If Aristotle had succeeded then rhetoric would have been concerned primarily with political decision and would doubtless have continued to subsume political strategy or heresthetics as well. But Aristotle failed and rhetoric became almost entirely a matter of eloquence. It was Cicero who settled the tradition for most of the next two thousand years. In the *Orator* (line 44) he says the rhetor "must consider three things, what to say, in what order, and in what manner or style to say it," but then he goes on to remark that he will treat the first two only briefly because, while important, they are a part of "ordinary intelligence rather than eloquence." Plainly, therefore, eloquence was in Cicero's mind the distinguishing feature of rhetoric and he banished all else, including what might have become heresthetic.

If this historical speculation is correct that rhetoric became simply persuasion—and the least rational kind of persuasion at that—then rhetoric could hardly sustain heresthetic, especially in the absence until modern times of deliberative assemblies where political strategy is easy to observe. While it is thus explicable that the subject of heresthetics has not been studied, it is nevertheless clear that the reason scholars have ignored it has nothing to do with its significance, but rather with the accident that it was excluded from the one tradition in which it might have survived.

V

In the previous section I sought to define heresthetics, to show its universality, and to explain why, despite its universality, it is unstudied. I turn now to a further explication of heresthetics by distinguishing it from rhetoric with which, given the relatedness of subject matter, it might be confused.

Rhetoric and heresthetic are both techniques of winning. But they are different kinds of techniques. Rhetoric is persuasion. It involves confronting a judge or jury in a courtroom, or voters on a committee or in a polity, or buyers in a marketplace, or friends or philosophers in dispute with sentences that may convince them that you are correct or believable. The sentences may convince because they are beautiful or sonorously uttered, or because of their irrefutable arguments, or because of their presentation of the situation in a way the auditors are predisposed to accept. But the essential feature, qua rhetoric, is that they convince. With heresthetic, on the other hand, conviction is at best secondary and often not even involved at all. The point of an heresthetical act is to structure the situation so that the actor wins, regardless of whether or not the other participants are persuaded.

The contrast between rhetoric and heresthetic is nicely seen in the dilemma, a form shared by the two fields. Rhetorically, the dilemma-maker succeeds because he convinces the auditors that, if his opponent cannot resolve the dilemma, then the opponent's position is intellectually weak. Hence the dilemma is a device for persuasion. Heresthetically, the dilemma-maker succeeds because he forces his opponent into a choice of alternatives such that, whichever alternative is chosen, the opponent will alienate some of his supporters.

Consider the best of the textbook examples of the rhetorical dilemma: It is the pair of dilemmas posed by Tisias and Korax. Korax, whose name means "crow," was the founder of the school of rhetoric at Syracuse, and was Gorgias' teacher. Tisias, who was also Korax's student, had undertaken to pay tuition when he won his first case; but he had neither practiced nor paid, so Korax sued. Tisias responded with this dilemma: "If I win the case, then I need not pay because I am freed by the judgment of the court. If I lose the case, then I need not pay because the terms of the contract will not have been satisfied. Since I must either win or lose, I need not pay." To this Korax replied: "If I win the case, then I must be paid because of the judgment of the court. If I lose the case, then I must be paid because the terms of the contract will have been satisfied. Since I must either win or lose, I must be paid." The judge dismissed the case, saying Tisias was a bad egg from a bad crow. Although Korax lost, the advertisement was so good that people still repeat it 2500 years later. Not only did Korax show that he could teach a student to present what appeared to be an absolutely convincing defense, he also showed that he then could himself tear it all down with an exact riposte.

Consider now an heresthetical dilemma, Lincoln's famous question to Douglas in the Freeport debate. During the senatorial campaign of 1858 Lincoln met Douglas, the incumbent, in debates in several Illinois cities, while both were soliciting support for candidates for the state legislature who were in turn pledged to support them for the Senate. Lincoln's question was: "Can the people of a United States Territory, in any lawful way, against the wish of any citizen of the United States, exclude slavery from its limits prior to the formation of a state Constitution?" (Lincoln, 1958, p. 108). To the contemporary reader this seems perhaps innocuous enough; but it is at the very center of the partisan dispute of the era and expresses exactly the raison d'etre of the Republican party.

The parties of the tradition of Federalist-National Republican-Whig-Republican did not do well throughout the first two-thirds of the nineteenth century. Indeed between 1797 and 1867 they elected only one President by a majority, while the Jeffersonian-Jacksonian Democratic parties probably elected ten by a majority. The main problem for the parties of the Federalist-Whig-Republican sequence was that they usually espoused a platform of commercial expansionism which appealed only to a minority; Democrats, on the other hand, espoused agrarian expansionism which often appealed to a majority. Naturally the Whig-Republican leaders searched constantly for a better platform and they finally found one in the combination of commercial expansionism with the limitation of slavery. This platform had the advantage of splitting the Democrats, who were well distributed in North and South, more than it did the Whigs, who were weak in the South. Lincoln's question exactly expressed this Republican strategy.

The Democratic defense was to cover up the slavery issue, to assert it was a local concern that should be banished from national politics. In the 1850s Douglas had been the main agent of this defense by sponsoring the Kansas-Nebraska Act. This Act satisfied the South because it rendered slavery local and it mollified those Northern Democrats who were tempted to oppose slavery because it allowed the territories to eliminate slavery. It failed, however, to localize the issue, especially after the ruling in the Dred Scott case (1857) placed slavery beyond the control of local legislators. But Douglas was still trying in 1858 to patch up the national Democracy by localizing the issue and Lincoln's question was a trap to encourage him to do so, thus:

If Douglas answered "yes" (that territories could exclude), then he would alienate Southern Democrats for whom the Dred Scott decision was the new status quo. Since he hoped and expected to be the Democratic candidate for President in 1860, to answer "yes" would be to reduce his Southern support and thus to jeopardize his chances in that election. At the same time a "yes" answer would placate Illinois Democratic voters with free soil principles and thus enhance his chances for reelection to the Senate.

If he answered "no" there would be converse results. He would alienate Illinois free soil Democrats and possibly lose his Senate seat, but he would win the loyalty of the South for the Presidential election of 1860.

Since he had to answer either "yes" or "no," he jeopardized either his election in 1858 to the Senate or in 1860 to the Presidency.

Douglas answered a kind of "yes." Without disputing the Dred Scott decision, he said "slavery cannot exist a day or an hour anywhere, unless it is supported by local police regulations," which, he argued, an anti-slavery territorial legislature need not adopt (Lincoln, 1858, p. 113). This was the answer Lincoln's advisors feared — they had opposed his asking the question — for it probably helped Douglas to reelection. But, as things turned out, Lincoln won in 1860, helped immeasurably by Douglas' shortsighted "yes." An intriguing question: Did Lincoln in 1858 see ahead to his own candidacy in 1860 or was he sacrificing himself for the greater Republican good?

Clearly the dilemma Lincoln posed was not intended to persuade the audience that Douglas' position was intellectually weak. Indeed, it did not depend for its effect on convincing anybody of anything. It was simply a stratagem to force Douglas to reveal to one of his incompatible groups of supporters that he was faithless to its cause. As such it was strictly a heresthetical device that set up a situation for subsequent decisions in such a way that at least one of the decisions would be to Lincoln's taste.

The essentially heresthetical character of Lincoln's act of posing the dilemma is underlined by the fact that, viewed another way, it is very similar to the heresthetical devices of Nicias or Demosthenes, which I described earlier. They raised a new fiscal dimension of judgment in order that voters would be less enthusiastic about the preparations for war so heartily approved on a military dimension of judgment. Lincoln's stratagem also involved raising a new dimension, slavery, to drive some voters to oppose the agrarian expansion they would otherwise approve. Douglas' response was to try to suppress the new dimension. Thus, although the Lincolnian device has the form of a dilemma, it has the substance of the generation of a new issue.

VI

The purpose of this essay is to recommend the study of heresthetic, not actually to study it. Nevertheless, in the hope of making my recommendation more persuasive, I conclude with a brief statement of what I have so far myself learned from the study of heresthetic.

In the study of politics and public policy we devote most of our attention to the analysis and interpretation of the platforms and policies of the winners of political disputes, elections, wars, and so forth. And this is quite proper because the preferences of the winners are the values that are authoritatively allocated. That is, the tastes of the winners are the actual content of social decisions and thus the content of the immediately subsequent present time. Conversely, we ignore the policies and platforms of the losers because these are the junk heap of history, the might-have-beens that never were. But we should not, I think, entirely overlook the losers and their goals for the losers provide the values of the future. The dynamics of politics is in the hands of the losers. It is they who decide when and how and whether to fight on. Winners have won and do not immediately need to change things. But losers have nothing and can gain nothing unless they continue to try to bring about new political situations. This provides the motivation for change. And the confirmation of this fact comes from the study of heresthetics. Losers are the ones who search out new strategies and stratagems and it is their use of heresthetics that provides the dynamic of politics.[7]

In my recent work, *Liberalism against Populism* (1982) I have discussed, mainly in chapters 6, 7, and 9, the way in which participants in an electoral system can manipulate electoral procedures to their advantage. Strategic manipulation is, of course, one important part of heresthetics. So the categories of manipulation used in that work are also categories of heresthetics. The categories I used were:

(1) strategic voting, which involves voting for a less preferred alternative (in lieu of a more preferred one) at some initial decision point in order that the voter can achieve (or improve the chance of achieving) an outcome at the final decision that the voter favors over the outcome expected from initially voting for the more preferred alternative;

(2) manipulation of the agenda, which is structuring the set of alternatives or the procedure of voting in such a way as to produce an outcome more favored by the manipulator than might otherwise have been achieved.

Within each of these two main categories are a number of kinds of examples, each of which has the property that the user of the particular heresthetical device must be a person who has lost a decision or reasonably anticipates losing one. Then the stratagem itself becomes a means either of winning on a new issue or of transforming the anticipated loss into a victory. Thus, strategic voters in each of the following examples are persons who anticipate losing if they do not adopt the stratagem:

(1) Avoidance of "wasted" votes: In plurality voting over three or more alternatives, a voter who most prefers some alternative other than the two most popular may nevertheless vote for his or her favorite among those two so that in the vote count the favorite (within the top pair) will have a better chance of winning than if the voter had "thrown away" his or her vote on the most preferred alternative. Clearly this heresthetic device is available only to supporters of the third most popular (or, in the case of more than three, the least popular) alternative;

(2) Creation of a voting cycle: When a motion as amended is so distasteful to some of the supporters of the original motion that they reject the amended motion, it is of course open to the opponents of the original motion to attach the amendment to the motion in the hope thereby of creating a cycle in which

(a) the status quo beats the amended motion

(b) the amended motion beats the original motion

(c) and the original motion beats the status quo.

In such a cycle, some opponents of the original motion are, as line (c) indicates, losers; but they can perhaps become winners if they can attach the amendment, as indicated by line (a);

(3) Vote-trading: Potential vote-traders are those who, on divisions on two motions, can expect to win on the motion less valuable to them and to lose on the more valuable one. If they can find enough persons oppositely situated so that they can, by trading, together reverse the outcomes, then the traders will win on their more valuable motions and lose on their less valuable ones. Manifestly, traders must be losers in order to gain by trade.

The same features are exhibited by examples of manipulation of the agenda:

(1) Arrangement of the sequence of decisions: Those directly in control of the agenda can, if they foresee an unfavorable outcome from the normal or customary agenda, rearrange the agenda so that alternatives more popular than their favored one are eliminated prior to the decision on their favorite. Hence they can improve its chances. They need to engage in this maneuver, however, only when they expect the "natural" vote to go against them;

(2) Introduction of new alternatives: Those who expect their preferred alternative to lose initially may introduce new alternatives, even as mere participants not leaders. Assuming the new alternative is at least better for them than the most popular alternative in the initial set and that some of the supporters of the popular alternative will prefer the new alternative, then the introducers improve their chances of defeating the initially most popular alternative. Obviously only those who initially expect to lose are motivated to use this strategy.

It seems clear, therefore, that, in the case of all the heresthetical devices I have examined, the users are persons who are not now winning but hope to become winners. Insofar as these devices involve a fairly wide range of political life, it also seems clear that losers are the instigators of political change and it is they who are thus motivated to exploit heresthetic and who become the agents of political dynamics.

A generalization of the sort just uttered is exactly the kind of theoretical payoff political scientists might expect to obtain from heresthetical categorization. It is in the hope of further such generalizations that I recommend the study of heresthetics.

NOTES

1. See Riker, 1977, 1980, 1982(a) for more detailed versions of this history.
2. This feature of Black's work is closely related to the Hotelling-Downs (1957) model of spatial equilibrium. For a survey of the development of work on that model, see Riker and Ordeshook (1973) and a forthcoming volume by Melvin Hinich and James Enelow.
3. One of my critics believes the statement in the text is too strong because all sorts of institutions impose constraints on outcomes and thereby preclude the possibility that "anything can happen." Of course, he is correct with respect to applications to the real world, as I indicate in section II of this paper. But it is important to note that, in the abstract without considering institutions, there is almost no likelihood of an equilibrium.
4. "Heretics" might be a better Anglicization of the Greek source, but that word is a form of the word "heresy," which has been co-opted by religion. Hence, I prefer the term I have chosen.
5. One of my critics defines my call for a new kind of data as a plea for us "to devote more systematic attention to the *dynamics* of collective decision making. A standard criticism leveled against existing political models is that they are static in nature. Even when the more ambitious among us attempt to model dynamic phenomena, the essentials of the model remain constant. Of course, we must learn to walk before we can learn to run and all that, but at some point a progressive political theory will begin to remove the basis of the criticism."

6. One of my critics believes that my implicit definition of heresthetics is too broad. He points out that I seem to be considering as heresthetical both the manipulation of preferences and the manipulation of alternatives. He suggests that I ought to restrict the reference to the latter manipulation (i.e., situations where preferences are constant and only alternatives change) because we already have names for the former manipulation. I hesitate to restrict reference in this way, however, because one of the things that happens in the manipulation of alternatives is that as a consequence the salience (and hence the content) of preferences are also changed.

7. One of my critics suggests that, by emphasizing the creative (perhaps artistic) element of heresthetics, I am, unconsciously or slyly, removing it from the range of science. I certainly do not intend to do so. While it is certainly true that human life involves artistic creations, we would deny the possibility of all social science by asserting that creativity cannot be scientifically described. Just as Von Neumann and Morgenstern discovered how to discuss analytically creative acts of choice among strategies, so I believe we can discover how to discuss analytically creative acts of structuring strategies themselves.

REFERENCES

Aldrich, John, & Rohde, David. The limitations of equilibrium analysis in political science. In Peter C. Ordeshook and Kenneth A. Shepsle (Eds.). *Political equilibrium.* Boston: Kluwer-Nijhoff, 1982, pp. 65-95.

Aristotle. *Rhetoric.* As interpreted in Larry Arnhart, *Aristotle on political reasoning.* DeKalb, Ill.: Northern Illinois University Press, 1981.

Arrow, Kenneth. *Social choice and individual values* (2nd ed.). New Haven, Conn.: Yale University Press, 1963. (Originally published, 1951)

Axelrod, Robert. *Conflict of interest.* Chicago: Markham, 1970.

Benzel, Richard F., & Sanders, Elizabeth. The effect of electoral rules on voting behavior: The electoral college and shift voting. *Public Choice,* 1979, *34,* 609-38.

Black, Duncan. On the rationale of group decision making. *Journal of Political Economy,* 1948, *56,* 23-24.

Black, Duncan. *The theory of committees and elections.* Cambridge: Cambridge University Press, 1958.

Black, Duncan & Newing, R. A. *Committee decisions with complementary valuation.* Edinburgh: William Hodge, 1951.

Black, Jerome. The multi-candidate calculus of voting: Application to Canadian federal elections. *American Journal of Political Science,* 1978, *22,* 609-38.

Bueno de Mesquita, Bruce. The war trap. New Haven: Yale University Press, 1981.

Butterworth, Robert. A research note on the size of winning coalitions. *American Political Science Review,* 1971, *65,* 741-45.

Cain, Bruce E. Strategic voting in Britain. *American Journal of Political Science,* 1978, *22,* 639-55.

Cicero. *Orator.* H. M. Turnbull (Ed.). London: Loeb Library, 1934.

Coase, R. H. Duncan Black: A biographical sketch. In Gordon Tullock (Ed.). *Toward a science of politics: Papers in honor of Duncan Black.* Blacksburg, Va.: Center for the Study of Public Choice, Virginia Polytechnic Institute and State University, 1981, pp. 1-10.

Cohen, Linda. Cyclic sets in multi-dimensional voting models. *Journal of Economic Theory,* Feb. 1979, *22,* 1-12.

Condorcet, Marquis de. *Essai sur l'application de l'analyse à la probabilité des décisions rendues à la pluralité des voix.* Paris, 1785.

Connor, W. Robert. *The new politicians of fifth-century Athens.* Princeton: Princeton University Press, 1971.

DeMeyer, Frank, & Plott, Charles. The probability of a cyclical majority. *Econometrica*, 1970, *38*, 345-54.

de Romilly, Jacqueline. *Magic and rhetoric in ancient Greece*. Cambridge: Harvard University Press, 1975.

DeSwaan, Abram. *Coalition theories and cabinet formation*. San Francisco: Jossey Bass, 1973.

Dionysius of Halicarnassus (pseudo.). *TEXNH PHEOPIKH*. (Heinrich Schott, Ed. and trans. into Latin). Leipzig: Engelhard, 1804.

Dodd, Lawrence C. *Coalitions in parliamentary government*. Princeton: Princeton University Press, 1976.

Downs, Anthony. *An economic theory of democracy*. New York: Harper, 1957.

Easton, David. *The political system: An inquiry into the state of political science*. New York: Knopf, 1953.

Farquharson, Robin. *Theory of voting*. New Haven: Yale University Press, 1969.

Fiorina, Morris P., & Shepsle, Kenneth A. Equilibrium, disequilibrium, and the general possibility of a science of politics. In Peter C. Ordeshook and Kenneth A. Shepsle (Eds.), *Political equilibrium*. Boston: Kluwer-Nijhoff, 1982, pp. 49-64.

Fishburn, Peter. *The theory of social choice*. Princeton: Princeton University Press, 1973(a).

Fishburn, Peter. Voter concordance, simple majorities, and group decision methods. *Behavioral Science*, 1973(b), *18*, 364-73.

Garman, Mark, & Kamien, Morton. The paradox of voting: Probability calculations. *Behavioral Science*, 1968, *13*, 308-16.

Gehrlein, William, & Fishburn, Peter. The probability of the paradox of voting. *Journal of Economic Theory*, 1976, *13*, 14-25.

Gibbard, Allan. Manipulation of voting schemes: A general result. *Econometrica*, 1973, *41*, 587-601.

Gilpin, Robert. *War and change in world politics*. New York: Cambridge University Press, 1981.

Hardin, Russell. Hollow victory: The minimum winning coalition. *American Political Science Review*, 1976, *70*, 1202-14.

Harsanyi, John C. *Rational behavior and bargaining equilibrium in games and social situations*. New York: Cambridge University Press, 1977.

Hempel, Carl G. *The philosophy of natural science*. Englewood Cliffs, N.J.: Prentice Hall, 1966.

Jaeger, Werner. *Demosthenes: The origin and growth of his policy*. Berkeley: University of California Press, 1938.

Kennedy, George. *The art of persuasion in Greece*. Princeton: Princeton University Press, 1963.

Kramer, Gerald. On a class of equilibrium conditions for majority rule. *Econometrica*, 1973, *41*, 285-297.

Lemieux, Peter. *The liberal party and British political change: 1955-74* (Doctoral dissertation, Massachusetts Institute of Technology, 1977).

Lincoln, Abraham. *The Illinois political campaign of 1858: A facsimile of the printer's copies of his debates with Stephen Arnold Douglas as edited and prepared for press by Abraham Lincoln*. Washington, D.C.: Library of Congress, 1958.

McKelvey, Richard D. Intransitivities in multi-dimensional voting models and some implications for agenda control. *Journal of Economic Theory*, 1976, *12*, 472-82.

Niemi, Richard. Majority decision making with partial unidimensionality. *American Political Science Review*, 1969, *63*, 489-97.

Niemi, Richard & Weisberg, Herbert. A mathematical solution for the probability of the paradox of voting. *Behavioral Science*, 1968, *13*, 317-23.

Pliny the Younger. *Letters*. Betty Radice (Ed.). Cambridge: Harvard University Press, 1969.

Plott, Charles. A notion of equilibrium and its possibility under majority rule. *American Economic Review*, 1967, *57*, 787-806.

Plott, Charles. Path independence, rationality, and social choice. *Econometrica*, 1973, *41*, 1075-91.

Popper, Karl. *Conjectures and refutations: The growth of scientific knowledge.* London: Routledge and Paul, 1963.

Redman, Eric. *The dance of legislation.* New York: Simon and Shuster, 1973.

Riker, William H. *The theory of political coalitions.* New Haven: Yale University Press, 1963.

Riker, William H., & Ordeshook, Peter C. *An introduction to positive political theory.* Englewood Cliffs, N.J.: Prentice Hall, 1973.

Riker, William H. The future of the science of politics. *The American Behavioral Scientist*, 1977, *21*, 11-38.

Riker, William H. Implications from the disequilibrium of majority rule for the study of institutions. *American Political Science Review*, 1980, *74*, 432-46.

Riker, William H. *Liberalism against populism: A confrontation between the theory of democracy and the theory of social choice.* San Francisco: W. H. Freeman, 1982(a).

Riker, William H. The two-party system and Duverger's law: An essay on the history of political science. *American Political Science Review*, 1982(b), *82*, 753-66.

Schelling, Thomas C. *The strategy of conflict.* Cambridge: Harvard University Press, 1960.

Schelling, Thomas C. *Arms and influence.* New Haven: Yale University Press, 1966.

Schofield, Norman. Generalized bargaining set for cooperative games. *International Journal of Game Theory*, 1978(a), *7*, 183-99.

Schofield, Norman. Instability of simple dynamic games. *Review of Economic Studies*, 1978(b), *45*, 575-94.

Schofield, Norman. Instability and development in the political economy. In Peter C. Ordeshook and Kenneth A. Shepsle (Eds.), *Political equilibrium.* Boston: Kluwer-Nijhoff, 1982(a), pp. 96-106.

Schofield, Norman. Political fragmentation and the stability of coalition governments in western Europe. Paper presented at the European Public Choice Society Meeting, Poitiers, France, March 22-27, 1982(b).

Shepsle, Kenneth. The size of winning coalitions. *American Political Science Review*, 1974, *68*, 505-18.

Smith, Richard A. *Lobbying influence in Congress: Processes and effects.* (Doctoral dissertation, University of Rochester, 1980.)

Thucydides. *The Peloponnesian War.* (Benjamin Jowett, trans.). In Francis Godolphin (Ed.), *The Greek Historians.* New York: Random House, 1942.

Weintraub, E. Roy. *Microfoundations: The compatibility of microeconomics and macroeconomics.* Cambridge: Cambridge University Press, 1979.

Wilcox, Stanley. The scope of early rhetorical instruction in Greece. *Harvard Studies in Classical Philology*, 1942, *53*, 121-55.

3

Toward Theories of Data:
The State of Political Methodology

Christopher H. Achen *

In one sense, political methodology in the early 1980s enjoys robust health. Applications of powerful econometric techniques — simultaneous equation estimation, time series methods, analysis of covariance structures — appear in political science journals on a frequent, if not yet routine, basis. *Political Methodology*, less than a decade old, prints a large fraction of the best empirical research done in political science. Perhaps most tellingly, the quantitative method has attained full legitimacy among serious scholars, including those who do not use it. Just a decade ago, a graduate student interviewing for an American politics position at a first-class liberal arts college could be asked whether his interest in mathematical techniques was some youthful fancy from which he might be expected to recover. Today, one trusts, no department with an eye to its reputation would do the same.

Yet if these are the best of times, they are the worst of times as well. Several decades after its beginning, political methodology has so far failed to make serious theoretical progress on any of the major issues facing it. Psychologists invented factor analysis and scaling methods to cope with mental tests; economists created structural equation estimation to deal with their models, especially the economy-wide macroeconomic theories; and even sociologists have contributed latent class analysis to the corpus of social scientific methodology. Political science has done nothing remotely comparable.

Political methodologists have largely occupied themselves with two activities. First, they have continued to develop the major quantitative research

*I am indebted to Greg Markus, George Rabinowitz, and Jim Stimson, who served as able discussants on the panel of the American Political Science Association 1982 Annual Meeting where an earlier version of this paper was presented. Doug Hibbs, Jerry Kramer, Neal Beck, and especially an anonymous reviewer with an inordinate fondness for aggregate data gave me trenchant comments and criticism. I would also like to thank John Sullivan, chairman of the methodology panels at the 1982 meeting, for inviting me to organize my thoughts on this topic, and Henry Brady for many conversations over several years on these and other methodological issues.

tool in the discipline, the opinion survey. Most issues of *Political Methodology*, for example, have at least one article exploring the reliability or validity of alternate survey techniques. Political methodologists also contribute regularly to the *American Journal of Political Science*, which often contains articles on survey research, and *Public Opinion Quarterly*, which covers the same topics almost exclusively. Unfortunately, nearly all this work has been atheoretical. Question wordings, interview design, and techniques for reducing nonresponse are invented as needed, with no overarching framework, so that every new topic must be tackled *de novo*. The result is a body of work that is certainly "methodological" in the broad sense of the term, and without it, empirical work in political science would be drastically impaired. But survey research remains a purely applied science. If judged by the standards prevailing elsewhere in the discipline, where good work is recognized for its contribution to theoretical understanding, survey methodology has achieved very little intellectual advance.

Second, political methodologists have expended much of their energies teaching the rest of the discipline new statistical techniques invented in other fields. In a typical publication of this kind, an intuitive exposition is combined with an illustration or two from political science. The new method may be compared favorably with an older, more common technique. The result is an article that can be assigned to graduate students needing both motivation and simplified mathematics to learn the material.

Intellectual middlemen have their uses, of course. Political science remains a field with woefully little methodological capital, and any successful investment scheme deserves praise. But remedial teaching is not scholarship, and popularization does not a methodologist make. Here as in survey research, there is no real intellectual achievement of our own to report.

Political methodologists as a class have largely avoided theoretical thinking. With few exceptions, we do not investigate carefully the properties of the new methodological procedures constantly appearing in the discipline. Certainly we rarely invent a legitimate estimator, prove consistency theorems, or derive confidence intervals. Instead we shop for hand-me-down techniques invented by statisticians, psychologists, and economists—techniques often meant for very different tasks. Empirical researchers then adopt the statistical ideas and methodological standards we have propounded. Is it any wonder that the pages of our journals frequently have the look of living rooms decorated at garage sales?

The general lack of interest in fundamental questions is particularly disquieting because it coexists with deep methodological conundrums specific to political science. One thing political methodologists *have* done is to show that measurement does matter. Apparently trivial differences in question wording can lead to large changes in response patterns. (Among many possible examples, two particularly striking cases appear in Bishop, Tuchfarber, and Oldendick, 1978; and Sullivan, Piereson, and Marcus, 1978.) Nor are the peculiarities confined to survey items. The ghastly results all too common in working with aggregate voting data are also well documented, and the "ecological fallacy" has destroyed the credibility of many well-intentioned projects. Indeed, skepticism about aggregate data is so widespread that the quantitative historical research once so common in the discipline has very nearly disappeared. Thus ignoring our methodological foundations because "they probably don't matter much in practice" is simply naive. Whatever else may be uncertain in methodology, there is ample evidence that the shaky foundation it provides has weakened intellectual structures across the discipline.

These puzzles in our data sets are not work-a-day procedural problems with administrative solutions. Better question writing and more careful data collection will make no more than a marginal difference. Only a better understanding of our processes of measurement can truly help us. Nor can we expect other disciplines to supply the necessary theory. In large part, the statistical questions posed by political data are of relatively little interest outside political science. No one is likely to solve them but ourselves. So far, we have not been much interested.

If political methodologists were to take up their main agenda, the first item of business would be the formulation of our troubles clearly enough that they could be diagnosed and treated. The remainder of this essay is meant to begin this formulation. Of course, remarks of this length cannot hope to cover the entire field. Political scientists are interested in simultaneous equation estimation, time series, discrete choice analysis, and a host of other interesting and important statistical methodologies not reviewed here in detail. None of these statistical fields, however, raises difficulties so much our own as the two long-standing research areas that are the focus of this article. The first is the issue of measurement error, the second the aggregation problem. Each illustrates in striking fashion the dimensions of the task before us.

MEASUREMENT ERROR

Quantitatively-trained political scientists are very much aware that measurement error can bias their findings. Most have at least a vague recollection from introductory econometrics that under some conditions, it can attenuate regression coefficients. Frequently, several other features of measurement error are "remembered" as well, for example:

(A) If some of the independent variables in a multiple regression are measured with error, all coefficients will be attenuated. Thus if one can establish the existence of an effect in spite of measurement error, the true effect must be even larger.

(B) Measurement error can be a serious problem in the bivariate regression case, but the more independent variables without error in the regression equation, the smaller the biases will be.

(C) If the measurement error variance in the independent variables is a small fraction of their total variance (high reliability), the bias in the coefficients will be a small fraction of their true size.

(D) In any case, discussions of all these questions are contained in any standard introductory text on econometrics.

All four statements are false. To take the last first, the surprising fact is that some of the best multiple regression texts ignore the subject of measurement error in the independent variables entirely (Kelejian & Oates, 1981; Dhrymes, 1970). Nearly all the rest discuss the bias only in very general terms (Johnston, 1972; Hanushek & Jackson, 1977; Pindyck & Rubinfeld, 1976; Rao & Miller, 1971; and Theil, 1971). The direction of bias for the coefficients is given solely for random error in the bivariate case—a single independent variable—where, of course, the effect is to drive the estimated coefficient toward zero. (Rao and Miller also reference, but do not discuss, an antique article by Theil that gives a rough approximation for the asymptotic bias when there are exactly *two* independent variables, one of which is observed with random error.) Only Maddala (1977) discusses non-random error (in the bivariate case), or random error in multiple regression (with just two independent variables, each observed with error).

None of these texts gives any explicit results when there are more than two independent variables. In fact, as late as 1973, *Econometrica* was still exploring the case of multiple regression with a single variable observed with random error, and finding the direction of the asymptotic bias only for the variable with error. (It is biased toward zero.) A complicated procedure was given for learning the direction of the biases in the other coefficients, but nothing could be said about their sizes (Levi, 1973). More recently, as part of a sophisticated and fairly lengthy treatment of random measurement error in regression, Dhrymes (1978, pp. 242-266) has shown that R^2 is driven downward in errors-in-variables regression, which implies that the F-test for the overall significance of the regression will also be depressed. But on the question of the direction of the bias in coefficients or t-ratios, apart from the usual bivariate regression result, he throws up his hands.

Apparently the only result in the literature more general than these was published in *Political Methodology* (Greene, 1978). In the ordinary multiple regression setup with k independent variables, each possibly observed with random error, let g_j be the fractional asymptotic bias (inconsistency) in the jth coefficient. For example, $g_j = -0.5$ means 50% attenuation. Then in effect, Greene's main result is that a certain weighted average of these biases must be negative. In particular, let β_j be the true jth coefficient and ω_j^2 the error variance of the corresponding independent variable. Then:

$$\sum_{j=1}^{k} \beta_j^2 \omega_j^2 g_j < 0. \tag{1}$$

Thus in some sense, the "average g_j" is negative, and measurement error drives coefficient estimates toward zero.

Note, however, that this result is limited in several respects. First, as Greene notes, it gives only an average direction of bias that may not apply to most of the coefficients in question. In fact, the theorem guarantees only that at least one of the coefficients will be driven down. The rest might actually be increased in absolute size. Moreover, no limits on the size of the biases are given. Nothing in the result guarantees that coefficients will be attenuated in the usual sense that they will fall somewhere between the truth and zero. We know that they will be driven toward zero, but nothing prevents their being driven right on through it to the other side. Finally and more importantly, independent variables with no error ($\omega_j^2 = 0$) are weighted zero in (1). That is, the inequality tells us nothing about the direction or size of the biases in variables observed without error. Thus the result covers only the variables with error. There appears to be no literature at all on the size of the biases in the other coefficients.

Returning to the other three "facts" researchers remember from econometric theory, one can see that the available literature neither supports nor contradicts them. Answers to them simply are not known, and in their most general form, the complexity of the mathematics will probably prevent much progress. However, a great deal can be done in certain simple cases.

Consider, then, the case of multiple regression with random measurement error in a single independent variable, the other independent variables being measured exactly. Then denote the variable with error by x_1, its error variance by σ_e^2, and its true coefficient by β_1. Finally, let the residual variance when the *true* first variable is regressed on the other independent variables be s^2. Then if $\hat{\beta}_1$ is the estimated coefficient for the variable with error, its "asymptotic value" (i.e., probability limit) is as follows (see the appendix):

$$plim\,(\hat{\beta}_1) = \frac{s^2}{s^2 + \sigma_e^2}\beta_1. \tag{2}$$

For any other estimated coefficient, say $\hat{\beta}_j$, its asymptotic value is:

$$plim\,(\hat{\beta}_j) = \beta_j + \frac{\sigma_e^2}{s^2 + \sigma_e^2}\beta_1 b_j, \tag{3}$$

where b_j is the coefficient on the jth independent variable when the true first independent variable is regressed on all the others.

With this machinery, the questions (A), (B), and (C) raised above can be addressed. Note first that the coefficient on the variable with error is indeed attenuated. Equation (2) shows that asymptotically, the estimated value of the coefficient will fall between zero and the truth. Nothing of the kind is true for the other coefficients, however. As seen in (3), other coefficients will "pick up" part of the explanatory power of the variable with error, with the size of the acquisition varying according to their correlation with it (b_j). Thus variables measured without error can have their effects increased or decreased; there is no net tendency for them to be attenuated.

Next, observe that the size of the bias depends inversely on s^2, the residual variance when the true first independent variable is regressed on the others. Now s^2 can be taken as a measure of collinearity: the more intercorrelated the independent variables, the smaller is s^2, until at perfect collinearity, $s^2 = 0$. It follows that high collinearity will induce relatively large asymptotic biases, *no matter how small the measurement error variance*. The coefficient for the variable with error, for example, can be driven arbitrarily closer to zero just by increasing collinearity, even if the reliability is 99%. Small error variances do not necessarily give much protection against large inconsistencies. And of course, this bias is particularly pernicious because it depends on the unexplained variance in the regression of the true first independent variable on the others, a quantity that cannot be computed due to the measurement error in the first variable.

Finally, note that s^2 is quite likely to become smaller and smaller as additional variables are added to the equation, simply because the more variables there are, the better that x_1 can be forecast and the smaller its residual variance s^2 will be. Thus additional independent variables will tend to reduce s^2 and raise the inconsistencies in (2) and (3), making the biases worse rather than better. Therefore, as promised, we have shown that all four statements (A)-(D) are false in general, since they are false for the simple case of one independent variable with error. Measurement error, then, is more dangerous than commonly believed.

So far only purely random measurement error has been considered. Unfortunately, political scientists can rarely be certain that their errors are uncorrelated with the true values and with other independent variables. In fact, in many applications just the reverse is suspected. For example, Ross and Duvall (1982) have reminded us once again of the treacherous nature of cross-national political information. They note that even the size of standing armies in modern nations is subject to gross errors. In 1965, for instance, one major source reports 132,000 men under arms in Norway, while another gives 36,000 as the correct figure (p. 31). Using sources like the International Institute for Strategic Studies and the U.S. Arms Control and Disarmament Agency, Ross and Duvall commonly find discrepancies of 50% or more in the estimates for the same country in the same year throughout the modern era, and the mean is almost 25%. Some sources correlate rather well with each other, others quite poorly. It seems unlikely that this kind of error is purely random.

Unfortunately, nonrandom error presents even more serious threats to inference than the random kind. Suppose that just one variable in a multiple regression is observed with error, and that the error may be systematic in the sense of being correlated with any of the independent variables. (Correlation with the disturbance term, which can only make matters worse, will be excluded.) Then we have this mathematically trivial but substantively significant result: no matter what the true regression coefficients, if there is systematic error in a single independent variable, ordinary regression can converge to *any* pattern of coefficient estimates.

Proposition. Let β^* be any given vector of dimension k. Then in the multiple regression setup with k independent variables, there exists a pattern of systematic measurement error in the first independent variable such that the OLS coefficients will tend asymptotically to β^*.

Proof. Let the true model be:

$$y = x_1\beta_1 + X_2\beta_2 + u, \tag{4}$$

where y is the n-dimensional column vector of observations on the dependent variable, the column vector x_1 contains the n observations on the first independent variable and the $n \times (k-1)$ matrix X_2 the observations on the other $k-1$ independent variables, u is a disturbance term, and β_1 and β_2 are a constant and a column vector, respectively, of coefficients to be estimated. This relationship is not observed. Instead, we have:

$$y = (x_1 + e)\beta_1 + X_2\beta_2 + u, \tag{5}$$

where e is the vector of systematic error in x_1. Now partition $\beta^{*\prime} = [\beta_1^* \ \beta_2^{*\prime}]$, where β_1^* is the first element of β^* (corresponding to x_1), and β_2^* is the vector of remaining elements (corresponding to X_2). Suppose that e has the following form:

$$e = (x_1\beta_1 - x_1\beta_1^* + X_2\beta_2 - X_2\beta_2^*) / \beta_1^*. \tag{6}$$

Now e is just a linear combination of the independent variables x_1 and X_2. Hence from standard regression theory, its only effect on the asymptotic values (probability limits) of the coefficients is to transform them accordingly. That is, suppose that the original relationship is:

$$y = X\beta + u.$$

Now suppose that the matrix of independent variables is linearly transformed, which we can represent as postmultiplication of X by the nonsingular square matrix A. Then regression theory tells us that the new coefficients will be given by $A^{-1}\beta$. The new setup can be written as:

$$y = (XA)(A^{-1}\beta) + u.$$

The obvious fact here is that $(XA)(A^{-1}\beta) = X\beta$. Given the transformed data matrix XA, then, we can find the new coefficients simply by solving for constants which, when multiplied by XA, will equal $X\beta$.

In the systematic error problem, the estimated coefficients will be those values of β_1 and β_2 which, when substituted in the transformed regression (5), make (5) the same as the original regression (4). Elementary algebra will show that when e is defined as above, (4) and (5) are equivalent when β_1 and β_2 are replaced by β_1^* and β_2^*, respectively. Thus, for any arbitrary coefficient vector β^*, there exists a systematic error structure (6) that will generate it. *This ends the proof.*

These developments make it clear just how dangerous to inference measurement error is. Tossing raw attitudinal measures of survey responses into regression equations or cross-tabulations is likely to lead to sensible conclusions only by chance. Correcting for measurement error in independent variables alone guarantees useful results.

A number of correction procedures for measurement error have been proposed. The first, and perhaps the most useful generally, is the set of techniques known as factor analysis or scaling. These methods all assume that the

researcher has available several different measures of the same true underlying variables. Strong distributional assumptions are then added (e.g., all
measures are normally distributed, the underlying true scores are normally
distributed, the measurement errors are normally distributed, or even, quite
commonly, all of the above). Estimates of the true variables are then
produced.

A wide variety of models are available, suitable for continuous or discrete
variables, one underlying dimension or many, and several different theories
of how the scores were produced. (The most complete source remains Lord &
Novick, 1968. See also Torgerson, 1958; and Rasch, 1980.) These theories
constitute an impressive armamentarium, and they are far too little used and
understood in political science. But we stand a great distance off from making
a theoretically-informed choice among them. Do survey respondents obey the
assumptions of any of these models, even approximately? The answer is surely
no. If they do not, how much difference does it make? Brady (1981) has
begun to explore factor analytic models with no assumptions about either the
distributional form of the errors or about the functional form that relates factors to observed variates. A great deal more work of that kind will be
necessary before one can have full faith in scaling and factor analytic
methods. Intensive, theoretically-informed research on these techniques
should have a prominent place among methodologists' priorities.

Scaling methods are not the sole route to correcting regressions for
measurement error. Attractive and relatively simple correction procedures
also exist, for example, when the error variances are known or when they are
estimable (Johnston, 1972, pp. 281-291). Procedures for computing the standard errors of the adjusted coefficients have also been derived (Warren,
White, & Fuller, 1974; for a cruder but simpler approach, see Achen, 1978).
Sometimes, as with well-known scholastic tests like the SAT or GRE batteries,
reliabilities have been published. In other cases, more elaborate estimation
procedures are required.

In one case, political scientists have expended considerable effort to
learn a set of error variances. Converse (1964) argued brilliantly that most individuals have little conception of political issues. As part of his evidence, he
showed that a set of standard political attitude questions from the Michigan
Survey Research Center's National Election Studies (NES) correlated quite
poorly with themselves over a two-year interval, with Pearson's r's often no
more than 0.4. Implicitly assuming that the reliability of the questions was
1.0, he said that responses with so little stability indicated a lack of real
understanding. By contrast, individuals showed considerably more stable
party identification, demonstrating that party loyalties were genuine in a way
that issue preferences were not.

Converse added other evidence as well, such as the higher inter-item correlations for elites than for mass samples, but his study (and virtually all such
elite-mass comparisons since) examined groups who were asked quite different questions. The elite questions were more precise, the mass items diffuse. Differences in the correlations would be expected on that basis alone.
Similar objections apply to the comparison of elite over-time correlations with
the corresponding mass correlations, as in Kinder (1983). For this reason, the

stronger part of Converse's argument has always been the mass over-time correlations considered on their own.

Since Converse's time, a series of scholars have tried to learn the reliabilities of the items to correct his correlations for measurement error. Constructing careful measurement models and exploiting the three measurements in the NES 1965-58-60 panel study, they have derived reliabilities for the data Converse considered. The uniform conclusion of them all (Asher, 1974; Achen, 1975; Erikson, 1975; Dean & Moran, 1977; Jackson, 1979) has been that, apart from the party identification question, reliabilities were quite low, on the order of 0.5. Correcting for them typically brought the over-time attitude stabilities to 0.90 or more, meaning that most respondents were quite stable in their true opinions. Moreover, respondents' measurement error variances did not diminish much as they became better educated or more interested in politics, indicating that measurement error was not primarily a matter of misunderstanding the questions.

All of these revisionist studies require that the response uncertainties constitute "measurement error" in the statistical sense. That is, instability must be due to the questions, not to the respondents. Confidence on this point is necessary if the corrected correlations are to be meaningful.

Several arguments blaming the respondents rather than the questions have been developed. For example, it is sometimes said that if the measurement error corrections are accurate, then the populace is very sophisticated about politics—too sophisticated to be believable. Hence the measurement models must be false. This argument misses the point of the revisionist literature. Nothing in the high over-time correlations implies that the citizenry has a good grasp of political life. As noted repeatedly by the revisionists, opinions may be stable for all sorts of unimpressive reasons. H. L. Mencken could accept the measurement models without changing his estimate of American intelligence.

In a similar fashion, some scholars have wondered whether the questions could have been as badly worded as the measurement models seem to imply (Converse & Markus, 1979; Kinder, 1983). But again, nothing in the measurement literature implies anything of the kind. Rather, the low reliabilities may simply reflect the difficulty of eliciting certain kinds of attitudes; difficulties that no opinion researcher can escape. Even in an interview with a foreign policy expert, for example, learning his general orientation toward American interventionism will be no simple matter. Inquiring after his party identification will be far easier. There is no reason to believe that all opinions are equally complex, even for individuals who understand them thoroughly. Thus the fact that most opinion reliabilities are low, while the party identification reliability is not, carries no necessary implication that the opinion questions are badly worded or that one item is better written than another. Objections based on those assumptions attribute a theoretical content to the models which they do not contain.

Other objections to the measurement literature have been based on collateral evidence. Thus Converse and Markus (1979) have argued that in two-wave panel studies, attitudes toward a political candidate correlate over time in proportion to the candidate's visibility. Feelings about Edward Kennedy are more stable than those about Henry Jackson. Since the question wordings are essentially identical, differences in stability must be due to differences in comprehension. Thus low correlations show low knowledge. Converse and Markus conclude that something similar must be going on with the original Converse items, so that the measurement models were mistaken in finding that true policy opinions were relatively stable. In their view, "measurement error" consists primarily of misunderstanding.

Converse and Markus's argument is inventive but not convincing. Its logic is this:

1. Low over-time correlations in candidate preference items are due to a lack of understanding on the part of respondents.
2. The revisionists' models imply that candidate preference items correlate poorly over time solely because of random measurement error.
3. Therefore the measurement models are mistaken.

The conclusion here certainly follows if the two premises are correct, and Converse and Markus make a good case for the first premise. Unfortunately, they present no evidence at all for the second one. They apparently assume that the measurement models would give the same result for candidate preferences as for policy views, so that the low correlations would be due to random error in both cases. But it is by no means clear that this supposition is true. Why should the rather precise notion of candidate preference have the same measurement characteristics as the necessarily nebulous policy attitudes? Without the second premise, the issue is not joined. It does no harm to the case for stable policy attitudes to point out that voters sometimes fail to learn much about unsuccessful Presidential candidates.

A serious indictment of the measurement models using the Converse-Markus data must support the second premise above: that the candidate preferences behave as policy preferences do. Two pieces of evidence are needed. First, the measurement models would have to be shown to yield high over-time stabilities for both visible and obscure candidates. Secondly, the measurement variances would have to be demonstrated to vary little with differences in education, political interest, or other relevant proxies for sophistication. Absent either one of these results, the measurement models would imply precisely what Converse and Markus say is true, namely that the differences in stabilities for candidates reflect genuine differences in understanding. Without these two findings, then, Converse and his critics agree on the analysis of candidate preferences, and those data are simply irrelevant. Since Converse and Markus provide no evidence on either point, the measurement models escape unscathed.

One is left, then, with the conclusion that the revisionists' case has yet to be seriously challenged. No one has been able to formulate a measurement model for Converse's data which supports his analysis. This consensus might seem to give hope to political scientists facing error-laden data. Unfortunately, matters are not so simple. All the available measurement models are closely related to a model of D. Wiley and J. Wiley (1970), in which attitude change over time is supposed to follow a first-order autoregressive law with purely random disturbances. In the Wiley-Wiley (1970) model, let observed survey responses (standardized to mean zero) at times 1, 2, and 3 be denoted by x_1, x_2, and x_3, and let u_1 be the true attitude at time 1. Let v_1 and v_2 be random disturbances in true attitude, and e_1, e_2, and e_3 be measurement errors at times 1, 2, and 3, both sets of which are assumed to have mean zero and to be distributed independently of the u's. In addition, the errors are assumed to have constant variance over time. Finally, let r_1 and r_2 be constants. Then the equations for the three time periods in the panel study are:

$$x_1 = u_1 + e_1$$
$$x_2 = r_1 u_1 + v_1 + e_2$$
$$x_3 = r_2(r_1 u_1 + v_1) + v_2 + e_3 \tag{7}$$

The six variances and covariances may be used to solve for the six parameters, namely, r_1, r_2, and the variances of u_1, v_1, and v_2, plus the error variance.

Other models can be imagined. For example, one might want to make the measurement errors slightly systematic, so that they were correlated over time. This corresponds to the notion that people may answer the same question the same way on two different occasions at least partly because the same extraneous forces impinge on them at both periods. For instance, the same interviewer may have come around again, the same election-time propaganda may have appeared on the doorstep, and so on. In short, individuals may be stable from one election to the next for reasons having little to do with the persistence of attitudes in their own minds.

A model of this kind has been proposed by J. Wiley and M. Wiley (1974). It differs from the D. Wiley-J. Wiley model in just two respects: first, the autoregressive parameter is fixed equal over the second and third time periods ($r_1 = r_2$); and second, the errors of measurement are assumed to obey a first-order autoregressive scheme with lag coefficient s. Thus the equations are as follows:

$$x_1 = u_1 + e_1$$
$$x_2 = r_1 u_1 + v_1 + se_1 + e_2$$
$$x_3 = r_1(r_1 u_1 + v_1) + v_2 + se_2 + e_3. \tag{8}$$

The six parameters here are the same as before, except that s replaces r_2, and they may be estimated in the same way.

The results of applying these two models to two of the questions used by Converse are given in Table 1. Both models fit the data exactly, in the sense of reproducing the variance matrix with perfect accuracy. Yet their conclusions are astonishingly different. If the first model, which is standard in the literature, is correct, the over-time stabilities are very nearly 1.0, more than twice as large as the raw correlations, making Converse dead wrong. On the other hand, if the second model is the truth, most of the over-time correlation is due to correlations between error terms, and the true stabilities are about 0.2, just half the size of the raw coefficients. In that case, attitudes at one time period statistically explain almost nothing in attitudes two years later (in no case more than 7% of the variance), so that Converse was even more right than he imagined.

With present knowledge, no grounds exist for choosing between these competing models. The rather dreary conclusion follows that even in the most heavily studied case, no confidence about the error variances is possible. In less trodden fields, the situation is inevitably more desperate. Bluntly put, political scientists do not know what survey responses are measuring.

The fundamental problem here is lack of a mathematical theory of the survey response. As a recent report of the National Academy of Science (Turner & Martin, 1981) has emphasized, we have little or no rigorous understanding of the effects of question wording, question order, and response error. And if these difficulties are severe in the case of ordinary surveys, they become crippling in the case of important international studies like Almond and Verba (1965), as was emphasized by Scheuch (1968). Real progress waits on basic theoretical research by political methodologists interested in surveys.

Even without a theory, a great deal could be learned by extending our current techniques to lengthier panel studies. For example, with just four waves of interviews, the two Wiley-Wiley models could be combined and tested. The new model would subsume (7) and (8) and extend them to a fourth wave in the obvious way, allowing for first-order autoregressive struc-

TABLE 1

Overtime Correlations of Political Attitudes Corrected for
Measurement Error Under Two Different Models
(Original Items Are from Converse, 1964)

	Guaranteed Jobs			Housing and Power		
	56-58	58-60	56-60	56-58	58-60	56-60
D. Wiley–J. Wiley Model (1970)						
raw r	.45	.47	.43	.37	.36	.37
corrected r	.95	.99	.94	.99	.99	.98
	56	58	60	56	58	60
reliability	.46	.49	.45	.38	.36	.38
	56-58	58-60	56-60	56-58	58-60	56-60
J. Wiley–M. Wiley Model (1974)						
raw r	.45	.47	.43	.37	.36	.37
corrected r	.25	.27	.07	.18	.18	.03
	56	58	60	56	58	60
reliability	.84	.85	.84	.88	.87	.88

tures in both true opinions and measurement errors, with the autoregressive parameters fixed equal over time for the errors. Thus the lag coefficients for true opinions would be r_1, r_2, and r_3, and the lag parameters for the errors would be s. Along with the measurement error variance and the variances of u_1, v_1, v_2, and v_3, there would be nine quantities to estimate, but ten variances and covariances in the data. Thus one could distinguish these two models (and many others) statistically and evaluate how well they fit. A better understanding of the Converse problem would result, and more importantly, clues would be provided as to how mathematical modeling of survey responses might proceed.

The urgency of theoretical research on the survey response bears emphasizing. Correcting for measurement error is the heart of any use of survey data. As yet, we simply do not know how to do that.

AGGREGATION BIAS

When political scientists doing empirical work are not using survey data, they are most often working with aggregate data of one sort or another: census information, voting returns by county or electoral district, crime statistics by state, and so on. These data are often cheaper to collect than survey information, and they extend back considerably further in time than do surveys. If one wants to know who voted for the Nazis, for instance, there is little alternative to working with aggregate elections returns. Moreover, even when surveys are feasible and affordable, aggregate information may be preferable. If one wants to study the effect of capital punishment on the murder rate, murder statistics are likely to yield more trustworthy conclusions than any possible survey. The answers to questions like "Have you ever murdered anyone?" or "Have you ever wanted to murder someone but were deterred by the thought of the electric chair?" would not be of much value.

Since Robinson (1951), social scientists have been painfully aware that ecological data were full of pitfalls. If one has a proposition cast at the individual level (e.g., Catholics were more likely to vote for the Nazis), voting returns from constituencies allow no direct test of it. Catholic constituencies might be more likely to vote Nazi even though individual Catholics are not. Robinson spoke of correlations, but his point is perfectly general. Goodman's (1953) "ecological regression" has the same problems.

Aggregation Bias as Contextual Effect

Two reactions are possible. In the first, one simply ignores the individual level of analysis. All explanations are cast at the constituency level, and the ecological inference problem disappears. In this model, single citizens do not vote; constituencies do. The statistical demand of this approach is that there be a unitary actor at the constituency level. Interactions among individuals do not suffice to create group-level explanations; processes of that kind can be formulated mathematically at the individual level (Erbring & Young, 1979). A legitimate "group mind" is needed to make the group-level explanation coherent.

Theories of group mind have always depended for their credibility on their imprecision. Stated clearly, they lack persuasive power. If the voting decision is truly made at the group level, one must come very near saying that the constituency rises sleepily on election day, rubs its eyes, takes thought, and says, "I imagine I will vote 37% Nazi." Researchers who find this a veridical theory of voting will be able to use logistic transformations of vote percentages —which destroy all chances of talking about the voters themselves (see Hannan, 1971, pp. 23-30)—and every other technique of quantitative analysis without qualm. No *statistical* difficulties occur.

For political scientists who cling to the conventional wisdom that individual citizens do the voting, more complex responses are needed. First, one may derive the conditions under which the ecological inferences will be the same as the individual-level ones. Theil (1954) considered the case of a single aggregate unit observed over time. His conclusions were extremely pessimistic. Roughly, every individual within the aggregate had to obey identical statistical laws or had to respond to changes in aggregate statistics in the same way. In practice, of course, neither is true.

Although no similar results are available for the cross-sectional case more common in political science, practical examples have been just as depressing as Theil's theoretical results. In Goodman's ecological regression model, for example, one might want to find the proportion of Democratic voters at time 1 who continued to vote Democratic at time 2, and the proportion of Republican voters at time 1 who switched to the Democrats at time 2. Call these proportions P and Q, respectively. Then if the fraction of Democratic votes at time 1 is denoted by D_1 and the same fraction at time 2 by D_2, and if everyone votes either Democratic or Republican, we have the simple accounting relationship:

$$D_2 = PD_1 + Q(1 - D_1). \tag{9}$$

If P and Q are constant across constituencies, or at least vary in ways that can be absorbed into a random disturbance term u, then (9) can be applied to a set of constituencies. Thus if i denotes the constituency number, we have from (9) in an obvious notation:

$$D_{2i} = Q + (P - Q)D_{1i} + u_i, \tag{10}$$

which has the form of a bivariate regression with intercept Q and slope $P - Q$. Thus one simply regresses the proportion Democratic at time 2 on the same proportion at time 1, and solves for P and Q from the resulting slope and intercept. It is quite easy to extend the model to multiple parties, abstention, controls for demographics, and so on, just by adding more terms to the regression and estimating additional regressions.

Computational experience with this model has been most unhappy. Commonly, the intercept is too small or even negative, and the slope is so large that the estimate of P is too high or even above one. Thus meaningless probabilities below zero and above one result. In fact, a substantial literature has developed to force the usual implausible estimates into the meaningful range from zero to one (e.g., Irwin & Meeter, 1969; Crewe & Payne, 1975). So far, the corrective treatments merely palliate the biases.

The standard interpretation of aggregation errors is to attribute them to "contextual effects." Ecological results are said to differ from individual findings because people influence each other. For example, heavily Democratic districts will produce Democrats who vote even more heavily Democratic than they otherwise would, simply because the environment drives them in that direction. Thus an individual-level—though, of course, not individualistic—explanation is used to account for the aggregate findings.

Much of this literature is not closely related to data, with predictable results. For example, literally dozens of articles have been written arguing that ecological regressions like Goodman's need a quadratic term. The argument goes that P and Q are not really constant across constituencies but instead depend on D_{1i}. Making P and Q linear functions of D_{1i}, and substituting in the original equation (10) yields a quadratic equation in D_{1i}. Unfortunately for this line of thinking, almost all ecological regressions exhibit strikingly linear relationships. The key to Goodman's woes must lie elsewhere.

The most specific and best grounded contextual argument is Butler and Stokes (1969, pp. 303-312). First, they give examples to show that the well-documented phenomenon of "uniform swing" in Britain is incompatible with Goodman's model. Their point holds generally. Formally, define uniform swing by the condition that for all i and some constant k, $D_{2i} = D_{1i} + k$. Taking expectations in (10) and rearranging:

$$k = Q + (P - Q - 1)D_{1i}. \tag{11}$$

Since k and Q are fixed, if (11) is to hold for all D_{1i}, we must have $P - Q - 1 = 0$, or:

$$P = Q + 1. \tag{12}$$

But then for any $Q > 0$, we have $P > 1$, which is impossible. Hence Goodman's model cannot be correct for any electoral system capable of uniform swing.

Butler and Stokes propose to modify Goodman by distinguishing two groups of voters. The first group attend to national media and thus respond to national forces, obeying Goodman's model. The second group are locally-oriented and take their cues from the partisan context of their local constituency. Butler and Stokes show that combinations of these two forces can produce uniform swing, and they give some evidence that in the 1964-1966 elections, the two groups exhibited the approximate qualitative behavior expected from the model.

Sad-to-say, the great difficulty of producing adequate models of contextual effects suitable to aggregate data can be illustrated even in this case. Formalize Butler and Stokes in the following way. Suppose that, in addition to the usual Goodman effects, a contextual force operates in proportion to the difference in the party strength. Following Butler-Stokes, let us measure this difference at the *previous* election. Then the contextual force is proportional to $D_{1i} - (1 - D_{1i})$, or $2D_{1i} - 1$. Letting its coefficient be G and adding this effect to the original Goodman equation (10), we have[1]:

$$D_{2i} = Q + (P - Q)D_{1i} + G(2D_{1i} - 1) + u_i,$$

or:

$$D_{2i} = (Q - G) + (P - Q + 2G)D_{1i} + u_i. \tag{13}$$

At first glance, Butler and Stokes appear to have broken through to high ground. Goodman's model tends to produce intercept terms too small and slopes too large, and equation (13) seems to explain why. The intercept is depressed by the amount G; the slope is increased by $2G$. The equation is perfectly linear, just as Goodman and the data had assured us, but the coefficients must be interpreted differently than Goodman had supposed.

Unfortunately, the model does not hold up upon closer examination. Return again to an electoral system with uniform swing. Under the Butler-Stokes model, two statements can then be made. First, in a constituency in which the two parties each received 50% of the vote at time 1, no contextual effect operates at time 2. That is, if $D_{1i} = 0.50$, $2D_{1i} - 1 = 0$, then the original Goodman model must fit. Making use of uniform swing gives (11) with $D_1 = 0.5$:

$$k = Q + (P - Q - 1)0.5. \tag{14}$$

Next, we note that (13) must also hold when averaged over constituencies. Letting $\overline{D_1}$ be the mean vote at time 1, exploiting the fact of uniform swing, and taking expectations:

$$k = (Q - G) + (P - Q + 2G - 1)\overline{D_1}. \tag{15}$$

The problem now becomes apparent. In any given election, P, Q, and G are parameters determined by the contests at times 1 and 2, plus the nature of the contextual effect. In addition, $\overline{D_1}$ is fixed. Thus these four factors can be taken as given. Among them, they determine the size of the uniform swing. Unfortunately, they do so in two distinct ways, (14) and (15). In general, the two equations are not consistent.

As an example, consider two elections with $P = 0.8$, $Q = 0.3$, $G = 0.1$, and $\overline{D_1} = 0.4$. (Incidentally, though it is beside the point, these are all quite reasonable values that might be expected to occur in an actual election.) Then (14) gives a swing of 5%, while (15) implies an 8% swing. Thus the model contradicts itself. Butler and Stokes cannot cope with uniform swing any more than Goodman can.

The dilemma cannot be escaped by making contextual effects dependent on the vote at the *second* time period. Though this assumption makes more sense substantively, essentially the same problem occurs. In this case, the Goodman model must fit constituencies where the vote at time 2 is 50%, plus fit a modified version of equation (15). Consistency again occurs only by chance.

As this example makes clear, even our most sophisticated aggregate-level contextual models have important lacunae. Contextual effects simply are not well understood. In spite of an enormous literature extolling their importance, almost no one has suggested explicit models by which they might operate. The key exception is Erbring and Young (1979), an article that summarizes and eviscerates an enormous amount of careless thinking on this topic. Although entirely focused on individual-level data, in principle this article proposes for the first time the explicit statistical models of social interaction that contextual theories assume. Whether its very heavy data demands will be met in the near future is questionable. But success at the individual level might make possible an inference to the aggregate-level model that is so badly needed.

Whether a contextual effect is there to be found remains an open question. As Prysby (1976) notes, even the best arguments in its favor are deeply flawed, and their evidence is certainly consistent with its absence. Weatherford (1982) finds that most people do not talk politics with their neighbors in any case, which eliminates the usual mechanism for communicating contextual effects. Finally, in one of the most direct tests of the contextual hypothesis, Tate (1974) showed that a large number of contextual variables proved to be useless in predicting individual-level British voting behavior. In short, the form of contextual effects, their internal logic, and even whether they exist at all remain unknown. Serious theoretical research on deriving an aggregate-level contextual model from empirically-verified assumptions about individual-level interactions should have a high priority for students of social context.

Aggregate Bias as Specification Error

Since Hanushek, Jackson, and Kain (1974), many researchers have taken up the view that aggregation error occurs because of specification errors. On this view, contextual effects may or may not exist, but aggregation bias would be expected in any case, simply because erroneous equations never yield the right answer. Hence the task is to properly specify the regression equations so that bias disappears. Hanushek *et al.* show that Robinson's original example is very nearly corrected by adding variables to the equation to specify it more accurately.

Needless-to-say, better specifications are always welcome. But one can question whether this formulation resolves the theoretical question. "Specification error" is often taken to mean a deviation from the one true causal law. On this logic, aggregation bias occurs because some of the causally important variables are omitted from the equation. Adding them, it is said, eliminates the bias.

A moment's thought will show that in this form, eliminating specification error is a hopeless task. For we are not very likely ever to have perfect knowledge. Causally important variables are omitted from *every* social science regression, simply because not everything is measurable. If good estimates from aggregate data wait on specifications with all causal factors included, no progress can be hoped for in our lifetimes. More importantly, adding a variable here and there may make marginal improvements, but no guarantee exists that the bias is thereby reduced. Statistical theory demonstrates that the one true model is better than any other, but not much more. An equation missing several key causal factors is not necessarily improved by adding one of them; the biases in fact may get worse.

If on the other hand, one takes "proper specification" of a regression equation to mean that its independent variables are uncorrelated with the disturbance term (the conventional statistical definition), the notion that the absence of specification error implies the absence of aggregation bias is simply false. Take the case of Goodman's model. It is purely descriptive and hence perfectly well specified at the individual level. With individual level data, its independent variables are necessarily uncorrelated with its disturbance, and accurate estimates result. However, with aggregate data, it often gives meaningless results, even with large amounts of data. Thus proper specification in this sense is not the answer either.

We are left then with just one possibility. "Proper specification" might mean that at the aggregate level, the disturbances are uncorrelated with the independent variables. Now of course this does guarantee asymptotically accurate results. But what are we to make of it? What sort of modification of our specifications is called for? Our theoretical knowledge is entirely at the individual level, and we rarely understand much of the grouping procedure that created the geographic districts. The advice to seek proper specification, interpreted in this fashion, is either tautological (Avoid bias!) or else quite difficult to interpret. *What characteristics of the individual-level specifications lead to uncorrelated disturbances at the aggregate level?* That is the central question for this point of view, and its answer is unknown.

What makes the aggregation problem so severe, then, is this dilemma. Aggregate data are often superior to individual-level information, even when no contextual effect or group mind is at work. But they commonly lead to severe biases, of whose solution we understand almost nothing. For serial correlation, selection bias, underidentification, or the other difficulties routinely encountered in non-experimental work, every textbook carries straightforward counsel on eliminating the biases. One may not always be willing or able to take the advice, but there is never any doubt about what should be done. One looks in vain for similar instruction on aggregation. At this stage in our knowledge, the aggregation problem simply is in a class by itself. Clearly, intensive theoretical research on this problem deserves high priority in methodologists' research programs.

CONCLUSION

The state of our knowledge in political methodology gives little cause for self-congratulation. The two principal topics that have concerned us, measurement error and aggregation bias, remain both poorly formulated and even more poorly understood. Enough data has been collected that one could surely recognize a successful solution to either one if it were presented. But the anemic mathematics that has been applied to both tasks is not likely to produce one.

More than anything else, what would help are formal theories with measurement models built into them. These have been common in psychology (see, for example, Atkinson, Bower, & Crothers, 1965) and sociology (see Berger, Cohen, Snell, & Zelditch, 1962) for two decades now. Political science remains dominated by fact-free theory of the verbal or rational-choice variety. In a charming exception, Enelow and Hinich (1983) have recently attempted to link the spatial theory of voting to factor analytic models of public opinion. Work of that kind remains all too rare.

LISREL-type models (Jöreskog & Sörbom, 1979) also constitute a partial exception. These sophisticated structures offer the opportunity to mesh substantive specifications with measurement models. In a very general way, they represent the direction in which empirical work must move, and political scientists have not been slow to exploit them. But here again our theoretical limitations are painfully obvious. First of all, we often have no knowledge of either the substantive or the measurement model, and so assume linearity without further argument. Doing so may be better than ignoring measurement altogther, but it creates additional doubt in what is usually a complicated specification with enough credibility problems to go around. No LISREL model abolishes the theoretical questions discussed earlier.

Even ignoring these first difficulties, LISREL models raise many inferential questions. They assume normal distributions for every variable in the equations, including both measured and unmeasured variables, plus disturbances. Thus one dummy exogenous variable will violate the postulates. No doubt the consistency of the estimates will survive such minor transgressions (though this has not been proved, to my knowledge), but the standard errors of the coefficients will not. Thus even if all the other assumptions held, it would be a safe bet that every LISREL standard error published in a political science journal is erroneous. Perhaps jackknifing the estimates would help; again, no such result is known.

Other limitations of the standard LISREL model have become clear in applications. All equations are assumed linear. No interaction effects can be employed, no quadratic terms, no transformations of variables already used untransformed elsewhere in the model. Moreover, variables must be continuous. Dichotomous or polychotomous endogenous variables are beyond the capacity of the system (except in rather specialized cases, e.g., all exogenous variables normally distributed). Brady (1982) has investigated the extension of LISREL models to discrete data, but very little else has been accomplished in political science. Here as everywhere else, there is much theoretical work remaining.

The progress that might be expected from more explicit attention to methodological theory became clear in the recent debate on how economic conditions affect the vote (Kramer, 1971; Kinder & Kiewiet, 1979; and others). Initially, one side used over-time aggregate data which implied strong economic effects on the vote, and the other studied survey responses which showed none. Since neither side had a measurement model, contradiction and confusion were the inevitable result.

Happily, however, Kramer (1983) has produced formal statistical models of the theories on each side. He assumes that citizens respond politically to *government-induced* changes in their income, while researchers can observe (with either survey or aggregate data) only the *total* income change. Thus a measurement error is generated. As his main finding, Kramer shows that, as one would expect under his assumptions, aggregate-level data largely wash out the errors. Though not unbiased, they are greatly superior to the individual-level survey responses. In this case, then, aggregate data are to be preferred, an iconoclastic finding reminiscent of Grunfeld and Griliches (1960). Similarly, Kramer shows that if voters respond to the true overall state of the economy rather than their own personal situations ("sociotropic voting"), an interpretation seemingly supported by some of the cross-sectional survey data, then in fact those data are hopelessly biased. Because there is no variance in the state of the economy at a single time period, a cross-section contains no statistical information about sociotropic voting. Once again, aggregate data are superior.

Kramer's powerful argument poses a severe challenge to the conventional wisdom about aggregate data. At a minimum, it dramatically raises the level of the debate, suggesting that our lack of understanding of aggregation may not be so debilitating after all. Yet the force of his conclusions can be questioned. As Kramer himself notes, aggregate data are inadequate in principle to disentangle self-interested from sociotropic voting. Regardless of whether citizens respond to their own income changes or to changes in national income, the effect at the aggregate level is the same: national income changes predict the vote. What Kramer shows is that if we must choose between individual-level cross-section data with uncorrectable errors and over-time aggregate data with the same weaknesses, the latter are to be preferred in studying economic effects on the vote. But since the aggregate data cannot answer the central question, and probably have biases beyond those Kramer mentions[2], his result shows only that in the land of the blind, the one-eyed man is king. If depth perception is needed, it may be best to find a new king.

Kramer's findings do leave an alternative open to the devotees of individual-level data: the estimation of a substantively plausible model taking account of measurement error in the survey responses (both Kramer's kind of error and ordinary response error). In theory, truly adequate estimates could be produced from a single cross-section, at least if we relax Kramer's assumption that in sociotropic voting, everyone acts on the same view of the national economy. In practice, however, panel studies seem more likely to be helpful, not only because they generate real variation in the national state of the economy and thus escape Kramer's critique, but also because they contain repeated measures and lagged instrumental variables to control measurement error. A panel study with individual-level survey responses and adjustments for measurement error would be greatly superior to aggregate data, even under Kramer's postulates. Most importantly, it would distinguish sociotropic from individualistic voting, which aggregate data cannot hope to do. Of course, as noted earlier, correcting for measurement error in the survey responses will be no trivial affair. The plausible substantive assumptions and analytic techniques that would guarantee consistent estimates are not yet evident. Certainly, intriguing methodological challenges on both sides of this topic remain to be investigated. Kramer's work demonstrates just how great the rewards of progress on our principal agenda might be.

Mounting a sustained attack on such questions across political science may demand some changes in our work habits. Fundamental research must come to take priority, at least some of the time, over applied work. It should be possible to get funding, publish respectably, and make a career studying the principal agenda of political methodology. And to provide for the future, much better mathematical training will have to be provided at both the graduate and undergraduate level.

Basic methodological research will not be of general interest to the profession. Almost by definition, any work simple enough to be understood widely will not dent the problems. *Political Methodology,* if it is to keep its leadership position in the field, will become more specialized and technical. To some degree this has already occurred, just as it did in economics and psychology in an earlier era. So long as it does not lead to sterile theorizing, the growing separation is a sign of health and progress.

In sum, the tenor of this essay should be taken as optimistic rather than pessimistic. Certainly it provides no excuse to abandon quantitative work. One does not escape logical gaps in an argument by becoming less rigorous, or by abandoning logic entirely. We have no choice but to find out how people answer survey questions, how national and international agencies produce cross-national data, and what aggregation bias amounts to.

A beginning has been made. Political methodologists may still be rewarded more for "substantive" (i.e., merely applied) work than for "technical" (i.e., theoretical) contributions, but their numbers grow and the product improves. *Political Methodology* may look like *samizdat,* but its sophistication steadily distances it from the more prestigious journals. And even the fact that our theoretical failings have led to so many anomalies gives cause for hope. For if we can come to face our weaknesses, then in the manner of the alcoholic standing up for the first time to confess his drunkenness, a major step toward improvement may have been taken.

APPENDIX

This appendix gives a proof of the inconsistency result for multiple regression when a single independent variable is observed with error. The true relationship is assumed to be

$$y = X^*\beta + u, \tag{A1}$$

where y is an n-dimensional vector of observations on the dependent variable, X^* is an n × k matrix of observations on the fixed true values of the independent variables, β is a coefficient vector to be estimated, and u is a disturbance term whose elements are mutually independent. The usual regression assumptions are made: the disturbances are assumed to have mean zero, constant variance, and zero correlation with the true independent variables. That is, $E(u) = 0$, $E(uu') = \sigma_u^2 I$, and $E(X^{*\prime}u) = 0$.

All but one of the independent variables are observed without error. The first true independent variable, x_1^*, is not observed but is related to an observed variable, x_1, as follows:

$$x_1 = x_1^* + e_1, \tag{A2}$$

where x_1, x_1^*, and e_1 are each n-dimensional vectors, and where it is assumed that the elements of e_1 are mutually independent, and that they have mean zero, constant variance, and zero correlations with the true independent variables and the disturbances. Thus $E(e_1) = 0$, $E(e_1 e_1') = \sigma_e^2 I$, $E(X^{*\prime} e_1) = 0$, and $E(u' e_1) = 0$. Finally, to guarantee that certain probability limits exist, it will also be postulated that $\lim X^{*\prime} X^* / n = \Omega$, a constant positive definite matrix, and that the elements of u and e_1 have uniformly bounded absolute fourth moments.

Letting $E = [e_1\ 0 \ldots 0]$, it follows that $plim\ E'E/n = \Sigma$, a matrix which is zero everywhere except for its upper left corner element, which is σ_e^2. Now let β_1 be the first element of β and let X be the matrix of observed independent variables, so that $X = X^* + E$. Then write (1) as:

$$
\begin{aligned}
y &= X\beta + u - E\beta \\
&= X\beta + u - \beta_1 e_1.
\end{aligned} \tag{A3}
$$

Then the OLS estimate is:

$$
\begin{aligned}
\hat{\beta} &= (X'X)^{-1}(X'y) \\
&= \beta + (X'X/n)^{-1}(X^* + E)'\ (u - \beta_1 e_1)/n.
\end{aligned} \tag{A4}
$$

Thus:

$$
plim\ (\hat{\beta}) = \beta + (\Omega + \Sigma)^{-1}
\begin{bmatrix}
-\beta_1 \sigma_e^{\ 2} \\
0 \\
\cdot \\
\cdot \\
\cdot \\
0
\end{bmatrix}. \tag{A5}
$$

Now partition the matrix of observed independent variables as $X = [x_1\ X_2]$ and similarly $\beta' = [\beta_1\ \beta_2']$. Thus x_1 is the first independent variable and β_1 is its coefficient, while X_2 is the matrix of all the other independent variables and β_2 is its coefficient vector. Set $b = (X_2' X_2)^{-1} X_2' x_1^*$ and $s^2 = [x_1^{*\prime} x_1^* - x_1^{*\prime} X_2 (X_2' X_2)^{-1} X_2' x_1^*]/n$. Hence b is just the coefficient vector when x_1^* is regressed on X_2, and s^2 is the corresponding residual variance. Now using standard results on partitioned inverses (e.g., Theil, 1971, p. 18), we find from (A5):

$$plim\ (\hat{\beta}_1) = \frac{s^2}{s^2 + \sigma_e^2}\ \beta_1. \tag{A6}$$

and

$$plim\,(\hat{\beta}_2) = \beta_2 + \frac{\sigma_e^2}{s^2 + \sigma_e^2}\,\beta_1\,b. \tag{A7}$$

The last equation is a relationship between vectors. Taking any single line from it, say the *j*th, gives the result (3) in the text.

NOTES

1. To avoid unnecessary complexity, the division of the population into locally and nationally oriented groups has been suppressed. If these groups have constant proportions across constituencies, for example, (13) can easily be rewritten to reflect the fact that the contextual effect applies only to the former group and the Goodman model only to the latter. As written, (13) absorbs the proportionality weights for the two groups into the parameters *P*, *Q*, and *G*.
2. Another of Kramer's assumptions is that in expectation, all citizens respond identically to income changes (in dollars), meaning that their regression coefficients are all equal. This postulate allows him to escape aggregation bias (Theil, 1954). However, systematic variation in political responses to income change seems quite likely, even within the rational-choice framework Kramer adopts. Diminishing marginal utility of income would generate it, for example. Thus his aggregate level estimates probably have additional biases beyond those he considers. Some random coefficient models also generate biases in cross-sectional or even panel data, of course, so that the relative magnitudes of the biases need investigation. The advantage of individual-level data is that more powerful statistical techniques can eliminate those biases. With aggregate data, the parameters of coefficient variation are hopelessly underidentified.

REFERENCES

Achen, Christopher H. Mass political attitudes and the survey response. *American Political Science Review*, 1975, *69*, 1218-23.

Achen, Christopher. Measuring representation. *American Journal of Political Science*, 1978, *22*, 475-510.

Almond, Gabriel A., & Verba, Sidney. *The civic culture.* Boston: Little, Brown, 1965.

Asher, Herbert B. Some consequences of measurement error in survey data. *American Journal of Political Science*, 1974, *18*, 469-85.

Atkinson, Richard C., Bower, Gordon H., & Crothers, Edward J. *An introduction to mathematical learning theory.* New York: Wiley, 1965.

Berger, Joseph, Cohen, Bernard P., Snell, J. Lauri, & Zelditch, Morris, Jr. *Types of formalization in small-group research.* Boston: Houghton Mifflin, 1962.

Bishop, George F., Tuchfarber Alfred J., & Oldendick, Robert W. Change in the structure of American political attitudes: The nagging question of question wording. *American Journal of Political Science*, 1978, *22*, 250-69.

Brady, Henry E. The factor analysis of ordinal preference data. Working Paper 106. Graduate School of Public Policy, University of California, Berkeley, 1981.

Brady, Henry E. Random utility models of primary preferences with latent variables and undecided voters. Paper presented at the meetings of the Public Choice Society, San Antonio, Texas, March 1982.

Butler, David, & Stokes, Donald. *Political change in Britain.* New York: St. Martin's, 1969.

Converse, Philip. The nature of belief systems in mass publics. In David E. Apter, Ed., *Ideology and discontent.* New York: Free Press, 1964, pp. 206-61.

Converse, Philip, & Markus, G. B. Plus ca change. . . The new CPS election study panel. *American Political Science Review,* 1979, *73,* 32-49.

Crewe, Ivor, & Payne, Clive. Another game with nature: An ecological regression model of the British two-party vote ratio in 1970. *British Journal of Political Science,* 1975, *6,* 43-81.

Dean, Gillian, & Moran, Thomas W. Measuring mass political attitudes: Change and unreliability. *Political Methodology,* 1977, *4,* 383-414.

Dhrymes, Phoebus. *Econometrics.* New York: Harper and Row, 1970.

Dhrymes, Phoebus. *Introductory econometrics.* New York: Springer-Verlag, 1978.

Enelow, James, & Hinich, Melvin J. *The spatial theory of voting.* Cambridge: Cambridge University Press, forthcoming.

Erbring, Lutz, & Young, Alice A. Individuals and social structure. *Sociological Methods and Research,* 1979, *7,* 396-430.

Erikson, Robert S. The SRC panel data and mass political attitudes. Paper delivered to the 1975 annual meeting of the American Political Science Association, San Francisco, September 1-5, 1975.

Goodman, Leo. Ecological regression and the behavior of individuals. *American Journal of Sociology,* 1953, *64,* 610-25.

Greene, Vernon L. Aggregate bias effects of random error in multivariate OLS regression. *Political Methodology,* 1978, *5,* 461-67.

Grunfeld, Y., & Griliches, Z. Is aggregation necessarily bad? *Review of Economics and Statistics,* 1960, *42,* 1-13.

Hannan, Michael T. *Aggregation and disaggregation in sociology.* Lexington, Mass.: D.C. Heath, 1971.

Hanushek, Eric A., & Jackson, John E. *Statistical methods for social scientists.* New York: Academic Press, 1977.

Hanushek, Eric A., Jackson, John E., & Kain, John F. Model specification, use of aggregate data, and the ecological correlation fallacy. *Political Methodology,* 1974, *1,* 89-107.

Irwin, Galen, & Meeter, Duane A. Building voter transition models from aggregate data. *Midwest Journal of Political Science,* 1969, *13,* 545-66.

Jackson, John E. Statistical estimation of possible response bias in close-ended issue questions. *Political Methodology,* 1979, *6,* 393-423.

Johnston, J. *Econometric methods* (2nd ed.). New York: McGraw-Hill, 1972.

Jöreskog, Karl G., & Sörbom, Dag. *Advances in factor analysis and structural equation models.* Cambridge, Mass.: Abt, 1979.

Kelejian, Harry H., & Oates, Wallace E. *Introduction to econometrics* (2nd ed.). New York: Harper and Row, 1981.

Kinder, Donald R. Diversity and complexity in American public opinion. This volume, 1983.

Kinder, Donald R., & Kiewiet, D. Roderick. Economic discontent and political behavior: The role of personal grievances and collective economic judgments in congressional voting. *American Journal of Political Science,* 1979, *23,* 495-527.

Kramer, Gerald H. Short-term fluctuations in U.S. voting behavior, 1896-1964. *American Political Science Review,* 1971, *65,* 131-43.

Kramer, Gerald H. The ecological fallacy revisited: Aggregate- versus individual-level findings on economics and elections, and sociotropic voting. *American Political Science Review,* forthcoming.

Levi, Maurice D. Errors in the variables bias in the presence of correctly measured variables. *Econometrica,* 1973, *41,* 985-86.

Lord, Frederic M., & Novick, Melvin R. *Statistical theories of mental test scores.* Reading, Mass.: Addison-Wesley, 1968.

Maddala, G. S. *Econometrics.* New York: McGraw-Hill, 1977.

Pindyck, Robert S., & Rubinfeld, Daniel L. *Econometric models and economic forecasts.* New York: McGraw-Hill, 1976.

Prysby, Charles L. Community partisanship and individual voting behavior: Methodological problems of contextual analysis. *Political Methodology,* 1976, *3,* 183-98.

Rao, Potluri, & Miller, Roger LeRoy. *Applied econometrics.* Belmont, Calif.: Wadsworth, 1971.

Rasch, Georg. *Probabilistic models for some intelligence and attainment tests.* Chicago: University of Chicago Press, 1980.

Robinson, William S. Ecological correlations and the behavior of individuals. *American Sociological Review,* 1950, *15,* 351-57.

Ross, Keith, & Duvall, Raymond. The size of armed forces: Dispelling some myths about cross-national data. *Journal of Conflict Resolution,* forthcoming.

Scheuch, Erwin K. Cross-cultural use of sample surveys: Problems of comparability. In Stein Rokkan, Ed. *Comparative research across cultures and nations.* Paris: Mouton, 1968.

Sullivan, John L., Piereson, James E., & Marcus, George E. Ideological constraint in the mass public: A methodological critique and some new findings. *American Journal of Political Science,* 1978, *22,* 233-49.

Tate, C. Neal. Individual and contextual variables in British voting behavior: An explanatory note. *American Political Science Review,* 1974, *68,* 1656-62.

Theil, Henri. *Linear aggregation in economic relations.* Amsterdam: North Holland, 1954.

Theil, Henri. *Principles of econometrics.* New York: Wiley, 1971.

Torgerson, Warren S. *Theory and methods of scaling.* New York: Wiley, 1958.

Turner, Charles F., & Martin, Elizabeth, Eds. *Surveys of subjective phenomena: Summary report.* Washington, D.C.: National Academy Press, 1981.

Warren, Richard D., White, Joan Keller, & Fuller, Wayne A. An errors-in-variables analysis of managerial role performance. *Journal of the American Statistical Association 69,* 1974, *348,* 886-93.

Weatherford, Stephen. Measurement problems in contextual analysis: On statistical assumptions and social processes. *Political Methodology,* 1982, *8,* 61-69.

Wiley, David E., & Wiley, James A. The estimation of measurement error in panel data. *American Sociological Review,* 1970, *35,* 112-16.

Wiley, James A., & Wiley, Mary Glenn. A note on correlated errors in repeated measurements. *Sociological Methods and Research,* 1974, *3,* 172-88.

4

Self-Portrait:
Profile of Political Scientists*

Naomi B. Lynn

This survey offers a current profile of the political science profession in the United States, drawing on a substantial number of studies that have been made over the years. What emerges can be termed a self-portrait. It is, however, no simple self-portrait of an individual against a neutral background. Rather it is a group picture which shows a profession resting on a somewhat fragmented foundation, grappling with current challenges--both individually and collectively--in order to build a viable future. Thus, the portrait is complex, more in the tradition of Hieronymus Bosch than Rembrandt.

At the 1978 meeting of the American Political Science Association Everett Carll Ladd, Jr. and Seymour Martin Lipset characterized political science as "a discipline in decline" (Ladd & Lipset, 1978, p. 21). This summary statement is an appropriate and proper backdrop for the self-portrait of the discipline. Decline, however, for political science is a new development; the profession has not suffered from any gradual, long-term loss of ideas or energy. On the contrary, the profession experienced recent periods of explosive growth. But the excitement of the intellectual currents and debates led us to ignore the impending demographic and economic forces that have shaped our current problems. The past half dozen years have been difficult ones for political science.

The Discipline's First Century Foundations:
Some Broad Currents

Political science, as an organized academic discipline in American universities and colleges, was one of the products of the flowering of higher

*The author is grateful to Seymour Martin Lipset for his criticisms and suggestions and to Walter B. Roettger, Margaret Conway, Eugene J. Alpert, David Finley, Thomas Mann and Neale Pearsons for their review comments. She also thanks Charles O. Jones and Austin Ranney for some perspicacious observations.

education in this country in the decades following the Civil War. In June of 1880 the School of Political Science was founded at Columbia University, under the leadership of John W. Burgess (Somit & Tannenhaus, 1978, p. 17). Interest in the subject grew at numerous other institutions; by December of 1903 the numbers of and the interactions between political scientists had reached the point that it was useful to establish the American Political Science Association. Thus our discipline is barely into its second century as an established field, while as an organized professional group we are an even younger phenomenon.

A Capsule Look at Some Major Intellectual Issues. The century following 1880 had many turbulent aspects as the field sought to define itself and to select its objectives and methods of reaching them. Lipset (1969, p. vii) has pointed out that the term *political science,* as originally used, meant what would now be called policy science; that is, it initially emphasized the structure and function of government and the concerns of authorities. Only later did political science also stress systematic generalizations based on empirical data and statistical analyses of the sort now familiar in all social sciences. This fluctuation of emphasis between the study of the polity on the one hand and the relationship of the polity to the society in which it operates on the other has been a main feature of the discipline. Such fluctuation can be frustrating for those who feel a need for an integrating model of the field. Greenstein and Polsby (1975) reflect on this when they observe that "Early in his career, the fledgling political scientist learns that his discipline is ill-defined, amorphous, and heterogeneous" (p. v).

The discipline of political science has problems: political scientists per se are highly differentiated from political philosophers on the one hand and pure mathematicians who may handle political data on the other; the discipline lacks a central paradigm and is unlikely to get one soon; political science relies mainly on conceptual schemes from such disciplines as economics, sociology, and psychology; there is a notable current lack of methodological concerns; political cleavages of the late 1960's and 1970's have left scars on the discipline; and finally, economic and demographic factors have adversely affected the environment within which political scientists work. We may draw, however, some comfort from a brief review of some of our field's past challenges.

One of the pioneer scholars, Charles E. Merriam of the University of Chicago, sought in the early 1920's to move toward a "science of politics" (Somit & Tannenhaus, 1967, p. 87). He wanted more scientific rigor, and his efforts led to the establishment in the American Political Science Association of a Committee on Political Research. (Dwight Waldo, 1975, p. 48 traces to Merriam's "school" many leaders in the behavioral movement of later decades.) In contrast, Thomas H. Reed of Harvard argued that the primary responsibility of political science was to educate citizens and to prepare students for careers in government. As Somit and Tannenhaus (1967) note "Though neither Merriam nor Reed captured the Holy Land, or came very close to it, both crusades left their mark on the discipline" (p. 88).

After the second World War, with the advent of computers,

"behavioralism" became the dominant intellectual force in political science. Behavioralists argued for a more scientific approach to the study of politics. They borrowed many of their models from the physical and natural sciences. By the 1960's the behavioral movement made extensive use of the sort of scientific approaches and systematic tools that Merriam had urged. It appeared that if behavioralism delivered on its major promises, it might become the "predominant paradigm" of political science (Somit & Tannenhaus, 1967, p. 210). This did not occur.

A survey of members of the American Political Science Association indicates that while behavioralism made important contributions, it did not establish hegemony; indeed, it appears that there is no consensus of commitment to it, nor great certainty about the meaning of the term (Roettger, 1978, p. 10). In part this reflects the deep doubt of most political scientists that the field has the capacity to become "scientific" in the sense of the natural sciences (Roettger, 1978, p. 14). More seriously behavioralism has been accused of developing "a number of blind and unquestioned ideological biases . . . that followed almost directly from the dominant belief that facts could and should be separated entirely from values, and that followed from the criterion that rigor always comes before relevance in questions of good political science" (Lowi, 1972, p. 14).

By the early 1970's the term behavioralism was often used in contradistinction to post-behavioralism (see Graham & Carey, 1972). The latter embodied the value orientations that were associated with the counterculture and the New Left (Waldo, 1975, pp. 113, 114). Post-behavioralism also incorporated other points, as David Easton observed in his 1969 presidential address to the APSA: Substance must precede technique; behavioral research must not lose touch with reality; knowledge must be implemented (Easton, 1969, p. 1052). In summary, post-behavioralism "supports and extends behavioral methods and techniques by seeking to make their substantive implications more cogent for the problems of our times" (Easton, 1969, p. 1061). Like the counterculture post-behavioralism left a noticeable mark, but it did not produce enduring basic changes in political science's intellectual and methodological underpinnings.

As political science ended its first century, it became increasingly clear that the search for a single paradigm was futile. Rather, each sub-specialty searches for its own unifying model. As it does so, it tries to incorporate appropriate scientific methodology, but it also seeks to discover meanings that "science" alone may miss (Baum, Griffiths, Mathews, & Scherruble, 1976, pp. 915-917). Baum *et al.* points out the need for the latter with a quotation from Charles Darwin's *Autobiography:*

> But for many years I cannot endure to read a line of poetry. My mind seems to have become a kind of machine for grinding laws out of a large collection of facts, but why this should have caused the atrophy of that part of the brain on which tastes depend, I cannot conceive. The loss of these tastes is a loss of happiness, and may possibly be injurious to the intellect, and more probably to the moral character, by enfeebling the emotional part of our nature (p. 917).

Other intellectual issues are also unresolved in the discipline. The dispute between rationalism and anti-rationalism is a notable example. Essentially rationalism contends that people are rational and seek to maximize stated goals in a calculating manner; this is the approach of economics. According to this formulation the bureaucrat seeks to maximize the budget, the voter tries to maximize expected utility, and the analyst attempts to formulate theories of collective choice (Barry, 1970; Frolich & Oppenheimer, 1978; and Goodin, 1976). The anti-rationalist view is more social-psychological in nature. It points out that irrationality is an inescapable feature of social experience and that feelings and needs defy rational examination (see Glass, 1978, pp. 63-92 in Frolich and Oppenheimer).

A parallel dispute arises over whether political scientists should seek to build deductive or inductive theories, or both. Similarly there is disagreement between some who downplay the role of the study of classical political philosophy, and others who consider that these roots are our rich foundation that should not be ignored.

Two decades of intellectual ferment have led to productive and exciting work. They have also exacted a price as David Finley (1982) points out:

> The hiatus of the methodological debates, squabbles and cabals of the 1960's, championing or reviling symbols of behavioralism and then post-behavioralism—essential as the underlying issues have been and remain—did forestall a lot of the substantive progress that the outside world (and governments and private foundations that want a product) had been encouraged to expect from the discipline. That generally undermined the popular respect for political science among important external constituencies on whom we still depend. The historical fact is a part of diagnosing the condition of the profession today. . . . We *do* suffer from the absence of an agreed paradigm, even if that absence is inevitable. (Comment made as panel member, APSA convention, Denver, 1982)

Indicators of Excellence. Political science is taught and learned at many hundreds of American colleges and universities. Political science research and writing have produced a voluminous literature. As in all academic fields, some schools, journals and individuals have achieved special prominence. The work that carries the mark of special excellence forms part of our common foundation.

Over the years there have been many ratings of the "top departments" in virtually all areas. Such ratings are subject to inevitable criticisms, chief among them that the underlying validity of the reputational perceptions on which most are based are doubtful. All measures are necessarily symptomatic, and they should not be taken too seriously. They seek signs which may be reasonable surrogates for excellence, but which are not excellence per se. Somit and Tannenhaus (1967), in their monumental study of our field, recognize that, "Full many a flower is born to blush unseen." They go on, however, to publish a comparative ranking shown here as part of an interesting 40-year comparison study in Table 1. These data show great consistency, even though some schools have gained (e.g. Yale) and some lost (e.g. Illinois) standing over the years. While a few position shifts have occurred, the striking fact that emerges is the stability in these ratings over a 57-year period.

This is especially significant when one observes that no two studies used exactly the same criteria and questions.

John S. Robey (1979) made a "productivity" study of departments that considered, not reputations, but publications by departments' faculty. This is shown in Table 2. Michigan is first in productivity—above its rating in the other studies. Ranked second through fifth are Kentucky, Florida State, Michigan State and Georgia, none of whom ranked in any of the reputational studies. While one would not want to claim that counting journal articles in the *American Political Science Review* and six regional journals is an ultimate criterion, it does suggest that excellence is more widely distributed than some suppose. It must, of course, be noted that many leading scholars publish most of their articles in books because they are under pressure to do so by people with project and/or conference money. (Robey did not count books, even highly important ones; he also did not control his numbers for department size.)

In a 1982 study McCormick and Bernick found results generally consistent with the earlier studies cited above. They controlled, however, for two things: the size of the authors' current departments and the number of recent graduates produced at the Ph.D. granting institutions (see Table 3).

The identification of prestigious journals is shown in Table 4. Data come from surveys from Somit and Tannenhaus with a later update by Roettger. The main change shown is the emergence of the *American Journal of Political Science* to "second tier" status, as it moved from its former regional (Midwest) identification (Roettger, 1978, p. 19).

The identification of the most outstanding contributors to the field of political science can be done both by reputation and by a count of others' citations to their work. Table 5 shows the results of Roettger's 1978 reputational study. Table 6 was compiled by John S. Robey; it is based on 1970-1979 citations. Also shown in this table are the schools where these scholars received their Ph.D.s and where they teach. It is noteworthy that the "elite" universities identified by the early reputational studies again show up prominently.

THE PROFESSION'S JOB MARKET

A full picture of the job market would have to include the observation that there are many political scientists among the tenured faculty at soundly financed universities. But, just as it is unemployment more than employment that reflects the economy's health, so our profession's economic situation is heavily influenced by the problem-ridden segments of the job market.

The Stagnation of Demand. The demand for academic political scientists is related significantly to the number of potential students who are able to pursue higher education. From the middle 1940's to the early 1960's a "baby boom" occurred. This produced a large number of college students from the 1960's to the early 1980's. There was general prosperity (with notable exception periods such as 1973-1975), and government-sponsored financial aid pro-

TABLE 1

Longitudinal Ranking of Graduate Departments of Political Science:
1925, 1957, 1963, 1964,* 1975-1976, 1982

1925 (Hughes)		1957 (Keniston)		1963 (Somit-Tannenhaus)	
1	Harvard	1	Harvard	1	Harvard
2	Chicago	2	Chicago	2	Yale
3	Columbia	3	California	3	California (Berkeley)
4	Wisconsin		(Berkeley)	4	Chicago
5	Illinois	4	Columbia	5	Princeton
6	Michigan	5	Princeton	6	Columbia
7	Princeton	6	Michigan	7	Michigan
8	Johns Hopkins	7	Yale	8.5	Stanford
9.5	Iowa	8	Wisconsin	8.5	Wisconsin
9.5	Pennsylvania	9	Minnesota	10.5	California
11	California	10	Cornell		(Los Angeles)
	(Berkeley)	11	Illinois	10.5	Cornell
		12	California	12	Johns Hopkins
			(Los Angeles)	13	Northwestern
		13	Stanford	14	Indiana
		14	Johns Hopkins	15	Illinois
		15	Duke	16	Minnesota
				17	North Carolina
				18.5	Duke
				18.5	Syracuse
				20	Pennsylvania

grams multiplied; thus the market demand was good. The birth rate peaked in 1957, so by 1975 the number of potential freshmen started downward. In 1973-1974 there were 291 new positons for political scientists; by 1974-1975 there were only 239 (Mann, 1976, p. 412).

In the 1980's the smaller number of college-age people and the lessened amount of financial aid create a market that can optimistically be called stagnant. A moderate recovery of the birth rate points toward some improvement by the year 2000, especially if prosperity then prevails.

The demand for academic political scientists affects the whole field, including the best paid tenured professors. In the 1960's the strong demand helped attract large numbers of highly talented students into undergraduate and graduate programs. Those with intellectual interest and high ability in political science could afford to pursue their interest, confident that with a Ph.D. they would be eagerly sought in the job market. We will never know exactly how many of the potential top contributors to our field will never enter it because of the present low level of demand, but surveys (e.g. Ladd & Lipset, 1978, pp. 9-12) suggest that it is a substantial number.

Doctoral Output. In most years of the mid-1970's, there were about 1000 firm candidates for academic positions (Mann, 1976, p. 413). This reflected in large part the dramatic increase in doctoral output that took place after 1960.

TABLE 1 (continued)

1964 (Cartter)		1975-76 (Roettger)		1982 (Jones, Lindzey and Coggeshall)	
1	Yale	1	Yale	1	Yale
2	Harvard	2	Harvard	2.5	California (Berkeley)
3	California (Berkeley)	3	California (Berkeley)	2.5	Harvard
				4.5	Chicago
4	Chicago	4	Chicago	4.5	Michigan
5	Columbia	5	Michigan	6	M.I.T.
6	Princeton	6	Stanford	7.5	Stanford
7.5	M.I.T.*	7	Princeton	7.5	Wisconsin
7.5	Wisconsin	8	Wisconsin	9	Princeton
9	Stanford	9	North Carolina	10.5	Minnesota
10	Michigan	10	Minnesota	10.5	Cornell
11	Cornell	11.5	California (Los Angeles)	12	Rochester
12	Northwestern			13.33	Columbia
13	California (Los Angeles)	11.5	Johns Hopkins	13.33	North Carolina
		13	Northwestern	13.33	Northwestern
14	Indiana	14	Columbia	16.5	Indiana
15	North Carolina	15	Cornell	16.5	California (Los Angeles)
16	Minnesota				
17	Illinois			18	Duke
18	Johns Hopkins			19.33	Illinois
19	Duke			19.33	Ohio State
20	Syracuse			19.33	Washington (St. Louis)

Source: 1925-1964 data taken directly from Albert Somit and Joseph Tannenhaus (1967), *The Development of Political Science: From Burgess to Behavioralism*, Boston: Allyn and Bacon, p. 164. 1975-76 data are from Walter B. Roettger (1978), "The Discipline: What's Wrong, and Who Cares?" Paper presented at the Annual Meeting of the American Political Science Association, New York City. 1982 data are from Lyle V. Jones, Gardner Lindzey and Porter E. Coggeshall (Eds.), *An Assessment of Research-Doctorate Programs in the United States: Social and Behavioral Sciences*, Washington, D.C.: National Academy Press, 1982.

*M.I.T. was not included in the 1925, 1957 and 1963 studies.

Table 7 shows the number of American doctorates produced in political science. The 1960-1970 production was absorbed fairly easily by the "baby-boom" induced demand, but the burgeoning output of the 1970's swamped the market. The post-behavioralists of the 1970's urged relevance and future orientation in their writings; perhaps too little attention was paid to these points in our graduate advising. By the last half of the 1970's the production of Ph.D.s started to slow down. Especially important was the dramatic reduction in the number of new Ph.D. students (see Table 8). Even with these reductions, there were still more new Ph.D.s than the academic market could absorb.

TABLE 2

Political Science Departments:
Top 20 Departments Ranked by Productivity

1. Michigan	11. Minnesota
2. Kentucky	12. Texas
3. Florida State	13. Arizona
4. Michigan State	14. Harvard
5. Georgia	15. California (Berkeley)
6. Iowa	16. Rochester
7. Wisconsin	17. Houston
8. Massachusetts	18. North Carolina
9. Ohio State	19. California (Los Angeles)
10. Indiana	20. Yale

Source: John S. Robey. Political Science Departments: Reputations Versus Productivity, PS, 1979, 12, p. 205.

Law schools apparently attracted many of the stronger students of the late 1970's who might have sought Ph.D.s in political science a few years earlier (Ladd & Lipset, 1978, p. 9). The growth in Masters in Public Administration programs also drained off some of the bright career-oriented students. About a third of political science departments have reported a decline in the quality of new Ph.D.s (Sheilah Mann, 1982, p. 91). Among sub-fields there have been moderate gains in the number of students in public administration and public policy as areas of concentration, and a decline in the students choosing comparative politics and political theory (Sheilah Mann, 1982, p. 91).

The Pay Record and Outlook. Academic folklore has long accepted as an enduring truth that there was low faculty pay in the field of political science. Thus it was surprising when Ladd and Lipset, using 1969 survey data, found that the pay of political scientists was relatively high; only law and medicine did better in the *elite* schools (Ladd & Lipset, 1974, pp. 21, 22). Salaries in political science relative to other fields dropped from 1969 to 1977, although similar drops occurred in other social sciences (Ladd & Lipset, 1978, p. 6).

The most recent expectation has been that incomes, adjusted for inflation, will drop in the future (Walker, 1978, p. 484). Given the imbalance between the number of openings and the number of people seeking academic positions, it could hardly be otherwise. The effects of low starting pay extend to all faculty ranks, as hard-pressed institutions are forced by state budget crises to economize. The outlook, even for those who have tenured jobs, is economically bleak. And since the median age of political science faculty was 37 in 1971 (Baker, 1971, p. 34), and it only rose to 42 by 1980 (Lane, 1982, p. 52), many of us could face decades of economic hardship.

In addition to the economic toll there are side effects which drastically alter professional and interpersonal relations in faculty departments.

TABLE 3

Comparative Rankings of Political Science Departments by Reputation
and Alternate Standardized Measures of Productivity

Reputational Rankings[a]	Graduate-Training Rankings I[b]	Graduate Training Rankings II[c]	Affiliation Rankings[d]	Affiliation Rankings (1974-1978 data)[e]
1. Yale	1. Iowa	1. Rochester	1. Florida Atlantic	1. Carnegie-Mellon
2. Harvard	2. North Carolina	2. Washington-St. Louis	2. Carnegie-Mellon	2. Michigan State
3. Berkeley	3. Vanderbilt	3. Kentucky	3. Kentucky	3. Kentucky
4. Chicago	4. Michigan State	4. Stanford	4. Emory	4. Iowa
5. Michigan	5. Syracuse	5. Vanderbilt	5. Rochester	5. Virginia
6.5. MIT	6. Yale	6. Brown	6. Florida	6. Rochester
6.5. Stanford	7. Rochester	7. Michigan State	7. Iowa	7. Ohio State
8. Wisconsin	8. Kentucky	8. Boston College	8. California-Riverside	8. Houston
9. Princeton	9. Minnesota	9. Yale	9. Michigan State	9. USC
10. North Carolina	10. Duke	10. North Carolina	10. Georgia	10. Wisconsin-Milwaukee
11. Columbia	11. Stanford	11. Duke	11. Cal. Tech.	11. Florida
12.5. UCLA	12. Illinois	12. Tulane	12. Ohio State	12. California-Riverside
12.5. Minnesota	13. Princeton	13. Georgetown	13. Stanford	13. Wisconsin
14.25. Cornell	14. Wisconsin	14. Minnesota	14. Minnesota	14. Michigan
14.25. Indiana	15. Tulane	15. Michigan	15. California-Irvine	15. Minnesota
14.25. Northwestern	16. Berkeley	16. New School	16.5. Arizona	16. Texas Tech
14.25. Rochester	17. Michigan	17. Case Western	16.5. Cincinnati	17. Duke
18.5. Iowa	18. Chicago	18. Houston	18. Vanderbilt	18. Rice
18.5. Oregon	19. Harvard	19. Pennsylvania	19. Michigan	19. Tulane
20.33. Illinois	20. Florida	20. Ohio State	20. Massachusetts	20. Arizona
20.33. Johns Hopkins				
20.33. Washington-St. Louis				

TABLE 3 (continued)

Source: Joseph M. McCormick and E. Lee Bernick. Graduate Training and Productivity: A Look at Who Publishes, *Journal of Politics*, 1982, *24*, 212-227.

[a]The reputational rankings are drawn from David R. Morgan and Michael R. Fitzgerald, Recognition and Production Among American Political Science Departments. *Western Political Quarterly*, September 1977, *30*: 348. The numbering for tied ranks has been changed slightly to conform with the convention and in other tied rankings.

[b]To obtain these graduate training ranks, the weighted department scores were standardized by the number of recent graduates. The figure used for each department was the average number reported in the *Guide to Graduate Study in Political Science* for the 1977 through the 1979 editions. Since the figure reported in each edition of the *Guide* is in itself averaged over the past three years, the figure ultimately employed in the analysis tends to cover the years of our study. [After controlling for number of graduates in Ph.D. programs, the authors weighted the journal articles on the basis of the estimated quality of the journal: *APSR* as 1.0, *JP* as .957, *AJPS* as .943, *Polity* as .843 and the *WPQ* as .829.]

[c]To obtain these graduate rankings, the weighted department scores were divided by the number of political scientists in the profession who received their graduate training from that institution (as determined by our systematic sample of the discipline).

[d]These standardized rankings come from Robey, "Political Science Department."

[e]To obtain these rankings, the weighted present affiliation scores were divided by the number of faculty members in a department. The figure used was the average of the number reported for 1976 and 1977 in the *Guide to Graduate Study in Political Science* and the 1978 figures from Robey, "Political Science Departments."

TABLE 4

Journal Ranking 1963 and 1976

Journal	1976		1963	
	Rank	Index	Rank	Index
American Political Science Review	1	2.75	1	2.78
Journal of Politics	2	2.42	3	2.31
World Politics	3	2.40	2	2.32
American Journal of Political Science	4	2.25	9	1.89
Public Administration Review	5	1.96	7	1.99
Political Science Quarterly	6	1.94	4	2.07
Public Opinion Quarterly	7	1.90	8	1.93
Administrative Science Quarterly	8	1.82	5	2.01
American Behavioral Scientist	9	1.84	10	1.73
Western Political Quarterly	10	1.81	6	2.00

Source: Table compiled by Walter B. Roettger. 1976 data were from a random sample drawn from APSA's Directory of Members; 1963 data from Somit and Tannenhaus, *American Political Science: A Profile of a Discipline*. See Walter B. Roettger, "The Discipline: What's Right, What's Wrong, and Who Cares?" Paper presented at the 1978 Annual Meeting of the American Political Science Association.

Caplow's *The Academic Marketplace* (1958) notes schisms prevailing in higher education in the 1950s: young turks vs. elderstatesmen; teachers vs. researchers, generalists vs. specialists; conservatives vs. liberals; pro-administration vs. anti-administration; humanists vs. scientists; and inbred vs. outbred. To these we would have to add—perhaps at the top of the list—tenured vs. non-tenured. It is not unfair to say that there are three distint classes of political scientists; tenured, those with hope of getting tenured, and those with little or no hope of getting tenure. This situation introduces a new stress on hierarchy within departments. Organizational hierarchy involves at least three modes of unequal allocation of resources: inequality in security, inequality in perceived punishment for deviance, and inequality of authority. In all cases non-tenured persons are at a disadvantage and those "without hope" are uniquely so. The result is an atmosphere scarcely conducive to stimulating the free exchange of ideas which traditionally has characterized the academic arena.

Academic and Non-Academic Prospects. Academics have always been the majority among political scientists. A 1970 National Science Foundation study showed the following occupational breakdown of political science Ph.D.s (quoted in Waldo, 1975, p. 120):

Academics	76.9
Business	1.8
Federal Government	5.4
Military	1.4
State and Local Government	3.5

TABLE 5

Ranking of Significant Contributors: A Longitudinal Perspective[a]

Pre-1945[b]		1945-1960		1960-1970		1970-1976	
Rank	Name	Rank	Name	Rank	Name	Rank	Name
1	Merriam	1	Key (35%)	1	Dahl (40%)	1	Lowi (18%)
2	Lasswell	2	Lasswell (32%)	2	Easton (19%)	2	Wildavsky (10%)
3	White	3	Dahl (20%)	3	SRC Group[c] (18%)	3	Dye (9%)
4	Beard	4	Easton (18%)	4	Deutsch (17%)	4	Dahl (8%)
5	Corwin	5	Morgenthau (18%)	5	Almond (16%)	5	Huntington (7%)
6	Bentley	6	Truman (16%)	6	Wildavsky (7%)	7	SRC Group[c] (6%)
7	Wilson	7	Strauss (8%)	7	Lowi (4%)	7	Verba (6%)
8	Herring	8.5	Deutsch (6%)	9	Lipset (4%)	7	Sharkansky (6%)
9	Wright	8.5	Simon (6%)	9	Wolin (4%)	10.5	Barber, Deutsch,
10	Ogg	10.5	Friedrich (5%)	9	Huntington (4%)		Left Radicals[d], Riker
		10.5	Schattschneider (5%)				

Source: Compiled by Walter B. Roettger, Strata and Stability: Reputations of American Political Scientists. *PS*, 1978, *11*: 9.

[a] Figures in parentheses represent the percentages of respondents designating the contributor. Sample size for 1945-1960 was 181; for 1960-1970, 179; and for 1970-1976, 113. The variation between periods (and the departure from the overall response level) is due to the failure of all respondents to designate significant contributors in each period.

[b] Taken from Somit and Tannenhaus, *American Political Science: A Profile of a Discipline*, New York: Atherton Press, 1964, p. 66.

[c] The "SRC Group" consists of Angus Campbell, Philip E. Converse, Warren E. Miller, and Donald E. Stokes. Mention of one or more of these persons was coded as "SRC Group."

[d] The "Left Radicals" include: Ira Katznelson, Herbert Marcuse, Ralph Miliband, C. Wright Mills, James O'Connor, and Bertell Ollman. Mention of one or more of these persons was coded as "Left Radicals."

TABLE 6

Rank Order of 20 "Most Significant Political Scientist Contributors"
by Number of Citations 1970-79,
Where They Received Degree and Where They Teach

Name	Number of Citations	Ph.D.	Teaching
1. Seymour Martin Lipset	3425	Columbia	Stanford
2. Herbert Simon	3425	Chicago	Carnegie-Mellon
3. Robert Dahl	2235	Yale	Yale
4. Angus Campbell	2184	Stanford	Michigan
5. Karl Deutsch	1870	Harvard	Harvard
6. Gabriel Almond	1799	Chicago	Stanford
7. David Easton	1644	Harvard	Chicago
8. Samuel Huntington	1511	Harvard	Harvard
9. Harold Lasswell	1410	Chicago	Yale
10. Philip Converse	1282	Michigan	Michigan
11. V. O. Key	1110	Chicago	Harvard
12. Theodore Lowi	913	Yale	Cornell
13. Charles Lindblom	958	Chicago	Harvard
14. Robert Lane	782	Harvard	Yale
15. Aaron Wildavsky	766	Yale	California, Berkeley
16. W. H. Riker	759	Harvard	Rochester
17. Thomas R. Dye	709	Pennsylvania	Florida State
18. Carl J. Friedrich	701	Heidelberg	Harvard
19. Sidney Verba	645	Princeton	Harvard
20. Ira Sharkansky	589	Wisconsin	Wisconsin

Source: Compiled from John S. Robey, Reputation vs. Citations: Who Are the Top Scholars in Political Science. *PS*, 1982, *15:* 200. Biographical data from *Who's Who in America.* Herbert Marcuse and C. Wright Mills were dropped from Robey's list because they were not political scientists.

TABLE 7

Production of Ph.D.s in Political Science

Year	Number of Doctorates Awarded in Political Science
1880-1960	3700
1960-1970	3836
1970-1980	8519

Source: 1880-1970 compiled from Walter B. Roettger. "I Never Promised You a Rose Garden: Career Satisfaction in an Age of Uncertainty." Paper presented at the Iowa Conference of Political Science, 1977. 1970-1980 data compiled from Sheilah Mann. Placement of Political Scientists, 1980-1981. *PS*, 1982, *15:* 85.

TABLE 8

Supply of Political Scientists, 1969-1981

New Students Beginning Ph.D. Study in Political Science		Graduate Student Enrollments in Ph.D. Programs in Political Science		Ph.D.s Awarded
Fall, 1981	1,042	1981-82	5,491	679
Fall, 1980	1,068	1980-81	5,756	729
Fall, 1979	1,100	1979-80	5,888	766
Fall, 1978	1,051	1978-79	5,742	851
Fall, 1977	1,182	1977-78	5,737	881
Fall, 1976	1,064	1976-77	5,462	885
Fall, 1975	1,174	1975-76	6,150	862
Fall, 1974	1,443	1974-75	6,150	907
Fall, 1973	1,414	1973-74	6,450	906
Fall, 1972	1,576	1972-73	*	811
Fall, 1971	1,695	1971-72	*	821
Fall, 1970	2,138	1970-71	*	634
Fall, 1969	2,487	1969-70	*	559

Source: Data obtained from "Political Science Degrees Awarded and Graduate Students Enrolled: 1982 Update." PS, 1982, 15: 459-460.

*Not available.

The remainder were presumably retired, unemployed, or not in the labor force. This suggests that, given a good job market, such as that of 1970, the great majority of political scientists prefer an academic position.

Even in recent job markets most of those who get positions find them in universities and colleges. In 1981 only 18 percent of Ph.D. placements were non-academic (less than in 1979 and 1980). The proportion of 1981 placements to temporary positions was 28 percent, down from all earlier surveys. The placement success percentage--81 percent--was the highest since 1974. The reason for this may well lie in the relatively low number of candidates, 697 (Sheilah Mann, 1982, p. 86).

Success in placement varies by sub-fields. Public administration, public policy and American government Ph.D.s fare better than those in comparative politics, international relations, and political philosophy (Sheilah Mann, 1982, p. 89). A shift in placement opportunity has resulted in the need for the Ph.D. to be completed; ABDs found many placements in the early 1970s, but later in the decade the completion of the degree was required for the majority of new positions (Mann, 1978, p. 27).

Some have suggested that the skills of political scientists fit them well for many non-academic positions. About one fifth of Ph.D. programs— particularly those of smaller departments—have sought to adapt themselves and prepare students for non-academic positions (Sheilah Mann, 1982, p. 85). Also, about 150 to 175 Ph.D.s (2 percent of the total) leave academia annually for outside jobs. The 1981 placement data suggest that non-academic placements are not becoming the solution to our profession's market problem. A few want such positions; others, such as those who do not gain tenure, must seek them. In some fields, such as government and lobbying, the political science degree is, of course, a distinct asset. For most people starting post-baccalaureate study, however, the alternative to being a political science Ph.D. teaching in a university is not being a political science Ph.D. at all. It is setting out for another educational and career objective in the beginning.

VIEWPOINTS

The views of political scientists have been noticeably different on the average from those of other academics. Certainly we are not a representative sample of the nation's population. We are drawn disproportionately from the middle class and almost half of us come from families where the father holds a professional or managerial position. Even when we compare ourselves to others in the academic community we are more advantaged. Only the students and faculty in the medical profession can claim a higher socio-economic background than political scientists (Ladd & Lipset, 1974, pp. 5-6). In terms of ethnocultural background it is worth noting that even though Catholics outnumber Jews by roughly nine to one in the general population, twenty-two percent of political science faculty is Jewish compared to 10 percent Catholic. Jews are also disproportionately represented at elite schools (Ladd & Lipset, 1974, pp. 7-9). In a 1982 survey of 637 political science departments it was found that women made up 11.17 percent of full-time tenure-track faculty. Blacks were 2.89 percent and 1.07 were Spanish surnamed Americans (American Political Science Association, 1982, p. 1). The political science professoriate is indisputably male, white and non-hispanic.

Political Views. Political views are taken with special seriousness by our profession. The major currents of these views have been consistent over a substantial period. A 1977 faculty study conducted by Ladd and Lipset indicates that 58 percent of social scientists identify themselves on the liberal side of the political spectrum (Lipset, 1981, p. 3). Among social scientists, economists are the most conservative; sociologists and anthropologists are the most liberal. Political scientists take a central position in this group, but are still liberal when compared to the average American (Lipset, 1981, p. 5). The *Christian Science Monitor* surveyed political scientists attending the 1981 American Political Science Association Meeting and 73 percent of those responding characterized themselves as "moderately liberal" or "very liberal" (*Christian Science Monitor* Survey, 1981).[1] This liberal stance is partially explained in terms of self-selection. Students with more liberal orientations are attracted to fields with a heavy focus on social problems and to fields where they feel ideologically comfortable (Ladd & Lipset, 1975, pp. 152-157). Ideology and partisan preference are determined more by adult socialization than by family background. Political scientists credit knowledge gained in the profession and the influence of colleagues as major determinants of their partisan preferences and ideologies (Turner & Hetrick, 1972, p. 365; Ladd & Lipset, 1975, pp. 157-159).

Political scientists are strongly Democratic, although there has been an increase in the number of Independents. This is evident in a comparison of the 1970 study of members of the American Political Science Association and those surveyed by the *Christian Science Monitor* in 1981 (See Table 9). It is obvious that the Democratic party's loss is not necessarily the Republican party's gain. Political scientists may become disillusioned and frustrated by the failure of the system to respond adequately to the problems confronting it—32 percent agreed that the American political system was not sound and needed many improvements or fundamental overhauling—but apparently they are not willing to join the Republican party to seek a solution. In the 1981 APSA convention survey respondents reportedly saw a conservative trend in the country, but 67 percent saw it as a brief phenomenon (*Christian Science Monitor* Survey, 1981).

Seymour Martin Lipset contends that the *leadership* of American political science is neoconservative. These neoconservatives support government action to curb social injustice and the welfare state, but they have serious misgivings about what they consider to be misguided efforts to achieve equal opportunity, and they are concerned about policies which fail to meet what they view as communist expansionism (Lipset, 1981, p. 5). It is likely that some variance does exist between these leadership views and those of the membership in general.

Franklin Delano Roosevelt was by far our favorite president. When asked to rank the best overall President from Roosevelt to Carter, 69.3 percent chose Roosevelt. The race for the worst president was won easily by Nixon who received 59.5 percent of the vote. His nearest competitor was Carter with 22 percent.

John F. Kennedy, who is one of the most popular presidents with the general public (Gallup, 1980, p. 27), does not have high standing among

TABLE 9

Party Preference of Political Scientists

Party Preferences	1959	1970	1976	1981
Republican	16.4	11.8	12	10.04
Democrat	73.7	73.4	74	61.19
Independent	8.0	12.5	12	22.39
Other	1.9	2.3	2	6.37

Source: 1959 data from Henry A. Turner, Charles G. McClintock and Charles B. Spaulding. The Political Party Affiliation of American Political Scientists, *The Western Political Quarterly*, 1963, *16:* 652. 1970 data from Henry A. Turner and Carl C. Hetrick. Political Activities and Party Affiliations of American Political Scientists. *The Western Political Quarterly*, 1972, *25:* 363. 1976 data furnished by Walter Roettger, Drake University, from unpublished Ph.D. dissertation, University of Colorado, 1977. 1982 data computed from *Christian Science Monitor*/American Political Science Association Survey, data obtained from the Roper Center, The University of Connecticut.

political scientists. Only 7.6 rank him as the best overall, and he is tied with Eisenhower in that rating. This is consistent with the earlier Ladd-Lipset finding that although Kennedy made a conscious effort to gain their support, he was never popular with intellectuals. Adlai Stevenson and Hubert Humphrey were much preferred for the 1960 Democratic nomination. Intellectuals disdained Kennedy's mediocre congressional record, and his failure to take a strong stand against McCarthy (Ladd & Lipset, 1975, pp. 22, 23). During Kennedy's term of office, James Reston of the *New York Times* discussed Kennedy's lack of support among intellectuals and said that they were describing his presidency as "the third Eisenhower administration" (quoted in Ladd & Lipset, 1975, p. 24). Some twenty years later Kennedy is still equated with Eisenhower among political scientists; for example, as best on foreign policy, 12 percent chose Eisenhower and 11.3 Kennedy. (Eisenhower and Kennedy rank on foreign policy behind Roosevelt, Truman and Nixon, in that order.)

Jimmy Carter's ranking among political scientists is low. Sixty-three percent rate him as the president who was least able to get things done. This is a consistent evaluation regardless of ideology, party preference, academic rank, gender or age. His predecessor, Gerald Ford, comes in second, but far behind with 20.6 percent.

When asked to compare Reagan with the past eight presidents 66 percent rate him as either not as good as most or worse than most. Political scientists do give him a grade of A, however, for his relations with Congress. From then on his grade point average begins to slip. He gets a majority of Ds and Fs on economic policy (58.4 percent), foreign policy (63.1 percent), social issues (73.8 percent), and over-all performance (51.1 percent). On all the scores mentioned above, women political scientists consistently rate Reagan lower than their male counterparts. Reagan's lack of relative popularity with women was manifested in the presidential election, which showed a significant sex difference in preference for Reagan.

As anticipated, political scientists exercise considerable "constraint" in their political ideologies. That is, their political positions and practices demonstrate a logical or systemic order (Ladd & Lipset, 1975, pp. 37-40). This constraint is shown by the fairly consistent positions taken by self-identified liberals and conservatives on major social issues in the *Christian Science Monitor* Survey. Self-identified liberalism/conservatism was the single most accurate predictor of policy position. It also confirms that political scientists are comfortably clustered at the liberal end of the political spectrum (see Table 10).

Educational Views. Clark Kerr has observed that "Few institutions are so conservative as the universities about their own affairs while their members are so liberal about the affairs of others" (quoted in Ladd & Lipset, 1975, p. 33). This has not been true of political scientists. The same consistency of ideas discussed above applied when political scientists were questioned on issues of student activism such as a broadened student role and the demands of blacks in the 1960's. Liberals were significantly more supportive of student positions (Ladd & Lipset, 1971, p. 138).

A major and controversial issue directly affecting higher education has

TABLE 10

Views on Selected Policy Issues of Political Scientists Attending the
1981 Meeting of the American Political Science Association

Issue	Political Scientists (n = 526)		Sample U.S. Population	
	Agree/ Approve	Disagree/ Disapprove	Agree/ Approve	Disagree/ Disapprove
Producing and readying the neutron bomb	34.5	65.4	48	44[a]
Reagan's handling of economic conditions	28.0	72.0	52	26[b]
Reagan's New Federalism	36.0	63.9	67	18[a]
Amendment to the Constitution that would permit prayers to be said in the public schools	7.9	92.03	76	15[c]
Equal Rights Amendment	83.04	16.9	63	32[d]

Source: Political Science data computed from data obtained from the Roper Center, University of Connecticut, *Christian Science Monitor*/American Political Science Association Survey. General population sample from:

[a] *Gallup Report* No. 193, October, 1981.

[b] *Gallup Report* No. 191, August, 1981.

[c] *Gallup Report* No. 177, April-May, 1980.

[d] *Gallup Report* No. 190, July, 1981.

been affirmative action. Among political scientists there has been a loss of support for affirmative action from 1969 to 1975. When asked about relaxing standards for the admission of minority students, 69 percent supported such measures in 1969 while only 43 percent did so in 1975; when asked similarly about minority faculty, support dropped from 40 percent in 1969 to 19 percent in 1975 (Ladd & Lipset, 1978, graph 3). The shift may be the result of a re-confirmation of the university as a meritocracy, but the shift in attitude away from minority faculty may also reflect a protective response to the tight academic market.

Political scientists are not, on the whole, well-satisfied with the product of their educational efforts. Data from 1969 show that 45 percent of the political science faculty at top schools disagreed with the proposition that graduate education in their field did a good job. The only field with a higher percentage of dissatisfaction was sociology (47 percent); by way of contrast, for business administration and chemistry the figures were 18 and 13 percent respectively (Ladd & Lipset, 1974, p. 35).

In a later study the attitudes remained about the same. Only half of the political science faculty said that graduate education did a good job, compared to three-fourths of all academics surveyed (Ladd & Lipset, 1978, p. 14).

This dissatisfaction may have several roots. One is that students must take courses from widely disparate fields, such as political philosophy and statistical applications. The sense of a unified whole may be apparent to only a few. The varieties of intellectual turnings may have caused some graduate students who need structure to lose confidence. Dissatisfaction is also nurtured now by the bleak job market outlook for many political science graduates. Perhaps we should not expect nor desire a high level of satisfaction with graduate education in political science at this time. Indeed, Charles O. Jones contends that, "We should probably be suspicious of a high level of satisfaction, since it could indicate that we have not kept up with the turns, twists and reversals which have characterized our discipline as it continues to undergo painful development" (Jones, 1982).

Views on Professional Satisfaction. This section can be summarized with Walter Roettger's (1978) conclusion that political science is not a very happy profession (p. 48). In all fields a minority of academics have always expressed regret concerning their choice of careers. Ladd and Lipset in 1973 found that 10 percent of political science faculty would not want to be professors, if they could start over again. This was about the same figure that applied to business, engineering, and the medical professionals (quoted in Roettger, 1978, p. 31). More relevant is the finding of statistically significant deterioration in career satisfaction from 1963 to 1976 among academic political scientists. Asked in a 1976 survey, "If you were able to start over and pick your profession again, would you still pick a career in political science?," academics gave these answers among others (Roettger, 1977, p. 12):

	Definitely yes	Definitely No
1963	41%	1%
1976	29%	7%

The main "pockets of optimism" were found in two seemingly disparate groups: public administration and political philosophy. The one is a growing field, and the other, perhaps, is a field that attracts those who care most for the joys of pure scholarship (Roettger, 1977, p. 33).

THE ASSOCIATION IN AN ERA OF STRESS

The membership of the American Political Science Association enjoyed the sort of post-World War II growth that characterized many fields of endeavor during that boom period. Its numbers went from 3300 in 1945 (Waldo, 1975, p. 54) to 15,758 in 1974 (Mann, 1982a). By 1982 the number had dropped to 11,597. This reflects economic conditions, but it also reflects a breakdown of shared consensus; Roettger (1978) reported many "can't say" answers in a 1978 survey that covered many educational, intellectual and professional issues that might inspire controversy, but hardly lack of opinion. A former executive officer of the American Sociological Association has stated that calling the ASA an "association" may be an overstatement, since not everyone is associating with everyone else (Demerath III, 1981, p. 87). The same description may be appropriate for the APSA.

The Association's stresses have been compounded by the controversies arising from behavioralism and post-behavioralism, by the emergence of policy oriented associations, and the growth of cognate organizations such as the American Society for Public Administration and the International Studies Association (the latter accompanied by a growing conviction that public administration and international relations ought to break off from political science), by the Viet Nam War, by the rise of the Caucus for a New Political Science, and by the emergence of women and minorities as groups with claims on the Association.

Preliminary results from a 1982 APSA survey of political scientists show some of the expressed reasons for discontent with the Association:

> Those who let their membership lapse did so because they thought the dues were too high, they didn't like the *APSR,* and they felt the APSA didn't serve their interests. Lapsed members most frequently agree with the statements that "The dues are unreasonably high" and that there is "too much emphasis on quantitative research." Moreover, lapsed members appear to be slightly less professionally active (in terms of memberships, journal subscriptions and publishing) and earn somewhat lower salaries than current members. (Mann, 1982c)

The Problem of Membership Decline. APSA membership peaked in 1974; by 1982 it was down 25 percent from that peak (Mann, 1982a). Annual meeting registration peaked before membership in 1969 at a level of about 4200 at the New York City meeting. Low points in registration of under 2500 were hit in 1973, 1976, and 1978. Both 1979 and 1980, however, showed growth (American Political Science Association, 1981, p. 610). The 1981 meeting totaled 2,887 which was the highest registration since the 1972 meeting (French, 1981, p. 786). Perhaps the meeting locations (Washington, D.C. and New York City) helped.

One reason for the membership and attendance decline is the emergence of specialized groups. This is related to the lack of a single paradigm discussed earlier. As political scientists have become more specialized, some members have concluded that their interests are better served by other organizations. A comparative government area specialist, for example, may find that he/she has more in common with economists, sociologists and anthropologists working in the area than with other political scientists. This may also decrease the value of the *American Political Science Review,* the most prestigious journal in the field. The journal may not be providing an adequate vehicle for exchanging ideas and concepts among those with similar interests. Scholars may find it more rewarding to publish in journals read by their "significant others" where they are more likely to be cited and where they may establish their national reputation more quickly. Specialization has devalued the two principal reasons for joining the APSA—the annual meeting and the journal.

Another problem is that of communication among members of the discipline, not only between areas of specialization, but also between scholars who have training such that they can comprehend research using quantitative methods or arguments presented in terms of formal logic and those who cannot.

The APSA has been generous in its approach to unaffiliated groups which meet at its annual meeting. The number of unaffiliated groups that got courtesy listings in APSA programs rose from six (with two and a half pages) in 1972 to 31 groups with 30 pages in 1982. Some have contended in the APSA Administrative Committee that unaffiliated groups were prospering at the expense of the APSA itself (Minutes, 1982). It seems unlikely, however, that non-cooperation with sub-groups would be an effective long-run strategy. In 1982 the Association developed guidelines for the establishment of sections. Sections will make it possible for groups of APSA members who share a common interest to meet, coordinate communications and receive help from the APSA national office in collecting dues and maintaining membership lists (American Political Science Association, Fall 1982b, p. 627). It is hoped that the establishment of sections will lead to restored integration of the discipline.

The Caucus for a New Political Science. The emergence and activities of the Caucus for a New Political Science have been among the most noteworthy features of the Association's history over the past two decades. The New Caucus was an organizational manifestation of the intellectual forces that led to the post-behavioral movement, with which it has significant ties. The Caucus for a New Political Science was convinced of the inseparability of politics and intellectual work. Beyond this the New Caucus was what one of its founders calls "an organized insurgency" (Lowi, 1972, p. 12) that believed that the APSA should have a strong stand against the Viet Nam War and racial discrimination and that it should actively support the "war on poverty" programs of the Johnson Administration (Lowi, 1972, p. 13). There were immediate negative reactions among those with the strong conviction that professional academic associations should not take policy positions on issues not directly related to the main function of the organization: promoting the intellectual and professional interests of the discipline and its members. The position of others can be summarized in a statement of a former president of The American Sociological Association reacting to the issue of taking policy positions within his organization, "The most that can be accomplished is to announce a policy position on an issue and thereby provide a catharsis for members who need it" (Hawley, 1981, p. 108).

In 1966 it was discovered that some APSA officials had worked with the CIA; this had a catalytic effect on the New Caucus' emergence. Lowi described the New Caucus' leaders efforts in the 1967 APSA Business Meeting as precipitating "probably the ugliest confrontation in the history of the profession" (Lowi, 1972, p. 13).

The groundwork was thus laid for a major schism in the Association. In the 1970's the New Caucus continued to attempt to take control of the APSA. Probably the high water mark of these efforts occurred in 1973. The New Caucus had a full slate of officers to compete with the slate offered by the APSA Nominating Committee. The final vote (which was taken by mail ballot) gave the New Caucus candidate for President, Peter Bachrach, 3191 votes; Austin Ranney, the choice of the Nominating Committee got 3803 votes (American Political Science Association, 1974, p. 36).

The New Caucus continues to function in the 1980's, although it does not issue the sort of challenges that it did in the 1970's. The appeal of the New Caucus has diminished with the end of the Viet Nam War, the worsening of the job market, and the declining role of the American Political Science Association resulting from the emergence of competing organizations. Partly in reaction to their recent lack of significant success in sponsoring candidates, and because the APSA Nominating Committee, in an effort to be more representative, has regularly nominated some New Caucus members, the New Caucus has stopped nominating its own slate. In 1978 the New Caucus proclaimed itsef a socialist organization; in 1979 it amended this to include socialist feminist. Its avowed objective is to create "a socialist center of gravity in the profession" (Caucus For A New Political Science, 1981). It has developed local chapters and is working with other groups, such as the Marxist Literary Group in sponsoring conferences. Its journal, *New Political Science,* deals with such topics as "The Left and Civil Liberties" and "The Socialist Academic: Between Theory and Practice." It meets annually as an unaffiliated group at the APSA convention. In 1982 it sponsored 25 panels. A major attraction of the New Caucus has been that of providing a forum and a critical means of support for those doing analysis of policy issues relevant to creating the social changes necessary to transcend capitalist society (Caucus For A New Political Science, 1981; Lankowski, 1982).

The Status of Women. Another important and related aspect of the challenge raised by the non-establishment groups in the late 1960's was the situation of women political scientists. In 1969, about 5 percent of APSA's members were women. About 8 percent of the faculty members in the field were women (Gruberg & Sapiro, 1978, p. 318); the lesser amount of membership may have reflected low pay, and temporary appointments.

In 1969 the Association adopted a resolution supporting equal treatment for women (American Political Science Association, 1969a, p. 671) and the Committee on the Status of Women was established (American Political Science Association, 1971, pp. 3, 10). In the same year women's concerns were organized through the establishment of the Women's Caucus for Political Science. In the 1970's the Women's Caucus ran candidates for APSA offices. Efforts to combine slates with the New Caucus were rarely successful because many women who were concerned with feminist issues did not share the New-Left ideology of the New Caucus.

The 1970's saw a dramatic percentage increase in the proportion of women in the field, except at the rank of full professor:

	% Women	
	1972	1981
Bachelor's degrees in Pol. Science	19%	37%
Master's degrees in Pol. Science	19%	28%
Ph.D. in Pol. Science	10%	20%
Assistant Professors	10%	20%
Associate Professors	8%	12%
Full Professors	4%	5%

Source: Data from Thomas Mann, Executive Director, American Political Science Association.

The APSA has never had a woman president. In 1979 the Women's Caucus nominated Betty Nesvold for president. The New Caucus also ran a candidate against the nominating committee's choice, Charles Lindblom. Although the Women's Caucus ran a vigorous campaign their candidate came in third and far behind the official nominee (813 to 2,335) (American Political Science Association, 1980, p. 42). Over the past decade Women's Caucus candidates who were also official Nominating Committee choices gained election to office. This has provided them with representation on the Executive Council of the Association.

In 1978 the Women's Caucus and other supportive groups, in an intensely debated motion before the Association's business meeting, passed a resolution calling on the Association not to hold its annual meeting in Chicago because the State of Illinois had not passed the Equal Rights Amendment to the U.S. Constitution. If the resolution had received less than a two-thirds majority it would have had to be ratified by the total membership by mail ballot. Those opposing the action argued that the ERA position violated the APSA constitution's ban on committing its members on questions of public policy. Others believed that the APSA should honor its hotel contract which had been made before the extension of the time period for ratification of ERA. They feared the law suit which ultimately occurred. Those supporting the business meeting action responded that in 1972 APSA had passed a resolution in favor of ERA and the Chicago boycott was simply an implementation of present policy. They also contended that one of the Association's main raisons d'etre is to promote and protect the interests of its members. As long as women members of the Association are victims of professional and employment discrimination, the Association has a responsibility and an obligation to take any and all steps necessary to help alleviate the situation.

The reaction of the Association's leadership was similar to its response in 1969 when it feared the New Caucus would take over the Association at business meetings. The 1969 response was to suggest a change in the Association's constitution so that candidates who were opposed had to be elected by a mailed secret ballot rather than at the business meeting which had been the earlier practice. The argument was that "temporary majorities" should not be making decisions for the vast majority of members. This was countered by the contention that members with sufficient interest to attend the annual meeting can adequately represent the membership (American Political Science Association, 1969b, pp. 269-302). There was thus a sense of deja vu in 1979 as the establishment moved to limit the power of the business meeting to take policy positions. A detached observer of the 1969 meeting made some observations which were equally applicable a decade later. Anthony King of the University of Essex, England commenting on the struggle between the New Caucus and the establishment wrote:

> One is bound to feel sorry for...(New Caucus spokesperson). The poor man claims to value democracy and participation. But he knows very well that the more democracy and participation there is in the Association, the worse the prospects for the Caucus, so he is reduced to extolling the virtues of the Annual Business Meeting which he knows can, with any luck, be controlled by a tiny unrepresentative minority...Meanwhile, the defenders of the status quo profess to be anxious to embody democratic principles in the Association's constitution, whereas they are really worried about the possibility of a Caucus takeover. It is all an act on both sides. The Establishment's act is marginally more enjoyable, if only because it is being played with such a straight face. (American Political Science Association, 1969b, p. 294)

In 1980 the Constitution was amended by a vote of 2400 to 887 so that controversial policy issues receiving one-third vote at the annual meeting must be submitted to the entire membership by mailed secret ballot (American Political Science Association, 1980, p. 42).

The influence of the Women's Caucus, however, has been felt, and women have influenced the Association in many significant ways. In 1981, women held 11 percent of all political science full-time positions (American Political Science Association, 1982a, p. 1). This represents progress, if not great strides. The outlook is that the percentage of women is likely to do little more than hold steady because of the small number of openings, lower Ph.D. output, and the lower attractiveness of academic careers.

Minority Members. The American Political Science Association had a Black President, Ralph Bunche, in 1954. Despite this milestone the inclusion of racial minorities in the discipline remained extremely low, relative to the population at large. In 1969 there were only 65 black American Ph.D.s in Political Science, well under one percent of the total (Prestage, *et al.,* 1977, p. 1). In 1969, however, two developments improved the situation. One was the establishment of a Committee on the Status of Blacks in the Profession; the other was the establishment in the APSA of a fellowship program for black graduate students. Evron Kirkpatrick, then Executive Director of APSA was prominent among those who worked to improve the status of blacks. By 1977 the number of black political science Ph.D.s reached 200 (Woodard, 1982).

In 1977 the Committee on the Status of Chicanos was established for similar reasons. This committee also encourages members of its group to enter the field, seeks aid for graduate students, and stimulates research.

Chun-tu Hsueh argues that Asian and Asian-Americans are under-represented and discriminated against in political science. To support this contention he observes that no Asian has ever served on the APSA Council and that the Council denied a 1976 request to establish a Committee on the Status of Asians. The Council, however, agreed to publish professional notices of special concern to Asians in *PS* and to make space available at annual meetings for meetings of Asian political scientists. The status of Asians in political science contrasts with their prestige in other disciplines such as physics. More Asian-American political scientists could serve as helpful role models for Asian and Asian American students; they could also offer useful insights into many issues (Hsueh, 1976-77, pp. 11-15).

Had the favorable market conditions of the 1960's persisted, the efforts of the committees established to improve the status of underrepresented groups in the profession would probably have yielded more positive results. As things have evolved, the profession was opened noticeably for minority groups at the time of the market decline. The placement success of blacks was 90 percent in 1978 and 96 percent in 1981; for Spanish surnamed political scientists it was 100 percent in 1980 and 67 percent in 1981. The reader is reminded that we are dealing with small numbers. Blacks were 4 percent of 1981's placement class of 696; Spanish surnamed candidates comprised only 2 percent. By contrast the placement of women in 1981 was 75 of 101 candidates (including women of all races); this was the same percentage as that of men of all races (Sheilah Mann, 1982, p 88)

Association Responses. The establishment of the committees on women, blacks and Chicanos was in itself a significant response on the part of the APSA and demonstrated the willingness of the Association to open itself more to the full participation of all members. All the recent Executive Councils have had women and minority officers. There are those who believe that the comparatively small number of women and minorities involved in leadership positions represents "tokenism" and object to the tendency to re-appoint the same small group instead of seeking to identify new talent.

One available measure of tangible progress is participation in the annual meetings. Progress by women has been dramatic in this respect. In 1970, for example, 5.6 percent of the papers presented at APSA meetings were by women; by 1980 the figure was 21.9 percent and in 1981 it was 18.8 percent (Gruberg, 1981, p. 725). Women are thus represented more as paper givers than as full-time faculty.

Blacks have had more uneven progress, due perhaps in part to their relatively small numbers. Black program participation rose from 14 items in 1969 to 23 in 1972, but it dropped back to 16 in 1976 (Prestage, 1977, p. 16). Unfortunately full data on minority representation on panels are not available.

STRIVING FOR QUALITY AND VITALITY IN A DECADE OF AUSTERITY: APPROACHES TO MEETING THE CHALLENGES

Political scientists in the 1980's must understand and accept the realities of their situation, but they also must be future-oriented. There are discouraging aspects to the stagnant job market and the low turnover of personnel. We should remember, however, that most academic fields share a similar environment. Non-academic fields — many in the private sector and some in the public — often look at mere stagnation with envy, as they fare worse.

This period of increasing scarcity may not be all negative. Some serendipitous results may come out of the experience. Let me suggest two: First, the cut in research funding may minimize what many consider to be a prostitution of academia. Some observers have seen instances in which new ideas in the area of pure theory were shunted aside because researchers found it more convenient to work on projects for which funds were more readily available. Perhaps more people will be making decisions on the basis of academic value rather than fund availability. Second, we may see a resurgence of an emphasis on teaching. Areas such as political theory which have been devalued because of limited outside funding sources may experience a renaissance. Third, we are witnessing what Thomas Mann has described as the "political mobilization of the social science community" (Mann, 1982a, p. 416). In response to the Reagan Administration's proposed cuts for social science research, the Consortium of Social Science Associations was established. This new organization has the potential for providing a unified and effective voice in representing social science interests in Congress and with the federal bureaucracy.

The prime responsibility for maintaining academic vitality must rest at the individual department level. We must accept the fact that we have relatively young faculties who will not be able to move away. Faculty development must attain a very high priority. Support for attendance at professional meetings and seminars must be augmented, perhaps with outside gifts. As the pattern of student interests inevitably shifts, our nearly "tenured-in" faculties will have to re-tool. We may need to encourage a network of faculty exchanges. We will need to make more productive use than ever of sabbaticals. Department heads and chairpersons must assume an appropriate leadership role in seeking adequate support from their administrations; then they must work together nationally — in large part through APSA and the regional associations — to share their thoughts and to learn what methods work most effectively. More attention needs to be given at national meetings to professional development, and it also merits more research attention.

The Association itself had demonstrated that it is capable of responding to changing conditions and membership concerns. It now must move beyond response toward future-oriented actions.

NOTES

1. The respondents are sufficiently close in overall profile to the membership of the American Political Science Association to warrant the use of the data shown. The results are also generally consistent with other sample surveys of members.

REFERENCES

American Political Science Association. Association notes. *PS*, 1969, *2:* 671. (a)

American Political Science Association. Special symposium: The governance of the association. *PS*, 1969, *2:* 269-302. (b)

American Political Science Association. *Women in political science: Studies and reports of the APSA Committee on the Status of Women in the Profession.* Washington, D.C.: American Political Science Association, 1971.

American Political Science Association. Reports of APSA Committees: 1973 Elections Committee. *PS*, 1974, *12:* 36.

American Political Science Association. Reports of APSA Committees: 1979 Elections Committee. *PS*, 1980, *13:* 42.

American Political Science Association. Annual meeting registration - 1967-1980. *PS*, 1981, *14:* 601.

American Political Science Association. *APSA departmental services program: 1981-82 survey of departments.* Washington, D.C.: American Political Science Association, 1982. (a)

American Political Science Association. Association news. *PS*, 1982, *15:* 627-628. (b)

Baker, Earl M. The political science profession in 1970: Basic characteristics. *PS*, 1971, *4:* 33-39.

Barry, Brian M. *Sociologists, economists and democracy.* London: Collier-MacMillan, 1970.

Baum, William C., Griffiths, G.N., Mathews, Robert & Scherruble, Daniel. American political science before the mirror: What our journals reveal about the profession. *The Journal of Politics,* 1976, *38:* 894-917.

Caplow, Theodore. *The academic market place.* New York: Basic Books, 1958.

Caucus for a New Political Science. *Convention program, statement of objectives.* New York, 1981.

The Christian Science Monitor/American Political Science Association survey. Data obtained from the Roper Center, University of Connecticut, Storrs, CT 06268, 1981.

Demerath, N. J. Assaying the future: The profession vs. the discipline? *The American Sociologist,* 1981, *16:* 87-90.

Easton, David. The new revolution in political science. *The American Political Science Review,* 1969, *63:* 1051-1061.

Finley, David. Draft of Comments made as panel discussant, Annual Meeting of the American Political Science Association, Denver, Colorado, 1982.

French, Eloise. Registration rises at annual meeting. *PS*, 1981, *14,* 786.

Frolich, Norman & Oppenheimer, Joe A. *Modern political economy.* Englewood Cliffs, N.J.: Prentice Hall, 1978.

Gallup Opinion Index. Report No. 182, 27, 1980.

Glass, James M. In Goodin, Robert E. *The politics of rational man.* New York: John Wiley, 1976.

Goodin, Robert E. *The politics of rational man.* New York: John Wiley, 1976.

Graham, George J. Jr. & Carey, George W. *The post-behavioral era: Perspectives on*

Greenstein, Fred I. & Polsby, Nelson W. Preface. In Fred I. Greenstein & Nelson W. Polsby (Eds.) *Political science: scope and theory* (Vol. 1) Handbook of Political Science. Reading, Massachusetts: Addison-Wesley, 1975.

Gruberg, Martin. Letters. *PS*, 1981, 14: 725-726.

Gruberg, Martin & Sapiro, Virginia. Participation by Women in Annual Meetings. *PS*, 1979, *12:* 318-324.

Hargrove, Erwin C. Can political science develop alternative careers for its graduates? *PS*, 1979, *12:* 446-450.

Hawley, Amos H. Whither the ASA? *The American Sociologist*, 1981, *16:* 108-110.

Hsueh, Chun-tu. Asian political scientists in America. Hong Kong University, *Political Science Journal*, 1976-77: 11-15.

Jones, Charles O. Correspondence with the author, 1982.

Ladd, Everett Carll, Jr. & Lipset, Seymour Martin. The politics of American political scientists. *PS*, 1971, *4*, 135-144.

Ladd, Everett Carll, Jr. Portrait of a discipline: The American political science community, part I. *Teaching Political Science*, 1974, 2, 3-39. (a)

Ladd, Everett Carll, Jr. Portrait of a discipline: The American political science community, part 2. *Teaching Political Science*, 1974, 2, 144-171. (b)

Ladd, Everett Carl, Jr. *The divided academy.* New York: McGraw Hill, 1975.

Ladd, Everett Carll, Jr. Us revisited. Presented at the Annual Meeting of the American Political Science Association, New York, 1978.

Lane, John C. The slow graying of our profession. *PS*, 1982, *15:* 50-52.

Lankowski, Carl. Telephone interview with the 1980-81 President of the Caucus for a New Political Science. June 23, 1982.

Lipset, Seymour Martin. Politics and the social sciences: Introduction. In Seymour Martin Lipset (Ed.) *Politics and the social sciences.* New York: Oxford University Press, 1969.

Lipset, Seymour Martin. The limits of social science. *Public Opinion*, 1981, *4:* 2-9.

Lowi, Theodore J. The politics of higher education: Political science as a case study. In George J. Graham, Jr. and George W. Carey (Eds.), *The post-behavioral era: Perspectives on political science.* New York: David McKay, 1972.

Mann, Sheilah. Placement of political scientists. *PS*, 1982, *15:* 84-91.

Mann, Thomas. Placement of political scientists. *PS*, 1976, *9:* 412-414.

Mann, Thomas. Placement of political scientists in 1977. *PS*, 1978, *11:* 26-29.

Mann, Thomas. Executive director's quarterly column. *PS*, 1981, *15:* 582-583.

Mann, Thomas. From the Executive Director: First year report. *PS*, 1982, *15:* 415-420. (a)

Mann, Thomas. Letter to the Council of the American Political Science Association, 1982. (b)

Mann, Thomas. Memo to the Council of the American Political Science Association, 1982. (c)

Minutes of the Administrative Committee of the Executive Council of the APSA, April 5, 1982.

Prestage, Jewel, Adams, Russell, Jones, Mack, Martin, Robert, Moreland, Lois & Willingham, Alex. Report of the conference on political science curriculum at predominantly black institutions. In Maurice C. Woodard (Ed.), *Blacks and political science.* Washington, D.C.: The American Political Science Association, 1977.

Prestage, Jewel, Adams, Russell, Jones, Mack, Martin, Robert, Moreland, Lois & Willingham, Alex. Quelling the mythical revolution in higher education: Retreat from the affirmative action concept. *Journal of Politics*, 1979, *41:* 763-783.

Robey, John S. Political science departments: Reputations versus productivity. *PS*, 1979, *12:* 202-209.

Robey, John S. Reputations vs citations: Who are the top scholars in political science? *PS*, 1982, *15:* 199-200.

Roettger, Walter B. I never promised you a rose garden: Career satisfaction in an age of uncertainty. Paper presented at the Iowa Conference of Political Science. Iowa, 1977.

Roettger, Walter B. The discipline: What's right, what's wrong, and who cares? Paper presented at the annual meeting of the American Political Science Association. New York, N.Y., 1978.

Roettger, Walter B. Strata and stability: Reputations of American political scientists. *PS*, 1978, *11:* 6-12.

Roettger, Walter B. & Winebrenner, Hugh. Professional knowledge and electoral behavior: The case of political scientists. Paper presented at the American Political Science Association convention. Washington, D.C., 1981.

Roose, Kenneth D. & Anderson, Charles J. *A rating of graduate programs.* Washington, D.C.: American Council on Education, 1970.

Rossi, Peter H. The ASA: A portrait of organizational success and intellectual paralysis. *The American Sociologist,* 1981, *16:* 113-116.

Somit, Albert & Tannenhaus, Joseph. *The development of political science: From burgess to behavioralism.* Boston: Allyn and Bacon, 1967.

Turner, Henry A. & Hetrick, Carl C., 1972, Political activities and party affiliations of american political scientists. *The Western Political Quarterly,* 1972, *25:* 361-374.

Turner, Henry A, McClintock, Charles G., Spaulding, Charles B., 1963, The political party affiliations of American political scientists. *The Western Political Quarterly,* 1963, *16:* 650-665.

Waldo, Dwight. Political science: Tradition, discipline, profession, science. In Fred I. Greenstein and Nelson Polsby (Eds.), *Political science: Scope and theory.* Reading, MA: Addison-Wesley Publishing Company, 1975.

Walker, Jack L. Challenges of professional development for political science in the next decade and beyond. *PS*, 1978, *11:* 484-490.

Woodard, Maurice C. Interview. Washington, D.C., July 12, 1982.

AMERICAN POLITICAL PROCESSES AND POLICYMAKING

5

The Scholarly Commitment to Parties

Leon D. Epstein

"American political parties" are the subject of this "state of the discipline" essay. The continuing tradition that constitutes my theme is the preponderant scholarly commitment to the desirability of parties in a democratic society, and particularly in a society that may now reject them. Although I shall discuss chiefly the views of party specialists, their views in this respect have also long been held by political scientists in related areas of American and comparative politics.

Enough talent and industry have been engaged in studying American parties so as to produce many more impressive works than can be noted in any essay. I hope that the portion cited to illustrate my theme is fairly representative of our profession's customary treatment of parties within the general area of American government and politics. Comparative studies are mentioned only tangentially.

My scope is "parties" instead of "parties and other political organizations." The latter, as I shall suggest at the end, may reflect a more fully appropriate intellectual perspective. But I want to stress the special concern of political scientists for the role of parties even when they also write about interest groups. In any case, the boundaries of the party field are not very firm, but expansible into other fields of America politics like voting behavior and congressional behavior as well as interest groups.

The professional commitment of political scientists to the desirability of political parties has a substantial history. In fact, the scholarly commitment to parties is old enough to have been at odds with strong American political trends well before the party decline of the last few decades. I am thinking of the first ten or twenty years of the century when progressive reforms first began to diminish the power of party organizations and when a good deal of respectable public opinion already displayed a preference for nonparty politics (Shefter, 1978). At the time, political scientists themselves were among the reformers of old-style political organizations, but they did not characteristically settle, at least in national or state politics, for the nonpartyism of municipal progressivism (Hays, 1964). Specialists in municipal administration seem exceptional in their nonpartisan preferences. More impressive is the fact that certain leading scholars even at the turn of the century admired conventional American parties, objecting only to plainly corrupt manifestations while treating their non-ideological and decentralized features as suited to the constitutional and social order. From that standpoint, the old American parties were successful enough to justify preservation. These defenders of the established parties, while important and prestigious in American political science, have probably attracted less attention than have the scholars who emphasized the inadequacies of existing organizational structures and advocated the development of more effective parties. The latter, belonging loosely to the responsible-party or responsible-party government school of thought, have conducted a familiar debate with the defenders of existing parties.

The debate has been a meaningful one, not yet ended, but it is of less interest to me here than the underlying agreement that effective parties are desirable and probably essential in American politics as in democratic politics elsewhere. I treat the scholarly commitment to parties as more than a matter of specialists valuing any subject they have chosen to study. The case for parties has an intellectual basis that can be seen in the positive evaluations of parties by many less specialized political scientists. I begin therefore with a brief examination of that intellectual basis before discussing the historical positions of the defenders of conventional American parties and the advocates of responsible party government. Subsequently, I shall come to recent manifestations of the common tradition and to a question about its survival.

I. INTELLECTUAL BASIS

The scholarly commitment to the usefulness of parties has both empirical and theoretical sources. The empirical is apparent at the start. When the systematic study of American politics began in the late nineteenth and early twentieth centuries, parties were well-established institutions whose development much earlier in the century had coincided with an enlarged electoral franchise. Parties thus appeared to be products and agencies of American democracy. Although seldom the subject of academic inquiry before the last decades of the nineteenth century, their importance was recognized once political science emerged as a separate discipline around 1890 or 1900. Accordingly, while Bryce's substantial description of parties was famously innovative, it was not long alone in its appreciation of parties as "the great moving forces" of American government (1891, p. 5). Like Bryce, many American scholars of the period thought that American parties were too strong, notably in their control of patronage, and too unprincipled. But a desire to purify parties was compatible with a belief that reform could make parties more useful. Even the direct primary, for the political scientists who accepted it, was not a means to destroy parties.[1]

To be sure, the acceptance of parties in political science was at first less enthusiastic than it became after the objectionable city machines had weakened. Nevertheless, the earlier scholars usually treated American parties as much more than necessary evils. The favorable tone is evident in the works of Wilson, Ford, Lowell, and Goodnow (Ranney, 1954). Moreover, in the

early decades of the twentieth century, it was evident that parties accompanied democracy elsewhere and not merely in the United States. As Bryce
wrote, "parties are inevitable. No free large country has been without them.
No one has shown how representative government could be worked without
them. They bring order out of the chaos of a multitude of voters" (1921, Vol.
I, p. 119). This is the view of parties that has subsequently been dominant in
our profession. Neither Croly's belief that we could do without parties, despite
their previously useful services, nor Ostrogorski's belief that a true democracy
should do without them, has commanded a large scholarly following.[2] The rejection of Ostrogorski's anti-partyism, despite respect for his detailed study of
British and American parties, is most telling. In Macmahon's authoritative
words, Ostrogorski's approach reflected a "vast naivete" (1933). Charles
Merriam also specifically rejected Ostrogorski's views in his parties text (1922,
pp. 380-81), and spoke for his fellow scholarly practitioners when he said that
party "is one of the great agencies through which social interests express and
execute themselves" (p. 391).

The observable fact that parties have everywhere developed when a large
population participates in competitive elections, though it helps to explain
the original commitment of political scientists, does not provide a fully satisfying theoretical basis for defending parties against their critics. Such a basis,
however, soon developed, and by the middle and late years of the twentieth
century it underlay the several otherwise differing arguments for parties.
Specifically, the political scientists' case for parties involves a theory of
democracy sharply different from the individualism that determined
Ostrogorski's anti-partyism. Insofar as individualism, identified with direct
popular government and sometimes with Rousseau, is regarded as the
classical democratic theory, those who depart from it are said to be revisionists seeking to reconcile popular participation with respresentative institutions, intermediary groups, and regularized leadership. The word "revisionists" suggests a dilution of democratic ideals even when it is not prefaced
with the pejorative "elitist." Naturally, however, those who are called revisionists do not believe that they are diluting democracy. Rather, they conceive of collectively organized representation as the only means by which the
will of the people can be made effective. Town-meeting style democracy they
see as impractical in a large national or regional community, and strictly individual representation in legislative bodies as less responsive to popular majorities than party representation. The latter tends to be built around a kind
of program or set of policies, but the most severe revisionist might be content
with a party competition involving no more than a choice of leadership teams
without clearly differentiated principles (Schumpeter, 1950, p. 283). In either
view, most citizens are assumed to play useful political roles by exercising a
choice at periodic elections as long as their choice is made meaningful by
party labels. Many citizens may also participate in party candidate-selection
and policy-making, as some pro-party writers advocate, but such participation, whatever its advantages or disadvantages, is not required in all versions
of the democratic theory justifying parties. The essence of that theory is that
voters should be able to choose between recognizable competing leadership
groups.

By mid-century, the theory was explicit in influential comparative studies whose treatment of parties, especially of strong British-style parties, was highly favorable. Finer (1949, pp. 274-282, 353-362), Friedrich (1946 pp. 257, 294, 347), and Neumann (1956, pp. 397, 421) are important examples. Parties, they asserted, were essential in order to organize effectively the multitude of diverse interests in a modern society. In particular, working-class interests needed such organization. Still more explicitly, Duverger perceived the scale, centralization, and discipline—even the oligarchical character—of the twentieth century's mass parties as well-suited to political purposes in contemporary society (1954, p. 427).

Significantly, neither Duverger nor most other political scientists, American or European, thought of interest groups as sufficient agencies of collective representation. They have not always attacked interest groups as overly powerful and narrowly self-serving, but even when recognizing them as legitimate and useful in a political system, they seldom regard them as adequate mobilizers of majority preferences on behalf of broad public purposes. Interest groups, often studied along with parties, retain much of the stigma of "factions" in relation to the general interest. On the other hand, parties, in political science, are distinguished from factions because of the broader purposes and roles that they are supposed to fulfill. The point is now spelled out most sharply by Sartori (1976), but it has been embedded in much of twentieth-century political science. A party, Sartori writes, is "a part of a whole attempting to serve the purposes of the whole, whereas a faction is only a part for itself" (p. 25). For Sartori, it is true, faction is by no means synonymous with interest group; rather he uses the term in an older and more limited sense. But what he says about party in relation to faction asserts the superiority of party to any more particularized group. That superiority follows from Sartori's definition of party as functionally meant to serve the whole community. He believes that party serves that purpose not so much by representation as by its provision of channels of expression. Parties, in his view, transmit demands backed by pressure (p. 28). So, it can be said, do interest groups. But parties, it is thought, are motivated to relate demands to public purposes if only because parties, by their nature, must seek broad electoral support.

Important though Sartori and other comparativists have been in stating the theoretical basis for the scholarly commitment to parties, similar views may be found in works limited to American politics. I cite here one leading and prestigious example, Robert Dahl. Writing not as a party specialist but as an analytical theorist in his American government text, Dahl had no doubt that parties made substantial contributions to the operation of a democracy like that of the United States. They facilitated popular control over elected officials, helped voters to make more rational choices, and aided in the peaceful management of conflicts (1967, p. 243). These contributions were not to be found in the internal affairs of parties but in their external effects— among which was their assistance for "the many to overcome the otherwise superior resources of the few" (p. 250). The last point is an important one for believers in the democratic virtue of parties. They customarily see the mass of people, and notably poor people, as underrepresented in interest-group politics, and also likely to be underrepresented in an electoral politics conducted exclusively in terms of individual candidacies. Only by collective and organized action, meaning in practice a party capable of mobilizing majority support, can the many obtain governmental policies suiting their interests. Most commonly, that view is advanced by those who hope for a more coherent majority party than Dahl's own pluralist approach provides (James, 1974, pp. 6, 260-262). But Dahl, though far from denying either the legitimacy or the efficacy of the diverse interests that parties seek to combine in winning electoral coalitions, nevertheless shares with more majoritarian-minded advocates of parties the assumption that parties have a special value for those people whose own individual political power is limited.

There may be some quarrel with the adequacy of the intellectual case that political scientists expound in behalf of parties in a democratic society, but there should be no doubt about its widespread scholarly acceptance. As Samuel Eldersveld wrote in his major study of party organization: "Intellectually, we have become committed to the position in the twentieth century that parties are central to our system. . ." (1964, pp. 20-21). His page of quotations from eminent scholars makes it clear that the "we" of his sentence means political scientists.

II. DEFENDERS OF INDIGENOUS INSTITUTIONS

Constituting one of two loosely defined categories of pro-party political science, the defenders of conventional American parties respect the indigenousness of the very characteristics that believers in more responsible governing parties find objectionable. Decentralization, limited ideological or programmatic appeals, porousness, relatively noncohesive legislative contingents, and the absence of mass-membership organizations are appreciated as natural in American political development and often also as party qualities especially useful in the social and constitutional circumstances of the United States. Even the patronage on which American parties were originally built has occasionally been defended except in its plainly corrupting forms. Of course, not every defender of American parties admires all of their various characteristics. Some are critical enough so that their inclusion among the defenders might be questioned. The categorization is necessarily rough here as it is for the responsible-party government school, whose ranks include advocates of greatly varying degrees of change in existing party characteristics. And at least one important parties specialist, V. O. Key, is so hard to classify that he may deserve a category of his own.

In treating the appreciators of American parties, it is important to emphasize at the outset that their favorable opinions are based on the historical roles of parties in the nineteenth century and the first half of the twentieth. The defenders derive no satisfaction from the widely perceived recent decline in party efficacy, nor from the results of old or new progressive reforms designed to weaken parties. These are not the developments regarded as well-suited to American circumstances although they too might strike us as indigenous. No believer in the usefulness of parties applauds their decline and possible demise. Although the defenders of conventional American parties think that we cannot have (and often that we should not have) strong parties resembling foreign models, they definitely want parties that perform at least as well as those they have observed in American history.

The political scientists' defense of American parties, like their positive evaluation of parties generally, coincides with the emergence of relevant scholarly study near the turn of the century. Admiration for British parties, though established early among intellectuals, did not lead every scholar to follow Woodrow Wilson in urging that something like those parties be substituted for the American model. Even A. Lawrence Lowell, who shared Wilson's belief in the superiority of Britain's more responsible parties, thought the less cohesive American parties better suited to the American constitutional preference for a government in which no majority, acting through a cohesive party, could gain complete control (Ranney, 1954, pp. 48-69). Fuller praise of American parties came from Henry Jones Ford (1898), who can be regarded as the founder of the twentieth-century defense of American parties. Although Ford, like Wilson and Lowell, was critical of the limited degree to which American parties assumed policymaking responsibility, his hopes for developing that responsibility did not preclude an emphasis on the considerable accomplishments of the country's historic parties. Sharing the view, also held by Lowell and Wilson, that American parties owed much of their special character to the separation of executive and legislative powers established by the Constitution, Ford argued that parties in fact made that difficult system work. They bridged, to a useful extent, the separation. The extensive extragovernmental apparatus of the nineteenth-century boss-run machines impressed Ford as understandable given the circumstances in which parties had had to develop in the United States.[3]

Ford's emphasis on the usefulness of traditional party organizations became a familiar theme for many political scientists as those organizations slowly declined in the early twentieth century. This was notably so for a relatively conservative defender of American parties like E. M. Sait. In the first edition of his text (1927, pp. 159-164), Sait quoted Ford approvingly with respect to the success of American parties and, in a section labeled the "Peculiar Importance of American Parties," praised their accomplishments in harmonizing organs of government, enabling the electorate to function, advancing national unity, checking religious intolerance, assimilating foreign elements, softening the clash of economic interests, and adopting similar consensual platforms. Like Ford, Sait was skeptical about the claims for the direct primary, but after its first two decades of operation, he did not view its impact as so destructive of party responsibility as political scientists would later more often discover it to be. Nevertheless, Sait was already concerned with the apparent decline of the old organizational loyalties, whatever the cause. The decay of partisanship, he said, "cannot be viewed without disquiet. The democratic regime can no more function satisfactorily without strong parties than parties can function without strong organization" (p. 373).

By the 1920s, it was not only the formerly much criticized organizational strength of traditional American parties that non-reformist political scientists appreciated. The absence of well-defined distinguishing principles, as between the major parties, now also became a kind of virtue in the American system. For example, Sait included the moderating and unifying contributions of American parties among the praiseworthy accomplishments already cited. Similarly, Arthur Holcombe, in his well-known exposition of American parties (1924), responded directly to the "empty bottles" criticism that went back at least to Bryce. To have any chance of winning elections in the diverse American nation, parties needed to make broad rather than particularized appeals, such as those of an exclusively capitalist or socialist party. By their broad appeals in the United States, Holcombe said, parties tended to conciliate social strife. "The wide extent and diversified interests of the major parties," he added, "are the best guarantee which the people possess that power will be used with moderation" (p. 384).

In the political science literature of the next several decades, the defense of America's loose and compromising parties emphasized their decentralized, federative character as better suited to a pluralist society and to pluralist values than a more cohesive national party could be (Banfield, 1964; Grodzins, 1964). The general point was fully argued by Ranney and Kendall in their textbook's extended effort to present a theoretical basis for understanding mid-century American parties. Although the authors were attracted by the logic of absolute majority rule, which would in principle support a more cohesive national party, they were convinced that the present parties were "appropriate to the governing system the American people really want" (1956, p. 500).

With good reason, many defenders of traditional American parties found their case at mid-century most fully and persuasively stated by Pendleton Herring. In a sophisticated pluralist exposition of American institutions (1940), Herring — very much in the mainstream of postwar political science — appealed to many political liberals as well as conservatives. He treated the New Deal legislation of the 1930s as an accomplishment of existing institutions and as evidence of their workability. Herring saw in presidential leadership, within the existing structure, an effective means of obtaining positive action when required. "The New Deal," he said, "demonstrated that rapidity of action was possible within the limits of present institutions" (p. 421). Rather than deploring the fact that neither major party was a unified national entity, Herring found advantages in having only "a loose confederation of state and local organizations" (p. 245). He treated these organizations as meaningful, the professional politicians at their center as usefully in control, and their regular followers and supporters as significant despite — or because of — their diverse interests and principles.

So highly favorable a view of the performance of American parties was not characteristic of most of their defenders after World War II. Even scholars who shared Herring's evaluation of the usefulness of parties in earlier American experience, including the 1930s, often found contemporary parties inadequate as a result either of their decline or their failure to change sufficiently to meet new demands. The line between defenders of indigenous institutions and more-responsible party advocates becomes harder to draw. I do so hesitantly when I consider V. O. Key among the defenders. He is rightly well-known for his belief in strengthening and making more effective the

American parties that he studied so intensively and insightfully in the two decades after World War II. But he suggested no foreign models for American parties to emulate. Insofar as he had models, they appeared to be modernized variations of successful American parties of the fairly recent past. In fact, Key often deplored the twentieth-century decline in organizational strength, and most emphatically its absence in particular places. The sense in which he wanted parties to be responsible, or at least responsive to voters, was very much within the limits imposed by the constitutional structure. He did not advocate the full-fledged responsible party government that he thought unachievable in American circumstances.[4] Nor did he advocate a mass-membership party of a type largely unfamiliar in the United States. Rather, like most defenders of American parties, Key looked to the self-interest of party leaders to produce a responsiveness to the electorate.

Indeed, it was crucial in Key's approach that there should be party leaders and specifically more than one set of leaders—that is, competing teams. In the American context, that meant two parties rather than one. His most famous study, of the South (1950), is an extended criticism of the short-comings of traditional one-party politics in which voters lack the clear-cut alternatives posed by competing teams bearing different party labels. Factional conflicts within parties, though fought out in direct-primary elections, do not provide a satisfactory continuity for voters or a sufficient association between gubernatorial and legislative candidates. One-party politics is issue-less and also, most significantly, without a plain electoral choice between well-defined groups of politicians, the ins and the outs. In the long run, Key believed, the have-nots in a society were the losers from a politics so disorganized as to preclude their effective influence.

Similar themes are stressed in Key's more general study of state politics. For the North as well as the South, party competition is the best means of enforcing accountability. Key associated its absence in certain northern states with the decay of party organization. The vigor of two-party competition had declined, he thought, during the first half of the twentieth century. One cause is the direct primary which often, Key believed, transfers competition from an inter-party basis to a less meaningful level of personalities. "The new channels to power placed a premium on individualistic politics rather than on the collaborative politics of party" (1956, p. 169). Here as in his other works Key reflected a good deal more dissatisfaction with existing American parties than is customary among their defenders. And, while he regarded them as having been more effective in the past, his praise for their historical record was unenthusiastic. On the whole, Key is best understood as defending traditional American parties only in the sense that, when organized and competitive, they were the best that we were likely to have. He found advantages in two-party competitive states and in such national two-party electoral competition as occurred despite the disadvantages of decentralized confederative organizations (1964, p. 334). But Key did not proclaim any virtue for the limits in strength and coherence that flowed from the indigenous development of American parties. Instead, he merely accepted these limits, or most of them, as painful necessities.

III. ADVOCATES OF RESPONSIBLE
PARTY GOVERNMENT

Political scientists whom I categorize as advocates of responsible party government are chiefly distinguishable by their desire for American parties to transcend the limits associated with indigenous institutions. Unlike defenders of traditional parties, who accept those limits either enthusiastically or resignedly, members of the party government school argue for parties that would assume collective responsibility for governmental policymaking in a manner so far uncharacteristic of American experience.[5] Although they might praise American parties of the past as much better than no parties at all, the advocates of party government do not regard them as satisfactory models. They seldom suggest entirely new parties, but they want to transform the existing Republican and Democratic parties into essentially different political institutions. In their minds, a democratic society requires not merely parties of one kind or another, but two strong and cohesive parties each offering the electorate policy commitments which it could fulfill after winning government offices.

Party responsibility thus has a special import here that differentiates it from the ordinary meaning of the phrase. After all, the defenders of traditional parties—indeed, all believers in the usefulness of parties—prefer responsibility in some sense. But the advocates of party government want parties to be so much more responsible as to make for a difference in kind and not merely in degree. They sharpen this difference both by a thorough-going criticism of existing parties and by arguments for basic changes. These arguments are often cast as moral imperatives for overcoming the American institutional and social obstacles in the way of effective parties. The transformation that party government advocates have in mind is principally at the national level. Although they also deplore the frequent absence of party responsibility in state and local politics, their emphasis is on the weakness and incoherence of national parties. Attention is fixed on the inability of either Republicans or Democrats to promise and deliver policies through party control of Congress as well as of the presidency. They want *national* party government.

With its emphasis on national politics, the party government school has existed as long as American scholars have studied parties. Woodrow Wilson, early in his academic career, propounded a version of the doctrine, specifically drawn from the British model, and others near the turn of the century were attracted by it (Ranney, 1954, pp. 25-47). Its more recent presence is heavily identified with E. E. Schattschneider, a champion of stronger parties from the 1930s through the 1960s. As he said of himself, "I suppose the most important thing I have done in my field is that I have talked longer and harder and more persistently and enthusiastically about political parties than anyone else alive" (Adamany, 1972, p. 1321).[6] During his career parties declined rather than becoming stronger, as he had hoped, but Schattschneider did not lack academic followers or influence. If for a time these views had less prestige among political scientists than those of pluralist defenders of existing parties, they were never disregarded and their popularity revived in the late 1960s and 1970s.

That popularity may be partly attributed to the sharpness with which Schattschneider stated the majoritarian premise of the party government position. Unlike his pluralist opponents, he was not satisfied with direct interest-group representation and with parties that sought only to accommodate diverse interests in coalitional representation. Schattschneider assumed that there was a legitimate and definable majority interest that a party should mobilize and represent. Hence, he put into the conclusions of his best-known book: ". . . party government is good democratic doctrine because the parties are the special form of political organization adapted to the mobilization of majorities. How else can the majority get organized? If democracy means anything at all it means that the majority has the right to organize for the purpose of taking over the government. Party government is strong because it has behind it the great moral authority of the majority and the force of a strong traditional belief in majority rule" (1942, p. 208). The majority, in Schattschneider's writing, has a more public purpose than do minority interest groups, and its superiority in this respect derives from its inclusion of the great mass of people whom he believes to be unorganized and unrepresented by pressure groups (1960, p. 35).

Interestingly, Schattschneider did not seek to strengthen American parties by participatory reforms. He favored neither the direct primary nor any other large-scale democratizing of party organizations. Instead, he accepted, much as did Key, the sufficiency of the competing-teams conception of party. "Democracy is not to be found *in* the parties but *between* the parties" (1942, p. 60). Voters need not be burdened with party affairs. Nominations could be settled by organizational activists and by the leaders themselves. So could party policies and issue-positions. Voters would be well served if given a choice between sets of leaders, each united in its commitment to a party and its program. The trouble was that such a choice did not really exist in American politics. Neither the Republicans nor the Democrats presented coherent leadership teams. Thus the two-party system did not fulfill its advantage by way of a real majority winner. Neither party's majority was cohesive enough. The apparent success of major American parties in electing candidates was not followed by their effective mobilization to govern as a united force (1948, pp. 29-30).

Schattschneider, in his own writing, provided little by way of blueprints for change. But there was one prominent theme: build a national party leadership that would not be dependent on state and local politicians. Decentralization of party authority was the enemy of responsible-party government at the national level. The major American party, as "a loose confederation of state and local bosses," meant agreement for but limited purposes—chiefly patronage (1942, pp. 132-133). A party built around state and local bosses lacked policy coherence. Most emphatically, Schattschneider preferred a national leadership strong enough not only to control congressional party majorities but also to cut off patronage to local bosses. Before and after elections, presidential and congressional candidates would share genuinely public purposes. When Schattschneider spoke of party government, he meant party centralization (1942, p. 207).

Considerably more specific proposals for achieving party government are made in the famous report of the American Political Science Association's Committee on Political Parties (1950). Schattschneider chaired the Committee, and its report reflected his intense belief in the democratic need for two competing national parties to present alternative governmental programs. Although the report's proposals for intra-party democracy are at odds with Schattschneider's earlier acceptance of a policy-making leadership, many of its other detailed suggestions are consistent with his approach. So too is the report's basic and explicit assumption that parties can be made responsible without formally changing the U.S. Constitution (pp. 35-36). In that respect, the APSA Committee spoke for much of the responsible-party government school during the post-war years. This is not to say that it spoke for most political scientists or even most parties specialists. Despite the Committee's unusual status as an agency of the professional association, its report, published as a supplement to the APSA's journal, evoked immediate dissent from the defenders of conventional American parties. And the report was subsequently criticized because its advocacy lacked the kind of empirical support that political scientists came to expect in later decades (E. Kirkpatrick, 1971). Many of its proposals, however, continued to appeal to responsible-party advocates even in the 1970s. Interest in the report remained high (Pomper, 1971). Virtually all students of American politics at least agreed that effective parties of some kind were necessary, and many well may have preferred the Committee's kind of effective parties although they did not always share the Committee's belief that they could be established in the United States.

In its proposals, the APSA report linked the responsible-party doctrine to the participation of issue-oriented organized activists both in selecting candidates and in party policymaking. Activists could be expected to endorse and help to nominate candidates willing to carry out party policies that their organizations had developed. The participatory membership would be a means for achieving coherently responsible party government despite the direct primary and other institutional obstacles. Accordingly, Schattschneider's acquiescence in the Committee's organizational recommendation was not incompatible with his principal purpose. It is true that he had said, in his previously published work, that his purpose could be accomplished without intra-party democracy—that large-scale citizen participation in a party's internal affairs was not a democratic essential as long as citizens had a clear inter-party choice. But he might well have viewed participatory activists as genuinely committed party organizational members, not so far removed from smaller leadership groups. Party activists were very different from mere party voters whose membership Schattschneider had treated as a fiction created by primary registration laws. At any rate, the Committee's preference for organizational activism remained an important element in the advocacy of responsible party government. Also in the 1960s and 1970s similar large-scale citizen participation in party affairs was advanced even by scholars who otherwise disassociated their arguments for more effective parties from certain other aspects of the APSA report (Saloma & Sontag, 1973).

Another persistent theme in responsible-party advocacy is presidential leadership. For some scholars, a national party is essentially the president's, or the presidential candidate's. Congressional members and candidates are treated as members of his team. The nature of the presidential-party relationship, however, is not perceived to be the same by all believers in responsible party government. Woodrow Wilson, for example, came to put so much emphasis on a president's own popular mandate, received directly and individually from the electorate, that he can be charged with a departure from party government altogether (Ceaser, 1979, p. 197). After all, party government implies collective rather than strictly personal leadership. Thus, stronger parties are often specifically advanced as a means to secure effective government without a too-powerful president governing independently of party or of other intermediaries between himself and the people. For the responsible party school, the president is important as the leader of a team, but he is responsible to others on that leadership team as well as to the voters.

Among recent responsible party advocates emphasizing presidential leadership, Burns is preeminent in his concern with both a strong party and a strong leader, each complementing the other (1978, chap. 12). Burns seeks a leader capable of mobilizing a party majority rather than a personal, independent, or bipartisan majority. And he conceives of such a party majority as effective only if headed by a strong president. Specifically, Burns wants a presidential party able to lead a congressional majority: ". . . each presidential party must convert its congressional party into a party wing exerting a proper, but not controlling or crippling hold on party policy" (1963, p. 326). He would also have his presidentially-led national party build a mass-membership organization, but undoubtedly most of his hopes for party policymaking rest on innovative leadership to which party members would actively respond by way of campaign efforts to elect congressional candidates committed to the program of the president's party (1965, p. 111; 1972, chap. 8).

IV. MAINTAINING THE COMMON TRADITION

By discussing Burns and also a few other currently active political scientists, I have not entirely neglected contemporary scholarship within the historical context. But I want at this point to demonstrate the continuity of the scholarly commitment to parties by separately considering a small portion of the massive literature of the last two decades. The common ground now occupied by parties specialists will be more apparent than it was in the historical narrative. Differences between the two schools of thought surely remain, notably over their preferred remedies, but the differences tend to be overshadowed by a mutual dissatisfaction with the state of American parties in the 1970s and 1980s. Perhaps dissatisfaction is not the best word for the views of contemporary students who do not themselves deplore the ineffectiveness of American parties but merely describe it. Yet they too represent the pro-party tradition insofar as their description of present-day parties measures them by the standard of more effective models derived from the American past or from elsewhere. Shortcomings are suggested even without any overt advocacy. And often there is at least an expressed hope or a search for stronger parties.

A good deal of the continuity in the scholarly commitment is explicable in the most literal sense. Not only do certain important mid-century carriers of the tradition—Ranney and Burns, for instance—maintain their positions, but other slightly earlier figures—notably Schattschneider and Key—are followed by former students, disciples, and admiring professional colleagues. In parties textbooks as well as in monographic literature, Schattschneider's and Key's themes persist. To cite only two of many contemporary examples, the responsible-party model is central in Everson's analysis (1980), and it is prominent in Sorauf's well-established text (1980a). Neither author, it is true, is optimistic about the model's prospects, and in this respect the presentation is like that of many contemporary scholars who retain the traditional frame of reference but not the faith. Hence, their perspective is closer to Key's than to Schattschneider's. So too has Key been followed in the now standard use of the analytical categories of electoral, organizational, and governmental parties that he had popularized in his textbook (1964, pp. 163-165).

To display more specifically the continuity of Key's research interests, the readiest example is provided by the literature on party competition. His influence here is unusually direct in that for over two decades numerous talented and highly trained political scientists have examined Key's hypothesis that two-party competition produced superior policy outputs to those of a single party's personal factionalism (Lockard, 1968). Using increasingly refined quantitative methods, they compare inter-party competitive states and one-party dominant states with respect to welfare, education, and other policies—often counting redistributional results as signs of superiority. By no means has all of the research tended to confirm the hypothesis; a good deal of it leads instead to the belief that socio-economic variables account for more of the differences between state policy outputs than do strictly political factors. This point is stressed in a methodological critique that also usefully summarizes much of the large volume of relevant literature (Lewis-Beck, 1977). Nevertheless, the quest for statistical confirmation has not been abandoned. Even if it were, the established preference for party competition in state as in national politics would not also be readily abandoned. For Key's followers as for other scholars, inter-party competition has advantages that do not require statistical confirmation. It must seem almost self-evident that a democratic belief in the usefulness of parties means a belief in inter-party competition.

Moreover, among American parties specialists, this means that two-party competition, not multipartism, is the alternative to a one-party system. Unlike students of European politics, where multipartism either exists or is thought likely to exist, observers of American politics, now even more than earlier, confront situations in which third parties are only interesting and often temporary aberrations. Accordingly, the American classification of state party systems ranges from degrees of one-party dominance to degrees of two-party competitiveness (Jewell & Olson, 1982, p. 27). In that context, no more than in American national politics, is it relevant to contrast two-party competitiveness, favorably or unfavorably, with multipartism. Instead, implicitly if not always explicitly, the literature treats two-party competitiveness as a desirable norm in contrast to one-party dominance. The treatment is striking in work on the development of Southern Republicanism (Bass &

DeVries, 1976). In presidential and congressional elections, increased Republican voting may suggest the emergence of more meaningful national party alignments; and in state elections, the slower but visible growth of Republican strength suggests the possibility of finally ending a century of one-party Democratic dominance. Indeed, the new Republican strength in the South, fitting as it does a generally more national and less sectional voting pattern, is one of the few recent developments encouraging to believers in effective parties. Understandably, however, close observers of the South, like most students of American politics, remain cautious about the extent to which recent Republican votes represent new party commitments as opposed to a decline in Democratic commitments and another version of candidate-centered politics (Strong, 1977). Rather than a new electoral alignment, or realignment, is there in the South, and elsewhere, mainly a dealignment?

The question leads to the vast and imposing literature on voting behavior. Although that literature belongs in a substantial field of its own, some of it is produced by party specialists and a much larger share is used in studies of parties. From its early days, the most influential research group analyzing sample-survey data has focused attention on party identification as a prime determinant of voting behavior (Campbell, *et al.*, 1960). I deal but briefly with work of this kind because of lack of space, not lack of relevance. After all, the analysts of voting behavior have been the definers of the electoral party, or the party-in-the-electorate, which is of such great concern to American parties specialists. Voters' party preferences were, and are, observed from election returns and official state registration totals, but they are most familiarly determined by party identifiers in sample surveys. Each of the artifacts called a major electoral party apparently consists of a substantial percentage of voters who identify themselves as Republicans or Democrats in response to survey questions. The standard form of these questions is now open to significant criticism (Dennis, 1981), but the elicited responses provide a widely accepted record of several decades of "membership" in the major electoral parties. With about three-quarters of American voters thus identified as Republicans or Democrats as late as the 1950s and early 1960s, electoral parties looked impressive, relative to their counterparts elsewhere, even if American organizational and governmental parties might not (Converse & Dupeux, 1962). Despite critical deviations, most party identifiers, it could be shown, usually voted for candidates similarly identified.

To be sure, party mobilization of voters was demonstrably less complete than it had been earlier in American history (Burnham, 1965), but the party identification figures suggested considerable stability. Hence, it was their drop after 1964 that most saliently signified the decline of parties. By the 1970s, with only about two-thirds rather than three-quarters of the electorate regularly identifying as Republicans or Democrats, and with a concomitant decrease in straight-ticket voting, something important had happened to the parties that were familiar to mid-century political scientists (Nie, Verba and Petrocik, 1976; Dennis, 1975). Not everyone agrees on the meaning of the change. It is variously interpreted as a prelude to realignment, a temporary though major break in an old alignment that can be largely re-established, a noncontinuing decline that leaves electoral parties only somewhat less pervasive, or telling evidence of a continuing process of dealignment or electoral decomposition (Miller & Levitin, 1976; Sundquist, 1973; Ladd & Hadley, 1978; Burnham, 1970, 1975; Lipset, 1981; Pierce & Sullivan, 1980). I note sources for the several interpretations without pausing to explore their variety. But I should emphasize the extent to which most scholars treat a regularized partisan alignment—old, new, or prospective—as a more or less desirable norm. Even while acknowledging an association of independent voting and high educational levels and thus a modernity about party switching and split-ticket ballots, political scientists rarely see virtues in weaker electoral parties. More often, they look hopefully for a renewed vitality, and when instead they find the likelihood of a continuing dealignment, doubts are expressed about its compatibility with a meaningful democratic process.

Relative to electoral parties, whose weakening in the last few decades has been so readily measured, extra-governmental party organizations occupy a less prominent place in the literature of recent party decline. Twenty or thirty years ago, these organizations, unlike parties-in-the-electorate, already looked relatively weak. With a few conspicuous exceptions, chiefly Chicago's, city machines—conventionally the most imposing American party organizations—were regarded as withering anachronisms where they had not completely disintegrated. It is true that some machine organizations, besides Chicago's, were shown to have more fully developed during or after the New Deal than earlier, thus contradicting established views of when and how the bosses had been destroyed (Stave, 1970; Dorsett, 1977). And patronage remained important enough to be studied in various settings (Tolchin, 1971). But by the 1960s the old machines ceased to be generally dominant. Moreover, they had not, in their heyday, been favorites of political scientists. Several studies had appreciated the usefulness of their organizational activities, but for the most part the machines themselves had not been attractive even to the general defenders of indigenous party institutions. And, as observed, responsible party advocates regarded local bosses as obstacles in the way of effective national parties. Accordingly, the decline of the old machines was not so much marked or mourned in the last few decades as was (and is) the still limited development of organizational alternatives.

A scholarly interest in new nonmachine organizations has been apparent since the late 1950s. Eldersveld's already cited study (1964) of Republican and Democratic parties in metropolitan Detroit is a leading example. Another is Wilson's book on Democratic activists in several large cities (1962). And there were several studies of the dues-paying membership organizations that developed in California and Wisconsin during the 1950s and early 1960s. Unlike Detroit's parties, these organizations started as voluntary or extra-legal parties as distinct from the highly regulated statutory parties which they sought to take over. Successful and persistent in only a few places, their ideologically-motivated memberships—amateurs rather than professionals—did not strike every scholar as so effective electorally as had the old patronage organizations. At any rate, by the 1970s it was apparent that the regularized dues-paying membership had not become a widespread party phenomenon in the United States and that ideological activists tended to be candidate-centered and issue-group oriented, rather than primarily party organizational in their commitments, even when they worked within party channels. Hence Wilson (1973, pp. 95-118), though less sympathetic to ideological activism than some other observers, represents a common view of its limited contribution to the effectiveness of late twentieth-century American party organizations. So too does Wilson present, in persuasive style, a widely accepted perception of the generally unsubstantial character of those party organizations relative to other kinds of political organizations in the United States.

This is not to say that students of parties have become content with the perceived limitations. Hopes for strengthening parties through organizational activism are apparent in very recent research on state parties. Three interesting examples appear in an important volume on party renewal (Pomper, 1980). Each of the three is about participatory efforts within established state party organizations rather than through extra-legal voluntary clubs alone. Lawson (1980) describes pro-party changes, including legal changes, in California; Marshall (1980) discusses the large-scale use in Minnesota of the caucus-convention system for policy resolutions and candidate endorsements; and Mileur (1980) explains the Democratic party's charter movement in Massachusetts as a means to secure meaningful convention decisions. The last of these developments, as the author notes, is related to the national Democratic party's charter of 1974. It too appealed to party revitalizers although it did not fulfill proposals for an enrollment of a regularized membership (Crotty, 1977, p. 252).

A related but different organizational hope at the state level is reflected in studies of party headquarters. Scholars have discovered welcome signs of greater professionalization and better-financed bureaucratic services. Huckshorn's work on state party leaders (1976, p. 254) shows that over 90 state parties maintained headquarters staffs in the mid-1970s and that over half of these had developed since the 1960s. Although Huckshorn does not believe that the new organizations dominate most campaigns, he describes their provision of services to some party candidates and their potential to provide technologically-advanced help that is too expensive for many individual candidates to buy for themselves (p. 263). The financial base need not and evidently does not usually rest on dues-paying members; rather, money comes largely from contributors who, while often numerous small givers, have a different status from organized activists. Party leaders and their staffs, in these circumstances, may well have considerable freedom from ideological constraints. Subsequent research concerning state party organization in the late 1970s tends to confirm Huckshorn's findings; professionalization and institutionalization continued to develop (Cotter, Gibson, Bibby, & Huckshorn, 1980). The evidence is not overwhelming, but it is thought significant particularly with respect to Republican developments (Jewell & Olson, 1982, p. 292).

More attention lately is being given to a similar but larger Republican development at the national level. Two scholars, Bibby and Cotter—who also study state party organizations—have stressed the importance of the growth of the Republican National Committee's headquarters since the late 1970s. In several works, they knowledgeably describe its staff, professional institutionalization, technical services, increasing involvement in congressional and state campaigns, help for state parties and candidates, close relations with the Republican congressional and Senate campaign committees, and thriving financial capacity thanks in large part to direct-mail solicitations (Cotter & Bibby, 1980; Bibby, 1979, 1980; Bibby & Cotter, 1980).

Although the RNC itself is still insistently a confederative party structure, its headquarters operation constitutes a much more substantial *national* party presence than any previously established. Significantly, the operation may be described as bureaucratic and leadership-dominated in that it does not rest on participatory activism (Longley, 1980). Money, to be sure, comes from numerous small contributions, as well as from larger ones, but the contributors are not members in the policy-making, activist sense. The RNC thus combines the conventional American cadre party's organization of leaders without dues-paying members, and the now characteristically successful financing of nonparty political organizations from solicited contributors. The pattern, as Kayden suggests in her analysis of nationalizing party trends, may represent the party of the future (1980). As such, it is more welcome among scholars content with strong leadership parties than it is among those preferring a more participatory model. Almost all party specialists, however, tend to appreciate any organizational improvement especially at the national level where parties have until the last decade seemed unsubstantial (Cotter & Hennessy, 1964).

Similarly, the different kind of strengthening of the Democratic national party has had a broadly favorable reception even among many political scientists critical of particular post-1968 reforms. The 1974 party charter, as noted already, is regarded as a positive development. So too is the establishment of the national party's authority over delegate-selection practices. For example, Ranney (1978, p. 226) treats the party's rule-making nationalization as a positive accomplishment although he dislikes the major results of the more general reform process of which the nationalization was a part. After all, national party authority, fortunately confirmed in U.S. Supreme Court opinions over-ruling contrary state regulations, might be used to achieve other preferred results. Apart from such possibilities, another more reform-minded political scientist sees the new power of the national party, relative to state parties, as "the most significant and far-reaching outcome of the entire reform era" (Crotty, 1978, p. 260). Not all scholars, it is true, are avid nationalizers; a few still prize the old confederative structure and, therefore, dislike overriding state parties. But the desire to strengthen national organizations is, as observed earlier, a long-standing one among party specialists.

However favorable the political science perception of the organization-enhancing potential of the Democratic national party's rule-making authority, it is not nearly so prominent as the adverse reaction to the development, or at least the accelerated development, of candidate-centered presidential nominating campaigns after 1968. Associating that development with the proliferation of primaries that was an evidently unintended consequence of party reforms, political scientists have become leading critics, especially within Democratic circles, of the party-weakening effects of the "plebiscitary" process of choosing presidential nominees (Ceaser, 1979, 1982; Ladd, 1980; J. Kirkpatrick, 1978; Ranney, 1975, 1978). The process, it is recognized, is used in practice by Republicans as well as Democrats. Although Republicans appear neither to have initiated the post-1968 reforms nor to have suffered electorally from the results of such reforms, their presidential nominees too have become the more or less popular choices of voters as expressed mainly in state-mandated primaries. Party organizational influences in determining nominations are thus observed by scholars to have been reduced in both parties. "Peer review" of candidates by leadership cadres—state and local party officials along with national figures in and out of Congress—is widely perceived as having been superseded by media-influenced campaigns among rank-and-file voters.

It is true that the old peer review had never won the support of those pro-party advocates who champion participatory activism by the ideologically committed. They prefer open caucuses in which activists, not merely leaders, can influence nominating contests. But they share with the defenders of nomination by regulars and professional politicians a dislike for the now-dominant presidential primaries—indeed for primaries altogether (Burns, 1980, p. 198). Whatever their other differences, almost all political scientists want to strengthen, in one way or another, party organizational roles in choosing nominees. This generalization holds even in the case of a scholarly observer who, untypically, does not plainly deplore the new nominating process; thus Kessel, while recognizing the problems of candidate-centered politics, finds in recent presidential nominating and election campaigns hopeful indications of continuing, meaningful national followings. He sees these "presidential parties"—campaign workers carrying over, often as local party officials, from one presidential candidate to another—as positive developments along with the increasingly important national party committees (1980, pp. 245, 265).

In the more usual pessimistic view of the plebiscitary nominating process, political scientists stress its impact on the capacity of presidents, once nominated and elected, to provide effective governmental leadership. Polsby and Wildavsky make the point sharply and familiarly when they discuss "the decline in the vital function of intermediation by parties." Parties are less able to perform this function "because the formal properties of plebiscitary decision-making, such as occurs in primary elections, leave so little room for the bargaining process" (1980, p. 281). A presidential nominee, not the choice of a coalition of politicians within a party, is unable to count on such a coalition to sustain his policies, notably in Congress after a winning election campaign. The political scientists' concern here is the traditional one of using party to bridge the constitutional gap between the two elected branches of American government. The old presidential nominating convention, while never helping as directly as the still older congressional caucus nomination might have done, now appears less unsuccessful than the plebiscitary system (at least for those more attentive to Carter's than to Reagan's experience). Because of the understandably special concern that there should be effective presidential leadership of congressional parties, or at least an effective cooperative relationship, some degree of return to peer review and a brokered convention is appealing. Presidential primaries, unlike direct primaries for most other party nominations, seem recent enough in many instances so that they or their influence might yet be curbed. Contemporary political scientists might also like to roll back direct primaries for other offices; more than earlier scholars, they are likely to regard all primaries as harmful to party organizations. But, realistically, political scientists concentrate on trying to limit the use of primaries in selecting the distinctively important presidential nominees. They hope thereby to make the presidential nominating convention again a striking exception to the prevalence, in this century, of the direct primary for choosing nominees for most American elective offices.

With or without the impact of plebiscitary presidential nominations, the problem of establishing effective governing parties has troubled political scientists recently as it has in the past. Perceived declines in effectiveness are attributed to many causes apart from the new presidential nominating procedures. From the imposing literature on congressional behavior and elections during the last two decades, a picture emerges in which individual Representatives and Senators, never entirely cohesive party followers, have become increasingly independent actors. Congressional parties still organize each house, still account for the roll-call votes of most members more often than anything else, and still maintain elaborate structures (actually more elaborate than before) to mobilize their forces. But members especially of the House have strongly candidate-centered relationships with their constituents and are able to conduct their own campaigns with the help of substantial non-party contributors (Mayhew, 1974; Fiorina, 1977; Mann, 1978; Hinckley, 1981; Jacobson, 1980). Moreover, the specialized professionalism of members, institutionalized in the decentralizing committee and subcommittee structure of Congress, contributes to independent behavior (Patterson, 1978). The tasks of party leaders are recognizably difficult. Ideological agreement plainly helps; party cohesion in roll-calls on certain sets of policy issues is greater than on others (Clausen, 1973).

I should not leave the impression that the authors of specialized studies of Congress are generally disappointed seekers of greater party cohesion. Many explain why Congress is not and perhaps cannot be dominated by stronger parties, and their studies sometimes emphasize the remarkable degree to which parties persist and effectively function within the limits imposed by the American system. Often, however, there is a note of satisfaction with reference to successful party performances of the past (Brady, 1978) and an apparent anxiety about any party decline. Furthermore, party specialists, when writing on Congress, tend to be alarmed about any diminished party cohesion (Burnham, 1975), and to search for new sources, notably an ideological realignment of members and voters, that would facilitate greater cohesion (Everson, 1980). Parallel concerns appear in the less well-known literature on state legislative parties (Jewell & Patterson, 1977, pp. 383-388).

V. AGAINST THE TIDE?

However incomplete my review of the recent literature relating to parties, it reveals, I trust, the continuity of the scholarly commitment established earlier in the century. The demonstration is hardly remarkable or even necessary insofar as it merely confirms that those who study parties think

them important. But in discussing recent work as well as in the earlier intellectual history, I have also stressed how the interest in the subject is
accompanied by a belief in the usefulness and desirability of parties. That
belief, though also familiar, strikes me as a significant characteristic of our
field. Not every other area of study is marked by anything like a parallel to the
persistent strength of the pro-party commitment. Interest groups present an
especially telling contrast; studies of that subject, while often accepting the
usefulness as well as the inevitability of interest groups in the political system,
are far from agreement on the desirability of making them more effective in
determining public policy. It is not unusual, now as in the past, for political
scientists to think that interest groups are already too effective in this respect.
Parties, on the other hand, are treated by our profession much as are those
governmental institutions—Congress, presidency, courts—whose strengthening is also frequently advocated by their specialized scholars.

The relative *in*effectiveness of contemporary American parties is now our
field's principal concern. Far from ignoring trends toward candidate-
centered politics, party scholars emphasize the decline in the party identification of voters, the weakening of the organizational power of state and local
leaders, the growing role of Political Action Committees especially in
financing campaigns, the personalizing impact of mass media and communications, the increasingly nonparty electoral bases of congressional incumbents, and the new nonorganizational routes to presidential nominations and
elections. Disputes occur over the reversibility of these trends and their potential for destroying parties altogether, and over ways of maintaining or re-
building parties. But common ground exists here as it has more generally for
the defenders of indigenous party institutions and the advocates of responsible
party government. These schools of thought, I have argued, represent two
strands of a scholarly pro-party tradition reacting to the candidate-centered
politics that has become increasingly popular among other Americans during
much of the twentieth century. Their differences, as the relevant literature indicates, lie in the means for strengthening parties. One group would restore
and rebuild party leadership structures (caricatured as the "back-to-the-
bosses" movement). The other would mobilize issue-oriented activists to exercise influence through caucus or other party participatory channels.

The differences, though consequential as they have always been, are contained within a Committee on Party Renewal that party specialists of various
persuasion formed in the late 1970s. Members include scholars who (like Ranney) look primarily to a restoration of the traditionally competing leadership
coalitions, others (like Burns) who remain identified with the advocacy of
responsible party government under presidential leadership, and still others
who emphasize large-scale participatory organizations. The Committee has
made its case for strengthening parties both within and outside the profession.
For example, it appeared before the Committee on House Administration
(1979, pp. 392-393) that was considering proposals for government financing
of House election campaigns, and urged that at least a substantial share of
any such financing be provided to parties rather than to candidates alone (as
the Representatives' own bills specified). In this as in other respects—like
presidential nominating conventions—the Committee on Party Renewal seeks

to rebuild parties as a counterforce to the now established candidate-centered politics. A leading member of the Committee, Gerald Pomper, edited a book devoted to arguments for party renewal as well as to useful studies, previously cited, of actual renewal efforts. The tone is clear in Pomper's introductory chapter: ". . . we must either acknowledge the mutual reliance of our parties and our democracy—or lose both" (1980, p. 5).

Pomper's language is more typical of responsible party advocates than it is of defenders of the old institutions, but the two schools of thought surely stand together as embattled champions of institutions which in one form the American public has never accepted, and which in the other form it has increasingly abandoned. Seldom do political scientists accept the decomposition of parties with equanimity. Now as always it is rare to find a scholar who rejects parties altogether—along with representative government—in the manner of Rousseau (B. Barber, 1980); it is nearly as infrequent for political scientists to express anything like satisfaction with relatively weak parties. Democratic politics without parties, or with much weaker parties than we now have, is almost always contemplated regretfully or fearfully when it is considered at all (Crotty & Jacobson, 1980). New kinds of political organizations, it is recognized, may be developing to perform certain party-type functions (Sorauf, 1980b), but these organizations are rarely seen as fully replacing parties even when they are regarded as potentially useful. Among political scientists, virtually no anti-party, or nonparty, school has arisen to correspond to the anti-party sentiment of a substantial portion of the larger community. Scholars do not reflect that sentiment though they may now have limited expectations with respect to party activities and accomplishments, particularly in policy-making spheres (King, 1969).

Are professional students of politics champions of a lost cause, trying with words to roll back a tide of American anti-partyism? So it sometimes appears as the scholarly devotion to parties has become more pronounced since mid-century while the power and public status of parties have visibly diminished. It might then follow that much less attention, in research and teaching, should be given to parties and more to other means of representation. The idea must occur to many political scientists, but, speaking now for myself, there are two reasons for not rushing to select this option.

First, I doubt that the pro-parties cause is irrevocably lost. Signs of decline can be acknowledged without thinking of them as overwhelming; newly developing national electoral alignments and organizational forms could suit the late twentieth-century American environment in ways that neither the old structures nor certain responsible-party models have done. I am thinking of the "presidential parties" and the broadly financed professional bureaucratic headquarters that scholars have recently examined, and also of the now-familiar evidence of a cohesive Republican governing party in 1981. Taking note of such developments, Harmel and Janda (1982, p. 132) write of what may be "the first steps on a path leading to a new vitality for the American party system." The suggestion is no less intriguing because it is made in the context of a work that typically and persuasively explains the constraints under which parties operate when trying to strengthen themselves. Possibly too there will be a broader tolerance for party strengthening than could have been expected when the old power and corruption of machine politics were more salient. No doubt, the earlier bad reputation of parties lingers generally, in middle-class attitudes particularly. But American parties may now have declined enough so as to allow a sympathetic public response to their revival in modern form. The signs of that kind of response are admittedly limited. A little pro-party sympathy may be detected in congressional legislation concerning campaign finance; although the major effect of that legislation has been to confirm candidate-centered financing, a few regulatory and public-funding provisions explicitly support parties (Kayden, 1980, p. 261; Alexander, 1980, p. 176). And there are proposals for more fully helping parties. Several states already do so through public funding (Jones, 1980). The popularity of the cause is enhanced by the greater contemporary reaction against Political Action Committees than against the weakened parties.

Secondly, I share, though a little skeptically, our discipline's long-established conception of the special importance of parties in a democratic society. I have used "they" for its various exponents principally to maintain a stylistic distance. I am myself impressed with the theoretical argument that parties are essential intermediaries for effective representation of a large and diverse electorate. Like other political scientists, I see no examples of a democratic political system, now or in the past, working without parties, or with much weaker, more porous parties than we now have.

Nevertheless, I do not believe that the established intellectual perspective or the limited indications of party revival should preclude the exploration of institutional alternatives to parties. Perhaps such exploration is already encouraged under the rubric used for APSA conventions, "Political Parties and Other Political Organizations." We know that Political Action Committees, in particular, are subjects of able scholarly work. They are not neglected even by party specialists who do not ordinarily conceive of them, any more than they conceive of the news media, as adequate to serve all of the purposes of parties. At most, it seems to me, the continuing scholarly commitment to parties may mean that they receive, compared to other political channels, more of our attention than their contemporary roles would seem to merit. The special attention is reflected not only in research but in courses and texts that concentrate on parties within an increasingly specialized discipline.[7] Concentrating in that way myself, I do not depart from the intellectual context of the continuing commitment that I have described. But the context along with the commitment may not be immutable.

FOOTNOTES

1. See Merriam and Overacker (1928) and Hannan (1923), reporting the views of political scientists among others in a special issue of the *Annals* devoted to the direct primary. Significantly, in 1923 a slight majority of the political scientists replying to Hannan's question favored convention nominations over the direct primary. Also among the several scholarly contributors to the special issue there were critics of the direct primary. Moreover, the political scientists who wrote in support of the direct primary did not make their case, as did Senator George Norris (another contributor to the special issue), on anti-party grounds. Altogether it seems from the 1923 col-

lection that political scientists already reflected a good deal of the skepticism about the direct primary's benefits that had been expressed earlier by the influential Henry Jones Ford (Ranney, 1954, pp. 85-87).

2. Ranney (1954) summarizes the arguments of Croly and Ostrogorski. The latter's major work, first published in English in 1902, is still widely admired for its scholarship by social scientists who nonetheless reject Ostrogorski's hostility to parties. Note, for example, S. M. Lipset's Introduction to an abridged paperback edition of Ostrogorski's study (1964). The other well-known European critic of parties, Michels, seems to have been no more influential than Ostrogorski in turning American political scientists away from their democratic hopes for parties; his argument, in any event, was not to dispense with parties but to realize their inevitable oligarchical nature (1949). Hence, in this essay I do put aside the interesting arguments against parties. By no means, however, am I suggesting that they have disappeared. Even if now rare among American political scientists, as I suggest in a later reference (B. Barber, 1980), the plainly widespread public hostility to parties has its contemporary intellectual champions as well as its staunch Washingtonian tradition. It may be uninfluential only among political scientists, but they and their study of parties constitute my subject.

3. I draw here not only on Ford's 1898 book, which I have cited, but also on Ranney's summary (1954, pp. 70-91) of Ford's later work.

4. Accordingly James (1974, pp. 9-28) treats Key as a proponent of a "responsible party" model rather than of a "party government" model in a classification that is probably more useful for some purposes than the simpler two-fold classification that I have adopted.

5. I have elsewhere discussed the part that British experience played in this advocacy (Epstein, 1980).

6. Adamany, in an appreciative review essay, cites *The Wesleyan Argus* (March 5, 1971, p. 2) as the source of the revealing quotation. For another insightful review of Schattschneider's work, see Boyd (1979).

7. Unlike Key (1964), several recent texts for parties courses do not include pressure groups or interest groups in their titles. Sorauf (1980a) is a case in point, but it should be noted that without devoting any chapters explicitly to interest groups, he does emphasize the limited roles of parties.

REFERENCES

Adamany, David. The political science of E. E. Schattschneider: A review essay. *American Political Science Review,* 1972, *66,* 1321-35.

Alexander, Herbert E. *Financing politics.* Washington: Congressional Quarterly, 1980.

APSA Committee on Political Parties. Toward a more responsible two-party system. *American Political Science Review,* 1950, *44* (Supplement).

Banfield, Edward C. In defense of the American party system. In Robert A. Goldwin (Ed.), *Political parties, U.S.A.* Chicago: Rand McNally, 1964.

Barber, Benjamin R. The undemocratic party system: Citizenship in an elite/mass society. In Robert A. Goldwin (Ed.), *Political parties in the eighties.* Washington: American Enterprise Institute, 1980.

Bass, Jack & DeVries, Walter. *The transformation of southern politics.* New York: Basic Books, 1976.

Bibby, John F. Political parties and federalism: The Republican National Committee involvement in gubernatorial and legislative elections. *Publius,* 1979, *9,* 229-36.

Bibby, John F. Party renewal in the national Republican party. In Gerald M. Pomper (Ed.), *Party renewal in America*. New York: Praeger, 1980.

Bibby, John F., & Cotter, Cornelius P. Presidential campaigning, federalism, and the federal election campaign act. *Publius*, 1980, *10*, 119-36.

Boyd, Richard W. Schattschneider, E. E. In *International encyclopedia of the social sciences*, 1979, *18* (Biographical Supplement). New York: Macmillan and the Free Press.

Brady, David W. Critical elections, congressional parties and clusters of policy changes. *British Journal of Political Science*, 1978, *8*, 79-99.

Bryce, James. *The American commonwealth* (Vol. II). Chicago: Sergel, 1891.

Bryce, James. *Modern democracies*. New York: Macmillan, 1921.

Burnham, Walter Dean. The changing shape of the American political universe. *American Political Science Review*, 1965, *59*, 7-28.

Burnham, Walter Dean. *Critical elections and the mainsprings of American politics*. New York: W.W. Norton, 1970.

Burnham, Walter Dean. Insulation and responsiveness in congressional elections. *Political Science Quarterly*, 1975, *90*, 411-35.

Burns, James MacGregor. *The deadlock of democracy*. Englewood Cliffs, N.J.: Prentice Hall, 1963.

Burns, James MacGregor. *Presidential government*. Boston: Houghton Mifflin, 1965.

Burns, James MacGregor. *Uncommon sense*. New York: Harper & Row, 1972.

Burns, James MacGregor. *Leadership*. New York: Harper & Row, 1978.

Burns, James MacGregor. Party renewal: The need for intellectual leadership. In Gerald M. Pomper (Ed.), *Party renewal in America*. New York: Praeger, 1980.

Campbell, Angus, Converse, Philip E., Miller, Warren E., & Stokes, Donald E. *The American voter*. New York: John Wiley & Sons, 1960.

Ceaser, James. *Presidential selection: Theory and development*. Princeton, N.J.: Princeton University Press, 1979.

Ceaser, James. *Reforming the reforms: A critical analysis of the presidential selection process*. Cambridge, Mass.: Ballinger, 1982.

Clausen, Aage R. *How congressmen decide: A policy focus*. New York: St. Martin's, 1973.

Committee on House Administration of the House of Representatives. *Hearings on public financing of congressional elections* (96th Congress, 1st Session). Washington, D.C.: U.S. Government Printing Office, 1979.

Converse, Philip E., & Dupeux, George. Politicization of the electorate in France and the United States. *Public Opinion Quarterly*, 1962, *26*, 1-23.

Cotter, Cornelius P., & Hennessey, Bernard C. *Politics without power: The national party committees*. New York: Atherton Press, 1964.

Cotter, Cornelius P., & Bibby, John F. Institutional development of parties and the thesis of party decline. *Political Science Quarterly*, 1980, *95*, 1-27.

Cotter, Cornelius P., Gibson, James L., Bibby, John F., & Huckshorn, Robert J. State party organizations and the thesis of party decline. Paper prepared for delivery at the Annual Meeting of the American Political Science Association, Washington, D.C., 1980.

Crotty, William J. *Political reform and the American experiment*. New York: Crowell, 1977.

Crotty, William J. *Decision for the democrats*. Baltimore: Johns Hopkins University Press, 1978.

Crotty, William J., & Jacobson, Gary C. *American parties in decline*. Boston: Little, Brown, 1980.

Dahl, Robert. *Pluralist democracy in the United States*. Chicago: Rand McNally, 1967.

Dennis, Jack. Trends in public support for the American party system. *British Journal of Political Science,* 1975, *5,* 187-230.

Dennis, Jack. On being an independent partisan supporter. Paper prepared for the Annual Meeting of the Midwest Political Science Association, Cincinnati, Ohio, 1981.

Dorsett, Lyle W. *Franklin D. Roosevelt and the city bosses.* Port Washington, N.Y.: Kennikat Press, 1977.

Duverger, Maurice. *Political parties.* New York: Wiley & Sons, 1954.

Eldersveld, Samuel J. *Political parties.* Chicago: Rand McNally, 1964.

Epstein, Leon D. What happened to the British party model? *American Political Science Review,* 1980, *74,* 9-22.

Everson, David H. *American political parties.* New York: Franklin Watts, 1980.

Finer, Herman. *Theory and practice of modern government.* New York: Henry Holt, 1949.

Fiorina, Morris P. *Congress: Keystone of the Washington establishment.* New Haven: Yale University Press, 1977.

Ford, Henry Jones. *The rise and growth of American politics.* New York: Macmillan, 1898.

Friedrich, Carl J. *Constitutional government and democracy.* Boston: Ginn and Company, 1946.

Grodzins, Morton. Party and government in the United States. In Robert A. Goldwin (Ed.), *Political parties, U.S.A.* Chicago: Rand McNally, 1964.

Hannan, William E. Opinion of public men on the value of the direct primary. *Annals of the American Academy of Political and Social Science,* 1923, *106,* 55-62.

Harmel, Robert, & Janda, Kenneth. *Parties and their environments: Limits to reform?* New York: Longman, 1982.

Hays, Samuel P. The politics of reform in municipal government in the progressive era. *Pacific Northwest Quarterly,* 1964, *55,* 157-69.

Herring, Pendleton. *The politics of democracy.* New York: W.W. Norton, 1940.

Hinckley, Barbara. *Congressional elections.* Washington, D.C.: Congressional Quarterly, 1981.

Holcombe, Arthur N. *The political parties of to-day.* New York: Harper & Bros., 1924.

Huckshorn, Robert. *Party leadership in the states.* Amherst: University of Massachusetts Press, 1976.

Jacobson, Gary C. *Money in congressional elections.* New Haven: Yale University Press, 1980.

James, Judson L. *American political parties in transition.* New York: Harper & Row, 1974.

Jewell, Malcolm E., & Patterson, Samuel C. *The legislative process in the United States.* New York: Random House, 1977.

Jewell, Malcolm E., & Olson, David M. *American state political parties and elections.* Homewood, Ill.: Dorsey Press, 1982.

Jones, Ruth S. State public financing and the state parties. In Michael J. Malbin (Ed.), *Parties, interest groups, and campaign finance laws.* Washington, D.C.: American Enterprise Institute, 1980.

Kayden, Xandra. The nationalizing of the party system. In Michael J. Malbin (Ed.), *Parties, interest groups, and campaign finance laws.* Washington, D.C.: American Enterprise Institute, 1980.

Kessel, John. *Presidential campaign politics.* Homewood, Ill.: Dorsey Press, 1980.

Key, V. O., Jr. *Southern politics in state and nation.* New York: Knopf, 1950.

Key, V. O., Jr. *American state politics: An introduction.* New York: Knopf, 1956.

Key, V.O., Jr. *Politics, parties, and pressure groups.* New York: Crowell, 1964.

King, Anthony. Political parties in western democracies. *Polity*, 1969, *2*, 112-41.

Kirkpatrick, Evron M. "Toward a more responsible two-party system": Political science, policy science, or pseudo-science? *American Political Science Review*, 1971, *45*, 965-90.

Kirkpatrick, Jeane Jordan. *Dismantling the parties*. Washington, D.C.: American Enterprise Institute, 1978.

Ladd, Everett C. A better way to pick our presidents. *Fortune*, 1980, *101*, 132-35, 138, 142.

Ladd, Everett C., & Hadley, Charles D. *Transformations of the American party system*. New York: W. W. Norton, 1978.

Lawson, Kay. California: The uncertainties of reform. In Gerald M. Pomper (Ed.), *Party renewal in America*. New York: Praeger, 1980.

Lewis-Beck, Michael S. The relative importance of socioeconomic and political variables for public policy. *American Political Science Review*, 1977, *71*, 559-66.

Lipset, Seymour Martin (Ed.). *Party coalitions in the 1980s*. San Francisco: Institute of Contemporary Studies, 1981.

Lockard, Duane. State party systems and policy outputs. In Oliver Garceau (Ed.), *Political research and political theory*. Cambridge: Harvard University Press, 1968.

Longley, Charles H. National party renewal. In Gerald M. Pomper (Ed.), *Party renewal*. New York: Praeger, 1980.

Macmahon, Arthur W. Ostrogorsky, Moisey Yakovlevich (1854-1919), *Encyclopaedia of the social sciences* (Vol. XI). New York: Macmillan, 1933.

Mann, Thomas E. *Unsafe at any margin*. Washington, D.C.: American Enterprise Institute, 1978.

Marshall, Thomas R. Minnesota: The party caucus-convention system. In Gerald M. Pomper (Ed.), *Party renewal in America*. New York: Praeger, 1980.

Mayhew, David R. *Congress: The electoral connection*. New Haven: Yale University Press, 1974.

Merriam, Charles E. *The American party system*. New York: Macmillan, 1922.

Merriam, Charles E., & Overacker, Louise. *Primary elections*. Chicago: University of Chicago Press, 1928.

Michels, Robert. *Political parties*. Glencoe, Ill.: Free Press, 1949

Mileur, Jerome M. Massachusetts: The democratic party charter movement. In Gerald M. Pomper (Ed.), *Party renewal in America*. New York: Praeger, 1980.

Miller, Warren E., & Levitin, Teresa. *Leadership and change*. Cambridge, Mass.: Winthrop Publishers, 1976.

Neumann, Sigmund. *Modern political parties*. Chicago: University of Chicago Press, 1956.

Nie, Norman H., Verba, Sidney, & Petrocik, John R. *The changing American voter*. Cambridge, Mass.: Harvard University Press, 1976.

Ostrogorski, M. *Democracy and the organization of political parties*. Garden City, N.Y.: Doubleday, 1964.

Patterson, Samuel C. The semi-sovereign Congress. In Anthony King (Ed.), *The new American political system*. Washington, D.C.: American Enterprise Institute, 1978.

Pierce, John C., & Sullivan, John L. (Eds.). *The electorate reconsidered*. Beverly Hills, Calif.: Sage, 1980.

Polsby, Nelson W., & Wildavsky, Aaron. *Presidential elections: Strategies of American electoral politics*. New York: Charles Scribner's Sons, 1980.

Pomper, Gerald M. Toward a more responsible two-party system? What, again? *Journal of Politics*, 1971, *33*, 916-40.

Pomper, Gerald M. (Ed.). *Party renewal in America*. New York: Praeger, 1980.

Ranney, Austin. *The doctrine of responsible party government*. Urbana: University of Illinois Press, 1954.

Ranney, Austin. *Curing the mischiefs of faction: Party reform in America*. Berkeley: University of California Press, 1975.

Ranney, Austin. The political parties: reform and decline. In Anthony King (Ed.), *The new American political system*. Washington, D.C.: American Enterprise Institute, 1978.

Ranney, Austin, & Kendall, Willmoore. *Democracy and the American party system*. New York: Harcourt, Brace, and World, 1956.

Sait, Edward M. *American parties and elections*. New York: Century Co., 1927.

Saloma, John S. III, & Sontag, Frederick H. *Parties: The real opportunity for effective citizen politics*. New York: Vintage Books, 1973.

Sartori, Giovanni. *Parties and party systems*. New York: Cambridge University Press, 1976.

Schattschneider, E. E. *Party government*. New York: Holt, Rinehart and Winston, 1942.

Schattschneider, E. E. *The struggle for party government*. College Park: University of Maryland, 1948.

Schattschneider, E. E. *The semi-sovereign people*. New York: Holt, Rinehart and Winston, 1960.

Schumpeter, Joseph. *Capitalism, socialism, and democracy*. New York: Harper & Brothers, 1950.

Shefter, Martin. Party, bureaucracy, and political change in the United States. In Louis Maisel and Joseph Cooper (Eds.), *Political parties: Development and decay*. Beverly Hills, Calif.: Sage, 1978.

Sorauf, Frank J. *Party politics in America*. Boston: Little, Brown, 1980(a).

Sorauf, Frank J. Political parties and political action committees: Two life cycles. *Arizona Law Review*, 1980(b), *22*, 445-64.

Stave, Bruce M. *The new deal and the last hurrah*. Pittsburgh: University of Pittsburgh Press, 1970.

Strong, Donald S. *Issue voting and party realignment*. University, Ala.: University of Alabama Press, 1977.

Sundquist, James L. *Dynamics of the party system*. Washington, D.C.: Brookings Institution, 1973.

Tolchin, Martin & Susan. *To the victor: Political patronage from the clubhouse to the White House*. New York: Random House, 1971.

Wilson, James Q. *The amateur democrat*. Chicago: University of Chicago Press, 1962.

Wilson, James Q. *Political organizations*. New York: Basic Books, 1973.

6

The Forest for the Trees: Blazing Trails for Congressional Research

Leroy N. Rieselbach

Research on legislatures is essentially a post-World War II phenomenon. As recently as the early 1950s, the legislature—its practices and politics—was an unexplored wilderness.[1] Much of the then-extant knowledge about Congress, for example, was codified in three influential texts that practitioners had produced (Gross, 1953; Galloway, 1953; and Griffith, 1951).[2] In the ensuing years, an ever-growing army of scholars marched boldly into this virgin territory, producing literally thousands of studies that illuminated many dark corners of the forest. This chapter, of course, is an attempt, no doubt idiosyncratic, to specify what these explorers have uncovered and, more importantly perhaps, to identify those obscure portions of the legislative terrain that remain largely unmapped.[3]

These forays into the unknown, mostly the efforts of individual researchers doing individual projects, have surveyed much of the legislative landscape, at least to a limited degree. Most have produced discrete, narrowly focused, analyses of particular features of congressional structure and performance (the "trees"). With respect to some topics—congressional elections and roll call voting, for example—this research cumulates to provide substantial insight; in other areas—committee behavior and political party influence, for instance—much remains uncharted.

At a more general level, in the past decade or so, some genuine progress at integrating the bits and pieces of single studies into "middle range theories" has been made. Not surprisingly, the best cartography pictures those portions of the legislature most thoroughly investigated (elections and roll call voting), but some insightful contributions deal with less malleable topics such as committee processes and political representation. It is particularly difficult to

*This is a revised version of a paper delivered at the 1982 Annual Meeting of the American Political Science Association. I have benefited enormously from the comments of Michael L. Mezey, Samuel C. Patterson, David W. Rohde, and Gerald C. Wright, Jr., but none of them bears responsibility for the arguments advanced here.

theorize about such complex but critical matters as member motivation, political communication, and power and influence.

Finally, at a still broader level, there remains little "grand theory" that encompasses the totality of congressional politics (the "forest"). There are some traces of both empirical theory ("purposive," organizational, and systems-role paradigms) and normative theory (executive force, responsible parties, literary, and congressional supremacy models), but neither front has witnessed much forward movement in recent years. Existing theories have not led to a clear formulation of Congress' place and performance in national policy making. The forest has proved difficult to penetrate because it is not fixed or immutable; no sooner is the underbrush cleared from one corner or another than there appears some new growth that makes existing maps obsolete.[4] Congress refuses to stand still for easy and permanent exploration.

I. THE TREES: WHAT WE HAVE DISCOVERED

Research on Congress has, of late, emphasized congressional elections and roll call voting in particular. There has been a cumulation of knowledge here, absent in other areas of concern, that reflects scholars' access to data as well as their perseverance in exploring variations on central themes. On other topics, by contrast, difficulties in data collection and the centrality of less tractable concepts (influence, for example) have made progress beyond description hard to achieve. Thus, we know considerably less about committee processes, political party performance, and the impact of informal norms on member behavior than we do about elections and roll call voting. Similarly, the interactions between the executive and interest groups, external to the legislature, and the members of Congress remain only dimly illuminated.

Congressional Elections

Voters. The pioneering efforts of the Survey Research Center led, in the 1960s, to the view that voters in congressional elections were relatively uninformed about candidates and their campaigns, tending to cast their ballots in keeping with their personal partisan identifications (Campbell *et al.*, 1966). When they defected from partisanship, citizens seemed to respond, in the aggregate at least, to national political trends, particularly the state of the economy and the standing of the president in the polls (Tufte, 1978; Kernell, 1977); thus the "outs" prospered at the midterm. More recently, individual level studies, however, found that voters were curiously indifferent to their personal economic circumstances in choosing congressional candidates (Kinder & Kiewiet, 1979).

These more current studies, which often use 1978 and 1980 Center for Political Studies congressional election data, suggest that local conditions, the essential features of single House or Senate contests, are more important than national developments. The voters respond, by this evidence, to a particular pair of candidates, influenced as much if not more by their familiarity with and evaluation of the opponents than by partisanship or national trends

(Mann, 1978; Mann & Wolfinger, 1980). The more they know about candidates and the more they admire them, the more likely they are to vote for those nominees, even if to do so requires abandoning their partisan commitments. Moreover, incumbents rather than their challengers are most likely to benefit from these voter propensities (Beth, 1981-82).

Campaigns. The primacy of local conditions and candidates squares with the major findings about campaign processes, strategy, and tactics (Kingdon, 1966; Leuthold, 1968; Hershey, 1974; Fishel, 1973). Given the general weakness of the national political party organizations, congressional candidates take nearly complete responsibility for their own campaigns.[6] They devise their own strategies, recruit their own volunteers, and raise their own funds. If they win, they feel beholden to no one, though they will act to keep their victorious coalitions intact. Such control of campaigns, however, does not breed a sense of security: on the contrary, candidates, including incumbents, run with considerable trepidation (Fenno, 1978). They are always worried, even if their seats seem safe, that disaster lurks around the bend; defeat comes often enough to arouse fear among those who survive (Erikson, 1976; Collie, 1981).

Incumbency. Incumbents most often succeed in locally focused, personally managed campaigns. Several factors seem to account for this result. While Tufte's (1973) claim that redistricting is a central explanation—state legislatures drew the lines to accommodate incumbents—has been discounted (Bullock, 1975; Ferejohn, 1977), other possibilities abound. For one thing, voters' orientations and attributes may have changed. They may vote the issues rather than the party (cf. Nie *et al.*, 1979, with Converse & Markus, 1979). Alternatively, while they may not be more "rational," citizens may simply recognize—when asked or when voting—the incumbent and cast their ballots for the more familiar figure. Moreover, incumbents have substantial advantages in making themselves well known: they can more easily raise campaign funds (Jacobson, 1980); they can use the perquisites of office—the frank, a monopoly of media attention, their ability to conduct "casework"—to "advertise" and "claim credit" (Mayhew, 1974; Cover & Brumberg, 1982; but see Johannes & McAdams, 1981); they can obtain the collaboration of cooperative bureaucrats (Fiorina, 1977; Arnold, 1979).

Finally, the explanation for incumbent success may be more a function of the absence of strong challengers than anything else. Unable to match the incumbents' resources, the out-party candidates cannot make themselves visible, and thus viable, alternatives to sitting members of Congress (Abramowitz, 1980; Hinckley, 1981). Whatever the reasons, truly competitive contests remain rare, especially for House seats (Cover & Mayhew, 1981). More than nine of ten incumbents seeking reelection to the House have won in recent years. Only when challengers can overcome all the obstacles, and become both visible and attractive, do they threaten incumbents. This possibility is greatest in Senate races—where new campaign technologies can be used to reach heterogeneous electorates—and since 1976, sitting Senators have become increasingly vulnerable.

In sum, two decades of research on congressional elections has revealed a good deal about the ways in which members of Congress win and retain their seats. We know little, however, about the forces that impel them to run in the first place; studies of recruitment have lagged well behind those of campaigns. Some candidates are presumably "self-starters," seeking a seat in Congress on their own initiative; others are reluctant and respond only to the importunings of local party and other interests. We would understand more about elections if we had better information about who runs and what motivates them to do so. In any case, the efforts of those who win nominations reflect individual actions in particular districts, characterized by varying voter configurations. Senators and representatives tailor their campaigns both to the district and to the opponent who emerges to challenge them at any particular time. Moreover, as Mayhew (1974) indicates, they structure their institution to meet these electoral needs.

Congressional Roll Call Voting

If scholars have obtained some understanding of the ways congressmen and women arrive and remain in Washington, they have also staked out some claim to comprehending the ways members make that most elemental of decisions—the roll call choice among various voting alternatives. Here, too, the availability of "hard" data as well as the existence of historical precedent (see, for example, Lowell, 1901; Rice, 1928; Turner, 1951) stimulated explanation of the *patterns* into which floor votes fall. Votes do not, it is important to emphasize, reveal members' motivations or preferences precisely, but they do record the basic alignments of supporters and opponents. (See Matthews & Stimson, 1975, pp. 5-12 on the rationale for studying roll calls.)

Member Characteristics. Votes on the floor of Congress may flow from members' personal attributes and experiences, which presumably antedate their election. Background characteristics give what Asher and Weisberg (1978) call a "long-term component" to legislators' outlooks and, thus, voting choices. Partisanship is most central; party has both psychological and organizational reality, and lawmakers prefer, other things equal, to support their party. Party "constitutes the single most important group loyalty for members of Congress" (Davidson, 1969, p. 147), and numerous studies document that they do indeed vote along partisan lines regularly (MacRae, 1958; Truman, 1959; Mayhew, 1966; Kingdon, 1981). Electoral realities, the need to satisfy similar sorts of constituents (Cooper *et al.*, 1977) or "shared policy attitudes" (Norpoth, 1976) may undergird partisanship, but whatever the motive, party retains a firm grip on its adherents even though that hold may have become somewhat weaker in recent years (Brady *et al.*, 1979).

When party cohesion declines, cleavage is likely to fall along ideological lines. One study (Schneider, 1979; see also Shaffer, 1980) argues that ideology provides the focal point around which most, if not all, congressional voting revolves. Whether this is, in fact, the case, remains problematic; it is clear, however that on some issues at least (Clausen, 1973), ideology is decisive. The conservative coalition, of course, is the most clearly visible manifestation of an ideological alignment that transcends partisanship (Manley, 1973; Brady & Bullock, 1980). It appears, in any event, that member attributes, party affiliation and ideological orientation, provide a benchmark—call it "judgment" or "conscience"—against which legislators evaluate issues that appear on their agendas.

Constituency Characteristics. Members also assess these matters as the representatives of particular constituencies; they act in the face of the influence, real or potential, of those "back home" whose support they need. Members may define constituency in different ways (Fenno, 1978)—as all voters (the "geographic constituency"), hardcore supporters (the "primary constituency"), or a small set of personal "intimates"—but they presumably cast their votes with a careful eye on the constituency as they perceive it.

Early roll call studies tended to adopt the broadest definition and uncovered some modest relationships between the demographic attributes of legislative districts and the voting stances the representatives of these constituencies adopted. For instance, differences appear among rural and urban legislators, Northern and Southern congresspersons, and those whose districts vary in class or ethnic composition on one or more issues confronting Congress (MacRae, 1958; Shannon, 1968; Turner & Schneider, 1970; Clausen, 1973). The reelection requisite apparently compels members to pay at least minimal attention to their constituencies, broadly conceived.

More recent research has sought to delineate constituency more narrowly and precisely. Jackson (1974) constructs measures of citizen preference and intensity, and finds constituency to be the most important correlate of senatorial voting, especially on issues salient to voters (see also Miller & Stokes, 1963). Where constituency pressures decline, members will join party coalitions, follow party leaders, or trade their votes in anticipation of reciprocal support on matters of significance to them. Fiorina (1974) goes a step further, arguing that, logically at least, members calculate their courses carefully in terms of constituency. Those from homogeneous, presumably safe districts, protect themselves electorally by voting consistently with the sentiments of the dominant local majority. Those from heterogeneous districts face more difficult choices; the best they can do is to vote with the constituency interest(s) they perceive as strongest.[7] In any event, congresspersons seem to cast their votes with a clear eye on district realities.

In short, research on roll call voting, like that on congressional elections, has been plentiful and cumulative. Members' votes appear to reflect a complex calculus that requires them to weigh and balance competing claims—reflecting their own experiences and commitments, constituency relations, and contacts with other participants both inside and outside the legislature—under conditions of imperfect information. The sum total of such individual calculations seems to shift from issue to issue and from one time period to another.

Some Darker Corners

If we know, relatively speaking, a good deal about congressional elections and roll call voting, some equally if not more important aspects of the congressional terrain remain ripe for additional investigation. Structural features such as committees, parties, and informal processes and congressional relations with external participants, particularly executives and lobbyists, have received less attention; work on such subjects has not often moved beyond description.[8] Two fundamental factors, at least, account for this situation. First, much of what we want to know involves informal, less visible, "off-the-record" sorts of communication that members do not reveal readily and that scholars are not always able to observe. Often, we simply cannot discover who said what to whom with what effect. Second, change has been especially rampant in recent years. Reform and evolution of practice, reflecting the unrest of the 1970s, have profoundly altered congressional politics. In consequence, our knowledge of these matters remains imperfect.

Committees and Subcommittees. Since Woodrow Wilson's (1885) time, observers have recognized the centrality of congressional committees, yet most studies have focused on single committees (e.g., Fenno, 1966; and Horn, 1970 on the Appropriations Committees; Manley, 1970, on House Ways and Means; and Robinson, 1963; and Matsunaga and Chen, 1976, on House Rules). The early work (summarized in Morrow, 1969, and Goodwin, 1970) emphasized the general: committees are autonomous, expert, and successful policy makers; their decisions most often become Congress' decisions.

More recent scholarship has moved beyond these sweeping generalizations about "the congressional committee." Truly comparative studies (Price, 1972; and Fenno, 1973; see also Price, 1981) make clear that the conventional wisdom may conceal more than it reveals. Committees differ, and in predictable ways. Panel members' behavior reflects their motivations and their places in the larger congressional system. They struggle to obtain desirable committee assignments (Shepsle, 1978; Bullock, 1979); they adapt to, and contribute to, distinctive patterns of committee leadership, structure, and process including partisanship and integration (Fenno, 1973; Parker & Parker, 1979; Dodd, 1972); and they learn to cope with a host of resource management problems, especially staff (Kofmehl, 1977; Fox & Hammond, 1977; Malbin, 1980) and computer technologies (Frantzich, 1979). Overall, individual committees appear to develop a characteristic modus operandi, to which members not only conform but also contribute.

As sophisticated and insightful as these studies are, there is much to learn about committee processes, and the task has proven to be extraordinarily difficult. Change has hit committees hard. Some change is "normal," or evolutionary: congressional turnover has been high (Cooper & West, 1981) and the Republicans have captured the Senate; new committee leaders have succeeded those whom the few committee studies have examined. Indeed, leadership is a phenomenon that has largely defied analysis. Little is known about the ways leaders deal with followers: who are the leaders, the chairs or other influentials? Which way does influence run: do leaders actually steer committee rank and file, or do they conform to on-going committee influence relationships? What strategies and tactics and what modes of resource use do leaders employ in dealing with followers? What impact does leadership have on follower behavior? These and other questions require answers, and it is probably safe to assume that they will get different ones at different times, and for different committees.[9]

In addition, intentional change, or reform, has had a major effect on congressional committees. The seniority system has been modified, and much authority, formerly lodged in full committees, seems to have devolved to sub-committees (Davidson, 1981). While preliminary evidence suggests that sub-committees have become "institutionalized" (Haeberle, 1978), and relatively independent of party leaders (Deering & Smith, 1981), the broader effects of "subcommittee government" remain to be investigated. What does subcommittee leadership look like? Do the same factors that seem useful in describing full committees help explain subcommittee performance? What is the range of variation in structure, process, and behavior across the multitude of House and Senate subcommittees? Here, too, there are far more unanswered than answered queries.[10] Given the obvious importance of committees and sub-committees, there remains much to do to specify their place in congressional politics.

Political Parties. Committees, by all accounts, constitute the major decentralizing influence in the Congress; political parties, by the same token, provide such propensities for centralization as exist. The standard generalization, of course, is that parties and their formal leaders possess limited resources that permit them to bargain for, but not to command, the loyalty of their fundamentally independent members. We have clear descriptions of party organizations—offices and committees—and party resources—members' psychological commitments and leaders' bases of influence (Peabody, 1976, 1981a, 1981b; Ripley, 1969; Jones, 1970; Dodd, 1979b).

Importantly, access to party leaders, in the House at least, has permitted observers to begin to describe and assess the ways in which party officials seek to lead (Waldman, 1980; Sinclair, 1981a). Thus, Westefield (1974) indicates that leaders use the committee assignment process to accommodate rank and file members whose support they seek. Similarly, the House Democratic leadership has employed ad hoc committees (Vogler, 1981) and Speaker's Task Forces (Sinclair, 1981b) to accommodate members' goals, and thus to secure their backing for party positions. In the same vein, Dodd and Sullivan (1981) chart leaders "vote gathering" strategies, and discover that efforts to generate party cohesion vary both with the nature of the issue and the character of those partisans at whom particular appeals are aimed.

Such studies are promising but they are only beginnings in the quest to comprehend leadership strategies, tactics, and effectiveness. Since these matters involve interpersonal contacts, they raise the same general issues as efforts to understand committee leadership. In the party context, as in the committee setting, we need to know more about what leaders offer (or their ostensible followers demand), what responses their initiatives engender, and what conditions facilitate rank and file support. Since much of the leader-follower communication is likely to be tacit rather than overt, scholars will have to infer and speculate in the absence of open covenants openly achieved. Here, too, change, both intended and inadvertent, has altered the circumstances of the parties: new leaders must work with new, younger, and more independent partisans; they have new, reform-generated resources that they have tested only partially. How they operate under changed conditions, and with what results, constitutes a challenging research agenda for students of Congress.[11]

External Participants: Executives and Lobbies

The congressional forest is only part of the political topography. Much of what Congress does occurs in response to actions of external participants, most notably the president, the executive branch, and interest groups. Once again, we confront a familiar set of research issues. We know a good deal about the general contours of the political scene, but little about the precise forms of behavior that occur within the known setting. With respect to the presidency, it seems clear that the Chief Executive largely controls Congress' agenda, at least the major items (Walker, 1977). He has a broad battery of weapons, formal and informal, with which to seek victory for his preferred positions (Wayne, 1978; Edwards, 1980), but his success depends on skillful persuasion because he cannot compel independent lawmakers to accept his initiatives (Neustadt, 1980).

Interest groups operate in a similar fashion. They possess a range of resources—money, campaign aid, expertise—that they can bring to bear through direct access to legislators (Truman, 1971) or indirectly through "grass roots lobbying" in the states and districts (Ornstein & Elder, 1978). If journalistic accounts credit lobbyists with substantial influence over legislators, neither group is prepared to acknowledge that the relationships are more than cooperative and voluntary. Group representatives insist that they employ mainly "soft-sell," persuasive techniques (Milbrath, 1963; Bauer et al., 1972); members of Congress claim that they can control their contacts with lobbyists without compromising their own independence (Matthews, 1960; Kingdon, 1981). Needless-to-say, however, both parties to any transactions are likely to be reticent about the exact nature of these arrangements. Moreover, group involvement in legislative politics has changed of late: changes in campaign finance, featuring the proliferation of political action committees, and the rapid rise to prominence of "single issue" groups that place a nearly exclusive emphasis on one topic such as abortion may render what little we know about group influence obsolete. Perhaps all that we can say is that interests are omnipresent but not necessarily omnipotent.

The connections between both executives and lobbyists, on the one hand, and Congress, on the other, raise the now-familiar influence problem. Knowing the general circumstances of these participants does not, in the absence of more direct and more systematic observation, permit generalization about the use of resources or their effects. On the executive branch, there is little beyond anecdote (but see, Jones, 1981a). With regard to groups, Bacheller (1977) has shown that different interests systematically vary strategies according to the type of issue and the legislative circumstances in which the matter is treated. Hayes (1981) argues that conflict is central to assessing group influence: where groups agree, they may often get their way; where they divide—where there are competing coalitions—legislators may gain considerable freedom by playing interests off against one another.[12] In fact, it is most difficult to determine the direction of influence between lobbyists and executives, on the one hand, and legislators, on the other. In most instances, we cannot easily ascertain who initiated contacts, what was exchanged in these contacts, which communicator, if any, yielded, or the net effect of such interaction over time. Untangling these complicated and reciprocal influence processes will require more sophisticated research than is presently available.

II. GETTING OUT OF THE WOODS: SOME EFFORTS AT SYNTHESIS

The partial listing of scholarly successes in identifying, describing, and analyzing specific aspects of Congress and congressional behavior does not exhaust the accomplishments of those studying the legislature. In a few areas— notably elections and roll call voting, but also committees, representation, and the "subgovernment" phenomenon—there have been valuable efforts to integrate the individual studies to produce "middle range theories." These achievements provide not only broader explanations for legislative phenomena but also explicit sets of hypotheses for further exploration.

Middle Range Theories

Elections. Research on congressional elections suggests some basic propositions: aggregate election results imply voter reactions to the president and the economy; individual choice, however, is largely independent of personal circumstance; incumbent candidates overwhelmingly win reelection, largely because they face weak challengers in their own districts. Jacobson and Kernell (1981) suggest a link, the strategic behavior of elites, that reconciles these disparate findings. The important campaign figures—the candidates and those who support, especially fund, them—*assume* that voters respond to national conditions. When those trends are favorable, attractive challengers choose to run, and attract strong support. When conditions favor the "ins," promising challengers avoid losing races and contributors seeking access or influence may donate to incumbents, who already possess all the advantages that the perquisites of office confer, virtually guaranteeing their success.

Voters face choices between pairs of candidates in their own states and districts that national economic circumstances affect through these strategic calculations of elites. Where prospects are promising, strong challengers wage strong campaigns; they emerge disproportionately in the party that economic conditions favor, but they tailor their campaigns to the constituencies in which they run. Candidate and contributor decisions "so structure the vote choice that electoral results are consonant with national level forces even if individual voting decisions are not" (Jacobson & Kernell, 1981, p. 3). Thus, though citizens choose in consequence of local conditions, the choice they confront reflects a larger economic reality, and the set of verdicts they render in the country at large translates that reality into the aggregate congressional returns. House incumbents win regularly because the circumstances that encourage strong challengers seldom appear; they occur more commonly in Senate contests, which accounts for the reduced success rates in the upper House.

Roll Call Voting. A multitude of studies suggests that members of Congress cast their roll call votes in light of their personal partisan and ideological commitments, their perceptions of constituents' sentiments, and their place in the congressional party and committee systems. They sort out competing claims on their votes under conditions of imperfect information; many matters fall outside their experience and competence. They make their choices, most studies indicate at least implicitly, through a process of "cue-taking," looking to trusted sources for guidance on subjects about which they are uncertain.

Kingdon (1981) imaginatively models this process: his interviews with House members inquired about the weights attached to cues from constituents, congressional colleagues, party and committee leaders, the executive branch, legislative staff, and the media and other information sources. He posits a "consensus mode" of decision making. Where members' "field of forces" is consistent, where there are few differences of opinion among those who provide advice, legislators simply vote for the majority position. Where consensus does not exist, representatives look first to selected informants, especially colleagues who specialize in the subject at issue, and with whom they tend to agree, i.e., who are of the same party or who are compatible ideologically. They also pay considerable heed, Kingdon finds, to their constituents, especially on visible votes on major matters. Other cues, while important periodically and on particular issues, are less significant than colleagues and constituents.[13] Note that cue-taking of this sort is entirely compatible with legislative norms such as reciprocity and members' reelection concerns.

The cue-taking perspective helps tie together other strands in the literature. Because cue-taking tends to recur and if successful be repeated, Asher and Weisberg's (1978) identification of a long-term component, a "voting history," rooted in partisanship, constituency, and ideology seems reasonable. Likewise, cue-taking patterns may vary from issue to issue (Clausen, 1973): party is important on "government management" questions; constituency on "civil liberties" (see also Miller & Stokes, 1963). Finally, enduring patterns of cue-taking explain why aggregate change in voting alignments seems related more to membership turnover than to individual opinion shifts: the newly elected bring new values and perspectives to Congress; those with longer service adhere to their standing vote decisions (Clausen & Van Horn, 1977; and Asher & Weisberg, 1978).[14]

Representation. Patterns of voting choice raise the fundamental question of representation, the connection between citizen preferences and needs on the one hand, and legislators' activities on the other. In policy terms at least, votes cast determine what the government does, which may or may not reflect what the public desires or requires. Following Miller and Stokes' (1963) empirical and Pitkin's (1967) philosophic revival of interest in this age-old topic, the rudiments of a middle range theory of representation have begun to emerge. At the most general level, representation is a reciprocal, but asymmetric, relationship between citizens and their elected lawmakers that involves several components (see Eulau & Karps, 1977). The link is reciprocal because communication, and thus influence, may begin at either end of the chain. Citizens may request (demand) that elected officials enact particular programs (policy representation) or perform specific chores such as engaging in "casework" for individuals or providing projects for the constituency (service representation). The ultimate sanction for such performance, of course, lies in the voters' ability to turn lawmakers out of office at the ensuing election. Alternatively, legislators may take the initiative, directing a variety of messages to the voters (symbolic representation) in order to structure constituents' views of them, and of the assembly itself (Fenno, 1978).

The representational link is asymmetric because any given communicative or influence effort does not automatically generate an "equal and opposite" effect. Residents of particular constituencies, and different classes of citizens within any district, may differ in the extent to which they make demands on their legislators. Members of Congress may vary widely—across issues and in terms of their electoral circumstances—in the degree to which they respond to citizen communications and to which they undertake symbolic representational activities (Cover, 1980; Johannes, 1980). Lawmakers must decide, as individuals, what representative stance to take toward their constituencies as they define them; how to allocate their limited resources among the types of representational activities; and, indeed, what commitment to make to representation generally as opposed to other claims they face.

Early work on representation adopted a policy "congruence" (or "concurrence") view that assessed the citizen-legislator link in terms of a match between preferences: legislators should act consistently with their own constituents' desires. Empirical work using this paradigm found representation to be far from perfect. Only on a few "hot" issues where citizens feel strongly and communicate clearly will legislators feel constrained to heed the "folks back home" (Miller & Stokes, 1963; Erikson, 1978; McCrone & Kuklinski, 1979). Subsequent research, however, suggests another standard. Weissberg (1978) proposes a criterion of "collective representation" that transcends congruence; "good" representation requires only that Congress enact what the nation as a whole wants. There is some evidence that it does (Backstrom, 1977; Monroe, 1979; but cf. Hurley, 1982).

These notions provide an approach to representation that moves beyond time, place, and single issues, although much empirical work remains undone. We need to know a good deal more about the conditions that induce members to listen to constituents and act accordingly. Alternatively, legislators' cultivation of constituents through symbolic representation needs clarification. The ways that members present themselves, and explain their actions, to citizens; the extent to which the former's initiatives win the latter's support and confidence; and the conditions under which they do so and the consequences, that is the policy making freedom, that flow from successful "home styles" are all central topics that deserve additional investigation.

Committee Decision Making. Recognizing the central place of committees, and more recently subcommittees, in congressional politics, scholars have charted, in general terms, the committees' contributions to a decentralized mode of legislative decision making. In a pioneering and deservedly influential book, Fenno has reoriented the study of congressional committees, stressing the differences rather than the similarities among them: ". . . [C]ommittees differ from one another. And . . . they differ systematically . . . with respect to five variables: member goals, environmental constraints, strategic premises, decision-making premises, and decisions" (1978, p. xiv). Examining six House panels, and their Senate counterparts, Fenno posits specifically that members' behavior reflects their *goals*—to seek reelection, power, or policy influence—and the particular *environmental constraints*—the chamber itself, the political party, the administration, and clientele groups—within which their committee operates. These variable antecedent conditions, in turn, shape distinctive committee *strategic premises* (or norms or decision rules) and specific *decision making processes* (partisanship, specialization, and leadership). All these committee attributes contribute to committee *decisions*, the result of panel deliberations.

Fenno's formulation has outstripped research on committees. The committees he examined (as well as those Price, 1972, studied) bear little resemblance, in composition and in performance, to their appearance a decade ago. His scheme has been applied comprehensively to few other committees (for exceptions, see LeLoup, 1979, on the House Budget Committee; and Perkins, 1980, on House Judiciary) and not at all to specific subcommittees, despite their increasing importance. In addition, there may be intra-committee variations that reflect the issues that comprise any panel's jurisdiction (see Price, 1978). Perhaps panels adopt different strategic premises or respond to different environmental actors when they deal with distinctive portions of their agendas. These and a host of similar inquiries constitute research possibilities sufficient to engage an army of congressional explorers.

The "Subgovernment" Phenomenon. Concerns about committees and the actors, executives and clienteles, in their environments merge in consideration of the subgovernment (or "cozy triangle," or "whirlpool") phenomenon. In conjunction with Lowi's (1964) distinction among distributive, regulatory, and redistributive policy arenas, scholars (Davidson, 1977; Ripley & Franklin, 1980) have identified a characteristic pattern of policy making, which appears frequently to dominate distributive (pork barrel) decision making. Within a narrow domain, cancer research funding or price supports for dairy products, for example, a cluster of participants— interested committee and subcommittee members, often with involved constituents; bureaucrats with program responsibilities; and interest group representatives—with clear stakes in particular policy results cooperate to control government decisions. Such arrangements are mutually reinforcing: they offer lawmakers an opportunity to achieve reelection, power, or policy goals; they provide executives with the possibility of defending if not enlarging their bureaucratic "turf"; and they offer outside interests the policies they seek to promote.

Where it can control conflict, keeping whatever policy opponents may exist (consumers, for example) unaware or disorganized, the subgovernment may well attain its policy objectives. Where controversy spills out into more visible and politicized arenas, where the potential "losers" perceive the costs they may be asked to pay on regulatory and especially on redistributive matters, cozy triangles are far less likely to prosper. Here, too, theory has outrun research: much of what we know is anecdotal (Ripley & Franklin, 1980) or contradictory (cf. Ferejohn, 1974; Arnold, 1979). We need, for example, clearer lines of demarcation among policy types. We need more detailed analyses of the contacts among subgovernment participants, the strategy and tactics cozy triangles employ, the conditions under which they are likely to succeed, and the results they are able to achieve. The subgovernment notion does tie together various strands of research on Congress, especially its committees, and the legislature's links to external actors, but it leaves a formidable research agenda to be addressed.[15]

Power and Influence: A Tangled Thicket

Lurking in the shadows, in both the narrower works and the efforts to synthesize them, is the thorny issue of *power*, influence, and authority—for simplicity, used interchangeably here. Much of what members do, and what Congress accomplishes, reflects the ability of some participants, inside and outside the legislature, to get others to accommodate their wishes by using methods that range from simple requests through complex bargaining to powerful pressure. Influence, of course, is reciprocal: executives and lobbyists wants legislators' support, but the latter often solicit aid from the former (Bauer *et al.*, 1972); citizens want representation, but legislators seek votes and trust from their constituents. Authority is also implicit: building credits does not require written contracts; behavior may reflect "anticipated reactions" that discourage lawmakers from engaging in actions that they do not expect to succeed.

Power, in short, is a nettlesome concept. Intuitively, we sense that some lawmakers have more authority than others, that they can win acquiescence from individual colleagues, and that they may even be able to bring about the legislative results they desire. Yet we remain uncertain about the ways, if any, that power operates in the congressional setting, and some clarification of its application seems essential (see Dahl, 1957; Riker, 1964; Oppenheim, 1978; and Baldwin, 1978). Research has identified many bases of authority, but generalizations about their use—how members employ them, under what conditions, and with what results—remain to be formulated. It will not be easy to extend the frontiers of knowledge here. There are numerous potential power-holders to consider; Congress is a complex and fragmented institution that diffuses power widely, but unequally, using formal and informal criteria.

Members are likely to dissemble, making observation of power difficult. They may act "strategically," professing positions contrary to their own in the hopes of extracting concessions for doing what they prefer to do in the first place, rather than "sincerely." If they succeed, they may claim exaggerated credit for their accomplishments; if they do not, they may be loath to reveal that they succumbed to more powerful forces.

It is far easier to call for a theory of congressional power and influence than to produce one, but the need is real. Unless and until we can learn more about authority and the exercise of it, our understanding of specific facets of congressional performance and our ability to cumulate our findings in more comprehensive explanations of legislative behavior will remain incomplete and unsatisfying.

III. THE FOREST:
EMPIRICAL AND NORMATIVE VIEWS OF CONGRESS

As a practical matter, scholarly investigation proceeds in small steps, but the ultimate goal of any discipline, or subfield, is to produce as complete an understanding as possible of the territory within its domain. In the final analysis, this entails a complete mapping of the terrain. For political science generally, and legislative politics more specifically, the presence of a normative dimension complicates the cartography. We want not only to describe and explain *how* the assembly works but also to assess *how well* it performs. To achieve these goals requires some integrative frameworks that encompass the full range of performance. Students of legislative politics have in fact generated such "models," which, while rudimentary, in the long run promise to yield a vision of the "big picture," of the forest that the trees constitute. Moreover, these views point in both empirical and normative directions.

Empirical Theories

Efforts to build empirical theories of legislative politics, not surprisingly, rest on the findings and speculations that narrower explorations have generated. Thus, these attempts are most often inductive, seeking to integrate the extant literature; alternatively, they may be "horizontal," looking to adopt and adapt approaches prominent in other social sciences. In either case, theorizing about legislatures emerged from two perspectives that have guided work on legislatures. An older view is *institutional* in focus; it looks at the legislature as a collectivity that produces certain products, and performs particular functions. Its concern is less with what individual legislators do or say and more with the quality and quantity of what legislative institutions produce (policy, oversight, representation). A more recent perspective is *individual* in focus; it treats the causes and consequences of lawmakers' behavior and sees the legislature's product as, in some sense, the sum of its members' activities.[16] These vantage points have stimulated three identifiable theoretical orientations to studying legislative politics: one, organization theory, stresses institutional performance; a second, purposive theory, emphasizes individual behavior; and a third, systems-role analysis, seeks to combine institutional and individual concerns. Each has its adherents, each singles out some central issues, but none has attained wide acceptance.

Organization Theory: The Legislature as Institution. In its simplest terms, organization theory posits that formal organizations—"social units (or human groupings) deliberately constructed and reconstructed to seek specific goals" (Etzioni, 1964, p. 3)—display behavioral regularities. Because they pursue their goals within complex, uncertain settings (environments), organizations seek to adapt (structure themselves) to environmental forces to achieve their specific purposes; thus they can be analyzed in terms of their relations to external forces, their internal requisites, their internal structure and processes, the links among external and internal attributes, and their ability to attain their goals (to survive). Organization theorists seek propositions that describe organizational behavior in these terms: for example, the more heterogeneous an organization's environment, the more decentralized its decisional structures (environmental-structure link), or the greater an organization's internal need for technical skills, the greater its dependence on expert members.

A few students of legislatures, notably Cooper (1977, 1981, inter alia; see also Davidson & Oleszek, 1976; and Froman, 1968), have begun to assess Congress as a complex organization seeking to survive and meet its objectives in a highly differentiated socio-political environment. Cooper (1977) suggests that the legislature, like other organizations, must meet basic internal needs for "division of labor, integration, and motivation." That is, Congress must develop expertise, through a division of labor; coordinate, through integration, what its structural components produce separately; and influence, through motivation, its members to perform appropriately.

Congress, Cooper continues, can satisfy these internal needs only with considerable difficulty, largely because its environment imposes substantial constraints on it. For one thing, unlike hierarchical organizations, it cannot centralize its operations; member independence, rooted in electoral arrangements and institutional commitments to formal equality and democratic norms, undermines the existence of centralizing (party) authority. The potential for an effective division of labor is thereby reduced: unable to control entry, the legislature must "make do" with those who win seats, however inexpert some may be. The lack of central authority also inhibits congressional capacity for integration: independent members cannot be compelled to conform; leadership rests on persuasion not formal power. Finally, decentralization limits motivation: lacking many material rewards, leaders may be hard pressed to induce members to commit their energies effectively.

Logically, the concepts of organization theory—internal needs (expertise, motivation), environmental forces, organizational patterns (centralization-decentralization)—provide a coherent and intellectually satisfying explanation of the congressional process: for example, the legislature is a decentralized institution that acts largely through bargaining mechanisms. Moreover, organizational notions sensitize the observer to possibilities for change; as conditions alter (e.g., new environmental conditions emerge), the organization will adapt (e.g., restructure its committee or party systems). But organization theory has not, in fact, stimulated much research, and its few practitioners have focused selectively on formal structures rather than on the less readily observable organizational processes (motivation, power, interactions with environmental forces). Thus, much theoretical clarification and empirical work remains to be done, especially with respect to the links between organizational attributes and legislative outcomes.

Purposive Models: The Legislator as Individual. The organizational paradigm minimizes attention to behavior on the individual level, and those who find legislators more fascinating than legislatures have looked elsewhere for theoretical guidance. The most fully developed alternative derives from the economic theories of individual choice. Whether labelled "rational," "social choice," or, as here, "purposive," these models view individual legislators as "goal-seeking agents who choose from available strategic alternatives to further their ends" (Ferejohn & Fiorina, 1975, p. 407). Fundamentally, the purposive perspective suggests that lawmakers employ some form of cost-benefit calculation to select a course of action that will maximize their ability to reach their chosen objectives. Positive "payoffs" encourage, and negative ones deter, specific behaviors whether they are campaign strategies, votes on bills and amendments or adherence to chamber norms.

For instance, Shepsle (1978) uses a purposive model to explain freshman House members' initial requests for committee assignments. In general, members seek positions that reflect their "interests" (the value to them in achieving their goals—reelection, power, policy influence—of a particular assignment) discounted by the probability of their winning the appointment —a probability shaped by the number of committee vacancies and the extent of the competition for them. Thus individual requests flow from an "expected value calculus." Shepsle's empirical analysis of Democratic representatives' actual requests is consistent with the model; within limits, members do engage in "rational choice" (1978, ch. 4). Similarly, Weingast (1979) and Panning (1982) suggest that conformity to folkways is consistent with rational calculation under certain circumstances. Voting, on amendments (Enelow, 1981) and more generally (Fiorina, 1974, ch. 5), also appears to reflect purposive choice.

Purposive models have attracted a somewhat larger following than organization theory, but inherent problems continue to limit the number of their adherents. It remains extraordinarily difficult to get an empirical, operational handle on many concepts, especially given the subjective, psychological character of individual calculation. Even direct access to, and intensive interviews with, legislators may not suffice to get measures of cost, benefit, utility, value, and maximization. Moreover, members of Congress act often under conditions of imperfect information. Calculations may vary widely among any set of lawmakers, making behavioral generalization problematic. In consequence, some applications of these models avoid data, that is they are purely deductive, or make inferences based on assumptions about individual calculations without directly observing them (Mayhew, 1974; Ferejohn, 1974; Arnold, 1979). Purposive models have unquestionably stimulated insightful

thinking about legislative politics, and it is no small accomplishment to conclude that members' behavior often seems consistent with, or looks "as if" it
results from, a specific cost-benefit calculus (see Moe, 1979).[17] Nonetheless,
while their potential remains great, economic models to date have not won
wide acceptance, perhaps because much hard empirical exploration remains
to be done in order to specify precisely the form and consequences of legislators' social choices.

Systems-Role Analysis: An Integrative Alternative. A third approach to
legislative politics, systems-role analysis, combines institutional and individual foci (Easton, 1965, 1979). Individuals act within structural constraints. Systems analysts see legislatures as (1) decision making structures
composed of formal elements like parties and committees, operating within
the mandates of written rules and informal norms, that (2) respond to communications ("inputs") originating outside the institution, from executives,
judges, organized interests, and the public, (3) to produce specific results
("outputs") such as policy, oversight, and representation. Legislative activities
may influence, through "feedback" processes, environmental forces to make
new or revised inputs to the assembly; these may require the legislature itself
to alter its structures, outputs, or both.

The role dimension of systems analysis suggests that legislators' behavior
reflects a series of choices ("role orientations") that they make about their
relationships to the structural features of the chamber and to the actors in its
environment. For instance, lawmakers must decide how to relate to their constituents. They may choose to speak for the district itself (the "district" orientation), a larger constituency (the "nation" orientation), or a combination of
the two (the "district-nation" orientation); in the same vein, they may act in
conformity to constituents' expressed preferences (as "delegates"), to their
own personal judgments (as "trustees"), or to one or the other as circumstances dictate (as "politicos") (see Wahlke *et al.*, 1962; Davidson, 1969). In a
similar fashion, legislators assume orientations toward legislative structures
and activities (Jewell & Patterson, 1977). Their choices reflect their own attitudes and the inputs they receive from external actors; the distribution of
their orientations shapes the legislature's performance.

While the systems-role view suggests numerous hypotheses—for example that "delegates" will seek out and reflect citizen preferences more closely
than "trustees" or "politicos"—it has generated only a modest quantity of
research (see Jewell, 1970, for a review and critique). Practical problems may
be responsible: legislators may be inaccessible and/or reluctant to respond
candidly. Moreover, the evidence that has been unearthed is, at best, inconclusive. It seems clear that lawmakers, when asked, can and do articulate
role orientations (Davidson, 1969), but the causal antecedent conditions that
lead to these choices remain largely unspecified. More importantly, it is far
from certain that role orientations explain representatives' behavior (Gross,
1978; Cavanagh, 1982). There is certainly no simple one-to-one relationship
between orientation and behavior; given the constraints that structural and
political circumstances impose, role is likely to be important only under certain, limited circumstances.[18] The challenge, of course, is to specify those

conditions precisely. In short, like organizational and purposive approaches, systems-role analysis has neither generated sufficient research to justify firm conclusions about its merits nor won wide acceptance as a roadmap of the congressional forest.

Normative Notions and Congressional Reform

Political scientists feel obliged not only to describe and explain legislative politics but also to evaluate legislative performance. With respect to the former, a consensual wisdom, mostly atheoretical, has appeared, largely from among the trees: Congress is a decentralized institution that diffuses influence and that, in consequence, acts incrementally through processes of bargaining and compromise. With respect to the normative task, there is less agreement. There are models of the "good" or "better" Congress (Davidson *et al.*, 1966), but neither outside observers nor practitioners promoting reform have made much sustained use of them. Yet each vision does provide the dissatisfied with a reform agenda that, if adopted, might move Congress in the directions they desire.

The Executive Force Theory. Proponents of the executive force model (e.g., Burns, 1963), accepting the conventional view of Congress as a policy maker, are pessimistic about the legislature's capacity to govern. They stress the need to solve pressing political, economic, and social problems, and despair that Congress can contribute meaningfully to policy formulation. The executive, by contrast, is likely to be the catalyst for progress. Congress, given its members, structures, and processes, can only impede innovation: a fragmented institution, representing multiple interests, especially the rural and small town constituencies of Middle America, it is incapable of acting decisively. It is better suited to oppose than to create, to react than to invent.

As a result, if policy making is to meet the nation's needs, the president must be permitted to lead, unobstructed by a recalcitrant Congress. Reform should reduce the legislative ability to frustrate presidential policy leadership. Independent sources of power, committees and subcommittees, for instance, should be curbed. Rules of procedure that permit minorities to block action require modification. In general, the path of presidential proposals through Congress needs to be smoothed substantially. The executive supremacy view, in sum, stresses presidential power and reduces Congress' role to legitimation, perhaps modification, and review after the fact. The president proposes and the legislature disposes according to his wishes.

The Responsible Parties Model. An alternative avenue to escaping congressional obstructionism is through the use of disciplined, cohesive, "responsible" political parties. If the majority party, given its command of the legislative terrain, as the chief organizational mechanism of the assembly, marched smartly and decisively forward in rank, its policy proposals would triumph at each and every stage of the lawmaking process. If, moreover, the president commanded the party troops, they would advance his—desirable and progressive—programs without risk of rear-guard delay or defeat.

Proponents of responsible parties (e.g., American Political Science Association, 1950) promote reforms to enlist rank-and-file members of Congress in the partisan armies. In general, they would empower the respective party's national committees to manage the electoral process. With the ability to control nominations, using a legal monopoly of campaign finance, for example, the central committees could control their elected representatives. To break ranks would, in effect, end the deserter's political career; the seat would be given to a more loyal recruit. Inside Congress, the rules would be rewritten to ensure that disciplined majorities could carry more easily the legislative day. In sum, in the responsible parties view, the president proposes and his loyal partisan army disposes consistently with his marching orders. Here, too, Congress would eschew policy making, emphasizing instead legitimizing and nonpolicy activities such as constituent services and oversight.

The Literary Theory. What appear as Congress' vices in the executive force and responsible parties models are virtues for the adherents of the literary theory (Burnham, 1959). They pay homage to "constitutional tradition," to checks and balances, and to separation of powers. In their view, Congress should restrain the power-seeking executive, in both policy formulation and implementation. Policy departures should come slowly, only after careful deliberation that considers all alternatives, and only after a genuine national consensus emerges. Thus, a decentralized legislature, to which all interests have access, and that can act only cautiously, is highly desirable.

These virtues have been lost in the twentieth century, the so-called age of executives, and reform is required to restore the status quo ante. To that end, literary theorists resist all centralizing mechanisms. They prefer an election system that protects legislators' independence; they fear disciplined political parties that might run roughshod over citizen sentiments; they distrust executive leadership; and, most important, they are predisposed to congressional procedures that promote the power of individual legislators to speak freely, slow action, deliberate carefully, and oversee the administration. Overall, they want Congress to propose and dispose, to make policy, to represent citizens, to police the bureaucracy, to countervail the executive. They seek to restore Congress to what they see as its rightful, legitimate place at the very center of the political process.

The Congressional Supremacy ("Whig") Model. The literary view pushed further becomes a model that stresses to an even greater extent the centrality of Congress. Legislative supremicists see Congress as "the first branch of government" (de Grazia, 1966), the prime mover in national affairs. They favor the reforms that the literary theorists advocate as well as other changes intended, in effect, to strip the chief executive of most major bases of authority. The whig view envisages a Congress that proposes and an administration (president and bureaucracy) that disposes in strict accordance with legislative desires. A supreme Congress will both make policy explicitly, on its own terms, and oversee the implementation of that policy.

Overall, then, there are models of the desirable Congress, each of which entails its own set of structural and procedural reforms. Each view could, theoretically, provide a standard against which to evaluate specific reform proposals: does a given suggestion move the legislature, or is it likely to do so, toward a clearly stated objective? The issue of legislative fragmentation is central to such assessment. Both executive force and responsible parties proponents stress the need for governmental action and they deplore a set of decentralized institutional arrangements that inhibit solutions to national problems; in stark contrast, the literary and congressional supremacy views focus on caution and consensus and they applaud structural mechanisms that deter policy changes until deliberation leads to agreement that new departures are desirable.

Reform in Reality. These normative formulations define more or less coherent visions of what the legislature should, and might, be. Reformers, in practice, are less often moved by such comprehensiveness; they tend to be legislators who seek to alter their institution in ways that advance their own, relatively narrow causes (Jones, 1977). They have, during the 1970s, in response to a series of legislative "crises," enacted a wide variety of changes, without much conscious effort to justify them as integral parts of any far-reaching plan to create a Congress of clear design.

In fact, four broad sets of reforms were adopted; those in the House were most prominent. A series of steps, including public committee meetings and recorded committee roll call votes, opened hitherto mostly invisible congressional processes to public scrutiny; together with ethics codes and financial disclosure requirements, these moves made it easier for citizens to know what their representatives were doing, and to hold them to account for their actions. Enacting the War Powers Resolution (1973) and the Budget and Impoundment Control Act (1974) armed Congress to challenge the executive branch for military and financial policy leadership. Third, the Speaker of the House obtained new influence—over bill referral and Rules Committee membership—and the Democratic Caucus seized control over committee assignments and chairpersons. Simultaneously, however, the rank and file members moved to "democratize" the House, adopting a "subcommittee bill of rights" that, in effect, created "subcommittee government" in Congress. (On these developments, see Sundquist, 1981; Jones, 1981b; Ornstein, 1981; Rieselbach, 1977.)

Research on the effects of these changes, sketchy as it is, seems to suggest that reformers alter current congressional conditions only with great difficulty. Moreover, the changes that have occurred often seem either unanticipated or undesirable. For instance, the accountability reforms do not appear to have had appreciable impact on congressional ethics—witness Abscam and the drug and sex allegations of 1982. Nor do citizens seem more aware of their elected representatives, either in general in terms of name recognition or recall or with respect to issue positions (Mann & Wolfinger, 1980). The "sunshine" reforms, however, may have contributed to an increased rate of retirement from Congress (Cooper & West, 1981). Whether they have made the legislative process more vulnerable to interest group influence—already difficult to assess—especially that of "single-issue" organizations, as some observers assert, cannot be answered without investigations that have not yet been undertaken.

Similarly, it is perhaps too soon to judge the effects of other reform thrusts. It is certainly hard to claim conclusively that Congress has greater control over the executive than in the pre-reform period. The War Powers Act has not been tested. The Budget Act has produced mixed results in practice; as the new procedures have shaken down, the legislature seems clearly to have restricted executive impoundments, but not necessarily to have altered the contours of fiscal and monetary policy (Ippolito, 1981; Schick, 1980; Wildavsky, 1979). The safest conclusion seems to be that Congress is better equipped institutionally to challenge the president, but is by no means firmly committed to engaging in combat.

Finally, the internal reforms seem to have cut in opposite directions. On the one hand, the parties are more powerful: the Speaker has made successful if infrequent use of his new powers, but with uncertain consequences. The Rules Committee regularly supports the leadership (Oppenheimer, 1981); multiple referral may both slow the legislative process and increase the likelihood that bills will be heavily amended; ad hoc committees, when created, have been circumscribed and only partially effective (Vogler, 1981; Oppenheimer, 1980). On the other hand, committee reforms on balance seem to have enlarged congressional decentralization: full committee chairpersons are on shorter leash, but much of their power has devolved to antonomous subcommittees (Davidson, 1981). Moreover, reform impinges differentially on individual panels; some (e.g., House Agriculture) seem immune to the reformers' prescriptions; others (e.g., Ways and Means) respond to drastic surgery (Ornstein & Rohde, 1977; Rieselbach & Unekis, 1981-82). Overall, at least some careful observers (e.g., Huntington, 1973; Dodd, 1980a, 1981) seem persuaded that Congress is more fragmented, more hard pressed to formulate coherent policy or to engage in careful oversight than a decade ago. In any case, the reform movement of the 1970s has done little to gladden the hearts of the executive force or responsible parties theorists.

In reality, then, reform—and research evaluating it—reflects the Congress; it has been pragmatic, inspired by practical politics not philosophical principles.[19] Yet models with normative import do exist, as do theories of empirical consequence. Pursuing the latter should provide data for assessing the former. Once we know how Congress operates, we may feel more comfortable in prescribing for any maladies we find afflicting the institution. However underdeveloped our models, both empirical and normative, at present, they do sensitize scholars to the need to look beyond the trees to the entire forest.

IV. CONCLUSION:
TRAILS BLAZED, AND FOR BLAZING

For a young subfield, legislative studies, especially work on Congress, has made remarkable progress in exploring the unknown. Scholars have blazed many trails. They have investigated, to at least a modest extent, virtually every aspect of congressional membership, structure, and performance. They have illuminated the terrain particularly with respect to congressional elections and roll call voting, and they also have begun to lay the groundwork for fuller mapping of committee and party processes and executive-legislative and interest group-lawmaker relationships. At a somewhat broader level, some integrative efforts have produced substantial enlightenment, in the form of middle range theorizing, about committees, representation, and subgovernments as well as elections and legislative voting. Understandably, grand theory has been slower to develop, but even here there are both empirical (organizational, purposive, and systems-role) and normative (executive force, responsible parties, literary, and congressional supremacy) perspectives that, while underdeveloped and too seldom used, constitute preliminary charts of the legislative territory. In short, research to date has staked out many trees, specified several stands of timber, and pointed toward some general pictures of the forest. These are unmistakably substantial and significant accomplishments.

There remain, of course, numerous challenges ahead. Future research might explore profitable areas where hard data are not so readily available. We need basic studies, for instance, of members' motives, perceptions, opinions, and even their personalities, and the ways in which such subjective factors shape legislators' behavior. We need to describe relatively unknown features of Congress more fully: staffing practices, support agencies, state delegations and other informal organizations, and the formal rules and their impact, inter alia. Most important perhaps, as noted, there is a need to deal with influence (power) processes, to chart the ways that various interactions— between executives and members of Congress, lobbyists and legislators, lawmakers and staff, representatives and constituents, and congresspersons and their colleagues—occur and the effects that these processes have on the participants' performance. These are difficult tasks, full of pitfalls, but unless we can cut through some of these tangles we will be unable to isolate and understand fully the causes and consequences of congressional behavior.

We also need to extend and apply the theorizing presently available. Fenno's useful approach to committee politics should be applied to the full range of panels. A comparable scheme for assessing political parties—encompassing the partisans and their motives, their relations to the electorate, their place in congressional party structures (e.g., the caucus), the organizations' modes of operation, and the character and effects of leadership strategies and tactics—would obviously have extraordinary value. A similar model of interest group politics would have equivalent importance. From such efforts, a theory of legislative influence might emerge; at least the centrality of interpersonal power relations in a decentralized institution argues for the effort to understand the exercise of authority in Congress.

Finally, while grand integrative theorizing may be quixotic, it remains appealing: mapping the forest is, after all, the ultimate goal. At the minimum, efforts to use, and thus to assess the utility of, the extant models should proceed. How far can organizational, purposive, and systems-role notions take us toward describing and explaining legislative politics? These models have not really been put to fair tests as integrative, heuristic, or predictive devices. Specifically, we might ask whether these, or alternative approaches, can provide a picture of the policy process. This, too, is no easy task; Congress is involved in each and every stage of policy—initiation, enactment, and implementation—though not always to the same degree. To model the entire process is, in effect, to model much of American politics. Nevertheless, some first steps seem clearly identifiable.

First, policy itself—the ultimate dependent variable—requires explicit specification. We need to move beyond issue domains (Clausen, 1973) and the classic Lowi (1964) categories (distributive, regulatory, redistributive). It has been particularly difficult to define the boundaries that distinguish among the latter. Having established what is to be explained, we can begin to look at variations in the origins of the different policy types. For instance, external actors may have greater opportunities to originate some forms of policy. Or legislators may assume differing role orientations with respect to separate policy categories. Similarly, we may eventually be able to specify more precisely distinct processes—with various outside forces and internal structures like committees and parties combining in particular ways—for given policy types. From this, it may prove possible to move on to assess more carefully the ways in which the legislature follows up on its actions; perhaps oversight varies for different policy types or processes.[20] These (and numerous other) possibilities suggest, however sketchily, a need to move forward, empirically and theoretically, to treat the total policy process.[21]

Future studies, whether narrow or broad, need to be conscious of change, evolutionary or intentional. Single propositions and general theories are at the mercy of events: international and domestic developments may raise new issues for congressional consideration; election results may alter the identities of executives who promote policy and of legislators who respond to new initiatives. Reform may alter structures, processes, and products in ways anticipated or unexpected. Scholars, in consequence, must reexamine basic generalizations; they must test their theories and models constantly to see not only whether their propositions remain accurate but also whether the variables they employ continue to constitute the full set of relevant considerations.

If the changing contours of Congress, trees and forest, can be charted carefully, then research may mesh with other developments in the legislative politics subfield. Understanding one legislature—and Congress is surely the assembly about which most is known—should encourage genuine comparative research. Indeed, complete comprehension of Congress requires comparative analyses within chambers (committees, majority and minority parties), between the House and Senate[22] (elections, norms, rules, policy product), and over time (change and reform). Accurate generalizations and useful models, partial or full, about Congress could provide hypotheses that can be tested in other legislative settings. While such propositions may be disconfirmed elsewhere—Congress may prove to be a unique assembly—testing them should point to characteristics of legislatures generally that any full theory must take into account. In the long run, we seek such a full theory, one that is truly valuable for comparative and longitudinal analysis. It is highly unlikely that theories of Congress will suggest most, or even any, of the elements of a complete model. But in conjunction with the developing research on cross-national and domestic state and local legislatures—which space considerations have made impossible to treat here—they may help advance the long-term search for a theory of legislatures.

Thus, congressional scholarship has covered considerable ground during a quarter century of renewed exploration, displaying an enormous substantive, theoretical, and methodological virtuosity in the course of these investigations. Still, there is probably only one safe conclusion to draw from this cursory and partial survey of the legislative terrain: there is no scholarly consensus, no widely preferred models or methods, about the most appropriate approach to the study of legislatures. Research has proceeded eclectically and empirically, frequently though decreasingly unencumbered by explicit theorizing, focusing both on structures and processes, in a venerable tradition of institutional analysis, and on the attributes and activities of individual lawmakers, in a more recent mode of behavioral analysis. There remains, however, enough unknown territory to engage the attention of as many scholars as care to study legislatures. We are not out of the woods yet.

FOOTNOTES

1. There were some classic clearings in the woods. See, inter alia, Wilson (1885); Brown (1922); Chiu (1928); and Follett (1896) on congressional leadership; and Herring (1929); Schattschneider (1935); and Truman (1951) on group politics. The fact remains, however, that the most significant work is of much more recent vintage.
2. Any serious effort to cover the full range of materials on legislative politics, as a subfield, within the confines of a single paper for a single panel, is doomed to fail. Thus, the focus here is on Congress, as the legislature about which most is known at present. This limited concern, needless-to-say, is in no way intended to minimize the substantial and important work on local and state legislative bodies or the innovative and integrative efforts to develop comparative perspectives on legislatures. But what we have learned about Congress should provide some direction for those interested in moving into these even less well charted areas.
3. For other efforts to assess the "state of the discipline," see Peabody (1969); Meller (1970); Eulau and Abramowitz (1972); Huitt (1976); Rohde and Shepsle (1978); and Cooper and Brady (1981). For broader, comparative views, see Polsby (1975); and Mezey (1979).
4. For instance, the congressional stability ("institutionalization") of the 1960s seems to have given way to a period of increasing flux in the 1970s. (Compare Polsby, 1968, and Cavanagh, 1980.)
5. Space considerations preclude extensive citation. Where possible, I have tried to cite studies that are basic contributions and that also summarize much of the literature. In consequence, a great number of quality studies are omitted here. For a monumental bibliography, listing more than 5500 citations, see Goehlert and Sayre (1982).
6. Recent party resurgence, especially by the Republicans, stressing central fund raising and modern campaign technologies, suggests that party influence may be greater in the 1980s than it was during the period covered in the literature.
7. Where these votes fall on the congressional voting continuum, in contrast to how accurately they reflect district opinion, is a more controversial matter. At issue, and unresolved, is whether members from "marginal" districts (defined variously)

take more moderate roll call positions than their "safe" colleagues. (See, inter alia, Fiorina, 1973, and Sullivan and Uslaner, 1978.)

8. This is not to denigrate description. Sound analysis must of course, rest on detailed understanding of "the facts." The forest, after all, *does* consist of trees.

9. For a preliminary effort to specify some of these issues, see Unekis and Rieselbach, forthcoming.

10. A similar set of problems exists with respect to committee member-committee staff interactions. We remain largely ignorant of the roles staffers play; the extent to which they influence, or are influenced by, their nominal principals; and the variations in staff-committee relationships and in the resultant panel performance across committees. (See Patterson, 1970; Price, 1971; and Salisbury & Shepsle, 1981.)

11. The place of informal norms (folkways) in congressional politics is equally cloudy. Again, interpersonal relations are central, and it is difficult to get a clear view of socialization processes, the content of the legislative "culture," and the ways in which custom and tradition impinge on member behavior. (See Matthews, 1960; Asher, 1973; Rohde *et al.*, 1974; Loomis & Fishel, 1981.)

12. For case studies that illustrate, typically or not, the problems of ascertaining groups' influence as distinct from their activities, see Gelb and Palley (1979), and Vogel and Nadel (1977).

13. Matthews and Stimson (1975) reach similar conclusions employing cue theory explicitly. The model, however, is not the full story, for as Weisberg (1978) demonstrates, as predictive devices, various analytic schemes, including cue-taking, do not move much beyond a simple "baseline model" of partisanship; projecting that members will vote with their party's majority yields almost equally accurate predictions.

14. This is not to suggest that short-term forces are irrelevant, or that individual representatives never shift their positions. Issues, such as abortion, may shift in salience. Or they may appear in new guises: civil rights seems less a "legal" than a "social" matter in the 1980s (see Deckard, 1976). Finally, lawmakers' situations may shift — a new committee assignment or leadership position, or a shift in the occupancy of the White House — and alter their perspectives on particular questions. What such change entails, of course, is a need to revise the cue-taking calculus; it does not undercut the utility of the approach.

15. For insightful efforts to broaden the treatment of subgovernments to encompass a wider variety of legislative circumstances, see Heclo (1978) on "issue networks," and Jones (1982, pp. 358-365), on "large sloppy hexagons."

16. To be sure, combining the institutional and individual perspectives has become increasingly common, but many studies remain squarely in one or the other of these two research traditions.

17. This, of course, is all that economic models claim to do. It is not necessary to stake out each tree in order to describe the forest.

18. For instance, McCrone and Kuklinski (1979) find that state legislators espousing the delegate orientation act consistently with it only when their constituents send them unambiguous messages.

19. It is, of course, true that normative judgments reflect individual values, and that political scientists have no special claim to either expertise or superiority in the realm of values. Still, congressional scholars have been loath to theorize, normatively or empirically; as a result, they have done less than they might have to pose the evaluative questions clearly and precisely. Michael Mezey and Gerald Wright (personal communications, 1982) suggest two causes of this reluctance. First, Congress is extraordinarily accessible; a superabundance of data about the legislature encourages careful but narrow empirical work (on the "trees") that

retards broader concern for theorizing (about the "forest"). Second, and probably as a consequence of the first, students of Congress come quickly to develop a great affection for the institution, and for their colleagues who research it. Thus, there is a consensus, favorable to Congress, within the scholarly community that discourages critical commentary, to say nothing of normative condemnation.

20. I have neglected oversight to a large extent, but it remains a basic, though elusive feature of the legislature's activity. For summaries of what we know to date, see Harris (1964); Ogul (1976); and Dodd and Schott (1979). Needless-to-say, there are innumerable facets of legislative-administrative relationships in need of exploration.

21. There have been some valuable beginnings here. In addition to case studies (e.g., Sundquist, 1968, and Reid, 1980), Orfield (1975) has tried to identify the conditions when Congress can exert its institutional influence most effectively. Similarly, Brady (1982, inter alia) and his collaborators have sought to specify the occasions (e.g., realigning eras) when the electoral process contributes to policy innovation in Congress. Nonetheless, these insights need to be integrated within broader theories.

22. The upper chamber has received less attention from contemporary scholars; there are fewer Senators, they seem to be less accessible, and their more heterogeneous constituencies are more difficult to categorize. The situation may be changing, however: see Baker (1980) and Foley (1980).

REFERENCES

Abramowitz, A. I. A comparison of voting for U.S. senator and representative in 1978. *American Political Science Review*, 1980, *74*, 633-640.

American Political Science Association, Committee on Political Parties. *Toward a more responsible two-party system.* New York: Rinehart, 1950.

Arnold, R. D. *Congress and the bureaucracy.* New Haven: Yale University Press, 1979.

Asher, H. B. The learning of legislative norms. *American Political Science Review,* 1973, *67,* 499-513.

Asher, H. B. and Weisberg, H. F. Voting change in Congress: Some dynamic perspectives on an evolutionary process. *American Journal of Political Science,* 1978, *22,* 391-425.

Bacheller, J. M. Lobbyists and the legislative process: The impact of environmental constraints. *American Political science Review,* 1977, *71,* 252-263.

Backstrom, C. H. Congress and the public: How representative is the one of the other? *American Politics Quarterly,* 1977, *5,* 411-435.

Baker, R. K. *Friend and foe in the U.S. Senate.* New York: Free Press, 1980.

Baldwin, D. A. Power and social exchange. *American Political Science Review,* 1978, *72,* 1229-1242.

Bauer, R. A., de S. Pool, I. and Dexter, L. A. *American business and public policy* (2nd ed.). Chicago: Aldine-Atherton, 1972.

Beth, R. S. 'Incumbency advantage' and incumbency resources: Recent articles. *Congress & the Presidency,* 1981-82, *9,* 119-136.

Brady, D. with Stewart, J., Jr. Congressional party realignment and the transformations of public policy in three realignment eras. *American Journal of Political Science,* 1982, *26,* 333-360.

Brady, D. and Bullock, C. S., III. Is there a conservative coalition in the House? *Journal of Politics,* 1980, *42,* 549-559.

Brady, D., Cooper, J., and Hurley, P. A. The decline of party in the U.S. House of Representatives, 1887-1968. *Legislative Studies Quarterly,* 1979, *4,* 381-407.

Brown, G. R. *The leadership of Congress.* Indianapolis: Bobbs-Merrill, 1922.

Bullock, C. S. III. Redistricting and congressional stability, 1962-1972. *Journal of Politics,* 1975, *37,* 569-575.

Bullock, C. S., III. House committee assignments. In L. N. Rieselbach (Ed.), *The congressional system: Notes and readings* (2nd ed.). North Scituate, MA: Duxbury Press, 1979.

Burnham, J. *Congress and the American tradition.* Chicago: Regnery, 1959.

Burns, J. M. *The deadlock of democracy.* Englewood Cliffs, N.J.: Prentice-Hall, 1963.

Campbell, A., Converse, P. E., Miller, W. E., and Stokes, D. E. *Elections and the political order.* New York: Wiley, 1966.

Cavanagh, T. E. The deinstitutionalization of the House. Presented to the Everett McKinley Dirksen Congressional Leadership Research Center-Sam Rayburn Library Conference, Understanding Congressional Leadership: The State of the Art. Washington, D.C., June 10-11, 1980.

Cavanagh, T. E. The calculus of representation. *Western Political Quarterly,* 1982, *35,* 120-129.

Chiu, C. *The Speaker of the House of Representatives since 1896.* New York: Columbia University Press, 1928.

Clausen, A. R. *How congressmen decide: A policy focus.* New York: St. Martin's, 1973.

Clausen, A. R. and Van Horn, C. E. The congressional response to a decade of change, 1963-1972. *Journal of Politics,* 1977, *39,* 624-666.

Collie, M. P. Incumbency, electoral safety, and electoral turnover in the House of Representatives, 1952-1970. *American Political Science Review,* 1981, *75,* 119-131.

Converse, P. E. and Markus, G. B. Plus ca change. . . ' The new CPS election panel study. *American Political Science Review,* 1979, *73,* 32-49.

Cooper, J. Congress in organizational perspective. In L. C. Dodd & B. I. Oppenheimer (Eds.), *Congress reconsidered* (1st ed.). New York: Praeger, 1977.

Cooper, J. Organization and innovation in the House of Representatives. In J. Cooper & G. C. MacKenzie (Eds.), *The House at work.* Austin: University of Texas Press, 1981.

Cooper, J. and Brady, D. W. Toward a diachronic analysis of Congress. *American Political Science Review,* 1981, *75,* 988-1006.

Cooper, J. and West, W. The congressional career in the 1970s. In L. C. Dodd & B. I. Oppenheimer (Eds.), *Congress reconsidered* (2nd ed.). Washington: Congressional Quarterly Press, 1981.

Cooper, J., Brady, D. W. and Hurley, P. A. The electoral basis of party voting: Patterns and trends in the U.S. House of Representatives, 1887-1969. In L. Maisel & J. Cooper (Eds.), *The impact of the electoral process.* Beverly Hills, CA: Sage, 1977.

Cover, A. D. Contacting congressional constituents: Some patterns of perquisite use. *American Journal of Political Science,* 1980, *24,* 125-134.

Cover, A. D. and Brumberg, B. S. Baby books and ballots: The impact of congressional mail on constituent opinion. *American Political Science Review,* 1982, *76,* 347-359.

Cover, A. D. and Mayhew, D. R. Congressional dynamics and the decline of competitive congressional elections. In L. C. Dodd & B. I. Oppenheimer (Eds.), *Congress reconsidered* (2nd ed.). Washington, D.C.: Congressional Quarterly Press, 1981.

Dahl, R. A. The concept of power. *Behavioral Science,* 1957, *2,* 201-215.

Davidson, R. H. *The role of the congressman.* New York: Pegasus, 1969.

Davidson, R. H. Breaking up those 'cozy triangles': An impossible dream? In S. Welch

& J. G. Peters (Eds.), *Legislative reform and public policy.* New York: Praeger, 1977.

Davidson, R. H. Subcommittee government: New channels for policy. In T. E. Mann & N. J. Ornstein (Eds.), *The new Congress.* Washington, D.C.: American Enterprise Institute, 1981.

Davidson, R. H. and Oleszek, W. J. Adaptation and consolidation: Structural innovation in the House of Representatives. *Legislative Studies Quarterly,* 1976, *1,* 37-65.

Davidson, R. H., Kovenock, D. M. and O'Leary, M. K. *Congress in crisis: Politics and congressional reform.* Belmont, CA: Wadsworth, 1966.

Deckard, B. S. Political upheaval and congressional voting: The effects of the 1960s on voting patterns in the House of Representatives. *Journal of Politics,* 1976, *38,* 326-345.

Deering, C. J. and Smith, S. S. Majority party leadership and the new House subcommittee system. In F. H. Mackaman (Ed.), *Understanding congressional leadership.* Washington, D.C.: Congressional Quarterly Press, 1981.

de Grazia, A. (coord.). *Congress: The first branch of government.* Washington, D.C.: American Enterprise Institute, 1966.

Dodd, L. C. Committee integration in the Senate: A comparative analysis. *Journal of Politics,* 1972, *34,* 1135-1171.

Dodd, L. C. Congress, the presidency, and the cycles of power. In V. Davis (Ed.), *The post-imperial presidency.* New Brunswick, N.J.: Transaction Books, 1979(a).

Dodd, L. C. The expanded roles of the House Democratic whip system. *Congressional Studies,* 1979(b), *6,* 27-56.

Dodd, L. C. Congress, the Constitution, and the crisis of legitimation. In L. C. Dodd & B. I. Oppenheimer (Eds.), *Congress reconsidered* (2nd ed.). Washington, D.C.: Congressional Quarterly Press, 1981.

Dodd, L. C. and Schott, R. L. *Congress and the administrative state.* New York: Wiley, 1979.

Dodd, L. C. and Sullivan, T. Majority party leadership and partisan vote gathering: The House Democratic whip system. In F. H. Mackaman (Ed.), *Understanding congressional leadership.* Washington, D.C.: Congressional Quarterly Press, 1981.

Easton, D. *A systems analysis of political life.* New York: Wiley, 1965.

Easton, D. *A framework for political analysis* (rev. ed.). Chicago: University of Chicago Press, 1979.

Edwards, G. C. III. *Presidential influence in Congress.* San Francisco: Freeman, 1980.

Enelow, J. H. Saving amendments, killer amendments, and an expected utility calculus of sophisticated voting. *Journal of Politics,* 1981, *43,* 1062-1089.

Erikson, R. S. Is there such a thing as a safe seat? *Polity,* 1976, *8,* 623-632.

Erikson, R. S. Constituency opinion and congressional behavior: A reexamination of the Miller-Stokes representational data. *American Journal of Political Science,* 1978, *22,* 511-535.

Etzioni, A. *Modern organizations.* Englewood Cliffs, N.J.: Prentice-Hall, 1964.

Eulau, H. and Abramowitz, A. Recent research on Congress in a democratic perspective. *Political Science Review,* 1972, *2,* 1-36.

Eulau, H. and Karps, P. D. The puzzle of representation: Specifying the components of responsiveness. *Legislative Studies Quarterly,,* 1977, *2,* 233-254.

Fenno, R. F., Jr. *The power of the purse: Appropriations politics in Congress.* Boston: Little, Brown, 1966.

Fenno, R. F., Jr. *Congressmen in committees.* Boston: Little, Brown, 1973.

Fenno, R. F., Jr. *Home style: Representatives in their districts.* Boston: Little, Brown, 1978.

Ferejohn, J. A. *Pork barrel politics: Rivers and harbors legislation, 1947-1968.*

Stanford, CA: Stanford University Press, 1974.

Ferejohn, J. A. On the decline of competition in congressional elections. *American Political Science Review,* 1977, *71,* 166-176.

Ferejohn, J. A. and Fiorina, M. P. Purposive models of legislative behavior. *American Economic Review Papers and Proceedings,* 1975, *65,* 407-415.

Fiorina, M. P. Electoral margins, constituency influence and policy moderation: A critical assessment. *American Politics Quarterly,* 1973, *1,* 479-498.

Fiorina, M. P. *Representatives, roll calls and constituencies.* Lexington, Mass.: Lexington Books, 1974.

Fiorina, M. P. *Congress—keystone of the Washington establishment.* New Haven: Yale University Press, 1977.

Fishel, J. *Party and opposition: Congressional challengers in American politics.* New York: McKay, 1973.

Foley, M. *The new Senate: Liberal influence on a conservative institution 1959-1972.* New Haven: Yale University Press, 1980.

Follett, M. P. *The Speaker of the House of Representatives.* New York: Longmans, Green, 1896.

Fox, H. W., Jr. and Hammond, S. W. *Congressional staffs: The invisible force in American lawmaking.* New York: Free Press, 1977.

Frantzich, S. E. Computerized information technology in the U.S. House of Representatives. *Legislative Studies Quarterly,* 1979, *4,* 255-280.

Froman, L. A., Jr. Organization theory and the explanation of important characteristics of Congress. *American Political Science Review,* 1968, *62,* 518-526.

Galloway, G. B. *The legislative process in Congress.* New York: Crowell, 1953.

Gelb, J. and Palley, M. L. Women and interest group politics: A comparative analysis of federal decision-making. *Journal of Politics,* 1979, *41,* 362-392.

Goehlert, R. U. and Sayre, J. R. *The United States Congress: A bibliography.* New York: Free Press, 1982.

Goodwin, G., Jr. *The little legislatures: Committees of Congress.* Amherst, MA: University of Massachusetts Press, 1970.

Griffith, E. S. *Congress: Its contemporary role.* New York: New York University Press, 1951.

Gross, B. A. *The legislative struggle.* New York: McGraw-Hill, 1953.

Gross, D. A. Representative styles and legislative behavior. *Western Political Quarterly,* 1978, *31,* 359-371.

Haeberle, S. H. The institutionalization of the subcommittee in the U.S. House of Representatives. *Journal of Politics,* 1978, *40,* 1054-1065.

Harris, J. P. *Congressional control of administration.* Washington, D.C.: Brookings Institution, 1964.

Hayes, M. T. *Lobbyists and legislators.* New Brunswick, N.J.: Rutgers University Press, 1981.

Heclo, H. Issue networks and the executive establishment. In A. King (Ed.), *The new American political system.* Washington, D.C.: American Enterprise Institute, 1978.

Herring, E. P. *Group representation before Congress.* Baltimore: Johns Hopkins University Press, 1929.

Hershey, M. R. *The making of campaign strategy.* Lexington, MA: Lexington Books, 1974.

Hinckley, B. *Congressional elections.* Washington, D.C.: Congressional Quarterly Press, 1981.

Horn, S. *Unused power: The work of the Senate Committee on Appropriations.* Washington, D.C.: Brookings Institution, 1970.

Huitt, R. K. Congress: Retrospect and prospect. *Journal of Politics,* 1976, *38,* 209-227.

Huntington, S. P. Congressional responses to the twentieth century. In D. B. Truman (Ed.), *The Congress and America's future* (2nd ed.). Englewood Cliffs, N.J.: Prentice-Hall, 1973.

Hurley, P. A. Dyadic and collective representation in 1978. *Legislative Studies Quarterly*, 1982, *7*, 119-136.

Ippolito, D. S. *Congressional spending*. Ithaca, N.Y.: Cornell University Press, 1981.

Jackson, J. E. *Constituencies and leaders in Congress*. Cambridge: Harvard University Press, 1974.

Jacobson, G. C. *Money in congressional elections*. New Haven: Yale University Press, 1980.

Jacobson, G. C. and Kernell, S. *Strategy and choice in congressional elections*. New Haven: Yale University Press, 1981.

Jewell, M. E. Attitudinal determinants of legislative behavior: The utility of role analysis. In A. Kornberg & L. D. Musolf (Eds.), *Legislatures in developmental perspective*. Durham, N.C.: Duke University Press, 1970.

Jewell, M. E. and Patterson, S. C. *The legislative process in the United States* (3rd ed.). New York: Random House, 1977.

Johannes, J. R. The distribution of casework in the U.S. Congress: An uneven burden. *Legislative Studies Quarterly*, 1980, *5*, 517-544.

Johannes, J. R. and McAdams, J. C. The congressional incumbency effect: Is it casework, policy compatibility, or something else? *American Journal of Political Science*, 1981, *25*, 512-542.

Jones, C. O. *The minority party in Congress*. Boston: Little, Brown, 1970.

Jones, C. O. How reform changes Congress. In S. Welch & J. G. Peters (Eds.). *Legislative reform and public policy*. New York: Praeger, 1977.

Jones, C. O. Congress and the presidency. In T. E. Mann & N. J. Ornstein (Eds.), *The new Congress*. Washington, D.C.: American Enterprise Institute, 1981(a).

Jones, C. O. House leadership in an age of reform. In F. H. Mackaman (Ed.), *Understanding congressional leadership*. Washington, D.C.: Congressional Quarterly Press, 1981(b).

Jones, C. O. *The United States Congress: People, place, and policy*. Homewood, Ill.: Dorsey Press, 1982.

Kernell, S. Presidential popularity and negative voting: An alternative explanation of the midterm decline of the president's party. *American Political Science Review*, 1977, *71*, 44-66.

Kinder, D. R. and Kiewiet, D. R. Economic discontent and political behavior: The role of personal grievances and collective economic judgments in congressional voting. *American Journal of Political Science*, 1979, *23*, 495-527.

Kingdon, J. W. *Candidates for office*. New York: Random House, 1966.

Kingdon, J. W. *Congressmen's voting decisions* (2nd ed.). New York: Harper & Row, 1981.

Kofmehl, K. *Professional staffs of Congress* (3rd ed.). Lafayette, Ind.: Purdue University Studies, 1977.

LeLoup, L. T. Process vs. policy: The House budget committee. *Legislative Studies Quarterly*, 1979, *4*, 227-254.

Leuthold, D. A. *Electioneering in a democracy: Campaigns for Congress*. New York: Wiley, 1968.

Loomis, B. A. and Fishel, J. New members in a changing Congress: Norms, actions, and satisfaction. *Congressional Studies*, 1981, *8*, 81-94.

Lowell, A. L. The influence of party upon legislation in England and America. *Annual Report of the American Historical Association*, 1901, *1*, 319-541.

Lowi, T. J. American business, public policy, case studies and political theory. *World Politics*, 1964, *16*, 677-715.

MacRae, D., Jr. *Dimensions of congressional voting.* Berkeley: University of California Press, 1958.

Malbin, M. J. *Unelected representatives: Congressional staff and the future of representative government.* New York: Basic Books, 1980.

Manley, J. F. *The politics of finance: The House Committee on Ways and Means.* Boston: Little, Brown, 1970.

Manley, J. F. The conservative coalition in Congress. *American Behavioral Scientist,* 1973, *17,* 223-247.

Mann, T. E. *Unsafe at any margin: Interpreting congressional elections.* Washington, D.C.: American Enterprise Institute, 1978.

Mann, T. E. and Wolfinger, R. E. Candidates and parties in congressional elections. *American Political Science Review,* 1980, *74,* 617-632.

Matsunaga, S. M. and Chen, P. *Rulemakers of the House.* Urbana, IL: University of Illinois Press, 1976.

Matthews, D. R. *U.S. Senators and their world.* Chapel Hill, N.C.: University of North Carolina Press, 1960.

Matthews, D. R. and Stimson, J. A. *Yeas and nays: Normal decision-making in the U.S. House of Representatives.* New York: Wiley, 1975.

Mayhew, D. R. *Party loyalty among congressmen: The difference between Democrats and Republicans, 1947-1962.* Cambridge: Harvard University Press, 1966.

Mayhew, D. R. *Congress: The electoral connection.* New Haven: Yale University Press, 1974.

McCrone, D. J. and Kuklinski, J. H. The delegate theory of representation. *American Journal of Political Science,* 1979, *23,* 278-300.

Meller, N. Legislative behavior research. In M. Haas & H. Kariel (Eds.), *Approaches to the study of political science.* Scranton, PA: Chandler, 1970.

Mezey, M. L. *Comparative legislatures.* Durham, N.C.: Duke University Press, 1979.

Milbrath, L. W. *The Washington lobbyists.* Chicago: Rand McNally, 1963.

Miller, W. E. and Stokes, D. E. Constituency influence in Congress. *American Poliical Science Review,* 1963, *57,* 45-56.

Moe, T. M. On the scientific study of rational models. *American Journal of Political Science,* 1979, *23,* 215-243.

Monroe, A. Consistency between public preferences and national policy decisions. *American Politics Quarterly,* 1979, *7,* 3-19.

Morrow, W. L. *Congressional committees.* New York: Scribners, 1969.

Neustadt, R. E. *Presidential power: The politics of leadership from FDR to Carter.* New York: Wiley, 1980.

Nie, N. H., Verba, S. and Petrocik, J. R. *The changing American voter* (enlarged ed.). Cambridge: Harvard University Press, 1979.

Norpoth, H. Explaining party cohesion in Congress: The case of shared policy attitudes. *American Political Science Review,* 1976, *70,* 1157-1171.

Ogul, M. *Congress oversees the bureaucracy: Studies in legislative supervision.* Pittsburgh: University of Pittsburgh Press, 1976.

Oppenheim, F. E. 'Power' revisited. *Journal of Politics,* 1978, *40,* 589-608.

Oppenheimer, B. I. Policy effects of U.S. House reform: Decentralization and the capacity to resolve energy issues. *Legislative Studies Quarterly,* 1980, *5,* 5-30.

Oppenheimer, B. I. The changing relationship between House leadership and the Committee on Rules. In F. H. Mackaman (Ed.), *Understanding congressional leadership.* Washington, D.C.: Congressional Quarterly Press, 1981.

Orfield, G. *Congressional power: Congress and social change.* New York: Harcourt Brace Jovanovich, 1975.

Ornstein, N. J. The House and Senate in a new Congress. In T. E. Mann & N. J.

Ornstein (Eds.), *The new Congress*. Washington, D.C.: American Enterprise Institute, 1981.

Ornstein, N. J. and Elder, S. *Interest groups, lobbying and policymaking*. Washington, D.C.: Congressional Quarterly Press, 1978.

Ornstein, N. J. and Rohde, D. W. Shifting forces, changing rules, and political outcomes: The impact of congressional change on four House committees. In R. L. Peabody and N. W. Polsby (Eds.), *New perspectives on the House of Representatives* (3rd ed.). Chicago: Rand McNally, 1977.

Panning, W. H. Rational choice and congressional norms. *Western Political Quarterly*, 1982, *35*, 193-203.

Parker, G. R. & Parker, S. L. Factions in committees: The U.S. House of Representatives. *American Political Science Review*, 1979, *73*, 85-102.

Patterson, S. C. Congressional committee professional staffing: Capabilities and constraints. In A. Kornberg & L. D. Musolf (Eds.), *Legislatures in developmental perspective*. Durham, N.C.: Duke University Press, 1970.

Peabody, R. L. Research on Congress: A coming of age. In R. K. Huitt & R. L. Peabody, *Congress: Two decades of analysis*. New York: Harper & Row, 1969.

Peabody, R. L. *Leadership in Congress: Stability, succession, and change*. Boston: Little, Brown, 1976.

Peabody, R. L. House party leadership in the 1970s. In L. C. Dodd & B. I. Oppenheimer (Eds.), *Congress reconsidered* (2nd ed.). Washington, D.C.: Congressional Quarterly Press, 1981(a).

Peabody, R. L. Senate party leadership: From the 1950s to the 1980s. In F. H. Mackaman (Ed.), *Understanding congressional leadership*. Washington, D.C.: Congressional Quarterly Press, 1981(b).

Perkins, L. P. Influence of members' goals on their committee behavior: The U.S. House Judiciary Committee. *Legislative Studies Quarterly*, 1980, *5*, 373-392.

Pitkin, H. F. *The concept of representation*. Berkeley: University of California Press, 1967.

Polsby, N. W. The institutionalization of the House of Representatives. *American Political Science Review*, 1968, *62*, 144-168.

Polsby, N. W. Legislatures. In N. W. Polsby & F. I. Greenstein (Eds.), *Handbook of political science* (Vol. 5). Reading, MA: Addison-Wesley, 1975.

Price, D. E. Professionals and 'entrepreneurs': Staff orientations and policy making on three Senate committees. *Journal of Politics*, 1971, *33*, 316-336.

Price, D. E. *Who makes the laws? Creativity and power in Senate committees*. Cambridge, MA: Schenkman, 1972.

Price, D. E. Policy making in Senate committees: The impact of environmental factors. *American Political Science Review*, 1978, *72*, 548-574.

Price, D. E. Congressional committees in the policy process. In L. C. Dodd & B. I. Oppenheimer (Eds.), *Congress reconsidered* (2nd ed.). Washington, D.C.: Congressional Quarterly Press, 1981.

Reid, T. R. *Congressional odyssey. The saga of a Senate bill*. San Francisco: Freeman, 1980.

Rice, S. A. *Quantitative methods in politics*. New York: Knopf, 1928.

Rieselbach, L. N. *Congressional reform in the seventies*. Morristown, N.J.: General Learning Press, 1977.

Rieselbach, L. N. and Unekis, J. K. Ousting the oligarchs: Assessing the consequences of reform and change on four House committees. *Congress & the Presidency*, 1981-82, *9*, 83-117.

Riker, W. H. Some ambiguities in the notion of power. *American Political Science Review*, 1964, *58*, 341-349.

Ripley, R. B. *Majority party leadership in Congress*. Boston: Little, Brown, 1969.

Ripley, R. B. and Franklin, G. A. *Congress, the bureaucracy and public policy* (rev. ed.). Homewood, IL: Dorsey Press, 1980.

Robinson, J. A. *The House Rules Committee.* Indianapolis: Bobbs-Merrill, 1963.

Rohde, D. W. and Shepsle, K. A. Taking stock of congressional research: The new institutionalism. Presented at the annual meeting of the Midwest Political Science Association. Chicago, IL, April 20-22, 1978.

Rohde, D. W., Ornstein, N. J. and Peabody, R. L. Political change and legislative norms in the U.S. Senate. Presented to the Annual Meeting of the American Political Science Association. Chicago, IL, Aug. 29-Sept. 2, 1974.

Salisbury, R. H. and Shepsle, K. A. U.S. congressman as enterprise. *Legislative Studies Quarterly,* 1981, *6,* 559-576.

Schattschneider, E. E. *Politics, pressures and the tariff.* New York: Prentice-Hall, 1935.

Schick, A. *Congress and money: Budgeting, spending and taxing.* Washington, D.C.: The Urban Institute, 1980.

Schneider, J. E. *Ideological coalitions in Congress.* Westport, CT: Greenwood Press, 1979.

Shaffer, W. R. *Party and ideology in the United States Congress.* Lanham, MD: University Press of America, 1980.

Shannon, W. W. *Party, constituency and congressional voting.* Baton Rouge: Louisiana State University Press, 1968.

Shepsle, K. A. *The giant jigsaw puzzle: Democratic committee assignments in the modern House.* Chicago: University of Chicago Press, 1978.

Sinclair, B. D. Majority party leadership strategies for coping with the new House. *Legislative Studies Quarterly,* 1981(a), *6,* 391-414.

Sinclair, B. D. The Speaker's task force in the post-reform House of Representatives. *American Political Science Review,* 1981(b), *75,* 397-510.

Sullivan, J. L. and Uslaner, E. M. Congressional behavior and electoral marginality. *American Journal of Political Science,* 1978, *22,* 536-553.

Sundquist, J. L. *Politics and policy: The Eisenhower, Kennedy, and Johnson years.* Washington, D.C.: Brookings Institution, 1968.

Sundquist, J. L. *The decline and resurgence of Congress.* Washington, D.C.: Brookings Institution, 1981.

Truman, D. B. *The governmental process* (2nd ed.). New York: Knopf, 1971. (Originally published, 1951.)

Truman, D. B. *The congressional party.* New York: Wiley, 1959.

Tufte, E. R. The relationship between seats and votes in two-party systems. *American Political Science Review,* 1973, *67,* 540-554.

Tufte, E. R. *Political control of the economy.* Princeton: Princeton University Press, 1978.

Turner, J. *Party and constituency: Pressures on Congress.* Baltimore: Johns Hopkins University Press, 1951. (Rev. ed., by E. V. Schneier, 1970).

Unekis, J. K. and Rieselbach, L. N. *Congressional committee politics: Continuity and change, 1971-1980.* New York: Praeger, forthcoming.

Vogel, D. and Nadel, M. Who is a consumer? An analysis of the politics of consumer conflict. *American Politics Quarterly,* 1977, *5,* 27-56.

Vogler, D. J. Ad hoc committees in the House of Representatives and purposive models of legislative behavior. *Polity,* 1981, *14,* 89-109.

Wahlke, J. C., Eulau, H., Buchanan, W., and Ferguson, L. C. *The legislative system: Explorations in legislative behavior.* New York: Wiley, 1962.

Waldman, S. Majority party leadership in the House of Representatives. *Political Science Quarterly,* 1980, *95,* 373-393.

Walker, J. L. Setting the agenda in the United States Senate: A theory of problem selection. *British Journal of Political Science,* 1977, *7,* 423-445.

Wayne, S. J. *The legislative presidency.* New York: Harper & Row, 1978.

Weingast, B. R. A rational choice perspective on congressional norms. *American Journal of Political Science,* 1979, *23,* 245-262.

Weisberg, H. F. Evaluating theories of congressional roll call voting. *American Journal of Political Science,* 1978, *22,* 554-577.

Weissberg, R. Collective vs. dyadic representation in Congress. *American Political Science Review,* 1978, *72,* 535-546.

Westefield, L. P. Majority party leadership and the committee system in the House of Representatives. *American Political Science Review,* 1974, *68,* 1593-1604.

Wildavsky, A. *The politics of the budgetary process* (3rd ed.). Boston: Little, Brown, 1979.

Wilson, W. *Congressional government.* Cleveland: World Publishing, 1885.

7

Judicial Politics: Still a Distinctive Field*

Lawrence Baum

The decade of the 1960s was a time of upheaval in the field of judicial politics. New ideas challenged old assumptions, and new kinds of research changed the field's contours. By late in that decade one could have predicted confidently that the field would look quite different fifteen years later. Indeed, the field has changed considerably. But that change has taken forms which few people in the 1960s might have expected.

This essay is an effort to sort out what has happened to the field of judicial politics in the last fifteen years. It is not a comprehensive analysis of the research in that period. Nor is it offered as a definitive interpretation of the state of the field; it is doubtful that such an interpretation is possible.

The field of judicial politics may be defined in terms of subject matter or in terms of a set of scholars who specialize in the field. It is most useful for this essay to define the field in subject-matter terms. My definition is broad, including within it all processes that involve the courts directly. It does not include "legal" concerns to which the courts are peripheral: police as administrators, prisons, lawyers as a profession, or constitutional issues outside the context of judicial interpretations.[1] The essay will also be restricted to judicial politics in the United States. The growth of literature on courts in other nations is very welcome. But, in order to keep this essay manageable, I will exclude that literature from consideration here.[2]

In one important respect the essay's domain has been defined in terms of a set of scholars. Because my interest is in the state of judicial politics as a field of political science, the essay will focus primarily on the work of political scientists—although a good deal of attention will be given to interdisciplinary links in the study of the courts. Moreover, much of this essay will interpret the

---

*In developing this essay I was aided immensely by the suggestions of a number of scholars. I benefited particularly from the comments of Beverly Cook, Ada Finifter, Sheldon Goldman, Leslie Friedman Goldstein, Herbert Jacob, Charles Johnson, John Kessel, Elliot Slotnick, Susette Talarico, and especially James Farr.

189

state of the judicial politics field in terms of the perspectives of those political scientists who specialize in it.

The essay is divided into three parts. In the first, I will examine three important trends in the field of judicial politics over the past fifteen years. In the second, I will suggest an interpretation for those trends. The final section will evaluate the current state of knowledge in the field in light of the directions that it has taken.

In preparing this essay I benefited a good deal from other surveys of the field.[3] In addition, the essay is based in large part on a quantitative analysis of the judicial politics literature in the 1962-81 period. That analysis focused on articles in six political science journals, three law and social science journals, and doctoral dissertations.[4]

THREE RECENT TRENDS

The field of judicial politics has changed in many ways over the past fifteen years. Three types of changes seem particularly important, in part because they may have been unexpected. The growing diversity of scholarship in the field stands out most prominently, and I will give it particular attention. But two other changes also will be examined: (1) the resurgence of an interest in judicial outputs and normative questions; and (2) the establishment of new ties with other disciplines.

Diversity. Judicial politics always has contained a considerable range of scholarly interests. In past eras, however, there seemed to be a core to the field around which most scholarly work clustered. This is no longer true.

For a considerable length of time, the core of the field was constitutional law, generally involving critical analysis of the Supreme Court's work as interpreter of the Constitution. The revolution that culminated in the 1960s shifted the core to judicial behavior, generally involving analysis of the forces that shape the Court's policy choices. In the latter half of the 1960s a large share of published research dealt with Supreme Court decision-making, and this subject was at the center of the field's concerns.

In the study of judicial behavior there was a central issue: the role of "political" factors, primarily judges' personal policy preferences, in judicial decisions. Much of the impetus for the systematic study of judicial decision-making was methodological, with students of the courts focusing on decision-making as a means to apply sophisticated quantitative methods to judicial politics. But at a theoretical level the judicial behavior movement had as its primary purpose the refutation of a mechanistic view of judicial decisions. Research on decision-making was aimed at establishing the importance of policy preferences as bases for decisional choices and ascertaining the ways in which preferences arose and influenced decisions. This research did support a non-mechanistic view of decision-making by showing the consistency with which particular judges took particular ideological positions, the significance of group dynamics on multi-member courts, and the relationship between judges' political party affiliations and their decisional tendencies (see Goldman & Jahnige, 1976, ch. 5).

Even at the height of the field's focus on judicial behavior, a good deal of research dealt with other subjects—quite aside from the continuing work in constitutional law. But most of this research shared a primary interest in the Supreme Court; certainly this was true of the developing bodies of work on the impact of court decisions ("judicial impact") and political litigation. Much of this research also reflected an effort to challenge legalistic assumptions about the judicial process. Judicial impact research questioned the assumption that Supreme Court decisions are implemented faithfully. Political litigation research implicitly challenged the view that litigation is activity undertaken by individuals for individual purposes.

Thus, as of the late 1960s the field had a core subject matter and something of a central theme. Neither has disappeared; both Supreme Court decision-making and the challenging of legalistic assumptions remain important. But the period since the 1960s has seen a great expansion of subject matter and a subtle movement away from a central theme. The field has taken with a vengeance C. Herman Pritchett's advice to "Let a hundred flowers bloom" (1968, p. 509).

Within the judicial behavior area the subjects of research have broadened. Most notably, an increasing volume of work studies courts other than the Supreme Court. Research on the federal courts of appeals, for instance, has proliferated (see Goldman, 1975; Howard, 1981). The sentencing decisions of trial judges have become a major focus for the study of judicial behavior (Gibson, 1978b; Levin, 1972; Kuklinski & Stanga, 1979).

A second expansion is in the stages and types of judicial decisions that are studied. At the appellate level research increasingly has examined decision points other than the decision on the merits (Rohde & Spaeth, 1976). A particularly large body of research now exists on the selection by appellate courts of cases to be heard. This research has demonstrated that policy preferences play a central role in this stage of court action (Provine, 1980; Ulmer, 1972, 1978; Baum, 1977). Trial court research has introduced other types of judicial decisions to the area. Predominant among them is sentencing, but other stages such as bail-setting have been studied also (Flemming, 1982).

Finally, there has been some broadening in the decisional influences that scholars study. Because of the issue that dominated the area in the 1960s, research in that era dealt primarily with policy preferences or with preference-related variables such as social backgrounds. This is somewhat less the case today. Most important, substantial research has been done on the impact of judges' external environments (Kuklinski & Stanga, 1979; Gibson, 1980). This development followed a movement away from the Supreme Court to lower courts whose environments could be compared in relation to their decisions. Much of this research has shown geographical differences in decisional patterns and suggested the importance of local political culture and public opinion in shaping judicial decisions. Of particular interest are two studies of the sentencing of selective service offenders during the Vietnam War era. The two studies differ somewhat in their findings but agree that district judges' decisions were heavily influenced by their political environments (Cook, 1977; Kritzer, 1978).

In the 1960s, as I have noted, considerable research was done in areas related to the core of the field. The most notable of these areas were political litigation and judicial impact. In both areas the anti-legalistic theme that provided a focus for early research has weakened, and this change has helped to broaden the subject matter of research.[5]

In the case of political litigation,[6] there continues to be some debate over the extent of interest group involvement in litigation (O'Connor & Epstein, 1981-82). But most scholars have assumed the importance of policy goals and group activity in certain areas of litigation rather than seeking to demonstrate it. Recent studies generally have abandoned the earlier focus on major Supreme Court cases, looking at litigation activity throughout the judiciary and sometimes linking it with interest group activity elsewhere in the political system (Sorauf, 1976; O'Connor, 1980; Olson, 1981). These studies have underlined the complexity of political litigation processes, and they have helped to dispel the idea that broad litigation campaigns are easily undertaken and coordinated.

Even more than political litigation research, early studies of the impact of judicial decisions constituted a challenge to conventional legal wisdom. The largest body of work focused on the resistance of lower courts and administrators to controversial Supreme Court decisions on issues such as school desegregation and criminal procedure. Through this research it became clear that willing implementation of judicial politics is neither automatic nor inevitable (see Wasby, 1970). Since that point was established, a steady stream of research has continued. Much of this research continues to examine the implementation of single major Supreme Court decisions (Canon, 1973), but some has moved beyond this focus. Most notably, the impact of lower courts has begun to attract research. One form of lower-court research concerns state tort doctrines; two such studies have provided evidence that doctrines promulgated by state courts influence spending on insurance and hospital room rates (Croyle, 1979; Canon & Jaros, 1979). An increasing volume of research deals with institutional relationships among courts or between courts and the other branches of government, outside the context of specific decisions. For instance, Stephen Wasby has shown the problematic character of communication from the Supreme Court to police officers (1976).

By far the most important move toward diversity in the field of judicial politics has been the growth of trial court research. Through the mid-1960s the study of judicial politics by political scientists was devoted overwhelmingly to appellate courts. The primary subject, of course, was the Supreme Court. But even when research ventured beyond the Court, it was generally to the federal courts of appeals and state supreme courts. Now all that has changed.

Significant political science interest in trial courts began on the criminal side, perhaps in part because of the growing concern with criminal justice in American society. Some of the diverse research on criminal trial courts already has been discussed. Not surprisingly, the most common areas of research have been sentencing decisions and plea bargaining.

The interest in sentencing followed naturally from the field's existing focus on judicial behavior; as noted earlier, some scholars have studied sentencing in order to probe issues in the determinants of judicial decisions. Others have joined the effort to examine normative issues such as group discrimination in sentencing (Uhlman, 1979; Spohn, Gruhl, & Welch, 1981-82). The results of that effort have been inconclusive, with disagreement among studies about the existence and extent of discrimination by race and sex.

Early social science research on plea bargaining was aimed primarily at establishing the centrality of bargaining in most criminal courts and determining the ways in which it worked. Much of the more recent work by political scientists has focused on explanations for the prevalence of bargaining. Work by Milton Heumann (1978) and Malcolm Feeley (1979, ch. 8), among others, has helped to establish that heavy court caseloads represent an incomplete explanation for plea bargaining; other motivations such as the desire to avoid uncertainty also play major—probably more important— roles. Another body of research has probed the assumption that defendants who plead guilty receive sentencing rewards, with little consensus emerging as to the validity of this assumption (Eisenstein & Jacob, 1977, ch. 10; Uhlman & Walker, 1979; Brereton & Casper, 1981-82).

Political scientists turned to the civil side of trial court activity even more recently. Marc Galanter's highly influential article on civil litigation and its outcomes (1974) is instructive. Galanter sought to demonstrate "why the 'haves' come out ahead" in court; he showed that the "haves" benefit from a series of basic structural advantages. One advantage that Galanter emphasized was the tendency for "haves" to be recurring litigants, while "have-nots" tend to use the courts infrequently. Although the article's concerns were avowedly political, its author was a law professor who drew relatively little from the work of political scientists.

At about the same time, political science research on civil litigation began to grow. Austin Sarat and Joel Grossman offered a major theoretical view of litigation decisions, discussing court usage in the context of other adjudicative institutions (1975). Craig Wanner examined the allocation of values by trial courts (1974, 1975), documenting the success of government and business organizations relative to individuals in three cities. A few studies have examined litigation patterns through analyses of court records, showing changes in the distribution of cases among areas of law over time (McIntosh, 1980-81) and urban-rural differences in litigation rates (Daniels, 1982). The interdisciplinary Civil Litigation Research Project produced a wealth of theoretical insights and empirical data (Special Issue, 1980-81). Among its important findings was the existence of a great variation among types of legal problems in the frequency of both the use of the courts and other kinds of actions to redress grievances (Miller & Sarat, 1980-81). While political scientists' contribution to the understanding of civil justice remains relatively limited, this area seems to have become an integral part of research in the field.

Trial court research has shared the anti-legalistic theme common to other bodies of research in the field. Both criminal and civil court studies have challenged assumptions about the use of formal procedures to resolve disputes and about even-handed application of the law. As in other areas of judicial politics, this theme began to fade once the defects in the traditional assumptions were established.

Outputs and Normative Issues. Aside from methodology, the study of

constitutional law and the study of judicial behavior differ in two fundamental ways. The first is the distinction between a focus on the policies that
courts produce and the process of making policy. The second is the distinction
between an explicit focus on normative issues and an approach intended to
minimize attention to those issues. Thus the shift in the core of the judicial
politics field that occurred in the 1960s was from outputs to process, from
normative to empirical concerns. The other types of work that emerged during the 1960s were process-oriented also, reflecting a deliberate shift in focus
(see Peltason, 1955, p. 1), and to a lesser extent they shared a limited interest
in normative questions. It may have appeared at the time that the field was
abandoning its historic interests in the substance of the courts' work and in
values.

This has not occurred. The lines between process and outputs and between empirical and normative are difficult to draw, but it is clear that
research dealing with outputs and normative-centered inquiries have survived. Indeed, both have enjoyed something of a resurgence in recent years.

First of all, constitutional law has maintained a foothold in the field.
Scholars continue to produce analyses and evaluations of Supreme Court doctrine from a variety of perspectives. It is particularly notable that this area has
attracted new practitioners from the generation trained since the 1960s (see
Baer, 1978; Binion, 1982), and it remains a staple of dissertation research.
But this scholarship has not remained static. Recent work in constitutional
law frequently reflects an effort to apply the perspectives and findings of
judicial process research. The change that this effort has brought about is
reflected quite clearly in some current constitutional law texts, which incorporate research on decision-making and the effects of decisions (Goldman,
1982; Grossman & Wells, 1980).

Analysis of judicial policy outputs has taken other forms as well, sometimes combining concerns that grow out of the constitutional law tradition
with newer interests. One small but important body of research in this vein involves linguistic analysis of court decisions. The importance of this work lies
largely in its partial challenge to one tenet of much of the work on judicial
decision-making, the assumption that judges manipulate legal language to
produce their preferred outcomes. Those who undertake linguistic analysis,
in contrast, emphasize the ways in which legal language directs and constrains
judges in their choices (Brigham, 1978; O'Neill, 1981).

There also have been several bodies of research that are concerned with
the general roles of courts in the making of public policy. The long-standing
debate about the propriety of judicial activism continues (Halpern & Lamb,
1982). That debate has acquired new life with Donald Horowitz's argument
that courts are limited in their capacities to make effective policy choices in
the area that he called "social policy" (1977). Several scholars have addressed
that argument, analyzing the issue of courts' policy-making capacities; most
disagree with Horowitz (Cavanagh & Sarat, 1980; Wasby, 1978).

On a different level, a few scholars have followed Robert Dahl (1958) in
examining the relationship between Supreme Court policy and the "lawmaking majority" in the other branches (Funston, 1975; Casper, 1976;
Adamany, 1973). Jonathan Casper's article was particularly important,

because it made a strong case that the Court plays a more significant independent role as a policy-maker than Dahl concluded. The same kind of question
has been addressed in even broader terms in research that explores the position of the courts in the political regime (Villmoare, 1982; Roelofs, 1982;
Balbus, 1973).

Many of the new forms of output research, such as the work on judicial
capacity, have a central normative concern. Some types of research on
judicial processes also have developed a strong normative tinge. Plea bargaining research, for instance, frequently deals with the propriety of bargaining as
a means of resolving cases. Another kind of normative interest is reflected in
the general movement to evaluate judicial policies and procedures through
empirical analysis of their actual or potential consequences. Political scientists increasingly have become involved in that movement (Stookey, 1980;
Roper, 1980; Dubois, 1982); perhaps their main contribution has been to
question and to probe assumptions about the beneficial effects of a variety of
judicial "reforms."[7]

Thus the new directions of the 1960s have come to co-exist with earlier
traditions in the field rather than obliterating them. Research concerned with
outputs and with normative issues has been influenced a good deal by the
newer tides, particularly in the heavier empirical component of recent work
with normative interests. But that research clearly has continued to thrive.

Interdisciplinary Links. The field of judicial politics traditionally has
had strong links with other scholarly disciplines. During the era in which constitutional law was the core of the field, the major links were with legal
scholarship and history. The relationship with legal scholarship was particularly strong, because the doctrinal analysis in which the field specialized
was very similar to the predominant form of research in the legal field.

These links weakened considerably in the 1960s. Most directly, they
weakened because of the growth of process-centered interests that were not
shared with law and history. This shift in subject matter also reflected a desire
to turn the field toward what seemed to be the mainstream of political science
and away from other disciplines. The new emphasis on judicial behavior, a
subject that fitted well in the mainstream and less well into other disciplines,
seemed to portend a limited importance for interdisciplinary ties in the
future.

Yet during the same period a new set of links with other disciplines was in
the process of formation. Political scientists began to develop ties with other
social scientists and legal scholars who shared an interest in the systematic
analysis of legal processes. These ties strengthened in the 1970s, and they have
become impressively strong. In some respects the study of judicial politics
within political science now appears to be just one loose category in social
science research on law and the courts. Indeed, the discussions of judicial
politics literature in this section seem artificially limited because of the exclusion of relevant work by scholars in other disciplines.

The development of a field of study that transcends disciplinary boundaries requires mechanisms for communication across those boundaries. In
this instance the most important mechanism has been the Law and Society

Association, which was founded in 1964. As the Association became better established and more visible, its meetings and journal provided places for political scientists to exchange ideas and information with colleagues from other disciplines. The *Law & Society Review* has become the most important journal for social science research on legal issues, and political scientists have contributed heavily to it.

Other institutions have served similar communication functions. Among them are several interdisciplinary journals. These include *Judicature*, which has become increasingly receptive to social science research, and some newer publications such as *Law & Policy Quarterly*. At some universities networks have developed among scholars who share legal interests.

The strengthening of links with other disciplines is closely related to the development of some new interests in the judicial politics field since the late 1960s. A continued focus on judicial behavior in appellate courts would have limited interdisciplinary ties, because this is not a subject of central interest in other social sciences. When political scientists became more interested in subjects that *were* of central interest in other disciplines, particularly subjects related to civil litigation and criminal court processes, a basis for closer relationships was established.

Of course, the links with other disciplines helped to bring about these new interests. Political science research on criminal courts, for instance, owes much to work by sociologists that preceded it (Blumberg, 1967; Sudnow, 1965). Expansions of interest within judicial politics were much easier because research in other disciplines provided a base from which to work.

More generally, scholarship in other disciplines has had a profound effect on research on the courts by political scientists. The influence of individual scholars such as Abraham Blumberg (1967) and H. Laurence Ross (1970) is easy to identify. Broader currents such as anthropologists' interests in dispute settlement mechanisms also have had major impacts (see Shapiro, 1981; Mather & Yngvesson, 1980-81).

In an earlier era the work of political scientists in the general area of constitutional law could be distinguished from the work of scholars in other disciplines by its greater emphasis on political motivations and the contexts of judicial policy (see Murphy & Tanenhaus, 1972, pp. 13-17). Can a similar distinction in tone or approach be found today? I do not think that any sharp distinctions exist. The adoption by political scientists of approaches and frameworks from other disciplines has helped to bring about commonalities in research on particular topics.[8]

The sharpest distinction that exists is in subject matter. A large share of political science research in judicial politics continues to fall into areas that are of limited interest to other disciplines. Foremost among them is decision-making in appellate courts, which remains a mainstay of the field. Another area which has been much more important to political scientists than to other scholars concerns relationships among courts and between courts and other public policy-makers. Because of this divergence, the judicial politics field cannot be viewed as fully integrated into a larger interdisciplinary field of study.

A DISTINCTIVE FIELD

The three trends discussed in the preceding section involve different aspects of the judicial politics field which have developed in unexpected ways. For that reason they raise broad questions about the directions that the field has taken and the reasons for its current form. These inquiries will be the concern of this section.

It seems to me that an understanding of the judicial politics field in political science must focus on its distinctive character. To a degree, this would be true of any field in the discipline. Each field develops a degree of isolation from others and, partly as a consequence, its own traditions and approaches to its subject matter. Thus fields come to be defined not only in terms of suject matter, but also in terms of the perspectives of the people who specialize in the study of that subject matter.

Judicial politics is no exception to this general rule. Indeed, within the broader field of American politics it seems to be unusually distinctive in that it is both more isolated and closer to unique in its characteristics than are most other fields. This was not always true; early in this century judicial politics by its various names was somewhere near the center of the study of politics, because of the legalistic approach that pervaded so many fields. But gradually the rest of political science drifted away from a concern with law, thereby severing a link with the judicial politics field. With that link gone, for several decades there has been something of a gulf between judicial politics and other fields of political science.

The primary cause of that gulf, I think, is another gulf — the one that is perceived to exist between the judiciary and the rest of the political system. In part, this perception may flow from a residue of the myth that courts are "non-political" — though presumably few political scientists accept that myth. More important are the real differences between courts and most other policy-makers, including the legal context in which judicial policies are made and the partial isolation of courts from certain external influences such as interest group lobbying. It also is important that the courts operate outside the "normal flow" of the policy-making process through the legislative and executive branches.

These characteristics inevitably help to produce a view that courts are to be studied separately and in their own terms. That view is reinforced by the intimidating effects of legal language and procedure on non-specialists. As a result of both factors, fields of study that might include courts in their purview instead have fenced them off.

The avoidance of courts by political scientists who specialize in other fields seems to have weakened in the past two decades, in part because of the growing activism of American courts and a growing general interest in the judiciary. One sign of change is an apparent increase in the number of political scientists whose work is primarily in other fields but who have contributed to research on judicial politics, either alone or in collaboration with judicial specialists (e.g., Hansen, 1980; Costantini & King, 1980-81; Spohn, Gruhl, & Welch, 1981-82). But these are exceptions; in general specialists in fields other than judicial politics continue to leave the courts aside.

A good example of this neglect occurs in the relatively new field of public policy. The courts fit well into most of the major concerns of this field, such as agenda-setting and implementation, and one might expect courts to be integrated into the field's work. Indeed, a good deal of public policy scholarship does take the courts into account, sometimes in an integral way (Anderson, Brady, & Bullock, 1978; Edwards, 1980). But the public policy field as a whole gives a great deal less than proportionate attention to the courts, and frequently they are ignored altogether.

Some other fields that could include courts in their research do so to an even more limited degree than does the public policy field. The study of political participation and voting behavior is a particularly good example. Students of voting behavior seldom deal with judicial elections, though this omission stems in part from the field's national focus. Even more notably, the "modes of participation"[9] that scholars in the field study seldom include litigation (see Zemans, 1983).[10]

The avoidance of the courts by most scholars has been matched by what Theodore Becker called "a fatal attraction" which they have held for others (1970, p. 381).[11] Particularly in earlier periods, many political scientists who chose to study the courts were attracted to that area because of what seemed to be unique about the judiciary: the legal mode of reasoning in litigants' arguments and judges' decisions; the explicit addressing of normative and constitutional questions in opinions. As a result, they were predisposed to deal with the courts in terms of those characteristics rather than as political institutions analogous to legislatures and bureaucracies. Moreover, because courts operate so much in terms of the law, it seemed appropriate to retain a somewhat legalistic approach to their study even when that approach had been rejected as too limiting for other institutions.

In combination with the attitudes of political scientists outside the field, the perspectives of judicial specialists brought about an unusually severe isolation and a particularly divergent approach to the study of politics. Almost inevitably, judicial politics "developed a vocabulary and a set of methods somewhat marginal to the mainstream of political science" (Vines, 1970, p. 140). Certainly it is significant that the field could maintain a focus on constitutional law, a subject quite different from the fodder of most other fields in American politics. The general use of "public law" as a title for the field underlined its separation from other fields of study in American politics and suggested an orientation toward law rather than political science.[12]

Beginning with the work of C. Herman Pritchett in the 1940s (1941, 1948), the field began to develop in a way that brought it closer to other fields of study in American politics. The growing acceptance of what Martin Shapiro called political jurisprudence (1964, p. 15) was important, because it meant that courts increasingly were viewed as political as well as legal institutions. Meanwhile, the new focus on judicial behavior brought to the field's core a subject matter that was similar to the subjects of some other fields in American politics and brought in research methods of the type that were gaining favor in the discipline as a whole. These two developments were at their strongest in the 1960s, and by late in the decade Joel Grossman and Joseph Tanenhaus could report that the field "is now fast returning to the fold" (1969, p. 3).

In some important respects the integration process has continued. For instance, students of judicial politics increasingly have adopted perspectives and methods that are similar to those used in other fields of American politics. But in other respects the process of integration into the broader American politics field has slowed or even reversed. The three trends discussed in the preceding section represent both causes and consequences of the field's limited integration; it will be useful to take a second look at these trends from that perspective.

The growing diversity of research in the field represents a basically healthy process: the breaking down of past limits on the scope of judicial research.[13] But the sources of this diversity are noteworthy, because they suggest the continuing isolation of the field. Research on new topics has come overwhelmingly from specialists in judicial politics, not from specialists in other fields for which particular judicial processes are relevant.[14] Public policy specialists have not been responsible for research on agenda-setting in the courts. Students of state politics have not analyzed the impact of state court doctrines. When the litigation explosion helped to publicize "ordinary" (i.e., non-political) litigation as a concern, it was not students of political participation who responded.

At least one aspect of the expansion in research concerns may have increased the field's isolation from other fields in American politics. The long-standing focus of the judicial politics field on Supreme Court decisions and decision-making had the advantage that this was an area with which many scholars outside the field had some familiarity. The growing interest in courts below the Supreme Court has moved research to sectors of the judiciary with which other political scientists generally are less comfortable. For many students of American politics, for instance, the mysteries of the federal court system are exceeded only by the mysteries of the state court systems.

The resurgence of interest in policy outputs and normative issues does not distinguish judicial politics sharply from other fields of political science. After all, outputs are a focus of study in public policy analysis, probably the field of greatest growth since the late 1960s. The policy field also shares with judicial politics a concern with normative questions. And the political philosophy field, for which that concern is central, continues to thrive.

But this resurgence has represented a turning away from the subject matter and methods that are most compatible with other institutional fields of study in American politics. Systematic analysis of the decision-making process fits fairly well into the concerns of other fields. Debates over judicial capacity, relevant as they ought to be to students of government institutions, do not fit so easily into those concerns. Of course, this is the case even more with the study of constitutional law. Thus the field has in effect re-emphasized some traditional themes at the cost of reducing the potential for full integration into other institutional fields.

Why has judicial politics taken directions that move it away from scholars and scholarship in other fields of political science? Part of the answer lies in the third trend, the development of new links with other disciplines. That trend in itself represents an important reversal of the integration process. While it hardly is unusual for a political science field to build close ties with counterpart fields in other disciplines, it is striking that the judicial politics field did so at a time when its commentators were calling for integration into the discipline of political science.

The trend toward interdisciplinary cooperation also helps to explain the other trends mentioned above. For instance, interdisciplinary links brought new ideas into the judicial politics field. As I have noted, trial court research in political science owes a great deal to the groundwork of other disciplines. A similar debt exists for some new forms of normative and output-centered research, which have been spurred by the practical concerns of the legal community.

Other disciplines and interdisciplinary forums also have provided a receptive audience for newer forms of research. The role of interdisciplinary journals has been particularly important. In the 1970s and early 1980s political science journals reflected little of the expansion of the judicial politics field, concentrating instead on areas of traditional interest and those relatively close to the mainstream of American political research. But journals such as *Law & Society Review* provided a ready forum for other kinds of work.[15] This pattern of publication has had an interesting and rather important effect: political scientists are increasingly likely to be unaware of the state of the judicial politics field on the basis of their reading of the discipline's own journals.

Another part of the explanation for the field's unexpected directions lies in the continuing hold of long-standing traditions. The strength of new interdisciplinary ties in the last two decades reflects the habit of looking to relevant scholars in other disciplines as a reference group. If the membership of that reference group has changed a good deal, its importance has not. The resurgence of concern with normative issues may well reflect the early identification of the judicial politics field with such issues as they grew out of court decisions.[16] The maintenance of interest in constitutional law, in some ways the most surprising feature of the field today, can be understood in part as a product of its institutionalization in the field—not least of all in the teaching done by scholars in the field.

Tradition also affects the place of judicial politics in the discipline as a whole. Scholars in other fields exclude the courts from their concerns in part because their fields' interest long ago became defined in that way. Judicial politics is treated as a "special" field separate from the rest of American politics largely because it developed an image as special decades ago. Those ways of thinking will not break down easily, no matter how the field itself changes.[17] For that reason, if for no others, judicial politics may be fated to remain a distinctive field.

ASSESSING THE STATE OF KNOWLEDGE

Thus far I have left aside the task of examining what the judicial politics field has accomplished. In this section I offer a limited assessment of the field's progress. I do so with some hesitation. Assessment of judicial politics scholarship as a whole is particularly difficult because of its great diversity of subject matter and interests; the field's literature cannot be treated as a single integrated body of work, and any generalization about it demands numerous exceptions. Still, even a limited and tentative assessment may be useful as another way of charting the field's current position.

My concern will be the state of knowledge about judicial politics: how much we know and how well we know it.[18] The answers to these questions, of course, depend in part on what one thinks it is important to know. Theoretically-minded scholars and those with practical goals such as system reform might evaluate the field quite differently. My own assessment will focus on three types of knowledge: our ability to describe the processes of judicial politics; our accomplishments in developing explanations for those processes; and our contribution to a general understanding of political processes.

The line between description and explanation, of course, is a thin one— particularly as applied to works of scholarship. It is possible, however, to distinguish between our knowledge about "what happens" in the judicial process and our knowledge about the basis for what happens. That distinction is useful in assessing where we stand.

Description. The description of political processes is not the most glamorous task of scholarship. But its importance as a basis for explanation and evaluation, as well as for teaching, is obvious. In the judicial politics field the task of description has remained relevant; in some other fields the accurate description of basic processes was largely accomplished years ago, but that is not true of judicial politics. As of the late 1960s scholars knew little about a great deal that went on in the courts. The political science literature provided a clear picture of only a small segment of judicial politics, primarily processes involving the Supreme Court.

For this reason the continued vein of descriptive scholarship in the field seems not only justifiable but necessary. Certainly research over the past fifteen years by political scientists and other scholars has expanded fundamentally what we know about judicial processes. The most dramatic expansion has concerned criminal courts, for whose processes we have advanced from a position of substantial ignorance to one of extensive knowledge. Our knowledge about other subjects such as the selection of judges and civil litigation also has grown a good deal.

Yet even today our descriptive understanding of judicial politics is far from complete. Any scholar who teaches about the courts could produce a list of important subjects on which our ignorance remains considerable. There is hardly any subject that has not been studied at all, but frequently research is so thin that it would be risky to generalize from existing findings. For instance, although there has been significant research on the "Missouri plan" for judicial selection,[19] one still would need to be quite tentative in reporting to a state legislature on how the system works in practice.

The thinness in our descriptive knowledge may be largely a legacy of the past. The formalism and resistance to empirical analysis that typified study of the courts for a long time meant that there was a relatively limited base of descriptive scholarship in some areas. For instance, serious study of plea bargaining was delayed by the assumption that cases followed formal procedures and by an absence of appellate decisions which belied that assumption (see Mayer, 1967, p. 90).

The existence of artificial boundaries to the judicial politics field in the past also had a major effect in limiting descriptive research. By focusing on Supreme Court decisions and decision-making, political scientists ensured that they would build knowledge about only a small part of judicial politics. When the boundaries fell, there was a broad expanse of new territory to cover. It has helped that scholars in other disciplines have been engaged in substantial judicial research, especially on trial courts.[20] But it has not helped that political scientists who specialize in other fields tend to avoid the courts, leaving an unusually broad domain for judicial politics specialists to cover.[21] A decade ago, Martin Shapiro warned that with certain expansions of the field "we may have a package that is just too big to handle" (1972, p. 417). With the expansions that have occurred the package certainly has become difficult to handle, and one result is that the job of describing important judicial processes is far from completed.

Explanation of Judicial Processes. The breadth of the judicial politics field is reflected in its efforts at explanation as well as in its descriptive work. Judicial politics is not a field with a single dominant dependent variable. For the past two decades the explanation of judges' decisions has stood out as a major concern of the field, but significant attention has been given to a diverse group of other issues. Inevitably, progress has varied from area to area. To provide some sense of the general picture, it will be useful to examine two rather different examples of efforts at explanation.

The first falls in the area of judicial impact research (see Canon, 1982). In this area, the primary dependent variable has been the extent to which judges and administrators implement higher-court decisions faithfully. Early research was devoted chiefly to description of this variable, in part because of the interest in documenting the existence of non-compliance with Supreme Court rulings. Explanations for findings often were offered and sometimes were insightful, but research seldom was designed with explanation as a primary concern.

Although the volume of research on the implementation process has slowed, more recent research has given a higher priority to explanation. Empirical studies increasingly undertake systematic testing of hypotheses (Tarr, 1977; Bond & Johnson, 1982). Scholars also have offered some impressive theoretical formulations (Brown & Stover, 1977; Johnson, 1979). Fragments of an explanation for implementors' behavior have developed, emphasizing policy preferences and institutional interests as sources of responses to judicial policies.

But we still cannot make very confident judgments about the forces that shape the implementation process. There is no firm consensus on what these forces are, and there is little basis for conclusions about the relative importance of those that scholars have discussed. To take one example, the evidence on reversal as a sanction producing obedience by lower-court judges remains almost entirely colloquial.

This picture is fairly typical of most phenomena that scholars in the field have sought to explain. Efforts at explanation have become more concerted and more systematic, and progress has been made in explaining what happens. But explanations generally remain fragmentary and imprecise. We certainly can say something meaningful about the basis for voters' decisions in judicial elections or about the circumstances under which political litigation succeeds, but what we can say does not add up to anything like a well-founded and coherent explanation.

A few areas of judicial research stand out because they have produced more extensive and focused efforts at explanation. The research on the causes of plea bargaining is one example, and research on decisions to litigate is at least in the process of becoming another. In these areas, the work of political scientists has been pooled with that of other scholars. As noted already, the explanation of judicial decisions has received particularly long and concerted attention specifically from political scientists, so it provides a useful second example of efforts at explanation.[22]

The literature on decision-making has produced a large quantity of empirical findings on a broad range of factors that may influence decisions. These findings often are solidly based, in part because of the cumulative character of much of this research; unlike some other areas of judicial research, later studies frequently have challenged and improved upon their earlier counterparts. Decision-making research has provided a good deal of information about several aspects of the decision process: alignments among appellate judges, especially on the Supreme Court (see Rohde & Spaeth, 1976); group processes on federal appellate courts (see Brenner, 1980; Atkins, 1973); the relationship between sentencing decisions and an array of independent variables in several jurisdictions (see Eisenstein & Jacob, 1977); the role conceptions of judges in a variety of courts (see Howard, 1981); and the relationship between background characteristics and decisions, particularly in appellate courts (see Tate, 1981). Associated with these empirical inquiries has been a body of theoretical formulations, particularly on the relationship between judges' policy attitudes and their decisions (Schubert, 1974; Rohde & Spaeth, 1976). Through this research we have gained considerable insight into the forces that shape judicial decisions.

Yet this body of research has not given us a very precise sense of what influences decisions how much under what circumstances. On every significant issue our understanding remains quite tentative and uncertain. The most central question has been about the impact of judges' preferences concerning public policy on their decisional choices. Research taking a range of approaches has established that this impact is considerable. But it is not clear just how much judges' policy preferences explain, in what ways their impact is modified by other factors, and whether their influence varies among courts or types of cases. Our certainty is no greater on other issues in this area. Explanation of judicial decisions has proceeded much further than explanation of most other judicial phenomena, but there still is a long way to go.

The limited progress of the judicial politics field in explanation must be measured against a realistic standard. Conclusive explanations of political behavior have proved to be quite elusive under the most favorable circumstances. For instance, the study of voting behavior has benefited from having primarily a single and relatively simple behavior to explain, from the ready availability of very extensive data, and from the efforts of a fairly large group of scholars. Yet fundamental uncertainties remain (see Niemi & Weisberg, 1976). Undoubtedly, most of the gap between what we would like to know about explanation of judicial phenomena and what we actually know stems from universal problems in social research rather than from characteristics of a particular field.[23]

But some special characteristics of this field do retard the development of explanation. The breadth of the field means that in most areas relatively few scholars are doing research, and the continuing need for description draws the attention of some of those scholars. As a result, the efforts devoted to explanation of particular phenomena tend to be relatively limited. Even in the study of judicial decision-making, which benefits from the largest concentration of scholars in the field, the array of decision types and courts to be studied has stretched scholarly resources a bit thin.

These problems have secondary effects as well. The gaps in our descriptive knowledge of some processes—such as implementation of decisions—complicate the task of theory-building. Further, when efforts at explanation are few in number they are likely to be scattered rather than cumulative, and this has been the general pattern in most areas of judicial research. One result is that flaws in research may not be challenged and corrected.

Another major weakness of most efforts to explain judicial phenomena is the narrowness of their research focus in terms of both what is to be explained and the factors used to explain it. This weakness may result in part from the limited base of knowledge about many judicial phenomena, in that the uncertainties that exist about a phenomenon may seem to demand a narrow focus for explanatory work. But the base of knowledge on decision-making is relatively solid, and here too the focus tends to be narrow; most research deals with single determinants of decisions in isolation from others (but see Howard, 1981; Gibson, 1978a; Cook, 1977) and with particular types of decisions in particular courts rather than with multiple decisional contexts (but see Ulmer, 1972). This pattern is puzzling as well as frustrating.

Perhaps the goal of working toward general explanations has never taken hold in the field. The strong normative interests of the judicial politics field do reflect an alternative set of goals. The anti-legalistic theme that motivated early research in so many areas may have helped to establish a pattern of narrow inquiries for illustrative purposes. In any case, the limited willingness of judicial specialists to work explicitly toward general explanations for judicial phenomena has aggravated other problems in explaining those phenomena.

In examining the limitations of what judicial research has explained it is easy to lose sight of what has been accomplished. Research in the last fifteen years has added impressively to our ability to explain judicial processes just as it has added to our descriptions of those processes. But we still have a long way to go.

Understanding Political Processes. One goal of political science research is to understand political processes as unitary phenomena. We seek to comprehend such processes as decision-making, recruitment of public officials, and political participation in broad terms, with the institutions and settings in which they occur serving as sources of variation and not as boundaries on analysis (see Gibson, 1978a, pp. 1-5). One criterion with which to measure what we have learned about politics is its contribution to that goal.

Research on judicial politics makes a particular contribution as a body of work. Because of special characteristics of the courts, many processes take unusual forms in the judicial branch. For this reason one gains a much fuller sense of the variation in processes and the sources of variation by taking the courts into account. The burgeoning of judicial research in recent years has provided a wealth of new raw materials with which to build a general understanding of politics.

This contribution of judicial research is enhanced when the processes that it studies are linked explicitly with their counterparts outside the courts. Studies of judges' role orientations do more to build general knowledge when they draw from research on other policy-makers' roles and put their findings in the context of what we know about legislators and administrators. Not so incidentally, establishing that kind of linkage strengthens judicial research in itself. Thus it is a positive sign that many students of the courts have taken this approach, and unfortunate that a great deal of judicial research continues to isolate itself from the non-judicial literature.[24]

Of course, the most direct means to build a general understanding of political processes is through research that compares processes in different institutional contexts. Where such research might compare the courts with other branches, however, it is discouraged by the gulf that separates the study of the courts from the rest of the discipline. Scholars who specialize in other fields might be expected to do little comparative research involving the courts, and indeed that has been the case (but see McMurray & Parsons, 1965).

Thus, the burden for such research falls primarily on students of judicial politics. Adding such a burden to the already long agenda of the field may seem unreasonable, particularly since scholars in the field have shown little taste for cross-institutional research even within the judiciary. It is notable, for instance, how little research compares federal and state courts (but see Canon, 1977; Grunbaum & Wenner, 1980; Haas, 1982). But, because the interest of judicial scholars in the rest of the political system tends to be stronger than the interest of other political scientists in the courts, most comparative research will have to come from that direction.

A small body of work by specialists in judicial politics that compares courts with other institutions does exist. Some of this work reports comparative empirical research, while some unifies what is known from the empirical studies of individual institutions.

A large share of this work concerns the process of making policy. Two studies have followed individuals from the legislature to the judicial branch and compared the factors that influence their behavior in the two contexts: David Danelski's study of Harold Burton in Congress and the Supreme Court (1970); and James Gibson's survey of California judges who had served as legislators (1978a). In more general examinations of the policy-making process Martin Shapiro sought to identify similarities and differences between courts and administrative agencies (1965; 1968, ch. 1), and J. Woodford

Howard compared legislative and judicial behavior in several aspects (1969). Particularly striking in Shapiro's analysis was his demonstration of a close connection between the courts' adherence to precedent and incrementalism as a general style of decision-making (see also Braybrooke & Lindblom, 1963, pp. 106-107).

Much of the research on the role of the courts as policy-makers has had a comparative element, particularly when the interaction of courts with other branches is part of the concern (Dahl, 1958; Casper, 1976; Henschen, 1983). A few studies have been particularly direct and explicit in comparing courts' roles with those of other institutions. Two empirical studies have focused on specific issues: the agendas of state senates and supreme courts (Rainey, 1975). Another study synthesized past research to compare the ability of legis-Health, Education, and Welfare in obtaining school desegregation (Giles, 1975). Another study synthesized past reseach to compare the ability of legislators and appellate courts to control the implementation of their policies (Baum, 1982). Thomas Dienes compared legislative and judicial roles more broadly in the context of a study of birth control policy (1972).

The recent interest in the capacities of courts as policy-makers already has led to some comparative examinations of capacity. In his book on judicial capacities Donald Horowitz made a brief comparative inquiry into the capacities of courts and other institutions (1977, pp. 293-298). Some commentators on Horowitz also have taken a comparative approach. In one noteworthy study Cheryl Reedy systematically compared Supreme Court and Congressional capacities in abortion policy, concluding that the Court did not display a more limited capacity to perform competently than did Congress (1982).

This body of cross-institutional research is valuable for the data and insights that it provides, but it does not add up to more than a beginning. As yet, specialists in judicial politics have shown rather limited interest in this kind of comparison. If students of the courts can increase their collective commitment to comparison, they will make a major contribution to our understanding of political processes. They also may reduce the gap between the field of judicial politics and other fields that study aspects of American politics.

CONCLUSIONS

In examining the judicial politics field I have emphasized its distinctiveness. As I have seen it, attitudes toward the courts separated judicial politics from other fields in American politics and took it in its own directions. In turn, the distinctive character that the field developed has shaped its recent history and its progress in description and explanation.

Some scholars who viewed the field two decades ago had a simple recommendation: integrate judicial politics more fully into the discipline. That recommendation has been followed to a degree, particularly in the methods of empirical research used in the field. But the integration has been incomplete and in some respects non-existent. In part this has been the result of the continuing hold of long-standing traditions in the field. But even if these traditions were overcome the integration would remain incomplete so long as the established attitudes of other political scientists toward the courts continued to exist.

It is easy to assume that the field's distinctive traits are unfortunate, particularly in light of its slow progress in amassing knowledge about the courts. But only a portion of that slowness can be explained by characteristics of the field, and some of those characteristics have to do with the size of the task it has undertaken rather than with its ways of seeking knowledge. Moreover, whatever its failings may be, the field has contributed heavily to an extraordinary growth in our understanding of judicial processes over the past fifteen years.

Furthermore, much of what makes the judicial politics field distinctive can be viewed positively rather than negatively. The development of strong interdisciplinary ties has strengthened the field's ability to build an understanding of the courts. The focus on outputs has enhanced the relevance of the field's scholarship for policy-makers. Thus, the defensiveness that may be detected in some of the field's self-analyses seems misplaced; different is not necessarily worse.

It is customary in this kind of essay to make recommendations for future work in the field, even if the impact of such recommendations is likely to be nil. My preferences for the field probably are clear by now, but I will recapitulate them briefly. Specialists in judicial politics, I think, do not need to be self-conscious about the field's place in the discipline—in part because that is something largely beyond the field's control. Researchers do, however, need to be more self-conscious about their work and how it is building toward a general understanding of courts and of politics. Given our limited scholarly resources, we ought to use them as effectively as possible.

But this does not mean that the domain of the judicial politics field should be narrowed, even though our resources have been spread thin. Ultimately we need to understand the courts in all their aspects, and a diverse field is more likely to advance toward that objective than one that is artificially narrow in its subject matter and perspectives. Moreover, the very diversity of the field helps to keep it interesting and attractive to scholars. Pritchett's advice about proliferating flowers remains appropriate, so long as we think about what kind of arrangement they make.

NOTES

1. Many specialists in judicial politics would include one or more of these concerns within the field as they define it.
2. In the foreign and comparative literature perhaps the outstanding contribution has been made by Martin Shapiro (1981). Other important works by political scientists include Ehrmann's analysis of legal cultures (1976) and the text on comparative constitutional law by Murphy and Tanenhaus (1977). Scholars in other disciplines have made a more extensive body of contributions to this work; a sampling may be found in the *Law & Society Review* over the years. The failure of the comparative literature to grow more rapidly reflects the limited scope of both the judicial politics and comparative politics fields in political science.

3. Past surveys of the field that were especially helpful include Vines (1970), Shapiro (1972), Grossman and Tanenhaus (1969), Pritchett (1968), Schubert (1972), and Murphy and Tanenhaus (1972). A new set of broad and narrow surveys appeared in 1982 through the organizing efforts of Harry Stumpf for the meetings of the Western Political Science Association and by Beverly Cook for the meetings of the American Political Science Association. See Stumpf *et al.* (1983), Provine (1982), Jacob (1982), Carter (1982), and Canon (1982).

4. I used a twenty-year period to provide a baseline for the identification of changes in the past fifteen years. The political science journals that I analyzed were *APSR, AJPS, JOP, WPQ, APQ,* and *Polity.* Of these, I gave primary attention to the first four. The law and social science journals were *Law & Society Review, Law & Policy Quarterly,* and *Judicature.* For these journals I restricted my survey to articles written by political scientists. In my analysis I borrowed ideas and some data from a survey by Thomas Hensley (1981). Missing from this survey were the "conventional" law journals, which continue to publish work by political scientists. Their exclusion probably produced an underestimate of the field's current interest in issues related to constitutional law, although those issues were found to maintain a considerable presence in the political science journals.

5. Research on the selection of judges, another long-standing interest, has taken a somewhat different and rather interesting path. It long has been understood that the selection process is "political," so in that respect there were no legalistic assumptions to challenge. But the legal community has developed a conventional wisdom that one mode of judicial selection, based on commission screening of potential nominees, elevates merit over politics. Some research since the late 1960s has aimed at testing or questioning this wisdom (Watson & Downing, 1969; Slotnick, 1982). Other political scientists have sought to demonstrate the virtues of the elective method that the legal community distrusts (Dubois, 1980). So long as the current debate over selection methods continues, it will provide a focus for research on selection processes, and something of an anti-legalistic theme probably will continue.

6. By political litigation I mean litigation brought and fought largely to further group purposes or to achieve policy goals rather than to win individual victories.

7. One good example is the work by political scientists on the "merit selection" of judges, which has questioned the view of the organized bar as to the desirability of that system. See note 5 above.

8. It does appear that political scientists are more likely to put court processes into broader political contexts by such means as linking trial court activity to local political cultures (Ryan, 1980-81; Levin, 1977). Within areas of interdisciplinary research there also are some specific foci whose study is dominated by political scientists, such as research on the relationship between plea bargaining and sentencing, and these may reflect differences in interests and perspectives that I have not identified.

9. The term is from Verba and Nie (1972), which is a striking example of a broad political participation study that does not deal with litigation.

10. It may be that the attitudes of political scientists toward the courts are reflected in their attitudes toward the field that studies them. The respondents to the survey by Somit and Tanenhaus in the early 1960s gave very low rankings to "public law" for the significance of its work (1964, p. 56). The survey was replicated in the mid-1970s; in that survey political scientists responded to all the changes that had occurred over the previous decade by dropping public law into last place among seven fields (Roettger, 1978, p. 22). These results may be interpreted in a variety of ways. But they probably stem in part from scholars' reaction to a field with which they are largely unfamiliar because of its alien subject matter.

11. Becker was referring to "the law," but I think that his observation applies to the courts as legal institutions.

12. Yet during the 1920s and 1930s there were several students of the courts, political scientists among them, whose interests and methods were remarkably "modern" (see Vines, 1970, pp. 127-129). That their work was isolated rather than a model for the field as a whole may indicate the power of the prevailing perspectives on the courts at that time.

13. The question as to why this process occurred is an interesting one. As I suggest later in this section, the field's interdisciplinary ties helped to expand its concerns. Also important was the popularity of systems analysis, which demanded a broad view of the judicial process and which called attention to areas in which little research had been done (see Goldman and Jahnige, 1971).

14. This dichotomization of scholars becomes problematical when applied to younger scholars, who may have begun to study judicial processes such as plea bargaining on the basis of broader conceptual interests but who nonetheless became identified as judicial specialists as a result. Yet it is significant that this labelling occurs, because it reflects the relegation of everything involving the courts to a single field.

15. These generalizations are based on the analysis of journals that is discussed in note 4. In political science journals from 1970 through 1981, a majority of articles dealt primarily with the Supreme Court, while fewer than 20 percent dealt with trial courts. The most popular subjects were judicial decision-making and judicial impact on other policy-makers—two topics relatively close to the mainstream—and the traditional subject of constitutional law. Meanwhile, political scientists' work in the interdisciplinary journals reflected the newer interests rather clearly, especially the interest in trial courts.

    It may be that the lack of change in the political science journals reflects the preferences of editors less than it does authors' assumptions about those preferences. The editors of the *American Journal of Political Science* provided me with the titles of judicial politics manuscripts submitted in 1979-81, and their subject matter differed little from that of articles published by *AJPS*. Moreover, most reviewers of judicial politics manuscripts are themselves specialists in the field. Thus there is little basis for concluding that the limited coverage of new areas in the discipline's journals reflects only the unwillingness of other political scientists to accept work in those areas. But I do suspect that it would have been difficult to obtain publication of articles in those areas in large numbers without the development of a new set of journals.

16. It also may be that it is difficult to study the judiciary meaningfully without attention to normative issues because such issues arise so clearly and explicitly in the work of the courts.

17. It is worth noting that in 1982 one questionnaire of the American Political Science Association to its members continued to list "American government and politics" and "public law" as separate fields, and the APSA adopted the same format for its placement newsletter in 1982. In both instances only public administration and (if defined as part of American politics) public policy received the same treatment. Not only the separate listing of the field but the continued use of a title that emphasizes the field's distinctiveness and that has lost popularity within the field (see Shapiro, 1972) is striking.

18. These questions exclude from a consideration an assessment of scholarship that is primarily normative in its goals. This exclusion seemed necessary to allow a more focused discussion, and it does not reflect a judgment that normative work is unimportant.

19. This research includes an extensive case study in Missouri (Watson and Downing,

1969) and multi-state studies of commission members (Ashman & Alfini, 1974) and retention elections (Jenkins, 1977; Carbon, 1980).

20. Other disciplines would have been even more helpful if resistance to empirical analysis had not survived in much of the work of legal scholars. For instance, articles on selection of judges are a staple of law reviews, but relatively few of these articles inquire systematically into the actual selection process.

21. The breadth of this domain merits some emphasis. Since all processes involving the courts basically are left to specialists in judicial politics, those specialists must cover more than counterpart groups in other institutional fields. For instance, the implementation and impact of statutes is not defined as part of the legislative politics field, but the implementation and impact of court decisions by default became part of the judicial politics field.

22. My thinking about this question has benefited a great deal from the analysis of the judicial behavior literature by James Gibson (1983).

23. One other comparison may be useful. The scholarly resources devoted to the explanation of organizational behavior have been enormous, but a recent critique of theory development and testing in that area concluded that "the field is not very far along" (Mohr, 1982, p. 1).

24. My survey of judicial politics articles by political scientists in the *American Political Science Review* and *Law & Society Review* over the last decade indicated that citations of non-judicial political science articles were relatively sparse, even ranking behind citations of judicial literature from other disciplines. This pattern probably is not unusual for a field, but it symbolizes a somewhat limited use of what has been learned in other fields. Judicial impact research, for instance, has drawn surprisingly little from the literature on policy implementation.

   A significant portion of judicial research, however, has utilized theoretical frameworks that also are employed to study non-judicial processes. Most prominent are organization theory, used most often in criminal court research (Nardulli, 1979), and role theory, used chiefly in the study of judicial decision-making (Howard, 1981). Use of these frameworks sometimes represents an explicit effort to link judicial and non-judicial research, and it facilitates integration of findings about different institutions.

REFERENCES

Adamany, David. Legitimacy, realigning elections, and the Supreme Court. *Wisconsin Law Review*, 1973, 790-846.

Anderson, James E., Brady, David W. & Bullock, Charles, III. *Public policy and politics in America.* North Scituate, MA: Duxbury, 1978.

Ashman, Allan & Alfini, James J. *The key to judicial merit selection: the nominating process.* Chicago: American Judicature Society, 1974.

Atkins, Burton M. Judicial behavior and tendencies toward conformity in a three-member small group: a case study of dissent behavior on the U.S. Courts of Appeals. *Social Science Quarterly*, 1973, *54*, 41-53.

Baer, Judith A. Sexual equality and the Burger Court. *Western Political Quarterly*, 1978, 31, 470-491.

Balbus, Isaac D. *The dialectics of legal repression: Black rebels before the American criminal courts.* New York: Russell Sage, 1973.

Baum, Lawrence. Policy goals in judicial gatekeeping: a proximity model if discretionary jurisdiction. *American Journal of Political Science*, 1977, *21*, 13-35.

Baum, Lawrence. The influence of legislatures and appellate courts over the policy implementation process. In James E. Anderson (Ed.), *Cases in public policymaking* (2nd ed.), pp. 178-192. New York: Holt, Rinehart and Winston, 1982.

Becker, Theodore L. *Comparative judicial politics: The political functioning of courts.* Chicago: Rand McNally, 1970.

Binion, Gayle. The disadvantaged before the Burger Court: The newest unequal protection. *Law & Policy Quarterly,* 1982, *4,* 37-69.

Blumberg, Abraham S. *Criminal justice.* Chicago: Quadrangle Books, 1967.

Bond, Jon R. & Johnson, Charles A. Implementing a permissive policy: Hospital abortion services after *Roe v. Wade. American Journal of Political Science,* 1982, *26,* 1-24.

Braybrooke, David & Lindblom, Charles E. *A strategy of decision.* New York: Free Press, 1963.

Brenner, Saul. Fluidity on the United States Supreme Court: A re-examination. *American Journal of Political Science,* 1980, *24,* 526-35.

Brereton, David & Casper, Jonathan D. Does it pay to plead guilty? Differential sentencing and the functioning of criminal courts. *Law & Society Review,* 1981-82, *16,* 45-70.

Brigham, John. *Constitutional language: An interpretation of judicial decision.* Westport, CT: Greenwood, 1978.

Brown, Don W. & Stover, Robert V. Court directives and compliance: A utility approach. *American Politics Quarterly,* 1977, *5,* 465-480.

Canon, Bradley C. Reactions of state supreme courts to a U.S. Supreme Court civil liberties decision. *Law & Society Review,* 1973, *8,* 109-134.

Canon, Bradley C. Testing the effectiveness of civil liberties policies at the state and federal levels: The case of the exclusionary rule. *American Politics Quarterly,* 1977, *5,* 57-82.

Canon, Bradley C. Studying the impact of judicial decisions: A period of stagnation and prospects for the future. Paper delivered at meeting of American Political Science Association, Denver, CO, 1982.

Canon, Bradley C. and Dean Jaros. The impact of changes in judicial doctrine: The abrogation of charitable immunity. *Law & Society Review,* 1979, *13,* 969-986.

Carbon, Susan B. Judicial retention elections: Are they serving their intended purpose? *Judicature,* 1980, *64,* 210-233.

Carter, Lief H. Models of public law scholarship and their payoffs. Paper delivered at meeting of American Political Science Association, Denver, CO, 1982.

Casper, Jonathan D. The Supreme Court and national policy making. *American Political Science Review,* 1976, *70,* 50-63.

Cavanagh, Ralph and Austin Sarat. Thinking about courts: Toward and beyond a jurisprudence of judicial competence. *Law & Society Review,* 1980, *14,* 371-420.

Cook, Beverly B. Public opinion and federal judicial policy. *American Journal of Political Science,* 1977, *21,* 567-600.

Costantini, Edmond and Joel King. The partial juror: Correlates and causes of prejudgment. *Law & Society Review,* 1980-81, *15,* 9-40.

Croyle, James L. The impact of judge-made policies: An analysis of research strategies and an application to products liability doctrine. *Law & Society Review,* 1979, *13,* 949-967.

Dahl, Robert A. Decision-making in a democracy: The Supreme Court as a national policy-maker. *Journal of Public Law,* 1958, 6, 279-295.

Danelski, David. Legislative and judicial decision-making: The case of Harold H. Burton. In S. Sidney Ulmer (Ed.), *Political decision-making,* pp. 121-146. New York: Van Nostrand Reinhold, 1970.

Daniels, Stephen. Civil litigation in Illinois trial courts: an exploration of rural-urban differences. *Law & Policy Quarterly,* 1982, *4,* 190-214.

Dienes, C. Thomas. *Law, politics, and birth control.* Urbana: University of Illinois Press, 1972.

Dubois, Philip. *From ballot to bench: Judicial elections and the quest for accountability.* Austin: University of Texas Press, 1980.

Dubois, Philip. *The analysis of judicial reform.* Lexington, MA: Lexington Books, 1982.

Edwards, George C., III. *Implementing public policy.* Washington, D.C.: Congressional Quarterly, 1980.

Ehrmann, Henry W. *Comparative legal cultures.* Englewood Cliffs, N.J.: Prentice-Hall, 1976.

Eisenstein, James & Jacob, Herbert. *Felony justice: An organizational analysis of criminal courts.* Boston: Little, Brown, 1977.

Feeley, Malcolm M. *The process is the punishment: Handling cases in a lower criminal court.* New York: Russell Sage, 1979.

Flemming, Roy B. *Punishment before trial: An organizational perspective of felony bail processes.* New York: Longman, 1982.

Funston, Richard. The Supreme Court and critical elections. *American Political Science Review,* 1975, *69,* 795-811.

Galanter, Marc. Why the "haves" come out ahead: Speculations on the limits of legal change. *Law & Society Review,* 1974, *9,* 95-160.

Gibson, James L. Decision making across institutions: Legislators and lower court judges in California. Paper delivered at meeting of Midwest Political Science Association. Chicago, IL, 1978(a).

Gibson, James L. Judges' role orientations, attitudes, and decisions: An interactive model. *American Political Science Review,* 1978(b), *72,* 911-924.

Gibson, James L. Environmental constraints on the behavior of judges: A representational model of judicial decision making. *Law & Society Review,* 1980, *14,* 343-370.

Gibson, James L. From simplicity to complexity: The development of theory in the study of judicial behavior. *Political Behavior,* 1983, *5,* 7-49.

Giles, Michael L. H.E.W. versus the federal courts: A comparison of school desegregation enforcement. *American Politics Quarterly,* 1975, *3,* 81-90.

Goldman, Sheldon. Voting behavior on the U.S. Courts of Appeals revisited. *American Political Science Review,* 1975, *69,* 491-506.

Goldman, Sheldon. *Constitutional law and Supreme Court decision-making: Cases and essays.* New York: Harper & Row, 1982.

Goldman, Sheldon & Jahnige, Thomas P. Systems analysis and judicial systems: Potential and limitations. *Polity,* 1971, *3,* 336-357.

Goldman, Sheldon & Jahnige, Thomas P. *The federal courts as a political system* (2nd ed.). New York: Harper & Row, 1976.

Grossman, Joel B. & Tanenhaus, Joseph. Toward a renascence of public law. In Joel B. Grossman & Joseph Tanenhaus (Eds.), *Frontiers of judicial research,* pp. 3-25. New York: John Wiley and Sons, 1969.

Grossman, Joel B. & Wells, Richard S. *Constitutional law and judicial policy making* (2nd ed.). New York: John Wiley and Sons, 1980.

Grunbaum, Werner F. & Wenner, Lettie M. Comparing environmental litigation in state and federal courts. *Publius,* 1980, *10,* 129-142.

Haas, Kenneth C. The comparative study of state and federal judicial behavior revisited. *Journal of Politics,* 1982, *44,* 721-746.

Halpern, Stephen C. & Lamb, Charles M. (Eds.). *Supreme Court activism and restraint.* Lexington, Mass.: Lexington Books, 1982.

Hansen, Susan B. State implementation of Supreme Court decisions: abortion rates since *Roe v. Wade. Journal of Politics,* 1980, *42,* 372-395.

Henschen, Beth M. Congressional response to the statutory interpretations of the Supreme Court. *American Politics Quarterly,* 1983, *11,* forthcoming.

Hensley, Thomas R. Studying the studies: Political science research on judicial politics, 1961-1980. Paper delivered at meeting of Midwest Political Science Association. Cincinnati, Ohio, 1981.

Heumann, Milton. *Plea bargaining: The experiences of prosecutors, judges, and defense attorneys.* Chicago: University of Chicago Press, 1978.

Horowitz, Donald L. *The courts and social policy.* Washington, D.C.: Brookings Institution, 1977.

Howard, J. Woodford, Jr. Adjudication considered as a process of conflict resolution: A variation on separation of powers. *Journal of Public Law,* 1969, *18,* 339-370.

Howard, J. Woodford, Jr. *Courts of Appeals in the federal judicial system: A study of the Second, Fifth, and District of Columbia Circuits.* Princeton: Princeton University Press, 1981.

Jacob, Herbert. Trial courts in the United States: The travails of explanation. Paper delivered at meeting of American Political Science Association, Denver, CO, 1982.

Jenkins, William, Jr. Retention elections: Who wins when no one loses? *Judicature,* 1977, *61,* 79-86.

Johnson, Charles A. Judicial decisions and organizational change: A theory. *Administration & Society,* 1979, *11,* 27-51.

Kritzer, Herbert M. Political correlates of the behavior of federal district judges: A "best case" analysis. *Journal of Politics,* 1978, *40,* 25-58.

Kuklinski, James H. & Stanga, John E. Political participation and governmental responsiveness: The behavior of California Superior Courts. *American Political Science Review,* 1979, *73,* 1090-1099.

Levin, Martin A. Urban politics and judicial behavior. *Journal of Legal Studies,* 1972, *1,* 193-221.

Mather, Lynn & Yngvesson, Barbara. Language, audience, and the transformation of disputes. *Law & Society Review,* 1980-81, *15,* 775-821.

Mayer, Martin. *The lawyers.* New York: Harper & Row, 1967.

McIntosh, Wayne. 150 years of litigation and dispute settlement: A court tale. *Law & Society Review,* 1980-81, *15,* 823-848.

McMurray, Carl D. & Parsons, Malcolm B. Public attitudes toward the representational role of legislators and judges. *Midwest Journal of Political Science,* 1965, *9,* 167-185.

Miller, Richard E. & Sarat, Austin. Grievances, claims and disputes: Assessing the *adversary culture. Law & Society Review,* 1980-81, *15,* 525-565.

Mohr, Lawrence B. *Explaining organizational behavior: The limits and possibilities of theory and research.* San Francisco: Jossey-Bass, 1982.

Murphy, Walter F. & Tanenhaus, Joseph. *The study of public law.* New York: Random House, 1972.

Murphy, Walter F. & Tanenhaus, Joseph. *Comparative constitutional law: Cases and commentaries.* New York: St. Martin's, 1977.

Nardulli, Peter F. Organizational analyses of criminal courts: An overview and some speculation. In Peter F. Nardulli (Ed.), *The study of criminal courts: Political perspectives,* pp. 101-130. Cambridge: Ballinger, 1979.

Niemi, Richard G. & Weisberg, Herbert F. (Eds.). *Controversies in American voting behavior.* San Francisco: W.H. Freeman, 1976.

O'Connor, Karen. *Women's organizations' use of the courts.* Lexington, MA: Lexington Books, 1980.

O'Connor, Karen & Epstein, Lee. Amicus curiae participation in U.S. Supreme Court litigation: An appraisal of Hakman's "folklore." *Law & Society Review,* 1981-82, *16,* 311-320.

Olson, Susan M. The political evolution of interest group litigation. In Richard A. L. Gambitta, Marlynn L. May, & James C. Foster (Eds.), *Governing through courts,* pp. 225-258. Beverly Hills: Sage Publications, 1981.

O'Neill, Timothy J. The language of equality in a democratic order. *American Political Science Review*, 1981, *75*, 626-635.

Peltason, Jack W. *Federal courts in the political process*. New York: Random House, 1955.

Pritchett, C. Herman. Divisions of opinion among justices of the U.S. Supreme Court, 1939-1941. *American Political Science Review*, 1941, *35*, 890-898.

Pritchett, C. Herman. *The Roosevelt Court: A study of judicial votes and values, 1937-1947*. New York: Macmillan, 1948.

Pritchett, C. Herman. Public law and judicial behavior. *Journal of Politics*, 1968, *30*, 480-509.

Provine, Doris Marie. *Case selection in the United States Supreme Court*. Chicago: University of Chicago Press, 1980.

Provine, Doris Marie. Research on the judicial process, 1970-82: What have we learned? Paper delivered at meeting of American Political Science Association. Denver, CO, 1982.

Rainey, R. Lee. Dimensions of policy-making in courts and legislatures. Paper delivered at meeting of American Political Science Association. San Francisco, CA, 1975.

Reedy, Cheryl D. The Supreme Court and Congress on abortion: An analysis of comparative institutional capacity. Paper delivered at meeting of American Political Science Association. Denver, CO, 1982.

Roelofs, Joan. Judicial activism as social engineering: A Marxist interpretation of the Supreme Court. In Stephen C. Halpern & Charles M. Lamb (Eds.), *Supreme Court activism and restraint*, pp. 249-270. Lexington, MA: Lexington Books, 1982.

Roettger, Walter B. The discipline: What's right, what's wrong, and who cares? Paper delivered at meeting of American Political Science Association. New York, 1978.

Rohde, David W. & Spaeth, Harold J. *Supreme Court decision making*. San Francisco: W.H. Freeman, 1976.

Roper, Robert T. Jury size and verdict consistency: "A line has to be drawn somewhere"? *Law & Society Review*, 1980, *14*, 977-995.

Ross, H. Laurence. *Settled out of court*. Chicago: Aldine, 1970.

Ryan, John Paul. Adjudication and sentencing in a misdemeanor court: The outcome is the punishment. *Law & Society Review*, 1980-81, *15*, 79-108.

Sarat, Austin & Grossman, Joel B. Courts and conflict resolution: Problems in the mobilization of adjudication. *American Political Science Review*, 1975, *69*, 1200-1217.

Schubert, Glendon. Judicial process and behavior, 1963-1971. In James A. Robinson (Ed.), *Political Science Annual* (Vol. 3). Indianapolis: Bobbs-Merrill, 1972.

Schubert, Glendon. *The judicial mind revisited: Psychometric analysis of Supreme Court ideology*. New York: Oxford University Press, 1974.

Shapiro, Martin. *Law and politics in the Supreme Court: New approaches to political jurisprudence*. New York: Free Press, 1964.

Shapiro, Martin. Stability and change in judicial decision-making: Incrementalism or stare decisis? *Law in Transition Quarterly*, 1965, *2*, 134-157.

Shapiro, Martin. *The Supreme Court and administrative agencies*. New York: Free Press, 1968.

Shapiro, Martin. From public law to public policy, or the "public" in "public law." *PS*, 1972, *5*, 410-418.

Shapiro, Martin. *Courts: A comparative and political analysis*. Chicago: University of Chicago Press, 1981.

Slotnick, Elliot E. Judicial selection systems and nomination outcomes: Does the process make a difference? Paper delivered at meeting of Midwest Political Science Association. Milwaukee, Wis., 1982.

Somit, Albert & Tanenhaus, Joseph. *American political science: A profile of a discipline*. New York: Prentice-Hall, 1964.

Sorauf, Frank J. *The wall of separation: The constitutional politics of church and state*. Princeton: Princeton University Press, 1976.

Special Issue. Dispute processing and civil litigation. *Law & Society Review*, 1980-81, *15*, 391-920.

Spohn, Cassia, Gruhl, John & Welch, Susan. The effect of race on sentencing: A re-examination of an unsettled question. *Law & Society Review*, 1981-82, *16*, 71-88.

Stookey, John A. Assessing the substantive policy consequences of granting discretionary access control to a state court of last resort. Paper delivered at meeting of Western Political Science Association, San Francisco, CA, 1980.

Stumpf, Harry P., Shapiro, Martin, Danelski, David J., Sarat, Austin, & O'Brien, David M. Whither political jurisprudence: A symposium. *Western Political Quarterly*, 1983, *36*, forthcoming.

Sudnow, David. Normal crimes: Sociological features of the penal code in a public defender's office. *Social Problems*, 1965, *12*, 255-276.

Tarr, George Alan. *Judicial impact and state supreme courts*. Lexington, MA: Lexington Books, 1977.

Tate, C. Neal. Personal attribute models of the voting behavior of U.S. Supreme Court justices: Liberalism in civil liberties and economics decisions, 1946-1978. *American Political Science Review*, 1981, *75*, 355-367.

Uhlman, Thomas M. *Racial justice*. Lexington, MA: Lexington Books, 1979.

Uhlman, Thomas M. & Walker, N. Darlene. A plea is no bargain: The impact of case disposition on sentencing. *Social Science Quarterly*, 1979, *60*, 218-234.

Ulmer, S. Sidney. The decision to grant certiorari as an indicator to decision on the merits. *Polity*, 1972, *4*, 439-447.

Ulmer, S. Sidney. Selecting cases for Supreme Court review: An underdog model. *American Political Science Review*, 1978, *72*, 902-910.

Verba, Sidney & Nie, Norman H. *Participation in America*. New York: Harper & Row, 1972.

Villmoore, Adelaide H. State and legal authority: A context for the analysis of judicial policy-making. *Law & Policy Quarterly*, 1982, *4*, 5-36.

Vines, Kenneth N. Judicial behavior research. In Michael Haas & Henry S. Kariel (Eds.), *Approaches to the study of political science*, pp. 125-143. Scranton: Chandler Publishing, 1970.

Wanner, Craig. The public ordering of private relations, part one: Initiating civil cases in urban trial courts. *Law & Society Review*, 1974, *8*, 421-440.

Wanner, Craig. The public ordering of private relations, part two: Winning civil court cases. *Law & Society Review*, 1975, *9*, 293-306.

Wasby, Stephen L. *The impact of the United States Supreme Court: Some perspectives*. Homewood, IL: Dorsey Press, 1970.

Wasby, Stephen L. *Small town police and the Supreme Court: Hearing the word*. Lexington, MA: Lexington Books, 1976.

Wasby, Stephen L. Book review—Horowitz: *The courts and social policy*. *Vanderbilt Law Review*, 1978, *31*, 727-761.

Watson, Richard A. & Downing, Rondal G. *The politics of the bench and the bar: Judicial selection under the Missouri nonpartisan court plan*. New York: John Wiley & Sons, 1969.

Zemans, Frances Kahn. Legal mobilization: The neglected role of the law in the political system. *American Political Science Review*, 1983, *77*, forthcoming.

8

Public Policy Analysis:
Some Recent Developments and
Current Problems

Susan B. Hansen

As I began work on this paper in early 1982, I received a fund-raising letter from Walter F. Mondale's Committee for the Future of America. On page 1, the former vice-president stated,

> In our struggles to develop programs to give [our] principles life, we made some errors, went up some blind alleys. These missteps gave our cynical opponents the opportunity to challenge our purpose. But making mistakes in the public eye, for all the world to see, and then learning from these mistakes is what government and politics is all about.

One may question the wisdom of stating such a theory of politics in a request for funds; presumably his party's mistakes are to be preferred to those of his opponents. Nevertheless, these comments made me wonder: have we, as a discipline, learned from our mistakes? If so, are there areas of research to which we can point as evidence of the maturing of policy analysis as a field of study? If not, is there any hope that such promise will emerge in the near future, given our current interests and investments, the state of our theories, and our methodological tools?

Let me begin with a bit of history and some quantitative indicators concerning the growth of policy analysis (as I shall define it) within the discipline of political science. I will then consider three of the more promising theoretical trends in the discipline: the "political economy" approach, formal organizational theory, and new ways of measuring and conceptualizing policy failure. I will turn next to a discussion of some research strategies which appear to have engaged the attention of political scientists doing policy analysis. These include attempts to focus on "tractable" problems, analysis of im-

*My thanks to the following kind persons for their comments and suggestions: Douglas Ashford, Philip Coulter, Elinor Ostrom, Ray Owen, Bert Rockman, and an anonymous referee.

plementation of evaluations, studies of policy termination, and comparative, cross-systemic research on post-industrial societies. I conclude with a brief consideration of the changing role of political scientists as policy analysts and policy makers within the political process, and of what we might learn about that role from the economics profession.

Let me make clear at the outset what I mean by policy analysis. As Salisbury (1968) has so well said, there is little in the discipline of political science which does not touch on policy because of our historical concern with public life, constitutional arrangements for decision-making, and the authoritative allocation of values. In those senses, policy analysis is centuries old. But as I shall use the term, policy analysis refers to an explicit, focused, systematic analysis of the outputs of governments and their effects on society. "Process" studies of Congressional committees, public opinion, party competition, and so forth, are not considered policy analysis unless the linkage to political outputs is made explicit. My emphasis, then, will be on efforts to measure and evaluate policy outputs, to compare policies with reference to structure and impact, and to look at the connections (direct, indirect, or reciprocal) between political processes and policy outputs.

The field of policy analysis is likely to be viewed quite differently according to one's perspective. Barnes and Dubnick (1980) list the uses of policy analysis as viewed by scientists searching for truth, professionals seeking to design better policies, political advocates seeking to justify their positions, administrators trying to implement policies effectively and efficiently, and citizens using all of these approaches to buttress arguments for their own policy preferences (p. 123). One could of course suggest other perspectives— those of politicians, consulting firms, business, the economics or legal professions, universities, or the students we teach in policy courses. This assessment will be based in part on my experiences over the past year as Chair of the policy analysis section for the 1982 APSA meetings in Denver; this experience gave me both the opportunity and the responsibility to think about what was going on in the field. My concern in this essay will be with the contribution of policy analysis to the discipline of political science and to the development of theory.

THE GROWTH OF POLICY ANALYSIS, 1967-1982

First, where have we been? Let us go back 15 years,[1] to the 1967 APSA annual meeting in Chicago. At that meeting, there was one panel on public policy, listed under the section on "American Politics, Local and National." The featured paper was by Alan Altschuler of MIT entitled "The Politics of Managing a Full Employment Economy". A perusal of the program yielded three other papers with some policy content or perspective. One was a roundtable, "Does the Hatch Act Need Revision?" Two were presented at a panel entitled "Research and Teaching on Policy Issues"; Charles O. Jones of the University of Arizona discussed "The Policy Making Approach: An Essay on

Teaching American Politics," and Michael D. Reagan of the University of California at Riverside discussed "Policy Issues: The Interaction of Substance and Process." Several papers were given in international relations and legal processes which touched on policy, but these emphasized process or normative concerns rather than policy analysis as I have defined it.

A glance at annual meeting programs over the subsequent 15 years shows that policy analysis has become an increasingly important segment of political science. 1970 was the first year in which policy was given a separate panel; 33 policy papers appeared at that meeting. In subsequent years the categories varied. At some meetings policy analysis was listed with panels on public administration or on state, local, or national government. In other years, policy was considered from the perspectives of social indicators, the impact of science on society, or specific problems such as Vietnam or the anti-ballistic missile.

But throughout this time period, the number of panels and papers grew, both in absolute terms and as a proportion of all conference papers. The magnitude of that growth may be indicated by the number of papers given in 1981 and 1982. I arrived at the number simply by counting those papers that had "policy" or the name of a policy (regulation, OEO, health care, etc.) in their titles, or those that indicated in their abstracts that they offered a systematic analysis of government outputs in a substantive policy area. I also included discussions of the theory or methodology of such studies. I excluded papers on judicial process or foreign policy which appeared to stress issues of law, process, or the internal workings of bureaucracy, but included those oriented toward policy outputs and effects. These distinctions are of course highly arbitrary, but since they have been applied consistently in 1967, 1970, and 1981-82, they afford us a basis of comparison that I trust will not tread too much upon the turf of other subfields.

In 1981, I counted 86 papers on policy out of a total of 432, or 20 percent. Seventeen of these appeared to be comparative cross-nationally. A total of 29 panels were oriented toward policy (substance, theory, or methodology). In 1982, 140 papers on policy analysis were given at the Denver meeting, at 36 official panels. This constituted 31 percent of the total of 459 papers. I should also note the growth of interest in comparative (cross-national) public policy: a total of 38 papers at the Denver meeting, or 27 percent of the total number of policy papers. The first section devoted entirely to comparative public policy appeared in 1979, with six panels, although in earlier years one or more individual panels was devoted to comparative policy analysis, in addition to diverse individual papers given under other panel headings. And I have not even mentioned the many policy-related papers given under the rubric of "Courtesy Listing of Unaffiliated Groups" such as the Conference Group on Political Economy, the Caucus for a New Political Science, the Disaster Policy Group, the Women's Caucus, etc.

Policy analysis has grown by a number of other indicators as well, as a glance at figures supplied by the Policy Studies Organization on membership, journals, publications, and conference papers will show.[2] In quantitative terms, policy analysis has had a major impact on the discipline, at least as indicated by papers given at annual meetings. Let this be a warning to anyone so bold as to assume the responsibility for setting up policy panels in up-coming years: I had nearly one hundred proposals to evaluate, and suspect the number will increase in the future. I wholeheartedly agree with Aaron Wildavsky (1979) that it is "impossible to keep up."

The substance of the papers given at the 1982 APSA meetings may pro-vide some idea of the current interests of persons involved in policy analysis. By my count, about half of the policy papers were concerned primarily with substantive issues: welfare, school desegregation, tax policy, natural and man-made disasters, environmental policy, budgeting, and international agricultural policy. Several in the policy analysis section focused on new ap-proaches, such as policy design, policy failure and deimplementation, risk and uncertainty, and productivity and public policy. A few were concerned with measurement and the methodology for assessing and comparing policies. One panel on the "limits of the economic paradigm" was explicitly concerned with metatheoretical issues, although many of the substantive and methodological papers also raised questions about the models and assump-tions we use.

Both qualitatively and quantitatively the changes in the relationship between political analysis and the discipline of political science since 1967 are considerable. Whether these changes offer evidence of disciplinary progress or maturity is an issue to which I shall return.

THREE PROMISING THEORETICAL TRENDS

"Political Economy": A Macrotheoretical Approach

Let me now turn to a survey of three emerging trends in policy analysis which show promise of making major theoretical contributions to the field of political science. Fifteen years ago, political scientists interested in policy were likely to focus on substantive issues, often using case studies of policy design, execution, and effects. But the ideas of David Easton (1965) and two em-pirical studies published in 1966 dramatically changed the field. Each posed broad questions about the relationships between the economic development or capacity of a political system and its policy outputs. The first of these was Thomas R. Dye's *Politics, Economics, and the Public,* easily the most widely cited and the most frequently criticized work in the growing field of policy. The second was Gabriel Almond and G. Bingham Powell's *Comparative Politics: A Developmental Approach.* The conclusions of these books differed considerably, as did their methods, data bases, and time periods. Dye's cross-sectional analysis of the American states found little relationship between political factors and policy outputs once economic and demographic factors were considered. But Almond and Powell's historical and cross-national analysis suggested a strong relationship between political development and political capacity in several areas (extraction, regulation, distribution); in their analysis political and economic development were clearly linked.

Each of these books raised questions about the relationships among policies, and between politics and economics, that have engaged the attention of considerable numbers of researchers since. What was clear from these two seminal works, and the discussions they provoked, was that David Easton's model of the political system had empirical validity; political processes and outputs depended on their environment, international as well as national, as was shown by the increasing interest in the domestic constraints on foreign policy. But if both politics and economics were important for policy, what exactly was the magnitude of the relationship and the direction of causality? Given the current state of each academic discipline, neither economics nor political science has the tools, theoretical or methodological, to disentangle these complex and reciprocal relationships.

Roger Benjamin (1982) stated the problem well:

> It is time to reconsider basic relationships between politics and economics in the context of the breakdown of the distinction between domestic and comparative/ international politics. This breakdown is especially important with respect to relationships between post-industrial and industrial states. . . . It is necessary to attack first-order questions such as how one should *conceptualize* the boundaries between economics and politics. (p. 75) (Emphasis added.)

Since the 1960s, there have been several attempts at such new concep- tualization under the rubric of political economy. This approach to policy analysis has attracted an increasing amount of attention, as indicated by fre- quency of use of this term in books, journal articles, and conference papers. A large number of panels, many well-attended and including persons closely identified with the Policy Studies Organization, have been presented at APSA annual meetings since 1977 under the auspices of the Conference Group on Political Economy in Advanced Industrial Societies, chaired by Stephen Elkin.

But what is political economy? Unfortunately for our students—and people who attempt to write papers on the "state of the subfield"—the term has almost as many definitions as practitioners. Basically, however, all ap- proaches examine the interrelationships between the political and economic systems. One orientation—widely used by Marxist scholars but by no means limited to them—considers the impact of economic factors on political power, structure, and processes. Studies of dependency theory, multinational cor- porations, corporatism, political development, and the distribution of wealth, all build on this orientation.

In the American and Western European contexts, another focus of political economy has been on the positive role of the nation-state. Under pluralism, the state is usually seen as a neutral umpire that enforces the rules of the game; it is in itself simply the vector of organized interests in the society. A political economy approach would focus more on what Easton termed "withinputs": policy preferences and political entrepreneurship by persons within government, seeking to maintain or increase their own power and to define social needs to suit their own interests. Examples include: Frolich, Oppenheimer, and Young's (1971) theory of political leadership; Hugh Heclo's (1979) account of issue networks in the executive establishment; Niskanen (1971) on bureaucracy; and Morris Fiorina's *Congress and the Washington Establishment* (1977). All view the state as a self-perpetuating system having an independent impact on society and the economy (see also discussion by Lindblom, 1982).

A major issue for policy practitioners as well as scholars concerns the ability of governments to control the economy. Do politicians in democracies manipulate macroeconomic policy in order to further their own goals, such as reelection (Tufte, 1978; Hibbs, 1977)? Or are secular trends in productivity, population, and resource shortages so compelling that politicians can make only minor adjustments in economic policy (Benjamin, 1980)? Or is the economy so complex that efforts to manage it—whether for political purposes such as reelection, or economic goals such as growth or price stability—are likely to fail and may even make things worse (Shultz & Dam, 1977; Buchanan & Wagner, 1977)? Or can governments bring about economic growth and increased revenues by doing less: cutting taxes, reducing deficits and spending, and returning to the gold standard, as proponents of supply-side economics claim? (See Fink, 1982, for an excellent collection of essays debating supply-side economics.) One can find a considerable literature backing each point of view; aspects of the debate hinge on the data bases, methodologies, and causal models used (see Beck, 1982, and Kramer, 1983, for recent summaries, and Barry, forthcoming, for a critique).

Although macroeconomic change remains problematic, political scientists have long been interested in the capacity of parties and politicians to make marginal policy changes to benefit their supporters or particular regions or interest groups. Morehouse (1981) finds that state political factors such as party coherence and powers of the governor are linked to a range of policies benefiting the "have-nots." Welch and Karnig (1981) show that black representation has affected the level and distribution of city services. Boneparth (1982) documents areas in which women's political activity has led to policies benefiting women. Rundquist's *Political Benefits* (1978) gives some theoretical coherence to such research and includes numerous examples. The differential regional impact of Reagan's economic policies offers convincing evidence of the potential for politicians to affect the distribution of economic costs and benefits, but their failure to date to reduce unemployment suggests the limitations of political influence on the economy (Palmer & Sawhill, 1982).

Clever research design can go a long way toward delineating more precisely the boundaries of political and economic choice. In their study of state planning agency response to federal LEAA grants, Gray and Williams (1980) essentially hold state socioeconomic characteristics constant since their policy was totally funded by the federal government. They thus focus on the political and organizational dimensions of state compliance with LEAA goals. Winters and Reidenberg (1983) investigate the presence of an electoral budgetary cycle by contrasting changes in spending in constituency-oriented agencies as opposed to agencies supplying more public and indivisible goods. The former exhibit far larger election-year increases. Clearly, however, further research is needed to specify more precisely the macro- and micro-economic dimensions of political decision-making.

The whole political-economy orientation can be criticized as simply a new intellectual fad. It has been accused of being cynical rather than normative, of stressing strategy over advocacy, and of becoming so technical and abstract in its methodology that any policy payoffs are increasingly remote. My purpose here is neither to resolve such arguments nor to attempt further review of this voluminous literature. I would simply suggest that the intellectual controversy generated has been good for policy analysis (and political science) in a variety of ways. One is the increasing willingness to challenge economics and the economic paradigm, whose rational models have too often been based on highly simplified assumptions which ignore the operations of political institutions. From the standpoint of "covering law" principles, rational models are not only invalid as scientific theories (Moe, 1979, p. 240), but can do serious damage when applied to policy. Few political scientists today could read Joseph Pechman's 1975 article on economic policy-making in the *Handbook of Political Science* without some sense of embarrassment — which he may well share — over his optimism about the possibilities of economic management. Not only have political scientists begun to pay more attention to economics, but those in the field of institutional economics have even ventured to learn something about political science (Schotter, 1980; Samuels, 1979). Our historical strength in the analysis of political institutions and processes may become increasingly relevant to the debate over the future of the economics of advanced industrial societies as well as the Third World.

Another implication of the interest in political economy is a growing recognition of the interdependence of policies. Changes in one area, based on the best available knowledge and noblest of intentions, may cause serious dislocations elsewhere (for many good examples see Haveman & Margolis, 1982). As Wildavsky, Heclo, Jones (1975), and many others have argued, policies create their own problems, and much of our collective energy must be devoted to putting out fires caused by previous policy choices.

Recognition of policy interdependence has had two consequences. On the one hand, we see discussion of government "overload" (Rose & Peters, 1978), of the adverse consequences of trying to do too much with limited resources. On the other hand, we see increasingly sophisticated attempts to model such interdependence. One example is Roger Benjamin's (1982) thoughtful essay on the product cycle and the need for new theories applicable to political and economic changes which have occurred in postindustrial societies. Another is Mancur Olson's analysis of the impact of interest group power on government growth and economic decline (forthcoming). A third is Sabatier and Mazmanian's (1980) outline of a theory of implementation which considers the secondary and tertiary effects of policies in political as well as economic terms. Existing theory and methodology may indeed be insufficient to deal with the sorts of policy issues we now face, but the gap between performance and expectations has spurred the development of new approaches in politics as well as academia.

Formal Theories of Organization

A second potential area for theoretical advance is that of formal models of the operation of complex organizations. The term political economy has been applied to these as well, but in these studies the level of analysis shifts to discrete organizations rather than political systems. Theories of the behavior of bureaucracies or Congress are based on assumptions about the goals and resources of the actors involved. Studies of the political economy of regulation, for example, consider regulative policy in terms of interactions among government commissions, regulated industries, and politicians or interest groups which endeavor to represent the public interest. The policy outcome is a function of the goals and strategies of each sector as well as economic constraints such as the costs of organization, information, and factor scarcity (Mitnick, 1980). Other prominent examples include Niskanen (1971) on bureaucracy and Anthony Downs (1957) and his critics and elaborators on economic theories of democracy.

Over the past decade, a vast new literature has developed examining the consequences of systems of social choice for policy outcomes. Riker (1980) argues that "prudence in research directs the science of politics toward the investigation of empirical regularities in institutions" (p. 432). The emphasis has shifted considerably from the methodological individualism of an earlier era of behavioralism, when social outcomes were explained on the basis of choices, tastes and values of individual voters or legislators. Plott (1976) cogently sums up the results of two decades of debate: the concept of social choice involves an "illegitimate transfer of the properties of an individual to the properties of a collection of individuals" (p. 525).

Instead, in organizational theory, the emphasis is on the consequences of specific structures and decision rules (majority rule, decentralization, interorganizational communication) on policy outputs. Tastes and preferences are still important, but they are analyzed as a consequence as well as a cause of particular political structures. If preferences and outcomes diverge, of course, a system or subsystem is likely to be unstable and changes in either preferences or institutions may be attempted to bring it back into equilibrium. As Shepsle (1979) has shown, in an example particularly relevant to the U.S. Congress, a stable set of decision-making patterns can evolve from routines based on committee decentralization and rules concerning jurisdiction and amendments, even if individual motives and preferences conflict.

This is not the place to attempt a summary of this literature, nor am I qualified to do so (for an excellent overview which integrates older and newer theories of organizations see Scott, 1981). Over the past decade, however, formal organizational theory has informed many empirically-oriented policy issues. Hanf and Scharpf (1978) discuss "limits to coordination and central control" with a useful theoretical introduction and examples of intergovernmental policy-making in the U.S. and Europe. Gray and Williams (1980) use state implementation of LEAA grants to test propositions concerning the conditions of influence of federal agencies over state agencies. Ostrom *et al.* (1978) and Parks and Ostrom (1981) have considered the administrative effectiveness of alternative institutional arrangements. Pommerehne and Schneider (1983) have explored the consequences of various voting rules and institutions for representation of voters' preferences. Hansen (1983) has explored some of the structural and institutional reasons why tax policy outcomes diverge so far from taxpayers' preferences, using examples drawn from the recent "tax revolt" as well as from historical federal and state tax innovations.

Many of these studies could also be described under more traditional categories of public administration, implementation, and representation. I mention them here in the context of formal organizational theory because they all illustrate some of the best features of such theory: core assumptions are stated precisely, alternative predictions are subject to rigorous empirical testing, and cumulative modifications are made in the underlying theories. The seminal works of Anthony Downs (1957) and William Niskanen (1971) have contributed greatly to this field. Even though many of the original predictions derived from their work were later challenged, modifications and extensions of their original theories on voting, budget size, and bureaucratic behavior have led to theoretical advances.

As Ashford (1983) notes, "because the ideas of complexity and interdependence figure so heavily in systemic-level theories of the modern state, the insights provided by organizational theory are especially valuable" (p. 26) in providing operational, intermediate-level generalizations more easily subject to empirical validation than either macro- or micro-theories. Comparative policy studies, whether cross-national or across states and cities, have too often neglected policy implementation and the study of bureaucracy. Such an emphasis is crucial particularly in an era when many policies are enacted nationally but implemented locally, and when they involve interaction among many actors and organizations (Gray & Williams, 1980, p. 3). Jones' *Clean Air* (1975) provides excellent illustrations of these points although it would not be classified as formal organizational theory.

Changing Conceptions of Policy Failure

A third area of major theoretical interest involves new ways of conceptualizing and measuring policy failure. This concept has undergone considerable redefinition over the past 15 years. Ranney in his seminal 1968 article suggested that policy analysts attempt comparisons of "good" and "bad" policies — such as the Marshall Plan and the Bay of Pigs invasion — to help develop criteria for evaluating policy processes and contents. This proved to be a difficult task. Wildavsky notes on page one of *Speaking Truth to Power* the "difficulty of finding programs that work well." All of us had our intuitive notions — often based on prejudice or ideology — of program successes and failures; some, like the Bay of Pigs, were self-evident. When Alice Rivlin asked in 1971, 'How do we know what works?" the answer she implied was that we did not. Many programs, particularly Great Society social programs, were never subject to systematic evaluation according to the canons of social science. If evaluations were done, they were often *post hoc* and lacking in experimental controls. Without some baseline measurement, some agreement on what was being measured, and planning for evaluation as part of program design, indications of progress or failure could be based only on political expedience and partisan considerations.

The problem is threefold.[3] The first is that of data and measurement. At one time we may have been optimistic about the prospects for social or economic engineering, but we have by now discovered that the evidence on large and complicated issues of public policy is frequently ambiguous or missing altogether. In the 1960s these data problems seemed capable of amelioration if not of solution. Requirements and funding for evaluation studies appeared more frequently in legislation; the EPA's mandates for environmental impact statements constitute one example. Organized groups such as the Social Science Research Council urged the development of social indicators, and publication of the bicentennial *Historical Statistics of the United States* by the Census Bureau spurred the search for historical measures of social change to use as benchmarks for program evaluation. Large-scale experiments were conducted, most notably those on guaranteed incomes (Palmer & Pechman, 1978).

But masses of expensive data, though necessary, were not sufficient to solve issues of policy evaluation. Scientists need to worry about operationalization and the underlying theoretical assumptions of our design and measurement techniques. Such subtleties are not always easy to communicate to practitioners. Miller (1981) discussed the poor fit between our mathematical models and our standards of policy judgment. Measures of efficiency (particularly in economics and management science) have been developed to a far higher degree than measures of equity or responsiveness. Her work developed alternative mathematical formulations for use in evaluating educational reform. In this same vein, Smeeding (1982) and Paglin (1980) have considered different ways of measuring poverty based on alternative interpretations of in-kind transfers. Researchers at the University of Wisconsin's Institute for Research on Poverty have suggested a variety of ways to interpret statistics on trends in income equality in the U.S. (for summary and review of the literature see Taussig & Danziger, 1976). Taussig and Danziger (1976) argue that the omission of all forms of non-money income from the census and other time series "invalidates all empirical statements about trends in inequality since World War II" (p. 21).

The second problem is that of values. Standards for judging policy failure have changed considerably over the past 15 years. In the 1960s, during a period of economic prosperity and governmental growth, standards tended to be based on "demand-side" ideals of policy equity and of broad-based participation in the process of decision-making. In the 1970s, emphasis shifted to "supply-side" elements of control, efficiency, and effectiveness within budgetary constraints. In the earlier period, market failure was a sufficient reason for policy intervention. By the 1980s, judgments of the failures of many public spending and regulatory programs led to demands for a return to market methods of allocation based on competition and price mechanisms. Wildavsky (1979) suggests that we may have been "doing better and feeling worse" with respect to many policy areas; "we need to ask if present standards for judging policies are appropriate" (p. 5). If public policies are to be judged against our own overblown expectations or the promises of politicians, they may well fall short.

The private sector has been rediscovered as an alternative solution to various social and technological problems and as a benchmark against which to measure public programs. In the 1960s, since few measures of productivity were available for the public sector, productivity was not considered as a part of either policy design or implementation. Since then, however, efforts have been made to develop such measures (Ostrom, 1975; Bahl & Burkhead, 1977; Nagel, 1983; see also the new journal *Public Productivity Review*). Although ideology still weighs heavily, assessment of policy alternatives in at least some areas (notably urban politics) has become an empirical question rather than an ideological one. In her 1982 *APSA* paper, Hughes compared proprietary and non-profit provision of nursing care and found advantages and disadvantages for each. The analytical task is to formulate problems so that implicit values can be turned into explicit criteria for gauging the likely effects of alternative policies (May, 1981).

Politics is not the only alternative to a free market; a broad range of government and independent corporations and regulatory agencies must be considered. Before 1970, these received little attention outside of the literature on pressure-group politics and regulatory agency "capture." A review essay (Thomas, 1976) noted only a handful of studies by political scientists on the politics of economic regulation. Sharkansky (1979) describes what he terms an intellectual crisis in political science because of "the profession's myopic preoccupation with formal institutions of the state" and its behavioral and individualistic perspective. But this may be changing, as evidenced by his own work on public/private institutional hybrids, Lindblom's *Politics and Markets* (1977), and the rapidly growing regulation literature by political scientists as well as economists (see Mead, 1977; Mitnick, 1980; and Stone, 1982, for excellent summaries of political and economic approaches to regulation).

A revival of interest in market solutions also poses problems for evaluating policy failure. First of all, many social scientists lack much experience with businesses, and may confuse the rational, goal-directed, hierarchical textbook corporation with the real thing. In fact, large corporations face the same problems of information and control as do bureaucracies in the public or non-profit sectors. Second, given international economic trends, businesses can no longer predict markets or factor prices and thus they cannot operate efficiently (Muller, 1980). As Michael Reagan argues, private-sector or free-market solutions to the energy crisis pose more serious costs in both the long and short run than do government regulations, even though the latter are far from perfect; several externalities (particularly the unequal distribution of rising energy costs) have no apparent market solution. Imperfect markets dependent upon OPEC are not necessarily preferable to imperfect political regulation.

Third, despite the many problems that political scientists and economists have found with regulation, deregulation is not necessarily the solution. It is already proving disastrous for the airlines (Thayer, 1977) and adverse impacts on trucking, occupational hazards, and banking are to be anticipated. The problem is one of better management and information; whether public, private or mixed approaches are preferable must be decided for each industry under specific market situations. And we know little as yet about the deregulation process (for preliminary assessments see Mitnick, 1980; and Brewer & DeLeon, 1983).

Despite the progress made in social indicator measurement, statistical techniques, and mathematical modeling, evaluations remain difficult to evaluate because of our many and conflicting notions as to what failure is (Ingram & Mann, 1980). If a program has a negative cost-benefit ratio, or if a policy's stated objectives are not met, judgments of failure may be fairly straightforward. But what if the program's objectives were ambiguous or unattainable in the first place? Is the program we are evaluating better or worse than doing nothing, better or worse than relying on the private sector, better or worse than other programmatic alternatives? Systematic evaluation alone can seldom answer such questions, particularly in response to short-term policy issues such as when to cut losses and terminate a program whose outlook for success is ambiguous.

The evidence needed to support decisions is all too frequently amassed after the fact. Neither public nor private econometric models of the U.S. economy included estimates of supply-side pricing and incentive effects until after Reagan's election and the implementation of his economic policy (Roberts, 1982). Political power conveys not only the authority to make decisions, but the ability to influence the gathering of data and the funding of research on which future decisions will be made. As social scientists, we deceive ourselves if we think we can conduct value-free evaluation research. Research trends over the past ten years suggest that the deployment of knowledge remains highly partisan. The gap may be widening between policy analysts who are expected to evaluate policies and social scientists conscious of the ambiguities of determining policy failure. But as measures and models improve and as evaluative criteria are made more explicit, autopsies of political failure should contribute to better theories of the boundaries of politics.

Certainly a new humility, an awareness of the limitations of policy, has affected many of us. I note recent titles such as *The Futility of Family Policy* (Steiner, 1981), *The Ungovernable City* (Yates, 1977), *The Collapse of Welfare Reform* (Leman, 1981), "The Impotence of Sex Policy" (Wasby, 1980), and *City Limits* (Peterson, 1981). This is a far cry from the positivist orientations of the 1960s. The political implications of this "strategic retreat from objectives" are obvious. Less obvious may be the impact on our students. At the end of my most recent graduate seminar on public policy at the University of Pittsburgh one student told me that, from her perspective, the course had been a detailed study of Murphy's Law and that she was too discouraged to continue the study of policy further.

Several interim strategies are possible. One strategy—to be discussed below—is to define more carefully the scope of problems to which policy analysis is applicable: to find more "tractable" problems to keep policy analysts busy and politicians happy. Another is to take advantage of the research opportunity to study policy termination and the organizational responses to failure, as Ingram and Mann (1980, p. 16) suggest; given current trends, this could keep political scientists busy for quite some time.

The failures of policy are not necessarily those of policy analysis, but both reflect to some degree our limited knowledge. They can lead us to formulate our problems in different ways, redefine our theories, and improve our methodologies. In Karl Popper's words, "it is through the falsification of our suppositions that we actually get in touch with reality. It is the discovery and elimination of our errors which alone constitute that 'positive' experience which we gain from reality" (cited in Wildavsky, 1979, p. 59).

THE PRESENT: RESEARCH STRATEGIES

The policy payoff, if any, from such emerging theoretical developments may not be apparent for some time. This time lag may lengthen further if available funds continue to flow to contract research on short-range solutions to small-scale problems. In the interim, however, policy analysts within political science have turned to other strategies which appear to offer more immediate gains in terms of their applicability to pressing social issues. These include: (1) efforts to focus on "tractable" problems which can be solved, thus conserving both our own and the society's resources; (2) emphasis on implementation and knowledge utilization; (3) studies of policy termination; and (4) a growing interest in comparative policy analysis. Each of these strategies has been pursued for good reasons; each offers at least some potential for improving policy outputs and policy analysis. However, each also has serious pitfalls for theoretical development.

First of all, what is a "tractable" problem, and how do we distinguish one from others which may be less tractable? To some extent this judgment must be *post hoc* rather than predictive. If certain policies worked well in the past, whatever mix of processes and resources used then should work again on similar problems, *ceteris paribus*. But this poses obvious difficulties if we find few successful paradigms to follow or if conditions have changed. Nevertheless, attempts have been made. One is Richard Nelson's insightful and widely cited essay *The Moon and the Ghetto* (1977). In this work Nelson moves far beyond the obvious differences between messy "social" problems (race, education, welfare) and structured technological issues such as air pollution or landing a man on the moon. A problem, he notes, is more manageable if we can define it precisely, can agree on its causes, and if its causes are factors reasonably under our control within the constraints posed by time and money. Thus some social issues (e.g. implementation of the 1965 Voting Rights Act) have proved manageable, while some technological problems (e.g. nuclear and hazardous waste disposal) are currently beyond our grasp. In the same vein Sabatier and Mazmanian (1980, p. 542) suggest an index of problem "tractability" based on: (a) the availability of valid technical theory, (b) the diversity of target group population, (c) the target group size, and (d) the extent of behavioral change required.

But problem tractability may be more an indicator of the state of our theories and methods than a factor inherent in problems themselves. Thus a few brave researchers have attempted to discover structures in messy problems. Simon (1974) considered the "structure of ill-structured problems." Rockman (1981) was able to model the behavior of "regulars" and "irregulars" in the State Department and the National Security Council, and to use this model to evaluate proposals for improving American foreign policy. Another promising effort is Cohen, March, and Olsen's (1974) "Garbage Can Model of Organizational Choice" in which they attempt to structure the conditions of choice faced by organized anarchies. An organized anarchy—their example is a university—is characterized by inconsistent preferences, choices looking for problems, solutions looking for issues to which they might be an answer, and decision-makers looking for work. From such unpromising assumptions they proceeded to model the behavior of large and small universities under different economic conditions using a matrix of choice situations solved with the help of 324 simultaneous equations. Many of us may be encouraged and intrigued by their results if we are not discouraged by the mathematics. If the behavior of universities and the State Department can be modelled successfully, perhaps other political problems are not altogether beyond hope (see also Sproull *et al.*, 1977).

As Wildavsky (1979) notes, "the age of decision is over; the era of implementation is passing; the time to modify objectives has come" (p. 43). There is both temptation and opportunity in concentrating on manageable problems rather than raising expectations about problems that no one yet knows how to solve. But if we focus on the most tractable and well-defined problems—assuming we can find some—it is easy to lose sight of the complex relationships among issues. As MacRae (1976) has suggested, one argument for policy analysis is the need to surmount disciplinary boundaries, to deal with problems that have no fixed constituency, or that are caused in part by an entrenched or rigid one (regulation frustrated by the operation of iron triangles, for example (p. 290). Well-developed issue networks (Heclo, 1979) may engage in turf battles in their efforts to find problems to which their particular expertise is a solution. Problems are defined politically so as to aid agency and budgetary growth, not necessarily to generate solutions (as Nelson, 1978, found for child abuse).

Even worse, we may end up concentrating scarce resources on less pressing issues. Cohen and Lee (1979) have devised an index of natural and man-made hazards, based on the degree of risk (damages, lives lost) and their probability of occurrence. Their purpose in doing so was to recommend a focusing of societal resources on the greater hazards. But Johnson (1981) found that, for the period from 1957 to 1978, Congressional effort (bills introduced and laws passed) was greater for "old" hazards with which Congress was familiar and had dealt successfully in the past, than for newer issues, however urgent. One suspects the same relationships would hold for appropriations as well. It is understandable that a society would concentrate its efforts on manageable problems that we know how to handle at fairly low cost; Congressional desires for "credit claiming" are only one reason for such behavior. But the long-run implications are rather chilling, since several large potential hazards (nuclear reactor accidents, dam failure, hazardous wastes) have only very recently attracted much attention. The fastest growing domestic policy area, health care, appears to be beyond anyone's control despite the many efforts to limit health costs now being discussed (Marmor & Christianson, 1982).

In short, a focus on "tractable" problems assumes that we know more than we do. Ingram and Mann (1980) suggest no simple answers: "there are few hard and fast rules about what makes for successful implementation, and what works in one setting often fails in another" (p. 25). Without clear standards and mechanisms for ensuring compliance, success or failure may be impossible to assess, as O'Brien (1980) found in his study of the mutually contradictory Freedom of Information and Privacy Acts. And, as Pressman and Wildavsky (1973) noted in their Oakland study, the process of implementing policy is so difficult that we should be favorably surprised when policies have any favorable accomplishments. Even minor improvements in efficiency in some areas of management may end up saving millions because of the absolute size of government expenditures. But Quade (1972) would exclude such operations-research problems from the purview of policy analysis altogether and confine that term to the more difficult — and interesting — issues of tradeoffs among programs, resource allocation, program evaluation, and budgeting (p. 16).

One might, in fact, question whether tractability is a viable structuring principle or simply a rationale for reducing the scope of government, or cutting particular programs. As Ingram and Mann note (1980), "politicians and political systems are expected to solve problems, not ignore them. Policy failure . . . may be evidence of a political system that responds to problems, even if knowledge may be limited and appropriate policy tools unavailable" (p. 3). Retrospective voting for Reagan over Carter in 1980 suggests that in that election popular preferences leaned toward efficiency rather than effort or equity as values by which to judge candidates, but that balance could shift in 1984, as it has in the past.

When governments are faced with budgetary cutbacks, are the less "tractable" programs the first ones to go? Not necessarily. A RAND corporation study (Lipson & Lavin, 1980) of cutbacks in California cities after passage of Proposition 13 found that traditional services, those with the most entrenched bureaucracies, and those which could be financed by user fees instead of taxes, were least likely to be cut. Clark and Ferguson (forthcoming) note considerable differences among Republican, Democratic, and populist city governments in their responses to fiscal stress. Again, politics rather than program "tractability" appeared to be the major factor. Given these patterns, it remains to be seen whether policy analysts' judgments of "tractability" will have much programmatic effect.

The second research strategy I detect is a focus on knowledge utilization. This approach basically seeks answers to the question that frustrated policy analysts have too often had to ask: "Why is our good advice so seldom followed?" Earlier in the 1970s the problem of implementation received considerable scholarly attention, particularly after Pressman and Wildavsky's (1973) study of how grand designs in Washington could be frustrated in the hinterlands (in their case, Oakland, CA). Around that same time, evaluation studies became big business, both for governments and for universities and contract-research facilities. Budgetary constraints in recent years have been a strong impetus for cost-benefit analyses to find the programs most efficient per dollar spent. The problem, however, is to combine the studies of implementation and evaluation — to put knowledge into practice.

The focus on implementation has put the skills of political scientists to good use, since their graduate training emphasizes the knowledge of government processes and organization which the scientists, lawyers, engineers, or economists who design policy often lack. The institutional decision-making approach continues to be well represented in both political science and policy analysis (Rourke, 1976; Ripley & Franklin, 1980; Weiss & Barton, 1979; Derthick, 1980). The focus is on organizational processes, jurisdictional rivalries, cognitive limits, and bounded rationality. "Muddling through" remains a viable organizing principle for policy-makers as well as analysts, although organizational theorists, as discussed above, have attempted to model these processes using a rational choice perspective on complex organizations. One could also mention here recent emphasis on the quantitative study of agency decisions, represented by the work of Beck (1982) and Moe (1982).

During the 1970s social scientists learned more about how to do evaluation; texts appeared; courses were taught; experiments designed. The need for evaluation had been recognized, and the "how-to's" provided in terms of data bases, computer facilities, and increasing methodological sophistication. The U.S. government financed large-scale experiments, spending over $10 million to evaluate the effects of various income maintenance alternatives on work and leisure.[4] Many fine studies were done, often with counterintuitive results; the growth of evaluation has certainly enriched the social sciences in terms of knowledge, theory-building, and methodology—to say nothing of the personal economic benefits accruing to researchers. But somehow this growth in evaluation was not able to help us tell success from failure, or to discover "tractable" problems.

Studies of implementation tell us that, first of all, organizations actively distrust evaluation efforts that pose threats to their personnel, budgets, or missions; they have devised numerous strategies to prevent or bias evaluations efforts (McLaughlin, 1975). There is a growing suspicion that the more sophisticated our tools for analysis and evaluation, the less likely we will be to find successful programs. Persons generally favoring social change have long suspected that, in Salamon's (1976) words, policy evaluations are "handmaidens of conservative powers that be" because they neglect the time bias against potentially promising programs that pose an immediate threat to the status quo (p. 282; see also Berk & Rossi, 1976). Social-service agencies perceive short-term evaluation as a threat which diverts scarce resources from clients' needs (Marcus, 1981). Finding that bilingual education is not helpful to minorities, or that fiscal equalization of school-district funding will not solve school problems (Bish, 1976), is unlikely to be greeted with much enthusiasm by the proponents of these programs. Conservatives also distrust evaluations that may work against them; as Conway (1982) notes, the Reagan administration has decided to eliminate a number of statistical series altogether, thus depriving potential critics of ammunition. The Congressional Budget Office and its director, Alice Rivlin, have come under attack by Congressional Republicans for providing budget analyses considerably less optimistic than those of the Reagan administration.

Second, evaluations (positive or negative) can have little effect if they are not communicated to persons in a position to act on them. Donna Shalala, formerly Assistant Secretary for Research at HUD, noted in a Spring 1980 address at the University of Michigan that the Department had commissioned hundreds of studies of housing and urban policy, but had never devised ways to communicate these results either within the organization or to outside scholars. The sheer mass of available information may preclude its use or analysis. Thousands of studies are indexed every year by the Congressional Information Service and the National Technical Information Service, but they are seldom subject to peer review and the data on which they are based may not be available to scholars for reanalysis. There is little evidence that they are used by policy makers.

The best policy analysis information can be lost or defeated by organizations, and social scientists have shown increasing interest in such organizational processes (Brewer, 1973; Bulmer, 1982; Sproull & Larkey, 1983; Feldman & March, 1981; Rich, 1981; Weiss, 1977; Meltsner, 1976; and papers presented at the 1982 Denver meeting by Ellwood, MacRae, Kelley, and Dunn). Wildavsky noted the dilemma of the tradeoffs in organizations between error recognition and error correction. Small errors are easy to correct, but may be difficult to detect until they have caused large-scale problems; major failures are highly visible, but by the time they are discerned they may be difficult to remedy (1979, p. 16 ff.). It might be more useful if evaluations could pick up small problems early, but it is also more difficult.

Third, "knowing what works" implies communicating results to decision-makers in a fashion that would give them leverage for dealing with social problems. MacRae stressed the importance of "actionable alternatives," a distinction between things we can and cannot control (1976, p. 284). A sophisticated, multi-dimensional evaluation might well find that the problem at hand is due to forces beyond the control of the organizations being evaluated. For example, the cause of many urban problems lies in Washington, state capitals, or corporate board rooms where local governments have little leverage (Peterson, 1981). The tools that educators can manipulate—classroom size, teacher salaries, new curriculae—are not those that affect the learning rates of culturally and economically deprived children (Comfort, 1980). Organizations can redefine their goals or clientele in efforts to justify their continued existence, but the basic problems may survive untouched if the solutions are beyond their control, are rooted in other political cultures, or would involve coercive methods that cannot be tolerated in a democratic society.

Fourth, evaluations would have more impact if they considered long- as well as short-term effects, indirect, secondary or tertiary implications of programs, the impact of changing circumstances, tie-ins with other policies, and changing expectations. Given the political obstacles to doing even limited evaluations of single programs, this is a tall order. John Grumm (1975) described the methodological difficulty well as that of one independent variable (the program) and a very large, perhaps infinite, number of dependent variables, or outcomes; it is hard to know when to stop. Evaluations usually require results in a finite time period with limited funding, but politicians, and voters, have to make decisions before all the results are in. Evaluations, however sophisticated, may become increasingly irrelevant to policy unless solutions can be found to the problems political science and public administration have raised about implementing them (for some suggestions, see Nagel, 1980, *Improving Policy Analysis;* and Wildavsky, 1979, on the "self-evaluating organization").

A major challenge, however, is to include implementation strategy as part of policy design and evaluation—the "missing link" as described by Hargrove (1975). Even if legislative efforts are made to clarify policy objectives, provide financial resources, and include incentives for compliance and oversight provisions, no statutory design can determine "the number of veto-clearance points, the formal access of various actors to the implementation process, [or] the probable policy predispositions of implementation officials" (Sabatier & Mazmanian, 1980, p. 540). A "fixer" or "political entrepreneur" who is committed to a program and has the time and other resources to devote to it, may be far more instrumental to its success than either formal evaluation or statutory effort at legislation and oversight (Lewis, 1980). Successful implementation can too easily become a matter of luck or personality —elements hard to control and of little use in theory or prediction.

Interest in implementation and evaluation may have peaked just as the focus of most governments switched to de-implementation and policy termination. According to ACIR (1982), local government spending reached a maximum in 1974, state spending in 1976, and federal domestic spending in 1978 (all figures in constant dollars). In the era of implementation, analysts had the opportunity to examine what bureaucracies did when they were faced with unobtainable goals: redefine those goals, find new clients, use old clients for new purposes, etc. As Comfort (1980) notes of educational bureaucracies, "since the original objectives set for the Elementary and Secondary Education Act were probably unobtainable, implementers had no alternative but to redefine objectives to meet what could be achieved" (1980, p. 19). But in the new era, hundreds of programs have had their budgets and personnel reduced drastically or have been eliminated altogether. Cameron's (1978) discussion of the deinstitutionalization of California state hospitals found that "potential consequences were not considered until they were experienced" (p. 322). He described a massive policy shift based less on evaluation results than on changes in the prevailing myths or ideologies concerning mental health, on the allure of budget cuts, and on political considerations such as greater job opportunities for professionals in community mental health. No systematic appraisal of the costs and benefits of alternative policies took place, and release of long-term patients was not so much "implemented" as simply allowed to proceed without planning for alternatives. Cameron foresees "disastrous" results if his example suggests a general model for policy termination, but Brewer and DeLeon (1983) describe some successful terminations in their new text. More models may be expected with more research experience.

A decade or so ago the "agenda-building" perspective attracted scholarly attention to the processes by which social problems move from the private to the public sectors, and externalities produced by collective goods came to be defined as government responsibilities. We as yet know little about the reverse process of privatization. Deimplementation—and its cousins deregulation and deinstitutionalization—may well become a major new focus for policy analysis; this trend is indicated by several recent articles and a number of papers at the 1982 APSA meeting on cutbacks resulting from Reagan administration policies.

Another research strategy could be to examine whether certain characteristics of agencies (organization, political support) help predict their ability to survive in the current era. One might anticipate that the first programs to be eliminated would be those with explicit redistributive aims that were the most difficult to enact in the first place. The Reagan administration has been far harder on means-tested social programs (Food Stamps, disability, etc.) than on other non-means-tested programs with primarily middle-class constituencies such as Social Security and veterans benefits (Palmer & Sawhill, 1982). After a generation of government growth, many programs clearly need to be terminated; no country could afford all the defense or social programs which public bureaucracies and private interest groups have supported. But as DeLeon notes (1978, p. 293), termination strategies which are not carefully formulated and implemented can undermine their purpose and create more problems than they resolve. Deregulation, for example, is no panacea. Breyer (1982) argues that regulatory failure may result, not simply from problems of implementation, but from poor choice of regulatory tools. He identifies six specific types of market failure and the appropriate range of regulatory approaches for each type.

I will briefly mention one last example of interim research strategies: comparative policy analysis (for a fuller assessment, see Donald Hancock's essay on comparative policy elsewhere in this volume; also Ashford, 1983). Comparative policy research is hardly new; researchers in state and local governments have been doing it for years. But cross-national comparisons usually offer a greater range of policy variation, and political scientists are more sensitive to the importance of political system variation than, say, economists. Wildavsky may be right that some of our problems have no solutions, but other political systems may do better than the U.S. at posing and implementing alternatives and at policy succession. On the other hand, if post-industrial societies are facing similar difficulties (rising welfare costs, declining productivity), this may suggest something about the range of alternatives open to politicians and perhaps lead us to either lowered expectations or searches for common solutions (Benjamin, 1980). For example, U.S. manufacturing industries have advocated trade restrictions and tariff barriers to solve their problems, but if other producers follow suit, the outcomes could be harmful to all (Walters, 1982).

In terms of theory-building, comparison can put our judgments about policy processes and outcomes in better perspective. In terms of concrete assistance to policy makers, however, comparative research on policy may not be of much help. Neither policies nor institutions may be directly comparable. There seem to be few powerful conceptual tools that cross cultural boundaries. One exception is Caiden and Wildavsky's *Planning and Budgeting in Poor Countries* (1974). Uncertainty and resource scarcity produce similar budget strategies in a variety of political settings. Conversely, very different institutional arrangements may produce similar policy outcomes; differences may appear in the consumption or the legitimization of policies rather than in their production (see Lundqvist, 1980, on air pollution; Kelman, 1981, on regulation; or Leman, 1980, on welfare).

The most serious problem, however, is that the major variables accounting for different policy outcomes may be due to historical or constitutional factors not readily manipulable by policy makers. The U.S. is unlikely to import responsible party government or corporatist systems of government/business economic planning on the Japanese or Italian models (Vogel, 1979; Holland, 1972; Schmitter & Lehmbruch, 1979). Yet recognition of such limitations on the range of choices may be of some use in directing policy efforts to problems whose amelioration may depend on policy levers that we can employ.

CONCLUSION

One issue that engaged the attention of political scientists early in the development of policy analysis continues to spark intellectual controversy. That is the issue of the ability of political scientists to make recommendations or take policy stands based on their disciplinary qualifications rather than as individuals or interested citizens. Ranney (1968) and Lowi (1979) suggest that political scientists do have special skills and perspectives to offer based on our traditional interests in public law, political theory, and the operation of institutions. But the problem is twofold. First, such knowledge does not constitute a tight analytic system on the model of economics; our theories are not developed to the stage where they permit predictions or concrete advice to policy makers. Second—and probably a result of the first—political scientists are seen as lacking legitimacy, as not having any special knowledge that is not shared by reasonably well-informed citizens, politicians, or bureaucrats. Both Ranney and Lowi caution against trying to "beat the subject-matter experts at their own game by becoming especially skilled hydrologists or welfare economists or astronautical engineers or whatever" (Ranney, 1968, p. 18), lest we become laughingstocks to those who are truly knowledgeable.

The controversy still rages, but behavior has changed, despite such warnings. Increasing numbers of political scientists are becoming policy experts. Joint degrees in political science and other areas are not uncommon; graduate programs in public policy often require or recommend extensive course work in subject areas. Even academic job descriptions now request political scientists with substantive knowledge in particular policy areas, and some departments may become as specialized in policy fields as large economics departments have been. One cannot write on subjects such as air pollution, earthquakes, nuclear waste disposal, urban land values, or taxation without acquiring considerable practical knowledge in these areas and often the academic or field-work credentials to substantiate that knowledge.

Perhaps because of this trend, political scientists appear to be more willing to offer specific policy recommendations concerning all phases of the policy-making process, following the recommendations of Easton (1969) for action and relevance. It is not that their credentials in specific policy fields give them the standing to compete with other experts—although some in our field may have become sufficiently knowledgeable to do just that. Rather, substantive knowledge of a policy area is required in order to gain access to decision-makers, attentive publics, or the research funds to enable one to do policy research at all. Once having gained both expertise and access, policy analysts can and have made recommendations in terms of political processes and social values as well as technological alternatives concerning specific policies and programs. Examples include Henry Kissinger and Jeane Kirkpatrick on foreign policy, Aaron Wildavsky (1980) on the balanced-budget amendment, Alexander George (1972) on multiple advocacy in foreign-policy decision-making, Allen Schick (1981) on the budgetary process, and Ted Lowi himself on the writing of laws for Congress.

Is this advice likely to be any good, or have any effect? That question cannot be answered *a priori,* but must be based on the actual experiences of political scientists and policy analysts in the field. Ballard, Brosz, and Parker (1980) suggest that social researchers can play a variety of roles (substantive expert, information processor, disciplinary scholar, change agent) depending on their own proclivities and the situations in which they find themselves. They may be effective in some roles more than others, in some situations more than others. Some research has already been done on the use, and misuse, of social science research and the recommendations of policy analysts; the evidence to date is mixed (see Weiss, 1977, for some positive examples; Szanton (1981), Brewer (1973), and Aaron (1978) for more negative views). But I find little analysis of the substance or effects of policy advice tendered by political scientists *qua* political scientists.

One symposium issue of the *Policy Studies Review* dealt with anthropologists in public policy. I was struck by a thoughtful article by Michael Agar (1981), "Strangers in a Strange Land: Anthropologists in Agency Settings." He gives a discouraging account of his own experiences of "culture shock" and the differences between agency and academic perspectives on policy research. But he nevertheless recommends that such involvement continue and that graduate training be changed to change the field itself. He concludes that "to move into non-academic settings will stimulate and enrich anthropology from basic premises to specific techniques." Will this be true for political scientists as policy analysts? I suggest that we do not yet know the answer to that question, but that it would be well worth finding out. One alternative, as suggested by Erwin C. Hargrove (*PS,* Spring 1982) is the development of closer professional ties with our students and colleagues who have entered non-academic employment. A symposium in the *Policy Studies Journal* or *Review* on the experiences of political scientists as policy experts or advocates might consider the short- as well as the long-term implications of their experiences for policy outcomes and for the discipline.

But we must be prepared to make mistakes, to have our cherished assumptions and theories questioned, to have our expert advice ignored, and even—like Dennis Palumbo—to be sued. We can also expect critiques such as Michael Nelson's (1979). He argues, using a graphic illustration based on CETA evaluations, that academic policy analysis, whether based on methodological erudition or advice given in terms policy-makers can understand and accept, is of little help in dealing with policy problems. Yet the outcomes of greater political involvement need not be entirely discouraging. Knorr (1980) finds evidence of mutual accommodation between policy analysts and policy-makers, rather than sycophancy by social scientists and domination—or rejection of experts' recommendations altogether—by political elites. The important point, according to Jones (1976), is that policy analysis is only one input, only one aspect of the political process. He strongly urges that that voice be heard, quoting John Gaus (1976): "for any achievement of gains, however slight, toward a reasonable solution of the problems of government contributes to a renewal of confidence in reason itself and a strengthening of nerve" (p. 286).

Many have argued against the involvement by political scientists, as political scientists, in applied policy analysis because we have not developed a workable model of the world, an all-encompassing theory that would permit prediction of political outcomes. As should be clear from this survey of the state of the field, the critics are probably right. We cannot tell success from failure in any scientific sense, nor can we tell policy-makers how to make such determinations. Our *post hoc* evaluations seldom have the theoretical base to permit predictions. The world is a far more complex place than we had thought; traditional and disciplinary distinctions between American and cross-national, domestic and international politics, cannot deal with policy decisions in an interdependent world. The political economy and organizational approaches suggest a movement toward theoretical integration, but we are only at the beginning, and the policy payoffs of such integrative theories are as yet far off.

In the interim, policy analysts in our profession have turned to a variety of short-term research strategies. Each of those I have summarized here has some potential for contributing to knowledge — and keeping policy analysts employed — but all pose problems for policy as well as theory development (Portis & Davis, 1982). The choice between training substantive experts and experts on processes and procedures is real. Perhaps the only area in which political science has a firm toehold on substance may be foreign policy. In other respects we are at a great disadvantage compared with economics. In addition, it may be much harder to understand institutional and decision-making processes than it is to understand policy outputs. Designing a proper decision system is like constitution making; one needs to make it effective for the moment but also flexible enough to accommodate new developments, including new information and values. Political scientists are much better as social critics than as developers of normative or explanatory policy theory.

As Charles Lindblom has said, however, "policy aims at suppressing vice even if virtue cannot be attained." Despite the variety of approaches and differences in methodological sophistication, policy analysts in political science are almost unanimous in their agreement on one principle: the inadequacy of economic theory and methods. Policy analysis has too long been regarded, by too many in this profession, as an instrumental orientation with emphasis on efficiency in an economic sense. The tools of economic analysis are powerful and can be extremely helpful for certain classes of problems; most public policy texts draw heavily on economic theory and methods. But how empirically useful are models whose behavioral assumptions are increasingly open to question and that pay little attention to real-world political institutions? Economics has little to say about the legitimacy or administrative effectiveness of alternative organizational structures (Mead, 1977), yet these are inextricably linked to goal attainment, as implementation analysis demonstrates. Our unstated behavioralistic or ideological assumptions may be just as unrealistic as those explicitly formulated in political economy or formal organizational theory (Boynton, 1982). But political scientists can at least pose questions about administrative effectiveness or organizational structures even if we cannot claim to have all the answers.

An irony of the present condition is that the dominance of economics in policy analysis and in policy-making in Washington coincides with considerable self-searching going on in that profession about failures to deal with macroeconomic policy, corporate behavior, consumer choice, energy, and other pressing social issues (Bell & Kristol, 1981; see also Eyestone, 1978, for a perceptive review of recent books by economists critical of their own field). A major contribution that political scientists could make to the policy process might be to communicate to decision-makers what is wrong with the economic approach, aided by our growing policy expertise, our understanding, however imperfect, of political institutions, and the profession's collective memory of government decisions that represented good economics but bad public policy. Most political scientists can easily think of examples (see Nagel, 1980, for several good ones), but because of our disciplinary self-doubts we have been unable or unwilling to share these with a wider audience.[5]

I must conclude by again stressing my debt to Karl Popper—and Walter Mondale. We may not know what works, but we are beginning to get some notions as to what does *not* work in the real world of politics. Perhaps it is time to convey some of this hard-earned humility to economists and decision-makers.

NOTES

1. This starting point is not intended to imply that political scientists' interest in policy analysis dates only from 1967. See Ranney (1968) for a capsule history of policy perspectives in the discipline.
2. According to the *Personnel Directory* of the Policy Studies Association, 68% of its 1100 members were political scientists (1979 data).
3. Special thanks to Bert Rockman for ideas for this section.
4. The income-tax experiments raise fascinating questions about the design of large-scale public policy experiments, their results, and their political implications. See Rossi and Lyall (1976) for a trenchant critique. As Steiner (1981, pp. 106-110) describes, the impact of tax payments on work effort was minimal, but one wholly anticipated result was increasing family instability. So many divorces and family breakdowns occurred among subsidized families—although the precise causal link was never specified—that it became politically impossible to implement the income maintenance experiment on a larger scale.
5. It is interesting to compare economists' and political scientists' writings on their duties as policy advisers or policymakers. I have been unable to discover any economist since Edwin Nourse, the first chairman of the Council of Economic Advisers, who questioned the right, duty, and obligation of their profession to participate in the making of public policy. As Pechman (1975) notes, economists argue among themselves in strongly partisan terms and have difficulties communicating their models to policymakers.

REFERENCES

Aaron, Henry. *Politics and the professors: The great society in perspective.* Washington, D.C.: Brookings, 1978.

Advisory Commission on Intergovernmental Relations. *Significant features of fiscal federalism 1980-81.* Washington, D.C.: U.S. Government Printing Office, 1982.

Agar, Michael H. Strangers in a strange land: Anthropologists in agency settings. *Policy Studies Review,* 1981, *1,* 133-147.

Almond, Gabriel & Powell, G. B. Jr. *Comparative politics: A developmental approach.* Boston: Little, Brown, 1966.

Ashford, Douglas. Comparing policies across nations and cultures. In Stuart Nagel (Ed.). *Encyclopedia of policy studies.* New York and Basel: Marcel Dekker, 1983.

Bahl, R. & Burkhead, J. Productivity and the measurement of public output. In L. Levine (Ed.). *Managing human resources: A challenge to urban governments.* Beverly Hills, CA: Sage, 1977, 253-270.

Ballard, S. C., Brosz, Allyn R. & Parker, Larry P. Social science and social policy: Roles of the applied researcher. *Policy Studies Journal,* 1980, *8,* 951-957.

Barnes, Barbara & Dubnick, Melvin J. Motives and methods in policy analysis. In Stuart Nagel (Ed.). *Improving policy analysis.* Beverly Hills, CA: Sage, 1980.

Barry, Brian. Does democracy cause inflation? A study of the political ideas of some economists. In L. Lindberg & P. Maier (Eds.). *The politics of global inflation.* Washington, D.C.: Brookings (forthcoming).

Beck, Nathaniel. Parties, administrations, and American macroeconomic outcomes. *American Political Science Review,* 1982, *76,* 83-93.

Bell, Daniel, & Kristol, Irving (Eds.). *The crisis in economic theory.* New York: Basic Books, 1981.

Benjamin, Roger. *The limits of politics: Collective goods and political change in post-industrial societies.* Chicago: University of Chicago Press, 1980.

Benjamin, Roger. The historical nature of social-scientific knowledge: The case of comparative political inquiry. In Elinor Ostrom (Ed.). *Strategies of political inquiry.* Beverly Hills, CA: Sage, 1982.

Berk, R. A. & Rossi, P. H. Doing good or worse: Evaluation research politically reexamined. *Social Problems,* 1976, *23,* 337-349.

Bish, Robert L. Fiscal equalization through court decisions: Policy-making without evidence. In Elinor Ostrom (Ed.). *The delivery of urban services: Outcomes of change.* Beverly Hills, CA: Sage, 1976.

Boneparth, Ellen (Ed.). *Women, power, and policy.* Elmsford, N.Y.: Pergamon Press, 1982.

Boynton, G. R. On getting from here to there. In Elinor Ostrom (Ed.). *Strategies of political inquiry.* Beverly Hills, CA: Sage, 1982.

Brewer, Garry D. *Politicians, bureaucrats, and the consultant: A critique of urban problem solving.* New York: Basic Books, 1973.

Brewer, Garry D., & DeLeon, Peter. *The foundations of policy analysis.* Homewood, IL: Dorsey, 1983.

Breyer, Stephen. *Regulation and its reform.* Cambridge, MA: Harvard University Press, 1982.

Buchanan, James M. & Wagner, Richard E. *Democracy in deficit: The political legacy of Lord Keynes.* New York: Academic Press, 1977.

Bulmer, Martin. *The uses of social research: Social investigation in public policy-making.* Boston: Allen & Unwin, 1982.

Caiden, Naomi, & Wildavsky, Aaron. *Planning and budgeting in poor countries.* New York: John Wiley, 1974.

Cameron, James M. Ideology and policy termination: Restructuring California's mental health system. In J. May & A. Wildavsky (Eds.). *The policy cycle.* Beverly Hills, CA: Sage, 1978.

Clark, Terry N. & Ferguson, Lorna C. *Political processes and urban fiscal strain.* Chicago: University of Chicago Press (forthcoming).

Cohen, Bernard L. & Lee, I-Sing. A catalog of risks. *Health Physics,* 1979, *26,* 707-722.

Cohen, Michael D., March, James G., & Olsen, Johan P. A garbage can model of organizational choice. *Administrative Science Quarterly,* 1972, *17,* 1-25.

Comfort, Louise. Evaluation as an instrument for educational change. In H. Ingram & D. Mann (Eds.). *Why policies succeed or fail.* Beverly Hills, CA: Sage, 1980.

Conway, M. Margaret. Reaganomics and the federal statistical programs. *PS,* 1982, *15,* 194-198.

DeLeon, Peter. A theory of policy termination. In J. May & A. Wildavsky (Eds.). *The policy cycle.* Beverly Hills, CA: Sage, 1978.

Derthick, Martha. *Policy-making for social security.* Washington, D.C.: Brookings, 1980.

Downs, Anthony. *An economic theory of democracy.* New York: Harper & Row, 1957.

Dunn, William. Political analysis and policy evaluation. Paper presented at the Annual Meeting of the APSA, Denver, CO, 1982.

Dye, Thomas R. *Politics, economics, and the public: Policy outcomes in the American states.* Chicago: Rand McNally, 1966.

Easton, David. *A systems analysis of political life.* New York: John Wiley & Sons, 1965.

Easton, David. The new revolution in political science. *American Political Science Review,* 1969, *63,* 1051-1061.

Ellwood, Richard. Studying the influence of policy analysis in the legislature. Paper presented at the Annual Meeting of the APSA, Denver, CO, 1982.

Eyestone, Robert. Economists and public policy: The relevance debate. *Public Administration Review,* 1978, 488-491.

Feldman, Martha, & March, J. G. Information in organizations as signal and symbol. *Administrative Science Quarterly,* 1981, *26,* 171-186.

Fink, Richard H. (Ed.). *Supply-side economics: A critical appraisal.* Frederick, MD: University Publications of America, 1982.

Fiorina, Morris. *Congress—keystone of the Washington establishment.* New Haven, CT: Yale University Press, 1977.

Frohlich, Norman, Oppenheimer, Joe, & Young, Oran R. *Political leadership and collective goods.* Princeton: Princeton University Press, 1971.

George, Alexander L. The case for multiple advocacy in making foreign policy. *American Political Science Review,* 1972, *66,* 751-785.

Gray, Virginia, & Williams, Bruce. *The organizational politics of criminal justice.* Lexington, MA: D.C. Heath, 1980.

Grumm, John. The analysis of policy impact. In Fred Greenstein & Nelson Polsby (Eds.). *Handbook of Political Science* (Vol. 6). *Policies and Policymaking.* Reading, MA: Addison-Wesley, 1975.

Hanf, Kenneth, & Scharpf, Fritz W. *Interorganizational policy making: Limits to coordination and central control.* Beverly Hills, CA: Sage, 1978.

Hansen, Susan B. *The politics of taxation.* New York: Praeger, 1983.

Hargrove, Erwin C. *The missing link: The study of the implementation of social policy.* Washington, D.C.: Urban Institute, 1975.

Hargrove, Erwin C. Career alternatives for political scientists. *PS,* 1982, *15,* 289-291.

Haveman, R. H. & Margolis, Julius (Eds.). *Public expenditures and policy analysis* (3rd ed.). Chicago: Markham, 1983.

Heclo, Hugh. Issue networks and the executive establishment. In Anthony King (Ed.). *The new American political system.* Washington, D.C.: American Enterprise Institute, 1978.

Hibbs, Douglas. Political parties and macro-economic policy. *American Political Science Review,* 1977, *71,* 1467-1487.

Holland, Stuart (Ed.). *The state as entrepreneur.* White Plains, N.Y.: International Arts and Sciences Press, 1972.

Hughes, Bette H. The impact of the profit motive on tax-supported human services. Paper presented at the Annual Meeting of the American Political Science Association, Denver, CO, 1982.

Ingram, Helen & Mann, Dean E. (Eds.). *Why policies succeed or fail.* Sage Yearbooks in Politics and Public Policy, Vol. 8. Beverly Hills, CA: Sage, 1980.

Johnson, Branden B. Congress and technological hazard policy: A review of selected federal legislation 1957-1978. Mimeo. Dept. of Geography, University of Pittsburgh, 1981.

Jones, Charles O. Policy analysis: Academic utility for practical rhetoric. *Policy Studies Journal,* 1976, *4,* 281-286.

Jones, Charles O. *Clean air.* Pittsburgh: University of Pittsburgh Press, 1975.

Kelley, E. W. Standardized testing effects and educational policy. Paper presented at the Annual Meeting of the APSA, Denver, CO, 1982.

Kelman, Stephen. *Regulating America, regulating Sweden: A comparative study of occupational safety and health policy.* Cambridge, MA: MIT Press, 1981.

Knorr, Karen D. The gap between knowledge and policy. In Stuart Nagel (Ed.). *Improving policy analysis.* Beverly Hills, CA: Sage, 1980.

Kramer, Gerald H. The ecological fallacy revisited: Aggregate versus individual-level findings on economics and elections and sociotropic voting. *American Political Science Review,* 1983, *77,* 92-111.

Leman, Christopher. *The collapse of welfare reform: Political institutions, policy, and the poor in Canada and the U.S.* Cambridge, MA: MIT Press, 1980.

Lewis, Eugene. *Public entrepreneurship: Toward a theory of bureaucratic political power.* Bloomington: Indiana University Press, 1980.

Lindblom, Charles E. *Politics and markets.* New York: Basic Books, 1977.

Lindblom, Charles E. Another state of mind. *American Political Science Review,* 1982, *76,* 9-21.

Lipson, Albert J. & Lavin, Martin. *Political and legal responses to Proposition 13 in California.* Santa Monica, CA: Rand Corporation, 1980.

Lowery, David, & Sigelman, Lee. Understanding the tax revolt: An assessment of eight explanations. *American Political Science Review,* 1981, *75,* 963-972.

Lowi, Theodore H. What political scientists don't need to ask about policy analysis. In Stuart Nagel (Ed.). *Policy studies and the social sciences.* Lexington, MA: D.C. Heath, 1979.

Lundqvist, Lennart J. *The hare and the tortoise: Clean air policies in the U.S. and Sweden.* Ann Arbor: University of Michigan Press, 1980.

Marcus, Isabel. *Dollars for reform: OEO neighborhood health care centers.* Lexington, MA: D.C. Heath, 1981.

Marmor, Theodore R., & Christianson, Jon B. *Health care policy.* Beverly Hills, CA: Sage, 1982.

MacRae, Duncan, Jr. *The social function of social science.* New Haven, CT: Yale University Press, 1976.

MacRae, Duncan. Value indicators and public policy: Democratic information systems. Paper presented at the Annual Meeting of the APSA, Denver, CO, 1982.

McLaughlin, Milbrey. *Evaluation and reform: The elementary and secondary education act of 1965/Title I.* Cambridge, MA: Ballinger, 1975.

Mead, Lawrence. Institutional analysis: An approach to implementation problems in Medicaid. Washington, D.C.: Urban Institute, 1977.

Meltsner, Arnold J. *Policy analysis in the bureaucracy.* Berkeley: University of California Press, 1976.

Miller, Trudi. Political and mathematical perspectives on educational equity. *American Political Science Review,* 1981, *75,* 319-333.

Mitnick, Barry M. *The political economy of regulation.* New York: Columbia University Press, 1980.

Moe, Terry M. On the scientific status of rational models. *American Journal of Political Science,* 1979, *23,* 215-243.

Moe, Terry M. Regulatory performance and presidential administration. *American Journal of Political Science,* 1982, *26,* 197-224.

Morehouse, Sarah M. *State politics, parties, and policy.* New York: Holt, Rinehart, and Winston, 1981.

Muller, Ronald E. *Revitalizing America: Politics for prosperity.* New York: Simon and Schuster, 1980.

Nagel, Stuart F. (Ed.). *Improving policy analysis.* Beverly Hills, CA: Sage, 1980.

Nagel, Stuart F. Productivity improvement and policy evaluation. In Nagel & Marc Holzer (Eds.). *Productivity and public policy.* Beverly Hills, CA: Sage, forthcoming.

Nelson, Barbara. Setting the public agenda: The case of child abuse. In J. May and A. Wildavsky (Eds.). *The policy cycle.* Beverly Hills, CA: Sage, 1978.

Nelson, Michael. What's wrong with policy analysis? *Washington Monthly,* 1979, *11,* 53-59.

Nelson, Richard R. *The moon and the ghetto: An essay in public policy analysis.* New York: Norton, 1977.

Niskanen, William. *Bureaucracy and representative government.* Chicago: Aldine-Atherton, 1971.

O'Brien, David M. Crosscutting policies, uncertain compliance, or why policies often cannot succeed or fail. In Helen Ingram & Dean E. Mann (Eds.). *Why policies succeed or fail.* Beverly Hills, CA: Sage, 1980.

Olson, Mancur. *The political economy of comparative economic growth in pluralistic societies.* New Haven, CT: Yale University Press, forthcoming.

Ostrom, Elinor. *Measuring urban services: A multi-mode approach.* Bloomington, IN: Workshop in Political Theory and Policy Analysis, Indiana University, 1975.

Ostrom, Elinor, Parks, Roger B., & Whitaker, Gordon P. *Patterns of metropolitan policing.* Cambridge, MA: Ballinger, 1978.

Paglin, Morton. *Poverty and transfers in-kind.* Palo Alto, CA: Hoover Institution, 1980.

Palmer, John L. & Pechman, Joseph A. (Eds.). *Welfare in rural areas: The North Carolina-Iowa income maintenance experiment.* Washington, D.C.: Brookings, 1978.

Palmer, John L. & Sawhill, Isabel V. (Eds.). *The Reagan experiment.* Washington, D.C.: Urban Institute, 1982.

Parks, Roger B. & Ostrom, Elinor. Developing and testing complex models of urban service systems. In Terry N. Clark (Ed.). *Urban policy analysis: Directions for future research.* Beverly Hills, CA: Sage, 1981.

Pechman, Joseph. Making economic policy: The role of the economist. In Fred Greenstein & Nelson Polsby (Eds.). *Handbook of Political Science* (Vol. 6) *Politics and Policy-Making.* Reading, MA: Addison-Wesley, 1975.

Peterson, Paul. *City limits.* Chicago: University of Chicago Press, 1981.

Plott, Charles R. Axiomatic social choice theory: An overview and interpretation. *American Journal of Political Science,* 1976, *20,* 511-596.

Pommerehne, Werner W. & Schneider, Friedrich. Does government in a representative democracy follow a majority of voters' preferences? An empirical examination. In Horst Hanusch (Ed.). *Anatomy of government deficiencies.* Detroit, MI: Wayne State University Press, 1983.

Portis, Edward B. & Davis, Dwight F. Policy analysis and scientific ossification. *PS*, 1982, *15*, 593-599.

Pressman, Jeffrey & Wildavsky, Aaron. *Implementation*. Berkeley, CA: University of California Press, 1973.

Quade, E. S. *Analysis for public decisions* (2nd ed.). New York: Elsevier, 1982.

Ranney, Austin. The study of policy content: A framework for choice. In Ranney (Ed.). *Political science and public policy*. Chicago: Markham, 1968.

Reagan, Michael D. Energy: Government policy or market result? Presented at the APSA Annual Meeting, Denver, CO, 1982.

Rich, Robert F. *Social science information and public policy making*. San Francisco: Jossey-Bass, 1981.

Riker, William H. Implications from the disequilibrium of majority rule for the study of institutions. *American Political Science Review*, 1980, *74*, 432-446.

Ripley, Randall, & Franklin, Grace. *Congress, the bureaucracy, and public policy*. Homewood, IL: Dorsey, 1980.

Rivlin, Alice M. *Systematic thinking for social action*. Washington, D.C.: Brookings, 1971.

Roberts, Paul Craig. The breakdown of the Keynesian model. *The Public Interest*, 1978, *52*, 20-33.

Rockman, Bert A. America's departments of state: Irregular and regular syndromes of policy making. *American Political Science Review*, 1981, *75*, 911-927.

Rose, Richard & Peters, Guy. *Can government go bankrupt? Political economy in the mixed welfare state*. New York: Basic Books, 1978.

Rossi, Peter & Lyall, Catherine. *Reforming public welfare: A critique of the negative income tax experiment*. New York: Russell Sage, 1976.

Rourke, Francis E. *Bureaucracy, politics, and public policy*. Boston: Little, Brown, 1976.

Rundquist, Barry S. (Ed.). *Political benefits*. Lexington, MA: D.C. Heath, 1978.

Sabatier, Paul & Mazmanian, Daniel. The implementation of public policy: A conceptual framework. *Policy Studies Journal*, 1980, *8*, 538-560.

Salamon, Lester M. Follow-ups, letdowns, and sleepers: The time dimension in policy evaluation. *Sage Yearbooks in Politics and Public Policy*, 1976, *3*, 257-284.

Salisbury, Robert H. The analysis of public policy: The search for theories and roles. In Austin Ranney (Ed.). *Political science and public policy*. Chicago: Markham, 1968.

Samuels, Warren J. (Ed.). *The economy as a system of power*. New Brunswick, NJ: Transaction Books, 1979.

Schick, Allen. *Congress and money: Budgeting, spending, and taxing*. Washington, D.C.: Urban Institute, 1981.

Schmitter, Philippe C. & Lehmbruch, Gerhard (Eds.). *Trends toward corporatist intermediation*. Beverly Hills, CA: Sage, 1979.

Schotter, Andrew. *The economic theory of social institutions*. New York: Cambridge University Press, 1980.

Scott, W. Richard. *Organizations: Rational, natural, and open systems*. Englewood Cliffs, NJ: Prentice-Hall, 1981.

Sharkansky, Ira. *Wither the state: Politics and public enterprise in three countries*. Chatham, NJ: Chatham House Publishers, 1979. (Reviewed *APSR*, 1980, *74*, 859.)

Shepsle, Kenneth A. Institutional arrangements and equilibrium in multidimensional voting models. *American Journal of Political Science*, 1979, *23*, 27-59.

Shultz, George & Dam, Kenneth. *Economic policy beyond the headlines*. Stanford, CA: Stanford University Press, 1977.

Simon, Herbert. The structure of ill-structured problems. *Artificial Intelligence*, 1973, *4*, 181-201.

Smeeding, Timothy. The anti-poverty effect of in-kind transfers. *Policy Studies Journal*, 1982, *10*, 499-522.

Sproull, Lee S., Weiner, Stephen S., & Wolf, David. *Organizing an anarchy*. Chicago: University of Chicago Press, 1977.

Sproull, Lee S. & Larkey, Patrick D. (Eds.). *Advances in information processing in organizations*. Greenwich, CT: JAI Press, 1983.

Steiner, Gilbert. *The futility of family policy*. Washington, D.C.: Brookings, 1981.

Stone, Alan. *Regulation and its alternatives*. Washington, D.C.: Congressional Quarterly Press, 1982.

Szanton, Peter. *Not well advised*. New York: Basic Books, 1981.

Taussig, Michael, & Danziger, Sheldon. Conference on the trend of income inequality in the U.S. Madison, Wis.: Institute for Research on Poverty, 1976.

Thayer, Frederick. And now . . . the deregulators . . . when will they learn? *Journal of Air, Law, and Commerce*, 1977, *4*, 661-689.

Thomas, Norman C. Political science and the study of macro-economic policymaking. In James E. Anderson (Ed.). *Economic regulatory policies*. Lexington, MA: D.C. Heath, 1976.

Tufte, Edward. *Political control of the economy*. Princeton: Princeton University Press, 1978.

Vogel, Ezra F. *Japan as number one: Lessons for America*. Cambridge, MA: Harvard University Press, 1979.

Walters, Robert S. The steel crisis in America: National politics and international trade. In Harold Jacobson & Dusan Sidjanski (Eds.). *The emerging international economic order*. Beverly Hills, CA: Sage, 1982.

Wasby, Stephen L. The impotence of sex policy. *Policy Studies Journal*, 1980, *9*, 117-126.

Weiss, Carol (Ed.). *Using social research in policy-making*. Lexington, MA: D.C. Heath, 1977.

Weiss, Carol & Barton, Allen (Eds.). *Making bureaucracies work*. Beverly Hills, CA: Sage, 1979.

Welch, Susan & Karnig, Albert K. *Black representation and urban policy*. Chicago: University of Chicago Press, 1981.

Wildavsky, Aaron. *Speaking truth to power: The art and craft of policy analysis*. Boston: Little, Brown, 1979.

Wildavsky, Aaron. *How to limit government spending*. Berkeley, CA: University of California Press, 1980.

Winters, Richard C. & Reidenberg, Joel. Appropriations politics and the political business cycle. Mimeo. Dartmouth College, Hanover, N.H., 1982.

Yates, Douglas. *The ungovernable city*. Cambridge, MA: MIT Press, 1977.

9

Federalism:
The Challenge of Conflicting Theories
and Contemporary Practice

David R. Beam, Senior Analyst
Timothy J. Conlan, Analyst
David B. Walker, Assistant Director
Advisory Commission on Intergovernmental Relations

FEDERALISM: ITS THEORETICAL STATUS*

Federalism represents America's greatest contribution to the science of government. It is, as Sheldon Wolin (1964, p. vii) observes, "an innovation in Western political theory and practice" that has been widely copied. Indeed, over the past four decades something of a "federalist revolution" has swept the globe, embracing a substantial portion of the world's population under systems based, at least in part, on this key invention of the Founders (Elazar, 1981, p. 5).

In its native territory, however, the subject has come on hard times. Troubled by ambiguity and inconsistency, as well as by an inability to marshall evidence to support key assertions, the theory of federalism has fallen into disrepair. Intergovernmental relations, its principal heir, has not yet proven to be an adequate substitute. That, at least, is the conclusion of many political scientists in the field. Hence, the clarification or reformulation of federal theory appears to be an urgent task.

---

*The views presented here are those of the authors and should not be attributed to the members or staff of the Advisory Commission on Intergovernmental Relations. However, some of the content is drawn from Advisory Commission on Intergovernmental Relations, *The Condition of Contemporary Federalism: Conflicting Theories and Collapsing Constraints* (Washington, D.C.: U.S. Government Printing Office, 1981), Chapter 1.

The Traditional View

Perhaps because the concept of federalism was so influential and so deeply rooted in the structure of American government, the fundamentals of federal theory long remained remarkably constant. Federalism, as traditionally understood, meant "dual" federalism: a system for dividing functions between the state and national governments that left each considerable autonomy within its own areas of jurisdiction. This was the concept implicit in the Constitution as elaborated in the *Federalist* (14, pp. 82, 83). It later found clear judicial sanction, as when the Supreme Court (*Abelman v. Booth*, 1859) declared:

> The powers of the general government, and of the state, although both exist and are exercised within the same territorial limits, are yet separate and independent of each other, within their respective spheres.

Although dual federalism lost its constitutional status during the New Deal era (Corwin, 1950), the underlying philosophical concept remained. In the 1950s, Wheare (1951) still defined federalism as "the method of dividing powers so that the general and regional governments are each, within a sphere, coordinate and independent" (p. 11). Two decades later, Martin Diamond (1976) continued to maintain that:

> . . . the American system is federal to the extent that governing functions are kept out of the center and remain constitutionally with the states, just as they would in a traditional federation. This division of functions between nation and states was always understood, at least in principle, as having been settled by the Constitution. To quote *Federalist* 39, . . . the jurisdiction of the proposed central government "extends to certain enumerated objects only, and leaves to the several States a residual and inviolable sovereignty over all other objects." (p. 189)

Theory in Disrepair

Over time, the practice of American government has increasingly departed from this idealized pattern. Especially after the New Deal and the Second World War, Washington was transformed from a sleepy backwater into the nerve center of a massive welfare state. The relative independence and autonomy of the different levels of government envisioned under dual federalism were replaced with "cooperative federalism" by the 1960s and extraordinary intergovernmental interdependence during the 1970s (Beer, 1973; Scheiber, 1978; Walker, 1981). Despite the development of new, more flexible forms of assistance—revenue sharing and consolidated block grants—federal aid programs continued to mount in number, functions, recipient jurisdictions, and dollar amounts, and were augmented by new regulatory "mandates" and a steadily increasing number of preemptive statutes.

Federal theory has never adjusted adequately to these changing circumstances. To be viable, a political theory should be *descriptive* of key facts; give rise to useful *generalizations;* and include a *normative component* that offers useful policy guidance (Mayo, 1960, p. 11). Accordingly, a theory of federalism should keep abreast of changing empirical realities and, from a normative perspective, should justify the existence of two independently constituted levels of government; offer guidance on the appropriate allocation of functions between levels; specify the areas and character of shared responsibilities; and indicate how power may be balanced between levels in a manner that preserves and sustains the federal arrangement.

Contemporary theories of federalism are often faulted on all of these grounds (Wright, 1978, pp. 16-20). Although recent scholarly efforts to keep pace with policy developments have produced many excellent descriptive accounts of intergovernmental practices, critics stress difficulties in generalizing from the results of program studies and in developing well grounded policy recommendations. From a normative standpoint, the highly prescriptive theory of dual federalism has been abandoned without a satisfactory replacement.

A considerable number of scholars of federalism — with distinctive theoretical commitments of their own — have decried the current status of inquiry. Daniel Elazar (1981), who remains the field's best recognized expert, believes that

> . . . there is a crisis in American thinking about federalism. Even a casual perusal of the literature on the subject of the past decade, explaining, justifying, or advocating particular courses of government action in the United States in the name of federalism, would indicate that this is so. (p. 15)

Patrick Riley (1973, p. 90) has agreed that "the theory of federalism is in a state of confusion," while historian Harry Scheiber (1980, p. 664) has declared it to be in "considerable disarray." William Riker (1969, p. 145) suggests that the belief that federalism makes any difference has resulted in much misdirected scholarly effort, including his own. And, after a comprehensive historical review of federalist thought, Rufus Davis (1978) glumly concluded that:

> . . . there has rarely been a time in the history of the subject when it has been in a more depressing and uncertain condition than it is now. And this is not because we know less about the facts of federal life; on the contrary, there has never been a time when so much has been known about the subject. . . . Only the more we have come to know about it, the less satisfying and less reputable has become almost the whole legacy of our federal theory. (p. 205)

The Shift to Intergovernmental Relations

After the outpouring of new legislative enactments during the "Great Society" era, many scholars openly proclaimed "the final burial . . . of traditional doctrines of American federalism" (Sundquist, 1969, p. 6). "Federalism — old style — is dead," Michael Reagan (1972, p. 3) concurred, naming intergovernmental relations as its successor. Federalism, he charged, was a static legal concept stressing the constitutional division of authority and functions between the national government and the states. Intergovernmental relations, agrees Deil Wright (1978), is a dynamic, political and pragmatic concept, emphasizing the actual administrative relationships between the levels of government in the day-to-day performance of shared responsibilities.

This new approach fit well with the discipline's growing empiricism and the turn away from institutional and normative problems. Students of intergovernmental relations made questions of administration, politics, and finance the chief foci of inquiry. Building upon the work of earlier students (Anderson, 1956, 1960; Graves, 1964), they examined closely the development and impact of new social programs, especially those involving the federal government in urban affairs.

There is no doubt that these studies have enormously deepened our understanding of the operation of major grants-in-aid (Sundquist, 1969; Derthick, 1972; Pressman & Wildavsky, 1973; Nathan, Manvel, & Calkins, 1975; Larkey, 1978) and clarified the contours of the aid system as a whole (Wright, 1968; Mushkin & Cotton, 1969; ACIR, 1978; Anton, Cawley, & Kramer, 1980). At the same time—partly, perhaps, because of the inherent difficulties in generalizing from case material—the theoretical contributions have been relatively meager. Sheldon Edner (1976) has declared intergovernmental relations to be a "virtual wasteland" from a theoretical standpoint:

> Much of the literature has been confined either to political rhetoric and speculative analysis or a fragmented, piece-by-piece look at some of the elements of intergovernmental relations—i.e., specific programs, . . . administrative and professional contact between levels, . . . and most thoroughly on the fiscal aspects of the system. Little, if any, work has been done to try and trace the policy implications of the results of these studies. (pp. 150-151)

To Van Horn and Van Meter (1976) most writers on intergovernmental relations

> . . . are less interested in prescribing the proper allocation of responsibilities than with charting existing relationships where the assignment of responsibilities is shared by various governmental units. The primary task of these works has been to provide a description of the intergovernmental system with emphasis on such concerns as the distribution of power, the sources of leverage held by each governmental jurisdiction, and the consequences of administrative centralization and decentralization.
>
> While this body of literature has alerted us to a number of important considerations, it has failed to provide an analytic framework promoting either tests of the significance of particular variable clusters . . . or the policy implications of a particular administrative arrangement. . . . Since most of these works lack a coherent theoretical perspective, the results of the analysis lack generality, and they tell us little about how public policy is implemented in the intergovernmental system. (p. 41)

Catherine Lovell (1979) summarizes the current "conceptual crisis" well in stating that

> We have slipped away from the search for models of federalism and into the more satisfactory, albeit as yet less rigorous, discussion of IGR. . . . The transi-

tion in theoretical focus from "federalism" to "IGR" has not answered many fundamental questions. (pp. 11-12)

CONFLICTING ASSESSMENTS OF AMERICAN PRACTICE

One good indication of the present confusion is provided by scholarly disagreements over the effect of new intergovernmental grant and regulatory programs on the balance of power between the states and the national government. On the one hand, there are those who view the recent growth of new federal programs with considerable alarm, believing that centralizing forces have compromised essential virtues of American federalism. In the judgment of Stephen Schechter (1982)

> Over the past fifteen years the United States has crossed the fault line from a federal system to a decentralized national system. . . . When it comes time to make policy, all eyes look to Washington, and federalism is viewed as one among many cross-pressures rather than as a pathway through them. When it comes time to implement policy, federalism is transformed into a managerial model in which the states and localities are cast in the roles of middle and lower echelons of management that cannot be trusted to follow orders without being paid off and reined in. The political idea of states as polities and localities as communities has all but disappeared. (p. 61)

Similarly, Daniel Elazar (1980) has answered his own question, "is the federal system still there?," by stressing the shift in policy determination from the states to Washington:

> [W]e have moved to a system in which it is taken as axiomatic that the federal government shall initiate policies and programs, shall determine their character, shall delegate their administration to the states and localities according to terms that it alone determines, and shall provide for whatever intervention on the part of its administrative agencies as it deems necessary to secure compliance with those terms. . . . Not only has the Constitutional theory of federalism been replaced by a half-baked theory of decentralization, but it is a vulgar and, at times, vicious theory as well. . . . (pp. 84-85, 86)

Theodore Lowi (1978) concurs, arguing that the development of new, more coercive regulatory and redistributive programs at the national level merits a change in nomenclature from the "United States" to the "United State" (p. 15). What he terms the "Second Republic" has a new constitutional foundation, rooted in the belief that "There ought to be a national presence in every aspect of American lives. National power is no longer a necessary evil; it is a positive virtue" (1979, p. xi). Finally, Martin Landau (1973) — while finding some resurgence of the federal principle in the myriad organizational entities at the local level — has concluded that

> . . . the nationalization or centralization of authority has all but stripped the states of their independence. If there are now two separate systems operating in distinct but parallel channels, the states are not one of them. (pp. 191-192)

In pointed contrast, other scholars believe the reports of federalism's demise—as Mark Twain said about his own obituary—are greatly exaggerated. To Donald H. Haider (1981),

> . . . federalism . . . is very much alive, though a bit battered from the past twenty years' experience. . . . Although complex and multifaceted, federalism is still susceptible to experimentation, flexibility, and change. (p. 30)

Drawing upon his monitoring studies of general revenue sharing and the community development and CETA block grants (see Nathan, 1982), Richard Nathan argues that much of the concern about intergovernmental relations is rooted in mythology, rather than facts. For example, he maintains that

> . . . local democracy in the United States is really quite healthy; the trend of the past decade toward broader and less conditional federal grants has aided and abetted localism as a basic value of our political system. . . . The odd man out in all of this lately has been the states, the all important middle-man of the federal system. However, the states have basically good prospects down the road (1981a, p. 535; see also Nathan, 1981b; and Anton, 1980, p. 74)

Catherine Lovell (1979) shares a similar view, suggesting that only "on the surface" does the intergovernmental system appear to be tilting to Washington. Counterbalancing the fiscal advantages of the national government, she suggests, are new political pressures:

> [T]he last decade has seen the failures of so much centralization and has brought intensified demands for devolution and decentralization. . . . New breeds of liberals have joined hands with traditional conservatives in Congress to enact general revenue and block grant forms which devolve responsibility and expand state and local flexibility in decisions about spending. . . . Local governments are alive and well and becoming more aggressive. (pp. 9-10)

These sharply conflicting assessments illustrate the limitations of current theories of federalism and intergovernmental relations and demonstrate the diversity of views that presently mark the field. Leading authorities cannot agree whether American federalism is "very much alive" or recently expired, having crossed the line to a unitary state. Such dissension has both empirical and normative roots. In part, the current "complexity of the American public sector has itself been a major obstacle to clear understanding" (Anton, Cawley, & Kramer, 1980, pp. 9-10) and, as Lovell argues (1979, p. 6), "intergovernmental processes have been modified . . . more rapidly than we have been able to understand them." Yet, earlier developments in both theory and governmental practice contributed equally to this confusion. The balance of this essay will examine both dimensions, tracing the dissolution of federal theory as it has developed over time. Three schools of federal thought, each rooted in classical defenses of federalism, are examined, with particular attention to the potential guidance each provides on current federalism issues. Finally, the paper identifies some promising directions for future research.

FEDERALISM AND DEMOCRACY

From the late eighteenth century to the present, two basic political claims have been advanced on behalf of federalism. One maintains that federalism provides the most advantageous governmental arrangement for reconciling the competing political advantages of large and small republics. The second emphasizes its role in preventing concentrations of governmental power and in promoting public access to government decision-making.

While powerful arguments were developed very early along these lines, there have been few recent advances in federal theory. Normatively, these political arguments do lend support for the concept of dividing governmental authority, but they provide little practical guidance for designing a workable federal system. Empirically, evaluations of the links between democratic values and federalism have produced mixed or inconclusive results. Moreover, democratic theories of federalism have lost much of their original descriptive value as intergovernmental administrative arrangements have proliferated and American politics has been nationalized during the twentieth century.

Governmental Size and Democracy

An essential element in the political theory of federalism stems from the view that genuinely democratic government can flourish only in a small political entity. This notion has exerted a powerful influence on American political thought from colonial times to the present. It arises ultimately from the physical constraints on direct democracy: a true democracy cannot exceed a size that will accommodate a decision-making assembly of its citizens. Even allowing for representation, many believe the association between democratic vigor and smallness to be strong. In a small community, citizens are thought to be more familiar with both issues and leaders. They may perceive a greater stake in governmental affairs and have a greater sense of political efficacy. Both motivationally and logistically, then, smallness often is thought to contribute to democracy by enhancing citizen participation in and control over government.

Initially, such reasoning drew heavily upon the writings of Montesquieu (1748/1961), who wrote that:

> It is natural for a republic to have only a small territory; otherwise it cannot long subsist. In an extensive republic there are men of large fortunes, and consequently of less moderation . . . the public good is sacrificed to a thousand private views; it is subordinate to exceptions, and depends on accidents. In a small one, the interest of the public is more obvious, better understood, and more within the reach of every citizen. (pp. 395-396)

In America, this theory found its most influential spokesman in Thomas Jefferson—although similar views were held by all the "anti-federalist" opponents of the Federal Constitution. Jefferson urged that American government be founded on a series of local "wards," so that "any citizen can attend, when called upon, and act in person" (1816). In the New England states, he observed, such wards or townships "are the vital principle of their governments, and have proved themselves the wisest invention ever designed by the wit of man for the perfect exercise of self-government, and for its preservation."

Despite the passage of time, this view has continued to exert a powerful and lasting effect on American political thought and rhetoric. Today, it is often expressed as the belief that local government is "closer to the people," but the concept itself has changed very little. Thus, the following statement by Richard Nixon (1971) might well have been spoken by a Jeffersonian Democrat:

> [T]he further away government is from people, the stronger government becomes and the weaker people become. . . . [L]ocal government is the government closest to the *people* and it is most responsive to the individual *person;* it is peoples' government in a far more intimate way than the government in Washington can ever be. (pp. 53, 59)

Carried to its logical conclusion, however, this argument favors confederation, not federalism, and was advanced by the antifederalists for this reason. It therefore raises all of the impracticalities and administrative ills of confederation identified and attacked in the *Federalist*. But there also is contained in the *Federalist* a deeper, philosophical challenge to the notion that small units of government are particularly suited to nourish democratic government. In his famous argument in *Federalist* 10, Madison turned the small republic theory on its head, arguing that small states actually are more, not less, susceptible than large ones to domination by a narrow faction:

> The smaller the society, the fewer probably will be the distinct parties and interests composing it; the fewer the distinct parties and interests, the more frequently will a majority be found of the same party; and the smaller the number of individuals composing a majority, and the smaller the compass within which they are placed, the more easily will they concert and execute their plans of oppression. (p. 60)

The greater diversity of a larger state mitigates this tendency and promotes freer, more representative government:

> Extend the sphere, and you take in a greater variety of parties and interests; you make it less probable that a majority of the whole will have a common motive to invade the rights of other citizens; or if such a common motive exists, it will be more difficult for all who feel it to discover their own strength, and to act in unison with each other. . . . [I]n the extent and proper structure of the Union, therefore, we behold a republican remedy for the diseases most incident to republican government. (p. 61)

A variety of modern scholars have come to share Madison's assessment of the relative disadvantages of local government. Grant McConnell (1966) argued that "the effect of a small constituency is to enhance the power of local elites. . . . Decentralization . . . does not make for democracy. . . . It creates conditions hostile to democracy" (pp. 109, 114). Likewise, Morton Grodzins (1963, pp. 9, 10) maintained the claims that local government is closer to the people are simply "meaningless."

Such reasoning might ultimately imply a unified national state, although it was developed in the *Federalist* in support of the proposed Constitution. Nevertheless, there has been a continuing and perhaps inevitable tension between the two schools of thought. For most of American history, the conventions of localistic democracy held sway among the populace-at-large (Croly, 1965; Beer, 1973). Not until the 1930s was the federal government widely perceived to be more democratic than subnational units of government. At this time, a series of developments unforeseen in the eighteenth century—the creation of a modern party system, welfare state, and a system of progressive federal taxation—contributed to the belief that a distant national government could become more representative of and responsive to a majority of its citizens.

However, the tensions between the competing theories subsumed under federalism did not diminish over time, nor have they been resolved by empirical evidence on the relative political merits of different levels of government. Though the record is sparse, it tends to yield mixed results. On the one hand, the national arena seems to possess advantages for organized electoral participation. As a rule, party competition appears to be stronger at the national level (Leach, 1970, p. 124). Moreover, the nationalization of the media means that political information is increasingly focused on the national government. Studies of governmental salience have found that people are more aware of the federal government (Jennings & Zeigler, 1970). Other studies show that more people can identify their national elected officials than their state and local officials (Reeves & Glendening, 1976), and electoral statistics demonstrate that voter participation is higher in national elections (Verba & Nie, 1972, p. 31; Dahl & Tufte, 1973, p. 57).

On the other hand, modern studies of public attitudes reveal that people believe local government is more understandable to them, and they feel more capable of affecting a governmental policy at the local level (Dahl & Tufte, 1973, pp. 53-61). With the apparent dissolution of our political parties, this sense of efficacy may become an increasingly important source of democratic stability. In addition, survey research indicates that people have more confidence in state and local government performance ("Opinion Roundup," 1982a, p. 36, 1982b, p. 28).

These varied results are generally supportive of the federal principle, with its efforts to utilize the merits of each level of government. But this is, at best, a very general concept. It offers little guidance for the actual assignment of governmental functions or for coping with the exigencies of governing. Within a balanced federalism, one might prefer a somewhat greater concentration of programs or authority at one level or another, but unless there is a clear link between citizen participation and representation in a certain function at a given level of government, democratic assertions about governmental size provide little basis for determining where individual programs should be placed or how they should be shared. This perspective does suggest, however, that a governmental system should be simple enough to facilitate citizen understanding and have clear channels of accountability.

Federalism and Pluralism

While challenging the small republic theory of democracy in *Federalist* 10, Madison suggested a second link between federalism and democratic government. Federalism, he argued, was one expression of the constitutional system of divided powers intended to safeguard individual liberty. As Madison argued in *Federalist* 51:

> In the compound republic of America, the power surrendered by the people is first divided between two distinct governments, and then the portion allotted to each subdivided among distinct and separate departments. Hence a double security arises to the rights of the people. The different governments will control each other, at the same time that each will be controlled by itself. (p. 339)

Thus, he provided a pluralistic defense for federalism based, not on the democratic merits of different levels of government, but on the constitutional protections afforded by the territorial division of governmental authority.

This justification of federalism has attracted many modern adherents (Elazar, 1968, p. 354), and, over time, it has been strengthened and elaborated by additional pluralist arguments. It is maintained, for example, that the multiple power centers and access points in a federal system may enhance governmental responsiveness and improve the process of representation (Truman, 1971, p. 507; and Beer, 1978, p. 15). In the study of comparative government, federalism has been viewed as a device for protecting and insulating territorial minorities in such ethnically divided countries as Canada, Switzerland, Yugoslavia, and Nigeria.

To be sure, most empirical research has failed to demonstrate any systematic relationship between a federal system and the protection of individual and minority rights. As William Riker (1964; see also Neuman, 1955, p. 54) has pointed out:

> Local self government and personal freedom both coexist with a highly centralized unitary government in Great Britain and the Vargas dictatorship in Brazil managed to coexist with federalism. (p. 140)

In the U.S., he stressed, federalism facilitated the oppression of blacks, first as slaves and later as a depressed caste (1964, p. 152). Similarly, Eric Nordlinger (1972, p. 31) found that "federalism may actually contribute to . . . the failure of conflict regulation [in] some deeply divided societies." Nonetheless, it is evident that federalism has assisted in avoiding undue concentrations of political power in the American context, and it probably contributes to protecting individual liberty when it is part of a broader fabric of constitutional representation and restraint. Most importantly, perhaps, the pluralist argument for federalism is one of the few theories that clearly justifies genuine federalism, with its autonomous and unalterable subunits, rather than simply administrative or political decentralization.

Federal Theory and Political Change

Possibly the most serious problem facing both political theories of federalism is that neither has been systematically adapted to account for dramatic changes in American governmental structure and operation over time. Moreover, in comparative politics, where scholars first attempted to modernize political theories of federalism, they launched a chain of reasoning that threatened to trivialize the subject altogether. Starting in the 1950s, a number of political scientists began to view federalism in behavioral terms, as a political "process" or "bargain" that was frequently an unstable phase of political development (MacMahon, 1955; Riker, 1964; Friedrich, 1968). As the often vague concept of the federal process was stretched to encompass "infinite variety" (Earle, 1968), however, one prominent scholar was led to conclude that the concept was simply meaningless and without value (Riker, 1975).

In the American context, one example of the growing disjunction between democratic theory and governmental practice is evident in Madison's argument for an extended republic in *Federalist* 10, which was premised on the difficulties of enacting legislation at the national level (Leach, 1970, p. 57). In *Federalist* 46, moreover, he argued that state interests would be abundantly represented in the Congress.

Until the 1960s, such assessments appeared to be substantiated by political scholarship replete with references to "veto groups," "deadlock" and the "obstacle course" in Congress. For its part, the political party system was described as the bulwark of state and local interests in the United States (Grodzins, 1966, p. 254). In the post-1960 era, such generalizations seem hopelessly anachronistic (King, 1978). A decentralized and entrepreneurial Congress has been transformed from a legislative burial ground into a principal source of federal program initiatives (Orfield, 1975; Price, 1972; ACIR, 1981a). Interest groups are now widely viewed as the clients and supplicants of new federal legislation. The decentralized party system has decomposed, replaced in part by an active national media and by nationally-based interest groups. Yet the implications that dramatic federal growth and the nationalization of politics hold for the political theory of federalism have barely been explored.

Similarly, federal theory has yet to come to grips with problems of political accountability once "cooperative" federalism becomes the rule instead of the exception. Established theories have explored the relative advantages of concentrating government decisionmaking at the national or local level, as well as the advantages of utilizing both levels in a federal structure and dividing governmental functions between them. But as more and more activities are shared—often among three or more levels of government—through an increasingly complex array of grant and regulatory programs, political accountability becomes increasingly diffused. Citizen and even scholarly understanding of the actual workings of government is eroded, and responsibility for program performance cannot be fixed. Thus, the links between public preferences, citizen involvement, and policy outcomes that federalism was designed to enhance have become attenuated, with little guidance for redressing the situation provided by static theories of federalism.

THE POLITICAL ECONOMY OF FEDERALISM

A second normative approach to the study of federalism applies the methodology of economic analysis to political behavior in a federal system. This approach, often referred to as fiscal federalism or rational choice theory, shares many of the concerns of the more traditional democratic theories of federalism. Both tend to define political behavior in simple majoritarian terms. Moreover, both are concerned with the influence of governmental structure on the relationships between citizen preferences and public policy. On this basis, rational choice theory argues convincingly that federalism matters—that the territorial organization of government affects the content of policy.

Although its origins have been traced back to the *Federalist* (Ostrom, 1971), rational choice theory has developed most fully only in recent years. It has made several notable contributions to the study of federalism, such as providing a general framework for assigning governmental functions. Ultimately, however, rational choice theory suffers many of the flaws of traditional democratic theory in failing to account adequately for many features of modern intergovernmental relations.

Government Structure and Public Preferences

The underlying justification for federalism in rational choice theory derives from the distribution of public preferences for various public goods. Given regional variations in the demand for a particular public good, government production of the good can more closely match the preferences of more individuals through a decentralized system of government. Each jurisdiction then can respond to local preferences precisely, rather than having the central government produce a uniform level of the collective good (Oates, 1972). This efficiency can be enhanced through the market-like conditions of residential mobility, allowing like-minded individuals to migrate to jurisdictions offering a "market basket" of public goods corresponding to their own preferences.

A basis for allocating governmental functions also can be found in the argument that welfare is maximized when individual preferences match jurisdictional boundaries. Mancur Olson calls this concept the "principle of fiscal equivalence." He suggests (1969) that inefficiencies will occur when:

> (1) the collective good reaches beyond the boundaries of the government that provides it; [or] (2) the collective good reaches only a part of the constituency that provides it. (p. 482)

Either case results in economic externalities (or "internalities") that may encourage suboptimal production of collective goods. When benefits from a local function extend to nonpaying residents outside a jurisdiction, incentives exist to support the program at levels below its total social value. On the other hand, if a portion of the costs flow to individuals on the outside, the jurisdiction may overproduce the good because it is not bearing the total costs of the program. Similar effects result from "internalities," wherein a public good reaches only a geographic subset of a jurisdiction's population.

Based upon these propositions, most economists assign the tasks of economic stabilization and income redistribution to the central government, due to the national scope of their impact and the constraints on decentralized responses to them (Oates, 1972, pp. 4-11, 31-33; see also Musgrave, 1959; Ladd & Doolittle, 1982). Other governmental functions are then assigned to various levels of government according to the geographical range of their benefits. On the basis of this principle, economist George Break developed a classification of 20 public services useful in making functional assignments. For example, police and fire protection were classified as local functions; pollution control and mass transit were described as regional; and education and income maintenance were placed in the federal category (Break, 1967, p. 69).

Carried to an extreme, however, optimizing the concurrence between individual service preferences and governmental jurisdictions would promote a vast array of special servicing authorities (Ostrom, 1973) and ultimately "a separate governmental institution for every collective good with a unique boundary" (Olson, 1969, p. 483; Tullock, 1976). To avoid this in cases where externalities are of only modest size or accurate functional boundaries are difficult to draw, rational choice theorists recommend the use of grants from surrounding or higher jurisdictions to compensate a provider government for its production of external benefits (Olson, 1969, pp. 485, 486; Break, 1967). Without such assistance, the producing jurisdiction would have economic incentives to underproduce the collective good involved.

Evaluating Economic Theory

This line of reasoning suggests that the territorial organization of governmental activity can have a significant and systematic effect on policy outputs and on governmental responsiveness to citizen preferences. In a period marked by behavioralist skepticism about the effect of government structure on behavior, this contribution alone is significant. In addition, rational choice theory establishes an explanation and justification for the growth of intergovernmental grants, and it helps to direct the assignment of functions.

Yet, there are a series of unresolved problems confronting rational choice theory. At the most general level, economic theory does not justify federalism but political decentralization (Oates, 1972, pp. 17, 18). The fixed jurisdictional boundaries of component states in a federal system are inconsistent with the economic objective of continuous jurisdictional adjustments to changing patterns of externalities (Beer, 1977, p. 27).

Moreover, the promise of rational choice as a tool for directing functional allocations has been largely unfulfilled to date. In many cases, the externalities resulting from governmental policies simply cannot be measured with any accuracy (Oates, 1977, p. 6; McKean, 1966, p. 54). This problem is exacerbated when various important but unquantifiable factors are included in the calculation of functional assignments. For example, the gains promised by fiscal equivalence may be eroded by countervailing advantages present in a simpler system of fewer, consolidated jurisdictions, such as administrative coordination and economies of scale. In addition, increased governmental fragmentation in a rational choice setting may impose sizable information costs even on the population of rational citizens inhabiting the world of public choice. Because such factors rarely can be measured, rational choice theory may lose much of its normative power when confronting the real world.

Partly because of such difficulties, the policy prescriptions of rational choice theorists often vary, especially between more traditional public finance economists and a newer school of "public choice" economists. The former often utilize the theory to justify increased use of federal grants (Break, 1967) and greater program centralization. As Alan Campbell (1975) observed: "To minimize the flow of externalities, a greater number of activities must be assigned to large jurisdictions—to metropolitanwide ones, to states, and frequently to the national government" (p. 36). In contrast, the public choice school has favored highly decentralized policies. Its advocates (Bish, 1971; Ostrom, 1961) look favorably on a great diversity of small local governments that can establish market-like conditions in public services, as each jurisdiction competes for resident taxpayers through its offering of services and its rate of efficiency and taxation. Public choice economists have also expressed strong opposition to governmental centralization in other forms. Ostrom (1974), Niskanen (1971), and Buchanan (1977), for example, have all stressed the administrative and representational weaknesses of large, centralized bureaucracies.

Ultimately, both schools resemble political theories of federalism in their failure to adequately address current patterns of federal politics and intergovernmental relations. Economic analysts generally assume drastically oversimplified models of political behavior. Thus, the median voter model of representative government often is used to link government behavior to externalities (Olson, 1969, p. 482), despite ample evidence that actual electoral behavior is poorly described by the model (Stokes, 1963). More recent attempts by public choice theorists to explain government growth on the basis of budget maximizing bureaucrats (Niskanen, 1971) also lack a strong empirical footing (Derthick, 1975; ACIR, 1981a, p. 20).

The relationships between rational choice theory and current intergovernmental practice are also inadequate. Although the theory does attempt to account for intergovernmental transfers, grants are often viewed as marginal adjustments to the system. Economic theories of federalism still assume that the normal pattern of governmental adjustment to externalities is for spillovers to be internalized within relatively autonomous jurisdictions. Moreover, close observers of the intergovernmental system note that grants often do not fit the economic model. Charles Schultze (1974) maintains that "most categorical grants for social programs are not based on this [spillover] rationale" (p. 182). Like others (Monypenny, 1960; Mushkin, 1960), he suggests that existing programs are products of quite different historical and political factors. Similarly, economic norms about the proper design of grants conflict sharply with administrative experience derived from operating programs (Beam, 1980). In short, the powerful normative thrust of rational choice theory, like traditional democratic theory, requires more empirical verification and descriptive validity in order to contribute more fully to policy issues, both now and in the future.

ADMINISTRATIVE PERSPECTIVES ON FEDERALISM

Another early rationale for federalism centered on administrative considerations. The Founders believed that the system of divided authority established by the Constitution would assure better management of public affairs than had occurred under the preceding confederation or would be possible under a wholly unitary state. This remained the dominant administrative premise for at least 140 years. Although political scientists and public administrators developed new theories of cooperative federalism to describe and justify the expansion of intergovernmental programs from the New Deal to the mid-1960s, many recent commentators stress the obstacles to effective management created by a federal division of authority and the extensive use of intergovernmental techniques. However, despite some promising recent suggestions, no widely accepted alternate theory has yet been devised.

The Premise of Functional Separation

As MacMahon (1972, p. 29) observes, the United States pioneered the principle of direct national administration in a federal system. In *Federalist* 23, Hamilton stressed that one of the principal failings of the Articles of Confederation was the dependence of the national government upon the states in such crucial areas as defense and finance. The national government, he argued, needed to be authorized to execute independently whatever functions were entrusted to it. Under the new Constitution, he contended,

> . . . the essential point . . . will be to discriminate the OBJECTS . . . which shall appertain to the different provinces or departments of power; allowing to each the most ample authority for fulfilling the objects committed to its charge. Shall the Union be constituted the guardian of the common safety? Are fleets and armies and revenues necessary to this purpose? The government of the Union must be empowered to pass all laws, and to make all regulations which have relation to them. The same must be the case, in respect to commerce, and to every other matter to which its jurisdiction is permitted to extend. . . . Not to confer in each case a degree of power, commensurate to the end, would be to violate the most obvious rules of prudence and propriety, and improvidently to trust the great interests of the nation to hands, which are disabled from managing them with vigour and success. (p. 144)

A century later, John Stuart Mill (1861/1958) endorsed this theory as well:

> Within the limits of its attributions, [the Congress] makes laws which are obeyed by every citizen individually, executes them through its own officers, and enforces them by its own tribunals. This is the only principle which has been found, or which is ever likely to produce an effective federal government. (p. 323)

On the other hand, the Founders—and many others since—also stressed the impossibility of effectively managing a large nation from a single center. Jefferson (1816/1939) bolstered his democratic arguments for federalism with a claim that a unitary system would invite maladministration:

> Our country is too large to have all its affairs directed by a single government. Public servants at such a distance . . . must . . . be unable to administer and overlook all the details necessary for the good government of the citizenry, and the same circumstance, by rendering detection impossible to their constituents, will invite the public agents to corruption, plunder, and waste. (p. 30)

Madison (*Federalist* 14) offered a parallel view. Indeed, he contended,

> [I]t would not be difficult to show that if [the states] were abolished the general government would be compelled, by the principle of self-preservation, to reinstate them in their proper jurisdiction. (p. 102)

Thus, important administrative arguments were offered in support of dual federalism, and early practice largely conformed to these dictates. Nearly all major functions of the time (the administration of justice, road building, care of the indigent, the chartering of businesses) fell primarily to local and state governments. The federal establishment of the early 1800s was "small almost beyond modern imagination," with a "Congress larger than its administrative apparatus" (Young, 1966, pp. 28, 31). Yet when needs arose within its own areas of competence, the federal government could and often did act independently to carry out its responsibilities (Walker, 1981, p. 51; MacMahon, 1972; Beer, 1982, p. 17).

Although Hamilton's early emphasis on an energetic executive set out a philosophy of administration that served the nation well, and was in many respects far in advance of its time, professional attention to the subject was almost entirely lacking during most of the nineteenth century (White, 1955, pp. 10, 14-15). Recognition of the managerial function as one requiring specialized expertise and technique did not occur until 1890 and thereafter. When it began, it began

> . . . in the cities, especially the big ones, not in theories of sovereignty or the state or separation of powers. The cities were where most government was, where most action was, where most problems were, where the services of public administrators could most demonstrably be made more effective, more honest, and less costly. (Mosher, 1975, p. 8)

New administrative doctrines, developed chiefly by municipal governments, spread to the states and to Washington. The focus of attention was on prescriptions that remain the heart of administrative orthodoxy—a strong chief executive with budgetary and appointive powers, hierarchical organization by function, and the separation of administration from politics—at *each* level: national, state, and local. Functional autonomy of these governments, as prescribed by dual federalism, was assumed, since this accorded well with predominant practice. Indeed, Lovell (1979, p. 15) notes that many administrative theorists—unwisely in her view—still continue to assume that most functions should be performed by one particular level of government.

In another respect, however, the newly emerging theory of public administration was inconsistent with the traditional understanding of federalism. Administrative doctrine requires the presence of a formal hierarchy, whereas federalism is incompatible with such a form of organization. Eventually, this hierarchical model was transferred from administrative relationships *within* each government to those *between* them, though the authoritative relations which make hierarchical structuring possible were absent in this setting. From the standpoint of conventional theory, as Ostrom (1974, p. 35) has charged, "Large jurisdictions are preferred to small. Centralized solutions are preferred to the disaggregation of authority among diverse decision structures." To be sure, operational considerations may require an element of decentralization in the execution of policies established at the top. But even decentralization may imply hierarchical relations, "a pyramid of governments with gradations of power flowing down from the top" (Elazar, 1976, p. 13).

The Rationale for Cooperation

Morton Grodzins (1966) and Daniel Elazar (1962) in particular have stressed that the actual allocation of functions in the American system never corresponded entirely with the dictates of dual federalism. For example, even before the Constitution was ratified, the national government offered land grants for public schools.

During the nineteenth century, the number of land and cash grants slowly mounted, and most of the features of the modern formula grant—with its plans, matching requirements, audits, and so forth—were in place by the 1920s (ACIR, 1978, pp. 16-17). Yet, no special place was provided for these programs in administrative theory. After all, the Hamiltonian vision of independent governmental levels, separately financed and administered, still applied in most fields. Even as late as 1927, state governments received only about 2% of their revenues through the 15 grant programs then operating (Walker, 1981, p. 62).

This changed during the New Deal. The enactment of permanent and temporary grant-in-aid programs generated outlays that, in 1939, were more than 15 times the 1933 total, and touched a host of new functional fields. Supreme Court decisions in that period gave the grant technique a firmer constitutional footing and eliminated long-standing barriers on the scope of Congressional action.

The range of new intergovernmental activity began to attract attention from some scholars (Key, 1937; Clark, 1938). Those who examined the administrative implications of grants-in-aid often found much to applaud in what seemed to be a practical device for shared responsibility and cooperative effort. An early study stressed its managerial advantages:

> The grant system builds on and utilizes existing institutions to cope with national problems. Under it the states are welded into national machinery of sorts and the establishment of costly, parallel, direct federal services is made un-

necessary. A virtue of no mean importance is that the administrators in actual charge of operations remain amenable to local control. In that way the supposed formality, the regularity, and the cold-blooded efficiency of a national hierarchy are avoided. (Key, 1937, p. 383)

Although intergovernmental mechanisms were generally regarded as exceptional by the public administration community (White, 1955, p. 138), and sometimes ignored entirely (Pfiffner & Sherwood, 1960), this positive view prevailed. The Commission on Intergovernmental Relations, which undertook the first comprehensive official assessment, regarded the administrative problems associated with the grant system as comparatively minor inconveniences, more matters of detail than basic design (1955, pp. 140-142). Indeed, the strength of federalism increasingly was said to lie in its capacity for collaborative, rather than separate, action. As Grodzins (1966) declared:

> The grant programs have supplied a cooperative method for achieving results that might never have been achieved if the grant technique had not been developed. . . . It made possible the allocation of responsibilities between the levels of government according to criteria of administrative and fiscal efficiency. These criteria can be simply stated: the national government assumed partial responsibility for supplying funds and primary responsibility for establishing minimum standards of service, because the national government possessed superior fiscal resources and was concerned with the general welfare of the residents of all states. The states (and their political subdivisions) assumed primary responsibility for administration, because they were in the better position to interpret and meet local needs. (p. 62)

Contemporary Crosscurrents

Through the 1950s, the model of "cooperative federalism" provided an excellent description of federal-state relations. Grant programs were manageable in number and concentrated chiefly in areas in which federal and state officials shared common goals and administrative perspectives. Beginning in the mid-1960s, however, both public officials and management experts began to recognize that this doctrine offered inadequate guidance on many emerging management issues. These concerns reflected the proliferation of categorical aids—more new grants were authorized between 1964-66 than in all preceeding years—as well as a broadening of recipient jurisdictions and changes in program requirements (ACIR, 1967, pp. 150-184).

In the wake of the Great Society, many state and local officials complained of administrative confusion and red tape resulting from the array of new programs (Haider, 1974, pp. 52-62). Such analysts as Sundquist (1968) noted that, while basic policy decisions had been made in favor of an expanded federal role, new administrative strategies were now required:

> Many of the new goals that have been proclaimed by the national government have to be achieved through the initiative and the administrative expertise of other governments, state and local, that legally are independent and political-

ly may be even hostile. The transformation of the federal system seems to have been accepted, but the mechanisms that will make it work have yet to be perfected. . . . If and when a new "Hoover commission" is created, these are the questions that need attention. (p. 536)

Sundquist's critical assessment was confirmed by many later evaluation and implementation studies. Pressman and Wildavsky (1973), in particular, noted the difficulty of translating intentions into results through the multiplicity of actors and long string of decision points typical of most intergovernmental programs.

Yet, for the most part, such calls for reform as first emerged did not challenge the fundamental premises of the system of shared responsibility. Rather, the stress was upon devices for improved program coordination (at the community, regional, and national levels) and for the consolidation of separate categorical programs into broader block grants. This latter strategy had earlier been proposed by the First Hoover Commission (1949), which in a short discussion of federal-state relationships had condemned the growing fragmentation, overlap, and duplication among aid programs in a manner parallel to its criticism of haphazard executive branch organization. Although the Hoover Commission's proposals for grant consolidation met with little success in Congress, leading some to question the theory upon which they were based (Mushkin, 1960), block grants became a major instrument of reform under the Nixon Administration's 'New Federalism" (Conlan, 1981). Throughout, however, the key issue was viewed as simply one of the appropriate degree of administrative centralization or decentralization, not the reallocation of functions between autonomous governmental levels.

Many implementation researchers contend, however, that federalism poses very serious obstacles to the effective operation of centrally designed programs. They also stress that potential administrative pitfalls need to be taken into consideration during the policymaking process and generally favor simple, direct techniques for the delivery of public services over complex grants-in-aid. Yet, as Elmore (1979) has commented, "implementation research is long on description and short on prescription" (p. 601). Certainly it provides no clear or consistent guidance on questions concerning the proper allocation of functions and powers among governmental levels or for managing intergovernmental programs. Many studies confine their findings and recommendations to the operation of a specific aid program (Dommel, et al., 1982; Mirengoff & Rindler, 1978; Nathan, Manvel, & Calkins, 1975). Those that do offer broader conclusions draw upon many different organizational models (Elmore, 1978) and often have conflicting policy views. Thus some writers believe that past failures of federal program initiatives resulted from a division of authority that

. . . made it hard for federal policy makers to know what must be done to achieve their objectives locally, and for federal administrators to bring federal resources . . . effectively to bear on local settings. The same characteristics largely account also for the federal tendency to set unrealizable objectives. (Derthick, 1972, p. 93)

At the same time, others attribute the weaknesses of program performance to

> . . . the federal system—with its dispersion of power and control—[that] not only permits but encourages the evasion and dilution of federal reform, making it nearly impossible for the federal administrator to impose program priorities; those not diluted by Congressional intervention, can be ignored during state and local implementation. (Murphy, 1971, p. 60)

The first diagnosis seems to point toward devolution, the second toward increased national control.

In very recent years, a few public administrators have begun to assert that the issues posed by the management of federal-state-local relationships may necessitate a reexamination of the basic premises of administrative theory. Frederick Mosher (1980) notes that:

> In decades gone by, most of what the federal government was responsible for and expended money for it did by itself through its own personnel and facilities. Consequently, much of the doctrine and lore of federal management . . . was based on the premise that its efficiency rested on the effective supervision and direction of its own operations. (p. 541)

In fact, he adds, less than 20% of the federal budget now is directed to domestic activities that the federal government actually performs itself. Changes in both the *content* and *means* of program operation suggest the need, Mosher argues, for a "truly new public administration."

Another writer, Lester M. Salamon (1981), concurs with this general thesis, noting that the federal government is now heavily dependent upon "third parties," including state and local governments, for the accomplishment of its objectives. These changes may well have rendered many of the traditional preoccupations of public administration obsolete. The key to developing a more useful theory of public management, Salamon believes, might be to focus research on developing a systematic body of knowledge about the alternative "tools" of public policy, including various forms of grants-in-aid, insurance programs, loan guarantees, and so forth. From the standpoint of contemporary intergovernmental relations, special attention should be paid to the host of new regulatory devices affecting state and local governments (Beam, 1981). In contrast to the older "economic regulation," much of the "new social regulation" (Lilly & Miller, 1977) is directed at or implemented by these jurisdictions. This change—like the earlier development of grants—has important fiscal, political, and legal implications (Dubnick & Gitelson, 1981; Lovell, *et al.*, 1979; Muller & Fix, 1980).

Such innovative efforts to guide the research agenda warrant consideration. At the same time, however, they are a clear admission that an adequate theory of administration in a modern federal system does not exist presently. Public administrators have consistently failed to recognize the full implications of an expanding array of intergovernmental programs for governmental management at every level. While the traditional normative theory of separated responsibilities was set aside long ago, largely because it failed to accurately describe actual practice, no new approach has yet been developed to take its place.

CONCLUSION

This paper has outlined the theoretical divergence and empirical deficiencies of three traditional schools of federal thought. The record is disquieting, for it suggests that contemporary research provides inadequate guidance concerning the nation's most important governmental invention and the resolution of some of its most pressing political issues.

This is not to agree, however, that the concept of federalism is outmoded — or that it is, as some writers have argued, simply a temporary way station on the developmental path toward a single national community and a unitary national government. Ironically, just as federalism was being abandoned by many specialists, the influence of federalism and intergovernmental relations was belatedly discovered in other fields of political science. Comparative studies disclosed differences in the character of intergovernmental relations in federal and unitary states (Rose, 1982, pp. 161-165). The federal context of city politics was stressed increasingly in urban studies (Yates, 1979; Peterson, 1981). The role of federal grants in encouraging a new pattern of independent Congressional behavior was dissected in legislative research (Mayhew, 1974; Fiorina, 1979; Arnold, 1979), and new conceptions of bureaucratic politics and public administration were built upon intergovernmental foundations (Salamon, 1981; Mosher, 1980).

Even more importantly, federalism remains a living political reality, changed in form but embodying history and popular attachment (Hamilton, 1978). In policy circles, federalism is constantly being reborn in both pragmatic and philosophical attempts to restructure American government and improve its performance. In pursuit of very different objectives, issues of federalism have formed the centerpiece of domestic policy under four of the last five Presidents. Many post-industrial nations are currently grappling with proposals for devolution and the United States is no exception.

Indeed, if the idea of federalism did not now exist, it might have to be reinvented. Recent American experience validates Woodrow Wilson's (1908) observation that "the question of the relation of the States to the federal government is the cardinal question of our constitutional system"—one that cannot be permanently resolved because "every successive stage of our political and economic development gives it a new aspect, makes it a new question" (p. 173). Just as the rigid legal compartmentalization of national and state responsibilities was properly set aside to meet the exigencies of the Great Depression, theories of cooperative federalism used to explain and guide the formulation of policy during the late 1950s and early 1960s may now require similar revision. After all, their ready acceptance occurred in an era of widespread prosperity, rapid economic growth, growing public sector revenues, and high public confidence, and reflected the comparatively limited intergovernmental system that then prevailed. Despite cold war tensions, America's leadership in much of the free world was then unchallenged. In contrast, the contemporary period has been one of economic stagflation and resource shortages at all governmental levels, rising public alienation, and a very large and complex system of intergovernmental programs. The U.S. faces increasing economic competition from abroad, a declining status in global affairs, and an increasing threat of nuclear catastrophe. The states, on the other hand, are in far better institutional shape to assume an active domestic policy role than they were 15 years ago (Elazar, 1974; Sharkansky, 1978; ACIR, 1982; Reeves, 1983). All of these factors suggest that questions about the allocation of governmental responsibilities will figure prominently on the political agenda of the 1980s and 1990s, as they have during the past two decades.

Partly because of such developments, some scholars now suggest that American federalism may be in need of fundamental legal and constitutional reforms. For instance, Robert B. Hawkins, Jr. (1982; see also Elazar, 1980; Buchanan, 1975; and Wildavsky, 1980) comments that

> . . . the Founding Fathers, if they were around today, would certainly look at to-day's problems as problems of constitutional design. For example, the inability of Congress to control spending would be seen as a constitutional defect requiring a constitutional change. (p. 251)

Certainly, the widespread perception that key constitutional issues have all been resolved in favor of national authority overlooks the lively debate that has occurred within the judicial branch over the past decade. During the 1970s a considerable number of federal regulatory statutes were challenged by state and local governments (or other interested parties) and the judicial branch has reemerged as an important arena for intergovernmental deliberation (Cappalli, 1979; Horowitz, 1977; Howard, 1982; Kaden, 1979; Frug, 1978; Cole, 1982).

Although both legal and emerging policy issues deserve scholarly attention, we would suggest that the most critical task may be theoretical in nature: the consolidation and revision of the three schools of federal thought outlined above in light of current empirical observations. Each has something useful to contribute to the rejuvenation of federal theory, but none is adequate to the task alone. Because each perspective tends to correct, at least in part, for deficiencies in the others, there is a pressing need for a greater degree of theoretical integration. Some of the most interesting and potentially valuable works in recent years have drawn upon two perspectives—for example, studies in public choice merge politics and economics and implementation blends politics and administration—but very few have attempted to combine all three (but see Peterson, 1981).

Democratic theories, as the foregoing account makes clear, provide the most compelling rationale for maintaining a legally rigid system of divided authority under federalism, as opposed to a unitary system with some measure of administrative decentralization, which can be justified on a number of other grounds. This aspect of "checks and balances," like the separation of executive, legislative, and judicial authority, remains a useful hedge against excessive concentrations of power. Although such considerations may seem remote from the day-to-day concerns of programs and policymaking episodes during the Vietnam War and Watergate suggest that the Founders were wise in providing some institutional protection against potential abuses. At the same time, the experience of other nations demonstrates that federalism alone is by no means an adequate safeguard of individual liberties.

Although Madison's theory of the extended republic retains a certain credibility in the area of individual rights and liberties, which in recent times seem to have been most consistently advanced by the national government, it has become increasingly less relevant to many issues of positive governmental action. Madison believed that the sheer size and diversity of larger jurisdictions would tend to prevent their domination by organized interests in opposition to the majority will. This position had a certain plausibility during the 1950s and early 1960s, when the obstacles to action at the national level were so severe that scholars warned against the "deadlock of democracy" (Burns, 1963).

More recent experience, however, has seemed to turn Madison's forecast on its head. It is at the national level that both scholars and other political observers now find evidence of rampant factionalism and hasty action (King, 1978; Fiorina, 1977; Huntington, 1975). Charges are rife that the federal government is biased toward excessive spending and regulation, hypersensitive to the demands of special interest lobbies, or dominated by self-serving bureaucrats and politicians. The state-centered political party system—which once was regarded as the backbone of federalism—has largely withered away (Sorauf, 1976; Crotty & Jacobson, 1980). At the same time—partly because of the success of national reapportionment and civil rights policies—state governments and politics are far more representative of their constituencies than they were two decades ago.

From the standpoint of political representation, then, a federal system has opposing virtues and liabilities, each of which may be differently revealed under differing circumstances. On the one hand, as pluralists stress, multiple decisionmaking centers do improve access to government and offer alternative channels for the redress of grievances (Beer, 1978). At different times, and in different fields, the national government or the states have been the principal contributors of policy innovations. But, recent experience suggests that too much overlap in responsibility among the governmental levels can obscure channels of accountability and reduce popular control over policy decisions and outcomes.

Democratic theories of federalism provide little guidance, moreover, for determining where functions should be fixed, or which should be shared. Rather, there is a tendency to abstain entirely from normative judgments in support of whatever outcomes are ratified by the mechanisms of popular and legislative consent.

In contrast, political economic theories provide the most compelling framework for addressing questions concerning rationales for governmental action and the assignment of functions within a federal system. First, many of the problems addressed by contemporary governments are explicitly economic in character, and many of the others are at least partially susceptible to economic analysis (Amacher, Tollison, & Willett, 1976). Second, decisions about governmental services cannot be separated from questions about the availability of necessary fiscal resources: federalism has an essential revenue component as well as a servicing dimension (Musgrave, 1959; Nathan, 1975). Third, and most importantly from the perspective of this review, economic analysis offers the strongest policy prescriptions on the allocation of responsibilities among national, state, regional, and local institutions. While most political scientists have turned away from this issue, many political economists still regard it as the basic question to be resolved by a theory of federalism (Breton & Scott, 1978, p. 41).

On the other hand, this paradigm offers almost an embarrassment of riches, as evidenced by the competing prescriptions derived from the public choice and more traditional public finance perspectives. Furthermore, policy proposals that appear desirable from the standpoint of economic efficiency often turn out to be politically or administratively infeasible. Economic policy prescriptions need to be much more carefully validated if their potential power is to be realized. For example, some students of fiscal federalism have recognized that certain intergovernmental programs involve goal conflicts between governmental levels, leading to behavior quite different from that hypothesized by economic theory alone (Break, 1980; see also Ingram, 1977, and Porter, 1973).

There is, then, a pressing need for a more thorough understanding of the administration of intergovernmental programs and of the overall managerial implications of an extensively intergovernmentalized domestic policy system. Yet, neither of the two major administrative perspectives on intergovernmental relations — that is, theories of cooperative federalism and the implementation studies — provide a sound basis for generalization and policy prescription. As Peterson and Wong (1982) comment,

> . . . the new implementation theory is as undifferentiated as the old marble-cake theory. Where the optimistic view of Grodzins and his students found few areas of government activity where conjoint activity could not be undertaken, implementation theory reaches almost exactly the opposite conclusions. (p. 5)

What is required, as they argue, is a more differentiated theory of federalism. Research should attempt to identify the determinants of relatively successful and relatively unsuccessful outcomes.

One potentially useful focus involves the nature of program goals. For Elazar (1981), the major difference between the programs of the 1960s and those of an earlier period is that the latter were directed toward shared objectives, while the former were aimed at purposes established in Washington. The resulting tension has led to programmatic failures and steadily increasing federal coercion in an effort to secure compliance. These observations are consistent with some case study findings, which stress the dependence of federal program results on the state acceptance of national objectives (Edner, 1976) or the degree of local leadership and commitment (Greenwood, Mann, & McLaughlin, 1975). Peterson and Wong (1982) attempt to elaborate by suggesting that intergovernmental relationships will be more complex and conflictual where assistance programs are redistributive in intent. In contrast, federal and state objectives are likely to be shared in developmental programs, which are aimed at enhancing recipient jurisdiction's economic position. On this basis, they suggest that redistribution be a federal prerogative, while a good deal of developmental activity may be left to the states and localities.

A second promising strategy is more concerned with means than ends. The crucial point, as noted above, is a fuller recognition that the national government now depends very heavily upon state and local governments and a variety of other "third parties" for the execution of its domestic initiatives. For this reason, many administrative problems cannot be eliminated through such traditional panaceas as departmental reorganization, stronger executive leadership, or improved staffing. In many cases, what is needed may be more thoughtful program design. As Kirlin (1978) comments:

> Alternative policies usually exist for the pursuit of any policy objective. Thus, one can seek to reduce environmental pollution through regulation employing standards, enforced by administratively or court-determined sanctions, or a policy employing taxes upon effluents can be developed. As another example, the goal of reducing poverty can be pursued alternatively by policies employing cash transfers, manpower training, or attempts to redistribute political power. . . . Most importantly for present purposes, policy strategies constrain the choice of programs, thus largely determining implementation processes. And implementation processes, the relationships among governmental units and with clientele, structure the intergovernmental system. (p. 11)

The emergent literature on policy tools, instruments, and strategies has the potential of offering guidance on the appropriate use of a variety of specific subsidy and regulatory techniques.

From both perspectives, problems of management are viewed as integral with basic policy choices. The need to link these two areas, long separated by the hoary politics-administration dichotomy, is the clearest lesson emerging from the new implementation research. From the standpoint of federal theory, administrative perspectives should be tied to an updated understanding of democratic values and contemporary political processes.

Here, as in other areas, new scholarly efforts could help to articulate a theory of federalism that is both descriptive of and prescriptive for the present intergovernmental system. Although the heritage of dual federalism was set aside principally on pragmatic grounds, pragmatism now suggests that contemporary theories are inadequate from both normative and empirical standpoints. A new functional theory, merging democratic, economic, and administrative elements, is needed to provide the conceptual means of narrowing the gap between intergovernmental practice and the traditional principles of federalism.

REFERENCES

Abelman v. Booth. 21 Howard 506 (1859).

Ackerman, Bruce A. & Hassler, William T. *Clean coal/Dirty air.* New Haven: Yale University Press, 1981.

Advisory Commission on Intergovernmental Relations. *Fiscal balance in the American federal system* (Vol. 1). Washington, D.C.: U.S. Government Printing Office, 1967.

Advisory Commission on Intergovernmental Relations. *Categorical grants: Their role and design.* Washington, D.C.: U.S. Government Printing Office, 1978.

Advisory Commission on Intergovernmental Relations. *An agenda for American federalism: Restoring confidence and competence.* Washington, D.C.: U.S. Government Printing Office, 1981(a).

Advisory Commission on Intergovernmental Relations. *The condition of contemporary federalism: Conflicting theories and collapsing constraints.* Washington, D.C.: U.S. Government Printing Office, 1981(b).

Advisory Commission on Intergovernmental Relations. *State and local roles in the federal system.* Washington, D.C.: U.S. Government Printing Office, 1982.

Amacher, Ryan C., Tollison, Robert D. & Willett, Thomas D. *The economics approach to public policy.* Ithaca, N.Y.: Cornell University Press, 1976.

Anderson, William. *Intergovernmental relations in review.* Minneapolis, MN: University of Minnesota Press, 1960.

Anton, Thomas J. Intergovernmental change in the United States: Myth and reality. Ann Arbor, Mich.: Ph.D. Program in Urban and Regional Planning, The University of Michigan, 1980.

Anton, Thomas J., Cawley, Jerry P. & Kramer, Kevin L. *Moving money: An empirical analysis of federal expenditure patterns.* Cambridge, MA: Oelgeschlager, Gunn & Hain, 1980.

Arnold, R. Douglas. *Congress and the bureaucracy: A theory of influence.* New Haven: Yale University Press, 1979.

Arnold, R. Douglas. Overtilled and undertilled fields in American politics. *Political Science Quarterly,* 1982, *97,* 91-103.

Babbitt, Gov. Bruce. On States' Rights. *New York Times,* September 9, 1980, p. 19.

Barfield, Claude E. *Rethinking federalism: Block grants and federal, state, and local responsibilities.* Washington, D.C.: American Enterprise Institute for Public Policy Research, 1981.

Beam, David R. Economic theory as policy prescription: Pessimistic findings on 'optimizing' grants. In Helen M. Ingram and Dean E. Mann (Eds.). *Why politics succeed or fail.* Beverly Hills, CA: Sage Publications, 1980.

Beam, David R. Washington's regulation of state and localities: Origins and issues. *Intergovernmental Perspective,* 1981, *7,* 8-18.

Beer, Samuel H. The modernization of American federalism. *Publius,* 1973, *3,* 49-95.

Beer, Samuel H. A political scientist's view of fiscal federalism. In Wallace Oates (Ed.). *The political economy of fiscal federalism.* Lexington, MA: D.C. Heath, 1977.

Beer, Samuel H. Federalism, nationalism, and democracy in America. *American Political Science Review,* 1978, *72,* 9-21.

Beer, Samuel H. Federalism: Lessons of the past; Choices for the future. In *Federalism: Making the system work.* Washington, D.C.: Center for National Policy, 1982.

Bish, Robert. *The public economy of metropolitan areas.* Chicago, IL: Markham, 1971.

Brandeis, Hon. Louis D. *New State Ice Company v. Liebmann,* 258 U.S., 262 (1932).

Break, George F. *Intergovernmental fiscal relations in the United States.* Washington, D.C.: The Brookings Institution, 1967.

Break, George F. *Financing government in a federal system.* Washington, D.C.: The Brookings Institution, 1980.

Breton, Albert & Scott, Anthony. *The economic constitution of federal states.* Toronto: University of Toronto Press, 1978.

Buchanan, James M. *The limits of liberty: Between anarchy and leviathan.* Chicago: University of Chicago Press, 1975.

Buchanan, James. Why does government grow? In Thomas Borcherding (Ed.). *Budgets and bureaucrats.* Durham, N.C.: Duke University Press, 1977.

Buenker, John D. *Urban liberalism and progressive reform.* New York: W.W. Norton, 1978.

Burns, James McGregor. *The deadlock of democracy: Four-party politics in America.* Englewood Cliffs, N.J.: Prentice-Hall, Inc., 1963.

Campbell, Alan. Functions in flux. In Advisory Commission on Intergovernmental Relations. *American federalism: Toward a more effective partnership.* Washington, D.C.: U.S. Government Printing Office, 1975.

Cappalli, Richard B. *Rights and remedies under federal grants.* Washington, D.C.: Bureau of National Affairs, 1979.

Clark, Jane Perry. *The rise of a new federalism: Federal-state cooperation in the United States.* New York: Russell & Russell, 1965. (Originally published 1938.)

Cole, Steven J. The federal spending power and unconditional and block grants to state and local governments. *Clearinghouse Review,* 1982, *16,* 616-654.

Colella, Cynthia Cates. The political dynamics of intergovernmental policymaking. In Jerome J. Hanus (Ed.). *The nationalization of state government.* Lexington, MA: D.C. Heath, 1981.

Commission on the Organization of the Executive Branch of the Government. *Federal-state relations; A report to the Congress.* Washington, D.C.: U.S. Government Printing Office, 1949.

Conlan, Timothy J. *Congressional response to the new federalism: The politics of special revenue sharing and its implications for public policy making.* Unpublished doctoral dissertation. Cambridge, MA: Harvard University, Department of Government, 1981.

Corwin, Edward S. The passing of dual federalism. *Virginia Law Review,* 1950, *36,* 1-24.

Croly, Herbert. *The promise of American life.* Cambridge, Mass.: Belknap Press, 1965. (First published 1909.)

Crotty, William J. & Jacobson, Gary C. *American parties in decline.* Boston: Little, Brown, 1980.

Dahl, Robert & Tufte, Edward. *Size and democracy.* Stanford, CA: Stanford University Press, 1973.

Davis, S. Rufus. *The federal principle: A journey through time in quest of meaning.* Berkeley, Calif.: University of California Press, 1978.

Derthick, Martha. *New towns in-town: Why a federal program failed.* Washington, D.C.: The Urban Institute, 1972.

Derthick, Martha. *Uncontrollable spending for social services grants.* Washington, D.C.: The Brookings Institution, 1975.

Diamond, Martin. The forgotten doctrine of enumerated powers. *Publius,* 1976, *6,* 187-193.

Dommel, Paul R., et al. *Decentralizing urban policy: Case studies in community development.* Washington, D.C.: The Brookings Institution, 1982.

Dubnick, Mel & Gitelson, Alan. Nationalizing state policies. In J. Hanus (Ed.). *The nationalization of state government.* Lexington, MA: D.C. Heath, 1981.

Earle, Valerie (Ed.). *Federalism: Infinite variety in theory and practice.* Itasca, IL: F.E. Peacock, 1968.

Edner, Sheldon. Intergovernmental policy development: The importance of problem definition. In Charles O. Jones & Robert D. Thomas (Eds.). *Public policy making in a federal system.* Beverly Hills, CA: Sage Publications, 1976.

Elazar, Daniel J. *The American partnership*. Chicago: University of Chicago Press, 1962.

Elazar, Daniel J. Federalism. In David Sills (Ed.). *International encyclopedia of the social sciences* (Vol. 5). New York: Macmillan, 1968.

Elazar, Daniel J. Cursed by bigness or toward a post-technocratic federalism. *Publius*, 1973, *3*, 293-298.

Elazar, Daniel J. The new federalism: Can the states be trusted? *Public Interest*, 1974, *35*, 89-102.

Elazar, Daniel J. Federalism vs. decentralization: The drift from authenticity. *Publius*, 1976, *6*, 9-19.

Elazar, Daniel J. Is the federal system still there? In Advisory Commission on Intergovernmental Relations. *Hearings on the federal role*. Washington, D.C.: U.S. Government Printing Office, 1980.

Elazar, Daniel J. The evolving federal system. In Richard M. Pious (Ed.). *The power to govern: Assessing reform in the United States*. New York: Academy of Political Science, 1981.

Elazar, Daniel J. Can the federal system be saved? Philadelphia: Temple University Center for the Study of Federalism, 1982.

Elmore, Richard F. Organizational models of social program implementation. *Public Policy*, 1978, *26*, 185-228.

Elmore, Richard F. Backward mapping: Implementation research and policy decision. *Political Science Quarterly*, 1979, *94*, 601-616.

Engdahl, David E. Preemptive capability of federal power. *University of Colorado Law Review*, 1973, *45*, 51-88.

Federalist. Alexander Hamilton, John Jay, James Madison. *The federalist: A commentary on the Constitution of the United States*. Nos. 1-85 (1787-88). Introduced by Edward Mead Earle. New York: Modern Library, 1937.

Fiorina, Morris P. *Congress: Keystone of the Washington establishment*. New Haven: Yale University Press, 1977.

Friedrich, Carl J. *Trends of federalism in theory and practice*. New York: Praeger, 1968.

Frug, Gerald E. The judicial power of the purse. *University of Pennsylvania Law Review*, 1978, *126*, 715-794.

Graves, W. Brooke. *American intergovernmental relations: Their origins, historical development, and current status*. New York: Charles Scribner's Sons, 1964.

Greenwood, Peter W., Mann, Dale & McLaughlin, Milbrey Wallin. *Federal programs supporting education change*, Vol. III: *The Process of Change*. Santa Monica, CA: Rand, 1975.

Grodzins, Morton. Centralization and decentralization in the American federal system. In Robert A. Goldwin (Ed.). *A nation of states: Essays on the American federal system*. Chicago: Rand McNally, 1963.

Grodzins, Morton. *The American system: A new view of government in the United States*. Daniel J. Elazar (Ed.). Chicago: Rand McNally, 1966.

Haider, Donald H. *When governments come to Washington*. New York: The Free Press, 1974.

Haider, Donald H. The intergovernmental system. In Richard M. Pious (Ed.). *The power to govern: Assessing reform in the United States*. New York: Academy of Political Science, 1981.

Hamilton, Edward K. On nonconstitutional management of a constitutional problem. *Daedalus*, 1978, *107*, 111-128.

Hastings, Anne. *The strategies of government intervention: An analysis of federal education and health care policy*. Unpublished doctoral dissertation. Charlottesville, VA: University of Virginia, College of Education, 1982.

Hawkins, Robert B., Jr. Conclusion: Administrative versus political reform. In Robert B. Hawkins (Ed.). *American federalism: A new partnership for the republic.* San Francisco: Institute for Contemporary Studies, 1982.

Horowitz, Donald L. *The courts and social policy.* Washington, D.C.: The Brookings Institution, 1977.

Howard, A. E. Dick. The states and the Supreme Court. *Catholic University Law Review,* 1982, *31,* 375-438.

Huntington, Samuel P. The United States. In Michael J. Crozier, Samuel P. Huntington, & Joji Watanuki (Eds.). *The crisis of democracy: Report on the governability of democracies to the trilateral commission.* New York: New York University Press, 1975.

Ingram, Helen. Policy implementation through bargaining: The case of federal grants-in-aid. *Public Policy,* 1977, *25,* 499-525.

Jefferson, Thomas. Letter to Samuel Kercheval, 1816. Quoted in Mason, A. T. *Free government in the making* (2nd ed.). New York: Oxford University Press, 1956, p. 372.

Jefferson, Thomas. Letter to Gideon Granger, 1800. In Saul K. Padover (Ed.). *Thomas Jefferson on democracy.* New York: New American Library, 1939.

Jennings, M. Kent & Zeigler, Harmon. The salience of American state politics. *American Political Science Review,* 1970, *64,* 523-534.

Kaden, Lewis B. Politics, money, and state sovereignty: The judicial role. *Columbia Law Review,* 1979, *79,* 847-897.

Kennedy, Sen. Edward. Senator Kennedy addresses conference on federalism. *Congressional Record,* 97th Cong., 2d sess., July 1, 1982, pp. S 7923-25.

Key, V. O., Jr. *The administration of federal grants to states.* Chicago: Public Administration Service, 1937.

King, Anthony (Ed.). *The new American political system.* Washington, D.C.: American Enterprise Institute for Public Policy Research, 1978.

Kirlin, John J. Structuring the intergovernmental system: An appraisal of conceptual models and public policies. Paper prepared for presentation at the Annual Meeting of the American Political Science Association, New York, 1978.

Krier, James E. & Ursin, Edmund. *Pollution and policy: A case essay on California and federal experience with motor vehicle air pollution, 1940-1975.* Berkeley, CA: University of California Press, 1977.

Ladd, Helen F. & Doolittle, Fred C. Which level of government should assist the poor? *National Tax Journal,* 1982, *35,* 323-336.

Landau, Martin. Federalism, redundancy and system reliability. *Publius,* 1973, *3,* 173-196.

Leach, Richard H. *American federalism.* New York: W.W. Norton, 1970.

Lilly, William III & Miller, James C. III. The new 'social regulation.' *Public Interest,* 1977, *47,* 49-61.

Lovell, Catherine. Where we are in IGR and some of the implications. *Southern Review of Public Administration,* 1979, *3,* 6-20.

Lovell, Catherine H. *et al. Federal and state mandating on local governments: An exploration of issues and impacts.* Riverside, CA: Graduate School of Administration, University of California, Riverside, 1979.

Lowi, Theodore J. Four systems of policy, politics, and choice. *Public Administration Review,* 1972, *33,* 298-310.

Lowi, Theodore J. Europeanization of America?: From United States to United State. In Theodore J. Lowi & Alan Stone (Eds.). *Nationalizing government: Public policies in America.* Beverly Hills, CA: Sage Publications, 1978.

Lowi, Theodore J. *The end of liberalism: The second republic of the United States.* New York: W.W. Norton, 1979.

MacMahon, Arthur W. (Ed.). *Federalism: Mature and emergent*. New York: Double-day, 1955.

MacMahon, Arthur W. *Administering federalism in a democracy*. New York: Oxford University Press, 1972.

Madden, Thomas J. The law of federal grants. In Advisory Commission on Inter-governmental Relations. *Awakening the slumbering giant: Intergovernmental relations and federal grant law*. Washington, D.C.: U.S. Government Printing Office, 1980.

Mayhew, David R. *Congress: The electoral connection*. New Haven: Yale University Press, 1974.

Mayo, Henry B. *An introduction to democratic theory*. Fair Lawn, N.J.: Oxford University Press, 1960.

McConnell, Grant. *Private power and American democracy*. New York: Vintage Books, 1966.

McKean, Roland. The use of shadow prices. In Samuel Chase (Ed.). *Problems of public expenditure analysis*. Washington, D.C.: The Brookings Institution, 1966.

Mill, John Stuart. In Curring Shields (Ed.). *Considerations on representative government*. Indianapolis, IN: Bobbs-Merrill, 1958. (First published 1861.)

Mirengoff, William & Rindler, Lester. *CETA: Manpower programs under local control*. Washington, D.C.: National Academy of Sciences, 1978.

Montesquieu. *The spirit of the laws*. In Michael Curtis (Ed.). *The great political theories*. New York: Avon Books, 1961. (First published 1748.)

Monypenny, Phillip. Federal grants-in-aid to state governments: A political analysis. *National Tax Journal*, 1960, *13*, 1-16.

Mosher, Frederick C. (Ed.). *American public administration: Past, present, future*. University, AL: University of Alabama Press, 1975.

Mosher, Frederick C. The changing responsibilities and tactics of the federal government. *Public Administration Review*, 1980, *40*, 541-548.

Muller, Thomas & Fix, Michael. Federal solicitude, local costs: The impact of federal regulation on municipal finances. *Regulation*, 1980, *4*, 29-36.

Murphy, Jerome T. Title I of ESEA: The politics of implementing federal education reform. *Harvard Educational Review*, 1971, *41*, 55-63.

Musgrave, Richard. *The theory of public finance*. New York: McGraw-Hill, 1959.

Mushkin, Selma J. Barriers to a system of federal grants-in-aid. *National Tax Journal*, 1960, *13*, 193-218.

Mushkin, Selma J. & Cotton, John F. *Sharing federal funds for state and local needs*. New York: Praeger Publishers, 1969.

Nathan, Richard. Federalism and the shifting nature of fiscal relations. *Annals of the American Academy of Political and Social Science*, 1975, *419*, 120-129.

Nathan, Richard. Federal grants—how are they working? In Robert W. Burchell & David Listokin (Eds.). *Cities under stress: The fiscal crises of urban America*. Piscataway, N.J.: Center for Urban Policy Research, Rutgers, The State University of New Jersey, 1981(a).

Nathan, Richard. 'Reforming' the federal grant-in-aid system for states and localities. *National Tax Journal*, 1981(b), *34*, 321-327.

Nathan, Richard. The methodology for field network evaluation studies. In Walter Williams (Ed.). *Studying implementation: Methodological and administrative issues*. Chatham, NJ: Chatham House, 1982.

Nathan, Richard P., Manvel, Allen D. & Calkins, Susannah E. *Monitoring revenue sharing*. Washington, D.C.: The Brookings Institution, 1975.

Neuman, Franz. Federalism and freedom: A critique. In Arthur Macmahon (Ed.). *Federalism: Mature and emergent*. New York: Doubleday, 1955.

Niskanen, William. *Bureaucracy and representative government.* Chicago: Aldine-Atherton, 1971.

Nixon, Pres. Richard. Annual message to the Congress on the state of the union, January 22, 1971. In *Public Papers of the Presidents of the United States, Richard Nixon, 1971.* Washington, D.C.: U.S. Government Printing Office, 1971.

Nordlinger, Eric. *Conflict regulation in divided societies.* Cambridge, Mass.: Center for International Affairs, 1972.

Oates, Wallace. *Fiscal federalism.* New York: Harcourt, Brace, Jovanovich, 1972.

Oates, Wallace (Ed.). *The political economy of fiscal federalism.* Lexington, Mass.: D.C. Heath, 1977.

Olson, Mancur, Jr. The principle of 'fiscal equivalence': The division of responsibilities among different levels of government. *American Economic Review,* 1969, *59,* 479-487.

Opinion Roundup. *Public Opinion,* December/January 1982(a), 36.

Opinion Roundup. *Public Opinion,* February/March 1982(b), 28.

Orfield, Gary. *Congressional power: Congress and social change.* New York: Harcourt, Brace, Jovanovich, 1975.

Ostrom, Vincent, *et al.* The organization of government in metropolitan areas: A theoretical analysis. *American Political Science Review,* 1961, *60,* 832-842.

Ostrom, Vincent. *The political theory of a compound republic: A reconstruction of the logical foundations of American democracy as presented in the federalist.* Blacksburg, VA: Virginia Polytechnic Institute, Center for the Study of Public Choice, 1971.

Ostrom, Vincent. Can federalism make a difference? *Publius,* 1973, *3,* 197-238.

Ostrom, Vincent. *The intellectual crisis in public administration* (rev. ed.). University, AL: University of Alabama Press, 1974.

Peterson, Paul E. *City limits.* Chicago: University of Chicago Press, 1981.

Peterson, Paul E. & Wong, Kenneth K. Comparing federal education and housing programs: Toward a differentiated theory of federalism. Paper prepared for delivery at the Annual Meeting of the American Political Science Association, Denver, CO, 1982.

Pfiffner, John M. & Sherwood, Frank P. *Administrative organization.* Englewood Cliffs, N.J.: Prentice-Hall, 1960.

Porter, David O. with Warner, David C. & Porter, Teddie W. *The politics of budgeting federal aid: Resource mobilization by local school districts.* Beverly Hills, CA: Sage Publications, 1973.

Pressman, Jeffrey L.& Wildavsky, Aaron B. *Implementation.* Berkeley, CA: University of California Press, 1973.

Price, David. *Who makes the laws? Creativity and power in Senate committees.* Cambridge, Mass.: Schenkman Publishing Co., 1972.

Reagan, Michael D. *The new federalism.* New York: Oxford University Press, 1972.

Reeves, Mavis Mann. Look again at state capacity: The old gray mare ain't what she used to be. *American Journal of Public Administration,* 1982, *16,* 74-89.

Reeves, Mavis Mann & Glendening, Parris. Area federalism and public opinion. *Publius,* 1976, *6,* 135-167.

Riker, William H. *Federalism: Origin, operation, significance.* Boston: Little, Brown, 1964.

Riker, William H. Six books in search of a subject—Or does federalism exist and does it matter? *Comparative Politics,* 1969, *2,* 135-146.

Riker, William H. Federalism. In Fred Greenstein & Nelson Polsby (Eds.). *Handbook of political science* (Vol. 5). Reading, MA: Addison-Wesley, 1975.

Riley, Patrick. The origins of federal theory in international relations ideas. *Polity,* 1973, *6,* 89-121.

Rose, Richard. *The territorial dimension in government.* Chatham, N.J.: Chatham House, 1982.

Rothman, Rozann. The ambiguity of American federal theory. *Publius,* 1978, *8,* 103-122.

Salamon, Lester M. Rethinking public management: Third-party government and the changing forms of government action. *Public Policy,* 1981, *29,* 255-275.

Schechter, Stephen L. The state of American federalism in the 1980s. In Robert B. Hawkins, Jr. (Ed.). *American federalism: A new partnership for the republic.* San Francisco: Institute for Contemporary Studies, 1982.

Scheiber, Harry N. American federalism and the diffusion of power: Historical and contemporary perspectives. *University of Toledo Law Review,* 1978, *9,* 619-680.

Scheiber, Harry N. Federalism and legal process: Historical and contemporary analysis of the American system. *Law and Society Review,* 1980, *14,* 633-722.

Schultze, Charles. Sorting out the social grant programs: An economist's criteria. *American Economic Review,* 1974, *64,* 181-189.

Schultze, Charles. *The public use of the private interest.* Washington, D.C.: The Brookings Institution, 1977.

Seidman, Harold. *Politics, position, and power: The dynamics of federal organizations.* New York: Oxford University Press, 1970.

Sharkansky, Ira. *The maligned states: Policy accomplishments, problems, and opportunities.* New York: McGraw-Hill, 1978.

Sorauf, Frank. *Party politics in America.* Boston: Little, Brown, 1976.

Stewart, William H. Metaphors, models, and the development of federal theory. *Publius,* 1982, *12,* 5-24.

Stokes, Donald E. Spatial models of party competition. *American Political Science Review,* 1963, *57,* 368-77.

Sundquist, James L. *Politics and policy: The Eisenhower, Kennedy, and Johnson years.* Washington, D.C.: The Brookings Institution, 1968.

Sundquist, James L. *Making federalism work.* Washington, D.C.: The Brookings Institution, 1969.

Truman, David. *The governmental process* (2nd ed.). New York: Alfred A. Knopf, 1971.

Tullock, Gordon. Federalism: Problems of scale. In Ryan Amacher, Robert Tollison, & Thomas Willett (Eds.). *The economic approach to public policy.* Ithaca, N.Y.: Cornell University Press, 1976.

Van Horn, Carl E. & Van Meter, Donald S. Deimplementation of intergovernmental policy. In Charles O. Jones & Robert D. Thomas (Eds.), *Public policy making in a federal system.* Beverly Hills, CA: Sage Publications, 1976.

Verba, Sidney & Nie, Norman. *Participation in America.* New York: Harper and Row, 1972.

Walker, David B. *Toward a functioning federalism.* Cambridge, MA: Winthrop, 1981.

Wheare, K. C. *Federal government.* New York: Oxford University Press, 1951.

White, Leonard D. *Introduction to the study of public administration* (4th ed.). New York: MacMillan, 1955.

Wildavsky, Aaron. *How to limit government spending.* Berkeley, CA: University of California Press, 1980.

Wilson, James Q. American politics, then and now. *Commentary,* February, 1979, pp. 39-46.

Wilson, James Q. (Ed.). *The politics of regulation.* New York: Basic Books, 1980.

Wilson, Woodrow. *Constitutional government in the United States* (paperback ed.). New York: Columbia University Press, 1961. (First published 1908.)

Wolin, Sheldon S. Foreword. In William H. Riker. *Federalism: Origin, operation, significance.* Boston: Little, Brown, 1964.

Wright, Deil. *Federal grants-in-aid: Perspectives and alternatives.* Washington, D.C.: American Enterprise Institute, 1968.

Wright, Deil. *Understanding intergovernmental relations.* North Scituate, MA: Duxbury Press, 1978.

Yates, Douglas. *The ungovernable city: The politics of urban problems and policy making.* Cambridge, MA: The MIT Press, 1977.

Young, James S. *The Washington community: 1800-1828.* New York: Harcourt Brace Jovanovich, 1966.

COMPARATIVE POLITICAL PROCESSES AND POLICYMAKING

10

Comparative Public Policy:
An Assessment*

M. Donald Hancock

Public policy studies are indeed a multiform menagerie: they are narrative, quantitative, cross-national, cross-sectional, single policy cross-nationally, several policies cross-nationally, not to mention the many volumes devoted to the metatheory and metapolitics of policy studies. Any day now we will surely have a tortured soul cry out: "Enough!" and present us with "A prolegomenon to any future. . . ." (Diamant, 1981, p. 103)

By the early 1970s comparative public policy had emerged as a recognized subdiscipline within political science. A significant milestone in this development was reached when the American Political Science Association designated Arnold J. Heidenheimer, Hugh Heclo, and Carolyn Teich Adams' book *Comparative Public Policy: The Politics of Social Choice in Europe and America* as the best political science publication on United States national policy in 1975. The citation noted: "Cross-national policy research is still in its infancy; the [Gladys M. Kammerer Award] will be well-used if it stimulates the development of this field" (*PS*, 1976, p. 441).

The Association's hopeful expectations have been amply realized. During the late 1970s and early 1980s, numerous additional policy-oriented volumes and hundreds of journal articles have appeared, many of them genuinely comparative. At least five journals devoted exclusively to policy questions have been established in the United States and Canada. Comparative policy courses have been incorporated in both graduate and undergraduate curricula throughout North America. An advanced textbook series published by Temple University Press is well underway. And specialized con-

*For their helpful suggestions and advice in the preparation and subsequent revision of this essay, I am indebted to Erwin Hargrove, Arnold Heidenheimer, Charles Anderson, John Sloan, Douglas Ashford, Benjamin Walter, Jonathan Hartlyn, and Peter Katzenstein. I am thankful, too, to Arend Lijphart for the original nudge.

ferences and panels on comparative policy themes have been sponsored by Cornell University, the Council for European Studies, and both the national and regional professional political science associations.

Yet the very proliferation of comparative public policy studies raises important intellectual issues. The first concerns the enormous diversity in the scope, emphasis, methods, and findings in the existing literature. In light of this diversity, Elliot Feldman (1978) recently concluded that comparative policy analysis is a non-field lacking a "guiding theory" to focus research. Feldman's contention raises the obvious, and essential, initial question of assessment: What *is* comparative policy analysis? The first part of this essay will attempt to answer this question by formulating a conceptual framework for classifying the myriad studies that comprise the comparative policy literature. Even more important, however, are issues concerning the *content* of comparative public policy research. As my second, and more substantive undertaking, I will, therefore, survey the principal research foci, methods, and policy evaluations used within the subfield on the basis of the classificatory framework presented in the first section. In my conclusion, I will suggest, in light of what has and has not been accomplished to date, some priorities for future research.

A FRAMEWORK FOR ANALYSIS

"Comparative public policy," Heidenheimer-Heclo-Adams assert, "is the cross-national study of how, why, and to what effect government policies are developed" (1975, p. v). Most toilers in the proverbial vineyard of policy analysis would presumably concur with this textbook definition. "Policy analysis," Thomas Dye has observed, "is finding out what governments do, why they do it, and what difference it makes" (1979, p. 652). More simply, Ira Sharkansky states: "Policies are actions taken by government" (1970, p. 1).

The first step in assessing comparative policy research involves disaggregating the "how," "why," and "to what effect" components of the definition. Some scholars emphasize the former component, others the second, still others the third, and yet others various tangential or more general aspects of the subject. This has led to the formation of a wide variety of classificatory schemes that encompass the topics that ostensibly comprise comparative policy analysis. The most parsimonious is a bibliography of comparative policy studies compiled by B. Guy Peters for the inaugural issue of *Policy Studies Review* (1981). In Peters' view, the major research categories within the subdiscipline include: (1) general and theoretical studies, (2) tax policy, (3) economic policy, (4) social policy, (5) public expenditure studies, and (6) health policy. A partially overlapping and slightly longer list (albeit one emphasizing domestic public policy) is that contained in Fred I. Greenstein and Nelson W. Polsby's edited volume on *Politics and Policymaking* in the *Handbook of Political Science* series (1975): (1) research in policy analysis, (2) economic policy, (3) science policy, (4) welfare policy, (5) race policy, (6) comparative urban policy, (7) foreign policy, and (8) policy evaluation.

Douglas E. Ashford, Peter J. Katzenstein, and T. J. Pempel also distinguish among eight policy categories in their *Comparative Public Policy: A Cross-National Bibliography* (1978): (1) administrative reform, (2) economic management, (3) local and regional reorganization, (4) labor relations, (5) race and migration, (6) social security, (7) higher education, and (8) science and technology. In their first edition of *Comparative Public Policy,* Heidenheimer-Heclo-Adams concentrated on a somewhat different catalogue of topics: (1) health care, (2) secondary education, (3) housing, (4) city planning, (5) local government, (6) transportation, (7) income maintenance, and (8) taxation. They have extended their inventory of comparative policy topics in the second edition of their book (1983) to include assessments of (9) "the politics of social choice, (10) "economic policy," and (11) "policy constraints in the welfare state." Finally, the compilers of the *United States Political Science Documents* utilize 19 reference categories to encompass domestic and comparative policy studies, of which "policy evaluation" and "policy implementation" regularly contain the largest number of entries.[1]

Each of these classificatory schemes serves the useful purposes of codifying previous research, reporting new findings and insights, and/or guiding the interested scholar to relevant bibliographical sources. None, however, captures the full scope of comparative policy analysis and the wide array of empirical, methodological, and theoretical concerns demonstrated by its practitioners. To that end, I propose a more detailed classificatory framework in the form of a commonsense taxonomy based on the diverse components of the policy process itself.

As illustrated in Figure 1, the taxonomy categorizes the general and theoretical perspectives characteristic of the subdiscipline as well as the central empirical and analytical foci of comparative policy research itself. The former encompass contrasting metatheoretical assumptions about society and the policy-making process as well as different methodological approaches. The latter range from the description and analysis of the "how" and "why" of policy-making—including principal determinants of policy initiatives and choices—to assessments of specific policy outputs and their short-term, historical, and other consequences (i.e., the "to what effect" components of the Heidenheimer-Heclo-Adams definition cited above). One advantage of the taxonomy is that it makes explicit the fact that comparative policy analysis is more than the sum of its parts. Instead, it is a microcosm of the conceptual, methodological, and analytical diversity within political science as a whole; it is distinctive largely because of its emphasis on the causes, different forms, and social consequences of government action, or nonaction, in a variety of historical and contemporary settings.

In the sections to follow, I shall utilize the various categories of the taxonomy as a means to structure my assessment of the dominant approaches, findings, and problems that distinguish comparative policy analyses. For reasons of manageability, I have restricted my survey—with several exceptions—to the Anglo-American political science literature. My assessment of specific books and articles embraces a relatively small number of representative studies drawn from more than 300 bibliographical citations which I compiled for this essay.[2] I have selected these studies on the basis of the signifi-

FIGURE 1

A Taxonomy of Comparative Policy Analysis

General and Theoretical Perspectives	Policy Determinants	Policy Outputs and Evaluation
Subject Matter		
Contrasting Concepts of Society	Levels of Economic Development	Policy Areas: health, pensions, incomes policy, education, housing, taxation, employment, etc.
Contrasting Definitions of Policy	Elites	
	Bureaucracy	
Contrasting Research Methods and Units of Analysis	The State	Contrasting Evaluations:
	Types of Political Regimes	(1) Short-term: policy "impact," effectiveness
	Political Parties	(2) Longer-term: systemic consequences, e.g., "crises" of democracy, the welfare state, and/or capitalism; emergence of varieties of corporatism
	Interest Groups	
		(3) Analytical: relevance of empirical findings and conceptual refinements for theory-building; explanations of "history," inter-system differences, etc.
		(4) Prescriptive
Illustrative Scholars		
Ashford (1977, 1978)	Anton (1980)	Hibbs (1977, 1982)
Cyr and deLeon (1975)	Cameron (1978, 1982)	King (1973, 1981)
Feldman (1978)	Castles (1978, 1979)	Kjellberg (1977)
Heclo (1972)	Flora and Heidenheimer (1981)	Lindberg (1975, 1977, 1982)
King (1973)	Heclo (1974)	Peters (1972, 1975, 1977)
Peters (1977)	Heidenheimer (1973)	Smith (1969, 1975)
Rose (1973)	Heidenheimer-Heclo-Adams (1975)	Wilensky (1975)

cance of their findings and/or their suggestiveness for future research. No doubt I have excluded authors whose work fully deserves equal attention to those whom I cite; I apologize in advance for such omissions. To do proper justice to a evaluation of the subject would require a book.

GENERAL AND THEORETICAL PERSPECTIVES

In an early assessment of comparative policy analysis as an emergent subdiscipline, Richard Rose (1973) compiled what has become a standard set of justifications for the comparative study of public policy. The first justification, he noted, derives from the consideration that

> [t]he major problems that face one Western government are often the same as those that face its neighbours. . . . Whether the existence of common or similar problems results in a similar response is a question os practical and theoretical importance. Men of affairs may see the justification for comparative policy studies in the prospect that their government will be able to borrow policies or institutions from another country for use in resolving domestic problems. . . . Scholars too have appreciated the "quasi-experimental" features of comparative research in circumstances in which controlled experiments are merely impossible. (pp. 68-69)

In addition, Rose suggested that comparative policy analysis helps scholars avoid "culture-bound generalizations" which might arise from single-country policy studies; identifies "nondecisions" by national leaders who fail to respond to issues that lead to policy action in other countries; raises new questions concerning the role and importance of governmental institutions; and enables the scholar to test the "significance of social and economic conditions for public policy. . ." in a variety of settings (pp. 68-70).[3] Feldman (1978) has added to Rose's inventory of basic justifications the hopeful expectation that comparative policy analysis will yield "embracing theories for politics, as well as policy, beyond the boundaries erected by the details of systems because comparison helps establish norms for judgment and helps distinguish the essential from the trivial' (p. 187).

Underlying such objectives is what Charles Anderson (1982) has characterized as an "implicit social democratic orientation" among most practitioners of comparative policy analysis. Virtually all of the scholars whose work is cited in this chapter tend to look with favor on the activist state and its twentieth century socioeconomic achievements. As Anderson observed in commenting on the initial draft of this overview of the subdiscipline:

> Except for Samuel Huntington, whose work does not seem to figure prominently in intellectual debate or research, few scholars have written explicitly from a neo-conservative point of view. Marxist analyses are often taken into account, but little comparative policy study generally recognized as important is written from a neo-Marxist perspective. The great enthusiasm for Scandinavian institutions and practices, the relative neglect of Southern Europe and economically conservative regimes rather gives the game away. Many have gone to Sweden in search of inspiration but there has been no similar pilgrimage of scholars to find out how Margaret Thatcher "does it." (p. 5)

Presumably most members of the subdiscipline would endorse the proclaimed objectives of a comparative approach to policy research and analysis. Basic difficulties lie, however, in achieving them. From the outset, students of comparative public policy have confronted a set of problems agonizingly familiar to all comparativists: the high personal and financial costs of research in a variety of national settings, the need for adequate linguistic and interpretive skills, the frequent absence of reliable or equivalent national data, and the difficulty of gaining access to relevant officials and offices. Even more fundamental, as Arthur Cyr and Peter de Leon have noted (1975), are problems involving contrasting conceptualizations, units of analysis, and research methods. These include the following basic differences among scholars and their approaches to comparative policy analysis:

1. *Contrasting views of society as a whole.* Most comparative policy analysis is based on a "liberal" concept of rational individual self-interest and social pluralism. Characterizing this mainstream approach to policy research is the utilization of economic or behavioral analysis to explore the policymaking process and its social consequences.[4] A minority view, however, is represented by Ashford, Katzenstein, Pempel, and others who employ varieties of structural analyses to explain policy outcomes. In Ashford's perspective, for example, the nature of the *state*—including its institutional arrangements and elite constraints on policy choice—plays the central role in determining policy outcomes. As Ashford observes: "The state is better described by its policies than by its principles and alleged norms of individual choice and preference" (1977, p. 572).

2. *Contrasting conceptualizations of policy.* Strongly influencing the dichotomy mentioned above are basic differences in underlying conceptualizations of the linkage between policy and politics. Consistent with their utilization of individual-pluralist units of analysis, the majority of comparativists interpret policy outcomes as the product of antecedent economic, social, or political factors. Policy, in their view, is thus a *dependent* variable, comparable to "outputs" in David Easton's systems model of the political system. In contrast, structuralists such as Ashford (1978, 1977, 1981, 1982) and Katzenstein (1978) have followed the lead of Theodore Lowi (1964, 1972) and Robert H. Salisbury (1968) in conceptualizing policy as an *independent* variable. Accordingly, Ashford approaches the study of both the British and the French political systems from the perspective of the "politics of policymaking" (1981, 1982). Similarly, T. Alexander Smith (1969, 1977) and Francesco Kjellberg (1977) agree with Lowi that expected policy outcomes determine the choice of different conflict arenas. (Each of these authors will be discussed below.)

Less deterministic than the preceding opposing views that policy is either the cause or effect of politics is Rose's notion of policy as process (1973, 1976). Concurring with Donald Schon (1971) that process models provide a useful means to learn from case studies and extrapolate them to other countries and new policy isues, Rose has devised an elaborate framework of analysis that is distinctive for its comprehensive scope and open-endedness. As his recommended agenda of comparative research, Rose urges policy specialists to analyze in sequence: (1) the "initial state" in a society prior to public recognition that a policy need exists; (2) how policy issues are placed on the "agenda of political controversy"; (3) how demands are advanced; (4) the importance of the form of government for policy deliberations; (5) available resources and existing constraints; (6) the move toward a policy decision; (7) the determinants of governmental choice; (8) the context of choice; (9) implementation; (10) the "production of outputs"; (11) policy evaluation; and (12) feedback.

3. *Case studies vs. comparative studies.* Traditionally, most comparative policy analysis has involved only one or at most a limited number of countries and/or policy areas. Important examples include the Heidenheimer-Heclo-Adams volumes (1975, 1983); Heclo's earlier *Modern Social Politics in Britain and Sweden* (1974); Ashford's *Policy and Politics in Britain* (1981) and *Policy and Politics in France* (1982); and Leon Lindberg's edited volumes on *Stress and Contradiction in Modern Capitalism* (1975) and *The Energy Syndrome* (1977). Common to all of the case study scholars is their reliance on "qualitative" analysis which seeks—through the utilization of diverse sources including historical evidence, official documents, legislative statutes, interview data, and descriptive socioeconomic statistics—to "interrogate" (in Heclo's apt phrase) the purposes and consequences of policy actions.

In contrast to the case study or configurative approach, other scholars have undertaken more broadly-based comparisons of a number of countries. They have typically utilized quantifiable public expenditures or similar hard data as indicators of policy choices and system performance. Prominent among them are Peters (1972, 1974, 1975, 1977, 1979), Douglas A. Hibbs (1976, 1977), and David Cameron (1978, 1982).

4. *Longitudinal vs. correlational analysis.* Among scholars who characteristically view policy as the product of economic, social, or political forces, a further distinction can be drawn between the utilization of *longitudinal vs. correlational analysis.* Anthony King (1981) has succinctly described this contrast in his assessment of the effects of electoral outcomes on policy choice. Longitudinal research, he notes, involves efforts by the scholar "to see whether changes in policy in each of the policy areas have coincided . . . with changes in the party or parties in power in the given country or countries. . . ." Correlational analysis, on the other hand, seeks to determine statistically which of various economic, political, and other factors "does the best job of explaining any variation that exists among the countries' policies" (p. 311).

Differences in conceptualization about society, units of analysis, and methods have determined in turn the contrasting research foci and policy evaluations that characterize the empirical components of the comparative public policy literature. These contrasts are the subject of the following two sections.

DETERMINANTS OF POLICY CHOICE

Common to the contrasting paradigms of comparative analysis is an effort to explain policy outcomes in terms of at least implicit causal models of the policy process. But there is a notable lack of consensus among policy analysts concerning the relative importance of the factors that ostensibly determine policy choices.

An early, and continuing, dispute concerns the relative importance of "economics" vs. "politics" in explaining policy outcomes. The instigators of this debate within political science were primarily students of American state politics whose innovative conceptualizations and research techniques—borrowed from orthodox economics—subsequently helped influence the emergence of comparative policy analysis as a distinct subdiscipline. Basing their conclusions on correlational analysis of the effects of various socio-economic and political variables on policy choices, Richard E. Dawson and James A. Robinson (1963), Richard Hofferbert (1966), Thomas Dye (1966), Charles F. Cnudde and Donald J. McCrone (1969), and others argued that levels of economic development were more important than the political characteristics of individual states in determining the provision of government services within the American political system. Their findings were sharply attacked by critics such as Herbert Jacob and Michael Lipsky (1968) who faulted Dye *et al.* on both logical and empirical grounds; nonetheless, they underscore the obvious point that differences in regional and/or national wealth make possible greater or lesser degrees of public investment in education, health programs, and other social provisions.

Numerous scholars have followed the lead of the American state politics specialists in employing correlational analysis to test the relative significance of various policy determinants. But only one comparativist of note, Harold Wilensky, has corroborated the centrality of economic development for the provision of general social services. In his *The Welfare State and Equality* (1975), Wilensky reports that aggregate cross-sectional analysis of linkages between levels of national development and public expenditures on education, housing, and the military in 64 countries reveals that

> economic growth and its demographic and bureaucratic outcomes are the root causes of the general emergence of the welfare state—the establishment of similar programs of social security, the increasing fraction of GNP devoted to such programs, the trend toward comprehensive coverage and similar methods of financing. (p. xiii)

Wilensky promptly amends this generalization by noting that important differences exist in the degree and organization of welfare services even among the rich nations as a group. He attributes them to "specific differences in political, social, and economic organization—by the degree of centralization of government, the shape of the stratification order and related mobility rates, the organization of the working class, and the position of the military" (p. xiv).

Most other students of comparative public policy, in contrast, assume without serious question the ascendancy of politics over economics in determining policy choices. To Anthony King (1973), for example, the most important policy determinant is ideology. His principal argument—in an article published in the early 1970s—is that *ideas*—specifically, the ideas of those who govern—have decisive political, social, and economic consequences. With reference to national American politics, King asserts categorically that "elites, demands, interest groups, and institutions constitute neither necessary nor sufficient conditions of the American policy pattern; ideas, we contend, constitute both a necessary condition and a sufficient one" (p. 423).

Without disputing King's central contention that politics are primary, other scholars have emphasized the various factors, either singularly or in combination, that King relegates to secondary importance after "ideas." Some, such as John Higley (1981) and Douglas R. Boulter (1980), have focused on the pivotal role played by national political elites in setting the policy agenda and deciding policy outcomes. Important contributions to the elite approach can be found in studies of participation by high-level civil servants in national policy decisions in Mattei Dogan's edited volume on *The Mandarins of Western Europe* (1975) and Thomas J. Anton's *Administered Politics* (1980). Other policy analysts have concentrated on political parties and/or organized interest organizations as key instigators of policy outcomes. One example is Francis Castles, who has persuasively argued that Social Democratic electoral and organizational strength is the principal determinant of Scandinavia's comprehensive and distinctive commitment to what he terms the "welfare state provision" (1978, 1979). My own work on Sweden and Germany substantiates Castles' findings with the important qualification that many of the Social Democratic reform initiatives—particularly in the area of industrial relations—follow prior initiatives undertaken by the affiliated national federations of labor (Hancock, 1982).

On a more comprehensive theoretical level, several European and American scholars have sought since the mid-1970s to reformulate group theory as a means to assess new economic policy-making linkages among government, business, and labor representatives that have emerged in recent decades in a number of advanced industrial nations (notably Austria, the Netherlands, West Germany, Sweden, and Norway). Established primarily to stabilize labor-management relations in the interest of maintaining economic growth, such linkages characteristically involve policy consultations among high-level policy actors concerning wage and price stability, taxation, employment, and social services. The linkages may be either institutionalized and conducted on a regular basis, as they were following the introduction of a trilateral consultative system in 1967 in West Germany in the form of *Konzertierte Aktion* "concerted action"), or they may be informal and sporadic, as has been the case since the official demise of concerted action in 1977.[5] Philippe Schmitter (1974, 1979), Gerhard Lehmbruch (1979, 1982), Leo Panitch (1980), and Ulrich von Alemann and Rolf G. Heinze (1979) are among those policy analysts who see in policy deliberations among national government and interest group officials the emergence of different forms of "societal," "liberal," "political" and/or "economic" corporatism. Their theoretical and empirical findings—to which I shall return in the conclusion to this chapter—constitute an important ongoing paradigmatic shift within the subdiscipline.

Still other comparativists emphasize the policy significance of institutional arrangements—or, more abstractly, "the state"—as their primary unit of analysis. As the leading exponent of the structural approach to comparative policy studies, Ashford has consistently eschewed descriptive statistical or correlational analysis in favor of critical assessments of policy outcomes in terms of their legitimizing function for the state as a whole. For Ashford, as previously noted, the organization of institutionalized power is the most important determinant of policy outcomes. He has applied this interpretation in his studies of both British and French politics (1981, 1982). A good example of a systematic comparative study of political determinants of policy outcomes is David Snyder's evaluation of the influence of organizational and political factors on strike activity in the United States, France, and Italy (1975).

A largely conventional pluralist view of policy determinants can be found in much of the comparative case study literature. A judicious use of diverse source material characterizes both Heclo's study of social politics in Britain and Sweden (1974) and the Heidenheimer-Heclo-Adams examination of social policies in seven advanced democracies (1975, 1983). In the former case, Heclo asserts categorically that

> policy patterns do not flow straightforwardly from analysis of general correlations among aggregated variables. The policy process seems too delicate for that. Understanding how, or whether, politics has affected the advent of modern social policy seems to depend less on statistically unearthing and more on inductively building up generalizations from less tidy accounts. (1974, p. 12)

Accordingly, both Heclo and his collaborators selectively assess multiple factors of policy choice and development over time, with particular emphasis on the role of political parties, institutions, and bureaucracies.

A more complex version of eclecticism is Leon Lindberg's edited volume on *Stress and Contradiction in Modern Capitalism* (1975). The book's 17 chapters were commissioned to reveal contrasting Marxist, pluralist, and elitist perspectives on policy processes and system change in advanced West European and North American democracies. The result is that the book's four co-editors and other contributors variously emphasize social class, political parties, ideology, multi-national corporations, intellectual paradigms, interest groups, and even the alleged "political ascendancy of the sports metaphor in America" as determinants of policy outcomes. In his later collection of invited essays on energy policies in seven countries (1977), Lindberg and a new set of collaborators employ a much more conventional descriptive-analytical approach to comparative policy research which focuses on the decision-making role of government agencies, public and private enterprise, and organized interest groups.

POLICY OUTPUTS AND EVALUATION

The relative utility of these contrasting interpretations of the policy process is best demonstrated through an asssessment of their substantive research findings and their analytical and prescriptive components. Few scholars have narrowly applied King's "primacy of ideas" thesis to explain policy choice. Instead, most comparativists have embarked on exploratory voyages of discovery designed to validate positive hypotheses or propositions concerning the policy significance of key political actors and/or the socioeconomic effects of specific policy outputs. Various policy analysts have simultaneously utilized cross-sectional and longitudinal statistical analyses to test the "primacy of economics" argument advanced on behalf of orthodox economists by some students of American state politics. The results of these dual research strategies have been, on balance, empirically and analytically productive.

A positive result has been the compilation of a good deal of basic descriptive information concerning the scope, organization, costs, and benefits of public actions affecting health services, education, housing, incomes, taxation, and other policy areas in various countries (mainly West European and North American). This is certainly the case with the books and articles that comprise the mainstream public policy literature, including the contributions already cited by Heclo, Heidenheimer, Peters, and Cameron. A second contribution of comparative policy research is the cumulative insight that, while levels of economic development obviously matter in facilitating or restricting the provision of social services in general, *political* acts, and omissions, by policy elites play the key role in determining the content, timing, and social purpose of specific policy choices. This is the consensual theme of empirical findings by scholars employing otherwise widely divergent approaches to comparative policy analysis—among them Cameron, Castles, Lindberg, and Ashford.

At the same time, the very existence of sharply divergent conceptualizations and research foci has severely inhibited cumulative scholarship within the subdiscipline as a whole. At most one can discern cumulative trends within each of the various conceptual and methodological approaches. As articulate and prolific representatives of the mainstream approach, Heclo et al. have been able to collaborate on three occasions in refining and extending their empirical findings. In the process they have contributed a wealth of empirical data and discerning analytical insights into the policy-making process in a number of West European countries and the United States. In terms of their evaluative purpose, both Heclo's *Modern Social Politics in Britain and Sweden* (1974) and the two editions of the Heidenheimer-Heclo-Adams text on *Comparative Public Policy* (1975, 1983) embrace three of the four categories under the "policy evaluation" heading in the taxonomy presented in Figure 1 above. Singularly and jointly, the three authors are interested in exploring the short-term effects of policy decisions and omissions on the lives of citizens in the various countries in question; they address systemic consequences of the "welfare backlash" in the concluding chapter of the *Comparative Public Policy* volume; and in both the latter instance and in an edited volume by Peter Flora and Heidenheimer (1981) they utilize comparative policy analysis to analyze the evolution and performance of various welfare states in Western Europe and America. The result of their successive studies is enhanced understanding—if not of critical alternatives to established institutions and policy outcomes, then of the subtle complexities of social policy as both historical development and imperfect achievement.[6]

Scholars employing longitudinal and correlational analysis have been, by definition of their methodological approach, more rigorous and systematic in their choice and manipulation of data. An early, somewhat inclusive example —one inspired directly by the work of the American state politics specialists—

is James Bennett Hogan's comparative examination of the influence of social structure on public policy in Mexico and Canada (1972). Hogan utilized step-wise regression analysis to explore simple, partial, and multiple correlations among six independent political variables and nine dependent policy measures in the two countries. He found that political factors (especially the nature of the party system) were more important in determining policy outcomes in Canada than in Mexico, where "decisions of state policy makers [similar to those in the United States] are responsive to stages of socio-economic development. . ." (p. 502). The evaluative component of Hogan's analysis is primarily analytical; unable to determine conclusively why Canadian policy patterns differ from those in Mexico, he concludes that "more 'methodism' is not the recipe for reducing remaining unexplained variables in state politics and policy. The answer, if there is one, lies in better theory and more rigorous conceptualizations" (p. 509).

Both of these qualities characterize influential articles published later in the decade in the *American Political Science Review* by Douglas Hibbs on "Political Parties and Macroeconomic Policy" (1977) and David Cameron on "The Expansion of the Public Economy: A Comparative Analysis" (1978). In the former case, Hibbs utilized aggregate data on levels of unemployment and inflation between 1960 and 1969 in 12 industrial democracies to test the policy significance of government by left, center, and right parties. He found a positive correlation between low unemployment/high inflation and executive rule by left parties and, conversely, high unemployment/low inflation and government by center-right parties. Thus, his findings seem to confirm that political parties in fact pursue socioeconomic objectives that correspond to the policy preferences of their core constituents.[7] With important implications for both the primacy of economics vs. politics debate cited earlier and the future efforts to devise better theories to guide comparative policy research, Hibbs concludes:

> Macroeconomic outcomes, then, are not altogether endogenous to the economy, but obviously are influenced to a significant extent by long- and short-term political choices. The real winners of elections are perhaps best determined by examining the policy consequences of partisan change rather than by simply tallying the votes. (p. 1487)

Cameron's purpose is analytically broader than that of Hibbs—namely, to explain the underlying causes and consequences of the dramatic increase between 1960 and 1975 in the economic role and extractive resources of governments in 18 advanced industrial democracies. Using correlational analysis, he found that political, institutional, and international factors were significantly more important factors prompting governmental growth in North America, Japan, and a variety of West European countries than economic or fiscal explanations. Specifically, he discovered a pattern of more rapid growth of the public economy in countries with centralized rather than federal political systems as well as in countries with "open" rather than closed economies.[8] Through regression analysis, Cameron demonstrates that "the openness of the economy is the best single predictor of the growth of public revenues relative to the economic product of a nation" (p. 1254).

While the evaluative intent of Cameron's analysis is obviously analytical, his findings—particularly those in a subsequent article on "The Limits of the Public Economy" (1982)—have powerful prescriptive implications. In the latter case, Cameron reports—on the basis of correlational analysis, this time of relations between government spending and rates of economic growth, unemployment, inflation, and capital formation in 19 industrial nations—that high levels of government spending and budget deficits have not been responsible for stagflation in Western Europe during the 1970s and early 1980s, as many fiscal conservatives have alleged. A key reason, he suggests, is that

> a large and expanding welfare state may be beneficial and helpful to a capitalist economy and to the very groups that are often most critical of it. Why? Because by socializing collective bargaining to a degree and offering a social wage as an inducement for wage moderation by workers, the highly developed welfare state assists in limiting labor's share of national income, thereby increasing corporate profits and the funds available for capital investment. (p. 58)[9]

A sharply contrasting use of theory to guide comparative research is evidenced in the "policy as independent variable" approach employed by Smith (1969, 1975); Kjellberg (1977); and Peters, John C. Doughtie, and M. Kathleen McCulloch (1977). Their contributions constitute another instance of cumulative scholarship within the subdiscipline in that all five scholars have sought, albeit in different ways, to modify Lowi's typology of different policy types for purposes of comparative policy research.

Smith's approach is to define policy outcomes as "bundles of government decisions based on issues. . ." (1975, p. 1) and to examine 12 cases of policy conflicts in five Western democracies under four policy headings. The latter, each of which involves different sets of legislative and executive actors and decision processes, include: (1) distributive policies, (2) sectorally fragmented policies, (3) emotive policies, and (4) redistributive policies. The result of Smith's labors is a set of informative case histories of diverse policy outcomes ranging from decisions on agricultural subsidies in West Germany and the 1930 Smoot-Hawley Tariff Act in the United States (which he depicts as examples of distributive policies) to the nearly-revolutionary events of May 1968 in France and the struggle in West Germany over codetermination (which involve redistributive issues). Smith concedes a number of problems with his approach, including the dual difficulties of fully operationalizing Lowi's typology and "relating participants and institutions to the precise level of conflict. . ." in the empirical assessments of specific cases (p. 167). An additional problem with Smith's analysis is that his case studies are not consistently comparable in either substance or historical timeframe and therefore do not readily lend themselves to generalizations about the policy process either in the individual countries included in the volume or cross-nationally.

A more promising, if highly abbreviated, attempt to modify Lowi's typology for purposes of comparative policy analysis is Kjellberg's imaginative article on "Do Policies (Really) Determine Politics? And Eventually How?" (1977). Kjellberg is interested in basically the same question as Smith—and indeed draws on Smith's 1969 *Comparative Politics* piece as one of his conceptual sources—namely: "in what way does policy—the content and form of governmental activity—affect the political pattern that evolves in different situations?" (p. 555). In seeking an answer to this question, Kjellberg substantially modifies Lowi's typology of policy types by substituting the concepts of "direct" vs. "indirect" policies for Lowi's categories of "distributive" and "regulatory" policies, respectively. Kjellberg defines the former type of public activity as one aiming "at a direct allocation of individual or private goods. . ." (p. 562). "Indirect" policies, in contrast, are those "[r]eferring to the establishment of standards and general principles of future allocations. . . . To put it differently," Kjellberg adds, "this kind of policy introduces a jointness of supply—according to rules based on criteria of equity or some other criteria—but does imply a jointness of consumption" (p. 562). He then weds his reformulation of Lowi's policy types to the fundamental distinction, derived from economic theory, between individual (private) and collective (public) goods. The linkage between different types of policies and private vs. public benefits is depicted in Figure 2, which is adapted from Kjellberg's article (p. 562). Kjellberg posits that policy-making patterns will differ in each of the cells because the anticipated outcomes will vary.

He tests his typology on the basis of quantitative data drawn from case studies of postwar municipal Norwegian policy development affecting welfare, housing, and general planning. Unfortunately, the brevity of his reported findings does not provide a sufficient basis for fully evaluating the utility of his typology; nonetheless, they are highly suggestive. Kjellberg concludes that welfare policies have shifted from the provision of direct individual benefits (cell 1) to indirect benefits (cell 2), while housing benefits have become increasingly indirect and collective (cell 3). A parallel development has not (yet) occurred with respect to local planning, allegedly because of the reluctance by government officials and interest group spokesmen to implement national planning directives. The most striking aspect of Kjellberg's analysis is that changes in the provision of welfare and housing benefits have altered the policy-making process itself. Two important consequences have been to "[strengthen] the bureaucratic-professional element in the decision-making process . . . and to close the process off from outside influence by moving decisions from wider political forums to committees and other restricted groups" (p. 565).

A third application of Lowi's policy categories is the attempt by Peters, Doughtie, and McCulloch (1977) to devise a research strategy that links dif-

FIGURE 2

Kjellberg's Typology Scheme for Public Activity

	Types of Benefits Provided	
Types of Allocation	Individual	Collective
Direct	1	3
Indirect	2	4

ferent policies and contrasting regime types. Seeking to construct a theoretical explanation of the relation between policy inputs and outcomes, they draw on both Salisbury's earlier modifications of Lowi's typology (1968, 1970) and Arend Lijphart's typology of democratic political systems (1968) to construct an integrated typology of political systems and public policies, as shown in Figure 3. The purpose of their own typology is to generate a series of hypotheses concerning the correlation between the posited mode of policy-making in each of the cells and the type of political system indicated.

Utilizing one-tailed t tests to test the significance of differences of means for each of the policy areas and types of political systems, Peters and his co-authors found that redistributive policies are indeed associated with "depoliticized" democracies (as well as with consociational systems), distributive policies with "centrifugal" systems, regulative policies with con-

FIGURE 3

An Integrated Typology of Political Systems and Public Policy[a]

		Input Behavior[b]	
		Integrated	Fragmented
	Integrated	Depoliticized Democracy: Redistribution (Ex.: Sweden)	Consociational Democracy: Regulation (Ex.: The Netherlands)
Decisional System			
	Fragmented	Centripetal Democracy: Self-Regulation (Ex.: United Kingdom)	Centrifugal Democracy: Distribution (Ex.: France)

[a]Adapted from Peters, Doughtie, and McCulloch (1977, p. 335).

[b]The distinction between "integrated" and "fragmented" forms of input behavior and decision systems refers to "the level of fragmentation of demands coming from the social and cultural environment" (p. 334). The authors follow Lijphart's lead (1968) in defining the characteristics of the different regime types as follows (pp. 330-331):

(1) *Depoliticized democracy:* coalescent elite behavior; inclusion of all major organized interest groups in the decision-making process; "low levels of politicization of important national issues."

(2) *Consociational democracy:* fragmented political culture mitigated by "coalescent or accommodate behavior of the political elites. . . ."

(3) *Centripetal democracy:* relatively homogeneous political culture; active competition among political elites and organized interest groups in efforts to shape or influence public policy.

(4) *Centrifugal democracy:* "lack of agreement and integration at both the elite and the mass level"; unrestrained political conflict; strong potential for political instability and turmoil.

sociational systems, and self-regulative policies with "centripetal" democracies. They conclude from their demonstration of a positive relation between different policy outcomes and political systems that a modified version of Lowi's typology in fact seems suitable for cross-national research.

Further applications of the Peters-Doughtie-McCulloch typology will be required to determine its full utility, as the authors themselves readily concede (p. 350). In its present form, the typology constitutes a conceptual advance over Smith's utilization of Lowi's policy types for comparative purposes, and can be usefully tested against the alternative approach sketched by Kjellberg. The statistical analysis employed by Peters and his colleagues in their initial evaluation, however, obscures many important aspects of the policy process—including its developmental dimensions and the interaction among identifiable institutional and group actors in the actual formation of policy.

The latter criticism hardly applies to Ashford's structural approach to policy analysis in his *Policy and Politics in Britain* (1981) and *Policy and Politics in France* (1982). Consistent with his theoretical views concerning the primacy of the state, Ashford combines historical, cultural, and institutional analysis in crafting complex mosaics of the politics of policy-making in both countries. In each case, he examines administrative reform, economic policy, industrial relations, local and regional policies, social security, and immigration. Not a table, figure, or graph accompanies his detailed evaluation of the inhibiting effects of social and political consensus and the institutionalized pattern of adversarial relations among policy elites on effective policy outcomes, in the case of Britain, and the process of institution-building through successive regimes in France. The result of Ashford's rich analysis—to complete the circle from the pluralist approach to his own structural paradigm—is remarkably similar to the contributions of Heclo, Heidenheimer, and other mainstream scholars: incisive descriptive-analytical understanding of the "how" and "why" of policy outcomes and their cumulative consequences for diverse patterns of historical development.

CONCLUSION:
SOME IMPLICATIONS FOR FUTURE RESEARCH

The preceding assessment of different conceptualizations, research methods, and findings which comprise contemporary comparative policy analysis both confirms and qualifies Feldman's critical view of the subdiscipline cited at the beginning of this chapter. He is correct in observing that comparative public policy lacks unity as a field. It could hardly be otherwise, given the considerable epistemological and methodological diversity within political science as a whole. But it does not follow that comparative policy analysis simultaneously lacks guiding *theories*. On the contrary, as I have sought to demonstrate, theories abound within the subdiscipline and have profitably helped focus research and analysis within each of the designated approaches.

Comparative policy theory has been most fully developed by scholars such as Smith, Kjellberg, Peters, and Ashford who in different ways have interpreted policy as an independent variable. Pluralist scholars such as Heclo and Heidenheimer have refrained from articulating explicit theories or abstract models of the policy process but their empirical research has proved, on the whole, more impressive in both descriptive and analytical terms than many of those who have. The most sophisticated combination of theoretical and methodological rigor is found in recent correlational analyses conducted with considerable success by Hibbs and Cameron. The sum of these achievements is that comparative policy analysis has proved far more productive in generating new data, explanations of social change, and analytical insights than some critics have been willing to concede.

This is not to imply, however, that the subdiscipline is without its weaknesses or conceptual and research gaps. These, too, abound, and must be systematically addressed if comparative policy analysis is to continue to develop. Among them are the following deficiencies or omissions:

1. Much work remains to be done in the comparative analysis of public policies in the third world. Admittedly, a number of excellent configurative third world policy studies have appeared in recent years, including Susan Kaufman Purcell's penetrating analysis of *The Mexican Profit-Sharing Decision* (1975) and a succession of edited volumes dealing primarily with Latin America. Among them are David Collier's *The New Authoritarianism in Latin America* (1979), Merilee S. Grindle's *Politics and Policy Implementation in the Third World* (1980), Abraham Lowenthal's *The Peruvian Experiment* (1975), James Malloy's *Authoritarianism and Corporatism in Latin America* (1977), and Alfred Stepan's *Authoritarian Brazil* (1973). But third world policy studies—especially of a genuinely comparative nature—are an exception within the subdiscipline. Moreover, they rarely find their way into the major political science journals (as opposed to more specialized publications such as those devoted to area studies). Among the titles surveyed for this study, an overwhelming majority—approximately 70 percent—dealt with the advanced industrial democracies of Western Europe and North America. In contrast, fewer than 10 percent explored the policy process in Latin America or Asia. Systematic policy studies on the Middle East and Africa are virtually non-existent.

2. A critical omission even in the literature on North America and Western Europe is the absence of rigorous conceptual and empirical attention to policy implementation. Ashford (1978) touches on this omission in his own overview of comparative public policy—but largely as a warning: "Examining how policies are transformed into state activities can lead to the unproductive study of mechanics of policy in the old-style public administration sense. It can also produce generalizations that defy empirical treatment." His recommended strategy for "treading this narrow path between inconsequential and the transcendent is to examine more closely how states pursue similar objectives by very different means" (p. 90).

Erwin Hargrove (1983) has made a preliminary move in the latter direction with his suggestion that policy implementation can usefully be analyzed in terms of Lowi's familiar typology of policy types. He writes:

> The assumption beneath the development of [a typology of different kinds of policies] is that processes of implementation will vary according to the character of the policy being implemented. It is assumed that it is possible to classify types of policies so that the categories can be used as a basis for predicting the implementation processes within each category.

Hargrove has formulated his proposal with an eye to domestic American policy implementation but logically it could be extended to comparative implementation studies as well.

3. An additional goal of future comparative policy research should be to broaden its object of inquiry. To date, most analysts have focused on what governments do; the absence of government policy in a given area has typically been cited as a nondecision and a corresponding indicator of either lagging national development or differences in the scope of government. Yet the absence of overt government activity does not necessarily mean the absence of policy activities. So-called nondecisions may well mask a significant array of private social and economic policies by corporations, charitable organizations, unions, and other non-government actors. Such activities are eminently worthy of systematic comparative investigation.[10]

4. Comparative policy analysis can be broadened usefully in another crucial way as well. As indicated under the output and evaluation column in Figure 1 above, most policy studies deal with various social outcomes. More recently, however, some scholars have begun to evaluate national economic outcomes from a political perspective as well. Among them are Cameron, Lindberg, and J. Rogers Hollingsworth (1982). For future reference, promising ventures—both of which explore a comprehensive range of economic management topics in various industrial democracies—include forthcoming co-edited volumes by Lindberg and Charles Maier on *The Politics and Sociology of Global Inflation* and Peter Merkl and Haruhiro Fukui on *The Political Management of Economic Change in Japan and the Federal Republic of Germany.*[11] What remains as a next step in project design and comparative research is to combine the analysis of social and economic outcomes into integrated assessments of, for example, contrasting policy and institutional responses to persisting conditions of stagflation in the international economy.[12] The rapidly growing literature on varieties of corporatism in advanced industrial democracies is of considerable theoretical import in this context. More than the principal guiding theories in comparative policy analysis itself, the corporatist literature emphasizes the systemic and developmental consequences of policy linkages and trade-offs among key political and economic actors.

The attempts by Schmitter, Lehmbruch, Merkl, Fukui, Lindberg, and others to explore complex modes of institutional-group interaction in order to determine economic and social outcomes constitutes an ongoing transformation of comparative policy analysis. From their initial emphasis on social policies and patterns of public expenditures, which characterized the emergence of the subdiscipline in the 1970s, scholars in both North America and Western Europe have become increasingly concerned in the 1980s with problems of comparative macroeconomic management. In part, as Anderson (1982) has suggested, this transformation reflects a "shifting climate of public concern" rooted in the changed international economic conditions of the 1970s and early 1980s (p. 4). However, it also reflects increasing conceptual and empirical sophistication on the part of comparativists as they delve ever more deeply into the intricate processes of policy-making with its developmental consequences in a variety of national settings.

Efforts to extend comparative policy studies to underexplored topics and new, more complex manifestations of institutional-group interaction will inevitably transform the subdiscipline into an even greater "multiform menagerie" in the years ahead. But for the full promise of comparative policy analysis—as sketched by Rose, Feldman, and others—to be realized, even more empirical research and theoretical refinements are essential before one can confidently proclaim "Enough!"

Notes

1. As comprehensive as these various classificatory schemes are, they nonetheless omit several policy areas which have been the object of recent comparative analysis such as employment policy, abortion policy, energy policy, and inflation.
2. Because of limitations of space, the attached references are restricted to the books and articles cited in this essay and some other especially relevant citations.
3. Similar arguments have been advanced by Arthur Cyr and Peter deLeon (1975) and Howard Leichter (1977).
4. This characterization of the mainstream approach is based on Douglas Ashford's earlier assessment of comparative policy studies (1977).
5. Haruo Shimada and I explore these contrasting modes of policy linkages in our chapter on "Wage Determination in Japan and West Germany: A Corporatist Perspective" in Peter Merkl and Haruhiro Fukui (Eds.), *The Political Management of Economic Change in Japan and the Federal Republic of Germany* (forthcoming).
6. A contrasting approach to the historical development of the modern welfare state can be found in Norman Furniss and Timothy Tilton's *The Case for the Welfare State: From Social Security to Social Equality* (1977). The authors depict Britain as a "social security state," Sweden as a "social welfare state," and the United States as a "positive state."
7. For critical assessments of some of Hibbs' findings, see Cameron (1982) and Nathaniel Beck (1982). Hibbs has recently extended his argument concerning the linkage between class voting and macroeconomic outcomes with particular reference to the British case (1982).
8. By the "openness" of a nation's economy to the world economy, Cameron means, inter alia, the degree to which a country is dependent on international trade to sustain productivity and growth.
9. Cameron has expanded on this theme in his chapter on "Taxes, Spending, and Deficits: Does Government Cause Inflation?" in Leon Lindberg and Charles Maier (Eds.), *The Politics of Inflation and Recession* (forthcoming).
10. Mark Nadel (1975) has previously underscored this point by observing: "Limiting the concept of public policy to government policy tends to trivialize political science in that such a narrow concept misses some of the most significant alloca-

tions of values for citizens. Furthermore, these non-governmental allocations are increasingly intertwined with the activities of formal government. To factor out only governmental outputs for research thus tends to make policy studies a heuristic exercise divorced from the real world of policy-making and policy impacts. Such a limited concept is analogous to prebehavioral political science, in which the focus was on the legal and formal institutions of government to the exclusion of much of the world of political behavior. Similarly, the challenge now is to analyze public policy—whatever its source" (p. 33).

11. The Lindberg volume, scheduled for publication in 1983 by the Brookings Institution, consists of 16 chapters arranged under three broad headings: (1) collective interests and policy outcomes; (2) states, citizens, and public choices; and (3) political economies in conflict. Country foci include the United States, Canada, West Germany, Sweden, and Japan. Merkl and Fukui conceive their comparative study of postwar Japan and West Germany as an empirical test of alternative explanations for economic outcomes in the two countries, among them: (1) the ideology of the ruling party leadership, (2) political pragmatism, (3) bureaucratic politics, (4) interest group pluralism, (5) neo-corporatism, and (6) international interdependence. Some 30 Japanese, West German, and American scholars are collaborating in the study; chapter topics range from economic and advisory systems to energy resources, public and private investment, prices and inflation, and regional and local economic change.

12. An important precedent for such an effort is Katzenstein's edited volume (1978) on the foreign economic policies of advanced industrial states. Katzenstein and seven collaborators explore the interplay between international and domestic factors of policy-making in the United States, Britain, West Germany, Italy, Japan, and France.

REFERENCES: A SELECT BIBLIOGRAPHY
OF COMPARATIVE PUBLIC POLICY STUDIES

Alt, James E. *The politics of economic decline, economic management and political behavior in Britain since 1964.* Cambridge: Cambridge University Press, 1979.

Altenstetter, Christa. *Health policy making and administration in West Germany and the United States.* Beverly Hills: Sage Publications, 1974.

Anderson, Charles. *The political economy of modern Spain.* Madison: University of Wisconsin Press, 1970.

Anderson, Charles. Comparative policy analysis: The design of measures. *Comparative Politics,* 1971, *4,* 117-131.

Anderson, Charles. Commentary on M. Donald Hancock's 'Comparative public policy: An assessment.' APSA convention, Denver, Colorado, Sept. 2-5, 1982.

Anton, Thomas J. *Administered politics: Elite political culture in Sweden.* Boston: Martinus Nijhoff Publishing, 1980.

Ashford, Douglas. Political science and policy studies: Toward a structural solution. *Policy Studies Journal,* 1977, *5,* 570-583.

Ashford, Douglas (Ed.). *Comparing public policies: New concepts and methods.* Beverly Hills: Sage Publications, 1978.

Ashford, Douglas. *Policy and politics in Britain: The limits of consensus.* Philadelphia: Temple University Press, 1981.

Ashford, Douglas. *Policy and politics in France: Living with uncertainty.* Philadelphia: Temple University Press, 1982.

Ashford, Douglas, Katzenstein, Peter J., & Pempel, T. J. (Eds.). *Comparative public policy: A cross national bibliography.* Beverly Hills: Sage Publications, 1978.

Bahry, Donna. Measuring communist priorities: Budgets, investments and the problems of equivalence. *Comparative Political Studies,* 1980, *13,* 267-292.

Beck, Nathaniel. Parties, administrations, and American macro-economic outcomes. *American Political Science Review,* 1982, *76,* 83-93.

Boulter, Douglas R. Setting speed limits . . . and comparing public policy-making. *Comparative Politics,* 1980, *13,* 79-102.

Bunce, Valerie. Elite succession, petrification, and policy innovation in communist systems: An empirical assessment. *Comparative Political Studies,* 1976, *9,* 3-52.

Bunce, Valerie. Changing leaders and changing policies: The impact of elite succession on budgetary priorities in democratic countries. *American Journal of Political Science,* 1980, *24,* 373-395. (a)

Bunce, Valerie. The succession connection: Policy cycles and political change in the Soviet Union and eastern Europe. *American Political Science Review,* 1980, *74,* 966-977. (b)

Bunce, Valerie & Echols, John M. III. Power and policy in communist systems: The problem of 'incrementalism.' *Journal of Politics,* 1978, *4,* 911-932.

Cameron, David R. The expansion of the public economy: A comparative analysis. *American Political Science Review,* 1978, *72,* 1243-1261.

Cameron, David R. On the limits of the public economy. *The Annals,* 1982, *459,* 46-62.

Castles, Francis B. The political functions of organized groups: The Swedish case. *Political Studies,* 1973, *XXI,* 26-34.

Castles, Francis B. *The social democratic image of society.* Boston: Routledge & Kegan Paul, 1978.

Castles, Francis B. Public welfare provision, Scandinavia and the sheer futility of the sociological approach to politics. *British Journal of Political science*, 1979, *9*, 157-171.

Castles, Francis B. & McKinlay, Robert D. Does politics matter? An analysis of the public welfare commitment in advanced democratic states. *European Journal of Political Research*, 1979, *7*, 169-186.

Cerny, Philip G. & Schain, Martin A. (Eds.). *French politics and public policy*. New York: St. Martin's Press, 1980.

Cnudde, Charles F. & McCrone, Donald J. Party competition and welfare policies in the American states. *American Political Science Review*, 1969, *63*, 858-866.

Collier, David. *Squatters and oligarchs: Authoritarian rule and policy change in Peru*. Baltimore: The Johns Hopkins Press, 1976.

Collier, David (Ed.). *The new authoritarianism in Latin America*. Princeton: Princeton University Press, 1979.

Coulter, Philip B. Comparative community politics and public policy: Problems in theory and research. *Polity*, 1970, *3*, 22-43.

Cowart, Andrew T. The economic policies of European governments, part I: Monetary policy. *British Journal of Political Science*, 1978, *8*, 285-311. (a)

Cowart, Andrew T. The economic policies of European governments, part II: Fiscal policy. *British Journal of Political science*, 1978, *8*, 425-439. (b)

Cyr, Arthur & deLeon, Peter. Comparative policy analysis. *Policy Sciences*, 1975, *6*, 375-384.

Dawson, Richard E. & Robinson, James A. Interparty competition, economic variables, and welfare politics in the American states. *Journal of Politics*, 1963, *25*, 265-289.

deLeon, Peter. Public policy and political development: The case of the SSRC. *Policy Studies Journal*, 1977, *5*, 596-615.

Diamant, Alfred. Bureaucracy and public policy in neo-corporatist settings: Some European lessons (review article). *Comparative Politics*, 1981, *14*, 101-124.

Dogan, Mattei (Ed.). *The mandarins of western Europe*. New York: John Wiley, 1975.

Dye, Thomas R. *Politics, economics, and the public: Policy outcomes in the American states*. Chicago: Rand McNally, 1966.

Dye, Thomas R. Politics versus economics: The development of the literature on policy determination. *Policy Studies Journal*, 1979, *7*, 652-662.

Enloe, Cynthia H. *The politics of pollution in a comparative perspective: Ecology and power in four nations*. New York: David McNay, 1975.

Esping-Anderson, Gosta. Social class, social democracy, and the state: Party policy and party decomposition in Denmark and Sweden. *Comparative Politics*, 1978, *11*, 42-58.

Feldman, Elliot J. Comparative public policy: Field or method? *Comparative Politics*, 1978, *10*, 287-305.

Feldman, Elliot J. & Milch, Jerome. *Technology versus democracy: The comparative politics of international airports*. Boston: Auburn House Publishing Company, 1982.

Flora, Peter & Heidenheimer, Arnold J. (Eds.). *The development of welfare states in Europe and America*. New Brunswick: Transaction Books, 1981.

Furniss, Norman & Tilton, Timothy. *The case for the welfare state: From social security to social equality*. Bloomington: Indiana University Press, 1977.

Grindle, Merilee S. (Ed.). *Politics and policy implementation in the third world*. Princeton: Princeton University Press, 1980.

Hancock, M. Donald. Productivity, welfare, and participation in Sweden and West Germany: A comparison of social democratic reform prospects. *Comparative Politics*, 1978, *11*, 4-23.

Hancock, M. Donald. The political management of economic and social change: Contrasting models of advanced industrial society in Sweden and West Germany. *The Annals*, 1982, *459*, 63-76.

Hargrove, Erwin C. *The missing link: The study of the implementation of social policy*. Washington, D.C.: The Urban Institute, 1975.

Hargrove, Erwin C. The search for implementation theory. In Richard Zeckhauser & Derek Leebaert (Eds.), *The role of government in the 1980s*. Durham: Duke University Press, 1983.

Hayward, Jack. The politics of planning in France and Britain. *Comparative Politics*, 1975, *7*, 285-298.

Heclo, Hugh. Review article: Policy analysis. *British Journal of Political Science*, 1972, *2*, 84-108.

Heclo, Hugh. *Modern social politics in Britain and Sweden: From relief to income maintenance*. New Haven: Yale University Press, 1974.

Heidenheimer, Arnold J. The politics of public education, health, and welfare in the U.S.A. and Western Europe: How growth and reform potentials have differed. *British Journal of Political Science*, 1973, *3*, 315-340.

Heidenheimer, Arnold J. (Ed.). Public policy comparisons: Scandinavia. *West European politics* (Vol. 3), Oct. 1980, 293-430.

Heidenheimer, Arnold J., Heclo, Hugh, & Adams, Carolyn Teich. *Comparative public policy: The politics of social choice in Europe and America*. New York: St. Martin's Press, 1975. (Sec. ed. 1983)

Heisler, Martin O., & Kvavik, Robert. Patterns of European politics: The 'European policy' model. In Heisler (Ed.), *Politics in Europe: Structures and processes in some post-industrial democracies*. New York: St. Martin's Press, 1974.

Hibbs, Douglas A., Jr. Industrial conflict in advanced industrial societies. *American Political Science Review*, 1976, *70*, 1033-1058.

Hibbs, Douglas A. Political parties and macroeconomic policy. *American Political Science Review*, 1977, *71*, 1467-1487.

Hibbs, Douglas A. with the assistance of Nicholas Vasilatos. Economic outcomes and political support for British governments among occupational classes: A dynamic analysis. *American Political Science Review*, 1982, *76*, 259-597.

Higley, John, & Moore, Gwen. Elite integration in the United States and Australia. *American Political Science Review*, 1981, *75*, 581-597.

Hofferbert, Richard. The relation between public policy and some structural and environmental variables in the American states. *American Political Science Review*, 1966, *60*, 73-82.

Hogan, James B. Social structure and public policy: A longitudinal study of Mexico and Canada. *Comparative Politics*, 1972, *4*, 477-510.

Hollingsworth, J. Rogers. The political-structural basis for economic performance. *The Annals*, 1982, *459*, 28-45.

Inglehart, Ronald. Policy problems of advanced industrial society: Introduction. *Comparative Political Studies*, 1977, *10*, 291-298.

Jackman, Robert W. *Politics and social equality: A comparative analysis*. New York: John Wiley, 1975.

Jackman, Robert W. Socialist parties and income inequality in western industrial societies. *Journal of Politics*, 1980, *42*, 135-149.

Jacob, Herbert, & Lipsky, Michael. Outputs, structure, and power: An assessment of changes in the study of state and local politics. *Journal of Politics*, 1968, *30*, 510-538.

Katzenstein, Peter J. (Ed.). *Between power and plenty: Foreign economic policies of advanced industrial states*. Madison: University of Wisconsin Press, 1978.

King, Anthony. Ideas, institutions, and the policies of governments: A comparative analysis. *British Journal of Political Science*, 1973, *3*, 291-313, 409-423.

King, Anthony. What do elections decide? In David Butler, Howard R. Penniman & Austin Ranney (Eds.), *Democracy at the polls: A comparative study of competitive national elections*. Washington, D.C.: American Enterprise Institute for Public Policy Research, 1981.

Kjellberg, Francesco. Do policies (really) determine politics? And eventually how? *Policy Studies Journal*, 1977, *5*, 554-570.

Lehmbruch, Gerhard. Liberal corporatism and party government. In Philippe C. Schmitter & Lehmbruch (Eds.), *Trends toward corporatist intermediation*. Beverly Hills: Sage Publications, 1979.

Lehmbruch, Gerhard. Introduction: Neo-corporatism in comparative perspective. In Lehmbruch and Schmitter (Eds.), *Patterns of corporatist policy-making*. Beverly Hills: Sage Publications, 1982.

Leichter, Howard M. Comparative public policy: Problems and prospects. *Policy Studies Journal*, 1977, *5*, 583-596.

Leichter, Howard M. *A comparative approach to policy analysis: Health care policy in four nations*. New York: Cambridge University Press, 1979.

Lewis-Beck, Michael S. The relative importance of socioeconomic and political variables for public policy. *American Political Science Review*, 1977, *71*, 559-566.

Lijphart, Arend. Typologies of democratic systems. *Comparative Political Studies*, 1968, *1*, 3-44.

Lijphart, Arend. Comparative politics and the comparative method. *American Political Science Review*, 1971, *65*, 682-698.

Lindberg, Leon (Ed.). *The energy syndrome: Comparing national responses to the energy crisis*. Lexington: Lexington Books, 1977.

Lindberg, Leon. The problems of economic theory in explaining economic performance. *The Annals*, 1982, *459*, 14-27.

Lindberg, Leon, Alford, Robert, Crouch, Colin, & Offe, Claus (Eds.). *Stress and contradiction in modern capitalism*. Lexington: Lexington Books, 1975.

Lowenthal, Abraham F. (Ed.). *The Peruvian experiment: Continuity and change under military rule*. Princeton: Princeton University Press, 1975.

Lowi, Theodore. American business, public policy, case studies, and political theory. *World Politics*, 1964, *XVI*, 677-715.

Lowi, Theodore. Four systems of policy, politics, and choice. *Public Administration Review*, 1972, *XXXIII*, 298-310.

Malloy, James M. (Ed.). *Authoritarianism and corporatism in Latin America*. Pittsburgh: University of Pittsburgh Press, 1977.

Martin, Andrew. Political constraints and economic strategies in advanced industrial societies. *Comparative Political Studies*, 1977, *10*, 323-354.

Mayntz, Renate, & Scharpf, Fritz W. *Policy-making in the German federal bureaucracy*. New York: Elsevier, 1975.

Nadel, Mark V. The hidden dimension of public policy: Private governments and the policy-making process. *Journal of Politics*, 1975, *37*, 2-34.

Panitch, Leo. Recent theorization of corporatism: Reflections on a growth industry. *British Journal of Sociology*, 1980, *31*, 159-187.

Pempel, T. J. *Policy and politics in Japan: Creative conservatism*. Philadelphia: Temple University Press, 1982.

Peters, B. Guy. Economic and political effects on the development of social expenditures in France, Sweden, and the United Kingdom. *Midwest Journal of Political Science*, 1972, *16*, 225-238. (a)

Peters, B. Guy. Public policy, socioeconomic conditions and the political system: A note on their developmental relationship. *Polity*, 1972, *5*, 277-284. (b)

Peters, B. Guy. The development of social policy in France, Sweden, and the United

Kingdom: 1850-1965. In Martin Heisler (Ed.), *Politics in Europe*. New York: David McKay, 1975.

Peters, B. Guy. Developments in comparative policy studies: A brief review. *Policy Studies Journal*, 1977, *5*, 616-628.

Peters, B. Guy. Bureaucracy, politics and public policy (review article). *Comparative Politics*, 1979, *11*, 339-358.

Peters, B. Guy. Comparative public policy (a bibliography). *Policy Studies Review*, 1981, *1*, 183-197.

Peters, B. Guy, Doughtie, John C., & McCulloch, M. Kathleen. Types of democratic systems and types of public policy. *Comparative Politics*, 1977, *9*, 327-355.

Pryor, Frederic L. *Public expenditures in communist and capitalist nations*. London: Allen and Unwin, 1968.

Purcell, Susan Kaufman. *The Mexican profit-sharing decision: Politics in an authoritarian regime*. Berkeley: University of California Press, 1975.

Ranney, Austin. The study of policy content: A framework for choice. In Ranney (Ed.), *Political science and public policy*. Chicago: Markham Publishing Company, 1968.

Rimlinger, Gaston V. *Welfare policy and industrialization in Europe, America, and Russia*. New York: Wiley, 1971.

Rose, Richard. Comparing public policy: An overview. *European Journal of Political Research*, 1973, *1*, 67-93. (a)

Rose, Richard. Concepts for comparison. *Policy Studies Journal*, 1973, *1*, 122-127. (b)

Rose, Richard. *The dynamics of public policy: Comparative analysis*. Beverly Hills: Sage Publications, 1976.

Salisbury, Robert H. The analysis of public policy: A search of theories and roles. In Austin Ranney (Ed.), *Political science and public policy*. Chicago: Markham Publishing Company, 1968.

Schmidt, Manfred G. Does corporatism matter? Economic crisis, politics and rates of unemployment in capitalist democracies in the 1970s. In Gerhard Lehmbruch & Philippe Schmitter (Eds.), *Patterns of corporatist policy-making*. Beverly Hills: Sage Publications, 1982.

Schmitter, Philippe C. Still the century of corporatism? *The Review of Politics*, 1974, *36*, 85-131.

Schmitter, Philippe C. & Lehmbruch, Gerhard (eds.). *Trends toward corporatist intermediation*. Beverly Hills: Sage Publications, 1979.

Schon, Donald. *Beyond the stable state*. New York: W.W. Norton, Co., 1971.

Sharkansky, Ira. *Wither the state?* Chatham: Chatham House, 1979.

Sharkansky, Ira & Hofferbert, Richard I. Dimensions of state politics, economics and public policy. *American Political Science Review*, 1969, *63*, 887-889.

Siegel, Richard L. & Weinberg, Leonard B. *Comparing public policies: United States, Soviet Union, and Europe*. Homewood: Dorsey Press, 1977.

Simeon, Richard. Studying public policy. *Canadian Journal of Political Science*, 1976, *9*, 548-580.

Sloan, John W. Comparative public choice and public policy in Latin America. *Journal of Developing Areas*, 1982.

Smith, T. Alexander. Toward a comparative theory of the policy process. *Comparative Politics*, 1969, *1*, 498-515.

Smith, T. Alexander. *The comparative policy process*. Santa Barbara: ABC-Clio Press, 1975.

Snyder, David. Institutional setting and industrial conflict: Comparative analyses of France, Italy, and the United States. *American Political Science Review*, 1975, *40*, 259-267.

Spalding, Rose J. Welfare policymaking: Theoretical implications of a Mexican case study. *Comparative Politics,* 1980, *12,* 419-438.

Steiner, Jurg. The consociational theory and beyond (review article). *Comparative Politics,* 1981, *13,* 339-354.

Stepan, Alfred (Ed.). *Authoritarian Brazil: Origins, policies, and future.* New Haven: Yale University Press, 1973.

Tufte, Edward R. *Political control of the economy.* Princeton: Princeton University Press, 1978.

Verner, Joel C. Socioeconomic environment, political system, and educational policy outcomes: A comparative study of 102 countries. *Comparative Politics,* 1979, *11,* 165-188.

von Alemann, Ulrich & Heinze, Rolf G. *Verbaende und staat: vom pluralismus zum korporatismus: analysen, positionen, dokumente.* Opladen: Westdeutscher Verlag, 1979.

Wilensky, Harold L. *The welfare state and equality: Structural and ideological roots of public expenditures.* Berkeley: University of California Press, 1975.

Wilensky, Harold L. *The 'new corporatism': Centralization and the welfare state.* Beverly Hills: Sage Publications, 1976.

Winkler, J. T. Corporatism. *Archives Europeenes de Sociologie,* 1976, *17,* 100-136.

11

Studying the Politics of
Development and Change:
The State of the Art

*Joel S. Migdal**

When Lerner (1958, p. 45) surveyed Middle Eastern societies thirty years ago, the word that came to mind as he sought to make sense of the many images he encountered was "chaos." It is not a term most social scientists would use very comfortably in describing any sort of situation. Lerner's initial bewilderment at the dizzying pace and scope of change, though, was not atypical, nor was his response to societies seemingly engaged in a headlong rush into confusion. As Eckstein (1982, p. 457) put it, "The development theorists tried, in essence, to find patterns in pervasive novelty and seeming flux—to get bearings in a world devoid of all fixity and precedents." Lerner's reaction, much like that of other social scientists, was to ferret out a pattern, a system—indeed, even to *impose* an intellectual order where social and political order could not be discerned. The term development came to denote the movement from social and political "chaos" in Africa, Asia, and Latin America towards some implicitly understood order.

From the beginning, the field of development and change was constitutive; it was the musings of scholars seeking the principles of political and social orders and the conditions initiating them. Although the study of formal constitutional process was already considered somewhat antiquated in political science by the end of the 1950s, writing on non-Western politics came to be nothing less than excursions into how societies and states might be constituted—or better yet, reconstituted.[1] The field of development, in some senses, housed the new successors to Hobbes, Montesquieu, and the other

*I would like to thank Bruce Cumings, Samuel Huntington, George Modelski, John Montgomery, Ronald Rogowski, James Townsend, Sidney Verba, and Aristide Zolberg for their helpful comments on an earlier draft of this paper.

political philosophers who had sought constitutive measures in a similarly chaotic Europe.

The flush of excitement associated with the changes in the world map from 1947 to 1965 gripped political scientists who were seeking to untangle the debris of the old to articulate new bases of order. Few scholars agreed on any one approach to this great challenge. Pye (1965) wrote an article enumerating the many meanings the term political development had already taken in the literature. Half a decade later Huntington (1971) seemed to throw up his hands, saying that as long as there is a lack of a precise definition, the term political development can have no analytic value. All it does, he asserted, is describe some common field hoed by scholars.

For all the intellectual diversity the field spawned, there were important shared perspectives about the nature of political and social change in the Third World. But, in the late 1960s and early 1970s, serious critics attacked some of these notions, including the teleology, unidirectionality, and evolutionary determinism in the development literature.[2] Those criticisms initiated a new era of vitality for the field, as many, but by no means all, older perspectives were jettisoned and new approaches blossomed.

In assessing the state of the field, it is worth looking back at some of the major shared notions. A number of these ideas continue to sway, even today, interpretations of how change occurs. We will then turn to three major currents that have greatly influenced research in recent years and close with a discussion of how this new scholarship has affected our understanding of first principles.

APPROACHING THE STUDY OF DEVELOPMENT AND CHANGE

Several landmark books, appearing within a few years of one another, inaugurated the fields of development and modernization across the social sciences (Almond and Coleman, 1960; Millikan and Rostow, 1957; Rostow, 1960; Lerner, 1958). The Almond and Coleman volume placed studies of the developing areas firmly into the subject matter of comparative politics writ large. It gave birth to a highly touted nine-volume series, "Studies in Political Development," which spanned a fifteen-year period. Both the Almond and Coleman work and the subsequent series grew out of the prestigious Committee on Comparative Politics of the Social Science Research Council. Oddly, though, these works had only a muted impact on the burgeoning field in the 1960s and 1970s. Certainly, the volumes were read, discussed, and reviewed (see, for example, Montgomery, 1969). They did make political scientists take the politics imbedded in kinship systems as seriously as those found in Western parliaments. But the volumes were also much ignored. No school developed; they did not shape ongoing research. An obligatory opening footnote citing the Committee's work would be encountered in many monographs and articles, but there would be little evidence that it made a contribution to method or substance.

The work that played the role of midwife to the several branches of the field of political development was by the sociologist, Lerner (1958).[3] All these new branches shared, in one way or another, a commitment to Lerner's "system" of modernity. The notion of a system rested on the belief that the seemingly diverse aspects of socio-political change are actually related in a pattern of high co-variation.

By the mid-1960s, many scholars accepted three key features found in the Lerner book without necessarily endorsing Lerner's central hypothesis. First, a general research focus in those years was on domestic change. The herald of such change may have been the rapid transformation of the international environment, but the internal transformations siphoned off almost all the interest of scholars. Second, at the macro-level, political scientists focused upon the creation of central institutions (the term "state" was not yet in vogue) and their ability to transform society. Third, at the micro-level they used surveys and other research tools to assess the process of individual change and its relationship to social processes, such as urbanization, industrialization, and the like. Deutsch's (1961) concept of social mobilization, with its stress on the relationship between the breakdown of personal commitments and these near-universal social processes, became the byword for interpreting aggregated individual change.

Understanding macro-change — the configuration of institutional transformations in an entire society — demanded a framework of a different order. Several such frameworks were employed often differing only in terminology. The most popular was the modern-traditional dichotomy used by Lerner (1958) and other important social scientists such as Almond and Coleman (1960), Apter (1965), Black (1966), Eisenstadt (1966), Levy (1966), and Shils (1960). Also widely employed was the metaphor of center and periphery (see, for example, Lerner, 1966, and Shils, 1975). Among the other concepts used to make fairly similar distinctions are: elite-mass (Mosca, 1939); diffracted-fused (Riggs, 1964); Great Tradition-little tradition (Redfield, 1960); and even, at times, urban-rural (Sjoberg, 1960; and Tilly, 1967). Some scholars added intermediate terms, such as transitional or prismatic, but the endpoints of the continuum were the most theoretically important concepts. A formal theory of the relationship between the two sectors was never developed, but it is worth looking for a moment at some of the widely shared assumptions held by those employing such dichotomies. Although there may be variability in the size and strength of the two components of each dichotomy, the dichotomies themselves were meant to be enduring analytic tools not bound by time or space. The intent in the field of political development was to use the tool to depict a beachhead imagery; that is, in contemporary societies the locus of "development" is the modern sector or center (or elite, Great Tradition, urban areas) — the beachhead of change — and the locus of the "underdeveloped" part of society is the traditional sector or periphery (or masses, little tradition, rural areas).

The modern sector or center was seen as activist and aggressive; its authority was the motor of social and political change. The strength of the center lay in its integration, a result of the high consensus among elites sharing modern values. (The meaning of "modern values" did not, for most authors, stray far from the instrumental side of Parsons', 1951, five pattern variables.) To political scientists, the array of public institutions — the state — should have been the most interesting component of the center. Yet, it was not until the latter 1960s and 1970s that the state qua activist organization, began to become a major subject of research (see Nettl, 1968; and Tilly, 1975c). Before then, a rather hazy image prevailed of interlocking authoritative institutions in the modern sector or center. But the importance of authority was clearly understood. The very need for authority implied a measure of resistance in the society. Values were not fully or equally shared throughout the society and did not impel everyone towards the same type of behavior; otherwise, there would have been no politics at all. Social and political control of imperfectly integrated parts underlay the use of the modern-traditional and center-periphery dichotomies.

The traditional sector or periphery consists not of those parts of the population that exercise authority, but "of those strata or sectors of the society which are the recipients of commands and of beliefs which they do not themselves create or cause to be diffused, and of those who are lower in the distribution or allocation of rewards, dignities, facilities, etc." (Shils, 1975, p. 39). Authority expands the modern sector into the traditional. The leadership is never satisfied to live and let live but wants everyone to obey and to accept the validity of its rules of the game. Rewards and punishments exercised through the modern sector's organizations are used by the elites to facilitate the acceptance of their decisions and views.

Indifference to the structure, resiliency, and autonomy of the traditional sector or periphery marked many of the earlier major political science works on development as well as many contemporary studies — though there have been, to be sure, important exceptions (see Dahl, 1971; Huntington, 1968; Cardoso & Faletto, 1979). The periphery, while capable of change, took on in the 1950s and 1960s, and frequently continues to wear, a two-dimensional visage.

The European experience, in which nationalism has been the crucial component of the belief system and people have become increasingly attached to the larger territory in which they live, served for many writers as a model of change for the rest of the world. The Western experience, portrayed in grossly oversimplified terms, was seen as a process of change that involved the major centers' winning over minor centers and a shift from unimposing bureaucratic empires and feudal systems to modern, dynamic, effective centers. And that process was then presumed to be universal. The *direction* of development, it was assumed, is away from the primordial (biological criteria of affinity) towards attachment to the larger territory; the *form* of development is away from weak, non-intrusive centers to active, dominant centers; the *substance* of development is towards a civil society, marked by modern values and procedures. It is true, a noted author (Shils, 1975) suggested, that many states in Asia and Africa "have *not yet* become societies in a modern sense because they do *not yet* have effective centers" (p. 44). Rulers face "a population which is *not yet* formed into a society but which consists of a number of proto-societies" (p. 89, emphasis added). Even on these continents, however, the evolution seemed to be clear, and what must be overcome was the lag.

What is lacking currently, it was implied, are the key ingredients of authority and power. Huntington (1968) noted that in many cases in Asia, Africa, and Latin America "governments simply do not govern" (p. 2). "Government implies power," wrote LaPalombara (1971) but "the most unequivocal and uncontestable statement one can make about most of the new nations today is how little power those at the center actually possess" (p. 53).

If Third World societies, in fact, lack the authoritative element, if governments really do not govern, then the field of development may have been not very different from Alice in Wonderland. The ideas developed to analyze macro-level change—modern and traditional or center and periphery—were geared to explain the impact of the authoritative sector of society on those that are the recipients of commands. The analytic lenses filtered a pattern of change in which the primary struggle was that between a relatively united, institutionally strong elite against an undifferentiated mass. But were the institutions and elites really what they appeared to be? The questions posed by political scientists of those years tended to be directed more towards what these elites and their institutions had *not yet* become, i.e., modern integrated sectors or strong centers, rather than to what they actually were. Without an authoritative center, with governments that did not govern, analysts seemed to be describing a non-existent situation. The challenge for political scientists was made all the more imposing because in much of the Third World there was an adoption of institutional forms and names from the West (states, parliaments, parties, and the like). It was seductive to assume that there *had been* a convergence of elites and values in these institutions and that the outputs would eventually be those that were expected. It was tempting to assume that a state, *any* state, was tied into other central institutions sharing with it important values and that such a state was activist and powerful.

Huntington (1968) had a clear and lasting impact on the field largely because he took institutions seriously. He looked at what the political institutions of societies actually were, not at what they had "not yet" become nor at what they formally were supposed to be. Questions concerning the real political capabilities of states, of the possibility of institutional decay or breakdown, now became central topics of concern. For political scientists, the political institutions were returned to the limelight, no longer subsumed within the broader category of center nor made the simple outgrowth of non-political events, as they were in Lerner's work.

Huntington's analysis was in some ways a technical one. The guiding question was what specific kinds of mechanisms maintain political stability even in the face of increased political demands—potentially destabilizing demands growing out of the near-universal process of social mobilization. The effective mechanisms, he answered, were political institutions, especially political parties: Institutions that are adaptable, complex, autonomous, and coherent. Still left to be answered, however, were the political-philosophical questions that had informed the field from the 1950s: What are the principles—rather than the mechanisms—of social and political order? Why have some societies generated effective constitutional principles and institutions while others have not? What are the processes of change involved in constituting new orders? If modern sectors or centers are not what they are supposed to be how can we explain order and change?

In the 1970s and 1980s the means chosen to answer these macro-level questions resulted in a number of startling changes in the development field. First, the field, which usually had been defined by a residual geographic area — *non*-Western, *non*-Communist, neither from the first nor second worlds but from a heterogeneous Third World — was now extended into all other geographic regions, including the West. Second, in a subdiscipline that had regarded itself as au courant, that had concentrated on the subject of becoming modern in the post-World War II era, there was now an unexpected return to history. And such history was not simply the obligatory background preceding the "real" analysis but was a primary subject of research. Third, in a field that had restricted itself almost exclusively to domestic concerns, that had placed itself firmly under the heading of comparative politics (see Rustow, 1968), there were now new frameworks that were as much international as comparative.

THREE MAJOR RESEARCH CURRENTS

From the Third World to the First (and Second)

An irony of the first change, the spreading influence of the development field beyond the Third World into Europe and North America, is that the study of non-Western societies has been saddled with so many handicaps compared to research elsewhere. Access is frequently limited. Government statistics are often haphazard and unreliable; other base-line materials are also scarce. Sampling is problematical because of the heterogeneity of the population. Nonetheless, the intellectual excitement of social scientists observing change in that momentous era of successful independence movements infected those studying other societies as well. Kesselman (1970), for example, toyed with Huntington's concept of institutionalization, weighing its usefulness for explaining French politics; Inglehart (1970) did much the same for Europe with Deutsch's notion of social mobilization.

In one sense, Europe was part of the development field from the outset. The very connection of social change to development, as Nisbet (1969) makes clear, goes back to the earliest European writings. And the Western notion of development gathered special force in the theories of the late nineteenth and early twentieth centuries. When it came to giving substance to words such as "developed" or "modern" in the Third World, writers both implicitly and explicitly fell back on those patterns typical of the West. In addition, they used their understanding of the processes of change in Western history to project along which route non-Western states and societies would evolve. Not only did they assume the content of modernity but also the nature of the process — development or modernization — that would bring societies to modernity. Most interesting is how these Western cases were incorporated into development models, for it could be argued that the American and European "models" that were used bore little resemblance to the *actual* processes of change that had taken place in the United States and Europe. It was not until the 1970s, however, that the European experience began to be examined more closely to see what kinds of distortion had crept into the models used in understanding processes of change in the Third World (e.g., Rokkan, 1973).

What some writers came to question was the utter confidence that infused the works of those who used the modern-traditional metaphor or other similar imagery. Had centers coalesced or states centralized in Western history as completely and smoothly as had been assumed? Have peripheries been as passive and malleable as has been thought? In an excellent monograph, Berger (1972) found that even as highly centralized a state as France found itself faced with a peasantry and "its imperfect insertion into the body politic" (p. 2). In France, there had arisen "corporative organizations" characterized by their efforts to regulate peasant matters fully without tying these matters into the politics of the state. The corporative organizations were able to build a reservoir of political loyalty by assuming functions important to the peasantry. They then jealously guarded this arena of conflicts and interests that lay beyond the reach of the centralized state and, as a result, they inhibited "change in the political system by withdrawing from the domain of parties and the state those issues on which alignments of interests and values are formed" (Berger, 1972, p. 168).

Berger's later work extended some of the conceptions which underlay this analysis to European cases besides France and to sectors besides the peasantry (Berger & Piore, 1980). Various segments of some European societies have continued to differ substantially from one another. These variations (or dualism) have not been "mere way stations to ultimate convergence" through the authority of centers or states. Rather "traditional" segments have endured "because of the ways in which [their] political and economic interests overlap with those of the modern sector" (Berger & Piore, 1980, pp. 3, 87). In this, European societies differ little from non-Western ones, "The evidence from both developed and developing countries suggests the persistence, not the disappearance, of the traditional or informal sector" (Berger & Piore, 1980, pp. 4, 5). As Rogowski and Wasserspring (1971) put it, even in advanced industrial societies, "nothing compels individuals . . . to become atoms, bonded only by the nexuses of cash and self-interest" (p. 44). Perhaps Europe looks more like the Third World than the Third World was thought to look like Europe.

Also reflecting the impact of Third World development literature on the understanding of the constitutive principles of European society and state is the growing corporatist literature. Although the term corporatism referred earlier in this century to the fascist states of Europe, in the post-War era it was applied almost exclusively to Iberian cultures and their offshoots, most notably in Latin America. Only after its elaboration in that context did the concept return to the advanced industrial states of West Europe, now in a much more benign form.

Corporatism for most writers meant something quite different from Berger's corpora*tive* organizations. For Berger (1972), the corporative organizations try "to acquire the power and authority to rule their own household" *outside the state* (p. 9). In the Iberian and Latin American literature and later in the materials for other parts of Europe, the corporatist organiza-tions are "recognized or licensed (if not created) *by the state*" (Schmitter, 1974, p. 93, emphasis added). The state has moved to center stage.

Researchers working on post-War Spain, Portugal, and Latin America resuscitated the term corporatism almost reluctantly after the ignominy it suf-fered by the time of the Nuremberg Trials. Even revived, it at first retained a negative taint. Corporatism, after all, was the historical antithesis of liberal-ism, placing the group—with its special bonds and rights—over the in-dividual. It was thought to exclude the ambrosia of the twentieth century, in-dustrialization and modernization. Corporatism was an atavistic survival in a world of more dynamic isms. "The Iberian and Latin American political systems have retained a mausoleum-like appearance" (Wiarda, 1976, p. 5). As Newton (1974) put it, "in the experience of the Atlantic world the cor-porate state is an anachronism, and a faintly tawdry one at that" (p. 35). The term corporatism came to be associated with states and societies mired in habits and institutions ill-fitted to the twentieth century. "Corporatism and the corporatist tradition," wrote Wiarda (1977), "are a 'natural,' almost in-herent part of the Iberic-Latin political culture" (p. 4).

By the mid-to-late 1970s, practically all these associations began to die. Rather than the antithesis of liberalism and democracy, corporatism began to appear in titles such as "Liberal Corporatism and Party Government" (Lehm-bruch, 1979), "The Development of Corporatism in Liberal Democracies" (Panitch, 1979), and "Corporatism, Parliamentarism and Social Democracy" (Jessop, 1979). No longer associated exclusively with Iberic and Latin Ameri-can cultures, corporatism blossomed into a tool of analysis for other parts of Europe, Japan and elsewhere. And instead of being the scourge of indus-trialization, corporatism has been heralded as the foundation for advanced industrial growth and adaptation (e.g., Katzenstein, forthcoming; Pempel, 1978). More and more, writers came to accept "that corporatism, like liberalism or socialism, may take a variety of forms, both as between nations and within a single nation over time" (Wiarda, 1977, p. 5). The new authoritarianism in Brazil following the coup of 1964 (Stepan, 1973), Salazar's old Portugal (Schmitter, 1975), the Portuguese shift towards socialism after the 1974 coup (Wiarda, 1977), Japan's corporatism without labor (Pempel & Tsunekawa, 1979), along with many other cases, all became subjects of corporatist analysis. The difficulty with the concept's success is that without proper specification and disaggregation, it may become little more than a residual category that is used to explain nearly all state-society rela-tionships. Such fears have already been expressed by some (e.g., Nedelmann & Meier, 1979; Pempel & Tsunekawa, 1979). As Schmitter noted (1974), "It has become such a vaguely bounded phenomenon that, like clientelism, it can be found everywhere and, hence, is nowhere very distinctive" (p. 86).

For political scientists, the return of corporatism has had a welcome by-product, the return of politics to the limelight. The field of development has been overshadowed from the beginning by economic issues and by the econo-mists (though within the discipline of economics, development has been fairly low in status of late). At the same time, sociologists from Talcott Parsons and Edward Shils, in the Weberian tradition, to Barrington Moore and Immanuel

Wallerstein, in the Marxist mode, had dominated macro-level approaches. Corporatism identified as central to both economic change and societal structure two interrelated types of organizations that lie clearly in the domain of the political scientist.

The first type of organization is that of interest representation. Corporatist analysis thus became part of a larger body of work within political science. It stood as one kind of interest representation among the several different sorts familiar to the discipline, pluralism being the most identifiable. Schmitter (1974) played an important role in "restricting the concept, so to speak, to refer only to a specific concrete set of institutional practices or structures involving the representation (or misrepresentation) of empirically observable group interests" (p. 87).

The second type of organization within corporatist analysis that falls within the political scientist's bailiwick is the state. Corporatism was not the only concept that reintroduced the state into analyses in the 1970s and 1980s, but it did follow in Huntington's path of extricating political institutions or processes from more general social phenomena. Of the criteria that Huntington gave for assessing the capabilities of political institutions, none so grabbed the imagination of political scientists as that of autonomy. A major focus of attention came to be the autonomous or semi-autonomous state (e.g., Nordlinger, 1981; Poulantzas, 1975).

What role does corporatism demand of the state? Here, scholars divided according to their regional interests. Those writing on West Europe disentangled corporatism from its illiberal and anti-democratic past. Now corporatism—sometimes used with qualifiers such as *neo, liberal,* or *societal* (Offe, 1981)—became a political-economic tool or structure that coexisted with, indeed, integrated into, parliamentary government. It was viewed almost exclusively in the industrial sector (but see Keeler, 1981) as that mechanism that could assure survival and even growth in a fast-paced, open international economy. Corporatism's great advantages for advanced industrial democracies are that it promotes tranquility in industrial and political relations and adaptation in sector investment in response to changing international economic circumstances. A corporatist political structure enables the state to advance domestic tranquility, at least in the short run, by negotiating among self-seeking groups that are at odds with one another and coopting them into collaborative policy arrangements. Labor and capital, especially, participate in national economic planning and incomes policy bodies (Panitch, 1980, p. 160). As Schmitter (1981) noted, "The relative ruliness and effectiveness of the outcome is impressive" (p. 318). Corporatism furthers industrial adaptation through national planning as the state modifies "the free operation of the market by incorporating into the public decision-making apparatus those groups that are affected by the unhampered operation of the market" (Hernes & Selvik, 1981, p. 104).

Those working on Latin America stood on a different understanding of corporatism, one laced with political authoritarianism. In these cases, the state does not merely negotiate with interest organizations in order to preserve social peace nor simply license and incorporate them into the policy-making apparatus so as to insure smooth industrial adaptation. Here, regimes incorporate, even reshape, groups to deal with the near-impossible task of maintaining political ossification, the continued operation of an antiquated elite system of rule along with class harmony, in the face of rapid industrial growth. These are states "within which populist interests and participatory politics are reduced in scope, distributional concerns ignored or placed in low priority, and the maximization of economic growth and rapid industrialization given a top priority" (Graham, 1982, p. 14). The corporatist structure does not just have the state mediate within voluntarist arrangements among existing functional groups, as in West Europe. In Latin American corporatism, the state creates these groups or, at the very least, imposes firm control over them. The tensions of social and economic change, then, have demanded substantial changes in politics as well, leading to a new sort of political system characterized by the bureaucratic-authoritarian regime.

Collier and Collier (1979, pp. 978-979) attempted to bridge the gap between European-style and Latin American-style corporatism by viewing the two types not as a dichotomy but as part of a continuum with considerable variation within each one. Their argument is that corporatism can be categorized for different societies by classifying the inducements and constraints employed by the state in respect to group representation. Nonetheless, the thrust of the literature on Latin America emphasizes the authoritarian character of the state. I will return to this literature, especially that on bureaucratic-authoritarianism, later in the essay when considering how some in the field have moved from such dichotomous paradigms as modern and traditional.

Here, it is worth noting that the revival of corporatism and the development of bureaucratic-authoritarianism in Latin America had reverberations for study far beyond Western Europe. Chirot (1980), for example, wrote an essay entitled "The Corporatist Model and Socialism." Though the article dealt largely with the case of Romania, it did raise the point that corporatism offers the same advantage of social and political stability to socialist states driving towards rapid industrialization that it provides for those in the Third World. Corporate structures have emerged to deal with the immediate problems generated by rapid social and economic change, despite the ideal of the Communist Party to create a unitary society.

Corporatism's application to Eastern Europe followed the spread of Third World development literature to other aspects of socialist politics. Indeed, Triska and Cocks (1977) noted "a growing need to integrate Communist studies more closely within a broader comparative politics framework" (p. xv). They focused their volume on political development, and a small but growing number of other scholars did likewise (e.g., Jowitt, 1971; Triska & Johnson, 1975; Connor, 1975; Paul, 1979). The Latin American materials also had an impact on work about socialist and non-socialist states in Asia. A workshop on the Political Economy of Taiwan run by Columbia University's East Asian Center in 1980, for example, focused on the relevance of a model of Latin American-style authoritarianism for Taiwan. Cumings (1981) wrote an essay, "Corporatism in North Korea," and another (forthcoming) on the relationship of politics and economics in the four industrial states of Northeast Asia: Japan, North Korea, South Korea, and Taiwan. For the latter two, Cumings suggested dropping the recently fashionable acronym NICs (Newly Industrialized Countries) for one that includes a political dimension and reflects the similarity to Latin American cases. That acronym is BAIRs, or Bureaucratic-Authoritarian Industrializing Regimes.

All in all, the influence of development literature beyond the specific regions to which it had originally applied has been truly dramatic. The impact has come unexpectedly from the study of areas considered to be world peripheries, the non-Western world, to shape the way social scientists have viewed those regions thought of as world centers, the Socialist bloc and especially Western Europe. Cumings (1981, p. 11) noted that the entry on "corporatism" in the *International Encyclopedia of the Social Sciences,* published in 1968, read simply, "see fascism." Since then, the term has gained considerable renown transcending its earlier association with European fascism. It has been transformed from a term concerned parochially with traditional Iberian and Latin American societies to one dealing with the dynamics of change in a number of regions. The decline of static conceptions associated with "the end of ideology" and "post-industrial societies" opened the door in the West for theories and frameworks stressing social and political transformation. It was this new emphasis on change that enabled approaches dealing with the Third World to have such a telling effect elsewhere.

The Return to History

Also influencing the Europeanists' new-found interest in Third World studies was the reconsideration of European history mandated by the development literature. Through the 1950s and 1960s, notions about where changes in the Third World were heading rested upon implicit assumptions about the previous course of "development" and "modernization" in Western Europe and the United States. Beginning in the late 1960s, there were voices of dissent against some of those suppositions, paving the way for a later reorientation of the field. Huntington (1968) gave a telling critique of the use of the U.S. as a model for the Third World, and Moore's (1966) landmark study was to serve as an example of macro-level historical analysis that looked closely at state-society relations.

It was not until the 1970s, though, that a concerted reexamination of European historical development got underway. As Merkel (1977) put it, "While taking maximal advantage of available historical—especially European—scholarship, we must attempt to bridge the gulf between historiography and theories of development" (p. 463). Until then, ideas used by those studying the Third World about cohesive centers and steady centralization in Europe went largely unquestioned.

Some of the most influential books joining theories of development with European history were edited volumes (Almond, Flanagan, & Mundt, 1973; Tilly, 1975a; Grew, 1978a). Almond was the most intent on maintaining the continuity of the field, even with its new departure into Europe and into history. Matter-of-factly, he wrote,

The logic of our undertaking was elementary. As the Western nations were in some sense modern, and the non-Western ones were in almost all cases not

modern but seeking to become so, the historical experience of the modern nations had some relevance for our understanding of the problems and prospects
of modernizing efforts among the new nations. . . . (p. 3)

Our search for a cure in history now took a more modest, empirically
grounded, form. The logic of our inquiry was simple. Since the development
that we were seeking to explain occurred in history, why not select several
historical episodes, examine them in great detail, try out our varieties of
developmental explanation, and see how they fit? (p. 22)

The volumes edited by Tilly and Grew demonstrated more skepticism
about the ability to skip back and forth easily between development theories
and actual historical circumstances and between the West's past and the
Third World's present. The irony of the questioning attitude one encounters
in these two books is that they are the last of the SSRC Committee on Comparative Politics' series, "Studies in Political Development." That series, after
all, had canonized some of the most important notions now questioned by the
Tilly and Grew books. Perhaps the doubts stemmed from the fact that Tilly is
a sociologist and Grew, an historian; indeed, almost all the authors in Grew's
volume are historians. The commissioning of the Grew book by the SSRC
Committee in the latter part of the 1960s may have reflected not only a renewed interest in history but also an attempt to confirm the universality of the
members' latest schema, the so-called "crisis" approach. Be that as it may, the
results of both the Grew and Tilly volumes did little to sustain the
Committee's earlier works.

Tilly departed from the Almond, Flanagan, and Mundt book in two important ways. First, Tilly (1975b) and his co-authors used the volume as an
opportunity to debunk "misconceived models of Western experience as the
criteria of political development" (p. 4). This reexamination of the European
experience challenged some sacred assumptions about the nature of change.
For example, the dichotomous model of change (e.g., center versus
periphery) was brought into serious question by the finding that "the Europeans of 1500 and later did not ordinarily expand from a highly organized
center into a weakly organized periphery" (p. 24). Second, the Tilly volume
raised doubts about the relevance of European political change for current
Third World states. At best, it argued, some broad inferences may be drawn
and some generalizations made about comparative processes of state-
building.

What seems to have been less obviously pursued after the appearance of
the Almond, Flanagan, and Mundt volume is the quest for a universal theory
of development that could explain European history as well as events in the
contemporary Third World. More and more, one sees a focus on specific
historical forces—whether in a single country or, as is increasingly the case,
in world historical terms linking the fate of nations—in order to explain the
root causes of differing types of social and political change.

There are, however, several promising paths that have been pursued
seriously in the last few years to get at such causes. The distant and not-so-
distant past, even outside Europe, now has become increasingly acceptable as
part of the purview of political scientists; the horizons of the field have
widened considerably. Excellent studies, such as those by Vital (1975, 1982)

on Zionism or Perry (1980) on China, seek to understand the political changes that have had deep ramifications in the post-War period by examining events in the nineteenth and early twentieth centuries. Dominguez (1980) took a longer look back at the insurrections that brought the end of Spanish rule in the Americas. In his introduction (pp. 1-2), he was explicit about the need for a dialogue between history and the viewpoint of contemporary political science.

Another path came directly from the questioning by some that a universal model of development could be created. As Almond (1973, p. 2) and others recognized, the concepts and classification schemes of the 1950s and 1960s were Western in character. Grew (1978b) noted, "To argue that modernization is 'a new type of "Great Tradition" ' pointing toward a worldwide civilization is at the same time to admit that the roots of the process lie in Western Europe" (p. 5). Scholars, especially in the Third World, have responded by creating alternative, indigenous models of change. These models, wrote Wiarda (1981) "represent serious and fundamental challenges to many cherished social science assumptions and understandings and even to the presumption of a universal social science of development" (p. 2). Among the works cited by Wiarda are those by Mehta (1978) and Véliz (1980). One could add Hyden's (1980) impressive work on Tanzania, among others.

The cure-in-history that Almond mentioned had an additional result linking European and Third World processes of change, even in the absence of a universal theory. The result was a revival of Gerschenkron's (1962) notions about late development found in his famous essay on economic backwardness. Gerschenkron's major premise ruled out a simple replication from country to country of historical processes—his own interest as an economist was industrialization—because the environment within which change has taken place has varied so markedly in different periods. Late developers, to achieve the same industrialization, had to apply "institutional instruments for which there was little or no counterpart in an established industrial country" (p. 7). Grew (1978b) pointed to the notion of late development as the most important link between European history and change in the Third World.

> Most European nations thought of themselves as late developers; many felt they had too long been a cultural or economic colony of others (Italy, Germany, Poland); nearly all experienced the contradictions between efficiency and equality, change and stability. More than the older monarchies or pressured states to the east, the centralized republics of southern Europe . . . have had an experience comparable to that of the Third World. (p. 35)

Gerschenkron's ideas had never gone completely out of fashion. Hirschman (1968) had applied them imaginatively to Latin American cases, speaking of their "late, late" industrialization. In recent years, however, there has been an increased interest in notions of late development, still mostly in Latin America. Kurth (1979), for example, drew the analogy between European and Latin American cases. Hewlett and Weinert's (1982) volume on Brazil and Mexico focused specifically on the implications, largely political, of late development. In that book, the article by Bennett and Sharpe (1982) is the most explicit about the need to understand the peculiar role of the state as banker and entrepreneur in terms of Gerschenkron's outlook. The late, late development in Latin America, they argued, had created problems greater in scope than those faced by the late developers in Europe and, therefore, has elicited different state responses.

One of the interesting outcomes of the cure-in-history, still largely inchoate, is a broad perspective emerging in the development literature on the nature of institutional change. The standard outlook on institutional change has been expressed best by the neoclassical economists (see North, 1981; Davis & North, 1971). Institutions are simply the established systems of rules within which people deal with one another. An institution changes, according to the neoclassical formulation, at the margins. That is, when certain parameters or environmental conditions change—the appearance of people with different abilities or of a shifting capital stock due to varying population numbers and human knowledge—there is a corresponding adjustment process in the rules.

Thus, institutions change incrementally; with each new benefit or cost accorded by varying conditions, rules for human behavior and interaction are transformed. People are willing to change the rules when the expected benefits of the new institutional arrangements outweigh the expected costs. A *system* of rules, or an institution, includes innumerable, individual prescripts, so that the system as a whole, bound by written laws as well as moral codes, will change slowly and at the margins. Long-term institutional structure and change, in North's own view (1981, pp. 201-209), derive from the tension between the benefits to be gained through organizational specialization of institutions and the costs coming from such specialization—as in setting up specialized bureaus. Nonetheless, North did not seem to deviate from the neoclassical perspective of institutional change taking place incrementally, along a fairly smooth curve, at the margins.

Implicitly, at least, it is precisely this view that has been brought into question in the return to history by political scientists. In the field of international relations, a new concern with long waves or long cycles (Modelski, 1978) drew from an earlier literature of economic thought, represented by Kondratieff (1935) and Schumpeter (1939), and from an even longer philosophical tradition in Western civilization (Nisbet, 1969, p. 211 ff). Others in international relations developed interesting notions about change in international regimes—a regime being none other than an international institution. Over time, Krasner (1982) argued, regimes face pressures that, contrary to the neoclassical vision, may build without bringing corresponding adjustments in the rules. A lag exists until the pressure is so great that there is a sudden, massive change. This image is not at all one of smooth curves and changes at the margins.

The development field, too, has begun to diverge from the neoclassical outlook in ways very similar to those set out by Krasner. Here, the word most often used to convey the inducement of sudden, massive change has been "crisis." The Social Science Research Council Committee on Comparative Politics introduced the term as a central concept in the field in 1971 with the publication of the seventh volume in the series, "Studies in Political Development" (Binder et al.). Crises, though, had an odd meaning in this book. They are not necessarily "critical, episodic, political upheavals" (Binder, 1971, p. 69); rather they denote "the functional requisites of a modern or developed political system" (p. 67). In fact, Verba (1971, p. 299) preferred the term "problem area" to "crisis." In any event, crisis implied little more in this volume than the movement from the traditional to the modern along a series of dimensions reminiscent of Parsons' pattern variables. There seemed to be no quarrel yet with the neoclassical interpretation of institutional change. Binder (1971) wrote that the crises are likely to appear as recurrent issues that "may be coped with by the *gradual* arrangement of certain standardized patterns of response" (p. 69, emphasis added).

Though the concept of crisis has continued to be vague in meaning (Sandbrook, 1975), it has been applied in recent years in ways that make it a promising complement to the neoclassical approach. Studies on the Third World (e.g., Stepan, 1978; Migdal, 1974a, 1982), on Western Europe (e.g., Berger, 1972; Gourevitch, forthcoming; Katzenstein, forthcoming), and on Europe *and* the Third World (Skocpol, 1979) focus on the consolidation of new institutional arrangements as a result of historical crises that erupted from building pressures. In all these cases, the model of institutional change was not a continuous curve representing incremental alterations at the margins. It was, rather, an image of history as discontinuous, as bursting at rare moments with catastrophic suddenness. Some of these authors emphasize elite actions in response to environmental change. Stepan (1978), for example, wrote of

> corporatism primarily as an elite response to crisis, a response that involves the attempt by elites who control the state apparatus to restructure the relationship between sectors of civil society and the state. This 'crisis response' explanation of the existence of corporatism competes with one in which corporatism is viewed as a function of historical continuity. (p. 47)

Others (e.g., Scott, 1976; Migdal, 1974a) are more interested in the response of non-elites, especially the peasantry, to important changes in their environment. No one has as yet culled from this material a theory or set of generalizations as formal as those in neoclassical economics. How and when new compacts emerge, creating whole classes of rules, is still shrouded in mystery. Nonetheless, the use by scholars of a still implicit, alternative interpretation of institutional change in diverse regions in itself suggests how attractive a more developed theory might prove to be.

Adding an International Perspective

"Is the traditional distinction between international relations and domestic politics dead?" Gourevitch (1978, p. 881), surveying the literature on the influence of international factors on domestic politics, opened his essay with this question. Certainly, if the mushrooming of research on the merging of these fields is any indicator, the answer is yes. Along with the two topics surveyed above—the geographical extension of development studies into areas other than the Third World and the growing importance of history—interest in the impact of international elements on domestic change has marked a major departure for the development field.

Gourevitch (1978) noted two aspects of the international system having powerful effects on the character of domestic regimes: the distribution of power in the state system and the distribution of economic activity and wealth in the international economy. "Put more simply, political development is shaped by war and trade" (p. 883). While some very interesting material has appeared on the distribution of power (e.g., Anderson, 1974; Skocpol, 1979), the real burgeoning of interest has come in the effects of international economic influence and control on domestic structures.

Unlike practically all other streams in the development field—indeed, in the social sciences generally—the dependency literature has not been an American invention, packaged and shipped off to eager academic consumers in the Third World. Latin American scholars, following in the footsteps of economist Raul Prebisch, created dependency explanations against the current of accepted works in development. The standard writings had anchored the field securely in the waters of comparative politics: domestic, immanent factors lie at the heart of any causal explanation of systemic political change, or lack of change. Only in the 1970s and 1980s, did the ideas and concerns of the dependency theorists begin "creeping into mainstream North American social science" (Fagen, 1978, p. 287) on Latin America and, to a much more limited degree, on Africa and Asia.[5]

Evans (1979) summarized the thrust of the dependency literature:

> The starting point is still relations with the external world. A dependent country is one whose development is "conditioned by the development and expansion of another economy" (Dos Santos, 1970, p. 236). Dependent countries are classically those whose histories of involvement with the international market have led them to specialize in the export of a few primary products. While the income from these few products is absolutely central to the process of accumulation in the dependent country, for the center each product represents only a tiny fraction of total imports, and can usually be obtained from several different sources. The development of the dependent country, however, requires the continued acceptance of its products in the center. Therefore, economic fluctuations in the center may have severe negative consequences for the periphery, whereas an economic crisis in the periphery offers no real threat to accumulation in the center.
>
> Complementing and often underlying dependence based on trade relations, is dependence based on foreign ownership of the productive apparatus of the dependent country. When the principal aspect of dependence is that key sectors of the local productive apparatus are integral parts of capital that is controlled elsewhere, then accumulation in the dependent country is externally conditioned more by the "development and expansion of center-based capital" rather than by the "development and expansion of another country." The asymmetry is there nonetheless.
>
> Dependence is then defined most simply as a situation in which the rate and direction of accumulation are externally conditioned. (pp. 26-27)

The danger of dependency is that it can become the residual variable that explains anything and everything, much the same as the role played by the term "traditional" in earlier models of development. The temptation of making international inequality a *deus ex machina,* which explains the true causes of all poverty, can lead to neglect of the complex linkages between out-side pressures and internal mechanisms. To be sure, the writing on dependency has been extremely uneven, much of it suffused with tendentious argu-ments. Frank (1967), for example, went beyond existing notions about dualis-tic societies in seeing underdeveloped sectors as modern creation ("the development of underdevelopment") and as products of international rela-tionships. At the same time, however, he squeezed Latin American events and anomalies into his framework and, even more so in his subsequent book (1981), mercilessly bent worldwide cases to the needs of his theory.

A body of research and theory has appeared under the dependency heading, nonetheless, that has been very provocative. Cardoso's (1973) work on associated-dependent development, as a case in point, took account of the phenomenal industrial growth, accompanied by immense foreign investment, in countries such as Brazil. The restructuring of politics after the 1964 coup in Brazil must be understood, he argued, as an outgrowth of the new economic realities there and their relationship to external capital. Evans (1979) took up much the same subject in an insightful analysis, trying to untie the three strands of a Gordian knot, the multinational corporations, local private entrepreneurs, and state-owned enterprises. In a somewhat confusing book, Cardoso and Faletto (1979) made a valiant effort to tackle the difficult prob-lem of analytically incorporating different domestic structures in Latin American societies as more than the mere playthings of international forces. The political struggles in a society, they stressed, must be weighed alongside political-economic structures of domination, both internal and external. Although an overwhelming share of the literature has concerned First World-Third World relations, several pieces have begun to explore the dependent role of some Socialist countries (e.g., Reitsma, 1982).

Probably, the most valuable contribution of the dependency literature was that it put the question of the change of social and political institutions into a world capitalist context. "The dependency framework, in other words, explicitly rejects the unified state as actor as a useful conceptual building block of theory" (Caporaso, 1978, p. 2). Many of the works in the 1960s and early 1970s were not concerned with what model might replace the one based on states-as-building-blocks. On the whole, scholars simply assumed a bilateral relationship between the U.S. and/or American-based multi-national corporations, on the one hand, and dependent Latin American societies, on the other.

In the mid-1970s, the notion of a world system did offer an alternative to the perspective of single societies or states as individual building blocks. The paradigmatic shift, as some have called it, owed much not only to dependency literature but also to work in the field of international relations. An impor-tant volume edited by Keohane and Nye (1970) marked a shift away from see-ing international relations solely as the interaction of independent states—the billiard ball model or what they termed the state-centric view of world affairs. They built on another, neglected tradition, that of transnational relations. Here, interactions are as likely to be peaceful as conflictual and lead to sorts of interdependence in a single transnational society undreamed of in the state-centric model.

The new literature on international regimes has been only one product of the paradigmatic shift. Modelski (1979) drew specifically on the transnational literature and on the "cure in history" to develop an approach to international relations based on the idea of the modern world system (Modelski, 1981). A world system perspective in the field of development and change also borrowed from other disciplines, such as Wolf's (1969) anthropological work dealing with the effects of nineteenth century capitalism on peasant societies. Most important of all, however, was the flowering of world system theory in sociology, especially in the work of Wallerstein (1974, 1980), but in that of others, as well (e.g., Chirot, 1976, 1977; Meyer & Hannan, 1979; Kaplan, 1978; Goldfrank, 1979; Skocpol, 1979). Their macrosociological views built on the point raised by the dependency theorists: that is, it is misleading to assume that once external "factors impinge on a society, the main consequences occur through the internal structural processes that maintain the coherence of the society as a bounded system" (Meyer & Hannan, 1979, p. 3). They rejected

the intellectual tradition [that] emphasizes the treatment of societies as real units of analysis. . . . This is clearly naive. The economies, states, and cultural systems of almost all national societies are historical creatures of the European political economy. . . . Further, the current evolution of most national societies is greatly affected by the economic, political, and cultural events which occur entirely outside their boundaries. Economic developments in Africa, the Near East, or Latin America are clearly resultants, for better or for worse, of dominant world markets and technologies. Similarly, political events in such areas (e.g., the Nigerian civil war, the creation of an independent Angola) are also creations of the world system. (Meyer & Hannan, 1979, pp. 11-12)

The advance by world system theorists beyond the dependency framework is illustrated by the term "system" itself. It denotes an entity, other than a single society, within which there is an established set of rules for human interaction, what some have referred to as an ongoing division of labor. The term "world" signifies that the area of such an entity extends beyond individual societies or culture-groups; it does not mean necessarily that such a system blankets the entire globe. Most world systems historically have been world empires, such as the Roman Empire. One world system, the one we live in, has had no unifying political structure but has maintained its rules or division of labor through market exchanges (capitalism); it is a world economy. This modern world system "flourished, expanded to cover the entire earth (and thereby eliminated all remaining mini-systems and world empires), and brought about a technological and ecological 'explosion' in the use of natural resources" (Wallerstein, 1976, p. 349).

World systems have beginnings and all besides ours have had ends. The momentary events and relationships in any society can be understood only in terms of the life history of the system as a whole. This premise of the world system theorists has dovetailed with the return to history by many political scientists to produce a growing trend counter to the cross-sectional analyses so common in comparative politics.

The level-of-analysis problem has bedevilled political scientists for decades, and the world system approach has only complicated matters by rejecting all the levels commonly used by comparativists. It is not surprising, then, that political scientists have shown rather cautious interest in the new theories. Wallerstein's economic determinism and his relegation of the state to secondary status have created concern. Uneasiness has also surfaced since Wallerstein's theory neglects any independent role for domestic institutions and culture in processes of change. Nonetheless, despite these and other reservations, a number of political scientists have begun to use the world system rather than single states or societies, as their point of departure (e.g., Modelski, 1978; Zolberg, 1982). It is likely that in the coming decade the level-of-analysis debate will intensify and that the old distinctions between comparative politics and international relations will continue to erode. The world system field is now a growth industry with its own journal (*Review*), an institute headed by Wallerstein (the Fernand Braudel Center), a series of annuals, and more. With this sort of infrastructural support, one can expect a paradigmatic battle, which may bring new vigor into the field.

BACK TO FIRST PRINCIPLES

For close to a decade, the field of development and change has undergone a rejuvenation, overcoming the inertia brought on by sterile definitional battles and, later, by the loss of faith in the U.S. as the model of the first new nation. Scholarship has been freed from the Procrustean notions that the future of the Third World is faithfully reflected in the mirror of Western history. Has the new vitality in the field also led toward some acceptance of new constitutive principles? Have the recent forays into the uncharted waters of history, new geographic regions, and international politics challenged the assumptions of the earlier theorists and their dichotomous models about the nature of order and the causes of change? The answer to both questions seems to be a qualified yes: qualified because so many of the ramifications coming from the new work are still inchoate and because important connections to past assumptions do survive.

The issue of authority has been at the heart of the field's concerns. Those relying on center-periphery or other such dichotomies to comprehend the twists and turns of political changes made suppositions about the source and direction of authority. They assumed flows from a society's central elites and their integrated institutions to the rest of the population, which was often seen as rather undifferentiated. Dependency and world system theorists departed from an essential tenet of that premise, the integrity of the society itself as a basis for interpreting the source and direction of authority. They construed the most important movements of authority to be those across national boundaries. In world system analysis, the flows lie in the unequal exchanges constantly reproducing the worldwide division of labor, enforced when necessary by strong states. Order and change depend not primarily on the mix of values, institutions, and elites in a society but on the niche of that society in a much larger configuration. The values, the institutions, and the elites reflect a world pattern and act to ensure in their small corner, at least, the conditions necessary for the constant reproduction of the world division of labor.

Ironically, world system theory, inspired by an even earlier borrowing of terms by Prebisch and others (United Nations, 1950), used the same center-periphery metaphor. Now, however, the center, or core as some call it, signifies the portion of the world that appropriates the lion's share of world surplus through the international market, with the added backing of strong state mechanisms. The periphery includes the politically weakest entities, where populations are organized to produce commodities needed by the center. Like earlier models the internationalized version construes change in largely dichotomous terms (though Wallerstein adds an intermediate category, the semiperiphery). The international model treats the periphery in much the same way as the earlier conception: the periphery is passive and malleable in the face of a strong, integrated center. The center is the repository of authority.

Even for those who have accepted the shift away from a single society to transnational society, the conditions of order and change in an individual society still are created at that society's center—now because of the local center's ties to the world core. Political scientists from both sides of the paradigmatic divide have given special attention to the state as the storehouse of authority. As Anderson (1967) put it, "There is a predisposition to see state action as a primary factor in the process of economic development" (p. 3) and, one could add, in countless other processes as well. "Many contemporary notions about development," Anderson added, "seem to posit government as a kind of 'omnipotent given' that could if it would set matters right" (p. 5).

Oddly, this state-centered view runs directly counter to a perspective that has been described as maintaining "a pervasive grip upon citizens, journalists and scholars alike" (Nordlinger, 1981, p. 1). This alternative outlook depicts authority flowing from society to state, not vice versa. Nordlinger calls this view society centered. It includes both pluralism and Marxism, which portray state officials as subject to the desires, even control, of interest groups or social classes embedded in civil society. One might account for the contradictions between state-centered and society-centered perspectives by pointing to the state-centered portrayals largely as ones of non-Western countries while the society-centered descriptions are of democratic, industrial countries. Even so, it might also be noted that the pendulum for scholars studying the West has also swung towards a state-centered interpretation, emphasizing the autonomy, or at least the relative autonomy, of the state (e.g., Nordlinger, 1981; O'Connor, 1973).

In the Third World literature, bureaucratic-authoritarian interpretations have, if anything, strengthened Anderson's observation of fifteen years ago; the state remains at the foundation of many causal theories of order and change. This conclusion is not as true of much of the empirical on-site literature, which often has stressed the disarray in many states. But, in the general theories, civil society has most often been presented as the clay in the hands of the potter, the state. The premises of the dichotomies in which strong, integrated centers mold weak, diffuse peripheries, seem as popular as ever. The most influential of the writers on bureaucratic-authoritarianism has been O'Donnell (1979). He contended that increasing industrialization in Brazil and Argentina activated the popular sector inducing more rigidity by other sectors and, eventually, unregulated conflict. These tensions combined with weakening political institutions to create a crisis alleviated only by a "coup coalition" that excluded the popular sector and established a bureaucratic-authoritarian regime. The new military-led governments adopted "a techno-cratic, bureaucratic approach to policy making (as opposed to a more 'political' approach through which policies are shaped by economic and political demands from different sectors of society, expressed through such channels as elections, legislatures, political parties, and labor unions)" (Collier, 1979, p. 4). In the bureaucratic-authoritarian literature, the state looms larger than before, more shielded from societal pressures and inputs (see O'Donnell, 1979). And, in this respect, this literature has blended in effort-lessly with the corporatist works discussed earlier. In both sorts of studies, the state "is characterized by strong and relatively autonomous governmental structures that seek to *impose* on the society a system of interest representation based on *enforced* limited pluralism" (Malloy, 1977, p. 4, emphasis added).

It remains highly questionable whether states are indeed so formidable. Indeed, one questions whether corporatist and bureaucratic-authoritarian theories portray accurately the roots of change and the maintenance of order. Like the nineteenth century German philosophers, such as Fichte and Hegel, who saw the state as the guide to social transformation, these theories assume all too glibly the endless capacity of the state to shape society. Some recent and some not so recent literature has implied that such state-centered per-spectives may veil important elements of change and order. These same works, however, would not give heart to theorists using pluralist, Marxist, or other society-centered outlooks mentioned by Nordlinger (1981). What may be hinted at in these other writings is a new understanding of the causes of change and the nature of constitutive principles, rejecting the notion of the state or center as the sole repository of authority and also spurning the tradi-tional society-centered approaches of the comparative politics field.

Grindle (1977) conducted a fascinating study of public policy in a state noted for its bureaucratic-authoritarianism and corporatism, Mexico. The results of the state's efforts in creating and pursuing a new rural development policy were less than glowing. At every step in the policy process formidable obstacles appeared, thwarting the intent of central policymakers. Grindle noted one community worker's response:

> "Going out and meeting with peasants can be a dangerous business in Mexico. It threatens a lot of people." In some remote areas, the *caciques* [local bosses] were considered to be an unassailable force, even by the party. In one state, the reac-tion of such local influentials had caused the governor to request that CONASUPO [the state agency] completely remove the Field Coordination Pro-gram from his state. (p. 160)

Influence or authority here does not appear to be the exclusive domain of the state at all. This conclusion echoes a point made by Anderson (1967) a decade earlier. In his research on Latin America, he found "limited government, limited not so much by constitutional arrangements, as that term is conventionally used, as by the resources which government has at its disposal, and the relations between its role and function in the social order and that of other institutions" (p. 5). Drawing heavily on African cases, another work portrayed political conditions not greatly different from those described by Anderson for Latin America. Heeger (1974) depicted the "chronically weak [political] institutions which hinge on fragile bargaining relationships between elites in the center *and* the periphery" (p. 9, emphasis added). He was deeply critical of studies on political consolidation, which

> mistook the organizational aspirations of the political elites for reality and posited a cohesion that simply was not there. . . . Elite-mass consolidation was viewed as being comprehensible in terms of but a single successful linkage between center and periphery—charisma, the party, etc. To put this in another way, where such linkages were seen to exist, the relationships they were seen as establishing were given more coherence than they possessed in reality. The actual multiplicity of such links and their possible contradiction were either obscured or ignored altogether. (p. 49)

One article addressed directly the corporatist literature on Latin America and its premise of states capable of molding societies. The consensual order at the center so important to dichotomous models of change, Hammergren (1977) suggested, is largely absent in Latin America, but corporatist writings persist in picturing "the convergence of political power at the center and top of corporations" (p. 448). Hammergren went on to note, "The tradition of local caudillos, caciques, or *gamonales,* especially in more isolated areas of the country, the presence of regional elites even in more developed areas, the maintenance of economic ties between internal and external groups with minimal participation by the state, all point to a very limited penetration of society by the national center" (p. 449).

All this should not lead one to dismiss the state too quickly. These criticisms do not necessarily lead us back willy-nilly to society-centered perspectives in which the state is little more than a stage for playing out of conflicts among the factions and segments of society. The state is limited, to use Anderson's term, but it is surely not dead. It has tremendous resources available from international sources in the form of foreign aid, direct investment of foreign capital, and international loans as well as, in some cases, political-military support. Internally, its ability to mobilize resources, to regulate society, indeed even to reshape society may be substantial in specific sectors, regions, or policy-areas. Theorists of corporatism and bureaucratic-authoritarianism rightly highlight the state's "elimination of a whole network of intermediary groups and actors" (Hammergren, 1977, p. 456).

It is an exaggeration of many cases to say governments do not govern (Huntington, 1968), as it is misleading to dismiss the Third World simply as consisting of proto-societies or of no societies at all. These are societies with distributions of authority that do not fit existing state-centered or society-centered models very well. And, one may add, if the authors quoted above— Tilly on the limits of European centers in history and Berger and Piore on the bounds of state authority in Europe today—are right, then these models are equally misleading for some cases outside the Third World. What we need to know is how to describe and assess these distributions of authority and how to understand the changes that brought them about. What caused different distributions of authority in different societies? In which areas can states use their extraordinary powers and in which areas may they be all but helpless against other authoritative bodies? If the state is not all-powerful, if elites in the periphery may at times predominate, what becomes of the dichotomous models of change and order? Where do we turn for constitutive principles?

Anderson (1967) wrote that the state "is not snyonymous with the social order, but is one institution among the many that make up organized human life. Government has an impact on other social institutions and in turn is affected by them" (p. 5). Social organizations of all shapes scattered throughout society may be repositories of authority. In many countries, varied groups have managed to maintain rules of behavior and ways of life in direct conflict with the codes of the state or the norms of the center. They have held onto their ways with leech-like tenacity despite the greater resources and the substantial determination of state leaders, and despite the international norms that have mandated these leaders' active role in fostering social change. Berger and Piore (1980) described the European situation: "Various segments of society organize around different rules, processes, and institutions that produce different systems of incentives and disincentives to which individuals respond" (p. 2).

States are in conflict with a heterogeneous flock of other social organizations that do not share the rules of the state. Whether and to what degree states can successfully triumph in their conflict with such organizations varies. These variations are rooted in the different ways world historical forces have been played out. Incisive studies on the United States and Europe treat states, not as "omnipotent givens," but as variable in their ability to effect social policy and reshape society (Krasner, 1978, p. 57; Katzenstein, 1978b). The specific types of order and change in a society are the outcomes of the struggles over the rules of the game among social organizations, including the organization that is usually the weightiest of all though not always strong enough to end the struggle altogether—the state. How that struggle has developed and how it will proceed depend not only on domestic factors but on important historical and contemporary actions and alliances originating in the larger world system.

NOTES

1. Very few authors acknowledged their connection or debt to the earlier constitutional writers. An exception came in one of the very best books written on Africa, that of Kilson (1966).
2. The most notable rejection of the idea of patterned change is found in Whitaker (1967). Among other serious, critical articles are Tipps (1973), Schwartz (1972), Gusfield (1967), Migdal (1974b), Skinner (1971), and Shiner (1975).
3. In Lerner's concept of empathy, we find the basis for the "psycho-cultural school," which has included such notable scholars as McClelland (1961) and Inkeles (1974); in Lerner's stress on communications, we find the beginnings of the "diffusion of innovation" literature, with important works by Pool (1963) and Rogers (1969); and

in Lerner's focus on the city as an engine for change in an entire country, we find the roots of the growing literature on urbanization and broad structural change in the Third World (e.g., McGee, 1971; Qadeer, 1974). In addition, Lerner's method, his use of formal, cross-national survey of such huge dimensions, paved the way for other major studies of this sort. Some prime examples include Almond and Verba (1963); Liebman, Walker, and Glazer (1972); Inkeles and Smith (1974); and Verba, Nie, and Kim (1978).

4. Although they take on somewhat different meanings for different writers and are most often left wholly undefined, the concepts of center and periphery have been accepted by a surprisingly broad spectrum of those writing of macro-sociological and political change.

5. It is interesting to note that dependency literature introduced the first serious challenge by Marxist and Neo-Marxist works of the dominant approaches in the U.S. to development and change. For a review of this literature and its relationship to modernization literature in the U.S., see Higgott (1978).

REFERENCES

Almond, Gabriel A. & Coleman, James S. *The politics of the developing areas.* Princeton, N.J.: Princeton University Press, 1960.

Almond, Gabriel A. & Verba, Sidney. *The civic culture: Political attitudes and democracy in five nations.* Boston: Little, Brown, 1963.

Almond, Gabriel A. Approaches to developmental causation. In Almond, Flanagan, & Mundt (Eds.), 1973.

Almond, Gabriel A., Flanagan, Scott C., & Mundt, Robert J. (Eds.). *Crisis, choice, and change: Historical studies of political development.* Boston: Little, Brown, 1973.

Anderson, Charles W. *Politics and economic change in Latin America: The governing of restless nations.* Princeton, N.J.: D. Van Nostrand, 1967.

Anderson, Perry. *Lineages of the absolutist state.* London: NLB, 1974.

Apter, David E. *The politics of modernization.* Chicago: University of Chicago Press, 1965.

Bennett, Douglas, & Sharpe, Kenneth. The state as banker and entrepreneur: The last resort character of the Mexican state's economic intervention, 1917-1970. In Hewlett and Weinert (Eds.), 1982.

Berger, Suzanne. *Peasants against politics: Rural organization in Brittany 1911-1967.* Cambridge, MA: Harvard University Press, 1972.

Berger, Suzanne (Ed.). Organizing interests in Western Europe: Pluralism, corporatism, and the transformation of politics. Cambridge: Cambridge University Press, 1981.

Berger, Suzanne & Piore, Michael J. *Dualism and discontinuity in industrial societies.* Cambridge: Cambridge University Press, 1980.

Binder, Leonard. Crises of political development. In Binder, *et al.,* 1971.

Binder, Leonard, Pye, Lucian W., Coleman, James S., Verba, Sidney, LaPalombara, Joseph, & Weiner, Myron. *Crises and sequences in political development.* Princeton: Princeton University Press, 1971.

Black, C. E. *The dynamics of modernization: A study in comparative history.* New York: Harper & Row, 1966.

Caporaso, James A. Introduction to the special issue of *International Organization* on dependence and dependency in the global system. *International Organization,* 1978, *32,* 1-12.

Cardoso, Fernando Henrique. Associated-dependent development: Theoretical and practical implications. In Stepan, Alfred (Ed.), 1973.

Cardoso, Fernando Henrique & Faletto, Enzo. *Dependency and development in Latin America.* Berkeley: University of California Press, 1979.

Chirot, Daniel. *Social change in a peripheral society: The creation of a Balkan colony.* New York: Academic Press, 1976.

Chirot, Daniel. *Social change in the twentieth century.* New York: Harcourt Brace Jovanovich, 1977.

Chirot, Daniel. The corporatist model and socialism. *Theory and Society,* 1980, *9,* 363-381.

Collier, David (Ed.). *The new authoritarianism in Latin America.* Princeton, N.J.: Princeton University Press, 1979.

Collier, Ruth Berins & Collier, David. Inducements versus constraints: Disaggregating "corporatism." *American Political Science Review,* 1979, *73,* 967-986.

Connor, Walter D. Revolution, modernization and communism: A review article. *Studies in Comparative Communism,* 1975, *8,* 389-396.

Cumings, Bruce. Corporatism in North Korea. Presented at the Annual Meeting of the American Political Science Association. New York, 1981.

Cumings, Bruce. The origin and development of the northwest Asian political economy: Industrial sectors and political consequences, 1900-1982. *International Organization,* forthcoming.

Dahl, Robert A. *Polyarchy: Participation and opposition.* New Haven: Yale University Press, 1971.

Davis, Lance E. & North, Douglass C. *Institutional change and American economic growth.* Cambridge: Cambridge University Press, 1971.

Deutsch, Karl. Social mobilization and political development. *American Political Science Review,* 1961, *55,* 493-514.

Dominguez, Jorge I. *Insurrection or loyalty: The breakdown of the Spanish American empire.* Cambridge, MA: Harvard University Press, 1980.

Dos Santos, Teotonio. The structure of dependence. *American Economic Review,* 1970, *60,* 235-246.

Eckstein, Harry. The idea of political development: From dignity to efficiency. *World Politics,* 1982, *34,* 451-486.

Eisenstadt, S. N. *Modernization: Protest and change.* Englewood Cliffs, N.J.: Prentice-Hall, 1966.

Evans, Peter. *Dependent development: The alliance of multinational, state, and local capital in Brazil.* Princeton, N.J.: Princeton University Press, 1979.

Fagen, Richard R. A funny thing happened on the way to the market: Thoughts on extending dependency ideas. *International Organization,* 1978, *32,* 287-300.

Frank, Andre Gunder. *Capitalism and underdevelopment in Latin America.* New York: Monthly Review Press, 1967.

Frank, Andre Gunder. *Crisis: In the Third World.* New York: Holmes and Meier, 1981.

Gerschenkron, Alexander. *Economic backwardness in historical perspective: A book of essays.* Cambridge, MA: Harvard University Press, 1962.

Goldfrank, Walter L. (Ed.). *The world-system of capitalism: Past and present.* Beverly Hills: Sage, 1979.

Gourevitch, Peter. The second image reversed: The international sources of domestic politics. *International Organization,* 1978, *32,* 881-912.

Gourevitch, Peter. *International organization.* Forthcoming.

Graham, Douglas H. Mexican and Brazilian economic development: Legacies, patterns, and performance. In Hewlett and Weinert (Eds.), 1982.

Grew, Raymond (Ed.). *Crises of political development in Europe and the United*

States. Princeton: Princeton University Press, 1978. (a)

Grew, Raymond E. The crises and their sequences. In Grew (Ed.). *Crises of political development in Europe and the United States,* 1981. (b)

Grindle, Merilee Serrill. *Bureaucrats, politicians, and peasants in Mexico: A case study in public policy.* Berkeley: University of California Press, 1977.

Gusfield, Joseph R. Tradition and modernity: Misplaced polarities in the study of social change. *American Journal of Sociology,* 1967, *72,* 351-362.

Hammergren, Linn A. Corporatism in Latin American polities: A reexamination of the "unique" tradition. *Comparative Politics,* 1977, *9,* 443-461.

Heeger, Gerald A. *The politics of underdevelopment.* New York: St. Martin's Press, 1974.

Hernes, Gudmond & Selvik, Arne. Local corporatism. In Suzanne Berger (Ed.), 1981.

Hewlett, Sylvia Ann & Weinert, Richard S. (Eds.). *Brazil and Mexico: Patterns in late development.* Philadelphia: Institute for the Study of Human Issues, 1982.

Higgott, Richard. Competing theoretical perspectives on development and under-development: A recent intellectual history. *Politics,* 1978, *13,* 26-41.

Hirschman, Albert O. The political economy of import-substituting industrialization in Latin America. *The Quarterly Journal of Economics,* 1968, *82,* 2-32.

Huntington, Samuel P. *Political order in changing societies.* New Haven: Yale University Press, 1968.

Huntington, Samuel P. The change to change: Modernization, development, and politics. *Comparative Politics,* 1971, *3,* 283-322.

Hyden, Goran. *Beyond Ujamaa in Tanzania: Underdevelopment and an uncaptured peasantry.* Berkeley: University of California Press, 1980.

Inglehart, Ronald. Cognitive mobilization and European identity. *Comparative Politics,* 1970, *3,* 45-70.

Inkeles, Alex & Smith, David H. *Becoming modern: Individual change in six developing countries.* Cambridge, MA: Harvard University Press, 1974.

Jessop, Bob. Corporatism, parliamentarism and social democracy. In Schmitter and Lehmbruch (Eds.), 1979.

Jowitt, Kenneth. *Revolutionary breakthroughs and national development: The case of Romania, 1944-1965.* Berkeley: University of California Press, 1971.

Kaplan, Barbara Hockey (Ed.). *Social change in the capitalist world economy.* Beverly Hills: Sage, 1978.

Katzenstein, Peter J. (Ed.). *Between power and plenty: Foreign economic policies of advanced industrial states.* Madison: University of Wisconsin Press, 1978. (a)

Katzenstein, Peter J. Conclusion: Domestic structures and strategies of foreign economic policy. In Katzenstein (Ed), 1978. (b)

Katzenstein, Peter J. *Corporatism and change.* Ithaca, N.Y.: Cornell University Press, forthcoming.

Keeler, John T. S. Corporatism and official union hegemony: The case of French agricultural syndicalism. In Suzanne Berger (Ed.), 1981.

Keohane, Robert O. & Nye, Joseph S. Jr. (Eds.). *Transnational relations and world politics.* Cambridge, MA: Harvard University Press, 1970.

Kesselman, Mark. Overinstitutionalization and political constraint: The case of France. *Comparative Politics,* 1970, *3,* 21-44.

Kilson, Martin. *Political change in a West African state: A study of the modernization process in Sierra Leone.* Cambridge, MA: Harvard University Press, 1966.

Kondratieff, N. D. The long waves in economic life. *The Review of Economic Statistics,* 1935, *17,* 105-115.

Krasner, Stephen D. *Defending the national interest: Raw materials investments and U.S. foreign policy.* Princeton, N.J.: Princeton University Press, 1978.

Krasner, Stephen D. Regimes and the limits of realism: Regimes as autonomous variables. *International Organization,* 1982, *36,* 497-510.

Kurth, James R. Industrial change and political change: A European perspective. In David Collier (Ed.), 1979.

LaPalombara, Joseph. Political science and the engineering of national development. In Monte Palmer & Larry Stern (Eds.), *Political development in changing societies.* Lexington, MA: D.C. Heath, 1971.

Lehmbruch, Gerhard. Liberal corporatism and party government. In Schmitter & Lehmbruch (Eds.), 1979.

Lerner, Daniel. *The passing of traditional society: Modernizing the Middle East.* New York: The Free Press, 1958.

Lerner, Daniel. Some comments on center-periphery relations. In Richard L. Merritt & Stein Rokkan (Eds.), *Comparing nations.* New Haven: Yale University Press, 1966.

Levy, Marian J. Jr. *Modernization and the structure of societies: A setting for international affairs.* Princeton, N.J.: Princeton University Press, 1966.

Liebman, Arthur, Walker, Kenneth N. & Glazer, Myron *Latin American university students: A six nation study.* Cambridge, MA: Harvard University Press, 1972.

Malloy, James M. Authoritarianism and corporatism in Latin America: The modal pattern. In Malloy (Ed.), *Authoritarianism and corporatism in Latin America.* Pittsburgh: University of Pittsburgh Press, 1977.

McClelland, David C. *The achieving society.* New York: The Free Press, 1961.

McGee, T. G. *The urbanization process in the Third World.* London: G. Bell and Sons, 1971.

Mehta, Vrajenda Raj. *Beyond Marxism: Towards an alternative perspective.* New Delhi: Manohar, 1978.

Merkl, Peter H. The study of European political development. *World Politics,* 1977, *29,* 462-475.

Meyer, John W. & Hannan, Michael T. (Eds.). *National development and the world system: Educational, economic, and political change, 1950-1970.* Chicago: The University of Chicago Press, 1979.

Migdal, Joel S. *Peasants, politics, and revolution: Pressures toward political and social change in the Third World.* Princeton: Princeton University Press, 1974. (a)

Migdal, Joel S. Why change? Toward a new theory of change among individuals in the process of modernization. *World Politics,* 1974, *26,* 189-206. (b)

Migdal, Joel S. Capitalist penetration in the nineteenth century: Creating conditions for new patterns of social control. In Robert Weller & Scott Guggenheim (Eds.). *Power and protest in the countryside: Studies of rural unrest.* Durham, N.C.: Duke University Press, 1982.

Millikan, Max F. and Rostow, W. W. *A proposal: Key to an effective foreign policy.* New York: Harper, 1957.

Modelski, George. The long cycle of global politics and the nation-state. *Comparative Studies in Society and History,* 1978, *20,* 214-235.

Modelski, George (Ed.). *Transnational corporations and world order: Readings in international political economy.* San Francisco: W. H. Freeman, 1979.

Modelski, George. Long cycles of world leadership. Presented at the Annual Meeting of the American Political Science Association. New York, 1981.

Montgomery, John D. The quest for political development. *Comparative Politics,* 1969, *1,* 285-295.

Moore, Barrington, Jr. *Social origins of dictatorship and democracy: Lord and peasant in the making of the modern world.* Boston: Beacon Press, 1966.

Mosca, Gaetano. *The ruling class.* New York: McGraw-Hill, 1939.

Nedelmann, Birgitta & Meier, Kurt G. Theories of contemporary corporatism: Static or dynamic? In Schmitter & Lehmbruch (Eds.), 1979.

Nettl, J. P. The state as a conceptual variable. *World Politics,* 1968, *20,* 559-592.

Newton, Ronald C. Natural corporatism and the passing of populism in Spanish America. In Pike & Stritch (Eds.), 1974.

Nisbet, Robert A. *Social change and history: Aspects of the Western theory of development.* London: Oxford University Press, 1969.

Nordlinger, Eric. *On the autonomy of the democratic state.* Cambridge, Mass.: Harvard University Press, 1981.

North, Douglass C. *Structure and change in economic history.* New York: W. W. Norton, 1981.

O'Connor, James. *The fiscal crisis of the state.* New York: St. Martin's Press, 1973.

O'Donnell, Guillermo. Tensions in the bureaucratic-authoritarian state and the question of democracy. In David Collier (Ed.), 1979.

Offe, Claus. The attribution of public status to interest groups: Observations on the West German case. In Suzanne Berger (Ed.), 1981.

Panitch, Leo. The development of corporatism in liberal democracies. In Schmitter & Lehmbruch (Eds.), 1979.

Panitch, Leo. Recent theorizations of corporatism: Reflections on a growth industry. *British Journal of Sociology,* 1980, *31,* 159-187.

Parsons, Talcott. *The social system.* Glencoe, IL: The Free Press, 1951.

Paul, David W. *The cultural limits of revolutionary politics: Change and continuity in socialist Czechoslovakia.* Boulder: East European Quarterly and Columbia University Press, 1979.

Pempel, T. J. Japanese foreign economic policy: The domestic bases for international behavior. In Peter J. Katzenstein (Ed.), 1978.

Pempel, T. J. and Tsunekawa, Keiichi. Corporatism without labor? The Japanese anomaly. In Schmitter & Lehmbruch (Eds.), 1979.

Perry, Elizabeth J. *Rebels and revolutionaries in North China 1845-1945.* Stanford: Stanford University Press, 1980.

Pike, Frederick B. & Stritch, Thomas (Eds.). *The new corporatism: Social-political structures in the Iberian world.* Notre Dame: University of Notre Dame Press, 1974.

Pool, Ithiel de Sola. The mass media and politics in the modernization process. In Lucian W. Pye (Ed.). *Communications and political development.* Princeton, NJ: Princeton University Press, 1963.

Poulantzas, Nicos. *Political power and social classes.* London: NLB, 1975.

Pye, Lucian W. The concept of political development. *Annals of the American Academy,* 1965, *358,* 1-13.

Qadeer, M. A. Do cities 'modernize' the developing countries? An examination of the South Asian experience. *Comparative Studies in Society and History,* 1974, *16,* 266-283.

Redfield, Robert. *Peasant society and culture.* Chicago: The University of Chicago Press, 1960.

Reitsma, Hendrik-Jan A. Development geography, dependency relations, and the capitalist scapegoat. *The Professional Geographer,* 1982, *34,* 125-130.

Riggs, Fred W. *Administration in developing countries: The theory of prismatic society.* Boston: Houghton Mifflin, 1964.

Rogers, Everett. *Modernization among peasants: The impact of communication.* New York: Holt, Rinehart, 1969.

Rogowski, Ronald & Wasserspring, Lois. Does political development exist? Corporatism in old and new societies. *Comparative politics series* (Vol. 2). Beverly Hills, CA: Sage, 1971.

Rokkan, Stein. Cities, states, and nations: A dimensional model of the study of contrasts in development. In S. N. Eisenstadt & Rokkan (Eds.). *Building states and nations* (Vol. I). Beverly Hills, CA: Sage, 1973.

Rostow, W. W. *The stages of economic growth: A non-communist manifesto.* Cambridge: Cambridge University Press, 1960.

Rustow, Dankwart A. Modernization and comparative politics: Prospects in research and theory. *Comparative Politics,* 1968, *1,* 37-51.

Sandbrook, Richard. The "crisis" in political development theory. *Journal of Development Studies,* 1975, *12,* 163-185.

Schmitter, Philippe C. Still the century of corporatism? In Pike & Stritch (Eds.), 1974.

Schmitter, Philippe C. & Lehmbruch, Gerhard (Eds.). *Trends toward corporatist intermediation.* Beverly Hills, CA: Sage, 1979.

Schmitter, Philippe C. Interest intermediation and regime governability in contemporary Western Europe and North America. In Suzanne Berger (Ed.), 1981.

Schumpeter, Joseph. *Business cycles* (Vol. I). New York: McGraw-Hill, 1939.

Schwartz, Benjamin I. The limits of "tradition versus modernity" as categories of explanation. *Daedalus,* 1972, *101,* 71-88.

Scott, James C. *The moral economy of the peasant: Rebellion and subsistence in Southeast Asia.* New Haven: Yale University Press, 1976.

Shils, Edward. Political development in the new states. *Comparative Studies in Society and History,* 1960, *2,* 265-292.

Shils, Edward. *Center and periphery.* Chicago: The University of Chicago Press, 1975.

Shiner, L. E. Tradition/modernity: An ideal type gone astray. *Comparative Studies in Society and History,* 1975, *19,* 245-252.

Sjoberg, Gideon. *The preindustrial city.* New York: The Free Press, 1960.

Skinner, G. William. Chinese peasants and the closed community. *Comparative Studies in Society and History,* 1971, *13,* 270-281.

Skocpol, Theda. *States and social revolutions.* Cambridge: Cambridge University Press, 1979.

Stepan, Alfred (Ed.). *Authoritarian Brazil: Origins, policies, and future.* New Haven: Yale University Press, 1973.

Stepan, Alfred. *The state and society: Peru in comparative perspective.* Princeton: Princeton University Press, 1978.

Tilly, Charles. *The Vendée.* Science Editions. New York: John Wiley & Sons, 1967.

Tilly, Charles (Ed.). *The formation of national states in Western Europe.* Princeton: Princeton University Press, 1975. (a)

Tilly, Charles. Reflections on the history of European state-making. In Tilly (Ed.), 1975. (b)

Tilly, Charles. Western state-making and theories of political transformation. In Tilly (Ed.), 1975. (c)

Tipps, Dean C. Modernization theory and the comparative study of societies. *Comparative Studies in Society and History,* 1973, *15,* 199-240.

Triska, Jan F. and Johnson, Paul M. *Political development and political change in Eastern Europe: A comparative study.* University of Denver Monograph Series in World Affairs, Vol. 13, Book 2, 1975.

Triska, Jan F. & Cocks, Paul M. (Eds.). *Political development in Eastern Europe.* New York: Praeger, 1977.

United Nations. *The economic development of Latin America and its principal problems.* New York: United Nations, 1950.

Véliz, Claudio. *The centralist tradition in Latin America.* Princeton: Princeton University Press, 1980.

Verba, Sidney. Sequences and development. In Binder, *et al.* (Eds.), 1971.

Verba, Sidney, Nie, Norman H. & Kim, Jae-on. *Participation and political equality: A seven-nation comparison.* Cambridge: Cambridge University Press, 1978.

Vital, David. *The origins of Zionism.* Oxford: Clarendon Press, 1975.

Vital, David. *Zionism: The formative years.* Oxford: Clarendon Press, 1982.

Wallerstein, Immanuel. *The modern world-system: Capitalist agriculture and the origins of the European world-economy in the sixteenth century.* New York: Academic Press, 1974.

Wallerstein, Immanuel. A world-system perspective on the social sciences. *British Journal of Sociology,* 1976, *27,* 343-352.

Wallerstein, Immanuel. *The modern world-system II: Mercantilism and the consolidation of the European world-economy, 1600-1750.* New York: Academic Press, 1980.

Whitaker, C. S., Jr. A dysrhythmic process of political change. *World Politics,* 1967, *19,* 190-217.

Wiarda, Howard J. Transcending corporatism?: The Portuguese corporative system and the revolution of 1974. Institute of International Studies, University of South Carolina, Essay Series, No. 3, 1976.

Wiarda, Howard J. *Corporatism and development: The Portuguese experience.* Amherst: University of Massachusetts Press, 1977.

Wiarda, Howard J. Toward a non-ethnocentric theory of development: Alternative conceptions from the Third World. Paper presented to the American Political Science Association. New York, 1981.

Wolf, Eric R. *Peasant wars of the twentieth century.* New York: Harper & Row, 1969.

Zolberg, Aristide R. Origins of the modern world system: A missing link. *World Politics,* 1981, *33,* 253-281.

12

Voting Behavior Research in the 1980s: An Examination of Some Old and New Problem Areas*

Herbert B. Asher

The field of voting behavior is often viewed as the area within political science that has made the greatest progress in the generation of an empirically based, cumulative body of knowledge. Voting behavior research has been characterized by careful elaboration of theoretical approaches, serious attention to conceptual and operational questions, and sophisticated statistical analyses. When one asks where is the "science" in political science, a common reply is to point the questioner to the field of voting behavior.

Despite the scientific status accorded to voting behavior research, the field is currently in great flux.[1] There have been ongoing controversies about the models appropriate to the study of voting behavior, the conceptualization and measurement of key concepts, the specification of the basic models, and the analysis strategies employed to study core phenomena. New areas of research are becoming prominent as witnessed by the growth in congressional election studies and the increased interest in economic variables as determinants of political behavior. Likewise, some old areas are undergoing a rebirth of scholarly interest as can be seen in the current efforts at reconceptualizing the central concept of party identification.

Hence, any effort to describe the status of a field as complex and changing as voting behavior must of necessity make some difficult choices; the scope of the project must be limited in order to make it manageable. In this essay, I will focus primarily on research that falls under the general rubric of the social psychological approach. This approach holds that an individual's attitudes are the most immediate determinants of voting behavior, yet it recognizes that attitudes develop in, and their effects are shaped by, the social and

---

*Acknowledgments: This paper has profited much from the insightful comments of Paul Abramson, Richard Brody, Ada Finifter, Warren Miller, and Raymond Wolfinger. I am very appreciative of the efforts of Mary Pat Helbig to prepare the final version of this manuscript under very hectic circumstances.

institutional contexts within which a person lives. With respect to vote choice, this approach focuses on three clusters of attitudes: partisanship, issue attitudes, and candidate evaluations. With respect to the decision of whether to vote, the immediate attitudinal determinants are a set of civic orientations that include such factors as political efficacy, interest in the campaign, general involvement in politics, sense of citizen duty, and others. These civic attitudes are influenced by a person's position within the social structure, and they condition the effects of institutional factors on turnout. The decision to emphasize the social psychological approach reflects its dominant position in the field as exemplified by such influential works as *The American Voter* (Campbell, Converse, Miller & Stokes, 1960) and *The Changing American Voter* (Nie, Verba & Petrocik, 1976). Moreover, much of the current controversy in the field of voting behavior takes place within the context of the social psychological tradition.[2]

This essay is also bounded by my decision to focus primarily on literature in which vote choice is the major dependent variable and to largely ignore materials in which turnout and other forms of participation are the foci of interest. This is in part an arbitrary decision that serves to keep the essay a reasonable length, but it also reflects my view that the more exciting developments in voting behavior research are occurring in the area of vote choice.

I have further limited the topic by emphasizing research on national elections and largely omitting state and local election research. This decision reflects the status of the field for it is the national election research that comprises a somewhat cumulative and comparable body of literature whereas the state and local election research is much more disparate in its approaches, core questions, and methods. Certainly the national election research has profited from an interacting, national community of scholars with common approaches and similar research agendas and from the availability of data sets, particularly the national election studies from the University of Michigan's Center for Political Studies, that facilitate in-depth analyses of a specific election and comparative analyses across elections. With respect to the state and local literature, a very useful intellectual endeavor at this juncture would be a literature review and propositional inventory that would highlight the commonalities in the field, suggest the next steps in a research agenda, and propose appropriate research strategies to study state and local elections.

Finally, this essay has a temporal boundary to it. I will focus for the most part on developments in the field in the past decade. I assume that the reader is familiar with developments in the field up through the early 1970s; there are a number of already published review essays that detail earlier developments in voting research. Jensen (1969) and Silbey, Bogue, and Flanigan (1978) discuss historical analysis and the historical development of electoral behavior research, while Rossi's "Four Landmarks in Voting Research" (1959) does a thorough and insightful job of analyzing four books that have very much shaped the contemporary study of voting behavior. Rossi's essay traces the field of voting behavior until just prior to the publication of *The American Voter;* the Prewitt and Nie essay (1976) picks up from this point and provides a thoughtful summary and critique of the subsequent election studies of the "Michigan School." Papers by Niemi and Weisberg (1976) and Pierce and Sullivan (1980) also serve to update developments in voting research; the former discusses contemporary controversies in voting research and lists the major election surveys and the research reports that have emerged from them, while the latter summarizes a body of substantive findings and also highlights a set of methodological considerations that have affected the field of voting behavior. Finally, Converse (1975) focuses on two current controversies in electoral behavior research: the determinants of individual vote choice, a topic which will be updated herein; and the sources of partisan realignment.[3]

Having established the boundaries of this essay, I would now like to present a brief overview of what follows. The essay begins with an examination of two classical questions of voting behavior research: what are the determinants of the vote choice—the three major determinants are party identification, issue attitudes, and candidate evaluation—and what is their relative importance? Recursive and nonrecursive models of vote choice are considered as are the conceptual and methodological problems inherent in measuring the determinants of vote choice and in separating out their effects on the vote decision. In the discussion of issues, special attention will be given to the rapidly growing body of literature on the electoral impact of economic conditions. The essay then turns to another "growth area" in the field of voting behavior—the study of congressional elections. The essay concludes with a brief summary of the key points and a discussion of how the notion of retrospective voting ties together many seemingly disparate themes in the essay in the context of a particular conception of democratic theory.

THE DETERMINANTS OF VOTE CHOICE

Introduction

A central concern in voting behavior research has been the identification of the determinants of vote choice and the assessment of the relative importance of these factors. This research agenda, of course, reflects enduring questions of democratic theory about the role, competence, and performance of a democratic citizenry. Indeed, the empirical analysis of voting behavior, itself shaped by longstanding normative concerns, has served to stimulate debate about the requirements for a democratic political system as evidenced by the concluding chapter of *Voting* (Berelson, Lazarsfeld, & McPhee, 1954).

In *The Voter Decides* (1954), Campbell *et al.* viewed partisanship, candidate evaluations, and issue attitudes as the most immediate attitudinal determinants of the vote. In *The American Voter* (1960), party identification was seen more explicitly as a long-term attitude not closely tied to any specific election context, while candidate and issue attitudes were considered to have more of a short-term component reflecting the candidates and issues prominent in a particular election. The authors of *The American Voter* divided issue and candidate attitudes into a set of six partisan attitudes and argued that party identification played a major role in shaping these six attitudes—

attitudes toward the Republican and the Democratic candidate, attitudes about the issues of foreign policy and domestic policy, group-related attitudes, and attitudes about the political parties as managers of government.

A simplified version of *The American Voter* model of vote choice is presented in the following diagram.

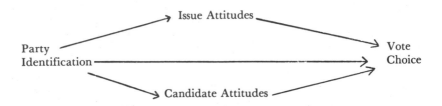

Using the terminology of causal analysis, we would label the above arrow diagram as a recursive (one-way causation) model. Party identification, issue attitudes, and candidate attitudes each have a direct effect on vote choice, but, according to the posited structure of the model, party identification also has indirect effects on vote choice via its effects on issue and candidate attitudes respectively. This model was the dominant one for characterizing voting behavior research through the early 1970s. Works by Goldberg (1966), Schulman and Pomper (1975) and Hartwig *et al.* (1980) analyzed variants of this core model and found that while the direct effect of party identification on vote choice declined somewhat in more recent elections, it still remained a strong predictor of vote choice, particularly when its indirect effects were considered. (Of course, the indirect effects of party identification on vote choice arise from the decision to have party identification influence candidate evaluations and issue attitudes.) The impact of issues varied dramatically over time, while candidate effects remained fairly strong consistently (Schulman & Pomper; Hartwig *et al.*). This basic model has come under attack along two broad fronts: (1) the recursive specification of the model has been challenged, and (2) the conceptualization and measurement of the explanatory components of the model have been criticized.

Recursive vs. Nonrecursive Formulations

The recursive model of vote choice was criticized almost from the beginning on the grounds that it failed to capture the richness of the possible relationships among the explanatory variables. For example, *The American Voter* explicitly recognized the possibility of a reciprocal (two-way causation) relationship between party identification and issue attitudes. Likewise, Goldberg (1966, p. 920) criticized his own revised dual mediation model in which party identification influenced partisan attitudes, but not the reverse; he argued that any plausible model should allow for partisan attitudes to have an impact on party identification. More recent critiques have argued for additional reciprocal linkages among the explanatory variables. Certainly it is plausible to argue for a reciprocal relationship between candidate and issue attitudes; a set of issue preferences held by a person might very well influence his or her evaluation of a candidate, while a preference for one candidate over another might well result in bringing one's own issue preferences into line with those espoused by one's preferred candidate. One can also argue for reciprocal relationships between the dependent variable of vote choice and each of the explanatory variables. For example, Brody and Page (1972) provide a very nice discussion of possible linkages between issue attitudes and vote choice: issue preference may influence vote choice (a case of issue or policy voting), but the causal flow can run in the other direction if issue preferences follow an already made vote choice. One can even envisage a situation in which vote choice affects party identification: a person who voted for a certain party may subsequently decide that he or she is an adherent of that party, a plausible linkage given attribution theory.

Hence, the possible relationships among our variables are much more complex; conceivably we might have a model that looks like this.

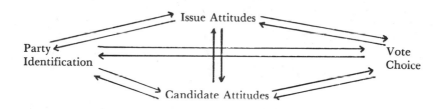

Such a model captures the full complexity of the relationships among our variables, but unfortunately the components of the model cannot be estimated since there is insufficient information to generate a unique set of estimates of the various linkages. Technically, we say that the model is underidentified; intuitively, we can think of underidentification as analogous to a system of equations in which we have more unknowns than equations.

Thus we now have a model that captures the plausible reciprocal relationships, but which cannot yield satisfactory estimates of the linkages among the variables. Fortunately, there are two general strategies available which enable us to work with models that incorporate mutual causation. The first strategy is to construct explicitly nonrecursive models, but build them in such a way that they can be estimated. The second strategy is to construct recursive models in which certain variables are measured at multiple time points. In such a system, we can represent a mutual relationship between two variables X and Y not by the direct reciprocal model $X \rightleftarrows Y$, but by a recursive, time lagged model $X_{t_1} \longrightarrow Y_{t_2} \longrightarrow X_{t_3}$. We will talk about each of these approaches, citing recent examples in the literature and discussing research design considerations entailed by each approach.

One of the earlier nonrecursive works was Jackson's (1975) analysis of voting in the 1964 presidential election in which he explicitly incorporated a reciprocal linkage between the voters' party identification and their evaluations of the policy positions of the candidates and political parties. The core of Jackson's model is depicted below.

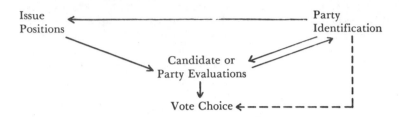

Note that there is a reciprocal link between party identification and evaluations and that no arrow directly links party identification and vote choice; the existence of this latter linkage is tested in the model.

Jackson estimates an elaborated version of this model and obtains results which suggest that

> party identifications are highly influenced by people's evaluations of what policies each party advocates relative to their own preferences, that party affiliations have little direct influence on the voting decision except for people who see little or no difference in the parties, that party identifications are important in determining what positions people take on domestic social welfare issues and how they perceive the positions of the parties on foreign affairs issues, and finally that party identification has little influence on either positions or perceptions on the civil rights issue. (pp. 176-177)

Jackson concludes that party identifications are primarily based on issue considerations and that party loyalties will change if people's positions on the issues change or if new issues arise which cut across the existing party cleavages. Hence, assuming the correctness of Jackson's results—to be considered in the discussion of the Page and Jones work below—his analysis departs from the classical voting model in that it puts a very heavy emphasis on the role of issues in party preference and finds little direct impact of party identification on vote choice. Party identification may be a relatively long-standing decision, but the mechanism is not simply an issueless, family dominated political socialization process characterized by the reinforcement over time of initial party loyalties. Instead, according to Jackson, the stability of party identification is a reflection of the stability of issue partisanship, and the development of partisanship is shaped by the issue foundation underlying parental partisanship. Hence, the inclusion of a nonrecursive linkage does result in interpretations and emphases quite different from the classical model. It should be noted that Jackson's interpretations go well beyond the direct evidence presented in his article.

Probably the most ambitious, cross-sectional, nonrecursive voting model is that proposed by Page and Jones (1979). The core of their model is shown below; note that it allows for reciprocal links among policy distances, party identification and candidate evaluations. Also note that no direct link is drawn between party identification and vote decision.

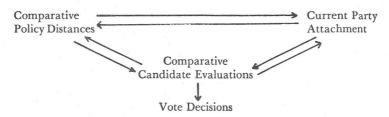

In estimating an elaborated version of this model, Page and Jones find that the relationship between policy distances and candidate evaluations is reciprocal. More importantly, they find that current party attachments are affected by the policy and candidate measures; indeed, for the 1976 election, the estimated effect of policy distance on party identification was .36, while the estimated effect of party identification on policy distance was .00. Hence, we again have evidence that party identification is more responsive to the current stimuli of politics than is suggested by the classical model.

The Jackson and Page and Jones works provide ample support that nonrecursive formulations are needed; recursive formulations by assumption rule out any findings such as those reported in these two articles. However, before accepting the Jackson, and Page and Jones findings as definitive, there are a number of cautionary notes that must be sounded. The first caveat is one appropriate for all pieces of data analysis, namely, do the measured indicators adequately tap the conceptual meaning of the variables? A more important set of considerations concerns the construction and estimation of nonrecursive models. The core models of Jackson, and Page and Jones depicted above are underidentified and hence cannot be estimated. In order to identify and then estimate these models, exogenous variables with certain properties must be formally incorporated in the model.[4] The selection of these exogenous variables is essentially a theoretical and substantive matter subject to certain statistical requirements; some desirable properties of the exogenous variables will be considered shortly.

In the real world of secondary data analysis, the selection and incorporation of exogenous variables is, of course, constrained by whatever variables happen to be measured in the data set being analyzed. This raises the possibility that the needed exogenous variables will not be in the data set or that the investigator will have to settle for less than satisfactory measures. The only way to be confident that the required exogenous variables will be available is to anticipate their need at the design phase of a research project. This requires the researcher to construct theoretical models prior to data collection, to determine whether these models are in fact identified, and to construct reliable and valid measures not only of the core variables but also of those exogenous variables needed to identify the model. Hence, a central task for those involved in the design of data collection efforts is to recognize and measure the variables needed to identify our nonrecursive models.

The Jackson, and Page and Jones articles are secondary analyses and hence dependent on whatever measures are already available in the data sets they are using. The reader should recognize that the choice of exogenous variables can very much affect the results obtained, particularly when good exogenous variables are available to identify one part (equation) of a model and less satisfactory measures are available to identify other parts. Fisher (1971, pp. 242-248) discusses at length two desirable properties of any variables that may be used to identify an equation in a nonrecursive model: first, the variable should be uncorrelated (in the probability limit) with the disturbance or error term in that equation; second, the variable should closely causally influence the variables which appear in that equation—this implies that a reasonable correlation exists between the exogenous variable and the other variables. The variables used by Page and Jones and by Jackson to identify their equations do not uniformly satisfy the criteria set out by Fisher and hence certain equations and linkages may be estimated "better" than others. Yet it is hard to fault the authors for this since they are constrained by the availability of measures in the data sets they are using. But it again suggests how important it is to give serious attention to the problem at the design stage of research; finding theoretically plausible exogenous variables with desirable statistical properties is a difficult task.

Nonrecursive models also create problems since ordinary least squares is not appropriate to estimate such structures; hence, the researcher proposing to analyze nonrecursive models will need to upgrade his or her statistical estimation skills. There are a variety of estimation procedures appropriate for nonrecursive models, assuming the equations to be estimated are either exactly or overidentified. One can talk of single equation models of estimation, examples of which are two stage least squares and limited information maximum likelihood estimation, and systems of equations methods of estimation, examples of which are three stage least squares and full information maximum likelihood estimation. These techniques are mentioned, not to intimidate the reader, but to suggest the kinds of statistical skills that might profitably be acquired and to show that a theoretical commitment to a nonrecursive model entails a statistical commitment to move beyond ordinary regression analysis. Fortunately, there is a technique available for exactly and overidentified nonrecursive models that is readily understandable—two stage least squares. But even here, the data analyst must be sensitive to special problems that arise in the use of the procedure; see Kritzer (1976) in particular for a discussion of the issues of standardization and multicollinearity in two stage least squares. One final point needs to be made about the estimation of nonrecursive, and recursive, models. The quality of the obtained estimates will be a function of a number of things including the availability of reliable and valid measures and the correct structural specification of the model. Model specification is primarily a theoretical and not a statistical enterprise. Incorrectly specified models can still be estimated; however, the obtained estimates may not be substantively meaningful. Hence, as one builds nonrecursive models and incorporates exogenous variables to help identify such models, specification should be grounded as firmly as possible in theoretical assertions about the processes being modelled. The importance of this point will become especially clear when we review the literature linking economic conditions and political behavior later in this chapter.

This essay has perhaps taken too much of a methodological and statistical turn. However, the theoretical decision to work with a nonrecursive model has some immediate consequences for the methodological and statistical decisions that must be made; it marvelously illustrates the interlocking nature of theoretical, methodological and statistical choices. This observation certainly holds for the other general strategy for representing nonrecursive relationships—using recursive models with variables measured at multiple time points. Probably the best substantive example of this approach in the field of voting behavior is the work of Markus and Converse (1979).

Markus and Converse construct a dynamic simultaneous equation model of vote choice that includes the usual set of explanatory variables, but which explicitly tries to model the social psychological processes by which the voter makes his or her vote choice. The model is dynamic in the sense that it examines political attitudes, not in the context of a single election, but instead over two elections on the premise that these attitudes are mutually dependent over time. For example, issue stands at time t depend on issue stands at time t-1; likewise, party identification at time t is influenced by party identification at t-1 and vote at t-1. Central to the Markus and Converse model is the assertion that issue preferences and candidate personalities do not affect vote choice directly; instead the authors argue that the major effect of these two attitudes—and also of party identification—is to jointly shape candidate evaluations that in turn directly affect vote choice. They build into their model a conditional relationship linking party identification to vote choice: party identification has more influence in shaping vote choice when the difference in candidate evaluations is small. When one candidate is much more highly evaluated than the other, the direct impact of party identification on vote choice vanishes, a notion very similar to the decision rule proposed by Kelley and Mirer (1974).

Markus and Converse found party identification to be fairly stable across elections, although previous voting behavior did have some effect on current party affiliation. Issue orientations, party identification, and candidate personalities were found to be important determinants of the evaluations received by Ford and Carter; moreover, the difference in evaluations of the two candidates enabled the authors to predict correctly the presidential choices of 90 percent of the voters. The authors emphasize that although the direct impact of party identification on candidate evaluations was less than the direct effects of issues and candidate personalities, its total effect was greater than the total effects of the other two variables because of party identification's indirect effects operating through candidate personalities. The authors conclude that candidate evaluations are the major determinant of vote choice, but stress that we must examine the causally prior effects of party loyalty and issue stands on candidate evaluations. Hence, we have further modifications of our classical voting model. And, again, some of these findings could not have been obtained had we stayed within the boundaries of a recursive, cross-sectional model.

The Markus and Converse approach obviously requires the use of a panel design. Panel data have certain advantages in the construction and testing of models. The temporal ordering among the variables often enables one to treat lagged measures of a variable as predetermined which means that such variables will be useful in identifying equations. More importantly, it seems that the representation of mutual dependence by a longitudinal formulation as opposed to a cross-sectional, nonrecursive model more faithfully reflects the processes the researcher is trying to model. For example, the model

probably does a better job of representing the mutual dependence of party identification and vote on each other than does the model

$$\text{party identification}_t \rightleftharpoons \text{vote}_t$$

At the least, there are questions about what a reciprocal linkage between variables measured at the same time actually means. Does the reciprocal linkage simply represent an average value of a process that has unfolded over time? Are the reciprocal estimates especially sensitive to the time point at which the investigator has gathered the observations? In general, more attention needs to be given to the interpretation of reciprocal linkages.

Of course, panel studies entail additional costs above and beyond the resources required for cross-sectional surveys, particularly in tracking the same respondents over time. Moreover, for many interesting research questions, a two wave panel would not be sufficient; three or more waves and the concomitant increase in costs would be required. It is not surprising that panel studies of national elections are infrequent. Furthermore, panel designs often use identical measures over time for the sake of comparability, yet in some instances in voting research, identically worded questions actually have different meanings over time as the social and political contexts change. Finally, panel designs are not panaceas. It is true that the temporal properties of the variables facilitate assigning causal priorities among them; however, as mentioned earlier, model construction is fundamentally a theoretical and substantive enterprise.

Despite the criticisms and limitations of nonrecursive and longitudinal models presented above, it is clear that these approaches are central to substantive advances in the field of voting behavior. Our standard cross-sectional and recursive models rule out by assumption too many substantively plausible linkages. The work of Jackson, Page and Jones, and Markus and Converse clearly demonstrates the substantive payoffs that come in using new approaches. However, before accepting the findings of Jackson, Page and Jones, and Markus and Converse as definitive, we should recognize that decisions about the conceptualization and measurement of variables and the specification and estimation of models have affected their substantive results just as these same decisions influenced the results of the earlier electoral research. Moreover, the findings of Jackson, Page and Jones, and Markus and Converse are not entirely congruent because of differences in specification, estimation, and operationalization. For example, Markus and Converse find that party identification is the most stable element of their model, even more so than issue attitudes, whereas Page and Jones conclude that policy distances, an issue measure, influence party identification rather than the reverse. Hence, it appears from these two pieces of research that the less stable variable is influencing the highly stable variable, a seeming anomaly. Since Markus and Converse explicitly incorporate a longitudinal element in their analysis while the Page-Jones work is cross-sectional and since different specifications are employed, both findings can be correct. As one tries to resolve this apparent anomaly, one needs to ask the fundamental question of how and where the different explanatory variables enter the process of vote choice. Given that evaluations of particular candidates tend to be specific to the election at hand—except perhaps for candidates who have been on the national scene for a long time—there is probably little controversy about having candidate evaluations in close temporal proximity to the vote decision. But a more long-term factor such as party identification could enter the vote decision process at many stages and its impact could be direct or indirect. Hence, it becomes extremely difficult to separate out the unique effects of party, candidate, and issue attitudes, the theme of the next section of the chapter.

Assessing the Effects of Party, Candidate and Issue Attitudes

A common goal in voting behavior research is to estimate the magnitude of the effects of party identification, candidate attitudes and issue preferences on vote choice. The typical strategy is to regress vote choice (Y) on party identification (X_1), candidate attitudes (X_2) and issue orientations (X_3) and examine the obtained regression coefficients. However, this procedure is flawed in two major ways. First, the regression equation

$$Y = b_0 + b_1X_1 + b_2X_2 + b_3X_3$$

is a model of direct effects only; it does not include any indirect effects of variables on vote choice. For example, the assertion that b_1 represents the effect of party identification on vote choice is an underestimation of its effect if partisanship also has indirect effects on vote choice via its impact on issue and candidate attitudes. In general, if one wishes to assess the total effects of variables on each other, one needs to move from direct effects regression models to more complex and interdependent causal systems such as those discussed in the first part of this essay.

Even if indirect effects did not have to be considered, the regression model depicted above would be unsatisfactory because of the operationalizations of party identification, issue orientations and candidate attitudes. Many of the measurement strategies that have been widely employed such as numerical counts of likes and dislikes of the parties and candidates, thermometer rating of the parties and candidates, and issue measures with a partisan or candidate proximity[5] component to them are problematic because they tap at least two of the explanatory variables simultaneously, thereby making it impossible to sort out the distinct effect of each variable. The classic example is the citizen who says that he or she voted against Carter because of his incompetence or against Goldwater because of his impulsiveness. How are these responses to be coded? Surely they are references to a candidate, but almost as surely, they likely have an underlying issue rationale to them. There is probably no simple answer to this problem since the variables are so inextricably linked.

Some analysts (Kirkpatrick et al., 1975; Nimmo & Savage, 1976; Miller & Miller, 1977; Shabad & Andersen, 1979; Kessel, 1980; Kinder & Abelson, 1981; and Miller et al., 1982) have been careful to sort out different kinds of candidate references. However, because of the conceptual overlap and mutual dependence among party, candidate and issue attitudes, it may be impossible to construct "pure" measures of each; hence, analysts should exercise caution in making claims about the unique effects of each of the explanatory variables. And, certainly, there should be continued efforts to develop measures that better tap the underlying constructs and clarify their meaning.

The research of Kinder and Abelson (1981) is an excellent example of the kind of work that is needed; their analysis of the trait judgments made by survey respondents about the presidential contenders yields two nearly independent dimensions: competence and integrity. They found perceptions of candidate competence to be a powerful predictor of presidential vote in 1980 and in particular found that citizens' assessment of *national* economic conditions strongly shaped their evaluations of Carter's performance. In their general vote model, candidate competence and integrity along with positive and negative affect toward the candidates were the most immediate determinants of the vote decision. The effects of policies, party identification and national economic conditions were indirect, channeled through appraisals of the candidates. Moreover, they found that over the course of the 1980 campaign, changes in perceptions of the candidates were associated with themes and developments in the presidential campaign.

The findings of Kinder and Abelson provide support for the Jackson, Page and Jones, and Markus and Converse models in which candidate assessments are the most immediate determinants of the vote. Miller et al. (1982) elaborate on the Kinder and Abelson work and argue that the criteria of competence and integrity are enduring ones that have structured candidate evaluations over the 1952-1980 period. Hence Miller and his colleagues assert that the standard treatment of candidate evaluations as "idiosyncratic responses to superficial criteria" needs to be drastically revised and propose a reconceptualization in which candidate assessments are based primarily on perceptions of how the candidate will perform, or has performed, in office. Hence, candidate based voting has a rational basis to it; it is not simply a gut reaction to a candidate's personality or appearance. This revised notion of candidate based voting serves as an example of prospective and retrospective voting, a topic developed at the end of this essay.

Kessel's (1980) analysis of the likes and dislikes of the parties and candidates expressed by samples of survey respondents does a good job of sorting out candidate, issue and party references, yet it also illustrates how intractable some of the problems are in disentangling issue and candidate effects. Kessel first examines citizens' responses under the general headings of candidate, party and issue references and then moves to a more refined classification. For example, the candidate references are divided into seven sub-categories of record and incumbency, experience, management, intelligence, trust, personality and a general category. Although this classification has major substantive payoffs in allowing one to map out candidate images in some detail, the seven categories are not as distinct as they initially appear to be. For example, under the management component of candidate attitudes are listed (for 1976) such responses as:

1. good/efficient/businesslike administration; balance budget; lower/ wouldn't increase national debt (reference 601 in the master code)
2. would spend less (than other side); would spend too little (reference 605 in the master code)

While these references certainly capture a management and/or efficiency dimension, they may also capture an issue dimension. Unfortunately, the NES surveys do not ask immediate followup questions that delve deeper into the respondent's concerns about spending. However, it is certainly plausible that the concern about spending is tied to specific policy preferences and support for specific programs. If so, these references are tapping an issue component as well as a candidate component, yet their treatment in the statistical analysis solely as a candidate reference would enhance the predictive power of candidate attitudes at the expense of issues. Although the problem is not at all serious in this particular example, the general problem of assigning a unique meaning to candidate, issue and party references is a difficult one.

Kessel employs maximum likelihood estimation procedures to assess the relative effects of the sixteen classes of responses (seven candidate, two party, and seven issue categories) on vote choice and finds that general candidate, general issue and party affect references tend to have the greater effects on vote choice. This conclusion is fine so long as one is careful to recognize that the obtained estimates measure direct effects only and not total effects. If one is interested in total effects, it will be necessary to posit a causal structure among the explanatory variables and assess the magnitude of the direct and the indirect effects. This again demonstrates the importance of the recursive and nonrecursive causal models of vote choice discussed in the first part of this chapter.

An exchange between Shaffer (1972; 1976) and Fiorina (1976) about the six component Michigan model (Stokes *et al.,* 1958; Stokes, 1966) is a useful starting point for suggesting new strategies for assessing the effects of partisanship, candidate evaluations and issue orientations on vote choice. Shaffer criticized the six component model on the grounds that all six components essentially tapped a single underlying party identification dimension and indeed were "simply six different ways of measuring the same thing" (p. 428). Fiorina correctly challenged this conclusion on a number of grounds. He observed that the first factor obtained in Shaffer's analysis accounts at most for 40 percent of the variance in the six components. Moreover, the factor loadings indicate that in most cases only about 30 to 40 percent of the variance of each component is accounted for by the common party identification factor. In addition, the correlations among the six components could not be reproduced very well by the common factor. Hence, Fiorina argued that the six components should be kept, even though they did have substantial variance in common. He claimed that although party identification may help shape these six components, there are other causal factors and more complex interrelationships involved. Shaffer rejoined that analysis in which the six components are entered into a regression equation and their separate effects compared can be very misleading, particularly when making cross-time and cross-variable comparisons.

I think a better way to view the Shaffer-Fiorina dispute is to recognize that party identification and issue and candidate attitudes are complex concepts — as we shall soon see — that cannot be adequately measured by a single indicator. Furthermore, the concepts of party identification, issue attitudes and candidate attitudes are latent (unmeasured) variables which we hope to tap adequately by means of our operational measures. The complexity of the concepts and the need to reproduce the true unmeasured variables requires a multiple indicators approach. Schematically, we might represent this situation by the following arrow diagram in which the circles represent latent or unmeasured variables, the rectangles measured indicators of the latent variables, and the u_is measurement error terms. Note in the diagram that there are multiple indicators of party identification and issue and candidate attitudes, but only a single indicator — reported vote — of the true vote choice.

The construction of indicators for each of our latent variables would be based on our conceptualizations of the unmeasured variables, although in the real world of secondary analysis we often have to make do with what is available. For example, one indicator of party identification might be the standard party identification question while other indicators might be thermometer evaluations of the parties or counts of the likes and dislikes of the parties expressed by citizens. Indicators of candidate attitudes might be thermometer ratings of the candidates and counts of the likes and dislikes of the candidates expressed by citizens. Finally, issue attitudes might be measured by a series of issue proximity measures.

This model can be estimated by a technique called LISREL (Jöreskog, 1970, 1973; Jöreskog & Sörbom, 1978). In fact, a model similar to the above in its logic but richer in its selection of indicators has been estimated by Dennis (1982); in particular, Dennis utilized the new party support measures in the 1980 national election survey as indicators of the true party identification. The LISREL approach is very powerful since it enables one to generate consistent estimates of the parameters of a given causal (structural) model *and* a measurement model from the observed variance-covariance matrix. Too often we have been content to estimate only the structural model and to ignore the measurement model altogether. Furthermore, LISREL places few restrictions on the kinds of structural and measurement models that can be estimated; for example, LISREL allows reciprocal linkages in the structural model and correlated errors in the measurement model. Its utility is further demonstrated by the fact that multiple regression, path analysis, and common factor analysis can all be subsumed under the general LISREL model. LISREL will undoubtedly become a more prominent model testing and analysis procedure in the study of voting behavior.

In the model depicted below, LISREL (particularly its factor analysis component) will enable the researcher to assess the convergent and discriminant validity of his or her measures. For example, with multiple measures of partisanship and candidate and issue attitudes respectively, we would certainly want the indicators designed to tap one latent variable to correlate more highly among themselves than with indicators tapping a different latent variable. If they do not, we might doubt our indicators (and/or our underlying conceptualization). Likewise, we hope that our indicators can discriminate among the latent variables.

In conclusion, the effort to sort out the unique effects of party identification, issue orientations, and candidate evaluations will be a difficult if not im-

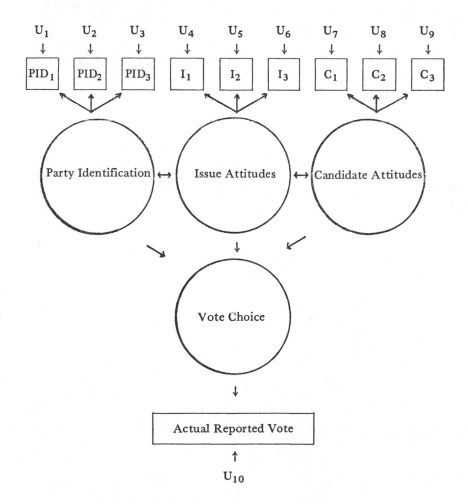

possible task. In order to accomplish this task, there must be sound conceptualization and measurement of each of our variables. However, there is currently great controversy about conceptual and measurement definitions, especially with respect to party identification, and it is to this topic that we now turn.

Party Identification

Party identification has been conceptualized as a psychological attachment to a political party. Citing reference group theory and small group influence processes, Campbell *et al.* (1960) viewed the political party "as the group toward which the individual may develop an identification, positive or negative, of some degree of intensity" (pp. 121-122). This identification is seen as structuring citizens' perceptions of politics, their evaluations of political objects, and their behavioral responses to political stimuli. Party identification has been important in the analysis of voting behavior for a number of reasons. First, it has been viewed as a major determinant of the political behavior of citizens. Second, party identification has been seen as a source of stability in the electoral cleavages characterizing the United States and as a dampener of electoral swings. Finally, party identification served as the core of the normal vote concept elaborated by Converse (1966) and as such provided a baseline from which to evaluate short-term partisan changes.

The traditional measure of party identification has been the two part question:

> Generally speaking, do you think of yourself as a Republican, a Democrat, an Independent, or what? Those who classified themselves as Republicans or Democrats were then asked, Would you call yourself a strong (Republican, Democrat) or a not very strong (Republican, Democrat)? Those who termed themselves Independents were then asked, Do you think of yourself as closer to the Republican or Democratic Party?

This two part question yields a seven category classification of party identification: strong Republican, weak Republican, Independent Republican, Independent, Independent Democrat, weak Democrat, and strong Democrat. This measurement strategy reflects a conceptualization of partisanship that assumes that Independent represents a neutral middle point along a unidimensional continuum ranging from strong Republican to strong Democrat and that Democrat and Republican identifications are polar opposite points along this continuum.

Currently, the unidimensional conceptualization and measurement of party identification are being challenged, and alternative conceptualization and measurement strategies are being proposed. Moreover, many of our empirical generalizations about party identification—such as its early development through a family-dominated political socialization process, its reinforcement and intensification over time and its concomitant stability—have been called into question. Hence, despite its pre-eminent role in the study of voting behavior, party identification is today being challenged on many fronts. (Also

see Shively, 1980, for a review of recent developments relevant to party identification.)

The Stability of Party Identification

The initial evidence about the stability of party identification came from
recall questions about past partisanship, but such recall information can be
very inaccurate (Niemi *et al.*, 1980). More direct and compelling evidence
about the stability of party identification is provided by panel data. An
analysis of the 1956-1958-1960 SRC panel data by Dreyer (1973) concluded
that the stability of partisanship was high and that whatever changes did
occur over time were random. Subsequent analyses by Dobson and St. Angelo
(1975), Brody (1977), and Howell (1981) have challenged this latter conclusion, arguing that changes in partisanship were indeed responsive to real
world events. For example, Dobson and St. Angelo found that Republicans
were less stable in their partisanship than Democrats between 1956 and 1958,
but that both groups behaved similarly between 1958 and 1960, a pattern
they attributed to the "Republican" recession of 1958. A similar pattern held
in the 1972-1974-1976 era with Republicans between 1972 and 1974 (the
Nixon resignation year) much more likely than Democrats to move away from
their partisanship, a party difference that practically vanished between 1974
and 1976. Brody argued that the economic climate and the low evaluation of
the Republican President's performance made Republican identifiers more
prone to changing their partisanship. Howell's analysis confirmed the responsiveness of party identification to short-term forces, although for Howell the
major short-term force was past voting behavior. Even here, however, issues
played a role in that their effects were channeled through past vote.
Hence there is much evidence accumulating that the conceptualization
of party identification primarily as a long-term force unresponsive to current
political stimuli is in need of revision. Party identification does respond to
short-term influences; indeed, this responsiveness is one reason why nonrecursive formulations that allow reciprocal linkages between party identification and issue and candidate attitudes are needed.
However, the assertion that party identification is sensitive to short-term
forces is *not* equivalent to saying that party identification is highly unstable;
to the contrary, party identification remains one of the most stable of political
attitudes. Converse and Markus (1979) find that partisan stability in the
1972-1974-1976 CPS panel far exceeded the stability of respondents' stances
on issues—moral issues being an exception. Moreover, direction of partisanship is more stable than strength of partisanship; the bulk of the observed
changes in the panel data are intra-party (e.g., from strong Republican to
weak Republican) rather than interparty. Various research findings suggest
that direction and strength of party identification can be viewed as conceptually distinct, the former being more stable and long-term and the latter
more responsive to the immediate political setting. (This distinction has implications for the processes by which partisanship is acquired; see Claggett,
1981.)[8]

Finally, the work of Jennings and Niemi (1978) provides an even stronger test of the stability of partisanship. The authors analyzed a sample of high school seniors and some of their parents in 1965 and reinterviewed much of this sample in 1973. Among the parental sample, partisan stability was very high with very little polar changes in partisanship. Among the youth sample, partisan change was much more common, particularly movement into the Independent category. The authors conclude that the partisanship of young adults is indeed susceptible to the dominant political forces of the time.

Alternative Conceptualizations of Party Identification

If party identification does respond to short-term stimuli, then at least a partial reconceptualization of partisanship may be required. Fiorina (1977; 1981) provides one such reformulation. He defines a person's identification with a party as the difference between the person's past experiences with that party minus the person's past experiences with the other party plus some adjustment representing the initial partisan bias the person brings into the political arena. This formulation is useful for it incorporates past experiences yet weights them less than current experiences, thereby allowing recent events to alter partisan predispositions. In effect, party identification becomes "a running tally of retrospective evaluations" (1981, p. 89). This formulation grounds party identification in reality and allows past experiences to anchor party identification somewhat, thereby giving to party identification some element of a standing decision even as it is responsive to current political stimuli. In fact, Fiorina (1981) explicitly states that "there is an inertial element (party identification) in voting behavior that cannot be ignored, but that inertial element has an experiential basis; it is *not* something learned at mommy's knee and never questioned thereafter" (p. 152). But overall, Fiorina rests party identification in evaluations of prior experiences and as such gives the acquisition of partisanship a more rational basis.

Shively (1979) also suggests a rational basis for the acquisition and retention of a party identification. His functional model argues very straightforwardly that party identification is acquired in order to make manageable the decisional burden facing the voter. Party identification is seen here as an economizing device that reduces the costs of decision-making. A person will be more likely to develop a partisanship if other economizing devices (e.g., class and group loyalties) are not available. Shively presents some evidence for his model and develops some interesting implications.

The Fiorina and Shively works are important because they move the discussion of party identification away from a long-term attitude acquired in childhood which would be likely to be devoid of issue and policy content and, instead, anchor party identification in the political reality experienced by the adult citizen. This does not deny child-adult party identification linkages, but it does suggest that the holding of partisanship is a more complex and dynamic process with a rational foundation.

There is still much evidence that party identification tends to be learned in childhood even before the party label has much issue content for the youngster. However, this early acquired partisanship does change in response to individual experiences and to the dominant political forces of the era. Howell's (1980) analysis of the effects of voting behavior on changes in partisanship reaches a similar conclusion; the development of adult partisanship "involves an interplay between the stable component of that attitude [party identification] and adult behavior [in Howell's case, voting behavior] which can be either reinforcing or nonreinforcing. Past behavior does influence future identification, but that influence is specified by both the stability and direction of the initial identification" (p. 298).

The Dimensionality of Party Identification

There are currently many questions being asked about party identification:

1. What actually is the object of party identification? What do citizens mean when they talk of political parties? Is party a set of ideas and issues, a set of elites, activists and candidates, a group of people like one's self or what?
2. What models can account for the development and acquisition of partisanship? Can the Fiorina and Shively notions be reconciled with the initial reference group conceptualization of partisanship?
3. What does party identification signify? Is it simply positive affect toward one party or does it also entail hostility toward the other party in a two party system? (Maggiotto & Piereson, 1977)
4. What does political independence mean? Is it indifference between the parties, support of both, or rejection of both? Assuming that we are working within the traditional unidimensional conceptualization and measurement of party identification, what about independent leaners: are they partisans or independents?[7]

Questions 3 and 4 lead into a discussion of the dimensionality of partisanship and the answers to these questions will in turn depend on and feed back into our conceptualization of partisanship. As mentioned above, the traditional party identification measure has been treated as unidimensional with strong Republicans and strong Democrats representing polar opposite points and independents representing a neutral midpoint along the scale. Presumably as one moved from strong Republican to strong Democrat across the categories of the scale, one was moving across increasingly Democratic categories.[8]

Early on, Petrocik (1974) observed that the seven fold party identification index did not behave as a unidimensional scale should. He found intransitivities in the scale as it related to other variables; for example, independent leaners were more likely than weak identifiers to be involved in politics, an anomalous result if one thinks of weak identifiers as having more intense partisan feelings which would result in higher levels of involvement. It turns out that independent leaners possess characteristics (e.g., higher education, higher income) generally linked to higher levels of involvement more than weak partisans do. Although the intransitivities uncovered by Petrocik dealt mainly with measures of involvement, inconsistencies also arise with respect to partisan-related measures such as evaluations of the parties and candidates (Asher, 1980, pp. 62-63) and past loyalty to one's party. Often the independent leaners do not fall between the weak identifiers and the pure independents as would be expected if the party identification index is unidimensional and the ordering of the categories correct. Keith *et al.* (1977) make similar points about independent leaners. They find that the pure independents score very low on measures of political activity, interest and knowledge, while the independent leaners score high. Moreover, the leaners tend to be more loyal than the weak partisans to their party's presidential nominees and indeed often resemble the strong partisans in their voting behavior, a pattern that again challenges the unidimensionality of party identification. Katz (1979) also provides evidence arguing against unidimensionality. In one part of his analysis of panel data, he finds that strong party identifiers who switched their party loyalty were more likely to move all the way to strong identification with a new party than to move to some intermediate position. This suggested to Katz that strong Democrat and strong Republican were actually close points and not opposite ends of a unidimensional continuum. One way in which strong Democrats and strong Republicans might be close in a partisan space would be if that space were characterized by two dimensions—the direction of partisanship and the intensity of partisanship.

Valentine and Van Wingen (1980) and Howell (1980) also argue for two dimensions of party identification—partisanship and independence. Van Wingen and Valentine argue that the problems inherent in interpreting the standard party identification measure arises from the fact that it is inadequately tapping two dimensions simultaneously. They therefore call for the development of direct unidimensional measures of partisanship and of independence.

Weisberg (1980) has also shown that the unidimensional view of partisanship does not fit certain empirical observations. For example, unidimensionality places Democrats and Republicans as polar opposites which implies that there should be a strong negative correlation between evaluations of the two parties; instead, the correlation in any year is at most slightly negative and in some years practically zero. Weisberg also examines the preference order given by respondents to the objects Democrat, Republican and Independent as measured by thermometer ratings and finds that almost half of the respondents give orderings incompatible with the unidimensional interpretation that would place Independents in the middle of the partisan continuum. Hence Weisberg rejects the unidimensional view of party identification and instead proposes a multidimensional conceptualization that entails three dimensions: attitudes toward the Democrats, attitudes toward the Republicans, and attitudes toward independence. He tested this conceptualization using some of the new party support measures in the 1980 National Election Study surveys. In a similar fashion, Dennis (1981a) also analyzes the new party support measures and finds three facets of partisanship: partisan direction, party system support, and political involvement. Valentine and Van Wingen, Weisberg, and Dennis show how moving beyond a unidimensional formulation helps one sort out intransitivities in the traditional party identification index; in particular, the seemingly anomalous behavior of independent leaners is better accounted for in more than one dimension. More generally, their analyses suggest that political independence is a complex phenomenon and that our traditional party identification measure may lump together as independents many different types of respondents.

Whither the Traditional Party Identification Measure

In an unpublished paper, Dennis (1981b) examined in great detail the properties of three measures of partisanship: the traditional party identification index, a partisan supporter typology based upon new items in the 1980 NES surveys, and a measure based on feeling thermometers toward the parties. He found that while the traditional measure did slightly better in tapping long term retrospective aspects of voting behavior such as regularity of party voting, it did no better than the other measures in relating to a set of criterion variables. Although the traditional measure had slightly higher stability and reliability coefficients and its marginal distributions were somewhat more stable from survey to survey, Dennis on balance comes down in favor of using the partisan supporter typology—except when studying long-term overall trends in partisanship.

Dennis' conclusion raises very directly the fundamental question of whether we can continue to use the traditional measure of partisanship. This standard measure has the advantages of familiarity, availability, and comparability over time and to give it up would impose hardships in many analyses. Nevertheless, it is clear that our underlying unidimensional conceptualization of partisanship is not very well reflected in our standard party identification item. Weisberg (1980, p. 49) takes the reasonable position that it would be silly to give up the traditional measure, even with its known flaws, unless alternative measures provide "real theoretical and substantive gains." Certainly in the area of understanding political independence the traditional measure needs to be supplemented if not replaced. But with respect to representing the partisan predispositions and locations of citizens, the traditional measure is still very powerful. Moreover, it is possible for a unidimensional measure to do a reasonably good job in representing the positions of people in a multidimensional space. Shively (1980) provides some tentative evidence suggesting that the traditional measure does not overly distort the ordering obtained in a two dimensional space. Likewise, Weisberg (1980) states that the traditional measure reduces "the three-space into a single partisan dimension with minimal violence" (p. 48). Hence, the case seems strong for the continued, but careful use of the traditional measure.

Fiorina (1981) takes the distinctive position that we should first decide on our conceptualization of partisanship and then develop appropriate measurement strategies. Hence, if we want party identification to be unidimensional with strong Democrat and strong Republican representing polar extremes and independence simply representing the absence of partisanship, we should design measurement strategies that will accomplish this. Just because the traditional measure has been shown to tap at least two dimensions does not mean that the conceptualization of party identification must change; it may be sufficient to alter the measurement strategies. Certainly at one level Fiorina is correct; conceptualization should guide measurement and not the reverse. However, as Weisberg (1982) argues, if reasonable empirical evidence indicates that citizens do not view parties as polar opposites along a unidimensional continuum, then we may have to reconceptualize party identification. (Fiorina would likely reject some of Weisberg's evidence as he views the party thermometers to be very contaminated measures.) Weisberg specifically proposes to conceptualize reactions to the parties as two separate dimensions.

The jury is still out in terms of which conceptualization and measurement strategies are preferable and under what circumstances. It is likely that different measures will be useful to address different substantive questions which means that in the future no single measure of partisanship will be expected to carry as much weight as the traditional measure has. Certainly questions about party identification will occupy a central place in the voting behavior research agenda for the foreseeable future. It is likely that the requirements of comparability and continuity will keep our traditional party identification measure in business even as work continues on new conceptualizations and measures. The works discussed herein represent a very promising start to a party identification dialogue, but one should be wary of allowing the new measures already developed to overly constrain future developments.

Candidate Attitudes

As discussed earlier, a number of recent models of presidential vote choice (e.g., Page & Jones, Kinder & Abelson, Markus & Converse) have posited candidate evaluations as the most immediate determinants of vote choice and as the variable through which other influences operate. Given the central importance of candidate assessments to the vote choice, it is surprising that research on candidate evaluations has lagged behind research on party identification and issue attitudes. Although we know from various pieces of research about the kinds of factors that shape candidate appraisals—party identification, issue preference, perceptions of national economic conditions and others—and we have some insights about the conditions under which different factors will be more or less important in shaping candidate assessments, until very recently we knew little about how candidate images develop and change over the course of the presidential campaign from the primaries to the general election.

The study of the development of candidate images of course requires a longitudinal design that spans the entire presidential selection process and not simply the general election campaign. After all, if as some recent analyses suggest, presidential elections are mainly candidate choices, and if most voters have made their vote choice weeks or months before Election Day in November, then the sources of candidate images must reside earlier in the selection process. Fortunately there are some new data sources that facilitate the study of candidate appraisals throughout the campaign period. For example, the various national surveys and the specific primary election exit polls conducted by such organizations as CBS News/*New York Times* (which are available to the social science community through ICPSR) are useful sources of information as are statewide polls conducted throughout the election period. Potentially important sources of data are the polls conducted for the presidential candidates, but these are not easily available to the social science community. Certainly one of the richest data sources available to election analysts is the 1980 National Election Studies conducted by the Center for Political Studies of the University of Michigan. The design of the NES/CPS surveys explicitly recognized the need to obtain observations throughout the presidential selection process. The complex design had a number of components: a panel of respondents interviewed in February, June, September, and post-election; a national cross-section interviewed in April and re-interviewed after the November election; and the traditional pre- and post-general election surveys.

These various data sets have contributed mightily to our ability to trace the development of candidate evaluations over time, yet even these sources have limitations that suggest how severe data problems can be in studying political phenomena longitudinally. The limitations of these data sets are partially a function of the fact that investigators have a diverse set of substantive questions on their agendas that cannot be adequately addressed by the same design. For example, one set of questions relevant to the primary election season would be the determinants of turnout and vote choice in presidential primaries. Such questions are best addressed by specific state surveys conducted in close temporal proximity to election day in those states. Another set of research questions might be the development of candidate evaluations during the primary season and the role of the media in nationalizing and publicizing the results of specific primary elections; here the optimal design might be national surveys, either cross-sections or preferably panels.

Obviously, it would be ideal to conduct specific state surveys to capture the contextual richness of the campaigns in specific states as well as to conduct repeated national surveys to detail the process of information diffusion about the candidates and the electoral consequences of this information. In the real world, however, resource constraints force investigators to make difficult choices. For example, one cannot conduct multiple surveys to capture all the important events and influences in a campaign. The first slices into an ongoing process will probably establish the baseline from which to evaluate subsequent change. For example, the first NES/CPS survey in 1980 was conducted in February after George Bush's popularity and public awareness as measured in the polls had jumped because of the major media coverage he received for his success in the Iowa precinct caucuses. Likewise, the first measurement of attitudes toward John Anderson in the 1980 NES/CPS surveys came in the April measurement, weeks after Anderson's strong showings in Vermont and Massachusetts and his concomitant increase in national visibility.

In a similar vein, resource constraints of both time and money force restrictions on the measures actually included in one's surveys. For example, the NES/CPS surveys asked certain followup questions about the 1980 presi-

the impact of economic conditions on voting behavior, a flawed collection of analyses that focus on one type of issue: the state of the economy.

On the methodological side, the development of new issue formats and the assessment of the consequences of question wording and question filters has immediate relevance to the issue voting—and the beliefs systems—controversy (see in particular the work of Aldrich *et al.*, 1982, and Bishop *et al.*, 1978a, 1978b, 1979 and 1980). On the substantive side, the work of Carmines and Stimson (1980) has distinguished between two kinds of issue voting, one based on "hard" issues and the other on "easy" issues. Hard issue voting results from a careful weighing of the alternatives (in a Downsian sense) and should be most prevalent in those citizens with the cognitive and conceptual skills to make such comparative assessments. Easy issue voting occurs for issues that are largely symbolic rather than technical, that deal with policy ends rather than means, and that have been on the political agenda for some time. Voters can respond to such issues on a gut level and hence need not possess any particular conceptual skills in order to cast an issue vote. Carmines and Stimson find that with respect to Vietnam, a hard issue, level of information (a measure of cognitive and conceptual abilities) affected the relationship between policy position and vote; issue voting was most pronounced among high information respondents. For desegregation, an easy issue, information level had much weaker effects. One conclusion the authors draw is that issue voting is not necessarily a sign of political sophistication since easy issue voting does not require any special intellectual skills. The Carmines and Stimson work will force future discussions of issue voting to be more careful about equating issue voting and citizen competence; high levels of issue voting do not necessarily indicate a highly competent electorate of rational decision-makers. In a related vein, the work of Rabinowitz *et al.* (1982) also provides insights about the properties and behavior of the electorate. The authors examined the effects of issue salience and, unlike some earlier studies, found that the salience of an issue to the voter did shape his or her political behavior. However, the one most salient issue for each voter did not dominate the vote decision; the electorate was not a collection of single issue voters. These recent works jointly suggest that when salient issues are also easy issues, the amount of issue voting in an election is likely to be high. However, these works also suggest that issues are only one of a number of influences on the vote decision and that the extent of issue voting will depend on the characteristics of the voters, the campaign emphases of the candidates and the nature of the issues themselves.

In many ways, the issue voting debate has been a stimulating one characterized by innovative conceptual, methodological and statistical contributions. Yet in some respects, the issue voting controversy has become sterile, in part because in our emphasis on social science methods and procedures, we have lost sight of the real world political questions motivating the debate in the first place. Issue voting occurs in the context of a campaign and election in which candidates seek support from the electorate, voters in some way respond to and impose constraints on candidates, and citizen-candidate interactions take place mainly within a media-dominated context. In essence, the campaign is a process of political communication, the major communication flow being from candidates to voters through controlled (e.g., partisan commercials) and uncontrolled (e.g., nightly news shows) media. (The communication flow can of course run in the opposite direction as citizens directly or indirectly express their preferences.)

If we think of the campaign as a communication process, then we want to know how well the candidate's mediated campaign is reaching the electorate; we literally want to know whether the campaign and the citizenry are on the same wavelength. This concern has a number of consequences for the issue voting controversy as well as for the debates on belief system constraint and levels of conceptualization. For example, if the campaign emphasizes certain issues, it is important to determine whether voters are responding to those issues. We can certainly study issues that are idiosyncratically important to citizens, but we would be remiss if we failed to assess citizens' reactions to the candidates' issue agendas. Thus, we should feel fully comfortable in querying voters about a set of issues that we as political scientists deem to be important in the campaign based on the emphasis given these issues by the candidates and the mass media. Likewise, criticisms of the use of certain measures such as the likes and dislikes of the parties and candidates on the grounds that these are partisan stimuli that are not as relevant to independents — and therefore make independents appear less competent — seem to me to ignore the very basic political fact that elections are candidate and party contests. Similarly, those who challenge the use of liberal-conservative terminology in studying levels of conceptualization and belief system constraint are ignoring the fact that such terminology is widely used by the candidates and media in discussing politics. Again, the campaign is a communication process and it is important to know whether candidates and political commentators are indeed speaking the same language as the voters.

The above argument does not deny that there are other appropriate ways of studying issue voting, belief system constraint, and the like. Certainly it is important to assess the substantive consequences of the measurement decisions we have made. And it certainly is important to know whether voters make decisions on the basis of issues idiosyncratically important to them or whether citizens employ their own unique frameworks in organizing their attitudes. However, these formulations of the questions often get so entangled in social science methodology that the political reasons for studying the topics in the first place get overlooked.

Economic Conditions and Voting

The bulk of the work on economic conditions and voting has been done in the context of congressional elections and, therefore, might have been included in the next section. I prefer to treat it under the rubric of issues, however, since the central theme of this research is how one particular cluster of issues — economic conditions — affects vote choice. In addition, much of this literature can be subsumed under the notion of retrospective voting. That is, a recurrent theme of these works is how voters' evaluations of the prior and current state of the economy shape subsequent vote decisions. This concern with the effects of economic conditions is pursued in both aggregate and individual level analyses, the latter better capturing the core elements of a retrospective voting model.

Congressional elections, especially the midterm election, have often been viewed as a referendum on the performance of the incumbent presidential administration with the state of the economy being a major factor entering into the voter's judgment of the President. A number of aggregate analyses seem to provide solid support for the contention that congressional election outcomes are responsive to national economic conditions. Kramer (1971) examined congressional elections in presidential and midterm years and found that increases in per capita personal income helped congressional candidates of the President's party and declines in personal income hurt them; changes in the inflation rate and unemployment levels did not seem to have any independent impact. Arcelus and Meltzer (1975) disagreed with Kramer's results, arguing that "with the possible exception of inflation, aggregate economic variables affect neither the participation rate in congressional elections nor the relative strengths of the two major parties" (p. 1238). Goodman and Kramer (1975) criticize Arcelus and Meltzer on a number of grounds and produce evidence which supports Kramer's earlier contentions. Bloom and Price (1975) contribute to this debate by suggesting an asymmetry in the effects of economic conditions; economic slumps hurt the party of the President, but economic upturns do not help.[10] Tufte (1975; 1978) flatly concludes that the midterm election is a referendum on presidential performance and the administration's handling of the economy. He argues that although the President's party almost always loses votes in the off-year election, that loss will be less if the President is enjoying high popularity or if the economy is going well or both.

Two more recent analyses that attempt to specify conditions under which economic effects will occur at the aggregate level arrive at contradictory conclusions. Owens and Olson's (1980) analysis runs counter to the bulk of the previous findings. They partially disaggregate the national analysis by examining economic conditions and vote outcomes at the congressional district level. They essentially find that voting in the 1972, 1974, and 1976 congressional elections was not affected by short run economic fluctuations and conclude that congressional elections outcomes are determined by the kinds of political factors discussed later. Hibbing and Alford's (1981) contribution is to examine economic effects within subgroups of candidate-defined districts. At the aggregate level, they find that the electoral margins of incumbents are more sensitive to economic conditions than is the case for non-incumbents; moreover, the effect is stronger for high seniority, in-party incumbents which makes sense if one thinks of those incumbents as having greater responsibility for the state of the economy. Hibbing and Alford's interpretation runs counter to the general direction of the incumbency literature which argues that incumbents immunize themselves and convert elections to local rather than national affairs. Hibbing and Alford's argument that incumbent electoral performance is more sensitive to economic conditions still does not result in incumbents being defeated. Because incumbents start with greater electoral margins, they can afford a downward shift in their electoral support and still have their vote percentage remain over the 50 percent mark.

The general thrust—with some notable exceptions—of these aggregate studies is that economic conditions—and presidential popularity—are strongly related to the overall distribution of the national House vote. However, when one moves from the aggregate to the individual level, the results are much more mixed, particularly in examining the effects of the personal as opposed to the national economic situation. Thus, Fiorina (1978) and Kinder and Kiewiet (1979) find scant effects of personal economic conditions on congressional voting—although Fiorina finds effects on presidential voting—while Weatherford (1978) and Klorman (1978) do observe such effects. Weatherford notes that working class citizens were more likely than middle class citizens to deviate from their expected vote in response to the personal economic difficulties associated with a recession. He attributes this finding to the simple notion that working class people feel the effects of recession more than middle class persons.

Hibbing and Alford (1981) and Kuklinski and West (1981) also find evidence of personal economic effects. Just as incumbency status affected the aggregate relationship uncovered by Hibbing and Alford, it also affected the individual level pattern: retrospective personal financial conditions influence vote choice, particularly for senior incumbents of the President's party. Kuklinski and West's contribution is to operationalize personal economic situations in terms of perceptions of future well being, as opposed to retrospective judgments, and to explicitly compare House and Senate voters. Overall they find a strong relationship between citizens' expected financial well being and vote choice in Senate elections but not in House elections. Kinder and Kiewiet (1979), in contrast, assert that it is only when economic variables are operationalized in terms of national economic conditions and perceptions of the parties' ability to deal with economic problems that economic variables will have an impact on the vote.

Critique and Conclusion

By now the reader should be overwhelmed by the range and disparities of the findings on economic effects. Indeed, this body of literature is a mess to disentangle for a number of reasons. First, there is often a lack of correspondence between theories, levels of analysis and data. For example, much of the literature is positing, at least implicitly, a rational economic voter, yet many of the analyses are on the aggregate rather than the individual level. Often there is a lack of clarity about whether the critical variable is objective economic condition or perceived economic condition.

Moreover, the various studies are non-comparable in a variety of ways. They often span different periods of time and examine different kinds of elections. They often focus on very different economic conditions such as inflation or unemployment or personal income. In general, model specifications differ in important ways across the various studies. Model specification is a serious problem in this body of literature since important non-economic variables are often omitted from equations which raises the possibility that the estimates of the effects of economic conditions are seriously biased. Finally, the economic effects one is trying to isolate may be relatively small and difficult to disentangle from errors of measurement, specification and sampling.[11]

There surely remains much to be done in assessing the effects of economic conditions on voting behavior. We presently have many discrete findings at the aggregate and individual levels which do not cumulate very well. Moreover, it seems likely that some of our findings are mainly artifacts of various model and measurement decisions rather than general statements about the linkages between economics and politics. In general, we need to do a better job of relating findings about economic effects to characteristics of the political system since some of the findings have potentially important normative implications for the operation of the American political system. Although the evidence about the consequences of personal economic situation for vote choice is mixed, there is some solid evidence (Rosenstone, 1982) that personal economic adversity reduces turnout. Hence those citizens most hurt by bad economic times may have the least to say about who will govern. And given that it is the already less well off who are hurt most by bad economic times, the biases in the election system and the economic system may be substantial. In the conclusion to this essay, I will pursue the notion of how retrospective voting, based on economic or non-economic issues, underlies one conception of democratic theory in which citizen influence is limited.

CONGRESSIONAL ELECTIONS

Introduction

The study of congressional elections is a growth area in the field of voting behavior as evidenced by two recent books on the topic (Hinckley, 1981; Jacobson, 1983) and scores of journal articles dealing with such subjects as incumbency advantages, midterm elections, issue voting in congressional elections, and others. Until this recent flurry of publications, our knowledge of congressional elections was dominated by two articles (Miller & Stokes, 1963; Stokes & Miller, 1962) based upon constituency and congressional data collected in 1958. These two articles suggested that congressional elections were low information events, that citizens had little knowledge of the candidates and issues. Fewer than half the respondents could identify which party controlled the Congress and almost half of the voters in contested House elections claimed to have voted without having heard anything about either candidate. Rather than being candidate and issue contests, voting in House elections was seen as a matter of partisanship; citizens supported candidates mainly on the basis of their party affiliations. Even the changes in the outcome of House elections from the presidential to the subsequent off-year election were not viewed in issue terms; instead, Campbell (1966) proposed a surge and decline explanation of House elections that relied heavily on differential turnout and defection rates in presidential and off-year elections and on the nature of the presidential election itself.

Today the dominant portrait of congressional elections is far different. No longer is the vote decision viewed primarily as a function of partisanship;

the central explanatory variables are candidate qualities and evaluations, particularly the differential awareness and strengths of incumbents versus challengers. The effects of party identification are weaker, in part because of the growth in the number of independents and because of the lessened loyalty of partisans to their party's nominee. In particular, the research of Cover, and Mann and Wolfinger has shown that the decline in party identification's impact on congressional voting can largely be attributed to the increased tendency of voters of the challenger's party to defect from their partisanship and support the incumbent. Even issues and ideology are being cited as sources of congressional voting.

Much of the evidence for this revised portrait has come from the 1978 congressional election survey conducted by the Center for Political Studies of the University of Michigan. The 1978 survey included a rich battery of items assessing the extent of citizen awareness of candidate qualities, activities, and issue stance. Moreover, the design of the 1978 survey used the congressional district rather than the county or SMSA as the primary sampling unit which facilitated the study of district level phenomena. The crucial contributions of the 1978 survey are evidenced by one very simple finding, noted by numerous analysts, that awareness of candidates is much higher when a test of name recognition is used rather than a test of name recall as was used in the 1958 survey. In addition to the 1978 survey, other important sources of data became available to congressional scholars in the 1970s, especially information about congressional perquisites and their utilization and reliable data about campaign financing.

Even before the availability of these new data sources, various investigators had noted trends that seemed to belie the portrait presented in the early studies based on the 1958 data. Certainly the core observation was the increase in incumbent electoral safety and the parallel decline in marginal congressional districts (Erikson, 1971; Mayhew, 1974). Numerous explanations of this phenomena were proposed and tested. Tufte (1973) suggested that reapportionment decisions were protecting incumbents, but Ferejohn (1977) showed that incumbent safety had increased in both redistricted and non-redistricted seats. Mayhew (1974) argued that incumbency advantages resided in the ability of incumbents to promote themselves and increase awareness through skillful use of perquisites such as the frank, and that this increased awareness on the part of the voters had electoral payoffs for incumbents. Ferejohn (1977) noted that if Mayhew's explanations were correct, one should observe over time an increase in the recognition levels of incumbents and an increasing gap between the recognition of incumbents versus challengers. Ferejohn found no such pattern, thereby calling into question Mayhew's explanation. Ferejohn then proposed a variation on Mayhew's theme and presented evidence indicating that party identification had become less of a cue to congressional voters. He suggested that incumbency was replacing partisanship as a voting cue, although he had no direct evidence for the reasons for the increased reliance on incumbency. Ferejohn noted that the decline in the effect of partisanship was not only due to the changed distribution of partisanship (i.e. the growth in the proportion of independents), but also to the tendency of partisans to be less loyal to their party's nominees.[12] This tendency was demonstrated dramatically by Cover (1977) who found that "since 1972 about half of those identifying with the challenger's party have deserted their party's congressional candidate in contested elections involving an incumbent" (p. 535). Hence for loyalists of the challenger's party, party identification or a coin flip would predict their votes equally well. Cover posits that the skillful use of congressional perquisites may be responsible for this incumbency advantage, but inspection of Gallup Poll data shows no pattern of increased incumbent recognition. Hence Cover concludes that incumbents have profited from changes in citizen behavior, but it is indeterminate as to whether incumbents played a significant part in generating these changes. Finally, Fiorina (1977a; 1977b) argued that the source of increased incumbency safety lay in the growth of the bureaucracy which can be electorally profitable for representatives as they intercede on behalf of constituents. This explanation does not require a growth in awareness of the incumbent, but only a change in the content of that awareness. If today congressmen are known more for their casework and constituency services, activities likely to be highly valued by constituents, whereas in the past congressmen were known more for policy stances which could be controversial and electorally costly, then the changed content of awareness could provide important electoral benefits to incumbents.

Most of the earlier works reviewed above pointed in some way to incumbency advantages and incumbent behavior as inducing behavioral change in voters, but little direct information was available about citizens' perceptions of the candidates. Fortunately, the 1978 CPS congressional election survey data permit one to assess in detail awareness of and information about the candidates and it is to these works that we now turn.

Incumbency Advantages and Comparative Candidate Assessments

The more recent literature on congressional elections can be organized around two general themes: the advantages of incumbency and the importance of comparative candidate evaluations. Initially it was the advantages of the incumbent that were emphasized, but as research has progressed, analyses have demonstrated that it was the comparative assessment of incumbents vis-a-vis their challengers rather than incumbency advantages alone that explained the electoral safety of incumbents. Thus, just as recent presidential vote models posit candidate evaluations as the immediate determinant of the vote, so some recent analyses of congressional voting argue for comparative candidate evaluations as the variable through which other influences operate. The relevant literature is voluminous and often repetitious and thus I will simply highlight some for the core findings.

Various works (Mann & Wolfinger, 1980; Abramowitz, 1980; Hinckley, 1980a, 1980b, 1981; Parker, 1980a, 1980b, 1980c, 1981; Goldenberg & Traugott, 1980, 1981; Epstein & Frankovic, 1982; Ragsdale, 1981; Jacobson,

1981; Cover & Brumberg, 1982; and Fowler, 1980) provide evidence supportive of the following assertions:

1. Incumbents are much better known and more highly evaluated than challengers.
2. The advantage the incumbent enjoys in terms of awareness is partially a function of the communication resources and constituency servicing opportunities available to the incumbent. There is some evidence directly linking perquisite utilization to increased saliency and more positive evaluations of incumbents. Overall, there is much more contact of various kinds between the incumbent and the voter than between the challenger and the voter.
3. The seriousness of the challenger in terms of political skills and experience, fund raising abilities, and awareness is a crucial determinant of the election outcome. Weak challengers are one type of incumbency advantage.
4. The disparity in recognition and resources between incumbents and challengers is much greater for the House than for the Senate. Senate challengers are much better able to attract resources, become known, and run credible campaigns, and hence Senate challengers enjoy a higher election success rate than House challengers. Moreover, Senate elections are more likely to entail explicit comparative assessment of the candidates by the voters, while House elections will have more incumbent-only based decision making.[13]
5. Ideology and partisanship seem to have a greater effect on assessments of Senate candidates than House candidates. In particular, House incumbents seem to be evaluated on the basis of personal qualities, voter contact activities, district servicing and the like and less on grounds of policy, ideology and the like (although see discussion below).
6. National forces such as presidential popularity and economic conditions play a relatively small part in House election outcomes (although see discussion below and the section on economic conditions and voting). House elections are primarily local events.
7. The effects of party identification on congressional, especially House, vote choice is more indirect than direct, often operating through candidate evaluation that itself is a function of personal and media contact with the candidate and recognition of the candidate. In general, candidate recognition is a function of the availability of information about the candidates; such information is more easily obtained for incumbents than for challengers, especially in the House.

Obviously not all the authors cited above would agree with all of these conclusions, but they seem to be a reasonable distillation of the current research. The above list ignores a number of other mechanisms affecting incumbent electoral performance that might be categorized as part of the strategic environment. Jacobson and Kernell (1981, 1982) argue that would-be candidates for Congress make their decisions about whether to run on the basis of the likely conditions that will exist at election time. In particular, if national economic conditions and presidential popularity are seen to favor the President's party nine months to a year before the election, then his party will attract highly qualified challengers. Likewise, if things seem bleak for the President's party, then the opposition is likely to attract strong challengers. Hence given what was said earlier about the electoral importance of the quality of the challenger, the Jacobson and Kernell thesis has much to say about the outcome of the November election.[14] Note that their argument views the impact of national economic conditions and presidential popularity on vote to be an indirect one mediated by the quality of the challenger emerging under differing economic conditions.

Payne (1980; 1982) also suggests a strategic component to congressional election outcomes. He argues that House members with aspirations to higher elective office work harder to increase their House electoral margins which may serve as a boost to their prospects for electoral advancement. Payne argues more generally that the personal election advantage of House incumbents has increased, particularly for the ambitious, upwardly mobile, publicity seeking representative who is successful in building a personal following. Payne suggests that one reason for the increase in incumbent's success may be a compositional change in House membership, that today a higher proportion of representatives are ambitious publicity seekers who act to enhance their electoral fortunes.

Issue and Ideology in Congressional Elections

Because they are scarce information, candidate-centered contests, the amount of issue voting in congressional elections is low. Mann and Wolfinger (1980) report on the basis of the 1978 CPS survey that "only 15% of all voters remembered how their representative voted on any bill in the past couple of years. Fewer than half could say whether they generally agreed or disagreed with the way that representative voted in Washington" (p. 629). In general, only a very small proportion of the open-ended comments about incumbents concerned their voting record and these were largely favorable. Hill and Hurley (1980) reach similar conclusions about the low level of issue awareness of the electorate, although they attribute part of the blame for this situation to the lack of clarity and distinctiveness of the representative's issue positions. Uslaner (1980) tried to assess what the maximum impact of issues might be under conditions most favorable to issue voting and generally concluded that House members had little to fear on issues, although there was some chance that issues could defeat an incumbent when confronted by a well financed challenger. For the Senate, however, Uslaner claimed that issues had greater electoral consequences for incumbents. An analysis of the 1974 congressional elections (Conway & Wyckoff, 1980) found that candidate variables and party identification were much more important influences on vote choice than were Watergate and economic attitudes. Hence, it seems that issues will normally play a very limited direct role in vote choice in congressional elections, especially for the House. Of course, salient issues can arise and be exploited effectively, particularly by well funded candidates, so that the potential for major issue effects remains.[15]

With respect to ideology, the available evidence suggests effects some-what stronger than those for issues. Abramowitz (1980; 1981) found that in Senate races in 1978 in which ideological clarity between the candidates was high, ideology had a substantial impact on vote decision; ideology played a small role in House elections. In particular, ideological proximity affected the Senate vote choice among independents and supporters of the challenger's party; if the incumbent Senator was ideologically distant from these groups, he lost votes. Using a measure of the discrepancy between the representative's and the district's ideology, Johannes and McAdams (1981) found that such a factor had significant effects on the member's re-election prospects. Finally, Jacobson (1981), using a different measure of ideological proximity in a dif-ferently specified equation, found the effects of ideological proximity lagged far behind those of candidate and party variables.

A reasonable summary conclusion is that congressional elections are can-didate and party affairs and that issue and ideological effects are generally weaker, operating at the margins and indirectly. Conditions may arise in which specific issues may become very important, but this is the exception rather than the rule. Of course, one need not have all citizens voting on the basis of issues in order to have dramatic election effects; a little issue voting could go a long way in determining partisan control of a congressional seat.

Critique and Conclusion

The research reviewed above has told us much about the factors influ-encing vote choice in congressional elections. However, there are a number of trends in the literature that are worrisome. Foremost among these is an ex-cessive concern with statistically estimating the relative effects of numerous independent variables on such dependent variables as vote choice, candidate recognition, candidate evaluations, and others. Although ultimately we should be testing and estimating complex multivariate models, it seems that some of the current efforts are premature on a number of grounds. For exam-ple, the justification for the specification of any particular model is often weak; different structures could be posited and different results would then be obtained. Hence, the obtained estimates are very much a function of a model that itself may be questionable, which suggests that we should not place too much weight on any particular estimated coefficient.

A closely related point is that some of the literature is insensitive to the consequences of entering different numbers of different classes of predictors into an equation. For example, if one estimates an equation for vote choice that has as independent variables one measure of partisanship, one measure of issue proximity, and four measures of candidate qualities, then under *ceteris paribus* conditions it is likely that any single candidate attribute will prove to be less important than partisanship or issue proximity, mainly because its contribution is being shared with the other measures of candidate qualities. This would not be a problem if the structural model being tested were the correctly specified one, but in most instances it is not; often the models tested are very much a function of the availability of measures. This is becoming more of a problem as more information about congressional utilization of perquisites becomes available; it is very tempting to plug a new indicator into a regression equation to assess its effect. Also contributing to the prematurity of some of our model estimation is the fact that many of our indicators are only crude surrogates for the true underlying causal variable; had we been able to collect better measures, our results might have been different. Certainly much of the debate between Johannes and McAdams (1981), Fiorina (1981) and McAdams and Johannes (1981) arises from placing too much reliance on an equation whose specification and measures can be questioned.

The above argument should not be read as a blanket condemnation of equation estimation. If the aim of such research is simply to suggest possible influences and provide admittedly crude estimates of their effects, then there is no serious problem. But too often the obtained estimates are treated as demonstrating generalizable and precise relationships when in fact the results are very much a function of the model construction and measurement decisions discussed above. It seems to me that the appropriate posture is demonstrated by Jacobson (1981) who after regressing vote on numerous independent variables and finding that party identification and likes and dislikes of the candidate have the greatest explanatory power concludes ". . . the most important message of this equation is that so many different factors contribute independently to the voting decision" (p. 197).

Currently there are many efforts being made to construct and test complex models of congressional vote choice analogous to the presidential vote models discussed earlier in this paper. A common characteristic of a number of these models is positing evaluations of the candidates as the most immediate determinant of vote choice. For example, Hinckley's (1980) schematic of congressional voting has evaluation of the candidates as the sole variable impinging on the vote, while the model of Goldenberg and Traugott (1980) has relative candidate recognition, relative candidate evaluation and party identification as the three direct determinants of the vote with party identification having an indirect effect through its impact on relative candidate evaluations. The Ragsdale (1981) model posits incumbent evaluations and challenger evaluations as the direct determinants of vote and allows for a reciprocal linkage between these evaluations. In turn, each candidate's evaluations are shaped by contact, media and recognition. Although these models differ in their various antecedents, at heart they are all candidate-centered models of congressional voting. Undoubtedly, the next phase of congressional voting research will be an elaboration and further testing of such decision-making models.

CONCLUSION

Some Methodological Considerations

We are witnessing in voting behavior research the ever increasing use of complex statistical procedures. More specifically, the field of electoral behavior has moved sharply in the direction of constructing and estimating explicit causal models of vote choice. This development means that future investigators will need a firm foundation in econometric estimation techniques in order to keep on top of the literature. Yet we should remain sensitive to the limitations of our statistical techniques and to those factors that can generate misleading results. Of particular importance is model specification; we must recognize that the estimation of poorly specified models may yield nonsense results, no matter how powerful the estimation procedure is. Since specification is a theoretical and substantive matter, it behooves us to devote more thought and care to model construction and not to jump too quickly to data analysis.

In a related vein, we should be careful not to frame our research questions in terms of false choices, e.g., is it incumbency or is it party identification? We need to employ analysis procedures such as nonrecursive path analysis that do not by assumption rule out plausible alternatives. And we should remind ourselves that many of the effects of interest to us may be small in magnitude but still of great substantive importance. Since many elections are decided in the 60%-40% range, small effects can dramatically alter election outcomes.

Finally, we must be careful that progress in a field not be overly data-driven and that we not allow ourselves to become trapped by specific measurement strategies. It is clear that the issue voting debate and congressional elections research have profited tremendously by the availability of carefully thought out new measures. However, we must continually ask ourselves whether current measurement strategies are hindering or helping us in addressing questions on our research agenda. And we must recognize that for certain questions such as the effects of economic conditions and the referendum interpretation of midterm elections, our models and data are inadequate in many respects and that research projects explicitly designed to study these topics are required.

Some Substantive Considerations

It seems clear that presidential and congressional elections have increasingly come to be viewed as candidate dominated choices with the effects of other variables such as party identification and issue attitudes increasingly viewed as being channeled through candidate evaluations. In particular, it appears that voters' perceptions of the performance of the presidential incumbent, and their relative awareness of the incumbent versus the challenger in congressional races, are major factors shaping election outcomes. Thus many observers argue that the Ford and Carter defeats in 1976 and 1980 resulted from negative evaluations of how these two incumbents had handled or mishandled the nation's economy.

This emphasis on candidate centered voting can be subsumed under the retrospective voting model, the core element of which is that voters evaluate the performance of the incumbent administration and, if dissatisfied with that performance, remove the incumbents from office. The notion of retrospective voting has a number of features that make it appealing to scholars of elections. First, it casts the vote decision in a rational, performance-based light and hence continues the effort begun by Key to redeem the competence of the American voter. At the same time, the demands placed on the individual voter by the retrospective model are not great. All the voter need be able to do is to place the blame for bad times on the incumbent administration; there is no requirement for full and complete information nor for a Downsian calculation of the relative payoffs to be obtained from various election outcomes. Furthermore, many different factors can be analyzed under the retrospective model. Economic conditions may most often serve as the basis for retrospective voting, but other issues could certainly result in performance-based voting. In addition, the retrospective model is appealing because it forces one to think in terms of an election period longer than the post-Labor Day campaign. Indeed, under the retrospective model, the entire administration of the incumbent may be evaluated, thereby injecting into the campaign questions of governance and performance. Finally, the retrospective model forces one to conceptualize candidate evaluations as central to the vote decision rather than to view candidate attitudes as a residual category to be considered after the effects of partisanship and issues are removed.

These latter three reasons are to me the payoff in utilizing the retrospective voting model. However, I think the first reason is potentially too beguiling to political analysts trying to salvage the voter's reputation and competence in democratic theory. One needs to be careful not to make too great claims for a democratic political system, even when it does satisfy the requirements of retrospective voting. Years ago, Joseph Schumpeter (1950) formulated a procedural conceptualization of democracy that fits the retrospective model well. Schumpeter wrote "the democratic method is that institutional arrangement for arriving at political decisions in which individuals acquire the power to decide by means of a competitive struggle for the people's vote" (p. 26). For Schumpeter, the key requirement of a democratic system was that there be free and open competition among competing sets of elites. If this condition was met, then voters dissatisfied with the performance of the incumbents could oust them at the next election. For Schumpeter, the primary function of the citizen's vote was to produce a government that in turn would have substantial discretion in formulating and instituting policies subject to the electorate's retrospective judgment at the next election. Hence, under Schumpeter's view, elections are not prospective affairs in which voters give policy mandates to guide the victorious party. Instead, the policy consequences of an election are quite minimal and the role of the voter very limited. Thus, the retrospective voting model, which clearly fits under the Schumpeter perspective, should not be viewed too optimistically as the salvation of the individual citizen. The retrospective model and Schumpeter's procedural view of democracy do not require much competence on the part of the voters.

In contrast to the retrospective model is a prospective model in which citizens are required to evaluate the various payoffs from the election of one party versus another and to choose appropriately among these choices. If such a model indeed operated in the real world, then the rational independent citizen of classical democratic theory would truly have been resuscitated. Moreover, with prospective voting, the possibility of electoral mandates and citizen influence is obviously enhanced, a sharp contrast to the retrospective model in which the victorious candidate and party have a nearly free rein in how they will address the problems that proved the undoing of the previous incumbent administration. Hence, the retrospective model does not necessarily elevate the citizen to a position of great influence and competence as its proponents might suggest. Citizens may select the government, but the policy implications of their vote beyond a rejection of the incumbents are difficult to ascertain.

There is an additional concern with performance-based explanations of voting and that is the potentiality for circularity. Although none of the authors discussed in this essay have fallen into the trap, it becomes a temptation to move from the election outcome back to an explanation of that outcome. That is, if the incumbent wins, the electorate must have been satisfied with the performance of the ins. One needs to be careful to keep the independent and dependent phenomena separate. In studying retrospective voting, the analyst will need to be careful to present evidence that demonstrates that evaluations of the incumbent had a causal impact on the election outcome.

In conclusion, the ferment that currently exists in the study of voting behavior is an indication that this is a subfield in which important work remains to be done. The prominence of new conceptualizations and models, the utilization of sophisticated analysis procedures, the employment of complex research designs, and the expansion of data sources all bode well for driving the field to a fuller understanding of the reasons for individual vote decisions and of the collective consequences of these individual choices.

FOOTNOTES

1. In his commentary on this paper, Warren Miller (1982) argues that in many respects the field of voting behavior does not merit the label of science. He attributes this to the fact that scholars in the field often treat questions of measurement, design, methodology, and substantive theory in a disjointed and discrete fashion. Such practices yield a portrait of confusion and the apparent non-cumulativity of research findings in the field even when results may actually be complementary.

2. The decision to emphasize the social psychological tradition, of course, results in the neglect of other important current strands of electoral behavior research. One notable omission is the rational choice perspective in which the voter is viewed as a rational actor choosing among party and candidate alternatives on the basis of the likely policy payoffs to be received by the election of one party vs. another. This approach portrays the voting act as more purposive, policy-oriented and rational than does the social psychological tradition.

3. Another criterion which delimits this paper is my decision to focus primarily on published literature since these works have in most cases undergone a peer review process which means that to some degree they represent a collective judgment about the state of the field. But, one cautionary note is in order. Having recently completed a three-year stint as co-editor of *American Journal of Political Science*, it seems to me that there is in the review and editorial process a bias that results in the published literature presenting a portrait of greater ferment and controversy in the field than does the unpublished literature. This occurs simply because the substantive results of many meritorious papers confirm the prevailing wisdom and

hence receive editorial decisions that their findings are not of sufficient importance to justify the allocation of always scarce journal space.

One could construct an argument that papers challenging the conventional wisdom would have greater difficulty in surviving the review and editorial process, particularly if such papers were disproportionately reviewed by scholars representing the prevailing wisdom. However, my distinct impression is that this is not the case, although perhaps had the challenge to the prevailing wisdom been more fundamental and threatening, reviewers would have been more likely to defend that status quo. Nevertheless, I am concerned that the one paper challenging the current wisdom is more likely to receive a wider audience through publication than the two or three or whatever number of papers which confirm the current wisdom.

4. Models generally contain two classes of variables—exogenous and endogenous. Exogenous variables are those that do not depend on any other *measured* variables in the model; endogenous variables are those that are influenced by other measured variables. Any model can be represented by a set of structural equations where there is one equation for each endogenous variable in the model. Each equation simply states which variables directly affect the endogenous variable in question. It is the coefficients of each equation that are to be estimated and the determination of whether a model is identified is made on an equation by equation basis. That is, it is possible that certain equations will be identified and hence be estimable, while other equations will be unidentified and not subject to estimation. See Asher (1983) for a fuller discussion of these points.

5. Proximity measures have been used widely in the past decade to study the impact of issues on vote choice. In essence, a proximity measure captures not only where the voter stands on an issue, but also where the voter perceives the candidate to stand on that issue. Thus, one can calculate a distance between the voter's and the candidate's stances; presumably the closer the voter is to the candidate, the greater the likelihood of voting for that candidate.

6. The fact that some party shifts are observed calls into question assertions about the early learning of partisanship and its subsequent intensification over the life cycle. The question of whether party identification intensifies over the life cycle or whether the observed age cohort differences in partisan intensities is a function of differential generational experiences has sparked a major controversy in recent years. It will not, however, be dealt with in this paper. See the work of Abramson (1976; 1979) and Converse (1976; 1979) for the definitive statement of the contending positions about this controversy.

7. Shively (1977) argues that independent leaners should be classified as independents despite the fact that they exhibit high loyalty to their party's nominees. He suggests the leaners are true independents who in response to the second part of the traditional party identification question are simply reporting their intended November vote. Hence, leaners under this notion would, of course, exhibit strong loyalty to a party. Shively (1980, pp. 234-235) presents additional evidence on behalf of treating leaners as independents; over time the "partisanship" of leaners seems to change in response to a change in vote intention whereas for genuine partisans, the rate at which their partisanship changed in the presence of changes in vote preference was much lower. Thus Shively argues that leaners do not behave very much like partisans and therefore should be treated as independents, although he readily admits that the evidence is not overwhelming.

There is additional evidence supporting the notion that leaners be treated as independents rather than as partisans. For example, Abramson *et al.* (1982, p. 17) show that in voting for Congress, independent leaners are less likely than weak partisans to support candidates of the party to which they lean. Moreover, a number of studies including Weisberg (1980) indicate that independent leaners are more likely to view themselves as Independents rather than as partisans. Finally, a number of socialization studies including Abramson (1983, p. 100) have shown that the transmission of partisanship from parents to children is more successful for weak partisans than for independent leaners.

Other analysts (Miller & Miller, 1977) view leaners more as covert partisans rather than true independents. With respect to evaluations of political stimuli and measures of partisan behavior, leaners often resemble weak and even strong partisans more than they resemble pure independents. For example, Wolfinger *et al.* (1976, p. 151) and Keith et al. (1977) show that in voting for President, independent leaners are more similar to strong partisans than they are to weak identifiers. Moreover, Asher (1980) and Keith *et al.* have challenged Shively's notions that leaning is simply an expression of vote intention. Keith *et al.* note that the number of cases on which Shively's conclusions rest is very small and that one reason for this is that most leaners were very stable in their vote intentions over two year periods. Asher (1980, p. 61) found that leaners were very stable in the direction of their leaning over a four year period; in some cases, vote intention changed over time but the direction of leaning did not. More importantly, Asher argued that if leaning is simply a matter of vote intention, then the frequency of independent leaners should increase as Election Day draws near and more independents have made their vote decision. However, an analysis of the distribution of partisanship in 1976 by time of interview showed no increase in the proportion of independent leaners among those respondents interviewed closer to Election Day. Hence, Asher argues that for purposes of understanding voting behavior, leaners should be treated as partisans.

Undoubtedly, the leaning category is actually a mix of partisans and independents and the problem is to sort out the relative size of the two groups. Clearly the traditional party identification measure encounters its greatest difficulty in the leaning category, a point emphasized further in the text.

8. Miller (1982) criticizes some of the recent literature on party identification on the grounds that it is not true to the conceptual meaning of the original measure. He asserts that one can always improve explained variance, but that this is not the overriding criterion in choosing one measure over another. Miller argues that many of the proposed revisions in the measurement of partisanship do not improve on the original measure's ability to capture the enduring long term component of party identification. Instead, according to Miller, the new measures do well in accounting for variance because they incorporate short term factors which were not part of the original conceptualization of party identification. Miller's argument parallels Fiorina's (1981) discussion in the text.

9. There are many additional points that can be made about the strengths and weaknesses of different data sources. The NES/CPS surveys are useful for tracing candidate awareness at the national level. But since the growth in candidate awareness is probably tied to the reporting of specific primary election outcomes, the timing of the NES/CPS surveys is not very suitable for picking up specific election effects. Any effort to use the NES/CPS surveys to study the reasons for vote choice in a particular primary or cluster of primaries would run into small N problems once respondents living in non-primary states and nonvoting respondents in primary states are removed from the analysis. In addition, given that the NES/CPS surveys were conducted in February, April and June, many citizens who did vote in particular primaries may have been interviewed weeks after their primary participation. Hence, their interview responses may have been shaped more by media reports of subsequent primaries and campaign events than by factors that affected their primary vote at the time it was cast.

The exit polls done by CBS/New York Times are tied to specific primaries and are useful for assessing the determinants of vote choice including the effects of specific campaign appeals made by the candidates. By definition, these polls cannot be used to study the determinants of turnout since only voters are interviewed. The exit polls include a very small set of measures and some of these are not repeated in surveys throughout the primary season; this limits the over time comparisons that can be made. Obviously, the various exit polls done in each state cannot be panels; the national surveys done by CBS/New York Times are also not panels. Without panel data, all one can do is assess the net amount of attitude change that has occurred and not the gross amount.

Repeated within-state surveys are useful for they enable one to trace the growth of candidate awareness and to assess the effects of media reporting of that state's primary. Although one must obviously be wary of generalizing from any single state, repeated measures within the same state might be a nice compromise between the NES/CPS and CBS/New York Times designs discussed above. It certainly would limit costs and would enable one to map the development of candidate awareness resulting from media reporting of other states' primaries and from the actual primary campaign effort made in that particular state. For a detailed discussion of the advantages and limitations of various data sources and for an excellent example of the creative use of multiple data sources to address the variety of substantive questions mentioned in the text, see Zukin and Keeter (1983).

10. This asymmetry notion has its analog in studies of the effects of presidential popularity on midterm voting. Kernell (1977) proposed a negative voting model such that a decline in presidential popularity hurts his party more than an improvement helps. Other studies on the effects of presidential popularity yield mixed results. Piereson (1975) found that evaluations of the President affected the vote of independents, not only for congressional offices, but also for state and local contests. Ragsdale (1980) however finds that presidential popularity has only weak effects on midterm elections when compared to other influences such as party identification and perceptions of the candidates. She argues that her analysis is preferable to others since her model is better specified than others due to its inclusion of other relevant variables.

11. Sigelman and Tsai (1981) present more specific criticisms of the research on the effects of personal financial status. They argue that too many studies search only for symmetric effects when the influence of economic variables could be asymmetric, depending upon whether the economy is improving or declining. They also argue that the typical question tapping personal financial situation—some perception of one's changing financial status—is not highly correlated with one's level of financial satisfaction. They try to remedy some of these deficiencies in their own study, but still find few effects of personal financial situation.

12. A similar argument has been made by Nelson (1978).

13. In a personal communication, Raymond Wolfinger emphasizes that caution should be exercised in making comparisons between the House and the Senate, mainly because a variety of problems exist with the Senate election data in the 1978 NES/CPS survey. Wolfinger points out that the sample entirely excluded a number of states with Senate elections and in some other states with Senate elections had a very small number of respondents. Moreover, most of the sample that voted in a Senate election in which an incumbent was running came from three states where GOP incumbents were challenged by strong Democratic opponents. Hence, the findings based on the Senate data may be misleading, particularly since a number of lop-sided contests in which the challenger fared poorly were not included in the sample.

14. Jacobson and Kernell (1982) add an intriguing party differential to their thesis. Since the Republican Party has been highly successful in fund raising and in providing support for its challengers, the willingness of Republican challengers to seek office should be less dependent on national conditions. Hence their argument would predict low net losses for the GOP in 1982, despite the poor state of the economy, in part because of the high quality of the Republican candidates. Moreover, the earlier work of Jacobson (1978, 1980) indicates that sufficient expenditures can purchase for the challenger a level of name recognition comparable to that for the incumbent. In general, the gains from campaign spending are greater for challengers than for incumbents. Hence, the prosperity of the GOP seemed to bode well for its challengers in 1982. In fact, Republican challengers did not fare well in 1982; only one challenger was successful in knocking off a Democratic incumbent. Nevertheless, the Jacobson and Kernell thesis is intriguing, although it may become less relevant should the national Democratic Party be successful in improving its fund raising and candidate support activities.
15. Songer (1981) presents evidence showing high awareness of the voting stands of congressmen in two Oklahoma districts. However, this evidence is not clearly linked to voting and hence says little directly about issue voting.

REFERENCES

Abramowitz, Alan I. A comparison of voting for U.S. Senator and Representative in 1978. *American Political Science Review,* 1980, *74,* 633-640.

Abramowitz, Alan I. Choices and echoes in the 1978 U.S. Senate elections: A research note. *American Journal of Political Science,* 1981, *25,* 112-118.

Abramson, Paul R. Generational change and the decline of party identification in America: 1952-1974. *American Political Science Review,* 1976, *70,* 469-478.

Abramson, Paul R. Developing party identification: A further examination of life-cycle, generational, and period effects. *American Journal of Political Science,* 1979, *23,* 78-96.

Abramson, Paul R. *Political attitudes in America.* San Francisco: W.H. Freeman and Company, 1983.

Abramson, Paul R., Aldrich, John H. & Rohde, David W. *Change and continuity in the 1980 elections.* Washington, D.C.: Congressional Quarterly Press, 1982.

Aldrich, John H., Niemi, Richard G., Rabinowitz, George, & Rohde, David W. The measurement of public opinion about public policy: A report on some new issue question formats. *American Journal of Political Science,* 1982, *26,* 391-414.

Alford, John R. & Hibbing, John R. Increased incumbency advantage in the House. *Journal of Politics,* 1981, *43,* 1042-1061.

Arcelus, Francisco & Meltzer, Allan H. The effect of aggregate economic variables on Congressional elections. *American Political Science Review,* 1975, *69,* 1232-1239.

Asher, Herbert B. *Presidential elections and American politics* (rev. ed.). Homewood, IL: The Dorsey Press, 1980.

Asher, Herbert B. *Causal modeling* (2nd ed.). Beverly Hills and London: Sage Publications, Inc., 1983.

Berelson, Bernard R., Lazarsfeld, Paul F., & McPhee, William N. *Voting.* Chicago: University of Chicago Press, 1954.

Bishop, George F., Oldendick, Robert W. & Tuchfarber, Alfred J. Experiments in filtering political opinions. *Political Behavior,* 1980, *2,* 339-369.

Bishop, George F., Oldendick, Robert W., Tuchfarber, Alfred J. & Bennett, Stephen E. Effects of opinion filtering and opinion floating: Evidence from a secondary analysis. *Political Methodology,* 1979, *6,* 293-309.

Bishop, George F., Tuchfarber, Alfred J., & Oldendick, Robert W. Change in the structure of American political attitudes: The nagging question of question wording. *American Journal of Political Science*, 1978, *22*, 250-269.

Bishop, George F., Oldendick, Robert W. & Tuchfarber, Alfred J. Effects of question wording and format on political attitude consistency. *Public Opinion Quarterly*, 1978, *42*, 81-92.

Bloom, Howard S. & Price, H. Douglas. Voter response to short-run economic conditions: The asymmetric effect of prosperity and recession. *American Political Science Review*, 1975, *69*, 1240-1254.

Born, Richard. Perquisite employment in the U.S. House of Representatives, 1960-1976: The influence of generational change. *American Politics Quarterly*, 1982, *10*, 347-362.

Brody, Richard A. Stability and change in party identification: Presidential to off-years. Paper delivered at the 1977 Annual Meeting of the American Political Science Association; Washington, D.C., September 1-4, 1977.

Brody, Richard A. & Page, Benjamin I. Comment: The assessment of policy voting. *American Political Science Review*, 1972, *66*, 450-458.

Campbell, Angus. Surge and decline: A study of electoral change. In Angus Campbell *et al. Elections and the political order.* New York: John Wiley and Sons, 1966.

Campbell, Angus, Converse, Philip E. Miller, Warren E. & Stokes, Donald E. *The American voter.* New York: John Wiley and Sons, 1960.

Campbell, Angus, Gurin, Gerald, & Miller, Warren E. *The voter decides.* Evanston, IL: Row, Peterson, 1954.

Carmines, Edward G. & Stimson, James A. The two faces of issue voting. *American Political Science Review*, 1980, *74*, 78-91.

Claggett, William. Partisan acquisition versus partisan intensity: Life-cycle, generation, and period effects, 1952-1976. *American Journal of Political Science*, 1981, *25*, 193-214.

Collie, Melissa P. Incumbency, electoral safety and turnover in the House of Representatives, 1952-1976. *American Political Science Review*, 1981, *75*, 119-131.

Converse, Philip E. Public opinion and voting behavior. In Fred I. Greenstein & Nelson W. Polsby (Eds.). *NonGovernmental politics, handbook of political science* (Volume 4). Reading, MA: Addison-Wesley Publishing Company, 1975.

Converse, Philip E. *The dynamics of party support: Cohort-analyzing party identification.* Beverly Hills and London: Sage Publications, Inc., 1976.

Converse, Philip E. Rejoinder to Abramson. *American Journal of Political Science*, 1979, *23*, 97-100.

Converse, Philip E. & Markus, Gregory B. Plus ca change. . .: The new CPS election study panel. *American Political Science Review*, 1979, *73*, 32-49.

Conway, M. Margaret. Political participation in midterm congressional elections: Attitudinal and social characteristics during the 1970's. *American Politics Quarterly*, 1981, *9*, 221-244.

Conway, M. Margaret & Wyckoff, Mikel L. Voter choice in the 1974 congressional elections. *American Politics Quarterly*, 1980, *8*, 3-13.

Cover, Albert D. One good term deserves another: The advantage of incumbency in congressional elections. *American Journal of Political Science*, 1977, *21*, 523-541.

Cover, Albert D. & Brumberg, Bruce S. Baby books and ballots: The impact of congressional mail on constituent opinion. *American Political Science Review*, 1982, *76*, 347-359.

Cover, Albert D. & Mayhew, David R. Congressional dynamics and the decline of competitive congressional elections. In Larry Dodd & Bruce Oppenheimer (Eds.). *Congress reconsidered* (sec. ed.). Washington, D.C.: Congressional Quarterly, 1981.

Dennis, Jack. On being an independent partisan supporter. Paper presented at the 1981 Annual Meeting of the Midwest Political Science Association, Cincinnati, April, 1981. (a)

Dennis, Jack. Some properties of measures of partisanship. Paper presented at the 1981 Annual Meeting of the American Political Science Association, New York, September, 1981. (b)

Dennis, Jack. New measures of partisanship in models of voting. Paper presented at the 1982 Annual Meeting of the Midwest Political Science Association, Milwaukee, April, 1982.

Dreyer, Edward C. Change in stability and party identification. *Journal of Politics*, 1973, *35*, 712-722.

Edwards, George C., III. The impact of presidential coattails on outcomes of congressional elections. *American Politics Quarterly*, 1979, *7*, 94-108.

Epstein, Laurily K. & Frankovic, Kathleen A. Casework and electoral margins: Insurance is prudent. *Polity*, 1982, *14*, 691-700.

Erikson, Robert S. The advantage of incumbency in congressional elections. *Polity*, 1971, *3*, 395-405.

Erikson, Robert S. Is there such a thing as a safe seat? *Polity*, 1976, *9*, 623-632.

Ferejohn, John A. On the decline of competition in congressional elections. *American Political Science Review*, 1977, *71*, 166-176.

Fiorina, Morris P. Partisan loyalty and the six component model. *Political Methodology*, 1976, *3*, 7-18.

Fiorina, Morris P. The case of the vanishing marginals: The bureaucracy did it. *American Political Science Review*, 1977, *71*, 177-181. (a)

Fiorina, Morris P. *Congress: Keystone of the Washington establishment*. New Haven: Yale University Press, 1977. (b)

Fiorina, Morris P. An outline for a model of party choice. *American Journal of Political Science*, 1977, *21*, 601-625. (c)

Fiorina, Morris P. Economic retrospective voting in American national elections: A micro-analysis. *American Journal of Political Science*, 1978, 22, 426-443.

Fiorina, Morris P. *Retrospective voting in American national elections*. New Haven and London: Yale University Press, 1981. (a)

Fiorina, Morris P. Some problems in studying the effects of resource allocation in congressional elections. *American Journal of Political Science*, 1981, *25*, 543-567. (b)

Fisher, Franklin M. The choice of instrumental variables in the estimation of economy-wide econometric models. In H. M. Blalock, Jr. (Ed.). *Causal models in the social sciences*. Chicago: Aldine-Atherton, 1971.

Fowler, Linda L. Candidate perceptions of electoral coalitions. *American Politics Quarterly*, 1980, *8*, 483-494.

Goldberg, Arthur S. Discerning a causal pattern among data on voting behavior. *American Political Science Review*, 1966, *60*, 913-922.

Goldenberg, Edie N. & Traugott, Michael W. Congressional campaign effects on candidate recognition and evaluation. *Political Behavior*, 1980, *2*, 61-90.

Goldenberg, Edie N. & Traugott, Michael W. Normal vote analysis of U.S. congressional elections. *Legislative Studies Quarterly*, 1981, *6*, 247-258.

Goodman, Saul & Kramer, Gerald H. Comment on Arcelus and Meltzer. *American Political Science Review*, 1975, *69*, 1255-1265.

Hartwig, Frederick, Jenkins, William R. & Temchin, Earl M. Variability in electoral behavior: The 1960, 1968, and 1976 elections. *American Journal of Political Science*, 1980, *24*, 553-558.

Hibbing, John R. & Alford, John R. The electoral impact of economic conditions: Who is held responsible? *American Journal of Political Science*, 1981, *25*, 423-439.

Hinckley, Barbara. Issues, information costs, and congressional elections. *American Politics Quarterly*, 1976, *4*, 131-152.

Hinckley, Barbara. The American voter in congressional elections. *American Political Science Review*, 1980, *74*, 641-650. (a)

Hinckley, Barbara. House reelections and Senate defeats: The role of the challenger. *British Journal of Political Science*, 1980, *10*, 441-460. (b)

Hinckley, Barbara. *Congressional elections*. Washington, D.C.: Congressional Quarterly Press, 1981.

Hinckley, Barbara, Hofstetter, C. Richard & Kessel, John H. Information and the vote: A comparative election study. *American Politics Quarterly*, 1974, 2, 131-153.

Howell, Susan E. The behavioral component of changing partisanship. *American Politics Quarterly*, 1980, *8*, 279-302.

Howell, Susan E. Short term forces and changing partisanship. *Political Behavior*, 1981, *3*, 163-180.

Hurley, Patricia A. & Hill, Kim Quaile. The prospects for issue-voting in contemporary congressional elections: An assessment of citizen awareness and representation. *American Politics Quarterly*, 1980, *8*, 425-448.

Jackson, John E. Issues, party choices, and presidential votes. *American Journal of Political Science*, 1975, *19*, 161-185.

Jacobson, Gary C. The effects of campaign spending in congressional elections. *American Political Science Review*, 1978, *72*, 469-491.

Jacobson, Gary C. *Money in congressional elections*. New Haven: Yale University Press, 1980.

Jacobson, Gary C. Incumbents' advantages in the 1978 congressional elections. *Legislative Studies Quarterly*, 1981, *6*, 183-200.

Jacobson, Gary C. *The politics of congressional elections*. Boston and Toronto: Little, Brown and Company, 1983.

Jacobson, Gary C. & Kernell, Samuel. *Strategy and choice in congressional elections*. New Haven and London: Yale University Press, 1981.

Jacobson, Gary C. & Kernell, Samuel. Strategy and choice in the 1982 congressional elections. *PS*, 1982, *15*, 423-430.

Jennings, M. Kent & Niemi, Richard G. The persistence of political orientations: An over-time analysis of two generations. *British Journal of Political Science*, 1978, *8*, 333-363.

Jensen, Richard. American election analysis: A case history of methodological diffusion. In Seymour Martin Lipset (Ed.). *Politics and the social sciences*. New York 1969.

Johannes, John R., & McAdams, John C. The congressional incumbency effect: Is it casework, policy compatibility, or something else? An examination of the 1978 election. *American Journal of Political Science*, 1981, *25*, 512-542.

Jöreskog, Karl G. A general method for analysis of covariance structures. *Biometrika*, 1970, *57*, 239-251.

Jöreskog, Karl G. A general method for estimating a linear structural equation system. In Arthur S. Goldberg & Otis Dudley Duncan (Eds.). *Structural equation models in the social sciences*. New York: Seminar Press, 1973.

Jöreskog, Karl G. & Sörbom, Dag. *LISREL IV—A general computer program for estimation of a linear structural system by maximum likelihood methods*. Chicago: National Education Resources, 1978.

Keeter, Scott & Zukin, Cliff. New images and old horses: The origin and development of citizens' image of presidential candidates. In Doris A. Graber (Ed.). *The President and the public*. Philadelphia: Institute for the Study of Human Issues, 1982.

Keith, Bruce E., Magleby, David B., Nelson, Candice J., Orr, Elizabeth, Westlye, Mark, & Wolfinger, Raymond E. The myth of the independent voter. Paper presented at the Annual Meeting of the American Political Science Association, Washington, D.C., September 1-4, 1977.

Kelley, Stanley, Jr. & Mirer, Thad W. The simple act of voting. *American Political Science Review*, 1974, *68*, 572-591.

Kenski, Henry C. The impact of unemployment on congressional elections, 1958-1974: A cross-sectional analysis. *American Politics Quarterly*, 1979, *7*, 147-154.

Kernell, Samuel. Presidential popularity and negative voting: An alternative explanation of the midterm congressional decline of the President's party. *American Political Science Review*, 1977, *71*, 44-66.

Kessel, John H. Comment: The issues in issue voting. *American Political Science Review*, 1972, *66*, 459-465.

Kessel, John H. *Presidential campaign politics: Coalition strategies and citizen response*. Homewood, IL: The Dorsey Press, 1980.

Key, V. O., Jr. *The responsible electorate*. Cambridge, MA: Belknap Press of Harvard University Press, 1966.

Kiewiet, D. Roderick. Policy-oriented voting in response to economic issues. *American Political Science Review*, 1981, *75*, 448-459.

Kinder, Donald R. & Abelson, Robert P. Appraising presidential candidates: Personality and affect in the 1980 campaign. Paper presented at the Annual Meeting of the American Political Science Association, New York City, September 3-6, 1981.

Kinder, Donald R. & Kiewiet, D. Roderick. Economic discontent and political behavior: The role of personal grievances and collective economic judgments in congressional voting. *American Journal of Political Science*, 1979, *23*, 495-527.

Kinder, Donald R. & Sears, David O. Political behavior. In E. Aronson & G. Lindsey (Eds.). *The handbook of social psychology* (3rd ed.). Reading, MA: Addison Wesley, 1982.

Kirkpatrick, Samuel A., Lyons, William & Fitzgerald, Michael. Candidates, parties, and issues in the American electorate. *American Politics Quarterly*, 1975, *3*, 247-284.

Klorman, Ricardo. Trend in personal finances and the vote. *Public Opinion Quarterly*, 1978, *33*, 31-48.

Kramer, Gerald H. Short-term fluctuations in U.S. voting behavior, 1896-1964. *American Political Science Review*, 1971, *65*, 131-143.

Krehbiel, Keith & Wright, John R. The incumbency effect in congressional elections: A test of two explanations. *American Journal of Political Science*, 1983 forthcoming.

Kritzer, Herbert M. Problems in the use of two stage least squares: Standardization of coefficients and multicollinearity. *Political Methodology*, 1976, *3*, 71-93.

Kuklinski, James H. & West, Darrell M. Economic expectations and voting behavior in United States House and Senate elections. *American Political Science Review*, 1981, *75*, 436-447.

Maggiotto, Michael A. & Piereson, James E. Partisan identification and electoral choice: The hostility hypothesis. *American Journal of Political Science*, 1977, *21*, 745-767.

Maisel, L. Sandy. Congressional elections in 1978: The road to nomination, the road to election. *American Politics Quarterly*, 1981, *9*, 23-47.

Mann, Thomas E. & Wolfinger, Raymond E. Candidates and parties in congressional elections. *American Political Science Review*, 1980, *74*, 617-632.

Markus, Gregory B. & Converse, Philip E. A dynamic simultaneous equation model of electoral choice. *American Political Science Review*, 1979, *73*, 1055-1070.

Mayhew, David R. Congressional elections: The case of the vanishing marginals. *Polity*, 1974, *6*, 295-317.

Mayhew, David R. *Congress: The electoral connection*. New Haven: Yale University Press, 1974. (b)

McAdams, John C. & Johannes, John R. Does casework matter; A reply to Professor Fiorina. *American Journal of Political Science*, 1981, *25*, 581-604.

Miller, Arthur H. & Miller, Warren E. Partisanship and performance: Rational choice in the 1976 presidential election. Paper presented at the 1977 Annual Meeting of the American Political Science Association, Washington, D.C., September 1-4, 1977.

Miller, Arthur H., Wattenberg, Martin P. & Malanchuk, Oksana. Cognitive representations of candidate assessments. Paper delivered at the 1981 Annual Meeting of the American Political Science Association, Denver, Colorado, September 2-5, 1982.

Miller, Warren E. Commentary on 'Voting behavior research in the 1980s: An examination of some old and new problem areas.' Paper presented at the Annual Meeting of the American Political Science Association, Denver, Colorado, September 4, 1982.

Miller, Warren E. & Shanks, J. Merrill. Policy directions and presidential leadership: Alternative interpretations of the 1980 presidential election. *British Journal of Political Science*, 1982, *12*, 299-356.

Miller, Warren E. & Stokes, Donald E. Constituency influence in Congress. *American Political Science Review*, 1963, *57*, 45-57.

Nelson, Candice J. The effect of incumbency on voting in congressional elections, 1964-1974. *Political Science Quarterly*, 1978, *93*, 665-678

Nie, Norman H., Verba, Sidney & Petrocik, John R. *The changing American voter*. Cambridge, MA: Harvard University Press, 1976.

Niemi, Richard G., Katz, Richard S. & Newman, David. Reconstructing past partisanship: The failure of the party identification recall questions. *American Journal of Political Science*, 1980, *24*, 633-651.

Niemi, Richard G. & Weisberg, Herbert F. The study of voting and elections. In Richard G. Niemi & Herbert F. Weisberg (Eds.). *Controversies in American voting behavior*. San Francisco: W.H. Freeman and Company, 1976.

Nimmo, Dan & Savage, Robert L. *Candidates and their images*. Pacific Palisades, CA: Goodyear Publishing Company, Inc., 1976.

Norrander, Barbara K. *Mass behavior in presidential primaries: Individual and structural determinants*. Ph.D. dissertation, The Ohio State University, 1982.

Owens, John R. & Olson, Edward C. Economic fluctuations and congressional elections. *American Journal of Political Science*, 1980, *24*, 469-493.

Page, Benjamin I. & Jones, Calvin C. Reciprocal effects of policy preferences, party loyalties and the vote. *American Political Science Review*, 1979, *73*, 1071-1089.

Parker, Glenn R. The advantage of incumbency in House elections. *American Politics Quarterly*, 1980, *8*, 449-464. (a)

Parker, Glenn R. Cycles in congressional district attention. *Journal of Politics*, 1980, *42*, 540-548. (b)

Parker, Glenn R. Sources of change in congressional district attentiveness. *American Journal of Political Science*, 1980, *24*, 115-124. (c)

Parker, Glenn R. Interpreting candidate awareness in U.S. congressional elections. *Legislative Studies Quarterly*, 1981, *6*, 219-234.

Patterson, Thomas E. *The mass media election: How Americans choose their President*. New York: Praeger Publishers, 1980.

Payne, James L. The personal electoral advantage of House incumbents, 1936-1976. *American Politics Quarterly*, 1980, *8*, 465-482.

Payne, James L. Career intentions and electoral performance of members of the U.S. House. *Legislative Studies Quarterly*, 1982, *7*, 93-99.

Pierce, John C. & Sullivan, John L. An overview of the American electorate. In John C. Pierce & John L. Sullivan (Eds.). *The electorate reconsidered.* Beverly Hills and London: Sage Publications, Inc., 1980.

Piereson, James E. Presidential popularity and midterm voting at different electoral levels. *American Journal of Political Science,* 1975, *19,* 683-694.

Prewitt, Kenneth & Nie, Norman. Election studies of the Survey Research Center. *British Journal of Political Science,* 1971, *1,* 479-502.

Rabinowitz, George, Prothro, James W. & Jacoby, William. Salience as a factor in the impact of issues on candidate evaluation. *Journal of Politics,* 1982, *44,* 41-63.

Ragsdale, Lyn. The fiction of congressional elections as presidential events. *American Politics Quarterly,* 1980, *8,* 375-398.

Ragsdale, Lyn. Incumbent popularity, challenger invisibility, and congressional voters. *Legislative Studies Quarterly,* 1981, *6,* 201-218.

Rosenstone, Steven J. Economic adversity and voter turnout. *American Journal of Political Science,* 1982, *26,* 25-46.

Rossi, Peter H. Four landmarks in voting research. In Eugene Burdick & Arthur J. Brodbeck (Eds.). *American voting behavior.* New York: The Free Press, 1959.

Schulman, Mark A. & Pomper, Gerald M. Variability in electoral behavior: Longitudinal perspectives from causal modeling. *American Journal of Political Science,* 1975, *19,* 1-18.

Schumpeter, Joseph A. *Capitalism, socialism, and democracy.* New York: Harper & Brothers, Publishers, 1950.

Shabad, Goldie & Andersen, Kristi. Candidate evaluations by men and women. *Public Opinion Quarterly,* 1979, *32,* 18-35.

Shaffer, William R. Partisan loyalty and the perceptions of party, candidates and issues. *Western Political Quarterly,* 1972, *25,* 424-433.

Shaffer, William R. Rejoinder to Fiorina. *Political Methodology,* 1976, *3,* 19-26.

Shively, W. Phillips. Information costs and the partisan life cycle. Paper presented at the 1977 Annual Meeting of the American Political Science Association, Washington, D.C., August 31-September 4, 1977.

Shively, W. Phillips. The development of party identification among adults: Exploration of a functional model. *American Political Science Review,* 1979, *73,* 1039-1054.

Shively, W. Phillips. The nature of party identification: A review of recent developments. In John C. Pierce & John L. Sullivan (Eds.). *The electorate reconsidered.* Beverly Hills and London: Sage Publications, Inc., 1980.

Sigelman, Lee & Tsai, Yung-Mei. Personal finances and voting behavior: A reanalysis. *American Politics Quarterly,* 1981, *9,* 371-399.

Silbey, Joel H., Bogue, Allan G. & Flanigan, William H. Introduction. In Joel H. Silbey *et al.* (Eds.). *The history of American electoral behavior.* Princeton, N.J.: Princeton University Press, 1978.

Songer, Donald R. Voter knowledge of congressional issue positions: A reassessment. *Social Science Quarterly,* 1981, *62,* 424-431.

St. Angelo, Douglas & Dobson, Douglas. Party identification and the floating vote: Some dynamics. *American Political Science Review,* 1975, *69,* 481-490.

Stokes, Donald E. Some dynamic elements of contests for the presidency. *American Political Science Review,* 1966, *60,* 19-28.

Stokes, Donald E., Campbell, Angus, & Miller, Warren E. Components of electoral decision. *American Political Science Review,* 1958, *52,* 367-387.

Stokes, Donald E. & Miller, Warren E. Party government and the salience of Congress. *Public Opinion Quarterly,* 1962, *26,* 531-546.

Tufte, Edward R. The relationship between seats and votes in two-party systems. *American Political Science Review,* 1973, *67,* 540-554.

Tufte, Edward R. Determinants of the outcomes of midterm congressional elections. *American Political Science Review,* 1975, *69,* 812-826.

Tufte, Edward R. *Political control of the economy.* Princeton, N.J.: Princeton University Press, 1978.

Uslaner, Eric M. Ain't misbehavin': The logic of defensive issue voting strategies in congressional elections. *American Politics Quarterly,* 1981, *9,* 3-22.

Valentine, David C. & Van Wingen, John R. Partisanship, independence, and the partisan identification question. *American Politics Quarterly,* 1980, *8,* 165-186.

Weatherford, M. Stephen. Economic conditions and electoral outcomes: Class differences in the political response to recession. *American Journal of Political Science,* 1978, *22,* 917-938.

Weisberg, Herbert F. A multidimensional conceptualization of party identification. *Political Behavior,* 1980, *2,* 33-60.

Weisberg, Herbert F. Party evaluations: A theory of separate effects. Paper presented at the 1982 Annual Meeting of the Midwest Political Science Association, Milwaukee, Wisconsin, April 29-May 1, 1982.

Wolfinger, Raymond E., Rosenstone, Steven J. & McIntosh, Richard A. Presidential and congressional voters compared. *American Politics Quarterly,* 1981, *9,* 245-256.

Wolfinger, Raymond E., Shapiro, Martin & Greenstein, Fred I. *Dynamics of American politics.* Englewood Cliffs, N.J.: Prentice-Hall, 1976.

Yiannakis, Diana Evans. The grateful electorate: Casework and congressional elections. *American Journal of Political Science,* 1981, *25,* 568-580.

Zukin, Cliff & Keeter, Scott. *Citizen learning in presidential nominations.* New York: Praeger, 1983.

13

Diversity and Complexity in American Public Opinion*

Donald R. Kinder

V. O. Key once wrote that "to speak with precision of public opinion is a task not unlike coming to grips with the Holy Ghost" (1961, p. 8). Key was right. Nevertheless, my audacious purpose here is to speak with precision of what we have learned about American public opinion over the last twenty years and what we might try to learn next.

The task seems even more difficult now than Key imagined because of the dramatic events that have marked American politics through the last two decades. It has been a tumultuous time, stained by assassinations, race riots, a bleeding war abroad that provoked deep divisions at home, flagrant violations of public trust, roller-coaster economics, and more. As these events unsettled American society, so too did they challenge conventional thinking about American public opinion. Much of what we thought we knew twenty years ago is now widely regarded as false, or at least as hopelessly outdated. Controversy, not progress, seems to have been the field's most important product.

---

*An earlier version of this essay was delivered as an invited "theme" address at the 1982 Annual Meeting of the American Political Science Association, Denver, Colorado, September 1-4, 1982, under the title "Enough Already about Ideology: The Many Bases of American Public Opinion." It is drawn from a more extensive analysis of public opinion and political action, written with David O. Sears, prepared as a chapter for *The Handbook of Social Psychology* (3rd edition), G. Lindzey and E. Aronson (Editors), 1983.' At one stage or another, many people commented on the project. I thank them all, especially Robert Abelson, Paul Abramson, W. Lance Bennett, Philip Converse, Ada Finifter, Morris Fiorina, John Jackson, M. Kent Jennings, D. Roderick Kiewiet, Jon Krosnick, Richard Lau, Gregory Markus, David Mayhew, Walter Mebane, Warren Miller, Steven J. Rosenstone, Randolph Wagner, Janet A. Weiss, and Robert Weissberg. The manuscript was prepared, again and again, with great competence and good cheer by Nancy Brennan, Maureen Kozumplik, Barbara Lohr, and Joyce Meyer.

But that verdict is too easy and too cynical. As I hope to demonstrate, we have in fact learned a great deal about American public opinion, in part *because* of the turbulence of the last two decades. Indeed, the period beginning with the assassination of John Kennedy and ending with the resignation of Richard Nixon represents, from the perspective of a science of public opinion, a splendid natural experiment. Progress, not controversy, is honored and recapitulated here.

My point of departure is provided by an observation made by Walter Lippmann (1922) more than half century ago. In *Public Opinion,* Lippmann declared that the trials and tribulations of daily life are compelling in a way that politics could never be. To expect ordinary people to become absorbed in the affairs of state, wrote Lippmann, would be to demand of them an appetite for political knowledge quite peculiar, if not pathological.

Over the years, Lippmann's thesis has aged with uncommon grace. According to countless surveys spread over more than five decades, Americans are in fact indifferent to much that transpires in politics, hazy about many of its principal players, lackadaisical regarding debates that preoccupy Washington, ignorant of basic facts that the well-informed take for granted, and unsure about the policies advanced by presidents and presidential hopefuls (Kinder & Sears, 1983). To be sure, a significant portion of this confusion and ignorance is not of the citizens' own making, but must be traced instead to the complexity of political life and to the ambiguity that governments often cultivate (see Bennett, 1975; Page, 1978). It is nevertheless true that the events of political life are, for most Americans, most of the time, peripheral curiosities.

This is a fundamental fact and one that should be kept in mind in the pages ahead, but it tells us little in detail about how everyday political thinking proceeds. Theories that presume that the public possesses a voracious appetite for political information should, of course, be greeted with great skepticism. But having said that, we are left with the mystery of how people arrive at those political opinions they do hold. What logic, if any, can be said to underlie public opinion?

This essay opens by taking up a possibility that has commanded monstrous attention: that the ordinary American's political beliefs may be derived from abstract ideological principles, sweeping ideas about how government and society should be organized. As we will see only too clearly, the ideology literature is laced with difficulties and entanglements. One conclusion is perfectly obvious, however: the field of public opinion has been far too occupied with the ideological possibility. Alternatives have suffered neglect, and the consequences have not been benign. The second part of the essay is therefore dedicated to promoting ways of understanding how Americans form and organize their political ideas other than through deductions from ideological principles: ways dominated by personal needs, by self-interest, by group identifications, by core values, and by inferences from history. The essay then closes with a general exhortation, accompanied by specific recommendations, in support of a livelier and closer interdependence between research on public opinion, on the one hand, and psychological theory, on the other.

IDEOLOGICAL INNOCENCE?

Perhaps Americans deduce their specific political opinions from general ideological principles. To many analysts, this has seemed an irresistibly appealing solution to the problem of political reasoning, for citizens and for governments alike. From the individual's perspective, deductions from abstract political concepts might substitute for the extensive acquisition of and rumination over political information—since that surely does not happen. Then political reasoning might be sophisticated, even if informationally thin. If Americans reason ideologically, then their grasp of politics is certainly substantial: "new political events have more meaning, retention of political information from the past is far more adequate, and political behavior increasingly approximates that of sophisticated 'rational' models, which assume relatively full information" (Converse, 1964, p. 227). From the governments' side, if ordinary citizens were to reason ideologically, as political elites presumably do, then the prospects for democratic control would be enhanced. That is, if leaders and general publics thought about politics along generally the same lines, there would be at least the possibility of genuine communication between them. Leaders would be better positioned to try to do what the public desired on those occasions when leaders ask for instruction. In short, the extraordinary interest in the possibility of ideological reasoning was and still is an expression of concern for the quality and very possibility of democratic forms of government.

However this may be, the possibility that Americans in large numbers might be moved by ideology was regarded as quite preposterous two decades ago. National surveys carried out in the late 1950s and early 60s turned up few full-fledged liberals or conservatives, much less more exotic political types. According to these early explorations, the vast majority of Americans were thoroughly innocent of ideology (Campbell *et al.*, 1960; McClosky *et al.*, 1960; McClosky, 1964; Prothro & Grigg, 1960).

In the past decade, however, consensus on this point has come undone. The field is now in "crisis" (Bennett, 1977). The cozy consensus of the past has been replaced by the often unfriendly arguments of today: some arcanely technical, some broadly methodological, some interpretational, and some plainly political. To be faithful to this complex and treacherous literature, I review it in four parts. First I quickly sketch the original claim—that the American public is largely innocent of ideology—particularly as realized in the writings of Converse (1963, 1964, 1975a, 1975b). I concentrate on Converse because his rendering of the ideological innocence argument is the most powerful and because it effectively set the terms for most subsequent work—indeed, for too much subsequent work. Though accepting his terms, research that followed Converse has often been critical of his conclusions; that revisionist literature is reviewed next. Then I take up proposals regarding ideology that lie largely outside the principal tussle between Converse and his critics, but bear obviously upon it. In the final section I draw the various pieces together and deliver a general verdict on the claim of ideological innocence.

The Original Claim

Converse approached the problem of ideology by trying to describe the public's general belief systems. These he defined as configurations ". . . of ideas and attitudes in which the elements are bound together by some form of constraint or functional interdependence" (1964, p. 207). Guided by this definition and making use of national surveys conducted by the Survey Research Center in 1956, 1958, and 1960, Converse concluded that dramatic, perhaps unbridgeable,. differences divided elites from masses. Turning from the political belief systems of activists to those of ordinary citizens, "constraint declines across the universe of idea-elements, . . . the range of relevant belief systems becomes narrower and narrower. Instead of a few wide-ranging belief systems that organize large amounts of specific information, one [discovers] a proliferation of clusters of ideas among which little constraint is felt. . ." (Converse, 1964, p. 213). Simultaneously, "the character of the objects that are central in a belief system undergoes systematic change. These objects shift from the remote, generic, and abstract to the increasingly simple, concrete, or 'close to home' " (p. 213).

Converse was led to these conclusions in part because of Americans' unfamiliarity with ideological concepts. Those questioned in the 1956 survey were asked to discuss the good and bad points of the two major political parties and, in a parallel series of questions, to comment on the major presidential candidates. According to Converse's coding, active use of ideological terms was confined to just 2.5 percent of the public. Near-ideologues, those who made some use of abstract concepts but appeared neither to rely upon them heavily nor to understand them very well, comprised another one-tenth of the national sample. This left fully 88 percent of the general public ideologically innocent.

Even the recognition of standard ideological terms was not widespread. The 1960 interview included a series of questions designed to ascertain citizens' understanding of liberalism and conservatism. Those interviewed were asked to assign these labels to the two parties—if they first indicated that there existed meaningful party differences—and then to explain what they meant. Just one-sixth of the public both assigned the labels properly and explained party differences in terms of broad ideological themes.

Of course, ideology might still flourish among the public, if it turned out that many people simply could not articulate or recognize the principles that in fact determined their beliefs. If many Americans really used ideological principles, but could not express them easily or quickly, their opinions on various issues should still exhibit consistency, tied together as they would be by underlying ideological principles. To test for such "constraint," Converse computed correlations between opinions on topical issues within two groups, both interviewed in 1958: a national cross-section of the general public, and a smaller group made up of candidates for the United States House of Representatives. Respondents in each group were asked their opinions on a series of domestic and foreign issues: aid to education, government guarantee of employment, military support for countries menaced by Communist aggression, and the like. Substantial constraint between opinions on such issues was apparent only for the candidates. Indeed, among the public, there was little consistency at all. Converse concluded that the opinions expressed by ordinary citizens on particular issues do not derive from widely-shared, general principles. Weak correlations across different topics reflected citizens' failure to master and employ the abstract ideological concepts that might have tied the topics together (Aberbach *et al.*, 1981, Chapter 5; Butler & Stokes, 1974; Converse & Pierce, 1983; Klingemann, 1979; Miller & Miller, 1976).

Not only did policy opinions appear largely insulated from one another, they also seemed to wobble capriciously back and forth over time. The policy questions included in the 1958 national survey referred to above were also posed to the same respondents two years earlier, in the 1956 survey as well as two years later, in 1960. Although there were virtually no aggregate shifts in opinion on any of these issues across this period, and despite precautions taken to discourage superficial replies, at the individual level change was the rule. Stability coefficients (Tau-Beta's) ranged from .28, in the case of the issue that perhaps best reflected the enduring philosophical dispute between liberals and conservatives—whether the federal government should have any role in the construction of housing and the production of electricity—to .43 and .47 in the case of policies that impinged upon blacks—the desirability of establishing a fair employment practice commission and the desirability of school desegregation, respectively. On the average, less than two-thirds of the public came down on the same side of a policy controversy over a two-year period, where one-half would be expected to do so by chance alone.

Oddly enough, the opinions on public policy expressed by survey respondents in 1960 could be predicted just as well by their opinions in 1956 as by their opinions in 1958. This pattern led eventually to Converse's "black and white" model of opinion change that partitioned the public on any particular issue into two groups: one composed of citizens who are quite indifferent to it and when pressed, either admit ignorance or invent a "non-attitude" (Converse, 1963); the other, of those who possess genuine opinions and hold onto them tenaciously. The heart of Converse's message here is that the real opinion holders are usually greatly outnumbered.

In short, most Americans approach the political world innocent of ideology: indifferent to standard ideological concepts, lacking a consistent perspective on public policy, and with authentic opinions on only a handful of policy questions. All this, according to the conventional wisdom of two decades ago.

Counter-claims

The most elaborate challenge to the conventional wisdom came in the form of Nie, Verba, and Petrocik's *The Changing American Voter* (1979). Nie and his associates argued that one of the several ways in which the American voter had changed since the 1950s was that he or she had become more ideological. Nie, Verba, and Petrocik looked at citizens' replies to the open-ended candidate and party questions, as had Converse, this time examining the series from 1952 to 1976. They reported that ideological reactions to candidates, virtually invisible in 1952, increased dramatically in 1964 and then

declined sharply in 1976.[1] They concluded that given proper circumstances —
like the ideologically polarized contest between Johnson and Goldwater — a
substantial fraction of the American public is capable of thinking ideologically, a conclusion that quickly became the new conventional wisdom (also see
Field & Anderson, 1969; Pierce, 1970).

There are serious deficiencies in the new wisdom, however. Nie and
associates worked not from verbatim readings of the original protocols, as had
Converse, but from replies already coded by the SRC staff. As a consequence,
Nie *et al.*'s measurement of ideological reasoning was reduced to tallying up
the incidence of ideological terms. A better test of the claim that American
voters had changed would require close replications of Converse's original
analysis. Several such painstaking efforts have recently been published. They
indicate that the American public's use of ideological concepts *has* increased
since the 1950s but that the increase has been glacial: from roughly 2½% in
Converse's analysis to about 7% in several analyses from the late 1960s and
early 1970s (Klingemann, 1979; Klingemann & Wright, 1973; Miller &
Miller, 1976; Pierce & Hagner, 1982). By these reports, ideological reasoning
seems to respond sluggishly if at all to fluctuations in the ideological character
of political debate.

What, then, should be made of the quite sensational changes reported by
Nie, Verba, and Petrocik? Presumably they reflect a facility on the public's
part to pick up the labels that ideologically-charged campaigns make prominent. The use of ideological vocabulary, of course, in no way guarantees that
the underlying ideas are deeply understood or even that the terms are correctly used. It appears that revisionists have demonstrated increases only in what
might be called the non-ideological use of ideological terminology (Levitin &
Miller, 1979; Smith, 1980; Nie, Verba, & Petrocik, 1981 say this is what they
meant all along). Such demonstrations do little damage to the original claim
of innocence.

Another challenge to the original claim comes from the recent finding
that when asked directly, many Americans are quite willing to describe themselves in ideological terms. Since 1972, those interviewed in SRC/CPS national election studies have been asked whether they think of themselves as
liberals or conservatives, and if so, to locate themselves on a 7-point scale,
stretching from extreme liberal (on the far left of the scale, naturally) to extreme conservative (on the far right). Self-professed liberals tend to favor
redistributive welfare policies, social change, and leftward leaning presidential candidates, while self-professed conservatives tend to express misgivings about racial integration, celebrate capitalism, and give their votes to
conservative candidates. These results are interesting (particularly as presented and interpreted by Conover and Feldman, 1981), but they do not
signify, as some have maintained (Holm & Robinson, 1978; Stimson, 1975),
the sudden emergence of an ideology ridden public.

This claim goes too far on a number of grounds. First, when provided the
opportunity, three Americans in ten concede that they never think of themselves as liberals or as conservatives (29% in 1972, 33% in 1976, 36% in
1980). Second, among those who do identify themselves in ideological terms,
large numbers embrace moderation. In 1976, for example, fully 39% of those

who declared some acquaintance with ideological terms selected the exact mid-point of the scale, labelled "moderate, middle-of-the-road." No doubt some of them were passionate centrists, but for many the middle may reflect ideological neutrality, perhaps even confusion (Levitin & Miller, 1979). Third, evidence regarding the political significance of self-professed ideology is underwhelming. Correlations with opinions on public policy issues seldom exceed .3 and are apparent in any case only among the most politically engaged of the public (Converse & Pierce, 1983; Levitin & Miller, 1979; Stimson, 1975). Fourth and finally, there is what citizens say they mean by their ideological choices. In Klingemann's 1974 survey of the United States, only one-third of those who characterized themselves in ideological terms also furnished definitions of any political depth, referring in most cases to social change or to fiscal prudence (*cf.*, Conover & Feldman, 1981).

In short, ostensibly ideological identification need not have genuinely ideological underpinnings, just as increases in the use of ideological vocabulary need not entail increases in ideological thinking. No doubt for some Americans, ideological identifications do summarize a general political stance: for government intervention or free enterprise; for social change or social stability. But not for most.

This brings us to the empirical centerpiece of the revisionist argument: the compelling demonstration of greater cohesion in the American public's beliefs on public policy beginning in the 1960s (Nie & Andersen, 1974; Nie, Verba, & Petrocik, 1979). Nie and his associates replicated Converse's original analysis of constraint in seven national surveys running from 1956 to 1972. Through the late 1950s and early 1960s, Nie *et al.* found—as had Converse—little constraint between opinions on issues of social welfare, equality of opportunity, foreign relations and the like. This changed in 1964. Suddenly opinion on school integration became aligned with feelings about big government; foreign policy views became linked to beliefs regarding the federal government's responsibility to subsidize medical care; and so on. Detected first in 1964, this new-found structure in public opinion persisted at about the same level through 1968, and has since slightly declined (see Miller & Miller, 1977; Nie, Verba, & Petrocik, 1979, p. 369). Nie and his colleagues interpreted these results to indicate a sea change in public thinking, provoked by the tumultuous events of the 1960s.

Not so. In 1964, coincident with the increase in cohesion in public thinking on policy matters, the formats of the public policy questions were altered. The changes seemed innocuous enough: from a conventional Likert format to an arrangement in which respondents were asked to choose between a pair of opposing alternatives; and from a gentle to a somewhat more insistent invitation to admit to no opinion at all. Could such subtle changes explain what Nie and Andersen took to be ". . . dramatic shifts in both the breadth and depth of liberal/conservative attitude structure. . ." (p. 571)? They could and probably did. (The most lethal weapon in this debate has been the experiment; see especially Sullivan, Piereson, & Marcus, 1978; Sullivan, Piereson, Marcus, & Feldman, 1979; a more complete bibliography can be found in Kinder & Sears, 1983.) It is now clear that most of the apparent change in opinion structure is artificial, produced not by political metamorphosis but by mundane alterations in question wording. This radically inverts the revisionists' message. Despite profound changes in American politics through the 1960s, the structure of public opinion changed not at all.[2]

Surely the most devastating element of the original claim of ideological innocence was how few people seemed to possess real preferences regarding public policy. Converse believed that the public's wandering over time from one side of a policy question to the other was symptomatic of the shallowness of opinion. Reluctant to admit their own ignorance, people invented evanescent opinions—liberal on one occasion, conservative on the next.

Well, maybe not. Converse's critics interpret instability to be a reflection instead of unclear questions; responses may not be stable, but the underlying opinions are. Instability reflects vague questions, not vague citizens (Achen, 1975, 1983; Converse, 1974, 1980; Erikson, 1979; Jackson, 1982; Judd & Milburn, 1980; Judd, Krosnick, & Milburn, 1981; Martin, 1981; Milburn & Judd, 1981; Pierce & Rose, 1974).[3]

If revisionists are correct, the original claim comes undone, at two points. Threatened first is the non-attitude thesis itself—that on many matters of public policy, most people possess no genuine preferences at all. Also threatened is the analysis of attitude constraint. Once purged of measurement error, the public's opinions on public policy questions no longer seem quite so feebly-structured (see Achen's, 1975, Table 3).

In adjudicating this conflict, much hinges on how instability is understood. According to Converse's interpretation, instability on any particular issue should vary from one person to the next. Stability should be comparatively high among people engaged by the issue and comparatively low among people whose political interests lie elsewhere. Testing this prediction was Achen's (1975) way of resolving the debate. Achen regressed his estimate of the measurement error associated with each policy question for each survey respondent against demographic characteristics (e.g., education, income, occupation) and measures of general political interest (e.g., concern over election outcome, interest in campaign, etc.), with feeble returns. Variation in education or in political engagement proved to be a weak predictor of error. Achen concluded that since unreliability was spread so evenly across the public, it should properly be ascribed not to citizen confusion but to questionnaire imperfection. (For comparable tests, see Erikson, 1979; and Judd *et al.*, 1981.)

But Achen's results are in fact compatible with a strict reading of Converse's argument. Converse emphasized the fragmentation of the public into narrow factions, each preoccupied with different policy matters. Demonstrating that *general* interest in politics fails to predict opinion stability does no damage to this view. A persuasive disconfirmation of Converse's claim requires showing, for example, that those citizens intrigued by matters of foreign policy do not differ from the rest of the population in the stability of their opinion on aid to foreign countries. Such evidence would be quite impossible to square with Converse's claim that instability reflects not measurement problems but weaknesses in opinion.

Comparisons of this sort are scarce, but those that have been reported favor Converse's original claim: policy-specific interest *does* seem to be associated with the durability of opinion over time (Converse, 1964, pp. 244-245; Schuman & Presser, 1981, Chapter 9). Moreover, collateral evidence of various kinds seems to contain serious anomalies for the critics of the non-attitude thesis. First, political elites appear to cling tenaciously to their own political beliefs. The best evidence of this now available is provided by Putnam and his associates (1979), in a panel study of Italian regional councillors. Interviewed first in 1970 and again in 1976, the councillors remained remarkably steadfast in their political opinions. On the question of government workers' right to strike, for example, councillors' opinions were substantially more stable across a six-year period (Pearson r = .75) than were the American public's belief across two years, on *any* of the policy questions included in either major SRC/CPS panel study. Does this radical contrast mean that Putnam and his associates have made historic breakthroughs in the formulation of questions, or does it reflect rather the greater attention and thought given to politics by Italian councillors than by average Americans? (For equally striking contrasts involving French Deputies and the French public, see Converse & Pierce, 1983.) Or consider that by simple correlations, identification with a political party is vastly more stable over time than are preferences on policy questions (Converse, 1964; Converse & Markus, 1979). Revisionists are forced to interpret this to mean that question writers have stumbled upon comparatively precise ways of asking respondents about their party affiliations, but haven't yet discovered how to ask questions about policy. This seems tortured, especially in light of recent agitation over the need to improve the measurement of party identification (see Weisberg, 1980).

In short, instability in political opinion cannot be reduced entirely to technical problems of measurement. Instability reflects both fuzzy measures *and* fuzzy citizens. When confronted with policy debates of great and abiding interest to political elites, many Americans can do no better than shrug. Instability largely reflects the fleeting attention commonly paid to politics, the preeminence of private desires over public ones.[4]

The durability of public opinion on policy matters also depends, finally, on the character of the policy itself. One of the clearest and least controversial lessons of recent research is that Americans are decisively more stable on some policy matters than on others. In particular, when policies become entangled with moral, racial, and religious values, indifference and non-attitudes may vanish altogether. In the mid-1970s, for example, nearly every American knew what the government should do about abortion, racial busing, and equal rights for women (Converse & Markus, 1979; Kinder & Rhodebeck, 1982). Whether Americans shrug or become impassioned when confronted with policy alternatives has therefore much to do with the nature of the times.

Altogether Different Claims

It is crude stereotyping on my part to refer to the diverse critics of innocence as though they belonged to the same club, but there is at least one kernel of truth to it. The promoters of the original claim and most of their critics share a common paradigm. However the revisionists tinker with method, or however their conclusions depart from ideological innocence, they nevertheless accept the basic terms established by Converse two decades ago.

Others do not. Converse's most persistent and able critic over the years has been Robert Lane (1962, 1969, 1973). Lane not only puts forward a powerful, layered attack on Converse's approach, he also argues for and illustrates in his own work an alternative approach, herein called *ideographic.*

Lane complains first of all that Converse, and nearly everyone else, examines only the products of political reasoning, not the process of reasoning. To learn about how people think about politics requires, according to Lane, radical departures from the conventional survey interview. Lane's *Political Ideology* (1962) was based upon a set of intensive, intimate, individually tailored interviews. Through what Lane calls a "contextual analysis" of these conversations, the process of political reasoning is supposedly revealed:

> An opinion, belief, or attitude is best understood in the context of other opinions, beliefs, and attitudes, for they illuminate its meaning, marks its boundaries, modify and qualify its force. Even more important, by grouping opinions the observer can often discover latent ideological themes; he can see the structure of thought: premise, inference, application. There is no other satisfactory way to map a political ideology. (Lane, 1962, pp. 9-10)

Lane also criticizes Converse for holding up his own ideas about how beliefs should be patterned as the uniquely appropriate standard for the public. (In one guise or another, this is the ideographic camp's favorite complaint; see Bennett, 1975, 1977; Brown, 1970, 1980; Conover & Feldman, 1980; Marcus, Tabb, & Sullivan, 1974.) According to Lane, Converse's "confusion" on this point—imposing his understanding of what political beliefs should belong with what other beliefs—slants his results. Such confusion gives priority "to the analyst's role in setting forth the idea-elements *he* thinks are important, developing the conceptual framework that the analyst regards as most likely to "govern" the more specific beliefs (exemplars), and thus providing a guided opportunity for measuring association and change. Equally important, this focus on the analyst gives him, but not the subject, an opportunity for talking about the patterns of idea-elements association" (Lane, 1973, p. 99). Lane avoids this problem in his work by providing his subjects with ample opportunity to express their own perhaps unique patterning of ideas in their own terms. Through such transactions, the definition of constraint allegedly passes from the analyst to the subject.

The confusion Lane ascribes on these matters to Converse in fact properly belongs mainly to Lane—a point that is itself usually confused. In the first place, Lane's criticism ignores Converse's analysis of the persistence of opinion over time. Such an analysis requires no assumptions regarding the particular ways in which beliefs should be patterned, only that they show reasonable stability. Indeed, this is a major reason why Converse undertook the analysis in the first place.

Secondly, although Converse does indeed impose his own standards elsewhere in his analysis, he does so deliberately. He may be wrong in his choice, but he is not at all confused. His choice is of course the standards imputed to characterize the thinking of political elites: reliance upon abstract, general principles. Lane is perfectly correct to insist that we should not conclude from the public's apparent failure to organize its policy preferences in these terms that the public therefore has no capacity to organize its political ideas at all. Converse did not—Lane's insinuation notwithstanding—nor should we.

And in the third place, Lane's cure for Converse's alleged confusion has problems of its own. Objectivity and replicability are hardly the hallmarks of contextual analysis. Although not without real virtues, Lane's approach is always vulnerable to the charge that he has not so much discovered the ideology of the "common man" (Lane's phrase) as he has unwittingly contributed to its momentary creation.[5]

Lane's most valuable contribution has been to insist on a broadened conception of political belief. In Converse's analysis, and in most that followed, opinions on public policy were given great attention—to Lane's way of thinking and to mine, inordinate attention. Political belief systems include policy preferences to be sure, but they also incorporate "the fundamental views which form the ideational counterpart to a constitution: ideas on fair play and due process, rights of others, sharing of power, the proper distribution of goods in society (equality), uses and abuses of authority. . ." (Lane, 1962, p. 15).

Lane's *Political Ideology* (1962) reflects his critique of the mainstream. He employed intensive contextual analysis and invited his subjects—15 working-class men of "Eastport"—to express their political beliefs in their own terms. Moreover, the interviews ranged well beyond public policy, touching on matters of equality, freedom, democracy and the like.

Consider, for illustrative purposes, Lane's discerning examination of the ordinary citizen's beliefs regarding equality. The uniquely egalitarian style of American social relations has struck observers from de Tocqueville to the present. Lane argues, however, that members of the working class generally do not want equality; that they are, in fact, afraid of it; and that inequality provides to them important gratifications: those that derive from identification with a just society, as well as the obvious satisfactions that result from comparisons with those lower in the social order. This was perhaps most plainly revealed in the subjects' uniformly fearful reactions to the possibility, posed to them by Lane, of a new social order in which inequality would be erased. Economic equality would deprive citizens of the goals of life; incentives would be destroyed; such a society could not long endure. For the common man, an egalitarian society would bring bewilderment and alienation, for "their life goals are structured around achievement and success in monetary terms. If these were taken away, life would be a desert" (1962, p. 78). Lane concluded that citizens do entertain genuine, occasionally deeply-felt political beliefs, not only about equality but about other fundamental political matters as well (Hochschild, 1981; Lamb, 1974; Sennett & Cobb, 1972; Ward, 1982).

Contrary to popular opinion, this conclusion in no way undermines Converse's original allegations. Because Lane and Converse (and hence, Lane and most everyone else) mean quite different things by ideology—Lane explores everyday notions of freedom, equality, and democracy while Converse worries about the public's appraisal of parties, candidates, and especially public policy—their conclusions touch each other only obliquely.

Rather than being a disconfirmation, it is far more appropriate and useful to regard Lane's findings as contributing another piece to the puzzle of political reasoning. If the ingredients of political ideology are broadened beyond conventional practice in the manner prescribed by Lane, then the ordinary American may properly be characterized as ideological. People make sense of equality, freedom, and democracy, though the sense is often personalized and idiosyncratic. It is an ideology not to be confused with that of the articulate, self-reflective, political sophisticate. But it is an ideology nevertheless: "There should be no doubt that in Eastport the common man has a set of emotionally-charged political beliefs, a critique of alternative proposals, and some modest programs of reform" (Lane, 1962, p. 15).

Although the relationship is predominantly complementary, there is one place where Lane's and Converse's arguments *do* directly intersect. To aid his description of the working-class man's political ruminations, Lane distinguished between two opposite modes of thought: "contextualizing," or thinking that places political events in topical, temporal, and historical perspective; and "morselizing," or thinking that considers events in isolation. Lane concluded that, with an occasional exception, morselizing was by far the dominant tendency: "This treatment of an instance in isolation happens time and again and on matters close to home: a union demand is a single incident, not part of a more general labor-management conflict; a purchase on the installment plan is a specific debt, not part of a budgetary pattern—either one's own or society's. The items and fragments of life remain itemized and fragmented. . ." (Lane, 1962, p. 353). As a consequence, constraint must be provided other than by deduction from abstract, general principles. In this way, but moving from a different conception of ideology and a radically different method, Lane simply reinforces the conclusion of ideological innocence.

Innocence Reappraised

"Belief systems have never surrendered easily to empirical study." So Converse began his seminal essay nearly two decades ago (Converse, 1964, p. 206); so it is today. Indeed, it would be difficult to imagine a more fitting tribute to Converse's assertion than the tangle of arguments and evidence spilled across the preceding pages. The difficulty of the subject, however, is not all that we have learned.

We have learned in the first place that ideological innocence is a fully appropriate verdict *if* by innocence we mean that few Americans make sophisticated use of sweeping ideological ideas; most are indifferent to standard ideological terminology. Even among those who claim an ideological identity, large numbers abandon the left and the right for the middle to embrace ideological neutrality. Although many Americans do pick up ideological labels when confronted with distinctively ideological presidential campaigns, they evidently do so without appreciating their political connotations. In fact, the proportion of the public making use of ideological concepts has grown glacially in twenty years, suggesting that genuine ideological reasoning may depend less on the occasional appearance of ideological campaigns and more on gradual compositional changes in the public.

Innocence of ideology is revealed also in the political connections Americans never make. Few Americans express consistently liberal, conservative or centrist positions on policy—either during the turbulent, ideological 1960s or during the serene Eisenhower years. In Lane's felicitous phrase, Americans "morselize" their political beliefs (1962, p. 353).

Morselization of opinion is of course different from having no opinion at all. And the non-attitude thesis, certainly the most controversial allegation in the original claim of ideological innocence, now seems less powerful. Opinion instability, it is now recognized, is partly the product of hazy questions. It has also become clear that issue publics need not be limited to narrow splinters of the general public: some issues engage the attention of nearly everybody. This leaves us somewhat more confident of the public's capacity to develop genuine political preferences than Converse was in 1964.

That the original claim of ideological innocence is largely sustained does not mean that the American mind is empty of politics; innocent as typical Americans may be of ideological principles, they are hardly innocent of political ideas. Such ideas, however, defy parsimonious description. Some beliefs are classically liberal, some classically conservative. There are some authentic opinions, tenaciously held; there are some non-attitudes, casually expressed. There are patches of knowledge and expanses of ignorance. "A realistic picture of political belief systems in the mass public, then" wrote Converse (1964, p. 247), "is not one that omits issues and policy demands completely nor one that presumes widespread ideological coherence; it is rather one that captures with some fidelity the fragmentation, narrowness, and diversity of these demands."

PLURALISTIC ROOTS OF POLITICAL BELIEFS

What are the sources of the fragmented, narrow, and diverse political demands that lurk in the American mind? On this point, the last twenty years of research have been more destructive than constructive. One prominent possibility—that political ideas are deduced from sweeping ideological principles—has been emphatically dispatched. This is important, but because of the field's fixation with the ideology question, we now know rather more about how Americans do *not* think about politics than about how they do.

The debate between Lane and Converse—between the ideographic camp and the defenders of the paradigm—revolves largely around the sources of constraint. Converse assumed that the roots of political belief are mainly social. According to Converse, ". . . the shaping of belief systems of any range into apparently logical wholes that are credible to large numbers of people is an act of creative synthesis characteristic of only a miniscule proportion of any population . . . to the extent that multiple idea-elements of a belief system are socially diffused from such creative sources, they tend to be diffused in "packages" which consumers come to see as natural wholes" (1964, p. 211).

Hence the politically engaged may manifest more consistency among their policy beliefs (Nie & Andersen, 1974; Barton & Parsons, 1977; Converse, 1975b; Judd, Krosnick, & Milburn, 1981) because they are more attentive to public life and therefore adopt combinations of political ideas that more faithfully reflect positions taken by well-placed leaders. In this sense, constraint is socially determined (*cf.* Abelson, 1975). In contrast, the ideographic tradition emphasizes the psychological sources of belief. Lane and others grant to ordinary citizens considerable autonomy to repackage ideas, to make them their own. The determination of constraint shifts from leaders' intellectual and rhetorical achievements to the ordinary citizens' own experiences, group relations, private needs and values. There is of course no need to choose between the social and psychological positions, and in the pages ahead, which are dedicated to sources of constraint other than ideological deduction, I try to respect both.

I will now take up in an illustrative way five alternative sources of constraint, from the intimate and concrete, to the remote and abstract. If not by a coherent ideology, perhaps the ordinary person's political thinking is shaped by (1) the expression of private needs and motives; (2) single-minded pursuit of self-interest; (3) identification with salient social groups, whose fortunes and prospects are seen to be affected by political decisions; (4) the affirmation of core values; and (5) inferences drawn from the unfolding of political history. My general purpose here is to direct attention away from the ideology question, so that we may begin to understand how citizens come to terms with the bewildering complexity that is modern political life.

1. Personality

According to Lane (1973), the analysis of political belief independent of personality is grotesque, for it "fails to take into account the individual's predispositions, his private 'decision rules,' the personal functions of a belief for his ongoing life strivings" (p. 91). Understanding the roots of a particular political belief requires, in his view, an appreciation of the part the belief plays in personality.

One general psychological tradition treats political opinions as though they were partly the playthings of the mind's inner conflicts. Smith, Bruner and White (1956) refer to the general process by which political beliefs come to stand for or express internal troubles as "externalization" (p. 43; *cf.* Katz, 1960). The externalization hypothesis was given grandest expression, of course, in *The Authoritarian Personality* (Adorno *et al.,* 1950). There is no need to recount in detail here the study itself or the methodological fusillade it set off. Hyman and Sheatsley's (1954) essay still stands as the most comprehensive and most damaging critique of the original work. But in effectively discrediting the evidence marshalled by Adorno and his colleagues, Hyman and Sheatsley did no necessary damage to the externalization hypothesis itself. In fact, evidence reported in the three decades following publication of *The Authoritarian Personality,* though it has come in a trickle, generally sustains Adorno *et al.*'s insistence that political belief and personality are intimately entwined (Brown, 1965; Kirscht & Dillehay, 1967; Wilson, 1973).

Lane (1962) also enlisted externalization in his discussion of working class men coping with the burdens of freedom. Lane suggested that those men who felt most troubled by freedom—who could not fully enjoy it themselves, who thought freedom dangerous, who worried extravagantly about its extension—were also those most uneasy about their own impulses. Apprehensions over sexual and aggressive appetites, over impulsive purchasing habits, over eating and drinking sprees, seemed to lead to hesitation and ambivalence about political freedom. "The burden of freedom for modern (and ancient) man," wrote Lane (1962, p. 55), "comes from relying on an inadequate system of personal controls. For him, therefore, the solution is the reinforcement of convention, the specification of behavioral codes, the demand for sanctions against behavior, the encroachment of the criminal code upon the area of individual choice."

Recent work on political intolerance reinforces Lane's point. Sullivan and his colleagues (Sullivan, Marcus, Feldman, & Piereson, 1981) defined political intolerance as a willingness to impose restrictions upon the activities of unpopular groups, through prohibiting their public gatherings, tapping their telephones, and so forth. They found that intolerance was especially common among those Americans who were "psychologically insecure"—who, on an omnibus measure of personality, were revealed to be dogmatic, misanthropic and authoritarian, low in self-esteem, and preoccupied with safety and sustenance. Thus personal inadequacies, which the psychologically insecure presumably have plenty of, are projected onto disreputable political groups. Such groups must be carefully monitored and controlled, lest they somehow spoil the American way.

By this scandalously brief review, the externalization hypothesis seems well supported. Ethnocentrism, conservative values, the burdens of freedom, political intolerance—all seem to have a partial basis in "inner troubles." Granted that personality is an elusive concept, and that it has routinely been mangled in application to politics. Nevertheless, it does appear that the roots of political belief do occasionally go this deep, reaching the murky province of intrapsychic conflict and desire.[6]

2. Self-interest

Nearly as intimate a basis of political belief as personality, and certainly one that political scientists feel more comfortable with, is self-interest. There is no more familiar presumption than that people support policies that promote their own material interests and oppose policies that threaten them. As *The American Voter* put it, beliefs on public policy are determined not by a coherent ideological stance but by "primitive self-interest" (1960, p. 205).

The presumption of self-interest is strong, but the evidence is not. For example, the economic predicaments of private life have only weak and intermittent effects on which policies citizens endorse. Neither losing a job, nor deteriorating family financial conditions, nor pessimism about the family's economic future has much to do with support for policies designed to alleviate personal economic distress (Denney, Hendricks, & Kinder, 1980; Kinder &

Kiewiet, 1981; Kinder, 1981; Lowery & Sigelman, 1981; Schlozman & Verba, 1979; Sears & Citrin, 1982; Sears, Lau, Tyler, & Allen, 1980). When economic self-interest does influence policy beliefs, moreover, the effects tend to be highly circumscribed. For instance, the unemployed, more than working people, believe that the national government should provide jobs, but they do not support unconventional or drastic solutions to unemployment, nor do they favor schemes to redistribute income (Schlozman & Verba, 1979). Consider another anomaly for self-interest: disruptions to private life occasioned by the sudden onset of energy shortages in 1974 seemed to have no ramifications for opinion on energy policy. People whose lives were most disrupted were no more likely to support greater conservation or the development of alternative energy sources than were their more fortunate counterparts whose personal lives went on unaffected by the crisis (Sears, Tyler, Citrin, & Kinder, 1978). Another: although war would seem to engage self-interest in an ultimate way, having close relatives or friends in Korea or Vietnam did not appear to affect opinion about the war (Mueller, 1973; Lau, Brown, & Sears, 1978). A final case, equally problematic for the self-interest presumption, comes from research on public opinion on school busing for racial desegregation. Opposition to busing, it turns out, has little to do with its personal consequences. Parents of children enrolled in public schools in neighborhoods affected by busing for desegregation are generally no more opposed to busing than any other segment of the public (Gatlin, Giles, & Cataldo, 1978; Kinder & Rhodebeck, 1982; Kinder & Sears, 1981; McConahay, 1982; Sears, Hensler, & Speer, 1979; Sears & Kinder, 1971).

Laid end to end, these studies do much to undermine the faith widely invested in material self-interest. As a basis for political belief, primitive self-interest seems to have been drastically overpromoted. Why this is so—why the links between self-interest and belief are so tenuous—is not yet clear. One possibility is that self-interest is typically overwhelmed by long-held, emotionally powerful predispositions. According to this "symbolic politics" account, people acquire predispositions (like racial prejudice or nationalism) rather early in life that shape their political views in adulthood. Interpretation and evaluation of political events are essentially affective responses to salient symbols that resemble the attitude objects to which similar emotional responses were conditioned in earlier life. Whether or not the event has some tangible consequence for the citizen's personal life is irrelevant; the pertinent personal stake is a symbolic one, which triggers long-held, affect-laden, habitual responses (Sears, Hensler, & Speer, 1979; Sears, Lau, Tyler, & Allen, 1980; Kinder & Sears, 1981).

A second general possibility directs attention to how people understand their own predicaments, particularly what they see as the causes for their problems, and how they think such problems could and should be solved. In the economic domain, Americans seldom blame themselves for their own predicaments, but neither do they blame government. Nor do they look to government for assistance in solving their economic difficulties. Instead, Americans see their predicaments as due to proximal, particularistic causes and rely on their own resources in seeking remedies. Thus people typically understand economic problems in ways that muffle their political ramifications. In so doing, the power of self-interest is eroded (Kinder & Mebane, 1983; Brody & Sniderman, 1977; Kinder & Kiewiet, 1979).

3. Group Identification

Can groups succeed where self fails? Perhaps political ideas reflect the web of allegiances and antipathies that individuals develop toward groups. From this perspective, political opinions are "badges of social membership": they are declarations, to others and to ourselves, of social identity (Smith, Bruner & White, 1956). Support for affirmative action reflects sympathy for the plight of blacks (Kinder & Sears, 1981); opposition to social welfare programs derives from hostility toward the poor (Feldman, 1983); support for war in Asia reflects fear of Communism (Mueller, 1973); enthusiasm for political repression hinges on whose phones are to be tapped (Sullivan *et al.*, 1981); and so forth.

Perhaps the most effective general demonstration of the important role played by social identity in political reasoning is the persistent prominence of social groups in Americans' appraisals of parties and presidential candidates. In Converse's original coding of open-ended replies in the 1956 SRC survey, citizens who made use of social groups comprised by far the largest single category — 42 percent of the entire public. Such citizens typically named benefits and deprivations that parties and candidates had visited upon social groups in the past or might deliver in the future. This is not ideology at work, according to Campbell *et al.* (1960), but "ideology by proxy," since there

> . . . is little comprehension of "long-range plans for social betterment," or of basic philosophies rooted in postures toward change or abstract conceptions of social and economic structure of causation. The party or candidate is simly endorsed as being "for" a group with which the subject is identified or as being above the selfish demands of groups within the population. Exactly *how* the candidate or party might see fit to implement or void group interests is a moot point, left unrelated to broader ideological concerns. (p. 234)

However unsophisticated the underlying process, the political meaning people find in social groups may be very powerful in shaping their beliefs. Moreover, Converse's (1964) original findings seem quite representative of other times and places. Many things have changed since 1956, but references to groups continue to occupy a central place in citizens' appraisals of parties and candidates — and not only in the United States (Kagay & Caldeira, 1980; Key, 1961; Klingemann, 1979; Stokes, 1966). But *which* group identifications are important?

One natural possibility is social class. According to Lipset, "the most impressive single fact about political party support is that in virtually every economically developed country the lower-income groups vote mainly for the parties of the left, while the higher-income groups vote mainly for parties of the right" (1963, p. 234). Indeed, middle and upper class Americans differ from their working and lower classes compatriots in the candidates they choose, the parties they support, and the social welfare policies they advocate (e.g., Alford, 1963; Centers, 1949; Converse, 1958; Hamilton, 1972; Ladd & Hadley, 1975).

At least as impressive as the regularity of the association between class and political preference in the United States, however, is its modesty. "Class struggle" is much too strong a phrase to impose on the rather anemic correlations typically reported; even "class conflict" may be too strong. Among Western democracies, the United States finishes close to last on measures linking class and political choice (Alford, 1963; Inglehart, 1977, p. 199). And while never very imposing, the link between class and political belief in the United States has in the past three decades steadily eroded (Abramson, 1974; Inglehart, this volume; Ladd & Hadley, 1975; Ladd & Lipset, 1981; Schlozman & Verba, 1979). Declining economic conditions may resurrect this weakening association, but in the meantime, we need to look at lines of conflict other than those defined by class.

Race is one obvious choice. Over the past four decades, whenever surveys have been taken, black and white Americans have differed systematically and often enormously in their support for open housing, federal assistance to "minorities," school integration, welfare, and on other matters of policy touching race. In a 1976 survey, for example, while blacks favored school integration by more than five to one, most whites declared that school integration was none of the federal government's business (this comparison and those that follow are taken from Converse *et al.*, 1980, and Miller *et al.*, 1980). Blacks and whites also divide deeply over perceptions of the progress American society has made in ridding itself of racial discrimination. Substantial differences emerge as well on questions that, while manifestly unrelated to race, nevertheless evoke the recent political experience of black Americans. Over the last several decades, for instance, far fewer blacks than whites worried that the federal government was too powerful. Similarly, in surveys conducted in the late 1960s and early 1970s, blacks were much more likely than whites to approve of protest as a legitimate means to political change.

The differences cited here seem primarily to reflect racial group membership and identification and not education, income, or other correlated characteristics: multivariate analysis sustains race as the preeminent predictor (Knoke, 1979). Moreover, political differences between blacks and whites rapidly diminish on questions that bear only obliquely on race. Although more blacks than whites support an activist federal government in the realms of employment, medical care, and housing, the differences are much less dramatic than on policies dealing directly with race. Thus, the power of racial group identifications is most pronounced on questions that bear directly and unambiguously on the fortunes of racial groups. This is no small thing, in a political system so deeply divided over race.

4. Values

Values are general and enduring standards. In theoretical reconstructions of belief systems, they are usually accorded a more central position than are attitudes. According to Allport (1961), attitudes in fact depend on preexisting social values (pp. 802-803). And according to Rokeach (1973), values ". . . lead us to take particular positions on social issues"; "predispose us to favor one particular political or religious ideology over another"; help us ". . . to evaluate and judge, to heap praise and fix blame on ourselves and others" (p. 13). Presumably the psychological machinery here is quite simple. Proposals and events are supported to the degree they are understood to further cherished values and to impede pernicious ones (Rosenberg, 1968; Dawson, 1979). Here I concentrate on a pair of values that seem particularly relevant to contemporary American politics: *individualism* and *egalitarianism* (Hofstadter, 1948; Huntington, 1981; Lipset, 1963; Merton, 1957; Myrdal, 1944; Pole, 1978; Verba, Orren, & Ferree, 1981).

To 19th century French writers in the aftermath of the Revolution, individualism meant the disintegration of social solidarity and the appalling collapse of social purpose. This was never the view in the United States. Here individualism has always stood for the beneficence of democracy and capitalism. As Lukes (1973) put it, American individualism is "a symbolic catchword of immense ideological significance," incorporating under one label "equal individual rights, limited government, *laissez-faire*, natural justice and equal opportunity, and individual freedom, moral development and dignity" (p. 20). For our purpose it is useful to examine in detail just one politically consequential strain of individualism, that which pertains to economic life.

Economic individualism includes a presumption against government regulation of economic conduct. It celebrates the virtues of hard work and sacrifice. It equates idleness with sin. Its most central element is the conviction that in America, the hard-working and talented, regardless of origin, will eventually find success.

Defined in these ways, economic individualism is widely endorsed by Americans—even by poor Americans, whose own experiences are evidently insufficient to shake support for the individualistic creed. " 'All men can better themselves': the circumstances of American life do not imprison men in their class or station—if there is such a prison, the iron bars are within each man." So argue the working-class men of Eastport (Lane, 1962, p. 61); the middle-class and the rich, naturally enough, agree (Feldman, 1983; Goodban, 1981; Huber & Form, 1973; Hyman, 1953; Schlozman & Verba, 1979).

Americans are also inclined to believe that the poor deserve their poverty. Explanations of poverty that emphasize exploitation, prejudice, or collapse of the educational system attract faint support. The primary causes of poverty are located instead within the poor themselves (Feagin, 1975; Feldman, 1983; Gurin, Gurin, Lao, & Beattie, 1969; Gurin, Gurin, & Morrison, 1978; Ryan, 1971; Strumpel, 1976). Popular *cures* for poverty also reflect the imprint of individualism. Economic hardships can (and should) be surmounted through individual diligence and discipline. Collective efforts are judged to be much less desirable—even by those crippled by economic deprivation (Feldman, 1983; Gurin *et al.*, 1969; Sniderman & Brody, 1977).

Each of these components of economic individualism has its parallel in Americans' racial beliefs. While acknowledging the existence of some racial discrimination, white Americans believe that opportunities are plentiful for blacks; that blacks are themselves largely to blame for their disadvantaged

economic position; and that blacks—like everyone else—can and should overcome poverty, discrimination, and other obstacles through individual effort,
not through collective efforts, and especially not through "government hand-
outs" (Feldman, 1983; Kinder & Sears, 1981).

Direct evidence on the consequences of individualism for political belief
is unfortunately mainly circumstantial, as in the discovery of a form of racial
prejudice—called "symbolic racism"—that seems to fuse conventional anti-
black sentiments with traditional American values, economic individualism
most of all. Symbolic racism appears to underly whites' opposition to welfare,
"reverse discrimination," "forced" busing, and other government programs
that violate individualism (Sears & Kinder, 1971; McConahay & Hough,
1976; Kinder & Sears, 1981). Whereas white Americans support compensa-
tory programs that foster equal opportunity for blacks, they strongly oppose
preferential treatment that guarantees racially equal results, since to do so
would amount to a desecration of individualism (Lipset & Schneider, 1981).
In these terms welfare represents government's betrayal of the effort and
sacrifice of those who do work—for the comfortable middle class of Orange
County (Lamb, 1973) as for the working class men of Boston (Sennett &
Cobb, 1972).

Common to these otherwise divergent investigations is the conclusion
that values—economic individualism in particular—shape opinions on
politics—social welfare and racial policy in particular. Also common to these
investigations, unfortunately, is their circumstantial quality. It is alleged that
economic individualism underlies political belief. But because the two are
never assessed independently, we remain uncertain about the connection that
supposedly joins them.

More direct efforts correct this limitation although they have problems of
their own. For instance, Feldman's (1983) analysis of the 1972 SRC/CPS National Election Study reveals consistent associations between economic individualism on the one hand and resistance to social welfare policy on the
other. Embracing the caricature of America as the land of opportunity appears to dull enthusiasm for government subsidized health care and employment. "Appears to" is used advisedly, for Feldman's analysis presumes that
values cause beliefs unilaterally. Perhaps they do; certainly his evidence that
Americans' beliefs about economic opportunity are impressively stable
between 1972 and 1976 is consistent with this point. But opinions on policy
questions might also influence the priorities people assign to values (this same
reservation applies as well to Conover and Feldman, 1980, and to Feagin,
1975). In short, more conclusive evidence on the power of individualism
awaits a more sophisticated analysis, one that allows for more complex causal
possibilities.

Individualism has often competed against egalitarianism in American
political history (Lipset, 1963; Ladd & Lipset, 1981). It is a competition that
egalitarianism has often lost. As Pole (1978) put it: ". . . only at comparatively
rare—and then generally stormy—intervals has the idea of equality
dominated American debates on major questions of policy. Equality is normally the language of the underdog. . ." (p. ix). The consequences of the
American commitment to egalitarianism are nevertheless apparent: in the

comparatively early institutionalization of universal suffrage, in Americans' widespread support for public education, and in the now nearly unanimous opposition among the white majority to racial discrimination (Lipset, 1963; Lipset & Schneider, 1981; Ladd & Lipset, 1981).

More pointed evidence on egalitarianism is difficult to obtain. The best, perhaps, is provided by Rokeach (1973). In a national survey undertaken shortly after the assassination of Martin Luther King, Rokeach found that the importance individual whites attached to equality was associated with their reactions to the King assassination—egalitarians more often reported anger and shame—and with their support for racial desegregation—egalitarians more often supported desegregation efforts. In the entire sample, moreover, egalitarianism was associated with sympathy for the poor, enthusiasm for social welfare policies, support for anti-Vietnam War student protests, and opposition to the war itself. Rokeach also found that equality was prized much more by blacks than by whites: in a list of 18 values, blacks ranked equality second while whites placed it 11th. All this evidence certainly sustains Pole (1978)—equality does indeed seem to be the language of the underdog—but cannot solve the causal question. Does egalitarianism lead to support for racial integration or is it the other way round?

Again we are left dangling. According to the most perceptive observers, individualism and egalitarianism are central to the American political tradition. They seem clearly implanted in American public policy and social practice, and they are somehow bound up with the public's political beliefs. But do values in fact drive the opinions people hold about politics? We do not know yet.

5. Inferences from History

The final alternative considered here, history, requires a change in perspective. So far I have tried to suggest the ways in which particular opinions might be derived from general dispositions, like group identification or core values. Now I want to introduce an explicitly dynamic component to public opinion and suggest how everyday thinking about politics is influenced by the unfolding of events.

The last ten years have seen an explosion of scholarly work on the impact of history on changes in American public opinion. Research has focused, variously, on the public's support for racial integration and racial equality (Greeley & Sheatsley, 1971; Taylor, Sheatsley, & Greeley, 1978); on the trust Americans place in their national government (Miller, 1974; Citrin, 1974); on opposition to war (Mueller, 1973); and on what problems the American public regards as important (Behr & Iyengar, 1982; Hibbs, 1979; MacKuen, 1981). Here, for illustrative purposes, I will concentrate on two especially consequential cases: the effects of events on changes in party identification and on changes in support for the president.

The American Voter defined party identification as a "durable attachment, not readily disturbed by passing events and personalities." Indeed, "only an event of extraordinary intensity can arouse any significant part of the electorate to the point that its established party loyalties are shaken" (p. 151).

Critics have since disagreed, arguing that party identification should be regarded *not* as a standing decision, but as a ". . . running balance sheet on the two parties" (Fiorina, 1977, p. 618). Is party identification responsive to new events or is it not?

A first point to make is that individual Americans do not take their commitment to party lightly. While two-year continuity coefficients for policy opinions hover around .35, the corresponding coefficient for party identification is about .85. Moreover, movement consists primarily of people traveling in and out of the Independent categories, rather than from one party to the other (Converse, 1964; Converse & Markus, 1979).

That party identification falls short of perfect stability, however, leaves room for the possibility that voters withdraw or invest support in the parties as their appraisal of events dictate. There is now good evidence that this does happen. Change in party identification does reflect a kind of running balance sheet on the performance of government—most notably, on matters of peace and war, unemployment and inflation, and civil rights (Fiorina, 1981; Kinder & Kiewiet, 1981; Rivers, 1980). For example, changes in Americans' intensity of party identification between 1972 and 1976 followed changes in their assessments of the parties' performance on economic matters. Across the four years, Democrats identified more strongly with their party when they took a dim view of the current (Republican) administration's economic performance; Republicans showed the complementary pattern, though not as consistently nor as strongly (Kinder & Kiewiet, 1981). These results support the revisionist position in principle without, however, doing much violence to the traditional conception of party identification as a standing decision. Although statistically respectable and theoretically important, the effects cited here are not large.

Policy disagreements may also motivate party change. In an analysis of the Jennings-Niemi 1965-1973 panel study, Markus (1979) found modest movement toward the Democratic Party among high school seniors in 1965 provoked by opposition to the Vietnam War and by support for racial integration. (For additional evidence of the impact of policy positions on party identification, see Jackson, 1975a, 1975b; Franklin & Jackson, 1981.)

Finally, voting for the opposition party's candidate also leads to shifts in party support. In this respect, Knoke's probing of the 1956-1960 SRC panel (1977, Chapter 6) fits nicely with Markus and Converse's (1979) exploration of the 1972-1976 panel. Both concluded that voting against party in one election diminishes identification with the party in subsequent elections. Again, however, the effects were modest. Conversion from one party to the other would require, by these estimates, an uninterrupted and extended *series* of contrary votes—a path few voters follow.

So party identification is *not* immovable; it is influenced by the performance of government, by policy disagreements, and by the emergence of new candidates. The loyalty citizens feel for party is at least partially a function of what governments and parties do, and what they fail to do.[7]

History also leaves its mark on the president's ability to muster support in the general public. Between election periods, the incumbent president's popularity soars and, much more often, declines. With the exception of

Eisenhower, every president since Franklin Roosevelt has departed from office less popular than when he entered it. This singular fact led Mueller (1973), who was the first to examine the dynamics of presidential support systematically, to include time in his regression equation. According to Mueller's estimates, a president's popularity suffers a bit during deep recessions and unpopular wars and is boosted temporarily during international crises. But the overriding determinant of a president's support is simply time. Mueller concluded that time erodes a president's support because more time means more opportunities to ". . . create intense, unforgiving opponents of former supporters" (1973, p. 205).

Mueller's pioneering procedure has since been criticized. Kernell (1978), among others (see, for example, Brody & Page, 1975), argued that time merely covers the events that are in fact responsible for fluctuations in presidential support and that to include time in prediction equations is necessarily to preempt the possibility of identifying those events.

With time removed, with more adequate measures of events, and with more appropriate estimation techniques, change in presidential support turns out to be closely tied to performance. A president's support depends first on the vitality of the nation's economy; high unemployment, rising prices, slow growth in real disposable income, all eat away at a president's support. So does American involvement in unpopular wars; as the number of Americans killed in action in Vietnam grew, public support for Presidents Johnson and Nixon deteriorated. Presidents also suffer when they flagrantly violate, or at least appear to violate, the public's trust. During the Watergate period, with each additional incriminating revelation, President Nixon's support dwindled. Finally, dramatic, sharply focused international crises involving the president typically boost his support. No doubt President Carter was the greatest recent beneficiary of this phenomenon. The seizure of the American embassy in Teheran followed by the Soviet invasion of Afghanistan produced an extraordinary surge in popular support for the President—enough of a boost, perhaps, for Carter to repel Kennedy's challenge in the primary season (Hibbs, Rivers, & Vasilatos, 1982a, 1982b; Kernell, 1978; Kernell & Hibbs, 1981).

Considered together, economic conditions, war, scandal, and international crises explain virtually all of the over time variation in presidential support. This implies that public opinion is sharply responsive in the aggregate to conspicuous national and international events.

Of course, history does not announce its lessons simply and neatly. Events must be interpreted. According to my earlier analysis, the meaning of events should be revealed in part as they are filtered through the citizen's own needs, group identifications, core values, and the like. Hints that this is so can be found in recent and more refined investigations into the dynamics of presidential support. Hibbs and his colleagues (1982b) examined approval trends within occupational groups. Blue and white-collar workers responded in highly similar fashion to international crises and to Watergate revelations. Elsewhere, however, interesting class differences emerged. First, the impact of mounting American casualties in Vietnam on presidential support was greater among the working class than among the middle class. And second, while the effect of change in the unemployment rate on presidential ratings was more pronounced among working class Americans than among the middle class, this was reversed for inflation: changes in prices influenced the president's support more among the middle class than among the working class.

These results may be seen in terms of self-interest. Thus the Vietnam findings "square with data indicating that the children of lower-status workers suffered a disproportionate share of the casualties" (Hibbs *et al.*, 1982b, p. 324). And the unemployment/inflation results are broadly consistent with the distribution of "the burdens and rewards conferred by fluctuations in aggregate economic conditions" (p. 326).

Both sets of results are compatible with other interpretations, however. Regarding the first, Schuman's (1973) investigation of American antiwar sentiment identified two forms of opposition to the Vietnam war: one moral, based on criticism of the war's goals and how it was conducted; and another pragmatic, based on disillusionment over failing to win it. The moral calculus was more prevalent among middle-class opponents; the pragmatic calculus motivated working-class opposition to the war. So the presidential approval results may reflect not class bias in the distribution of casualties (and therefore, self-interest), but class differences in the logic by which the war was evaluated.

That the working-class seems especially sensitive to changes in the unemployment rate in their presidential evaluations while the middle-class is influenced especially by changes in inflation may also be interpreted in terms other than self-interest. For one thing, Americans whose personal lives have been visited by serious economic difficulties are generally no more likely to disparage the president's performance than are the economically untroubled (Kinder, 1981). For another, while the Democratic party draws its supporters disproportionately from the working-class, the Republicans do better among the middle-class. And in the post-war period at least, the Democratic Party has championed the maintenance of full employment, while the Republican Party has worried more about restraining inflation. Hence the class difference may conceal what is really a partisan difference. Indeed, when the presidential approval model is re-estimated within *party* groups, the unemployment/ inflation differences are greater than in the social class analysis. That is, changes in unemployment affect the support given to the president by Democrats more than by Republicans, while changes in prices affect the support of Republicans more than Democrats, and these differences are more pronounced than the corresponding class differences (Hibbs *et al.*, 1982b).

In short, while the particular processes that underlie the dynamics of presidential support are not yet clear, there can be no doubt about the general point: that the lessons of history are filtered through the citizen's own individual dispositions. Furthermore, the basic relationship at the aggregate level seems well established. Changes in presidential support are driven by salient and consequential changes in national and international life.

Summary

The sources of Americans' political beliefs are pluralistic. Political beliefs are, in the first place, badges of social membership; I have stressed the allegiances people develop to class and race. Political beliefs also reflect other social characteristics that at certain moments, on certain public questions, become politically relevant: ethnicity (e.g., Greeley, 1975), religion (e.g., Converse, 1966; Lipset, 1963), gender (e.g., Klein, 1983), union membership (e.g., Converse & Campbell, 1968), and more. This list of course does not solve the persistent mystery of how sociological categories are transformed into psychological identifications, or how identifications, once formed, are successfully mobilized. Nor does it make clear the point at which group interest ends and self-interest begins. These are serious problems for future research.

Political beliefs also seem to reflect the values citizens embrace. Underneath Americans' continuing ambivalence toward race, welfare, affirmative action, and income redistribution, is a more fundamental struggle between egalitarianism and individualism. Political beliefs sometimes have still deeper, more personal roots; they may occasionally be resolutions of needs or the symptoms of inner distress. Political ideas of a fundamental sort are also driven by the "lessons of history"; war, recession, and other lesser events leave their imprint on the attachments Americans develop to their parties and their presidents. Finally, for a thin slice of the American public, political beliefs are governed by ideology; they are deductions from elaborate and abstract ideas about the nature of government and society.

When set against all this evidence, the earlier conclusion of ideological innocence must be modified. Americans are not creatures of coherent, wide-ranging ideologies. But their ideas do seem to reflect, in complex ways, preferences of modest scope. They are for some groups, and against others. They desire some values, and oppose others. In this sense, Americans' political beliefs *are* ideological. More generally, American public opinion is of many and diverse pieces, a mosaic of partisan attachments, social relations, values, and personality.

MOVING ON

Twenty years ago, V. O. Key could complain, with considerable justification, that the study of public opinion had been taken over by social psychologists. The result, according to Key, was "a large body of research findings characterized often by methodological virtuosity and on occasion even by theoretical felicity, [but] whose relevance for the workings of government is not always apparent" (1961, p. vii). In this final section I argue on the side of the angels—for methodological virtuosity and especially for theoretical felicity. Unlike Key, I recommend a deeper penetration of public opinion research by psychological concepts. The penetration should proceed along two lines: (1) by exploiting recent developments that emphasize the tacit theories (or "schemas") people hold about their world; and (2) by applying recent work on emotion, under the assumption that the underpinnings of political opinion are not only informational but also affective.

Prototypes, Stereotypes, and Scripts

An honorable and useful tradition in public opinion research is to treat people as if they were collections of discrete opinions. The interesting research puzzles then have to do with the strength and durability of the connections between opinions. People do more than take positions on specific topics, however. One other thing they do is try to understand what is going on, whether it be crisis in the Mideast, revolution in Central America, or recession at home. Trying to understand the persons, events, and circumstances that constitute political life is a noble and, to a certain degree, natural goal on the citizen's part. Understanding how citizens go about this would also seem to be a noble and natural goal for the public opinion analyst.

Those so inclined would be well advised to take advantage of a general theory of understanding being developed in cognitive science (see Anderson & Bower, 1973; Schank & Abelson, 1977). This theory—more precisely, this *family* of theories—takes understanding to be a process whereby new events are interpreted in terms of old knowledge. Happenings are understood to the degree that they are recognized as particular instances of familiar general types. Thus the news that the Reagan administration is stepping up military assistance to El Salvador may be understood by some as one more doomed, imperialist misadventure. Understanding the particular event comes through the eliciting of a general interpretive framework.

In psychological parlance, such frameworks are customarily referred to as "schemas" (Bartlett, 1932; Taylor & Crocker, 1981). Schemas are informal, tacit theories people hold about the world—about other people (called "prototypes": Rosch, 1977; Cantor & Mischel, 1979), about groups in society ("stereotypes": Hamilton, 1981), and about sequences of events ("scripts": Abelson, 1981; Schank & Abelson, 1977). Schemas provide the context within which new developments are understood.

In principle, schemas do this efficiently. They serve the average person much as formal, explicit theories serve the scientist. They provide explanations. They clear up ambiguities. They furnish predictions. They supply proposals for intervention and reform.

There is, of course, every reason to expect that the tacit theories of ordinary men and women will be less complete and less internally consistent than the formal theories of professional scientists. The ordinary person's sometimes extraordinary notions about, say, how the economy works, or the meaning of communism, or what a Democratic presidential candidate is likely to believe about energy conservation, may be utterly wrong. And even if not wildly incorrect, schemas are necessarily simpler than the events that evoke them. Nuanced and textured appreciation for a particular event gets sacrificed to the economies that accrue with the event's classification as a general type. Schema-based understanding is efficient, and given the peripheral place of politics for most people, perhaps irresistible, but it has its limitations.

If approaching political understanding from the perspective afforded by "schema theory" is sensible, then research on the *content* of political schemas is overdue. As Schank and Abelson (1977) put it:

> There is a very long theoretical stride . . . from the idea that highly structured knowledge dominates the understanding process, to the specification of the details of the most appropriate structures. It does not take one very far to say that schemas are important: one must know the content of the schemas. (p. 10)

Jervis (1976) has taken an effective step in this direction in his analysis of foreign policy decision-makers. According to Jervis, the scripts held by diplomats and other experts derive from superficial analysis of cataclysmic historical events (e.g., the "Munich script"). Once learned, such scripts are applied rather indiscriminately. In their interpretation of events, foreign policy decision-makers honor their scripts too much while paying too little attention to the events themselves.

Jervis tells a convincing story about diplomats, but he has nothing to say about ordinary folks. Several recent demonstrations, however, imply the promise of the schema concept for the general public as well. These include studies of the assumptions people make about the attributes of Democratic and Republican candidates, using testing and measurement procedures borrowed from cognitive psychology (Bastedo & Lodge, 1980); the theories ordinary people hold about the relations between economics and politics, which emphasize assumptions both about the causes of economic problems (national and personal) and their solutions (Kinder & Mebane, 1983); computer simulation of ordinary understanding of international events (Carbonell, 1978; also see Abelson, 1963); and the normative prototypes people hold about the characteristics of an ideal president (Kinder, Peters, Abelson, & Fiske, 1981). These results hint that schema may eventually become a standard part of the public opinion analyst's vocabulary.[8]

Opinion and Affect

Another custom in research and writing on public opinion over the last twenty years has been to treat people as if they were accountants. The typical American is portrayed as a bloodless calculator, who arrives at opinions by computation. "Which position advantages my group, promotes my values, reflects my ideology?" Americans ask themselves.

The accountant metaphor has its roots in the general rational tradition in Western thought. It is nourished also by the growing enthusiasm in political science for economic styles of analysis. The style is illustrated best in Downs' (1957) enormously influential *An Economic Theory of Democracy*, which presumes that citizens come to their political choices through a careful calculation of benefits and costs. That is, they approach "every situation with one eye to the gains to be had, the other eye on costs, a delicate ability to balance them, and a strong desire to follow wherever rationality leads" (Downs, 1957, pp. 7-8). The accountant metaphor has been aided and abetted also by what Tompkins (1981) called "cognitive imperialism" in psychology, the tendency to reduce all of mental life to the management and processing of information.[9]

The metaphor has its uses, but it is drastically incomplete. It ignores emotion. The underpinnings of opinion are partly informational, but also partly affective. Though perhaps not often, and hardly ever for everyone, politics entails passion: grief, when a president is assassinated; anxiety, when one resigns; hope, when a new president takes office; anger, when an American embassy is overrun; indignation, over racial injustice; fear, at the prospect of nuclear war. Where do such feelings appear in contemporary accounts of public opinion? They scarcely appear at all.

They may appear eventually, however, thanks in part to a renaissance of theorizing about emotion currently underway in social psychology. Particularly provocative in this respect is Zajonc's (1980) allegation that the evaluations people make are determined by two largely independent systems: a crude and fast affective one, and a slower, more detailed, cognitive one. Zajonc suggests further that the affective system may often dominate the cognitive one.

Political events no doubt differ widely in the degree to which they elicit affective response. Affect may be greatest when events bear on group identity and threaten core values. One promising place to investigate the affective underpinnings of public opinion seems therefore to be in the public's reactions to presidential candidates, whose campaigns, after all, attempt to mobilize group identity and exploit core values. Candidate popularity should be based not only on citizens' analysis of the candidate's personal traits and policy positions but also on the affective reactions the candidate evokes. According to several recent national surveys, affective reactions to presidential candidates were in fact widespread; particular candidates elicited distinctive profiles of affective response—Edward Kennedy elicited anger and sadness; Jimmy Carter, frustration and unease. The inclination to report positive feelings for a particular candidate was only faintly related to the failure to report negative feelings (i.e., *mixed* feelings were the norm). Most important, affective reactions were not at all redundant with trait judgments or policy opinions; affect contributed independently and powerfully to overall evaluation (Abelson, Kinder, Peters, & Fiske, 1982; Kinder & Abelson, 1981; on the last point, for parallel results in a different domain, see Tyler, 1980).

Postscript

The considerable commotion over public opinion reviewed in the preceding pages is usually justified on the assumption that, somehow or other, public opinion influences what government does. As Key (1961) put it, the study of public opinion is "bootless unless the findings about the preferences, aspirations, and prejudices of the public can be connected with the workings of the governmental system" (p. 535). But it might also be said that the study of public opinion will always be bootless if we cannot manage to get the basic findings straight. In this essay I have tried to straighten out our understanding of some findings, to describe where the study of public opinion has been, and to suggest where it might travel next—all this, so that we might be better equipped to take on, as Key prescribed, the deeper mysteries of citizens and their governments.

FOOTNOTES

1. Chapters 7, 20 and Appendix 2C of the "enlarged edition" of *The Changing American Voter* should not be read without consulting the corrections furnished by Nie, Verba, and Petrocik (1981).

2. This conclusion does not go to whether structure is estimated better by the old-style questions or by the new. With Sullivan and his colleagues (1978), I favor the latter, both because they encourage acquiescence less (Jackson, 1979), and because they capture better the essence of classical liberal-conservative debate. Hence Converse's original analysis understated the public's capacity to develop consistent issue positions.

3. Opinion instability may also reflect either real attitude change—citizens may change their minds on matters of public policy—or change in attitude objects—opinions may change when the meaning of the policy changes, as the intrusion of racial busing has changed the meaning of school desegregation. Converse and his critics suppose these changes to be empirically improbable. In the first place, the policy questions under examination reflect long-standing debates between political elites. On issues like federal aid to schools, the basic arguments were stated decades ago and have not much changed. Second, if the sources of instability were to be located in real change—either in attitude or in attitude object—then such change should cumulate. As conservative tides run throughout the country, citizens should move predominantly in a conservative direction across a set of policy questions. But this does not happen. For the periods and policies examined, about as many citizens drift leftward as turn to the right. As a consequence, the robust circulation of opinion at the individual level cancels at the aggregate level. The juxtaposition of the two—stability in the distribution of opinion in the aggregate coupled with substantial shuffling of opinion among individuals—leads to the suspicion that turnover at the individual level should *not* be ascribed to real change.

4. This conclusion is supported by the observation that public opinion is sensitive to the context of opinion elicitation. Opinion varies as a function of question wording (Bennett, 1975, chapter 4; Mueller, 1973, p. 44; Schuman & Presser, 1981; Tversky & Kahneman, 1981) and question order (Bishop *et al.*, 1982; Sears & Lau, 1983; Schuman & Kalton, 1983; Turner & Kraus, 1978). The sometimes striking susceptibility of public opinion to context implies that Americans often fail to supply their own.

5. Of course, the ideographic approach need not—and has not—relied exclusively on in-depth interviewing. More objective data collection and analysis procedures that still permit a measure of idiosyncracy in belief organizations have also been used, such as individual difference multidimensional scaling (Marcus *et al.*, 1974) and Q-methodology and factor analysis (Bennett, 1975; Brown, 1970, 1980; Conover & Feldman, 1982). These approaches center attention on *personalized* systems of beliefs, trying with some success to demonstrate, as Bennett (1975) put it, that "all people don't make sense of politics in the same way, but most people make sense of politics in some way" (pp. 18-19).

6. One of the embarrassments of this literature is the relentless way social scientists have pursued the neurotic underpinnings of *conservative* beliefs. On the authoritarianism of the left, see Rokeach, 1960.

7. I do not mean to press this too hard, however. Although party identification does respond to political events, it does so sluggishly. It is one thing for Republicans to feel less enthusiastic toward their party after a period of sustained national difficulty presided over by a Republican administration; it is quite another to embrace the opposition. The latter seldom happens. In this respect, the running balance sheet metaphor is quite misleading.

8. To speak of *the public's* prototype or stereotype or script implies a uniformity that I do not intend. Schemas no doubt vary from one citizen to the next in their inferential richness. There are those among us who find intrigue and high drama in even minor political developments. There are many others, who, out of cynicism, apathy, or a preoccupation with other activities, could scarcely care less. Schemas held by the politically expert are likely to be more elaborate, more easily evoked, and put to more sensitive use, than are those held by citizens less enchanted by politics (Fiske & Kinder, 1981).

9. Prototypes, schemas, and scripts of course contribute to cognitive imperialism, and, therefore, indirectly to the metaphor of the accountant.

REFERENCES

Abelson, R. P. Computer simulation of "hot cognition." In S. Tompkins & S. Messick (Eds.), *Computer simulation of personality.* New York: Wiley, 1963.

Abelson, R. P. Social clusters and opinion clusters. In P. W. Holland & S. Leinhardt (Eds.), *Perspectives on social network research.* New York: Academic Press, 1975.

Abelson, R. P. The psychological status of the script concept. *American Psychologist,* 1981, *36,* 715-729.

Abelson, R. P., Kinder, D. R., Peters, M. D., & Fiske, S. T. Affective and semantic components in political person perception. *Journal of Personality and Social Psychology,* 1982, *42,* 619-630.

Aberbach, J. D., Putnam, R. D., & Rockman, B. A. *Bureaucrats and politicians in western democracies.* Cambridge, MA: Harvard University Press, 1982.

Abramson, P. R. Generational change in the American electorate. *American Political Science Review,* 1974, *68,* 93-105.

Achen, C. H. Mass political attitudes and the survey response. *American Political Science Review,* 1975, *69,* 1218-1231.

Achen, C. H. Toward theories of political data. In A. W. Finifter (Ed.), *Political science: The state of the discipline.* Washington, D.C.: American Political Science Association, 1983.

Adorno, T. W. Frenkel-Brunswick, E., Levinson, D. J., & Sanford, R. N. *The authoritarian personality.* New York: Harper and Row, 1950.

Alford, R. R. *Party and society: The Anglo-American democracies.* Chicago: Rand McNally and Co., 1963.

Allport, G. W. *Pattern and growth in personality.* New York: Holt, Rinehart and Winston, 1961.

Anderson, J., & Bower, G. *Human associative memory.* Washington, D.C.: Winston-Wiley, 1973.

Bartlett, F. C. *Remembering.* Cambridge: Cambridge University Press, 1932.

Barton, A. H., & Parsons, R. W. Measuring belief system structure. *Public Opinion Quarterly,* 1977, *41,* 159-180.

Bastedo, R. W., & Lodge, M. The meaning of party labels. *Political Behavior,* 1980, *2,* 287-308.

Behr, R. L., & Iyengar, S. Television news, real-world cues, and changes in the public agenda. Paper delivered at the Annual Meeting of the American Association of Public Opinion Research, Hunt Valley, Maryland, 1982.

Bennett, W. L. *The political mind and the political environment*. Lexington: Lexington Books, 1976.

Bennett, W. L. The growth of knowledge in mass belief studies: An epistemological critique. *American Journal of Political Science*, 1977, *21*, 465-500.

Bishop, G. F., Oldendick, R. W., & Tuchfarber, A. J. Political information processing: Question order and context effects. *Political Behavior*, 1982, *4*, 177-200.

Brody, R. A., & Page, B. I. The impact of events on Presidential popularity: The Johnson and Nixon administrations. In A. Wildavsky (Ed.), *Perspectives on the presidency*. Boston: Little, Brown, 1975.

Brody, R. A., & Sniderman, P. M. From life space to polling place: The relevance of personal concerns for voting behavior. *British Journal of Political Science*, 1977, *7*, 337-360.

Brown, R. *Social psychology*. New York: Free Press, 1965.

Brown, S. R. Consistency and the persistence of ideology: some experimental results. *Public Opinion Quarterly*, 1970, *34*, 60-68.

Brown, S. R. *Political subjectivity*. New Haven: Yale University Press, 1980.

Butler, D., & Stokes, D. *Political change in Britain* (2nd ed.). New York: St. Martin's Press, 1974.

Campbell, A., Converse, P. E., Miller, W. E., & Stokes, D. E. *The American voter*. New York: Wiley, 1960.

Cantor, N., & Mischel, W. Categorization processes in the perception of people. In L. Berkowitz (Ed.). *Advances in experimental social psychology* (Vol. 12). New York: Academic Press, 1979.

Carbonell, J. G. POLITICS: Automated ideological reasoning. *Cognitive Science*, 1978, *2*, 27-51.

Centers, R. *The psychology of social classes*. Princeton, N.J.: Princeton University Press, 1949.

Citrin, J. Comment: The political relevance of trust in government. *American Political Science Review*, 1974, *68*, 973-988.

Conover, P. J., & Feldman, S. Belief system organization in the American electorate: An alternative approach. In J. C. Pierce & J. L. Sullivan (Eds.). *The electorate reconsidered*. Sage: Beverly Hills, 1980.

Conover, P. J., & Feldman, S. The origins and meanings of liberal/conservative self-identifications. *American Journal of Political Science*, 1981, *25*, 617-645.

Conover, P. J. & Feldman, S. How people organize the political world: A schematic model. Paper presented at the Annual Meeting of the American Political Science Association, Denver, CO, 1982.

Converse, P. E. The shifting role of class in political attitudes and behavior. In E. E. Maccoby, T. M. Newcomb, & E. L. Hartley (Eds.). *Readings in social psychology* (3rd ed.). New York: Holt, Rinehart and Winton, 1958.

Converse, P. E. Attitudes and non-attitudes: Continuation of a dialogue. Paper presented at meeting of the International Congress of Psychology, Washington, D.C. Published in 1970 in E. R. Tufte (Ed.). *The quantitative analysis of social problems*. Reading, MA: Addison-Wesley, 1963.

Converse, P. E. The nature of belief systems in mass publics. In D. E. Apter (Ed.). *Ideology and discontent*. New York: Free Press, 1964.

Converse, P. E. Religion and politics: The 1960 election. In A. Campbell, P. E. Converse, W. E. Miller, & D. E. Stokes. *Elections and the political order*. New York: Wiley, 1966.

Converse, P. E. Comment: The status of nonattitudes. *American Political Science Review*, 1974, *68*, 650-660.

Converse, P. E. Public opinion and voting behavior. In F. Greenstein & N. Polsby

(Eds.). *Handbook of political science* (Vol. 4). Reading, MA: Addison-Wesley, 1975. (a)

Converse, P. E. Some mass elite contrasts in the perception of political spaces. *Social Science Information*, 1975, *14*, 49-83. (b)

Converse, P. E. Comment: Rejoinder to Judd and Milburn. *American Sociological Review*, 1980, *45*, 644-646.

Converse, P. E., & Campbell, A. Political standards in secondary groups. In D. Cartwright & A. Zander (Eds.). *Group dynamics* (3rd ed.). New York: Harper and Row, 1968.

Converse, P. E., Dodson, J., Hoag, W. J., & McGee, W. H. *American social attitudes data sourcebook, 1947-1978*. Cambridge, MA: Harvard University Press, 1980.

Converse, P. E., & Markus, G. B. Plus ca change. . . : The new CPS election study panel. *American Political Science Review*, 1979, *73*, 32-49.

Converse, P. E., & Pierce, R. *Political representation in France*. Unpublished manuscript, ISR, University of Michigan, 1983.

Dawson, P. A. The formation and structure of political belief systems. *Political Behavior*, 1979, *1*, 99-122.

Denney, W. M., Hendricks, J. S., & Kinder, D. R. Personal stakes versus symbolic politics. Paper delivered to the Annual Meeting of the American Association for Public Opinion Research, Cincinnati, Ohio, May 29-June 3, 1980.

Downs, A. *An economic theory of democracy*. New York: Harper, 1957.

Erikson, R. S. The SRC panel data and mass political attitudes. *British Journal of Political Science*, 1979, *9*, 89-114.

Feagin, J. R. *Subordinating the poor*. New York: Prentice-Hall, 1975.

Feldman, S. Economic individualism and mass belief systems. *American Politics Quarterly*, 1983, *11*, 3-29.

Field, J. O., & Anderson, R. E. Ideology in the public's conceptualization of the 1964 election. *Public Opinion Quarterly*, 1969, *33*, 380-398.

Fiorina, M. P. An outline for a model of party choice. *American Journal of Political Science*, 1977, *21*, 601-626.

Fiorina, M. P. *Retrospective voting in American national elections*. New Haven: Yale University Press, 1981.

Fiske, S. T., & Kinder, D. R. Involvement, expertise, and schema use: Evidence from political cognition. In N. Cantor & J. Kihlstrom (Eds.). *Personality, cognition, and social interaction*. Hillsdale, N.J.: Erlbaum, 1981.

Franklin, C. H., & Jackson, J. E. The dynamics of party identification. Unpublished manuscript, Center for Political Studies, Institute for Social Research, University of Michigan, 1981.

Gatlin, D. S., Giles, M. W., & Cataldo, E. F. Policy support within a target group: The case of school desegregation. *American Political Science Review*, 1978, *72*, 985-995.

Goodban, N. A. *Attributions about poverty*. Unpublished thesis, Department of Psychology and Social Relations, Harvard University, Cambridge, Mass., 1981.

Greeley, A. M. A model for ethnic political socialization. *American Journal of Political Science*, 1975, *19*, 187-206.

Greeley, A. M., & Sheatsley, P. B. Attitudes toward racial integration. *Scientific American*, 1971, *223*, 13-19.

Greenstein, F. I. Personality and politics. In F. I. Greenstein & N. W. Polsby (Eds.). *Handbook of political science* (Vol. 2): *Theoretical aspects of micropolitics*. Reading, MA: Addison-Wesley, 1975.

Gurin, P., Gurin, G., Lao, R., & Beattie, M. Internal-external control in the motivational dynamics of Negro youth. *Journal of Social Issues*, 1969, *25*, 29-53.

Gurin, P., Gurin, G., & Morrison, B. M. Personal and ideological aspects of internal and external control. *Social Psychology,* 1978, *41,* 275-296.

Hamilton, D. L. (Ed.). *Cognitive processes in stereotyping and intergroup behavior.* Hillsdale, N.J.: Erlbaum, 1981.

Hamilton, R. F. *Class and politics in the United States.* New York: John Wiley, 1972.

Hibbs, D. A., Jr. The mass public and macro-economic performance: The dynamics of public opinion toward unemployment and inflation. *American Journal of Political Science,* 1979, *23,* 705-731.

Hibbs, D. A., Jr., Rivers, R. D., & Vasilatos, N. On the demand for economic out-comes: Macroeconomic performance and mass political support in the United States, Great Britain, and Europe. *Journal of Politics,* 1982, *44,* 426-462. (a)

Hibbs, D. A., Jr., Rivers, R. D., & Vasilatos, N. The dynamics of political support for American presidents among occupational and partisan groups. *American Journal of Political Science,* 1982, *26,* 312-332. (b)

Hochschild, J. L. *What's fair? American beliefs about distributive justice.* Cambridge, MA: Harvard University Press, 1981.

Hofstadter, R. *The American political tradition.* New York: Vintage, 1948.

Holm, J. D., & Robinson, J. P. Ideological identification and the American voter. *Public Opinion Quarterly,* 1978, *42,* 235-246.

Huber, J., & Form, W. H. *Income and ideology.* New York: The Free Press, 1973.

Huntington, S. P. *American politics: The promise of disharmony.* Cambridge, MA: The Belknap Press, 1981.

Hyman, H. H. The value systems of different classes. In R. Bendix & S. M. Lipset (Eds.). *Class, status, and power.* Glencoe: Free Press, 1953.

Hyman, H. H., & Sheatsley, P. B. The current status of American public opinion. In D. Katz, D. Cartwright, S. Eldersveld, & A. M. Lee (Eds.). *Public opinion and propaganda.* New York: Holt, Rinehart, and Winston, 1954.

Inglehart, R. *The silent revolution.* Princeton, N.J.: Princeton University Press, 1977.

Jackson, J. E. Issues and party alignment. In L. Maisel & P. M. Sacks (Eds.). *The future of political parties.* Beverly Hills, CA.: Sage, 1975. (a)

Jackson, J. E. Issues, party choices, and presidential votes. *American Journal of Political Science,* 1975, *19,* 161-185. (b)

Jackson, J. E. Statistical estimation of possible response bias in close-ended issue questions. *Political Methodology,* 1979, *6,* 393-423.

Jackson, J. E. The systematic beliefs of the mass public: Estimating policy preferences with survey data. Unpublished manuscript, Center for Political Studies, Institute for Social Research, University of Michigan, 1982.

Jervis, R. *Perception and misperception in international politics.* Princeton, N.J.: Princeton University Press, 1976.

Judd, C. M., & Milburn, M. A. The structure of attitude systems in the general public: Comparisons of a structural equation model. *American Sociological Review,* 1980, *45,* 627-643.

Judd, C. M., Krosnick, J. A., & Milburn, M. A. Political involvement and attitude structure in the general public. *American Sociological Review,* 1981, *46,* 660-669.

Kagay, M. R., & Caldeira, G. A. A "reformed" electorate? Well, at least a changed electorate, 1952-1976. In W. J. Crotty (Ed.). *Paths to political reform.* Lexington, MA: D.C. Heath, 1980.

Katz, D. The functional approach to the study of attitudes. *Public Opinion Quarterly,* 1960, *24,* 163-204.

Kernell, S. Explaining presidential popularity. *American Political Science Review,* 1978, *72,* 506-522.

Kernell, S., & Hibbs, D. A., Jr. A critical threshold model of presidential popularity. In D. A. Hibbs, Jr., & H. Fassbender (Eds.). *Contemporary political economy.*

Amsterdam: North-Holland, 1981.

Key, V. O., Jr. *Public opinion and American democracy.* New York: Knopf, 1961.

Kinder, D. R. Presidents, prosperity, and public opinion. *Public Opinion Quarterly,* 1981, *45,* 1-21.

Kinder, D. R., & Abelson, R. P. Appraising presidential candidates: Personality and affect in the 1980 campaign. Paper delivered at the Annual Meeting of the American Political Science Association, New York, 1981.

Kinder, D. R., & Kiewiet, D. R. Economic discontent and political behavior: The role of personal grievances and collective economic judgments in Congressional voting. *American Journal of Political Science,* 1979, *23,* 495-527.

Kinder, D. R., & Kiewiet, D. R. Sociotropic politics. *British Journal of Political Science,* 1981, *11,* 129-161.

Kinder, D. R., & Mebane, W. R., Jr. Politics and economics in everyday life. In K. Monroe (Ed.). *The political process and economic change.* New York: Agathon, 1983. •

Kinder, D. R., Peters, M. D., Abelson, R. P., & Fiske, S. T. Presidential prototypes. *Political Behavior,* 1980, *2,* 315-337.

Kinder, D. R., & Rhodebeck, L. A. Continuities in support for racial equality, 1972 to 1976. *Public Opinion Quarterly,* 1982, *46,* 195-215.

Kinder, D. R., & Sears, D. O. Prejudice and politics: Symbolic racism versus racial threats to the good life. *Journal of Personality and Social Psychology,* 1981, *40,* 414-431.

Kinder, D. R. & Sears, D. O. Public opinion and political action. In G. Lindzey & E. Aronson (Eds.). *The handbook of social psychology* (3rd ed.). Reading, MA: Addison-Wesley, 1983.

Kirscht, J. P., & Dillehay, R. C. *Dimensions of authoritarianism.* Lexington, KY: University of Kentucky Press, 1967.

Klein, E. D. *Consciousness and group politics: The rise of the contemporary feminist movement.* Cambridge: Harvard University Press, forthcoming.

Klingemann, H. D. Measuring ideological conceptualizations. In S. H. Barnes & M. Kaase et al., *Political action: Mass participation in five western democracies,* Beverly Hills, CA: Sage, 1979.

Klingemann, H. D., & Wright, W. E. Modes of conceptualization and the organization of issue beliefs in mass publics. Paper presented at the World Congress of the International Political Science Association, Montreal, Canada, 1973.

Knoke, D. *Change and continuity in American politics. The social bases of political parties.* Baltimore: The Johns Hopkins University Press, 1977.

Knoke, D. Stratification and the dimensions of American political orientations. *American Journal of Political Science,* 1979, *23,* 772-791.

Ladd, E. C., Jr., & Hadley, C. D. *Transformations of the American party system.* New York: W.W. Norton, 1975.

Ladd, E. C., Jr., & Lipset, S. M. Public opinion and public policy. In P. Duignan & A. Rabushka (Eds.). *The United States in the 1980's.* Stanford: Hoover Institution, 1981.

Lamb, K. A. *As orange goes.* New York: W.W. Norton, 1974.

Lane, R. E. *Political ideology.* New York: The Free Press, 1962.

Lane, R. E. *Political thinking and consciousness. The private life of the political mind.* Chicago: Markham, 1969.

Lane, R. E. Patterns of political belief. In J. Knutson (Ed.). *Handbook of political psychology.* San Francisco: Jossey-Bass, 1973.

Lau, R. R., Brown, T. A., & Sears, D. O. Self-interest and civilians' attitudes toward the Vietnam War. *Public Opinion Quarterly,* 1978, *42,* 464-483.

Levitin, T. E., & Miller, W. E. Ideological interpretations of presidential elections. *American Political Science Review*, 1979, *73*, 751-771.

Lippmann, W. *Public opinion*. New York: MacMillan, 1922.

Lipset, S. M. *The first new nation*. New York: Basic Books, 1963.

Lipset, S. M., & Schneider, W. *From discrimination to affirmative action: Public attitudes 1935-1980*. Washington, D.C.: American Enterprise Institute, 1981.

Lowery, D., & Sigelman, L. Understanding the tax revolt: Eight explanations. *American Political Science Review*, 1981, *75*, 963-974.

Lukes, S. *Individualism*. Oxford: Basil Blackwell, 1973.

MacKuen, M. B. Social communication and the mass policy agenda. In M. B. MacKuen & S. L. Coombs (Eds.). *More than news: Media power in public affairs*. Beverly Hills: Sage, 1981.

Marcus, G. E., Tabb, D., & Sullivan, J. L. The application of individual differences scaling to the measurement of political ideologies. *American Journal of Political Science*, 1974, *18*, 405-420.

Markus, G. B. The political environment and the dynamics of public attitudes: A panel study. *American Journal of Political Science*, 1979, *23*, 338-359.

Markus, G. B., & Converse, P. E. A dynamic simultaneous equation model of electoral choice. *American Political Science Review*, 1979, *73*, 1055-1070.

Martin, S. S. New methods lead to familiar results. *American Sociological Review*, 1981, *46*, 670-675.

McClosky, H. Consensus and ideology in American politics. *American Political Science Review*, 1964, *58*, 361-382.

McClosky, H., Hoffman, P. J., & O'Hara, R. Issue conflict and consensus among party leaders and followers. *American Political Science Review*, 1960, *54*, 406-427.

McConahay, J. B. Self-interest versus racial attitudes as correlates of anti-busing attitudes in Louisville. *Journal of Politics*, 1982, *4*, 692-720.

McConahay, J. B., & Hough, J. C., Jr. Symbolic racism. *Journal of Social Issues*, 1976, *32*, 23-46.

Merton, R. K. *Social theory and social structure*. New York: The Free Press, 1957.

Milburn, M. A., & Judd, C. M. Interpreting new methods in attitude structure research. *American Sociological Review*, 1981, *46*, 675-677.

Miller, A. H. Political issues and trust in government: 1964-1970. *American Political Science Review*, 1974, *68*, 951-972.

Miller, A. H., & Miller, W. E. Ideology in the 1972 election: Myth or reality? *American Political Science Review*, 1976, *70*, 832-849.

Miller, A. H., & Miller, W. E. Partisanship and performance: "Rational" choice in the 1976 Presidential election. Paper presented at the Annual Meeting of the American Political Science Association, Washington, D.C., 1977.

Miller, W. E., Miller, A. H., & Schneider, E. J. *American national election studies data sourcebook, 1952-1978*. Cambridge, MA: Harvard University Press, 1980.

Mueller, J. E. *War, presidents, and public opinion*. New York: John Wiley, 1973.

Myrdal, G. *An American dilemma*. New York: Harper and Row, 1944.

Nie, N. H., & Andersen, K. Mass belief systems revisited: Political change and attitude structure. *Journal of Politics*, 1974, *36*, 540-591.

Nie, N. H., Verba, S., & Petrocik, J. R. *The changing American voter*. Enlarged edition. Cambridge, MA: Harvard University Press, 1979.

Nie, N. H., Verba, S., & Petrocik, J. R. Reply. *American Political Science Review*, 1981, *75*, 149-152.

Page, B. I. *Choices and echoes in presidential elections*. Chicago: University of Chicago Press, 1978.

Pierce, J. C. Party identification and the changing role of ideology in American politics. *Midwest Journal of Political Science*, 1970, *14*, 25-42.

Pierce, J. C., & Rose, D. D. Nonattitudes and American public opinion. *American Political Science Review,* 1974, *68,* 626-649.

Pierce, J. C., & Hagner, P. R. Conceptualization and party identification: 1956-1976. *American Journal of Political Science,* 1982, *26,* 377-387.

Pole, J. R. *The pursuit of equality in American history.* Berkeley, CA.: University of California, 1978.

Prothro, J. W., & Grigg, C. M. Fundamental principles of democracy: Bases of agreement and disagreement. *Journal of Politics,* 1960, *22,* 276-294.

Putnam, R. D., Leonardi, R. & Nanetti, R. Y. Attitude stability among Italian elites. *American Journal of Political Science,* 1979, *23,* 463-494.

Rivers, D. The dynamics of party support in the American electorate, 1952-1976. Paper delivered at the Annual Meeting of the American Political Science Association. In P. N. Johnson-Laird & P. C. Wason (Eds.). *Thinking.* Cambridge, MA:

Rokeach, M. *The open and closed mind: Investigations into the nature of belief systems and personality systems.* New York: Basic Books, 1960.

Rokeach, M. *The nature of human values.* New York: The Free Press, 1973.

Rosch, E. Classification of real-world objects: Origins and representations in cognition. In P. N. Johnson-Laird & P. C. Wason (Eds.). *Thinking.* Cambridge, Mass.: Cambridge University Press, 1977.

Rosenberg, M. J. Hedonism, inauthenticity, and other goads toward expansion of consistency theory. In R. P. Abelson *et al.* (Eds.). *Theories of cognitive consistency: A sourcebook.* Chicago: Rand McNally, 1968.

Ryan, W. *Blaming the victim.* New York: Random House, 1971.

Schank, R. C., & Abelson, R. P. *Scripts, plans, goals and understanding.* Hillsdale, N.J.: Erlbaum, 1977.

Schlozman, K. L., & Verba, S. *Injury to insult.* Cambridge: Harvard University Press, 1979.

Schuman, H. Two sources of antiwar sentiment in America. *American Journal of Sociology,* 1973, *78,* 513-536.

Schuman, H. & Kalton, G. Survey methods and interviewing. In G. Lindzey and E. Aronson (Eds.). *The handbook of social psychology* (3rd ed.). Reading, MA: Addison-Wesley, 1983.

Schuman, H., & Presser, S. *Questions and answers in attitude surveys. Experiments on question form, wording, and context.* New York: Academic Press, 1981.

Sears, D. O., & Citrin, J. *Tax revolt: Something for nothing in California.* Cambridge, MA: Harvard University Press, 1982.

Sears, D. O., Hensler, C. P., & Speer, L. K. Whites' opposition to "busing": Self-interest or symbolic racism? *American Political Science Review,* 1979, *73,* 369-384.

Sears, D. O., & Kinder, D. R. Racial tensions and voting in Los Angeles. In Werner Z. Hirsch (Ed.). *Los Angeles: Viability and prospects for metropolitan leadership.* New York: Praeger, 1971.

Sears, D. O., Lau, R. R., Tyler, T., & Allen, H. M., Jr. Self-interest versus symbolic *American Journal of Political Science,* forthcoming.

Sears, D. O., Lau, R. R., Tyler, T., & Allen, A. M., Jr. Self-interest versus symbolic politics in policy attitudes and Presidential voting. *American Political Science Review,* 1980, *74,* 670-684.

Sears, D. O., Tyler, T., Citrin, J., & Kinder, D. R. Political system support and public response to the energy crisis. *American Journal of Political Science,* 1978, *22,* 56-82.

Sennett, R., & Cobb, J. *The hidden injuries of class.* New York: Vintage, 1972.

Smith, E. R. A. N. The levels of conceptualization: False measures of ideological sophistication. *American Political Science Review,* 1980, *74,* 685-696.

Smith, M. B., Bruner, J. S., & White, R. W. *Opinions and personality.* New York: Wiley, 1956.

Sniderman, P. M., & Brody, R. A. Coping: The ethic of self-reliance. *American Journal of Political Science,* 1977, *21,* 501-522.

Stimson, J. A. Belief systems: Constraint, complexity, and the 1972 election. *American Journal of Political Science,* 1975, *19,* 393-418.

Stokes, D. E. Some dynamic elements of contests for the presidency. *American Political Science Review,* 1966, *60,* 19-28.

Strumpel, B. Economic life styles, values, and subjective welfare. In B. Strumpel (Ed.). *Economic means for human needs.* Ann Arbor, MI.: Institute for Social Research, 1976.

Sullivan, J. L., Marcus, G. E., Feldman, S., & Piereson, J. E. The sources of political tolerance: A multivariate analysis. *American Political Science Review,* 1981, *75,* 92-106.

Sullivan, J. L., Piereson, J. E., & Marcus, G. E. Ideological constraint in the mass public: A methodological critique and some new findings. *American Journal of Political Science,* 1978, *22,* 233-249.

Sullivan, J. L., Piereson, J. E., Marcus, G. E., & Feldman, S. The more things change, the more they stay the same: The stability of mass belief systems. *American Journal of Political Science,* 1979, *23,* 176-186.

Taylor, D. G., Sheatsley, P. B., & Greeley, A. M. Attitudes toward racial integration. *Scientific American,* 1978, *238,* 42-49.

Taylor, S. E., & Crocker, J. Schematic bases of social information processing. In E. T. Higgins, C. A. Herman, & M. P. Zanna (Eds.). *Social cognition.* Hillsdale, N.J.: Erlbaum, 1981.

Tomkins, S. S. The quest for primary motives: Biography and autobiography of an idea. *Journal of Personality and Social Psychology,* 1981, *41,* 306-329.

Turner, C. F., & Kraus, E. Fallible indicators of the subjective state of the nation. *American Psychologist,* 1978, *33,* 456-470.

Tversky, A., & Kahneman, D. The framing of decisions and the psychology of choice. *Science,* 1981, *211,* 453-458.

Tyler, T. Impact of directly and indirectly experienced events. *Journal of Personality and Social Psychology,* 1980, *39,* 13-28.

Verba, S., Orren, G. R., & Ferree, D. Influence, income and equality: A study of elite attitudes. Paper delivered at the Annual Meeting of the American Political Science Association, New York, 1981.

Ward, D. Genetic epistemology and the structure of belief systems. Paper delivered at the Annual Meeting of the American Political Science Association, Denver, CO, 1982.

Weisberg, H. A multidimensional conceptualization of party identification. *Political Behavior,* 1980, *2,* 33-60.

Wilson, G. D. *The psychology of conservatism.* London and New York: Academic Press, 1973.

Zajonc, R. B. Feeling and thinking: Preferences need no inferences. *American Psychologist,* 1980, *39,* 151-175.

MICROPOLITICAL BEHAVIOR: AMERICAN AND COMPARATIVE

14
Changing Paradigms in Comparative Political Behavior*

Ronald Inglehart

I. OVERVIEW

Two waves of major developments in comparative political research have taken place since World War II. With each new wave the shift in perspective has been so great that one could speak of a paradigm change. At first glance, the overall trend may appear curvilinear; on closer examination it seems more like a spiral.

Starting from a traditional focus on political institutions, research first moved toward a micro-analytic emphasis; and then back again, so that today some of the most exciting current research again emphasizes structural factors. But it treats them in a more sophisticated fashion than it did before, striving to integrate macro and micro level variables into dynamic models of political behavior. While political science in general has shown similar trends, they are particularly evident in comparative research.

Until the post-war period, comparative politics focused almost exclusively on the role of political institutions. Since reliable measurements of individual-level factors were not available, they almost necessarily were ignored or assumed to be constant. The prevailing concepts of representative democracy were based on the optimistic assumption that all citizens would, or should, behave according to a rational-activist model, in which informed citizens considered the issues and candidates, and selected representatives who supported their position on the key issues. The fact that similar institutions functioned differently in different societies was not ignored, but prior to the development of such concepts as political culture, and the development of techniques to gather the relevant empirical data, researchers fell back on static stereotypes like "national character" to explain such phenomena.

---

*I am indebted to Paul Abramson, Robert Jackman, Joseph LaPalombara and Robert Putnam for helpful comments on an earlier version of this chapter; and to an anonymous panel of specialists who responded to a questionnaire on key developments in the field.

The behavioral revolution brought fundamental changes in the prevailing concepts of how political systems operate. Three landmark volumes published in the 1960s had a profound impact on the study of comparative politics, each of them stimulating an entire school of research: *Political Man* (1960), *The American Voter* (1960), and *The Civic Culture* (1963). The development and application of new techniques such as survey research and computer analysis provided fresh and sometimes startling insights into the ways in which individuals actually behave politically; micro-analytic research became the central focus of political science.

But the behavioral revolution entailed a still more profound change: argumentation shifted from a given author's impressions and insights, supported by anecdotal illustrations, to testable hypotheses supported or disproven by quantitative empirical data. Thus, while some of the key research —on the social requisites of democracy, for example—continued to focus on the macro-political level, it increasingly utilized quantitative indicators.

The empirical findings posed a severe challenge to the rational-activist model of representative democracy. In a cross-national perspective, viable democracy seemed to be linked with—and to a large extent *limited* to— nations having relatively high levels of economic development. And at the individual level, participation proved to be the exception, not the rule; moreover participation was shown to be highly skewed according to education and income. Furthermore, the typical citizen proved to be dismayingly ill-informed about political issues and the candidates' positions on them. Few citizens took part in politics in any way other than voting; and voting itself seemed to be shaped mainly by group loyalties, such as social class, religion, ethnic affiliations, and above all, by party identification.

Political behavior seemed to be determined more by the milieu into which one was born and by one's early socialization, than by the individual's rational assessment of current issues. To be sure, the political alignments prevailing in a given society could usually be traced back to earlier religious, class or regional conflicts, but to a large extent, the cleavages that prevailed when mass political parties were established seemed to become "frozen" and were transmitted to the individual either by intergenerational political socialization (Campbell *et al.*, 1960; Converse & Dupeux, 1962) or by organizational networks—which, in turn, seemed to be determined by the person's milieu more than by individual choice. Comparative political behavior came to emphasize the study of political socialization, more than the study of issue conflicts. The analysis of political behavior as an issue-free process reached an extreme case with Converse's (1969) model of the development of the strength of party identification, interpreted as the result of intergenerational transmission, plus the amount of time one had voted in free elections. The model was remarkably elegant but it pushed parsimony to its limits, explaining a major aspect of political alignment as virtually parthenogenic.

A new wave of research in comparative political behavior emerged in the 1970s. Stimulated by evidence that the impact of social class, religion, and political party identification was declining, while the importance of issue voting was growing, this research emphasized the role of political leadership, political institutions, and economic events.

It was not simply a return to a macropolitical focus, however. The frontier where critical new insights are most apt to be found now seems to be in the analysis of the linkages between macropolitical and micropolitical phenomena. This shift of focus was facilitated by the fact that in the 1970s, for the first time, adequate time series data became available to permit dynamic analyses of these interactions. While in the 1960s, one could rarely go beyond impressionistic speculation about relationships between structural variables and individual behavior, in the 1980s it is becoming feasible to test hypotheses about these interactions, using dynamic quantitative models.

The renewed emphasis on societal level variables has been accompanied by renewed interest in rational choice models, and attempts to resurrect the rational-activist model. The credibility of this approach seems enhanced by findings that rising levels of education and improved communications technology are conducive to the development of better informed, more issue-oriented publics. But its appeal also seems strengthened by the fact that the world tends to look more rational when viewed from a macro perspective.

One of the most impact-laden findings of the 1960s was the discovery of remarkably low levels of constraint or ideological coherence in the belief systems of mass publics (Converse, 1964). The correlations between attitudes, or between attitudes and reported behavior among mass publics, tend to be low; unless inflated by methods effects—such as a long series of similar questions in a similar format—relatively "strong" product moment correlations in survey research generally fall in the .3 to .4 range; most correlations are far below this. But at the aggregate level, relatively "strong" correlations generally fall in the .6 to .9 range. Frequently, one can explain several times as much variance in a given set of variables by simply aggregating them from the individual to the group level; doing this eliminates the idiosyncratic variance of individuals around the group mean. Whether this variance is due to non-attitudes among a large share of the public, or to error in measurement in survey research, the result is a much clearer structure at the aggregate level. This clarity is not a misrepresentation. Groups *do* behave more rationally—or, at least, more predictably—than individuals. The tendency for rationality to be more evident at the macrosocietal level may be further enhanced by the fact that groups are guided by elites—and at the elite level, one frequently *does* find well organized ideological views. In survey research based on elites, correlations among attitudes often fall in the .4 to .7 range (Aberbach *et al.*, 1981, pp. 125-134).

Now, as earlier, we are the prisoners of our data base. Much of the available macrolevel time series data is economic data, and the current models tend to emphasize economic variables. This is useful, but it is not enough. For the results of recent behavioral research suggest that, while economic and institutional factors play a significant part in shaping political behavior, their effects are conditioned by values and skills that can only be measured directly at the individual level. Similarly, voting statistics or reported voting intentions are the political variable for which data are most readily available, and some of the most fruitful recent models have focused on the relationship between economic variables and voting patterns (Kramer,

1971; Tufte, 1975, 1978; Hibbs, 1977; Alt, 1979; Hibbs & Vasilatos, 1982). But recent research indicates that voting is a relatively poor indicator of one's propensity to participate in other forms of political action, such as campaign activity or political protest; furthermore, quite different causal processes underlie the various types of political action (Verba, Nie & Kim, 1978; Barnes, Kaase *et al.*, 1979). Nevertheless, current macro-level research tends to focus on voting behavior and party support, in part simply because few other variables offer a long-term data base.

The research agenda calls for the development of interactive models. We will need to gather comparative time series data at both the individual level and the societal level, in order to understand not only voting behavior, but issue-oriented participation, and unconventional or violent political action. This is an ambitious goal, but its attainment seems essential if we are to move toward a more rational and effective steering process through which democratic systems can cope with economic, social and political change. Its success is seriously jeopardized by recent cutbacks in the funding of social research by both public and private agencies.

* * * * *

In recent years major contributions have been made toward increasing our understanding of political life through comparative analysis of political behavior. Having taken a brief overview of major trends, let us examine some of the specific findings. The literature has grown immensely; it is an impossible task to survey it all in one essay. I will focus, therefore, on three streams of research relating to three key variables: (1) participation, (2) cleavages, and (3) linkages between individual political behavior and societal level variables.

Participation is, in a sense, the first question of political science. One of the most basic characteristics of any political system is the extent to which decisions are shaped by a narrow elite stratum, or by input from a large share of the population. The related question, what *kind* of input, it also crucial for mass participation may range from purely symbolic actions, controlled and stimulated by elites, to actions originating among the public itself, designed to force elites to change their plans. Elite-challenging actions tend to be at least mildly disruptive; but if they become too disruptive or too violent, political institutions may be unable to function; differentiating between various kinds of political participation is vital.

If "who governs?"—or "who participates, and how?"—is the first political question, the second is "why?" This question is central to another distinct stream of research that we will call the research on political cleavages. Assuming that people *do* participate, what social ties, goals and values motivate them to do so?

Finally we will deal with the ways in which structural factors—above all the political and economic institutions of a given society—shape political behavior and outcomes. We are now at a stage where research on the interactions between structural and individual level variables is critical for advancing our understanding of comparative political behavior. The examination of some recent findings in the first two areas will demonstrate this point.

II. POLITICAL PARTICIPATION

The central question facing comparative political research in the post-war era was: What are the conditions under which democracy can survive and flourish?

Traditional research had focused on the role of institutions, with an implicit assumption that democracy was essentially a question of having the right type of constitution. But the cataclysmic failure after World War I of efforts to implant democracy in those European nations that had been governed by authoritarian regimes indicated that constitutional engineering by itself was not enough. The Weimar Republic had been an ideal democracy—on paper. But it failed to survive—partly, it seemed, because its democratic institutions were inconsistent with an underlying authoritarian political culture.

The Civic Culture (Almond & Verba, 1963) analyzed data from five nations: two established democracies, Britain and the United States; two previously fascist nations with new democratic institutions, Germany and Italy; and one developing country, Mexico, that was officially committed to democracy, but placed severe restrictions on opposition parties. It was a landmark research effort that applied concepts drawn from sociology, social psychology and psychological anthropology, and utilized survey research techniques in a cross-national analysis addressing the central research question of its time. And it suggested an answer: democracy failed in Germany and Italy, in large part, because they lacked a participant political culture.

Literally hundreds of subsequent studies have criticized virtually every aspect of *The Civic Culture,* from theory to methodology (an excellent overview appears in Almond & Verba, Eds., 1980). The criticism *The Civic Culture* engendered is a testimony to its fruitfulness; in the 1980s, it remains one of the most frequently cited works in comparative political behavior.

Two concepts were central to the "civic culture." First, the idea that political opposition must be acceptable; it could be tolerated, provided there was an underlying sense of trust bridging political cleavages. This outlook was found to be considerably more widespread in the two long-established democracies than in the other countries. This specific empirical finding—as well as some others—have become outdated by subsequent developments; one of the major phenomena of later years was the dramatic decline of trust in government in the United States (Miller, 1974; Abramson, 1983) and (apparently) in Great Britain (Marsh, 1977). On the other hand, political satisfaction and pride in political institutions has become markedly stronger in Germany (Baker *et al.,* 1981); political trust, however, remains very low in Italy (Inglehart & Rabier, 1982). These contrasting developments appear to be linked with the relative effectiveness of governmental performance in the respective systems. But, while specific findings have become outdated, the basic idea that a linkage existed seems to have been correct.

The second key concept emphasized "subjective political competence" as a major factor facilitating democratic politics; only in so far as the citizen feels that he or she is capable of influencing political decision makers, is he or she apt to play a participant role rather than that of an obedient "subject" or a politically irrelevant "parochial." The authors trace the development of this outlook in great detail. Among other things, they find that more educated persons are likelier to have a sense of "subjective political competence" and, therefore, to be political participants. Numerous other studies in various countries have established this point: citizens of higher socioeconomic status are more apt to participate in politics. (A useful overview of these findings is provided by Milbrath & Goel, 1977.)

But is this relationship due to the fact that higher education is linked with higher social status, or to the fact that education is conducive to the development of cognitive skills—a process that has been referred to as cognitive mobilization (Inglehart, 1977; Dalton, 1982)? Are those of higher status likelier to take part in politics (1) because of their greater capacity to process political information and their better knowledge of how to press their demands; *or* (2) because they have better social connections, more money, and because officials defer to the upper classes?

It seems clear that wealth and personal connections are relevant. But if we are interested in long-term changes, cognitive variables are particularly interesting. By definition, there will always be upper, middle, and lower socioeconomic strata. But pronounced changes have occurred in *absolute* levels of education, information, and political sophistication, and they may be changing the nature of the political process. Nie, Powell, and Prewitt (1969) argue that economic development leads to higher rates of political participation, but it does so chiefly because of its impact on a society's class structure and organizational infrastructure. Economic development increases the size of the middle class, which in turn leads to higher rates of membership in formal organizations. The middle class also tends to have civic attitudes (like "subjective political competence") which encourage participation.

Verba and Nie (1972) conclude that those with higher socioeconomic status are relatively likely to participate in politics—partly because they tend to have a particular set of "civic orientations." These orientations include a sense of efficacy, attentiveness to politics, and high levels of political information. The impact of social status *per se* is modest. Although the two tend to go together, when we take both into account, "civic orientations" explain *eight times* as much of the variance in overall political activity as does social status. Political skills seem more crucial than social class *per se*.

Verba, Nie and Kim (1978) carry this analysis farther, linking it with institutional factors in seven nations. Their central question is: Why is the relationship between socioeconomic status strong in some nations, but relatively weak in others? The authors develop two key analytic distinctions. First, they differentiate between individual propensities to participate, and institutional constraints on participation. Secondly, they distinguish between "easy" types of activities such as voting, and "difficult" ones, such as campaigning or cooperating with others to solve local problems. They find that political parties and voluntary associations can increase the participation rates of their members; and that they have their greatest impact on those lacking the personal motivation or skills for participation that education and economic resources provide—a fact which tends to equalize participation rates across socioeconomic strata. But the impact of institutional mobilization is considerably greater in relation to voting than to the "difficult" modes of participation. Variation in the amount of institutional affiliation by itself does not account for cross-national differences in the strength of the relationship between socioeconomic status and participation; for example, the proportion that is strongly affiliated is relatively high in the United States, but this is largely offset by the absence of clearly articulated conflict between social groups that are closely linked to specific political parties and voluntary associations—the importance of which is confirmed by the aggregate-level findings of Powell (1981). As Rokkan (1970) demonstrated earlier, lower classes participate more where class conflict is intense, and where specifically class-oriented parties exist.

Verba, Nie and Kim conclude, somewhat optimistically, that members of the lower socioeconomic strata can become participants by joining organizations even without changes in basic attitudes or skills. This is true in a sense, but it depends on what *kind* of participation one has in mind. Organizational membership, for the most part, seems to encourage *elite-directed*, rather than *elite-challenging*, forms of participation. It may not reflect the translation of public preferences into elite decisions so much as the effective mobilization of the public *by* elites in pursuit of goals largely chosen by the latter. As DiPalma (1970) pointed out, Italy consistently shows extremely high rates of voting turnout, but a *low* rate of participation in the more difficult, or elite-challenging, forms of action. Their electoral turnout of over 90 percent does *not* ensure that Italians get what they want out of politics; quite the contrary, Italians consistently show the lowest rate of satisfaction with the way their political system is functioning of any European Community public (Rabier, 1981).

Inglehart and Klingemann (1979) argue that participation springs from two fundamentally different processes, one being an older elite-directed mode of political participation, the other a newer elite-challenging mode. The institutions that mobilized mass political participation in the late nineteenth and early twentieth century—labor union, church, and mass political party—were hierarchical bureaucratic organizations in which a small number of leaders led masses of disciplined troops. They were effective in bringing large numbers of newly enfranchised citizens to the polls in an era when universal compulsory education had just taken root and the average citizen had a low level of political skills. But while these organizations could mobilize large numbers, they usually produced a relatively low qualitative level of participation—generally not going much beyond voting.

The predominance of elite-directed mass participation in politics reached extremes in the Soviet Union under Stalin, and in Nazi Germany. In both cases, voting rates, participation in rallies, and organizational membership rates were extremely high. But this sometimes frenzied participation was almost completely controlled from above, reflecting the effective mobilization of the masses to support the goals of a small, disciplined elite group, rather than the input of political influence from the masses. These were extreme cases, however. Skilling and Griffiths (1971), Hough (1972, 1976) and Friedgut (1979) argue that in the post-Stalinist era, various interest groups have attained increasing autonomy and exert a certain amount of independent influence on the policy process in the USSR. Bunce (1976, 1980) concludes that top Soviet leaders are relatively responsive to public preferences when they first come to power—at which point they emphasize consumer goods—in order to build public support. Gitelman (1982) finds that Soviet citizens have little or no opportunity to influence policy *making,* but do have some influence on policy *application,* and concentrate their efforts on the latter. On the other hand, La Palombara (1975, 1974) takes a skeptical view about the comparability of political participation between political systems as different as Western democracies and the Soviet bloc. Voting rates, for example, are extremely high throughout the Soviet sphere, but the highest rates tend to be found in the most authoritarian and *least* pluralistic states.

Elite-challenging participation is capable of expressing the individual's preferences more effectively and with far greater precision than are elite-directed modes of participation. It is a more issue-oriented form of participation, less likely to be based on established bureaucratic organizations than on *ad hoc* groups. It aims at attaining specific policy changes, rather than simply supporting the leaders identified with a given group. And, partly because it is issue-specific, this mode of participation requires relatively high levels of cognitive skills.

The "new" mode of political participation tends to be far more issue-specific and is likelier to function at the higher thresholds of participation than was true of traditional elite-directed politics. It is new in that it relies less heavily on a permanent—and hence relatively rigid—organizational infrastructure. It is new in that it is apt to employ relatively disruptive "unconventional" forms of political participation. It is new in that it depends on exceptionally high levels of ideological conceptualization among mass publics. And it is new in that it reflects emerging "Post-materialist" value orientations which accord top priority to self-expression and the quality of life, rather than to economic and physical security (Inglehart, 1977).

Like Verba, Nie and Kim (1978), Barnes, Kaase *et al.* (1979) conclude that there is a basic distinction between voting and the more "difficult" forms of political participation. But they also differentiate between conventional and unconventional (strongly elite-challenging) political participation. Comparing their cross-national data with earlier results from Almond and Verba (1963), Barnes, Kaase *et al.* (1979) find that there has been a substantial increase in the prevalence of unconventional political action. This form of participation is linked with the presence of relatively high levels of cognitive skills, and with Post-Materialist values, rather than high socioeconomic status *per se.* It does *not* seem to reflect a sense of relative deprivation, as hypothesized earlier by Davies (1962) and Gurr (1970). Barnes, Kaase *et al.* (1979) converge with Groffman and Muller (1973), Muller (1979), and Kinder and Sears (1983) in finding no support for the relative deprivation explanation of political protest. On the contrary, those with steadily rising expectations show the *highest* protest potential; they not only rank higher than those whose expectations are falling, but also higher than those whose expectations rose and then fell.

Moreover, an underlying potential for elite-challenging political action seems to be increasing gradually. Summing up the findings of the *Political Action* study (Barnes, Kaase *et al.,* 1979), Kaase and Barnes conclude: "We interpret this increase in potential for protest to be a lasting characteristic of democratic mass publics and not just a sudden surge in political involvement bound to fade away as time goes by. . . . The dependence of unconventional political behavior on education, cognitive skills and Post-Materialism displays too much of a structural component, and therefore permanence, to be considered just a fad of the young" (p. 524).

This was a rather bold conclusion in the late 1970s when reports of political protest had virtually disappeared from the newspapers. But in the 1980s, massive numbers of demonstrators are again on the march in Western Europe, protesting against nuclear power plants, airport construction, installation of nuclear missiles in Europe and other targets. Current political activism seems more widespread in Europe than in the United States. But even here, evidence from a second wave of panel interviews in the *Political Action* study indicates that there was a significant *increase* in protest potential among the American public from 1974 to 1981. Evidence based on macro-events is a useful but, by itself, inadequate guide for the analysis and forecasting of political behavior. It needs to be supplemented by investigations of underlying propensities, values and skills.

III. POLITICAL CLEAVAGES

The cleavage structures underlying politics in Western nations have changed profoundly during the past few decades.

Political cleavages can be viewed as relatively stable patterns of polarization in which given groups support given policies or parties, while other groups support opposing policies or parties. For almost a generation the nature of both the groups and the policy issues connected with support for change have been changing.

According to the classic model of industrial society, political polarization is a direct reflection of social class conflict. The working class is considered the natural base of support for the Left—that is, of support for change in an egalitarian direction. And the key issue underlying the Left-Right polarization is conflict over ownership of the means of production and the distribution of income.

As industrializing society gives way to advanced industrial society, there is a growing tendency for politics to polarize along a new dimension that cuts across the conventional Left-Right axis. Increasingly, support for social change comes from a segment of the modern middle class. This group has raised a new set of issues that tend to dominate the contemporary political agenda. The environmentalist movement, the opposition to nuclear power, the peace movement, the women's movement, the limits to growth movement, the consumer advocacy movement, all of these are manifestations of a political cleavage dimension that is only remotely related to conflict over ownership of the means of production and traditional social class conflict. The fact that these movements have taken the center of the stage in contemporary politics seems to reflect a long-term shift in the basic motivations of Western publics.

Thus far, this new axis of polarization has had only a limited impact on *voting* behavior; long-established political party loyalties, reinforced by party organizations and institutional linkages with labor unions and churches, are highly resistant to change. People continue to vote for the parties prevailing in their milieu that their parents or even grandparents may have supported. To a considerable degree, Lipset and Rokkan (1967) were correct in speaking of a freezing of party alignments dating back to the era when modern mass party systems were first established. But although deep-rooted political party alignments continue to shape voting behavior in many countries, they generally do not reflect the dynamics of the new politics. Voting is highly institutionalized and, in most countries, is constrained by party systems that were established many decades ago. The new axis of conflict is more likely to give rise to active protest and support for change than the older axis based on social class and religion. Hence, elite-challenging behavior is far more likely to reflect current political issues, than is electoral behavior.

This disparity between traditional political party alignments and the dynamics of contemporary issue-polarization places existing party systems under chronic stress. For extended periods of time, the traditional party systems may appear to be in business as usual, until suddenly a basic restructuring occurs. Sometimes the change manifests itself in the emergence of new political parties, as has recently happened in a number of West European countries. But established voting patterns and established organizations are not discarded lightly. Consequently, party alignments tend to lag behind social change—sometimes until the major ideological cleavage cuts almost orthogonally across established party spaces. When this happens, the alternatives are Realignment or Dealignment; the parties must either reorient themselves, risk being split, or suffer a gradual erosion of partisan loyalties. In many Western nations, that situation prevails today (Dalton, Flanagan & Beck, Eds., 1984).

The idea that politics is a struggle between rich and poor can be traced back to Plato. But unquestionably the most influential modern version of this idea is Karl Marx's argument that throughout industrial society, social class conflict is inevitably the central fact of political life, and the major mechanism by which society changes, with the proletariat constituting the base for change in industrial society.

The idea that politics in industrial societies is a class struggle has received strong support in the findings of empirical social research. Thus, in his classic and immensely influential work, *Political Man,* Lipset (1960) concludes that "The most important single fact about political party support is that in virtually every economically developed country the lower income groups vote mainly for the parties of the Left, while the higher income groups vote mainly for the parties of the Right" (pp. 223-224).

In another influential study based on data from four English-speaking democracies, Alford (1963) found that in virtually every available survey, manual workers were more likely to vote for parties of the Left than nonmanual workers. Calculating a "class-voting index" (obtained by subtracting the percentage of non-manual respondents voting for the Left from the percentage of manual respondents voting for the Left) Alford found a mean index of + 16 for the United States, and one of + 40 for Great Britain.

The electoral impact of social class has been demonstrated in more countries than that of any other variable, although it may be dominated by ethnic cleavages such as religion, language or race when they are present (de Jong, 1956; Rose & Urwin, 1969; Lijphart, 1971, 1979; Rose (Ed.), 1974; Sidjanski *et al.*, 1975). Nevertheless, there were grounds for believing that the paramount role of social class voting was not an immutable fact of political life. Campbell *et al.* (1960) argued that class voting in the United States, to a considerable extent, reflected a cohort effect: it was most pronounced among the generation that came of age during the Great Depression, and weaker among both older and younger groups. They speculated that class voting may vary inversely with prosperity, with substantial time lags due to cohort effects. Inglehart (1971, 1977, 1981) carried this line of reasoning farther, presenting evidence of a pervasive intergenerational shift from Materialist to Post-Materialist value priorities among the publics of advanced industrial society. The Post-Materialist outlook is linked with having spent one's formative years in conditions of economical and physical security; hence it is far more prevalent among the post-war generation than among older cohorts in Western nations; and it tends to be concentrated among the more prosperous strata of any given age group. Since the original investigation, studies by numerous other investigators have produced and analyzed evidence of an intergenerational shift from Materialist to Post-Materialist values in 16 different West European countries together with Poland, Hungary, the United States, Japan, Turkey, Israel and Australia (see Ike, 1973; Kerr & Handley, 1974; March, 1975, 1977; Kmieciak, 1976; Lafferty, 1975; Knutsen, 1982; Hildebrandt & Dalton, 1978; Zetterberg, 1977; Watanuki, 1979; Kaase & Klingemann, 1979; Jennings, Allerbeck & Rosenmayr, 1979; Pesonen & Sankiaho, 1979; Kemp, 1979; Flanagan, 1979, 1980, 1982; Nardi, 1980; Baker, Dalton & Hildebrandt, 1981; Leonardi, 1983; Fietkau & Kessel, Eds., forthcoming).

The political implications are significant and at first seem paradoxical. Post-Materialists give top priority to such goals as a sense of community and the non-material quality of life, but they live in societies that have traditionally emphasized economic gains above all. Hence, although they tend to come from relatively privileged backgrounds, they tend to be dissatisfied with their society, and relatively favorable to social change. Though recruited from the higher income groups that have traditionally supported the parties of the Right, they themselves tend to support the parties of the Left.

Conversely, when Post-Materialist issues (such as environmentalism, the women's movement, unilateral disarmament, opposition to nuclear power, etc.) become central, they may stimulate a Materialist reaction in which much of the working class sides with the Right to reassert the traditional Materialist emphasis on economic growth, military security and domestic law and order.

The rise of Post-Materialist issues, therefore, tends to neutralize political polarization based on social class. Although long-established party loyalties and institutional ties link the working class to the Left and the middle class to the Right, the social basis of *new* support for the parties and policies of the

Left tends to come disproportionally from middle class sources. But, at the same time, the Left parties become vulnerable to a potential split between their Post-Materialist Left, and their traditional Materialist constituency.

In 1972, this phenomenon temporarily split the Democratic Party in the United States, when a Post-Materialist wing captured the Presidential nomination. Throughout the past decade, a somewhat similar cleavage threatened to split the West German Social Democratic Party, torn between a Post-Materialist "Young Socialist" wing, and the labor-oriented main body. In The Netherlands, Scandinavia and Italy this phenomenon had already given rise to small but influential Post-Materialist parties in the 1970s (Lijphart, 1981; Leonardi, 1981). In West Germany, similar parties were unable to break through the 5 percent barrier at the national level until the 1983 elections. Leftist and Environmentalist in policy orientation, their electorate is largely middle class and heavily Post-Materialist (Burklin, 1981; Muller-Rommel, 1982). The environmental activists and political elites are even *more* heavily Post-Materialist than their electorate (Wildenmann *et al.*, 1982; Fietkau & Kessel, 1982; cf. Cotgrove & Duff, 1980, 1981).

After a lull in the middle 1970s, West European politics again show widespread political upheaval. And despite the economic difficulties of the present period, Post-Materialist issues continue to play a major role. Major recent political demonstrations have generally *not* been concerned with wages, unemployment or other economic issues; most of them have aimed at preventing the construction of nuclear power plants, highways, airports, military installations, hydroelectric dams and other projects that might provide jobs. Labor continues to be concerned with unemployment, wages, and inflation, but current political activism reflects mainly Post-Materialist concerns. Recent economic uncertainty seems to have slowed the growth of Post-Materialism in Western Europe but not stopped it: a Post-Materialist value type was more widespread at the end of the 1970s than at the start of that decade, and had shifted from being predominantly a student phenomenon, to being an important influence among young elites (Inglehart, 1981).

Our hypotheses concerning the emergence of a Post-Materialist Left imply a long-term decline in social class voting. Has it taken place? Alford (1963) examined this possibility himself, and concluded that "There had been no substantial shift in the class bases of American politics since the 1930's, despite the prosperity since World War II and despite the shifts to the Right during the Eisenhower era" (p. 226).

Alford seems to have been correct in his interpretation of the evidence he examined; indeed, social class voting in the United States actually *rose* during the period he dealt with, peaking about 1948 as the generation of the New Deal matured. A roughly similar pattern may apply to Western Europe; although reliable survey data for the years prior to 1948 are rare or non-existent for most countries, it seems that European electorates—newly enfranchised, in large part—were relatively volatile in the first decades of this century, with high levels of class voting coming *later*. But more recent studies by Glenn (1973), Abramson (1975, 1978b), Books and Reynolds (1975), Inglehart (1977), Pedersen (1979b), Borre (1980), Baker, Dalton and Hildebrandt (1981), Barnes, Kaase *et al.* (1979), Sani (1981), Stephens (1981),

Crewe, Sarlvik and Alt (1977), Crewe and Sarlvik (1982), Rose (1980, 1982), Capdevielle *et al.* (1981) and Lancelot (forthcoming) support the conclusion that during the past few decades there has been a secular decline in social class voting, not only in the United States but throughout much of the Western world.

There is not a unanimous consensus on this point. Franklin and Mughan (1978) argue that the decline of class voting in Britain has been exaggerated. And Hibbs with Vasilatos (1982) conclude that British class polarization has not declined at all, but has merely had cyclical ups and down in response to current economic conditions. Their diverging conclusion partly reflects the fact that Hibbs and Vasilatos use 1962 as their starting point; this happened to be the low ebb of British class voting from 1950 to 1969, which minimizes subsequent decline. Moreover, instead of measuring class polarization with the Alford Class Voting Index, they use other indicators, some of which seem less straightforward—the most dubious one lumps support for the Liberals together with support for Labour. Nevertheless, this ingenious analysis demonstrates that the evidence can, plausibly, be interpreted in alternative ways. In the same vein, Jackman and Jackman (1982) find that, while political polarization between manual and non-manual occupations may have declined, this dichotomy is only a poor indicator of *subjective* feelings of social class identity, which remain strong for most Americans. However, if we are content to use the simple but straightforward and relatively objective Alford Index as our indicator, it seems clear that class voting has been declining in many countries during the past few decades.

This tendency is probabilistic, not deterministic. A variety of factors affect the voters' choice: long-term party loyalties—sometimes transmitted from one generation to the next—religious and other group ties, the personalities of given candidates, the current economic situation and the relative positions of the various parties on key issues among others. These factors can cause large fluctuations in class voting from one election to the next within a given nation, and help account for wide variations in class voting between countries. But a growing body of evidence points to the conclusion that, underlying these fluctuations and cross-national differences, a long-term decline in class voting took place from 1950 to 1980. Thus, in the revised edition of *Political Man* Lipset (1981) updates his own earlier conclusions about social class voting with a new chapter discussing the evidence shown in Figure 1. This figure is limited to four nations for which particularly reliable time-series data exist (Abramson *et al.*, 1982; Books & Reynolds, 1975; Finer, 1980; Stephens, 1981; Zetterberg, 1983; Baker, Dalton & Hildebrandt, 1981; Dalton, 1984), but available evidence from other advanced industrial societies tends to be similar.

The fluctuations we see in Figure 1 are substantial, but the overall downward trend is unmistakable and seems to have continued despite recent economic setbacks. As Figure 1 demonstrates, class voting in the United States fell from a peak in 1948, to a low point in 1972 when the McGovernites captured the Democratic Presidential nomination, mobilizing the Post-Materialist constituency but engendering a massive desertion of working-class voters. Many of the latter returned to their traditional party allegiance under

ALFORD INDEX OF CLASS VOTING

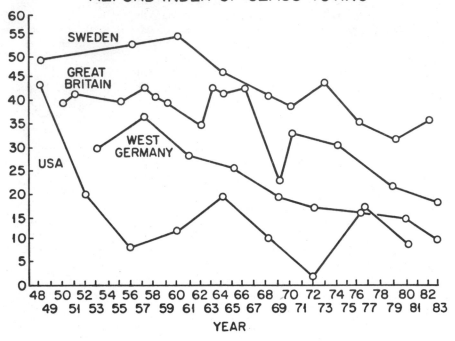

FIGURE 1

The Trend in Class Voting in Four Western Democracies, 1948-1983

Adapted from Seymour Martin Lipset, *Political Man* (second edition). Baltimore: Johns Hopkins University Press, 1981, p. 505. Updated with results from last two Swedish and German elections by present author. Sources: British data, Books and Reynolds (1975), Finer (1980), class voting in 1983 British election estimated by author from Euro-Barometer 19 data (April, 1983); Swedish data, Stephens (1981), Zetterberg (1983); German data, Baker, Dalton and Hildebrandt (1981), Dalton (1984); American data, based on whites only, Abramson *et al.* (1982).

a centrist candidate in 1976, but class voting in the United States remains low —and even this modest level largely reflects its persistence among older voters: A generation ago, Campbell *et al.* (1960) found that social class voting was strongest among the "generation of the New Deal" (then about 40 years old) and weaker among younger and older groups. Today, social class voting is strong only among the older cohorts. Among the youngest American age cohorts, it is close to zero (Abramson, 1978a). West European data show a similar pattern (Butler & Stokes, 1974; Baker, Dalton & Hildebrandt, 1981; Inglehart, 1984): for the nine European Community countries as a whole, during 1976-1979 the class-voting index for those more than 54 years old was +24; for those aged 18-34, it was only +15. The phenomenon seems to reflect a gradual intergenerational change.

If social class voting has been declining, one might expect a similar decline in religious voting since church attendance has been falling in most Western countries. This, together with other evidence of an intergenerational decline in the strength of religious ties (Schmidtchen, 1972, 1979; Barnes, 1974) would lead one to expect that the electoral impact of religion is decaying. But the evidence on this point is surprisingly mixed. A general decline in the place of the church and religious faith in people's daily lives *did* precede the dramatic weakening of religious voting which took place in The Netherlands in the 1970s (Miller & Southard, 1975; Dutter, 1978). The collapse came suddenly; voting for Confessional parties had been high for decades, with 63 percent of the Dutch electorate voting for Confessional parties as recently as 1963. By the 1972 elections, it had dropped to 36 percent. In Belgium, the vote for the Social Christians showed a similar decline, from 47 percent in 1958 to 34 percent in 1974. The underlying individual-level basis of religious voting may gradually decay, for a long time, before it becomes manifest at the institutional level.

Church attendance rates have also been falling in Germany and Italy— both of which are characterized by strong and remarkably persistent religious voting. In a multivariate analysis of West German electoral data from 1953 to 1976, Baker, Dalton and Hildebrandt (1981) find no weakening of religious voting; they conclude that social determinism is diminishing and issues are becoming more important, but the weakening of social determinism is mainly due to an intergenerational decline in social class voting. In Italy, a general secularization of society is manifest (Barnes, 1974, 1981; LaPalombara, 1982). The church seems to have lost its influence on how the Italian electorate votes on issues like divorce and abortion. But religion remains the dominant cleavage, and the Christian Democrats actually made modest gains in the 1979 elections. One factor in the persistence of strong linkage between religious affiliations and electoral behavior may be the fact that the rise of Post-Materialist politics has an inherent tendency to neutralize class-based political cleavages, but it does *not* have that effect on religious cleavages; on the contrary, conflict over cultural issues may even give them a new lease on life (Inglehart, 1977, pp. 217-222). In the long run, the decline of religiosity tends to undermine the individual-level basis of religious voting. But the rise or fall of any given political party can not be explained through reference to individual-level data alone; it requires the interactive mode of analysis that is now developing.

The decay of social determinism has stimulated revived interest in rational-activist models of voting. From this perspective, the decline of political party identification is even more crucial than the weakening of social class and religious voting. For political parties can acquire an independent influence on politics, even if their original role was determined by social structure. In the absence of clear and enduring class or religious voting, party identification may take on major importance as a determinant of electoral choice and of political behavior in general.

The pioneering empirical voting studies showed that a majority of voters made up their minds long before an election campaign began; these studies interpreted such long-standing decisions as largely determined by social structure—in particular, religion, occupation and urban-rural residence (Lazars-feld *et al.*, 1948; Berelson *et al.*, 1954). These writers tended to discount the independent influence of candidates and issues, emphasizing the extent to which voters assimilated candidates' issue stands in ways that were consistent with their own preferences. But social background variables seemed in-adequate to account for the long-term continuities in voting patterns found in subsequent research.

The concept of party identification was developed by Campbell *et al.* (1954, 1960) as a tool to distinguish between the short-term effects of the cam-paign itself (candidates and issues) and long-term factors (social background and, above all, party identification). Party identification was seen as a long-lasting, emotionally-rooted psychological membership in a political party, often transmitted from one generation to the next. The concept implied that, although the voter's choice in a given election may be influenced by issues and candidate preferences, in the long run most voters would tend to support the party with which they identified. Analysis of American data supported these assumptions, revealing party identification to be an extremely powerful ex-planatory variable. Moreover, it seemed to be learned at an early age (Green-stein, 1965; Easton & Dennis, 1969; Langton, 1967), and the correlation between parents' and childrens' party identification was on the order of .5 (Jennings & Niemi, 1968).

Serious doubts were expressed about the applicability of party identifica-tion to other countries, but Butler and Stokes (1974) and Crewe, Sarlvik and Alt (1977) demonstrated its usefulness for the interpretation of British politics. Similarly, early investigations suggested that stable, long-standing partisan affiliations were uncommon in West Germany (Kaase, 1967; Pappi, 1976); but more recent analyses tend to support its applicability to the West German setting, although they utilize modified measurement techniques (Norpoth, 1978; Baker *et al.*, 1981; Falter & Rattinger, 1982). Borre and Katz (1973) found party identification to be an important factor in Nor-wegian politics, and Sani (1977) concludes that party identification is a key variable in Italian politics, provided it is interpreted in the context of a broader Left-Right orientation. Analyzing data from nine countries, Budge and Farlie (1976) find that party identification is a much stronger predictor of vote than any of the standard socioeconomic variables such as occupation, income, education, religion, age, sex, region or urban-rural residence.

It seems equally clear, however, that party identification is a declining influence in many settings, including the country where it was discovered. Throughout the 1950s and early 1960s, about 75 percent of the American electorate identified with one of the two major parties as measured by the SRC/CPS election studies. This figure declined to 63 percent by 1972; more-over, among younger voters (under 25 years of age) only about half said they identified with one of the major parties, suggesting the possibility of inter-generational change. Nie, Verba and Petrocik (1976) and Miller and Levitin (1976) found widespread changes in the social correlates of party identifica-tion with a decline of regional, religious and class-based cleavages, and a ris-ing importance of race.

From 1960 to 1980, the American electorate became much more likely to mention issues, rather than party ties, when asked to evaluate what they liked or disliked about the presidential candidates (Verba, Nie & Petrocik, 1976; Eldersveld, 1982). Moreover, the National Election Study data also seem to indicate that the public's attitudes toward politics have become more salient and more strongly linked to voting behavior (Nie & Andersen, 1974; Verba, Nie & Petrocik, 1976, chapter 7; Pomper, 1972; Boyd, 1972; Brody & Page, 1972; Kessel, 1972; RePass, 1976; Jackson, 1975; Miller, *et al.*, 1976). These findings have been disputed (Niemi & Weisberg, 1976; Margolis, 1977; Sullivan *et al.*, 1978; Bishop *et al.*, 1978). Carmines and Stimson (1980) resolve an important part of this debate by distinguishing between "easy" and "hard" issues; only the latter demand high levels of cognitive skills and information in order to have an impact on one's political behavior. While the ideological sophistication of the electorate changes only gradually, through an "education-driven" process (Converse, 1972), rapid increases in issue voting can occur, provided the choices are simplistic. Carmines and Stimson conclude that issue voting *has* been increasing, but most of the sudden increase that occurred in the early 1960s was based on the growing salience of racial issues — an "easy" issue, in their terms. But rising levels of education imply that, in the long run, issues will tend to play a more important role in shaping political behavior, and, accordingly, that long term partisan loyalties will decline relatively.

Butler and Stokes (1974) and Crewe, Sarlvik and Alt (1977) demonstrated that partisan dealignment has been taking place in Great Britain also —a finding that foreshadowed the splitting of the Labour Party and the founding of the Social Democratic Party in 1981. At the 1964 general election, 40 percent of the British electorate "very strongly" identified with one of the two major parties; by the 1979 election, this figure had fallen to 20 percent (King, 1982). This phenomenon seems linked with a long-term weakening of the class alignment, leading to declining public support for the traditional class-based issue positions of both major political parties, aggravated by their failure to solve economic problems (Butler & Stokes, 1974; King, 1982; Rose, 1982). As Crewe, Sarlvik and Alt (1977) put it, "The electorate was well aware of the return to the politics of class conflict — and did not like it" (p. 172).

Thomasson (1976) found partisan identification to be less stable than voting preference in The Netherlands in the early 1970s, a finding that he traces to the breakdown of religious attachments as a cue to political choice during that period. Evidence can be found in numerous other countries of growing electoral volatility (Pederson, 1979a) and of partisan dealignment (Dalton, Flanagan & Beck, Eds., forthcoming). Understandably, there has been a growing interest in rational choice models of electoral behavior (Goldberg, 1969; Riker & Ordeshook, 1973; Fiorina, 1981; Himmelweit *et al.*, 1981).

Himmelweit *et al.* (1981) illustrate the difficulties involved. Drawing on a panel survey of English respondents interviewed repeatedly from 1959 to 1974, they provide convincing support for the view that attitudes do influence electoral behavior. Those whose political attitudes didn't match their original electoral choice were relatively likely to change their voting behavior on subsequent occasions; those whose attitudes changed during the course of the study were relatively likely to change their subsequent voting behavior, bringing it in line with their issue preferences. Interpreting voting as a process of rational choice, based on calculations about which party upholds one's issue position better than others, the authors demonstrate that political attitudes not only predict voting behavior far better than social class or religion, they even predict it better than party identification or past vote. At the same time, the authors go to extreme lengths in discounting the importance of party loyalties.

It is clear that political party identification has declined in Britain. But rumors of its death seem greatly exaggerated. For one thing, the sample used by Himmelweit *et al.* (1981) is skewed in ways that tend to favor their conclusions; a panel consisting mainly of well-educated, middle class males living in the capital seems relatively apt to vote according to issues, rather than social background or party identification. But, even in this sample, there is evidence of important long-term party identification effects. When the respondents were first interviewed in 1951, among those whose parents reportedly voted Conservative, more than 60 percent said that they themselves would vote for that party. Twenty-three years later, in 1974, more than 50 percent of this group reported that they actually had voted Conservative in the last election — rather than abstaining or voting for Labour, the Liberals, or some other party.

Evidence from other countries indicates that the decline of political party identification is by no means a universal tendency. In the United States, the decline has not reversed itself, but it seems to have leveled off; in the 1980 National Election Study, 64 percent of those interviewed identified themselves as Republicans or Democrats — about the same figure as in 1972. In West Germany, Baker, Dalton and Hildebrandt (1981) found an *increase* in the distribution of partisanship from 1961 to 1976, with a growing proportion of partisans who reported that they always voted for the same party. Similarly, Cameron (1972) and Inglehart and Hochstein (1972) found rising levels of party identification in France from 1958 to 1968, largely attributable to the growth of attachment to the newly-established Gaullist party. In keeping with these findings, Pedersen (1979a) reports that, while electoral volatility increased from 1948-59 to 1970-77 in many European party systems (including those of Great Britain, The Netherlands and Scandinavia), it decreased dramatically — falling to less than half its former level — in both West Germany and France.

The decline of long-term party loyalties is not inevitable. It seems to reflect an interaction between the issue preferences of electorates, and the issues emphasized by party elites. In a situation of "strong ideological focus" (Stokes, 1966), where one issue dimension is dominant *and* party distances correspond to this dimension, voters can be mobilized to form party attachments. This situation seems to have existed in France, during the Gaullist era (Inglehart & Hochstein, 1972). But if the dominant issue dimension cuts across the main dimension of party space, voters have less motivation to identify with existing parties, and may be attracted to new parties or split away from old ones. This situation seems to have prevailed recently in the United

States (Weisberg & Rusk, 1970; Rusk & Weisberg, 1972); and in Great Britain (Crewe, Sarlvik & Alt, 1977; King, 1982; Rose, 1982).

In the long run, party elites have strong incentives to adapt their strategies to the preferences of their electorates; otherwise, they may lose their voters, or be replaced by more responsive leaders. Thus, as the educational levels of electorates continue to rise, we can probably anticipate a gradual rise in issue voting and a diminishing dependence on party loyalties; for as Dalton (1982) demonstrates, cognitive mobilization seems conducive to partisan dealignment. But there is no reason to expect that party spaces will remain permanently incongruent with issue dimensions. The long-established party systems of Britain and the United States did so for many years, and experienced a decline in party identification. But the newer party systems of West Germany and France reflected contemporary issues more closely, and party identification seems to have risen there in the past few decades. Long-term political party loyalties will probably continue to be a major factor in voting for the foreseeable future.

This poses a serious problem for rational choice theorists since one of the crucial assumptions of rational choice models is that the parties are free to maneuver in policy space (Ordeshook, 1976). The party identification continuum from "strong Democrat" to "strong Republican" does *not* constitute such a space; it is defined by the parties themselves in such a way that the Republicans are not free to move to the "strong Democrat" position. Superficially, a Left-Right continuum based on party preferences might seem to resemble Downs' (1957) policy space, but it, too, is bounded by the parties themselves; even the content-free Left-Right ideological scale frequently used in mass surveys proves to reflect political party loyalties at least as much as policy preferences (Deutsch, Lindon & Weill, 1966; Barnes & Pierce, 1971; Converse & Pierce, 1973; Inglehart & Klingemann, 1976; Sani, 1977; Pierce, 1981). This dimension can be useful in predicting the parties to which given voters are likely to transfer their votes, or which coalitions are most feasible, but it does not constitute the sort of policy space required by formal models of rational choice.

Insofar as long-term commitments to political parties remain a major factor in electoral behavior, this behavior cannot be explained adequately by rational choice alone. Less formal—but more realistic—models have attempted to take this factor into account by introducing party identification as one dimension of a multi-dimensional policy space (Robertson, 1976), or by using a party-defined space that is capable of measuring *both* long-term predispositions such as party identification, and short-term influences, such as issue and candidate preferences (Budge & Farlie, 1976, 1982; Feldman & Zuckerman, 1982). Although Feldman and Zuckerman (1982) eliminate "party identification" from their analysis, they reintroduce a modified version of it that is similar to the partisan-affect scale used by Converse (1974) and Baker *et al.* (1981). This modification seems an improvement, both in its applicability to a wider range of political systems and in its accuracy of measurement. But it remains an indicator of attachments to given political parties that seem quite stable over time (Baker *et al.*, 1981, pp. 199-208). From a normative standpoint, it is attractive to interpret political behavior as purely a matter of rational policy choice. Empirically, it is difficult to do so without taking into account long-term influences that may have very little to do with immediate policy options.

Current issues definitely do count, and they may count for more in the future. In an innovative study based on content analysis of the issues emphasized in authoritative accounts of election campaigns, together with voting statistics, Budge (1982) makes a quantitative estimate of the net shifts in voting produced by the issues emphasized by political parties in 23 democracies. He concludes that they account for a net shift of 1 to 3 percent of the vote in most Western nations, and about 2 to 6 percent in the United States. These results converge with earlier estimates by Kramer (1971) that a "large" change in real income produces a 4 to 5 percent change in American electoral results, and by Tufte (1975, 1978) that it produces a change of approximately 6 percent for the incumbent party in off-year elections. Moreover, Budge's results for Britain approximate estimates by Studlar (1978) that the immigration issue—the key electoral issue in the early 1970s—produced a net shift of about 2.5 percent. In the long term, cumulative shifts of this size can have structural consequences; even in the short run they may be enough to win or lose an election. But there seems to be far more continuity than change in electoral behavior in most established democracies.

Concepts dealing with long-term orientations, such as party identification or political culture, will continue to be an essential part of any adequate explanation of political behavior. One can emphasize rational interpretations of those concepts, as has been done in an interesting and effective manner by Rogowski (1976), Fiorina (1981), and Katz (1981). Clearly, an important rational component is involved. But this component may reflect the rational responses one made a decade or two ago; it may even reflect the rational evaluations made by one's parents or grandparents, for the evidence of generational effects on political behavior, and intergenerational transmission of some orientations is too massive to ignore (Jennings & Niemi, 1974, 1981; Butler & Stokes, 1974; Richardson, 1974; Abramson, 1975, 1983; Inglehart, 1971, 1977, 1981, forthcoming; Barnes, Kaase et al., 1979; Dalton, 1977, 1980, 1981; Baker, Dalton & Hildebrandt, 1981; Conradt, 1980; Kaase & Klingemann, 1979; Aberbach et al., 1981; Szabo, Ed., 1983).

IV. ELITES AND MASS PUBLICS

Empirical elite research has produced a vast and varied literature. Herein, as with the research on mass publics, we will not attempt a comprehensive review, but will simply focus on the findings that are most relevant to our two key questions: Who participates?; and Why: what values and loyalties influence them?

Traditionally, the first of these questions has dominated elite research. Until rather recently, elite research concentrated overwhelmingly on the analysis of elite social background, with the implicit assumption that it determined elite attitudes and behavior, and that these, in turn, determined political outputs. Hence, if one knew the social background of a given system's elites, one could predict how that system operated. Today, a massive body of empirical findings converge in making two basic conclusions rather clear: (1) The classic social background factors, together with some psychological variables, *do* strongly influence elite recruitment; and (2) Social background does *not* determine elite attitudes or behavior.

The first of these findings parallels the findings on mass participation; everywhere — East and West, in industrial nations and in developing ones — elites are recruited disproportionately from the upper strata of society. This is even more true of administrative elites than of political elites, and truer still of business elites. Moreover, the higher the elite role, the more heavily the upper strata are overrepresented (Brzezinski & Huntington, 1964; Bonilla, 1970; Barton, Denitch & Kadushin, 1973; Putnam, 1976; Wildenmann, 1971, 1973; Friedgut, 1979; Aberbach *et al.*, 1981).

Although all elites tend to come from the more privileged strata of society, there are significant developmental differences, with the importance of family ties declining and that of education rising as a society becomes economically and technologically more developed (Dogan & Scheffer-Van der Veen, 1957-1958; Dogan, 1961; Clubok, Berghorn & Wilensky, 1969).

The second set of findings is more recent, intuitively less obvious, and runs counter to early expectations; nevertheless it now rests on a solid empirical base: the social background of elites has only a limited impact on their attitudes, issue preferences and behavior. This holds true partly, but only partly, because selective recruitment constrains the variation in social background, reducing its potential explanatory power. Knowledge of elite social background is essential in order to assess equality of opportunity in a given society, but it does not go very far toward explaining a nation's decision-making processes (Edinger & Searing, 1967; Prewitt, Eulau & Zisk, 1966-1967; Searing, 1969; Lodge, 1969, 1973; Barton, 1973; Wellhofer, 1974; Suleiman, 1974; Putnam, 1973, 1976; Aberbach *et al.*, 1981; Von Beyme, 1982). For example, a recent study of elites in Great Britain, West Germany, Italy, France, The Netherlands and the United States, found path coefficients between the respondent's social class and ideological position of only .10 among politicians, and .03 among bureaucrats (Aberbach *et al.*, 1981, pp. 161-164). Analyzing governmental decisions in the Federal Republic of Germany from 1949 to 1976, Von Beyme (1982) concludes that changes in the social composition of the parliaments do not explain variations in governmental output. These findings imply that the relative weight of adult role socialization, as compared with early political socialization, is greater for elites than for the general public — where family background *is* an important influence. This is not entirely surprising; elites receive far more adult political socialization in their roles as officials or politicians than does the general public.

One of the most basic features of modernization has been a long-term shift from role recruitment based on ascriptive characteristics toward an increasing emphasis on achievement (Almond & Coleman, 1961). The declining importance of family ties and the rising emphasis on education noted above seems to be part of this broad trend; but elites are distinctive in possessing a wide variety of skills, with technical expertise becoming increasingly prominent as a society becomes technologically more advanced (Dogan, 1961;

Blondel, 1963; Prewitt, 1970; Quandt, 1970; Bell, 1973; Rose, 1974; Putnam, 1973, 1976).

Elites tend to be much more politicized than non-elites. They are not only more educated and better informed about politics, but their political belief systems are more constrained and ideologically consistent than those of mass publics (Converse, 1964; Budge et al., 1972; Putnam, 1976).

Elites are, by definition, politically more influential than the average member of the general public. But the question of how much impact they have, and why, is one of the major areas demanding further research. Far too little is known about the linkages between masses, elites, and political outcomes. Elite analysts tend to avoid dealing with the difficult question of linkages by implicitly assuming that (1) elite behavior is not greatly influenced by mass pressures; but (2) elite preferences do determine political outcomes.

An extreme example of elite determinism is provided by Nordlinger (1981), who argues that public officials are largely autonomous from societal pressures, and are able to impose their own goals upon nominally democratic societies. Another example is Field and Higley's (1982) provocative interpretation of political change as almost completely due to the degree to which a nation's elites are unified or disunified. At the opposite extreme, aggregate analyses by Schmidt (1982) suggest that it doesn't make much difference what type of elite governs a society. Elite determinism remains an empirical question that has not been answered.

With most everyday issues elites, no doubt, do enjoy a great deal of freedom from mass pressures. But the exceptions tend to be crucial, as the Civil Rights movement, the opposition to the war in Vietnam, the anti-nuclear power movement and the current Peace Movement in Western Europe all suggest. Moreover, there are indications that the potential for more active mass political intervention has been increasing (Barnes, Kaase et al., 1979). Empirical analysis of elite-mass linkages is difficult, complex and expensive. But it is crucial to understanding the political process. To date, only a few studies have been completed (Miller & Stokes, 1963; Converse & Pierce, forthcoming). The findings indicate that constituencies do shape their representatives' views, but the extent to which this is true varies a good deal from issue to issue. Miller and Stokes (1963) found that, with foreign policy and social welfare issues, elite-mass linkages were weak; but in the area of civil rights, American Congressmen voted according to their perception of constituency attitudes — and these perceptions were pretty accurate.

Analyzing whether electorates influence the policy positions taken by their party, Inglehart (1984) examines data based on interviews with candidates for the European Parliament, from 66 different parties in France, Italy, Britain, Germany, The Netherlands, Belgium, Luxembourg, Denmark and Ireland. These candidates' positions indicate the issue positions taken by their parties, not only in the European Parliament but also in the respective national parliaments — in which many of them also hold seats. Analysis of these elite-level data, together with the results from samples of their electorates, reveals substantial correlations between the issue preferences of political elites and those of their electorates, many of them falling in the .5 to .7 range. We must bear in mind that these correlations are based on aggregated data (using the party as the unit of analysis); however, the strength of these correlations tends to support a rationalist interpretation of political behavior. But the *direction* of the causal linkages is unclear; does this close fit between the policy preferences of elites and electorates reflect the influence of the electorates on political leaders, or vice versa, or both? Or could these correlations be, in part, the joint result of some antecedent variable?

It is difficult to determine the direction of causality in the relationship between these elite and mass issue preferences. But we also have measures of constituency characteristics—such as the social class composition or the church attendance rate of a given electorate—that are *antecedent* to the issue positions taken by both elites and electorates. Here, the causal direction is relatively clear. One can plausibly argue that political elites take a "Left" policy position because their electorate is predominantly working class, or predominantly non-religious, or that a given social group supports a given party because its candidates take the Left position on given issues—each of which implies a different type of constituency influence. But one can *not* plausibly argue that a given electorate became working class, or ceased attending church, because its candidates favored the Left issue position. Similarly, Materialist or Post-Materialist value priorities tend to be long-term characteristics of given groups (Inglehart, forthcoming); it seems more plausible to view them as an influence on candidates' issue positions, than as caused by them.

Figure 2 shows the mean product moment correlations between constituency characteristics and elite policy preferences on two types of issues: (1) a set of three economic issues—concerning attitudes toward further nationalization of industry, a greater government role in the economy, and more equal distribution of income; and (2) a set of three non-economic issues—concerning support for building nuclear power plants, increased defense expenditures, and more severe measures against terrorism.

The social class composition of the electorate is linked with elite positions on economic issues in the expected direction: candidates of parties with a relatively high proportion of manual workers are relatively favorable to nationalization of industry, a greater government role in the economy, and more equal distribution of income. But the strength of these correlations is far weaker than the relationship with church attendance rates; elites whose electorates attend church frequently are very likely to support the conservative position on these issues. Moreover the social class composition of the electorate seems to have virtually no effect whatever on non-economic issues. These findings reinforce the individual-level evidence cited above that social class is no longer the dominant influence on political behavior. Conversely, the relatively powerful correlation between the religious orientations of the electorates and the issue positions of the candidates supports survey-based findings that religion remains a surprisingly strong political variable. However, the fact that the church, generally speaking, ceased intervening on economic issues some decades ago, suggests that much of the mass-elite issue congruence reflects the persisting influence of distinctive political cultures. Throughout most of Western Europe, church attendance is part of a long-standing political culture of the Right. Its effects seem remarkably pervasive

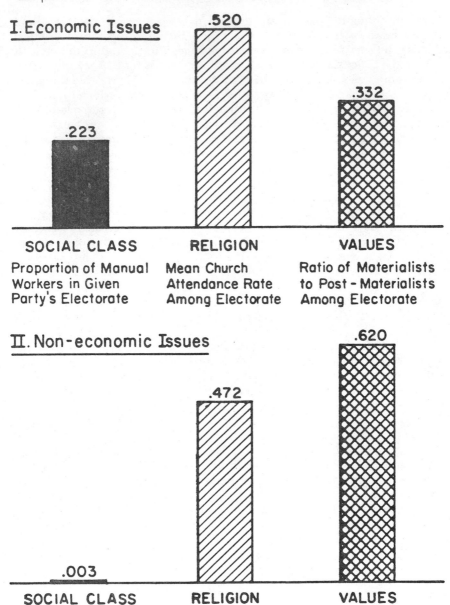

FIGURE 2

Correlates of Issue Positions Taken by Candidates of 66 Parties
from Nine West European Countries

Source: Issue battery included in survey of 742 candidates to European Parliament
interviewed in spring, 1979 (see Inglehart *et al.*, 1980); and data on electorates from
cumulative results of Euro-barometer surveys 3-12.

and durable; it outweighs the impact of social class, even on specifically economic issues.

The distribution of Materialist/Post-Materialist values among the electorate ranks far behind religion in its apparent impact on elite positions on economic issues. But with regard to the non-economic issues, the electorates' value priorities are the strongest predictor of all. Theoretically, Post-Materialism has emerged as an important political force only recently; and the empirical evidence supports this assumption. Political elites whose electorates include high proportions of Post-Materialists, tend to take the "Left" position on both types of issues, but the linkage is far stronger with the relatively new non-economic issues, than with the traditional Left-Right economic issues. The newness of the values cleavage, together with the newness of the noneconomic issues as they are formulated today, suggests that the elite-mass linkage found here does *not* simply reflect a long-standing political culture shared by elites and mass—such as the relationship between mass church attendance and elite issue positions. Current influences must be invoked to account for the correspondence between elite policy positions and the values of their electorates.

The strength of these linkages reinforces the interpretation that constituency preferences *do* influence elite policy positions. It may be that the relatively modest findings to date concerning the impact of mass policy preferences are partly due to the fact that we have been looking at only part of the picture. The analyses carried out so far have, of necessity, usually focused on voting, and have tended to use economic indicators as the independent variables. This does not reflect a blind spot on the part of the investigators; it is simply a consequence of the fact that other types of data have not been readily available. The findings presented here suggest that we would uncover stronger evidence of rationality in mass behavior if: (1) we were to examine dependent variables other than voting—which is far more heavily constrained by institutionalized party loyalties than is true of issue preferences or elite-challenging political behavior; and (2) we were to focus on the *new* issues that tend to be central to political controversy today, rather than the traditional Left-Right economic issues that remain important but are now deeply embedded in the political culture and party loyalties of industrial societies.

It is easier to propose such a research strategy than to carry it out. For if our interpretation is correct, we are *not* data-rich; we are suffering from a serious lack of certain types of data—above all, data on non-electoral cleavages at both the elite and mass levels. In the long run, information on individual attitudes and behavior must be incorporated in models that integrate both individual characteristics, and institutional and macroeconomic variables. In order to capture a maximum amount of institutional variation, these models should utilize cross-national time-series data. Many of the conceptual tools exist; we have only begun to gather the data.

V. TOWARD INTERACTIVE ANALYSIS

One of the central questions of comparative political behavior has been, "Who participates in politics?" But this question, itself, is meaningful only if we assume that political action has an impact—that those who participate most, are most likely to get what they want. Both mass and elite research are built on the assumption that they do.

This is the ultimate "So What?" question; Does political participation make any difference? Does it result in a higher share of the national income, or a higher life expectancy for the given group? Does it influence public policy, bringing it closer to the given group's goals? These are questions that individual-level research—whether it focuses on publics or elites—is ill-equipped to answer. In order to answer, one must be able to treat relative shares of income and other public policy outputs as variables—over time or cross-nationally; the dependent variable is a macro-phenomenon. Measuring the impact of given groups' values, preferences and skills on political outputs, requires the integration of micro- and macro-level data for aggregate-level data and individual-level data have complementary strengths and weaknesses. Using the latter alone, one can only assume that individual actions have an impact on systemic outputs; while using the former alone, one can only assume that values, goals and skills are monolithic and unchanging attributes of given groups. Neither set of assumptions is justifiable a priori.

One-shot survey research has rightly been criticized on the grounds that it takes the "So What?" question for granted. It could turn out that the behavior it studies does not have any real impact on one's standard of living, life expectancy, personal freedom, quality of life, or the other goals that people seek to attain through political action. In one of the few analyses that integrates survey data with policy measures, Page and Shapiro (1983) find that changes in American public opinion from 1935 to 1979 usually were followed by changes in public policy, and that public opinion seemed to influence policy more than policy influenced opinion. Nevertheless, the impact of public opinion has not yet been demonstrated in any conclusive manner.

But it is equally clear that most of the macro-level research undertaken so far, tends to take the "Why?" question for granted: it assumes that everyone is, and always has been, attempting to maximize the same utilities—with the implicit assumption usually being that they are maximizing personal economic gains. The research on values cited above indicates that (1) this is true of many, but by no means all people—with the exceptions being disproportionately active politically; and (2) it is much less true today than it was a few decades ago.

Thus far, aggregate-level studies have shown a good fit between macro-economic conditions and election outcomes (Kramer, 1971; Tufte, 1975; Fair, 1978), but survey-based research has found only weak linkages between the two at the level of the individual voter (Fiorina, 1978; Kinder & Kiewiet, 1979). Kinder and Kiewiet interpret this disparity as resulting from "sociotropic" behavior on the part of many voters: their choice is determined, not by how well they have done personally, but by how well they think the nation has fared. Rejecting this idea, Kramer (1983) argues that the disparity exists because individual-level data are heavily contaminated with exogenous influences that should be disregarded because they are politically irrelevant. Hence, in this case, individual-level behavior (voting) is best investigated with aggregate-level data.

Kramer, no doubt, is correct in concluding that individual-level behavior has a large idiosyncratic component. In part, the disparity between findings from the two levels reflects the inherent tendency, noted above, for behavior to seem more rational (i.e., explainable) when viewed at the aggregate level than at the individual level. However, the poor fit may also reflect the fact that personal economic gains are not necessarily the dominant influence on political behavior, although one *is* influenced by one's perceptions of how society as a whole is doing. Moreover, economic determinism seems to have been declining. If so, individual-level analysis based on recent surveys would show relatively little evidence of it—although its impact would still be large in macroeconomic analyses based on a long time series.

Both micro and macro analysis provide essential information. Economic rationality seems to have a significant impact on elections, as macroeconomic analyses indicate. But to view human motivations as a constant, and disregard individual-level evidence concerning them, seems unwise and unwarranted.

Does political participation tend to get the participants what they want, or what they are assumed to want? Some of the most significant recent research has addressed this question using aggregate-level data. The answer is not yet clear. Analyses by such scholars as Hewitt (1977), Cameron (1978), and Hibbs (1977) indicate that political participation *does* make a difference —a conclusion that is disputed by Parkin (1971), Jackman (1975, 1980) and Schmidt (1982).

A relatively small but growing set of comparative behavioral analyses have continued to focus on structural variables when the key innovations seemed to be emerging from individual level analysis. Gurr (1970) pioneered in the empirical analysis of political violence, elaborating a typology of domestic and external violence and attempting to explain it in terms of economic and institutional factors. In subsequent work, Gurr and Duvall (1973) and Gurr and Lichbach (1979) have developed a formal model with an impressive capacity to explain the magnitude and properties of civil conflict at the national level.

Lipset (1960) addressed the same basic question that concerned Almond and Verba (1963)—the social conditions favorable to democracy—but approached it through the analysis of aggregate statistical data and historical materials. He concluded that stable democracy requires a reasonably high level of economic development, plus legitimacy (the belief that the existing institutions are appropriate) and effective performance. Subsequent research has extended the scope of the original study and introduced far more sophisticated techniques, including time series analysis. But Lipset's basic findings have largely been upheld. Although Lipset tended to ignore the distinction between how *democratic* a nation is, and how *stable* a democracy is (Bollen, 1980), economic development does seem conducive to stable democracy (Cutwright, 1967; Dahl, 1971; Jackman, 1975; Hewitt, 1977). The extent to which democratic practices prevail in a country is linked with its per capita wealth and level of industrialization (Adelman & Morris, 1967; Jackman, 1973; Bollen, 1979). Also concerned with the preconditions of democracy, but focusing on communication variables, McCrone and Cnudde (1967) concluded that urbanization leads to the spread of education; education in turn leads to the development of communications networks; these in turn are conducive to the emergence of democratic government—perhaps as a consequence of processes similar to those *The Civic Culture* emphasizes.

The foregoing studies take it for granted that democracy is a good thing. But does it make any difference, in terms of economic equality, or might democracy be interpreted as a sham, from a purely materialistic viewpoint? Jackman (1975) finds that democracy is positively associated with income equality, but that this relationship is spurious. For there is a strong linkage between economic development and income equality, and between economic development and the presence of democracy; the association between democracy and equality disappears when the level of economic development is taken into account. Adelman and Morris (1973), Paukert (1973) and Wilensky (1975) reach similar conclusions. Hewitt (1977) develops this analysis farther, finding that while democracy, in itself, has only limited impact on income equality, government by social democratic parties *does* have a significant effect.

Similarly, Kramer (1971), Nordhaus (1975), Hibbs (1976, 1977), and Tufte (1975, 1978) analyze the impact of elections on macroeconomic policies and outcomes, such as economic growth, employment rates, and inflation rates. Moving beyond simple economic determinism, these investigators find that electoral behavior not only *responds* to economic events, it is also a major *influence* on them. Their results indicate, for example, that when parties of the Left are in office, they tend to emphasize full employment at the cost of higher inflation. In the same vein, Cameron (1978) finds that the more a nation has been governed by Social Democratic parties, the greater is the rate of growth in the public sector of the economy—although dependence on foreign trade is an even stronger predictor.

In striking contradiction to these authors, however, Jackman (1975, 1980) and Schmidt (1982) conclude that the partisanship of the government has little or no impact on the policy outputs of Western democracies. Reexamining the hypothesis that Socialist governments tend to reduce income inequality, Jackman (1980) notes that Hewitt (1977) included in his analysis an extreme outlier, South Africa; this country has (1) nearly twice as much income inequality as any other of the 15 nations analyzed, and (2) no significant socialist party. Removing this one outlier reduces the correlation between socialism and income equality from an impressive level to an insignificant one. This, and other considerations, lead Jackman to conclude that overall, social democratic governments do not produce greater income equality than more conservative regimes.

Schmidt (1982) broadens this argument. Reanalyzing Hibbs' (1977), evidence that social democratic governments reduce unemployment at the cost of higher inflation, he *adds* several deviant cases: relatively socialistic nations with high unemployment (such as Israel) or low inflation (Austria and Switzerland); or nations rarely or never governed by socialists, with low unemployment (Japan and New Zealand). This expanded data base shows a much weaker correlation between socialist participation in government and economic outcomes. Applying a similar critique to the findings of Cameron

(1978), Schmidt (1982) finds strikingly different correlations for the period 1960-1975, as compared with 1950-1959. He concludes that social democratic parties *per se* have little impact on the policy outcomes of capitalist societies. Only when a number of other preconditions are present—such as a strong, unified labor movement and a divided Right—do social democratic regimes reduce unemployment and expand the public sector of the economy; otherwise, they make little difference.

If Schmidt's basic conclusions are correct, the implications are far-reaching. From one perspective, they could be taken as evidence that democracy is largely meaningless in a capitalist society; the capitalist economic system dominates politics so totally that social democratic parties are either co-opted or rendered ineffectual (Offe, 1972). Full employment and full economic equality can only be attained by rejecting capitalism altogether.

Another interpretation is that the surprisingly small long-term differences between the economic outputs of socialist and conservative governments could reflect a tendency for market-oriented advanced industrial societies to move toward a predictable equilibrium point in the compromise between labor and capital (Przeworski & Wallerstein, 1982). In the most advanced societies, even those elites and publics that were once most favorably disposed toward egalitarian social policies become less and less change-oriented as they approach this point. Thus, although they helped develop one of the world's most advanced social welfare systems, Sweden's Social Democratic bureaucrats and politicians today are among the *least* change-oriented elites in the Western world (Anton, 1980; Aberbach, *et al.*, 1981). Similarly, the Danish public has supported the emergence of a highly developed welfare state, but today shows relatively little desire to expand it farther (Inglehart, 1984). Nevertheless, even if advanced welfare societies like Sweden and Denmark have experienced diminishing polarization on economic issues, we would *not* expect policy conflict between political parties to disappear; instead, it would show an increasing tendency to focus on emerging noneconomic issues.

The controversy seems far from settled, however. Analysis of the relationship between economic outputs and the political parties in power has produced some fascinating and provocative interpretations; it has not yet come up with definitive answers. One reason for the diverging results obtained so far is a problem inherent in using the nation as a unit of analysis: the small number of cases. If one is analyzing the importance of partisanship in industrialized democracies, for example, one has at *best* two to three dozen cases—assuming generous definitions of "industrialized" and "democracy." As we have seen, the addition or subtraction of a few cases—because of defensibly different interpretations of how a given case should be classified—can change the overall pattern dramatically. In order to alleviate this problem— and because the basis of political conflict or consensus seems to change over time—it is likely that research on this topic will increasingly utilize time series analysis. The third, updated edition of the *World Handbook of Political and Social Indicators* (Taylor & Jodice, 1983) should be of great value to this enterprise.

In a particularly interesting analysis that integrates macro-level and micro-level data, Powell (1981, 1982) examines the social, economic and political roots of effective democratic political performance. He concludes that performance has three distinct dimensions: (1) citizen participation, (2) stable government, and (3) political order. Each of these dimensions reflects different causal processes, shaped by different independent variables. Multivariate analysis of data from 29 democracies indicates that: nations with small populations tend to have low per capita rates of rioting and deaths from political violence; the level of economic development—though not economic growth rates—affects voting participation and death rates; ethnic homogeneity affects executive stability and deaths; and the type of party system affects voting rates, executive stability and deaths. On the whole, Powell's findings indicate that political factors—particularly party system characteristics and cleavage structures—are more important than economic influences on governmental performance.

In summation, after an era of relative quiescence, the macroanalysis of political phenomena has re-emerged with a vengeance. It has brought renewed attention to some of the most basic and significant aspects of political life, seeking answers to questions about the ultimate societal consequences of individual-level behavior. Its models are more complex than those commonly used in the analysis of individual-level data; they almost invariably explain a much higher proportion of variance in the data. Though they are still rare, the most fruitful studies combine data or insights from the macroanalytic and microanalytic level in interactive fashion, examining the linkages between political culture, political institutions, economic and social phenomena.

Recent trends place renewed emphasis on structural factors, and it has redressed the balance fruitfully, because institutions always were and still are important. But much of the research done so far reflects an unexamined assumption that economic variables are either the dominant influence on political behavior, or the only indicator worth considering for whether political action has significant consequences. Behavioral research has made the primacy of economics increasingly dubious.

While economics is an important factor in politics, it is by no means the only one. Some of the most significant other variables seem to be individual-level orientations and skills that we have only begun to measure in a standardized form suitable for quantitative comparative analysis. We must move farther in this direction. For the wave of the future does not seem to be a one-sided reliance on either macro-level analysis or individual-level analysis alone, but in the task of integrating both in more complex but more adequate models of politics.

REFERENCES

Aberbach, Joel D., et al. Bureaucrats and politicians in western democracies. Cambridge: Harvard University Press, 1981.

Abramson, Paul R. Generational change in American politics. Lexington, MA: Lexington Books, 1975.

Abramson, Paul R. Class voting in the 1976 election. Journal of Politics, 1978, 40, 1066-1072. (a)

Abramson, Paul R. Generational replacement and partisan dealignment in Britain and the United States. *British Journal of Political Science,* 1978, *8,* 505-509. (b)

Abramson, Paul R. *Political attitudes in America: Formation and change.* San Francisco: Freeman, 1983.

Abramson, Paul R., Aldrich, John H. & Rohde, David. *Change and continuity in the 1980 elections.* Washington, D.C.: Congressional Quarterly Press, 1982.

Adelman, Irma & Morris, Cynthia Taft. *Economic growth and social equity in developing countries.* Stanford: Stanford University Press, 1973.

Alford, Robert R. *Party and society: The Anglo-American democracies.* Chicago: Rand, McNally, 1963.

Almond, G., & Coleman, J. (Eds.). *The politics of the developing areas.* Princeton Princeton University Press, 1961.

Almond, Gabriel A. & Verba, Sidney. *The civic culture.* Princeton, N.J.: Princeton University Press, 1963.

Almond, G. A. & Verba, S. (Eds.). *The civic culture revisited.* Boston: Little, Brown, 1980.

Alt, James E. *The politics of economic decline: Economic management and political behavior in Britain since 1964.* Cambridge: Cambridge University Press, 1979.

Anton, Thomas. *Administered politics: Elite political culture in Sweden.* New York: Martinus Nijhoff, 1980.

Baker, Kendall L., Dalton, Russell & Hildebrandt, Kai. *Germany transformed.* Cambridge: Harvard University Press, 1981.

Barnes, Samuel. Religion and class in Italian electoral behavior. In Richard Rose (Ed.). *Electoral behavior: A comparative handbook.* New York: Free Press, 1974.

Barnes, Samuel. Elections and Italian democracy: An evaluation. In Howard Penniman (Ed.). *Italy at the polls, 1979.* Washington, D.C.: American Enterprise Institute, 1981.

Barnes, Samuel, Kaase, Max, et al. *Political action: Mass participation in five western democracies.* Beverly Hills: Sage Publications, 1979.

Barnes, Samuel & Pierce, Roy. Public opinion and political preferences in France and Italy. *Midwest Journal of Political Science,* 1971, *15,* 643-660.

Barton, Allen H. Determinants of leadership attitudes in a socialist society. In Allen H. Barton, Bogdan Denitch, & Charles Kadushin (Eds.). *Opinion-making elites in Yugoslavia.* New York: Praeger, 1973.

Barton, Allen H., Denitch, Bogdan & Kadushin, Charles (Eds.). *Opinion-making elites in Yugoslavia.* New York: Praeger, 1973.

Beck, Paul & Jennings, M. Kent. Political periods and political participation. *American Political Science Review,* 1979, *73,* 737-750.

Bell, Daniel. *The coming of post-industrial society: A venture in social forecasting.* New York: Basic Books, 1973.

Berelson, Bernard R. et al. *Voting—A study of opinion formation in a presidential campaign.* Chicago: The University of Chicago Press, 1954.

Berger, Manfred et al. Die bundestagswahl 1976: Politik und sozialstruktur. *Zeitschrift für Parlamentsfragen,* 1977, *8,* 197-231.

Bishop, George F. et al. Change in the structure of American political attitudes: The nagging question of question wording. *American Journal of Political Science,* 1978, *22,* 250-269.

Blondel, Jean. *Voters, parties, and leaders: The social fabric of British politics.* Harmondsworth, England: Penguin Books, 1963.

Bollen, K. A. Political democracy and the timing of development. *American Sociological Review,* 1979, *44,* 572-587.

Bollen, K. A. Issues in the comparative measurement of political democracy. *American Sociological Review,* 1980, *45,* 370-390.

Bonilla, Frank. *The failure of elites*. Cambridge, MA: M.I.T. Press, 1970.

Books, John W. & Reynolds, JoAnn B. A note on class voting in Great Britain and the United States. *Comparative Political Studies*, 1975, *8*, 360-375.

Borre, Ole & Katz, Daniel. Party identification and its motivational base in a multi-party system. *Scandinavian Political Studies*, 1973, *8*, 69-111.

Borre, Ole. The social bases of Danish electoral behavior. In Richard Rose (Ed.). *Electoral participation: A comparative analysis*. Beverly Hills, CA: Sage Publications, 1980.

Boyd, Richard W. Popular control of public policy: A normal vote analysis of the 1968 election. *American Political Science Review*, 1972, *66*, 429-449.

Brody, Richard A. & Page, Benjamin I. Comment: The assessment of policy voting. *American Political Science Review*, 1972, *66*, 450-458.

Brzezinski, Zbigniew & Huntington, Samuel. *Political power: USA/USSR*. New York: Viking, 1964.

Budge, Ian. *Agreement and the stability of democracy*. Chicago: Markham, 1970.

Budge, Ian, Brand, J. A., Margolis, Michael, & Smith, A. L. M. *Political stratification and democracy*. Toronto: University of Toronto Press, 1972.

Budge, Ian. Electoral volatility: Issue effects and basic change in 23 postwar democracies. Unpublished paper, University of Essex, 1982.

Budge, Ian & Farlie, Dennis. A comparative analysis of factors correlated with turnout and voting choice. In Ian Budge, Ivor Crewe & Dennis Farlie (Eds.). *Party identification and beyond*. London: Wiley, 1976.

Budge, Ian & Farlie, Dennis. *Voting and party competition: A spatial synthesis and a critique of existing approaches applied to surveys from ten democracies*. London and New York: Wiley, 1982.

Bunce, Valerie. Elite succession, petrification, and policy innovation in communist states: An empirical assessment. *Comparative Political Studies*, 1976, *9*, 3-42.

Bunce, Valerie. The succession connection. *American Political Science Review*, 1980, *74*, 966-977.

Bürklin, Wilhelm. Determinanten der wahlentscheidung fur die 'Grünen.' *Politische Vierteljahresschrift*, 1981, *22*, 4.

Butler, David & Stokes, Donald. *Political change in Britain* (2nd ed.). New York: St. Martin's Press, 1974.

Cameron, David R. Stability and change in patterns of French partisanshp: A cohort analysis. *Public Opinion Quarterly*, 1972, *31*, 19-30.

Cameron, David R. The expansion of the public economy: A comparative analysis. *American Political Science Review*, 1978, *72*, 1243-1261.

Campbell, Angus, Gurin, Gerald & Miller, Warren E. *The voter decides*. Evanston/White Plains: Row, Peterson,1954.

Campbell, Angus et al. *The American voter*. New York: John Wiley, 1960.

Capdevielle, Jacques et al. *France de Gauche vote à droite*. Paris: Fondation nationale des Sciences Politiques, 1981.

Carmines, Edward G. & Stimson, James A. Two faces of issue voting. *American Political Science Review*, 1980, *74*, 78-91.

Clubok, Alfred, Berghorn, Forrest, & Wilensky, Norman. Family relationships, congressional recruitment and political modernization. *Journal of Politics*, 1969, *31*, 1035-1062.

Coleman, James S. The political systems of the developing areas. In Gabriel A. Almond & James S. Coleman (Eds.). *The politics of the developing areas*. Princeton: Princeton University Press, 1960.

Conradt, David P. Changing German political culture. In Gabriel Almond & Sidney Verba (Eds.). *The civic culture revisited*. Boston: Little, Brown, 1980.

Converse, Philip E. The nature of belief systems in mass publics. In David E. Apter (Ed.). *Ideology and discontent.* New York: The Free Press, 1964.

Converse, Philip E. Of time and partisan stability. *Comparative Political Studies,* 1969, *2,* 139-171.

Converse, Philip E. Change in the American electorate. In Angus E. Campbell & Philip E. Converse (Eds.). *The human meaning of social change.* New York: Russell Sage, 1972.

Converse, Philip E. Some priority variables in comparative electoral research. In Richard Rose (Ed.). *Electoral behavior: A comparative handbook.* New York: Free Press, 1974.

Converse, Philip E. *Political representation in France.* Cambridge: Harvard University Press, forthcoming.

Converse, Philip E. & Dupeux, Georges. Politicization of the electorate in France and the United States. *Public Opinion Quarterly,* 1962, *26,* 1-23.

Converse, Philip E. & Pierce, Roy. Die mai-unruhen in Frankreich: Ausmass und konsequenzen. In Klaus Allerbeck & Leopold Rosenmayr (Eds.). *Aufstand der Jugend?* Munich: Juventa, 1971.

Cotgrove, Stephen & Duff, Andrew. Environmentalism, middle class radicalism and politics. *Sociological Review,* 1980, *28,* 333-351.

Cotgrove, Stephen & Duff, Andrew. Environmentalism, values and social change. *British Journal of Sociology,* 1981, *32,* 92-110.

Crewe, Ivor, Sarlvik, Bo, & Alt, James. Partisan dealignment in Britain 1964-1974. *British Journal of Political Science,* 1977, *7,* 129-190.

Crewe, Ivor, Sarlvik, Bo, & Alt, James. Reply to Abramson. *British Journal of Political Science,* 1978, *8.*

Crewe, Ivor & Sarlvik, Bo. *Voting in Britain.* Cambridge: Cambridge University Press, 1982.

Cutwright, Phillips. Inequality: A cross-national analysis. *American Sociological Review,* 1967, *32,* 562-578.

Dahl, Robert A. *Polyarchy: Participation and opposition.* New Haven, CT: Yale University Press, 1971.

Dalton, Russell J. Was there a revolution? *Comparative Political Studies,* 1977, *9,* 459-473.

Dalton, Russell J. Reassessing parental socialization: Indicator unreliability versus generational transfer. *American Political Science Review,* 1980, *74,* 421-431.

Dalton, Russell J. The persistence of values and life cycle changes. In Hans Klingemann & Max Kaase (Eds.). *Politische psychologie,* special issue of *Politische Vierteljahresschrift,* 1981, *12,* 189-207.

Dalton, Russell J. Partisan dealignment and cognitive mobilization in advanced industrial democracies. Presented at the ECPR Workshop on Problems of Party Government, Aarhus, Denmark, March 29-April 3, 1982.

Dalton, Russell J. The German party system: Between two ages. In Russell Dalton, Scott Flanagan & Paul Beck (Eds.). *Electoral change: Realignment and dealignment in industrial societies,* forthcoming.

Dalton, Russell J., Flanagan, Scott & Beck, Paul (Eds.). *Electoral change realignment and dealignment in advanced industrial democracies.* Princeton: Princeton University Press, forthcoming.

Davies, James C. Toward a theory of revolution. *American Sociological Review,* 1962, *27,* 5-18.

deJong, J. J. *Overheid en onderdaan.* Wageningen: Zomer en Keunings, 1956.

Deutsch, Emeric *et al. Les familles politiques aujourd'hui en France.* Paris: Editions de Minuit, 1966.

Dogan, Mattei. Political ascent in a class society: French deputies 1870-1958. In

Dwaine Marvick (Ed.). *Political decision-makers.* New York: Free Press, 1961.

Dogan, Mattei & Scheffer-van der Veen, Maria. Le personnel ministeriel Hollandais (1848-1958). *L'annee sociologique* (3rd ser.). 1957-58, 95-125.

Downs, Anthony. *An economic theory of democracy.* New York: Random House, 1957.

Dutter, Lee E. The Netherlands as a plural society. *Comparative Political Studies,* 1978, *10,* 555-588.

Easton, David A. & Dennis, Jack. *Children in the political system.* New York: McGraw-Hill, 1969.

Edinger, Lewis J. & Searing, Donald D. Social background in elite analysis: A methodological inquiry. *American Political Science Review,* 1967, *61,* 428-445.

Eldersveld, Samuel J. *Political parties in American society.* New York: Basic Books, 1982.

Fair, R. C. The effects of economic events on vote for president. *Review of Economics and Statistics,* 1978, *60,* 159-175.

Falter, Jurgen W. & Rattinger, Hans. Parteien, kandidaten und politische streitfragen bei der bundestagswahl 1980: Moglichkeiten und grenzen der normal-vote analyse. In Max Kaase & Hans D. Klingemann (Eds.). *Wahlen und politische kultur: Studien zur bundestagswahl 1980.* Opladen: Westdeutscher Verlag, 1982.

Feldman, Stanley & Zuckerman, Alan S. Moving beyond party identification. *Comparative Political Studies,* 1982, *15,* 197-222.

Field, G. Lowell & Higley, John. The states of national elites and the stability of political institutions in 81 nations, 1950-1982. Paper presented at the meeting of the American Political Science Association, Denver, CO, 1982.

Fietkau, Hans-Joachim & Kessel, Hans (Eds.). *Die gruene zukunft.* Frankfurt: Campus Verlag, forthcoming.

Fietkau, Hans-Joachim & Tischler, Wolfgang. *Umwelt im spiegel der offentlichen meinung.* Frankfurt: Campus Verlag, 1982.

Finer, Samuel E. *The changing British party system, 1945-1979.* Washington, D.C.: American Enterprise Institute, 1980.

Fiorina, Morris P. *Representatives, roll calls, and constituencies.* Lexington, MA: Lexington Books, 1974.

Fiorina, Morris P. *Retrospective voting in American national elections.* New Haven, CT: Yale University Press, 1981.

Fiorina, Morris P. Economic retrospective voting in American national elections: A micro-analysis. *American Journal of Political Science,* 1978, *22,* 426-443.

Flanagan, Scott C. Value change and partisan change in Japan: The silent revolution revisited. *Comparative Politics,* 1979, *11,* 253-278.

Flanagan, Scott C. Value cleavages, economic cleavages, and the Japanese voter. *American Journal of Political Science,* 1980, *24,* 177-206.

Flanagan, Scott C. Changing values in advanced industrial society. *Comparative Political Studies,* 1982, *14,* 403-444.

Franklin, Mark N., & Mughan, Anthony. The decline of class voting in Britain: Problems of analysis and interpretation. *American Political Science Review,* 1978, *72,* 523-534.

Friedgut, Theodore. *Political participation in the U.S.S.R.* Princeton: Princeton University Press, 1979.

Gitelman, Zvi. Politics on the output side: Citizen-bureaucrat interaction in the U.S.S.R. Paper presented at annual meeting of the American Political Science Association, Denver, CO, 1982.

Glenn, Norval D. Class and party support in the United States: Recent and emerging trends. *Public Opinion Quarterly,* 1973, *33,* 17-33.

Goldberg, Arthur S. Discerning a causal pattern among data on voting behavior.

American Political Science Review, 1969, *60*, 913-922.

Greenstein, Fred. *Children and politics.* New Haven, CT: Yale University Press, 1965.

Groffman, Bernard & Muller, Edward N. The strange case of relative gratification and potential for political violence: The V-curve hypothesis. *American Political Science Review*, 1973, *67*, 514-529.

Gurr, Ted R. *Why men rebel.* Princeton: Princeton University Press, 1970.

Gurr, Ted R. & Duvall, R. Civil conflict in the 1960s: A reciprocal theoretical system with parameter estimates. *Comparative Political Studies*, 1973, *6*, 135-170.

Gurr, Ted R. & Lichbach, M. I. Forecasting domestic political conflict. In Michael D. Wallace & J. David Singer (Eds.). *To augur well.* Beverly Hills: Sage, 1979.

Hewitt, Christopher J. The effect of political democracy and social democracy on equality in industrial societies. *American Sociological Review*, 1977, *42*, 450-464.

Hibbs, Douglas A. *Mass political violence.* New York: John Wiley, 1973.

Hibbs, Douglas A. Political parties and macroeconomic policy. *American Political Science Review*, 1977, *71*, 467-487.

Hibbs, Douglas A. On the political economy of long-run trends in strike activity. *British Journal of Political Science*, 1978, *8*, 153-175.

Hibbs, Douglas A. with Nicholas Vasilatos. Economic outcomes and political support for British governments among occupational classes: A dynamic analysis. *American Political Science Review*, 1982, *76*, 259-279.

Hibbs, Douglas A., Rivers, Douglas & Vasilatos, Nicholas. The dynamics of political support for American presidents among occupational and partisan groups. *American Journal of Political Science*, 1982, *26*.

Hildebrandt, Kai & Dalton, Russell J. The new politics: Political change or sunshine politics? In Max Kaase & Klaus von Beyme (Eds.). *Elections and parties: Socio-political change and participation in the West German federal election of 1976.* Beverly Hills, CA: Sage Publications, 1978.

Himmelweit, Hilde *et al. How voters decide.* London and New York: Academic Press, 1981.

Hofferbert, Richard I. *The study of public policy.* Indianapolis and New York: Bobbs-Merrill, 1974.

Hough, Jerry. The Soviet system: Petrification or pluralism? *Problems of Communism*, 1972, *21*, 24-45.

Hough, Jerry. Political participation in the Soviet Union. *Soviet Studies*, 1976, *28*, 3-20.

Ike, Nobutaka. Economic growth and intergenerational change in Japan. *American Political Science Review*, 1973, *67*, 1194-1203.

Inglehart, Ronald. The silent revolution in Europe: Intergenerational change in post-industrial societies. *American Political Science Review*, 1971, *65*, 991-1017.

Inglehart, Ronald. *The silent revolution: Changing values and political styles among western publics.* Princeton, N.J.: Princeton University Press, 1977.

Inglehart, Ronald. Post-materialism in an environment of insecurity. *American Political Science Review*, 1981, *75*, 880-900.

Inglehart, Ronald. The changing structure of political cleavages in western society. In Russell J. Dalton, Scott Flanagan & Paul Beck (Eds.). *Electoral change: Realignment and dealignment in advanced industrial societies.* Princeton: Princeton University Press, 1984.

Inglehart, Ronald. Stability change and constraint in mass belief systems: The level of analysis paradox. Forthcoming.

Inglehart, Ronald, Gordon, Ian, Rabier, Jacques-René, & Sorensen, Carsten. Broader powers for the European parliament? The attitudes of candidates. *European Journal of Political Research*, 1980, *8*, 113-132.

Inglehart, Ronald & Hochstein, Avram. Alignment and dealignment of the electorate in France and the United States. *Comparative Political Studies*, 1972, *5*, 343-372.

Inglehart, Ronald & Klingemann, Hans. Party identification, ideological preference and the left-right dimension among western mass publics. In I. Budge, I. Crewe & D. Farlie. *Party identification and beyond*. New York: Wiley, 1976.

Inglehart, Ronald & Klingemann, Hans. Ideological conceptualization and value priorities. In Samuel Barnes, Max Kaase *et al. Political action: Mass participation in five western democracies*. Beverly Hills: Sage, 1979.

Inglehart, Ronald & Rabier, Jacques-René. Trust between nationalities. Paper presented at the meeting of the International Political Science Association, Rio de Janeiro, August, 1982.

Inglehart, Ronald & Sidjanski, Dusan. The left, the right, the establishment and the Swiss electorate. In I. Budge, I. Crewe & D. Farlie. *Party identification and beyond*. New York: Wiley, 1976.

Jackman, Mary R. & Jackman, Robert W. *Class awareness in the United States*. Berkeley: University of California Press, 1982.

Jackman, Robert W. On the relation of economic development to democratic performance. *American Journal of Political Science*, 1973, *17*, 611-621.

Jackman, Robert W. *Politics and social equality: A comparative analysis*. New York: Wiley, 1975.

Jackman, Robert W. The predictability of coups d'etat. *American Political Science Review*, 1978, *72*, 1262-1275.

Jackman, Robert W. Socialist parties and income inequality in western industrial societies. *Journal of Politics*, 1980, *42*, 135-149.

Jackson, John E. Issues, party choices and presidential votes. *American Journal of Political Science*, 1975, *19*, 161-185.

Jennings, M. Kent & Niemi, Richard G. The transmission of political values from parent to child. *American Political Science Review*, 1968, *62*, 169-184.

Jennings, M. Kent & Niemi, Richard G. *The political character of adolescence* Princeton: Princeton University Press, 1974.

Jennings, M. Kent and Niemi, Richard G. *Generations and politics*. Princeton: Princeton University Press, 1981.

Jennings, M. Kent, Allerbeck, Klaus & Rosenmayr, Leopold. Generations and families: General orientations. In Samuel Barnes, Max Kaase *et al. Political action*. Beverly Hills: Sage, 1979.

Kaase, Max. *Wechsel von parteipräferenzen*. Meisenheim: Anton Hain, 1967.

Kaase, Max & Klingemann, Hans D. Sozialstruktur, wertorientierung und parteiensysteme. In Joachim Matthes (Ed.). *Sozialer wandel in Westeuropa*. Frankfurt: Campus Verlag, 1979.

Katz, Richard. *A theory of parties and electoral systems*. Baltimore: Johns Hopkins University Press, 1981.

Kemp, David A. The Australian electorate. In Howard Penniman (Ed.). *The Australian national elections of 1977*. Washington, D.C.: American Enterprise Institute, 1979.

Kerr, Henry & Handley, David. Conflits des générations et politique étrangère en Suisse. *Annuaire Suisse de Science Politique*, 1974, 127-155.

Kessel, John H. Comment. *American Political Science Review*, 1972, *71*, 459-465.

Kinder, Donald R. & Kiewiet, D. R. Sociotropic politics: The American case. *British Journal of Political Science*, 1979, 11, 129-161.

Kinder, Donald R. & Sears, David O. Public opinion and political action. In G. Lindzey & E. Aronson (Eds.). *The handbook of social psychology* (3rd ed.). Reading, MA: Addison-Wesley, 1983.

King, Anthony. Whatever is happening to the British party system? *PS*, 1982, *15*, 10-17.

Klingemann, Hans. Issue-kompetenz und wahlentscheidung. *Politische Viertel-jahresschrift*, 1973, *14*, 227-256.

Kmieciak, Peter. *Wertstrukturen und wertwandel in der Bundesrepublik Deutsch-land*. Gottingen: Schwartz, 1976.

Knutsen, Oddbjorn. *Materialisme og post-materialisme i Norge*. Oslo: Institutt for Samfunnsforskning, 1982.

Kramer, Gerald H. Short-term fluctuations in U.S. voting behavior, 1896-1964. *American Political Science Review*, 1971, *65*, 131-143.

Kramer, Gerald H. The ecological fallacy revisited: Aggregate versus individual-level findings on economics and elections. *American Political Science Review*, 1983, *77*, 92-111.

Lafferty, William M. Basic needs and political values: Some perspectives from Nor-way on Europe's 'silent revolution.' *Acta Sociologica*, 1975, *19*, 117-136.

Lancelot, Alain. *Les classes moyennes et la politique*. Forthcoming.

Langton, Kenneth P. Peer group and school and the political socialization process. *American Political Science Review*, 1967, *61*, 751-758.

LaPalombara, Joseph. *Politics within nations*. Englewood Cliffs, N.J.: Prentice-Hall, 1974.

LaPalombara, Joseph. Monoliths and plural systems. *Studies in Comparative Communism*. 1975.

LaPalombara, Joseph. Socialist alternatives: The Italian variant. *Foreign Affairs*, 1982, *60*, 924-942.

Lazarsfeld, Paul F. *et al. The people's choice*. New York: Columbia University Press, 1948.

Leonardi, Franco. Valori o stereotipie etico-sociali? Riflessioni sulla 'nuova sinistra' di Ronald Inglehart. *Sociologia*. Forthcoming.

Leonardi, Robert. The Italian parliament in the 1979 elections. In Howard R. Penniman (Ed.). *Italy at the polls, 1979*. Washington, D.C.: American Enterprise Institute, 1981.

Lijphart, Arend. *Class and religious voting in the European democracies*. Occasional paper No. 8, Survey Research Center, University of Strathclyde, 1971.

Lijphart, Arend. Religion vs. linguistic vs. class voting: The 'crucial experiment' of comparing Belgium, Canada, South Africa, and Switzerland. *American Political Science Review*, 1979, 442-458.

Lijphart, Arend. Political parties: Ideologies and programs. In David Butler *et al.* (Eds.). *Democracy at the polls: A comparative study of competitive national elections*. Washington, D.C.: American Enterprise Institute, 1981.

Lipset, Seymour Martin. *Political man: The social bases of politics*. Garden City: Doubleday, 1960.

Lipset, Seymour Martin. The changing class structure and contemporary European politics. *Daedalus*, 1964, *93*, 271-303.

Lipset, Seymour Martin. *Political man: The social bases of politics* (2nd ed.). Balti-more: Johns Hopkins University Press, 1981.

Lipset, Seymour Martin & Rokkan, Stein. Introduction. In S. M. Lipset & S. Rokkan (Eds.). *Party systems and voter alignments*. New York: Macmillan, 1967.

Lodge, Milton. *Social elite attitudes since Stalin*. Columbus, OH: Charles E. Merrill, 1969.

Lodge, Milton. Attitudinal cleavages within the Soviet leadership since Stalin. In Carl Beck *et al.* (Eds.). *Comparative communist political leadership*. New York: David McKay, 1973.

Margolis, Michael. From confusion to confusion: Issues and the American voter (1956-1972). *American Political Science Review*, 1977, *71*, 31-43.

Marsh, Alan. The silent revolution, value priorities, and the quality of life in Britain. *American Political Science Review*, 1975, *69*, 1-30.

Marsh, Alan. *Protest and political consciousness.* Beverly Hills and London: Sage, 1977.

McCrone, Donald J. & Cnudde, Charles F. Toward a communications theory of democratic political development: A causal model. *American Political Science Review,* 1967, *61,* 72-79.

Michelat, *Guy & Simon, M. Classe, religion et comportement politique.* Paris: Editions Sociales, 1977.

Milbrath, Lester W. *Political participation.* Chicago: Rand McNally, 1965.

Milbrath, Lester W. & Goel, M. L. *Political participation* (2nd ed.). Chicago: Rand McNally, 1977.

Miller, Arthur H. Political issues and trust in government: 1964-1970. *American Political Science Review,* 1974, *68,* 951-972.

Miller, Arthur H., Miller, Warren E., Raine, Alden S. & Brown, Thad A. A majority party in disarray: Policy polarization in the 1972 election. *American Political Science Review,* 1976, *70,* 753-778.

Miller, Warren E. & Stokes, Donald E. Constituency influences in Congress. *American Political Science Review,* 1963, *57,* 45-56.

Miller, Warren E. & Southard, Philip C. Confessional attachment and electoral behavior in The Netherlands. *European Journal of Political Research,* 1975, *3,* 219-258.

Miller, Warren E. & Levitin, Teresa E. *Leadership and change: The new politics and the American electorate.* Cambridge, MA: Winthrop, 1976.

Muller, Edward N. *Aggressive political participation.* Princeton: Princeton University Press, 1979.

Müller-Rommel, Ferdinand. Ecology parties in Western Europe. *West European Politics,* 1982, *1,* 68-74.

Nardi, Rafaella. Sono le condizioni economiche a influenzare I valori? Un conrollo dell'ipotesi di Inglehart. *Rivista Italiana di Scienza Politica,* 1980, *10,* 293-315.

Nie, Norman & Andersen, Kristi. Mass belief systems revisited: Political change and attitude structure. *Journal of Politics,* 1974, *36,* 540-591.

Nie, Norman H., Powell, G. Bingham & Prewitt, Kenneth. Social structure and political participation: Developmental relationships, Parts 1 and 2. *American Political Science Review,* 1969, *63,* 361-378, 808-832.

Nie, Norman, Verba, Sidney & Petrocik, John R. *The changing American voter.* Cambridge, MA: Harvard University Press, 1976.

Nordhaus, William D. The political business cycle. *Review of Economic Studies,* 1975, *42,* 160-190.

Nordlinger, Eric A. *On the autonomy of the democratic state.* Cambridge, MA: Harvard University Press, 1981.

Norpoth, Helmut. Party identification in West Germany: Tracing an elusive concept. *Comparative Political Studies,* 1978, *11,* 36-61.

Offe, Claus. *Struktur probleme des kapitalistischen staates.* Frankfurt, 1972.

Ordeshook, Peter C. The spatial theory of elections: A review and a critique. In Ian Budge *et al. Party identification and beyond.* London and New York: Wiley, 1976.

Page, Benjamin I. & Shapiro, Robert Y. Effects of public opinion on policy. *American Political Science Review,* 1983, *77,* 175-190.

Palma, Giuseppe di *Apathy and participation.* New York: The Free Press, 1970.

Pappi, Franz Urban. Sozialstruktur und politische konflikte in der Bundesrepublik. Cologne: Habilitationsschrift, 1976.

Parkin, Frank. *Class, inequality and political order.* London: MacGibbon and Kee, 1971.

Paukert, Felix. Income distribution at different levels of development. *International*

Labor Review, 1973, *108,* 97-125.

Pedersen, Mogens N. The dynamics of European party systems: Changing patterns of electoral volatility. *European Journal of Political Research,* 1979, *7,* 1-26. (a)

Pedersen, Mogens N. Denmark: The breakdown of a working multiparty system. Unpublished paper, Odense University, 1979. (b)

Pesonen, Pertti & Sankiaho, Risto. Kansalaiset ja Kan sanvalta: Suommalaisten kasityksia poliittisesta toiminnasta. Helsinki: Werner Soderstrom, 1979.

Pierce, Roy. Left-right perceptions, partisan preferences, electoral participation and partisan choice in France. *Political Behavior,* 1981, *3,* 117-136.

Pomper, Gerald M. From confusion to clarity. *American Political Science Review,* 1972, *66,* 415-420.

Powell, G. Bingham, Jr. Party systems and political system performance: Participation, stability and violence in contemporary democracies. *American Political Science Review,* 1981, *75,* 861-879.

Powell, G. Bingham. *Political performance in contemporary democracies.* Cambridge, MA: Harvard University Press, 1982.

Prewitt, Kenneth. *The recruitment of political leaders: A study of citizen-politicians.* New York: Bobbs-Merrill, 1970.

Prewitt, Kenneth, Eulau, Heinz & Zisk, Betty. Political socialization and political roles. *Public Opinion Quarterly,* 1966-67, *30,* 569-582.

Przeworski, Adam & Sprague, John. Final analyses: Electoral socialism project. Unpublished manuscript, Washington University, St. Louis, 1981.

Przeworski, A. & Wallerstein, Michael. The structure of class conflict in democratic capitalist societies. *American Political Science Review,* 1982, *76,* 215-238.

Putnam, Robert D. *The beliefs of politicians: Ideology, conflict, and democracy in Britain and Italy.* New Haven, CT: Yale University Press, 1973.

Putnam, Robert D. *The comparative study of political elites.* Englewood Cliffs, N.J.: Prentice-Hall, 1976.

Putnam, Robert D., Leonardi, Robert & Nanetti, Raffaella Y. Polarization and depolarization in Italian politics. Paper delivered at the 1981 Annual Meeting of the American Political Science Association, New York, September, 1981.

Quandt, William B. *The comparative study of political elites.* Beverly Hills, CA: Sage Professional Papers in Comparative Politics, vol. 1, no. 01-004, 1970.

Rabier, Jacques-René. Opinions et attitudes des Européens: Dix années de recherches internationales comparatives. *Futuribles,* 1981, 3-20.

RePass, David. Comment: Political methodologies in disarray: Issues and American voters, 1956-1968. *American Political Science Review,* 1976, *70,* 814-831.

Richardson, Bradley M. *The political culture of Japan.* Berkeley and Los Angeles: University of California Press, 1974.

Riker, William & Ordeshook, Peter C. *Positive political theory.* Englewood Cliffs, N.J.: Prentice Hall, 1973.

Robertson, David. *A theory of party competition.* London and New York: Wiley, 1976. (a)

Robertson, David. Surrogates for party identification in the rational choice framework. In I. Budge, I. Crewe & D. Farlie (Eds.). *Party identification and beyond.* New York: Wiley, 1976. (b)

Rogowski, Ronald. *A rational theory of legitimacy.* Princeton, N.J.: Princeton University Press, 1976.

Rokkan, Stein. *Citizens, elections and parties.* New York: David McKay, 1970.

Rose, Richard. *Electoral behavior: A comparative handbook.* New York: Free Press, 1974.

Rose, Richard. Class does not equal party: The decline of a model of British voting. *Studies in Public Policy No. 74.* Glasgow: University of Strathclyde, 1980.

Rose, Richard. From simple determinism to interactive models of voting. *Comparative Political Studies,* 1982, *15,* 145-169.

Rose, Richard & Urwin, Derek. Social cohesion, political parties and strains in regimes. *Comparative Political Studies,* 1969, 7-67.

Rusk, Jerrold G. & Weisberg, Herbert F. Perceptions of presidential candidates: Implications for electoral change. *Midwest Journal of Political Science,* 1972, *16,* 388-410.

Sani, Giacomo. The Italian electorate in the mid-1970s: Beyond tradition? In Howard R. Penniman (Ed.). *Italy at the polls: The parliamentary elections of 1976.* Washington, D.C.: American Enterprise Institute, 1977.

Sani, Giacomo. Italian voters, 1976-1979. In Howard Penniman (Ed.). *Italy at the polls, 1979.* Washington, D.C.: American Enterprise Institute, 1981.

Sartori, Giovanni. *Parties and party systems.* New York: Cambridge University Press, 1976.

Schmidt, Manfred. *Wohlfahrtstaatliche politik unter bürgerlichen und sozialdemokratischen regierungen.* Frankfurt: Campus, 1982.

Schmidtchen, Gerhard. *Zwischen kirche und gesellschaft.* Freiburg: Herder Verlag, 1972.

Schmidtchen, Gerhard. *Was den deutschen heilig is.* Munich: Kosel Verlag, 1979.

Searing, Donald D. The comparative study of elite socialization. *Comparative Political Studies,* 1969, *1,* 471-500.

Sidjanski, Dusan et al. *Les Suisses et la politique.* Berne and Frankfurt: Lang, 1975.

Skilling, H. Gordon & Griffiths, Franklyn. *Interest groups in Soviet politics.* Princeton, N.J.: Princeton University Press, 1971.

Stephens, John D. The changing Swedish electorate: Class voting, contextual effects, and voter volatility. *Comparative Political Studies,* 1981, *14.*

Stokes, Donald E. Spatial models of party competition. In Angus Campbell et al. *Elections and the political order.* New York: Wiley, 1966.

Studlar, Donley T. Policy voting in Britain: The colored immigration issue in the 1964, 1966 and 1970 general elections. *American Political Science Review,* 1978, *72,* 46-64.

Suleiman, Ezra H. *Politics, power, and bureaucracy in France: The administrative elite.* Princeton, N.J.: Princeton University Press, 1974.

Sullivan, John et al. Ideological constraint in the mass public: A methodological critique and some new findings. *American Journal of Political Science,* 1978, *22,* 233-240.

Szabo, Stephen F. *The successor generation: International perspectives of postwar Europeans.* London: Butterworth, 1983.

Taylor, Charles & Jodice, David A. *World handbook of political and social indicators: III.* New Haven, CT: Yale University Press, 1983.

Thomas, John C. Ideological trends in western political parties. In Peter Merkl (Ed.). *Western European party systems: Trends and prospects.* New York and London, 1980.

Thomassen, Jacques. Party identification as a cross-national concept: Its meaning in The Netherlands. In Ian Budge, Ivor Crewe, & Dennis Farlie (Eds.). *Party identification and beyond: Representations of voting and party competition.* New York: Wiley, 1976.

Tufte, Edward. Determinants of the outcome of midterm congressional elections. *American Political Science Review,* 1975, *69,* 812-826.

Tufte, Edward. *Political control of the economy.* Princeton: Princeton University Press, 1978.

Van Deth, Jan. Value change in The Netherlands: A test of Inglehart's theory of the silent revolution. *European Journal of Political Research,* 1983, *11.*

Verba, Sidney & Nie, Norman. *Participation in America: Social equality and political democracy.* New York: Harper & Row, 1972.

Verba, Sidney, Nie, Norman, & Kim, Jae-on. *Participation and political equality.* Cambridge: Cambridge University Press, 1978.

Verba, Sidney, Nie, Norman, & Petrocik, John. *The changing American voter.* Cambridge, MA: Harvard University Press, 1976.

Von Beyme, Klaus. Elite input and policy output: The case of Germany. In Moshe Czudnowski (Ed.). *Does who governs matter?* DeKalb: Northern Illinois University Press, 1982.

Watanuki, Joji. *Politics in postwar Japanese society.* Tokyo: University of Tokyo Press, 1979.

Weisberg, Herbert F. & Rusk, Jerrold G. Dimensions of candidate evaluation. *American Political Science Review,* 1970, *64,* 1167-1185.

Wellhofer, E. Spencer. Political parties as 'communities of fate': Tests with Argentine party elites. *American Journal of Political Science,* 1974, *18,* 347-363.

Wildenmann, Rudolf. Germany 1930/1970: The empirical findings. In Rudolf Wildenmann (Ed.). *Sozialwissenschaftliches Jahrbuch fur Politik* (vol. 2). Munich: Gunter Olzog, 1971.

Wildenmann, Rudolf. Towards a socio-political model of the German Federal Republic. Paper read at the Ninth Meeting of the International Political Science Association, Montreal, Canada, August 1973.

Wildenmann, Rudolf et al. *Fuhrungsschicht in der Bundesrepublic Deutschland.* Mannheim: University of Mannheim, 1982.

Wilensky, Harold L. *The welfare state and equality: Structural and ideological roots of public expenditures.* Berkeley: University of California Press, 1975.

Zetterberg, Hans. *Arbete, livsstil och motivation.* Stockholm: Svenska Arbetsgivareforeningen, 1977.

Zetterberg, Hans. Class voting in Sweden, 1979-1982. Stockholm: personal communication, 1983.

Zuckerman, Alan S. New approaches to political cleavage. *Comparative Political Studies,* 1982, *15,* 131-144.

Zuckerman, Alan S. & Lichbach, M. I. Stability and change in European electorates. *World Politics,* 1977, *29,* 523-551.

15

The Elusive Paradigm
Gender, Politics and Political Behavior:
The State of the Art

Marianne Githens

With the exceptions of Sophonisba Breckinridge's study (1933) of American women's political, social and economic activities, Maurice Duverger's treatise (1955) on women and politics and *The American Voter* (1960) which deals at some length with women's voting behavior, there was little systematic research on women and politics prior to the late 1960s. Although an extensive body of literature on political behavior had emerged by that time, the variable of sex had been largely ignored.[1] When studies did touch on the role of women in politics, they either simply confirmed or justified the limited participation of women (Lane, 1959; Barber, 1965). Otherwise, all that existed were a number of earlier, highly emotional, polemic pieces arguing the merits of women's suffrage. As a consequence, little was really known about modes of female political participation or the factors that might explain them.

This situation has substantially changed. A number of studies have appeared over the past decade and a half, and some have been highly praised in political science journals (Freeman, 1974; Kirkpatrick, 1974; Jaquette, 1974; Githens & Prestage, 1977; Diamond, 1977; Boles, 1979; Baxter & Lansing, 1980). This essay will attempt to review some of the contemporary research, examine its contribution to an understanding of the role of American women in politics — particularly in terms of their political behavior — and evaluate its implications for the discipline of political science. The kinds of research that have been done will be examined, and the problems shared by much of this gender related research will be identified. Then, the relationship of this research to the discipline of political science will be discussed, and recommendations will be made with regard to the future interface between gender related research and the discipline as a whole.

Two sets of propositions are offered to clarify the focus of this essay. The first set deals with gender related research itself, while the second set is concerned with the relationship between gender research and the discipline of political science.

471

The first set of propositions relating to the nature of gender related research itself are:

1. Since so little attention had been paid to the topic of women and politics, and since the prevailing assumptions about women's political behavior were largely drawn from conventional wisdom rather than from empirically tested hypotheses, the first gender related studies were devoted to filling in "information gaps" about the distinctive political behavior of women and were, as a consequence, primarily descriptive in nature rather than analytical.

2. Although at the present time a greater emphasis is being placed on public policy (Freeman, 1974; Gelb & Palley, 1982), the role of the women's movement in shaping women's political behavior and policy concerns (Boles, 1979; Evans, 1980; Rossi, 1983), and the interface of feminist theory and political philosophy (Orkin, 1979; Elshtain, 1981; Hartsock, 1981), gender related research has focused primarily on identifying the characteristics of women or the characteristics of the political system that have affected patterns of traditional political participation.

3. In more recent research where analysis has been attempted, findings have often been interpreted within existing frameworks and conceptualizations that were developed prior to the emergence of gender related research. The use of existing definitions, conceptualizations and frameworks to explain women's political behavior often obfuscates more than it illuminates; furthermore, it has circumscribed the research by measuring women's political participation and performance against norms predicated on male behavior (Berenice Carroll, 1979; Diamond & Hartsock, 1981). For example, initial efforts at analysis of women's political behavior drew heavily upon the concept of political socialization that is based on traditional, male definitions of the public, or political, sphere; they measured women against essentially male norms and found them wanting. Although studies of the political socialization of women and minority groups, such as blacks, have led to a more sophisticated understanding of the political socialization process, the norms for defining the public sphere on which political socialization research is based remain virtually unchanged. Using the definitions and conceptualizations formulated in order to identify men in the political elite, female political elite studies have focused on women holding traditional elective or appointive public office, rather than on women wielding some influence and power by virtue of their positions in social movements. As a consequence, the parameters of the female elite are artificially narrowed. Comparisons of women with men in the traditional political elite did give rise to some experimentation with analytic frameworks such as marginality, sex stratification and measurement of status, but the basis for comparison remains the majority male. Even studies dealing with issues closely linked to social movements, such as the ERA, are examined in terms of various existing conflict models.

4. Since financial support for research on women and politics has been limited, much of the empirical research dealing with women has tended to use relatively small subsets of women both in the political elite and at the citizen level. Much of the data about women in the political elite, for example, is drawn from a particular local community or state. Similarly, research

on behavioral and attitudinal characteristics has tended to use relatively small, unrepresentative subsets of adult and preadult women. Because studies of women and politics have often dealt with small subsets, conclusions about women's behavior in general are open to question. Conflicting and confusing results reported in different studies cannot be easily reconciled.

5. Problems in evaluating research findings are further complicated by the fact that the research has been done within a relatively short time span. Consequently, the relationship between a particular time frame or the characteristics of the general political environment of a period and specific patterns of women's political behavior is unclear. Thus, despite the conclusions reached in some of the research, it is difficult, if not impossible, to determine characteristics universal to women as a group over time.

The second set of propositions deals with the present interface between gender related research and political science itself. These propositions are:

1. The basic problems and flaws in gender related research are intensified by, and to a large extent the product of, the orientation of political science itself which has tended to view gender related research as an addendum to the discipline and to interpret women's political behavior within a broadly defined conceptual framework of deviance.

2. The norms against which women's political behavior are compared are not generic, but male specific. The second point requires some elaboration. In two essays, "Das Relative und das Absolute im Geschlechterproblem" and "Weibliche Kultur," Georg Simmel asserted that:

> The requirements of art, patriotism, morality in general and social ideas in particular, correctness in practical judgment and objectivity in theoretical knowledge . . . all these are categories which belong as it were in their form and their claims to humanity in general, but in their actual historical configuration they are masculine throughout. (1919, as quoted in Horney, 1935.)[2]

He then went on to note that values are "not neutral, arising out of the difference of the sexes, but in themselves essentially masculine." Further, he claimed "inadequate achievements are contemptuously called feminine, while distinguishing achievements on the part of women are called 'masculine' as an expression of praise." Parenthetically, one might add that in the case of American political science at least, masculine must be construed as white male, for the treatment of racial and ethnic research is similar to that of gender related research.

The problems posed for gender related research by the male norms and the models and standards based upon them have been noted previously (Berenice Carroll, 1979; Hartsock & Diamond, 1981). In her review essay of American politics and political behavior Carroll observed that:

> If it seemed in 1974 that the women's movement had introduced "possibilities for profound changes in the way in which the discipline studies women and the way in which it defines political activity," five years later there is little evidence that these possibilities have been realized or, indeed, pursued. The hopeful, if cautious, tone of earlier reviewers now seem (sic) largely premature, and their efforts to delineate the kinds of research and theoretical developments needed appear to have fallen on deaf ears. (p. 289)

The problem, as Carroll sees it, stems from a tendency to accept existing premises and theoretical frameworks that take neither women nor sex into account, failure to look more closely at the private sphere and instead to focus on the conventionally defined "public" or political sphere, and to force the analyses of issues such as the ERA into preformulated models. As a result, Carroll argues, women's efforts and struggles within their own contexts are ignored.

Diamond and Hartsock also point out the problems imposed on the study of women and politics by the approaches of political science. In their response to Sapiro's article (1981), "When Are Interests Interesting?" they write:

> Though Sapiro clearly holds that the state is not neutral vis-a-vis women, her conceptual tools do not permit her to develop this insight. . . .
>
> In sum, we are not saying, as Sapiro does, that recent scholarship in women's studies can show that political science has been studying the actions of only half of humanity, and that the subject matter of political science should be expanded. Instead, we are suggesting that the focus on the activity of only half of humanity is fundamental to what has been understood as political life for the last 2500 years. To include women's concerns, to represent women in the public life of our society might well lead to a profound redefinition of the nature of public life itself. (pp. 720, 721)

Taking into account the issues raised by Carroll and Diamond and Hartsock, this essay will attempt to show that although there are, in fact, a number of specific problems with gender related research to date, it is the equation, "objective = masculine" (Simmel, 1919), that condemns much gender related scholarship to oblivion by trivializing its findings, limiting its conceptual framework and restricting its potential contribution to a better understanding of politics and political life.

CONTEMPORARY GENDER RELATED RESEARCH[3]

There are a number of equally valid ways of dividing gender related research dealing with the political behavior of women. Efforts to explain particular patterns of female political participation have generally dwelt on categories of constraints: differential political socialization; biological and life cycle characteristics; unequal access to resources, especially educational, professional and financial; lack of prestige associated with traditional employment fields for women both within the home and outside; role strain and conflict stemming from interior-exterior orientations; and institutional sexism and discrimination. It is certainly possible to classify the literature this way, although other schemes for classification are probably equally valid. However, a division of the research into three categories—socialization, women's political behavior at the citizen level, and women in the political elite—seems more straightforward and useful for this essay.

Socialization

Since political socialization studies of the late fifties and early sixties suggested important sex differences, they provided a base for many of the initial studies of women and politics. Indeed, political socialization dominated discussion of women's role in politics for almost a decade. Therefore, it seems most logical to begin a survey of the literature with a review of the socialization studies.

In 1959 Herbert Hyman offered data suggesting that boys showed greater interest in politics than did girls. Fred Greenstein (1965) subsequently presented findings along similar lines. He found that boys were more political than girls, scored higher on political information, were better able to name news stories and were more interested in national news. In addition, his data showed boys to be more likely than girls to select a public figure whom they most admired. Finally, both boys and girls in his study tended to prefer their fathers as sources of political advice.[4] Sex differences were also reported by Easton and Dennis (1969). The Hess and Torney study (1967), which is perhaps the most comprehensive of all the socialization studies in terms of sample size and the diversity in SES and racial background of its respondents, reported that girls were more attached to personal figures in the political system and had a higher level of trust and reliance on the inherent goodness of the political system than boys who were more inclined to be task oriented and to see benefits in conflict and disagreement. Lynn Iglitzen (1974) in a much smaller study of the political socialization of Seattle school children found boys to be oriented more toward economic issues, while girls were more interested in peace, honesty and integrity. She also found that although girls were as likely as boys to want to be President, a sizable number of the boys wanted to be mayor; not a single girl chose this position. Instead, popular choices for girls were the school board and the judiciary.

More general studies of socialization tend to support these findings. Bardwick and Douvan (1971) found different processes and behavior norms existed for boys and girls. Studies using psychoanalytic theory, as well as identification theories based on it (Mussen, 1969; Kagan & Moss, 1962; Biller, 1971), have reported sex differences, although the findings of these and other studies have raised questions about the theoretical assumptions undergirding the research. Studies utilizing learning theory have also noted sex differences (Maccoby & Jacklin, 1974, 1975; Parsons *et al.*, 1976; Lambert *et al.*, 1971; Block, 1977; Hartley, 1960, 1964; Dweck, 1975; Etaugh, Collins & Gerson, 1975; Frueh & McGhee, 1975). Cognitive developmental theories, too, confirm the existence of gender differences (Liebert, McCalland, Hanratty, 1971; Perry & Perry, 1975). These cognitive development studies, in particular, tend to support the idea of the acquisition of sex role and of sex role appropriate behavior in children. Even more recent studies, such as Bearison's (1979) and Kelly and Boutilier's (1978) have continued to find sex linked patterns of socialization important.

The research on learning sex roles and sex role appropriate behavior in children, in combination with observed gender related differences noted in the earlier literature on the political socialization of chidren, was initially accepted as an explanation for differences in adult female political behavior at both the citizen and elite level. Indeed, one researcher attempted to identify the particular childhood socialization experiences of women in the political elite that differentiated them from women in general (Rosenberg, 1972).

Several basic problems have emerged, however, that open to question the usefulness of socialization theory as an explanation for women's political behavior. The first, and perhaps most serious, is that several of the more recent studies of political socialization have found gender differences to be insignificant, minor or relatively limited. Merelman (1971), for example, found few large or consistent differences between girls and boys. Similarly, Orum, Cohen, Grasmuck and Orum (1974) reported only minor differences between girls and boys. In Jennings and Niemi's study of high school students (1974) little appreciable differences between the sexes were found, although in a subsequent study they found more sex differentiation among their respondents than had existed earlier.[5] Some studies of political socialization in other countries (see, for example, Keller, 1978) report no gender related differences, while others (Jennings, 1982) suggest that socialization has an impact on the sixteen through twenty year age group in eight nations.

On the other hand, Rapoport (1981) reported substantial gender differences with females exhibiting lower levels of political information. Citing the Jennings and Niemi research (1978) that found a high correlation for the political knowledge of respondents of both sexes over time, Rapoport suggests that adolescent gender differences in political information are indeed important. Linking political knowledge with attitude expression and political persuasion, Rapoport argues that "increasing political knowledge among adolescents would increase levels of attitude-holding and lessen sex differences" (p. 44). Differences in political information have also been noted by others, especially Duncan and Duncan (1978) who examined sex role changes over time.

Given the items used to measure political information (the length of the term of a U.S. senator and representative, for example) in studies such as Duncan and Duncan (1978), one wonders, however, just how significant this information gap really is and whether or not the inferences drawn from such measures are warranted. Even more fundamentally at issue is the current distinction between the public, or political, and the private sphere. By continuing to use traditional definitions of the public, or political, sphere and then testing the respondent's knowledge about that political sphere, an understanding of the scope of girls' and women's knowledge about a somewhat differently defined public sphere may be obscured. In turn, conclusions drawn about the likelihood for political action by women based upon their knowledge of the traditionally defined political sphere may well be incorrect. Indeed, the discrepancies in research findings about women's political participation in one area, and lack of it in another—discussed more extensively below—may well stem from invalid initial assumptions about what constitutes political information and political activity for women.

Recent studies that reported minor, insignificant or limited gender differences weakened the initial supposition that women's political behavior could be explained by differential socialization alone. Furthermore, the relationship of early socialization to adult behavior has come under more critical scrutiny. A number of studies suggest that the linkage between the two is not as clear as was once assumed. In fact, some research indicates that childhood socialization to a given set of norms may be modified by learning experiences occurring later in the life cycle and by subsequent situational factors (Corbett, Rudoni & Frederickson, 1981; Fischer & Narus, 1981; Hall & Frederickson, 1979). The findings of this research, however, are challenged by other studies. Kelly and Boutilier (1978) argue on the basis of their analysis of women in a variety of political and private roles that "mother's occupation, education, income status and behavior directly affected the political socialization of the daughter" (p. 442).

A variety of explanations have been offered for the conflicting findings of studies dealing with socialization, as well as speculations on the relationship of socialization to behavior. Baer (1978) argues that while the sexism of the 1950s may be a factor in explaining the differences in the findings of the earlier and later political socialization studies, there is also considerably "different interpretations given to similar levels of gender linked differences" (p. 18). She goes on to say that "while the evidence does suggest some early learning of gender roles, for the most part, it is assimilated in an inconsistent fashion" (p. 18). Continuing, Baer contends:

> The social context within which gender role learning takes place is not nearly so uniform as adult notions of logical consistency would suggest. The socialization process is, instead, fundamentally an ambiguous and an ambivalent one. (p. 18)

Going still further, Welch (1977) questioned the value of socialization as an explanation of women's political behavior and characterized it as "irrelevant." Indeed, she concluded: "we . . . see little to support the socialization explanation. . . . Why many political scientists favor childhood political socialization explanation as reason for so much of adult political behavior is unclear" (p. 728).

Yet despite the position taken by Welch and others, some socialization research does continue to find gender differences. How can such divergent conclusions be explained? In a few cases the data base is extremely narrow, and the findings, therefore, are suspect. The time at which the study was done may also explain differences between some of the earlier and later findings. In still other instances, conflicting conclusions about the extent of gender differential socialization may be attributed to the interpretation given the data. Certainly Greenstein's work has been criticized on these grounds. In some other studies contradictory findings and conclusions may be the result, at least in part, of a failure to distinguish political socialization clearly enough from overall socialization, socialization to sex role and socialization to sex role appropriate behavior and to spell out the specific relationship of one to the others.

It is not easy to account for contradictions reported in other studies, however. Here, perhaps the concept of socialization itself offers some clue. The concept of socialization is predicated on the existence within a given society of universal norms transmitted to all. At the same time, the existence of group specific norms is acknowledged by the concept of majority/minority and the notion of a subculture wherein a group internalizes some but not all of the societal norms.

It is perfectly legitimate to investigate the extent to which minorities or subcultures have internalized dominant norms. However, it must be clearly understood that a dominant norm is one held by the majority or dominant group, whereas a universal norm is one shared by all groups in a society. It is crucial to recognize the distinction between the two because not all dominant norms are universal, although all universal norms are, of course, incorporated into dominant as well as minority or subcultural norms. This means that if dominant norms are the standard against which a minority or subculture is being measured, it is very likely that universal norms but not minority or subculture specific norms will surface in the research. Furthermore, an approach focusing on dominant norms as the standard says something about the social distance of the minority or subculture from the majority or dominant group but nothing about the desirability or appropriateness of dominant norms for the particular subculture or minority. Indeed, conditions springing from minority status or the environment of the subculture may make it highly undesirable for members of the minority group or subculture to internalize certain dominant norms.

In socialization research a problem often arises when empirically tested universal norms relevant to the political order are not specifically identified. Instead, majority or dominant norms based on the concept of the ideal citizen as *he* has been defined by political philosophers or on norms prevalent among males are assumed to be universal. Therefore, some discrepancies reported in the findings may be explained by the fact that some studies that find little gender differentiation in socialization are emphasizing norms that are universal while others reporting differences are tapping dominant norms. Similarly, women's unexpected involvement in certain kinds of political activity may reflect their socialization to group specific norms that have not been identified by approaches focusing on dominant norms. Such an explanation for the contradictions in socialization research findings is clearly speculative, but it may well be one that deserves further investigation.

Women's Political Participation at the Citizen Level

Early studies of political participation at the citizen level were devoted almost exclusively to voting or to behavior directly related to voting, such as party identification, political attitudes and their implications for voting behavior, and the effects of political trust, efficacy, cynicism and alienation on voting patterns. Verba and Nie (1972) in their study of political participation suggested a rather broad range of activities that might legitimately fall within the proper scope of political behavior. Following the lead of the discipline, early studies of women's behavior focused heavily on female voting behavior and related issues. With some exceptions (Stewart, 1980; Reid, 1977; Boneparth, 1978) most studies have accepted as the parameters of citizen participation traditional political activity, e.g., voting, party identification, political attitudes, etc. Early studies of women's voting behavior all noted different overall turnout rates for males and females (Campbell, Converse, Miller & Stokes, 1960). More recent studies, however, report a narrowing in the voting gap between men and women (Stucker, 1977; Cavanagh, 1981) or point to the fact that for a number of reasons, including decreased voter participation by men, a majority of voters are now women (Baxter & Lansing, 1980). Cavanagh (1981) in his study of voting turnout between 1964 and 1976 also notes the increased voting participation by women and goes on to observe:

> Gender was once a potent determinant of turnout, but its impact has all but vanished with the passage of time. The sex differential stood at 4.9 percent in 1964 Census Bureau survey on turnout, by 1976 it was negligible .8 percent. (p. 61)

In contrast, the voting participation of black female voters has equalled that of black males since 1964, and in 1976 they voted at slightly higher rates (Baxter & Lansing, 1980; Lansing, 1977). Pierce, Avery and Carey's study of black political participation and beliefs (1977) also found minimal gender differences in participation. Where there were differences, lower income black women were both more likely to participate and to be involved in both traditional and nontraditional politics than lower income black men. Furthermore, in terms of political beliefs black women were not more likely than black men to look favorably on people in politics, although they were less likely to feel politically efficacious than their male counterparts.

A number of studies have offered explanations for female voting. Primarily they have centered around the effects of the variables of age, education, region, occupation and income (Baxter & Lansing, 1980; Stucker, 1977; Verba & Nie, 1972; Milbrath & Goel, 1977; Soule & McGrath, 1977; Andersen, 1975; Scott, 1970). In fact, *The American Voter* (1960) itself found these variables to affect voting turnout rates. Certainly there is adequate documentation to confirm the importance of these variables on female voting behavior; in the case of voting turnout of college educated women in the professions, participation has been consistently high since 1952. Cavanagh's data (1981) shows similar turnout levels for males and females within given occupational categories in both 1964 and 1976. As Baxter and Lansing have concluded about recent voting behavior data: "Simply looking at gender as the determinant of turnout is unwise" (p. 38).

From the beginning of research touching on women and politics, limited female participation in areas of traditional political activity other than voting has been noted. Attempting to account for gender differences in participation, many studies have suggested that situational factors constrain female political participation. One often cited situation variable is the demands of motherhood. Both Campbell *et al.* (1960) and Lynn and Flora (1974) viewed the role of home and family, especially in the case of women with younger children, as affecting political participation. Jennings (1979), like Lynn and Flora (1974), found that parenthood, and particularly motherhood, affected interest in school politics. On the other hand, Jennings also found in this same study that parenthood, including motherhood, had little effect on national political participation.

Other situational factors including education, socioeconomic status and employment have also been advanced as an explanation for women's limited participation. *The American Voter* (1960) points out that voting participation differences between college educated fathers and mothers with young children are small, that the dip in participation among mothers of small children does not appear to be matched by a slackened political involvement, and that there are no gender differences in intensity of party loyalty, nor in sense of citizen duty. Elsewhere the authors report that "women are somewhat less likely to express a sense of involvement in the current situation. This discrepancy is clearest at the lowest levels of education, being fairly well obliterated or reversed among college educated men and women" (p. 261). In her study, Lee (1977) points to socioeconomic status as more critical to political participation than motherhood. She found that more affluent mothers who could afford things like baby-sitters were more likely to participate than mothers who lacked these resources. Flora (1977) found employment outside the home as well as socioeconomic status affected patterns of participation. Other studies (such as Verba, Nie & Kim, 1978; Jennings & Farah, 1981, that will be discussed below), although questioning the ability of situational factors alone to explain women's patterns of political participation, have noted that these factors do have some measurable effect on it.

Using SRC data for 1952, 1964 and 1972, Welch (1977) contends that there are in fact no systematic differences in political participation that cannot be attributed to situation variables. She writes:

> Our analysis has shown that the stereotype of the politically passive woman simply is untrue. Women as a whole participate as much as men when structural and situational factors are considered. . . . Women participate in the aggregate less than men not because of some belief they hold about the role of women in politics, but largely because they are less likely to be found in the categories of people who participate in politics; the employed and highly educated in particular. . . . (p. 726)

It is interesting to note that somewhat similar conclusions about the effects of education and income are reached by Ross and Thadani (1980) who in their study of political participation in Kenya concluded that inequalities between the sexes increase as males attain higher education and income.

On the other hand, some other recent studies have raised serious questions about the importance of situational variables. For example, in Verba, Nie and Kim's cross-cultural study (1978) even when situational factors were taken into consideration, women's interest in politics did not translate into the same level of political activity as men's did. Similarly, Jennings and Farah (1980) in their cross-cultural study of the effects of gender on political ideologues found differences between men and women, especially in the case of Germany, that, they contend, cannot be explained by situational variables.

Much attention has been directed to the issue of women's interest in politics. Until recently a number of stereotypes dominated all discussion of women's political activity. Generally speaking, women were described as essentially conservative in their outlook, more likely to vote Republican, more irrational in their reasons for choosing a candidate to vote for—for example, women are influenced by a candidate's good looks—and more likely to follow their husbands' lead in their voting behavior. Furthermore, women were depicted as having low levels of political efficacy, and less knowledge about politics. Campbell *et al.* (1964) describing women's political interest and knowledge wrote:

> The wife who votes but otherwise pays little attention to politics not only tends to leave the sifting of information up to her husband but abides by his ultimate decision about the direction of the vote as well. . . .
> The dependence of a wife's vote upon her husband's partisan predispositions appears to be one reason why the entrance of women into the electorate has tended to make little visible difference in the partisan distribution of the electoral vote. (p. 260)

This conception of the passive, submissive woman is reiterated in a much later study by Rapoport (1981) who maintains that while gender differences have decreased in terms of electoral participation, "women remain more passive in their voting behavior in that they are less likely to persuade others how to vote than are men" (p. 46).

Research on party identification has also tended to reinforce the idea of the passive woman who follows the lead of her husband. Robinson (1976), Beck and Jennings (1975) and Weiner (1978) conclude that husbands still influence their wives' party identification more than wives do their husbands'. However, De Fronzo (1981) found that although working wives describe their social status in terms of their husbands, their occupational attainment did have an independent effect on party identification.

The findings reported by De Fronzo are especially interesting in that they implicitly raise questions about the importance of shared socioeconomic status for husbands' and wives' party identification. It may well be that studies that have found husbands' and wives' party identification to be the same are really reflecting the congruent socioeconomic interests of both spouses. Perhaps some wives, especially those not employed outside the home, see their socioeconomic interests as identical to those of their husbands and, therefore, choose the same party as their husbands because of those shared socioeconomic interests. On the other hand, working women, although continuing to identify with the social status of their husbands, may develop special interests resulting from their employment outside the home that do not mesh with those of their husbands. As a consequence, working women whose employment outside the home is inconsistent with the socioeconomic interests of their husbands may adopt a party identification different from that of their husbands. Despite the considerable methodological problems in looking at husbands' and wives' socioeconomic status separately, some research on party identification that takes the socioeconomic interests of both spouses into account is probably now needed.

Although the linkage of ideological political orientations to gender has been widely assumed, research findings suggest a more varied relationship than has been previously believed. For example, Hershey and Sullivan (1977) have sought to clarify the relationship of masculine, androgynous and feminine sex role identity to political ideology. While their findings suggest that people who identify primarily with characteristics considered "appropriate" for members of their biological sex also tend to be more conservative in their political attitudes, the pattern is somewhat mixed. Corbett, Frankland and Rudoni (1976) found a relationship between sexism and political attitudes in males, but traditional females were not as tender hearted as they hypothesized. While Soule and McGrath (1977) found women in the political elite to be much more liberal than their male counterparts, their data also show women at the citizen level to be slightly more conservative than similarly situated males. However, the lack of extensive gender differences at the citizen level requires a reconsideration of their attachment of the label "conservative" to women.

Perhaps the most ambitious of all scholarly efforts to sort through the conflicting research on women's political participation at the citizen level is that of Baxter and Lansing (1980). In looking at their data they contend that although women trail men in a sense of political efficacy, women's lower sense "may be a more perceptive assessment of the political process" (p. 51). In terms of attitudinal differences on policy issues, they point out that the data show women to have a greater interest in peace and claim that women's support of Eisenhower reflected their approval of his position on the Korean War rather than their emotional response to his personality and charisma as is so often claimed. They also find that women are more wary of "extremist" candidates than men. At the same time, they argue that the data indicate a growing politicization of women and that "in terms of the attitudes known to be predictive of political behavior, women and men show little differences. . ." (p. 181).

In their research on male/female candidate evaluation, Shabad and Andersen (1979) found that there was little evidence that women were more personality and less issue oriented than men. They report that both sexes view and evaluate candidates by much more multidimensional criteria than previous research "by virtue of its conceptual framework" had suggested. They further argue that by lumping together a wide range of variables extending from looks and life style to leadership capabilities and by classifying all of these as personality characteristics, important dimensions of leadership are implicitly relegated to the category of trivial and politically irrelevant; this impoverishes an understanding of the interaction of the masses and the elite.

With the exceptions of Baxter and Lansing (1980) and Pomper (1975) who noted that gender affects attitudes on war and peace, scant attention has been paid to differences in public opinion between men and women. Indeed, until very recently the possibility of such differences existing over time was rejected (Berelson, Lazarsfeld & McPhee, 1954; Campbell et al., 1960; Pomper, 1975), but polling data gathered over the past two years suggest the existence of a "gender gap." Writing on the "gender gap," Frankovic (1982) has pointed to opinion differences; the disparities between men and women in candidate preference in the 1980 election and in the subsequent evaluations of Reagan's performance reported in a number of public opinion polls have been widely discussed and hotly debated in the mass media.

Women's negative assessment of Reagan and his performance and their apparent preference for the Democratic Party have, of course, received the greatest popular attention. From the perspective of the study of women's political behavior, however, what is more interesting is that on traditionally defined women's issues gender differences are not great. Rather, it appears that it is a configuration of peace, the environment, Reaganomics, social issues and a general sense of fair play that distinguishes women's preferences and opinions from those of men. It is too early to determine the effect of this "gender gap" on election outcomes and to tell whether or not specific political interests on the part of women will be translated into effective political activity. Nevertheless, the apparent lack of articulated gender differentiation on traditionally defined women's issues and the configuration of issues that distinguishes women's positions from those of men may indicate that women's views of what constitutes critical policy questions are somewhat different than was previously believed. Here again, some research on what women themselves consider to be important issues and what they believe to be the appropriate role of the political order is now needed. Perhaps if this area were investigated more fully, there would be a better understanding of the dimensions of women's political activity.

If women's views of the political order are somewhat different than the research to date suggests, it may also indicate the degree to which their interest in school and local politics reflects only situational constraints. This might also shed some light on research findings which show that, in spite of the reported political passivity of women, adults as well as adolescents are more often in agreement with their mothers than their fathers in terms of party identification (Jennings & Langton, 1969; Jennings & Niemi, 1974).

The differences that appear between the political activity of white males and females do not hold in most respect for the political behavior of black Americans. Perhaps a reason for this is that for black Americans there are common minority norms that cross gender lines. In the case of white males and females there is a less comprehensive set of shared norms. Until specific norms for the behavior prevalent among white women are identified and matched against norms for white males, however, black/white gender differences must remain an enigma.

In conclusion, it would seem that a major problem with research on women's political participation to date is the fact that the norms for judging and measuring effective political participation at the citizen level are based on dominant, male norms. By defining political activity more broadly and taking into account non-traditional political behavior—not just protest politics, but involvement in groups concerned with community affairs as well —a rather different picture of women's political participation might well emerge.

Women in the Political Elite

All research has pointed to one glaring, undisputed gender difference. Women are minimally represented in the political elite. Underlying almost all research on women in the political elite is an effort to account for that absence. Broadly speaking, the literature on this topic has focused on the characteristics of women in the elite: personal, demographic and attitudinal-situational factors affecting these women, consequent role strain or role conflict, and their performance. Moreover, research on this topic has tended to be quite adventuresome in trying to develop or utilize theoretical approaches or frameworks to explain the position of women in the elite (Kirkpatrick, 1974; Diamond, 1977; Githens & Prestage, 1977; Kelly & Boutilier, 1977).

Before proceeding with an overview of the research, however, a few words should be said about the term "political elite" itself. Political elite is, used in its narrowest sense, the holding of some elective or appointive political office. At the outside, political elite may be extended to include an important, independent, political influential, but such latitude in the use of the term is rare. When the research speaks of the paucity of women in the political elite, it is referring to their lack of representation in elective or appointive governmental or party office.

Empirical research on the characteristics of women in the political elite is fairly extensive (Werner, 1966, 1968; Werner & Bachtold, 1974; Gruberg, 1968; Costantini & Craik, 1972; Githens, 1977; Soule & McGrath, 1977; Bullock & Heys, 1972; King, 1977; Githens & Prestage, 1978, 1979; Jennings & Thomas, 1968; Kirkpatrick, 1974, 1976; Jennings & Farah, 1981; Johnson & Stanwick, 1976; Johnson & Carroll, 1978). All these studies note certain basic similarities in the kind of women recruited to the political elite. At the same time, each explores particular facets of these characteristics, such as background, personality, skill areas, etc. Based on the data these studies present, a picture of the woman recruited to the political elite emerges. She is recruited in her forties, is most likely to be married and to have children, is middle class and is drawn from a somewhat different range of occupations, including that of employment within the home, than is her male counterpart. In addition, she is more likely than women at the citizen level to possess a configuration of "masculine" personality characteristics. This means that she is more liberal in her attitudes, more unconventional and more adventuresome than women in the general public. While she does share some values with women at the citizen level, she is, nonetheless, different in the extent of her liberalism and adventuresomeness. In these characteristics she resembles more her male peers.

Some recent research, however, raises questions about the accuracy of this description of women in the political elite. Jennings and Farah (1981) using survey data on Michigan delegates to national party conventions found sex differences dwindling with regard to social background, political status, political careers and perceptions of the political process, although they do report differences in terms of ambition and aspirations. Using survey data on women state legislators, Githens and Prestage (1981) found these women to have less distinctive characteristics and attitudes than earlier studies suggested. The women seemed neither particularly unconventional nor adventuresome as a group. Indeed, the only characteristic they seemed to exhibit as a group was an acceptance of fatalism as opposed to a belief in personal efficacy.

Much of the discussion of women's limited participation in the political elite has centered around the multiple role demands that confront women in politics. A number of explanations are based on notions of role strain and role conflict which arise from the emphasis given by women in the political elite to their roles of wife and mother, and from the barriers to their political participation that arise from societal definitions of the obligation of these roles (Lee, 1977; Lynn & Flora, 1977; Githens & Prestage, 1977, 1978, 1979; Curry, 1977; National Women's Education Fund Survey, 1981; Kirkpatrick, 1974, 1976; Mandel, 1981; Sapiro, 1982). In fact, the application of the theory of marginality to women in politics initially focused rather heavily on the strains created by the role of politician on the one hand and the role of wife and mother on the other.

Subsequent research, however, seems to suggest that the conclusions drawn earlier about the effects of role strain may be overblown. Recent analyses of data testing the hypothesis of marginality (Githens & Prestage, 1980, 1981, 1982) indicate that the strains female legislators experience may be much more dependent on their aspirations to be accepted as unhyphenated politicians by their male peers and their perceptions of their male colleagues as continuing to see them as a distinctive and unequal subgroup than on strains arising from the conflicting demands of the roles of wife/mother and politician. Taking a somewhat different tack, Stoper (1977) argues that the conflicting roles of politician and parent/spouse may not be sex specific. Survey data gathered recently supports Stoper's interpretation by showing that the dual demands of home and politics may effect heavy costs on men as well as women.

Research on women in the political elite has also focused on the structural constraints on participation. Diamond (1976, 1977) has pointed out that women are more likely to be successful in those states where political offices are viewed as relatively less desirable by men, where they are associated with low pay and considered less professional. Interestingly, in a study of women mayors in Brazil, Blay (1979) comes to a similar conclusion; her findings show that women are most likely to be elected in the poorest, least industrialized and least urbanized states. MacManus (1976), Kirkpatrick (1974), Githens (1977), Githens and Prestage (1980) and Welch (1977) have all pointed to differences in skill areas as a constraint on the full participation of women in the political elite. A predilection of women to choose the amateur as opposed to professional role in politics has been suggested by Lynn and Flora (1977) as another form of constraint, although they argue that the choice of this role is motivated by perceptions of societal punishment for political participation.

In an examination of the relationship of gender role and party role, Fowlkes, Perkins and Rinehart (1979) found gender differences in ambition and activity among party members but did not see these as a constraint imposed on women by the political party. Rather, they conclude:

> According to our research, men are more ambitious than women, an expressive/ instrumental differential that comports well with recent evidence that the under-representation of women in elective office is more a result of a paucity of women candidates than discrimination against them at the polls. (p. 7)

Similarly, Darcy and Schramm (1977) found sex to have no effect on election outcome, except in the case of Democratic incumbent women who do significantly better than their male counterparts.

Sapiro and Farah (1980) have also looked at the issue of gender differences in ambition. Their data suggests that the development of political ambition in women is dependent upon a variety of factors: home, family, employment roles and feminism. They conclude that "women's lives shape the type of ambition women develop and the style of activism women pursue" (p. 33). Exploring the issue of volunteerism, they believe that traditional female roles in combination with gender ideology may mean that women move into political roles that are consistent with their orientation to service and civic responsibility.

Like the preceeding research on women in the political elite discussed above, the findings and conclusions drawn about structural constraints are contradictory. As was shown, Fowlkes *et al.* and Darcy and Schramm basically argue against constraints stemming from the political party and the electorate. Rinehart (1978) does not find women more likely than men to be clustered in amateur or semiprofessional roles. Githens and Prestage (1980) find women lawyers to be the most disadvantaged of all female state legislators in terms of office held in their legislative chamber and in their party organization in the legislature. In fact, after controlling for length of time in the legislature their findings show that women with high school diplomas hold more offices within their legislatures than more highly educated women. Welch (1978) in her analysis of the recruitment of women to public office concludes that:

> While women do not yet possess the same educational and occupational levels as men, their overall achievements in these areas would lead one to expect a greater percentage of female legislators than actually exists. Thus, if this were a "sex blind" but occupation and education sensitive process, about one quarter of the legislators would be female. Thus, structural characteristics are an important set of factors keeping women out of this kind of public office. (p. 379)

She does, however, go on to suggest, as Fowlkes and others have, that political socialization accompanied by active discrimination may reduce the number of female candidates.

Similarly, findings on the role and performance of women holding public office do not permit general conclusions to be drawn. Gehlen (1977) and Gruhl and Welch (1981) have found no gender differences, Kincaid (1976) found few differences between Congresswomen appointed to succeed their deceased spouses and those elected initially in their own right. Bers (1978) asserts that although there are differences in what stimulates males and females to seek membership on school boards — women rely more heavily on their own initiative — differences in male/female orientations to community service, and differences in perceived contributions to board activity, individual women behave in various ways and cannot be grouped on any basis other than sex. Bartol and Wortman (1979) conclude that there are few differences between male and female leaders in behavior, organizational outcomes or job performance.

Some research on women judges, however, indicates that although there are few gender differences in terms of personality characteristics, there are some other important differentiations. For example, Cook (1977) found that in simulated cases male and female Democratic judges expressed similar views toward the women's movement, but their behavior differed. She concluded that "women voters can vote for women candidates with as much profit as men have voted for party" (p. 237). Elsewhere Cook (1980) found women judges to be conscious of institutional constraints and more favorably disposed toward new social roles for women who demand them than are women in the general population.

At the same time, Deaux's study (1979) of differences in managers shows that men perceive their jobs as more difficult than women and that men report both more approval for their work and better relations with their coworkers and subordinates. If these findings extend to other occupations and professions, one wonders about their ramifications for women in political positions. Furthermore, research on sex stratification indicates the possibility of other gender related differences affecting the role and performance of women in politics. Broadly speaking, studies on sex stratification have found that low status people gain legitimacy by being assigned to leadership positions or proving their interest in a group's welfare (Meeker & Weitzell-O'Neill, 1977). This interest in the group's welfare is manifested by providing approval and encouragement to others. Indeed, women holding public office so often allude to the importance of this that it is tempting to believe that it may be a crucial component of their behavior. If this is true, the apparent absence of gender related differences may simply represent women's efforts to legitimize themselves and, in fact, confirm important gender differences in terms of access to power.

The validity of research findings on sex stratification seems to be supported elsewhere. In "Sex and Games," Sapiro (1979) reviews the literature on single and mixed sex dyads playing the prisoner's dilemma game. She points to the role that oppression plays in the strategies used by women both in games played with other women and with men. In mixed sex dyads cooperation rather than competition, she notes, results from a combination of female deference and male chivalry. She concludes:

> The theories and evidence . . . show that the psychological dependence instilled in an oppressive relationship may make rational actors turn against themselves and help maintain their low status. 'Happiness' is the act of choosing against themselves in an attempt to choose for themselves. . . .
>
> [O]ppression of women and female dependence are so ubiquitous they appear natural to women and men alike. (p. 406)

Finally, there is a body of research dealing with women in the political elite and feminism. Perkins and Fowlkes (1980) found attitudes of group and gender role to be

> of secondary importance in the choice between the men and women. The attitudes toward the legitimacy of groups in the political process is related only to the choice between the sexes. . . . Attitude toward gender roles is washed out in the fact of a choice between the sexes that activates instead an attitude about the legitimacy of groups in the political process. (p. 101)

At the same time, in Sapiro's view the public perceives an alliance between women and the young who are seen as more egalitarian in their attitudes than the older generation. From this she concludes that although there will be a struggle for more than incremental change, the public is prepared for a future in which there is greater equality between the sexes. Miller *et al.* (1981), on the other hand, distinguish between group identification and group consciousness. Their exploration leads them to conclude that when group consciousness is politicized it motivates its members to bring about change through participation in traditional types of political activities. Speculation about the development of a woman's voting block (Baxter & Lansing, 1980; MacManus, 1976) is largely based on assumptions about growing group consciousness among women, although Fulenwider (1979) does not see this as the case for black women.

At the same time, the mere presence of women in public office is seen as no guarantee of support for women's issues (Mezey, 1976, 1977; Carver, 1979). Almost all data collected on the subject indicates that women in the political elite give little priority to feminist issues over any others; do not define themselves as primarily representing the interests of women; and refrain from running as a feminist. Carroll (1979), on the other hand, has argued that it is elite politics that gives rise to this appearance and forces women to stay in the closet; Cook's work suggests that despite constraints, women in the judiciary, whether feminist or not, are more responsive than their male peers to issues of concern to women.

Research on women in the traditional political elite has, without doubt, not only provided useful information but also empirically tested many of the assumptions about women and their behavior drawn from conventional wisdom. What has emerged from the numerous studies is a picture of women not radically different from their male colleagues in terms of many "personality" characteristics. At the same time, research has depicted women as a group subjected to a variety of structural, situational and socialization constraints that have affected patterns of recruitment, performance and advancement. Continued research is obviously needed. More important though is the development of new approaches to the study of performance. Could it be, for example, that the findings on women judges' responsiveness to women's concerns are a function of the power of an individual judge to determine an outcome? Are elected women officials because they are a part of a much larger group more restricted in what they can do, as some research suggests? (Frieze & Ramsey, 1976; Ruble & Higgins, 1976). Does the number of women holding an elective office in, for example, a state legislature, make a difference in performance? Right now we really do not know what difference, if any, these conditions may make. One thing is certain, however, existing methods for assessing performance are not geared to evaluating the role of women or other minorities. Furthermore, there must be a reformulation of existing notions of what constitutes the political elite in order to include participants in social movements and other groups influencing the political order.

THE STATE OF THE ART
FOR GENDER RELATED RESEARCH

What, if anything, can one say about the status of gender related research? First of all, this research has provided us with a wealth of information that did not previously exist; if it did no more than this, it would have performed an invaluable service to the discipline of political science. Thus, whatever its flaws in conceptualization or methodology, it has provided empirical data about a little over half the American population. Without this body of information, one cannot speak accurately about political life or political behavior. The discipline owes a debt of gratitude to those who have added so significantly to information about the ways in which just over one-half the population behaves in the political arena.

But, although the gender related research has filled in "information gaps," it has not provided us with any clear unequivocable explanation of women's political behavior at either the citizen or elite level. To the contrary, it has presented us with a mass of conflicting data and interpretations, as the preceding review of the literature demonstrates. The scholar who wishes to take women's political behavior into account can only experience confusion and uncertainty about what, if any, conclusions can be drawn. Perhaps, it is this that encourages all but those deeply committed to gender related research to ignore the research altogether or to treat it with skepticism or derision.

This confusion stems partially from the nature of the research projects undertaken to date. Lack of financial resources has, no doubt, led many researchers to focus on small, basically unrepresentative national samples or localized subsets. As a result, the findings are probably idiosyncratic to the populations investigated. Perhaps, Costantini and Craik's findings on California women in the political elite differ from those of Jennings and Farah's on Michigan women because California is not Michigan; these conclusions might be invalid for women in other states. Alternatively, the time lapses between studies may account for the differences in findings; this, rather than a particularized region, may explain the differences in the findings of Costantini and Craik and of Jennings and Farah. Similarly, the differences in the findings of socialization studies may, at least in part, result from the representativeness of the samples investigated and the time lapses between studies.

There is little doubt that a more comprehensive investigation of women's political behavior is needed at least to clarify some of the ambiguity current in gender related research. But, the argument being advanced here is that even a more systematic and less fragmentary study of women's political behavior will not resolve the basic problems encountered in gender related research. The fundamental problems have little to do with the representativeness of the subsets under investigation. They will not be solved by more sophisticated or less sexist interpretations of the data or more scholarly rigor in drawing conclusions from the data under consideration. Furthermore, these difficulties are not even the result of the general confusion in political science about the linkage of attitude and behavior. Rather, they stem from the gestalt of the discipline of political science itself which encourages and supports a particular weltanschauung. From this spring a number of constraints which seriously distort both the nature of the research undertaken and the conclusions that can be drawn about both gender and race related research.

These constraints are assumptions about: the nature and diversity of intra-group relations, dealt with in some detail by Jones (1972); the parameters of political activity; the value implicitly attached to certain kinds of political activity; and the definition of political elite.

The problems arising from the present definition of political elite are so strikingly dramatic that it might be best to start with them. If one restricts a definition of political elite to public office holding, one finds few women. Vastly outnumbered, their ability to affect governmental policy outcomes is limited. Realizing that their small numbers may limit their impact, some have suggested alternative measures of performance. However useful alternative modes of evaluating minority performance in governmental or party office may be, they still fail to deal with the critical issue. Both black Americans and women have produced leaders who, although they did not hold office, exerted tremendous political power and affected public policy outcomes that far surpassed those of many white male public office holders defined as politically powerful. In the case of women, there are people like Jane Addams, Emily Balch and Julia Grace Wales, none of whom held any public office, but two of whom received the Nobel Peace Prize, and all of whom profoundly affected the processes of American diplomacy. It was the proposals of these women, and the Women's Peace Party that were the basis for Wilson's Fourteen Points. Kissinger's shuttle diplomacy, Haig's efforts to resolve the Falkland Island Crisis, Carter's Camp David Accords and recent Israeli-Lebanon negotiations are little more than the implementation of Wale's plan for continuous negotiation by neutrals. In 1915 Addams, Balch and Hamilton along with several European women commanded enough power to be received by the European political heads of state and foreign ministers of fourteen nations, including Great Britain and Germany. The American women, as well as others in the Women's Peace Party, were invited to meet with Woodrow Wilson to discuss their views on a number of occasions. Given the inclusion of their proposals in his Fourteen Points, their meetings with President Wilson may hardly be dismissed as perfunctory or social in nature. Additionally, the Women's Peace Party of this period was a politically active group with a membership high of some 40,000. Similarly, women like Florence Kelley, Alice Hamilton, Madeleine Doty, Lilliam Wald, Grace Abbott and Margaret Sanger, along with a host of supportive, primarily female organizations, were able to effect far reaching changes in social policy affecting the poor and the working class. Yet, because political science equates membership in the political elite with office holding which, parenthetically, may be appropriate in the case of more economically privileged white males, the role of many politically powerful women is ignored. As a result, the role of men in politics is artificially inflated, while the role of women is artificially deflated.

The consequence of this omission of women's non-traditional political activity is most fully spelled out by Gittell and Shtob (1980). They write:

In reporting on women's participation, few social scientists questioned the reasons for low participation, attributing it to inherent female characteristics or offering no explanation at all. Few were aware of the political role of women in the urban political reforms of the Progressive Era. Given this approach to research on women's political activity, many social scientists see the participation of middle-class and working-class women in activist community organization in the 1960s and 1970s as a complete reversal of their "normal" behavior. (p. 73)

The same is obivously the case for black leaders. In the face of the activities of individuals like Tubman, Hammer, King, Garvey, Rustin, Malcolm X and DuBois and the support they generated, descriptions of limited political participation at both the elite and citizen level are absurd. It is as ridiculous to draw conclusions about limited political participation of women and blacks based on the criteria of public office holding as it would be to conclude that based on their participation in the Women's Peace Party or Garvey's movement, more affluent white males participated minimally in politics.

The emphasis given to certain types of political activity further distorts the contribution of women to political life. The designation of peace and social justice as "soft" issues of peripheral concern to the political community while economic policy is pivotal focuses attention on those areas where males have dominated the political arena. While no one can deny the centrality of economic policy to human survival, economic well-being is scarcely possible in a war torn nation whose population has been decimated. The lack of importance attached to political activity for peace makes no sense at all. Similarly, women's involvement in local or community affairs may represent a much more realistic appraisal of where intervention will have the greatest impact. Lipsky's work on street level bureaucracy suggests that emphasis on community level politics may not be as peripheral as had been once supposed. Yet, the implicit or explicit value associated with certain types of political activity persists in the discipline.

What one is confronted with in gender and race related research is a series of norms for participation in politics based on the behavior of more affluent white males. When blacks and women are not found to participate in the same way, there is a search for explanations of their overall limited political participation. These explanations are predicated on group differences stemming from socialization, role orientation, and so forth.

Implicit in the research is also the assumption that groups are homogeneous. Yet the research demonstrates that the groups are in fact not as homogeneous as was supposed nor are the range of differences between groups as great as was anticipated. Yet, one tortured explanation after another is formulated to explain the findings and the confusion grows. The solution to this difficulty lies not in continuing this vicious cycle, but in rethinking and reformulating the issues altogether.

The notion that there is one mode of political participation must be rejected; recognition of the fact that there is a variety of modes of participation is essential. A new construct based on more than just the political activity of affluent white males is now needed. Without a new concept of political activity, research can only show us that women, blacks and those disadvantaged by reason of ethnicity, as well as the economically disadvantaged, are not affluent white males, which is something we already know. Meanwhile, the more interesting and compelling issues about how groups like women and blacks do participate, what they have or can accomplish by alternative modes of participation, and what factors influence the selection of modes of participation are ignored.

Gender and race related research to date has already made an important contribution by providing information about the ways in which both these groups have participated in one form of political activity. Now, these research findings require political scientists to recast their conceptualizations. Although it cannot be expected that the discipline will respond without regrets or tension, it must meet the challenge posed if political science is to move forward in the most productive way. What is now needed is a new research agenda focusing on what women define as political and what they see as appropriate political behavior within this context. To achieve this, methodological tools, frameworks and concepts to pursue such investigation must be developed. The effort involved is great, but the result for the discipline as a whole will be more than worth it.

NOTES

1. An example of this is the questionnaire used in Wahlke, Eulau, Buchanan and Ferguson's study of legislature behavior, where there is no item whatsoever referring to the sex of the respondent.
2. Georg Simmel. *Philosophische kultur.* Leipzig: Werner Klinkhardt, 1919. There are no English translations of Simmel's essays. "Das Relative und Das Absolute im Geschlechterproblem" and "Weibliche Kultur." The English translation of the quotes used here is taken from an essay, "The Flight from Womanhood: The Masculinity Complex in Women as Viewed by Men and by Women" by Karen Horney. (*Psychoanalytic Review*, 1935, *12*, pp. 241-257.)
3. The use of the term gender deserves comment. Clearly what is implied is research relating to women, although the definition of gender does not restrict its meaning in this way. In fact research focusing on male behavior—which was the typical case until very recently—is also gender research. Yet, it has never been designated as such. The fact that only studies of female behavior or comparative male/female behavior are described as gender research quite vividly illustrates the accuracy of Simmel's observation.
4. Criticisms of his interpretation of the data have been made as will be discussed later in this essay.
5. Apropos of this is Larwood, Glasser and McDonald's study of male/female cadets' attitudes toward military sex integration (1980). They found that attitudes toward equality deteriorated over time, and after increased interaction between the male and female ROTC cadets.

REFERENCES

Baer, Denise. Theoretical issues in political socialization: The identification of a crucial learning stage using gender roles as a paradigm case. Paper delivered at Southern Political Science Association Annual Meeting. Atlanta, Georgia, 1978.
Barber, James David. *The lawmakers: Recruitment and adaptation to legislative life.* New Haven: Yale University Press, 1965.

Andersen, Kristi. Working women and political participation. *American Journal of Political Science*, 1975, *19*, 439-455.

Bardwick, Judith M. & Douvan, Elizabeth. Ambivalence: The socialization of women. In Vivian Gornick & Barbara K. Moran (Eds.). *Woman in sexist society: Studies in power and powerlessness.* New York: Basic Books, 1971.

Bartol, Kathryn & Wortman, Max S. Jr. Sex of leader and subordinate role stress: A field study. *Sex Roles*, 1979, *5*, 513-518.

Baxter, Sandra & Sansing, Marjorie. *Women and politics: The invisible majority.* Ann Arbor: University of Michigan Press, 1980.

Bearison, David J. Sex linked patterns of socialization. *Sex Roles*, 1979, *5*, 11-18.

Beck, P. A. & Jennings, M. Kent. Parents as 'middle persons' in political socialization. *Journal of Politics*, 1975, *37*, 87-99.

Berelson, B. R., Lazarsfeld, P. F., & McPhee, W. N. *Voting: A study of opinion formation in a presidential campaign.* Chicago: University of Chicago Press, 1954.

Bers, Trudy Haffron. Local political elites: Men and women on Boards of Education. *Western Political Quarterly*, 1978, *31*, 381-391.

Biller, H. B. *Father, child and sex role: Parental determinants of personality development.* Lexington: Heath Lexington Books, 1971.

Blay, Eva Alterman. The political participation of women in Brazil: Female mayors. *Signs*, 1979, *5*, 42-59.

Block, J. H. Another look at sex differentiation in the socialization behaviors of mothers and fathers. In J. Sherman & F. Denmark (Eds.). *Psychology of women: Future research.* New York: Psychological Dimensions, 1977.

Boles, Janet. *The politics of the equal rights amendment: Conflict and the decision process.* New York: Longman, 1979.

Boneparth, Ellen. The impact of commissions on the status of women in the policy making process: A California case study. Paper delivered at American Political Science Association Annual Meeting, Chicago, Ill., 1976.

Boneparth, Ellen. *Women, power and policy.* New York: Pergamon Press, 1982.

Breckinridge, Sophonisba. *Women in the twentieth century: A study of their political, social and economic activities.* New York: McGraw Hill, 1933.

Bullock, C. S. & Heys, P. F. Recruitment of women for Congress: A research note. *Western Political Quarterly*, 1972, *25*, 416-423.

Campbell, Angus, Converse, Philip E., Miller, Warren, & Stokes, Donald E. *The American voter.* New York: John Wiley & Sons, 1960.

Carroll, Berenice A. Political science part I: American politics and political behavior: Review essay. *Signs*, 1979, *5*, 289-306.

Carroll, Susan. Women candidates and support for women's issues: Closet feminism. Paper presented at the Midwest Political Science Association Annual Meeting. Chicago, Ill., 1979.

Carver, Joan. The ERA in Florida. Paper delivered at the Southern Political Science Association Annual Meeting, 1979.

Cavanagh, Thomas E. Changes in American voter turnout, 1964-1976. *Political Science Quarterly*, 1981, *96*, 53-65.

Cook, Beverly B. The personality and procreative behavior of trial judges: A biocultural perspective. *International Political Science Review*, 1980, *3*, 51-70. (a)

Cook, Beverly B. Women judges and public policy in sex integration. In Debra W. Stewart (Ed.). *Women in local politics.* Metuchen, N.J.: Scarecrow Press, 1980. (b)

Cook, Beverly B. Will women judges make a difference in women's legal rights? A prediction from attitudes and simulated behavior. In Margherita Rendel (Ed.). *Women power and political systems.* London: Croom-Helm, 1981.

Corbett, Michael, Frankland, E. Gene, & Rudoni, Dorothy. Explorations into the impact of sexist attitudes on other politically relevant attitudes: A research note.

Paper delivered at Southern Political Science Association Annual Meeting, Atlanta, Georgia, 1976.

Corbett, M., Rudoni, D., & Frankland, E. G. Change in stability in sexism among 1981 college students: A three year panel study. Sex Roles, 1981, 7, 233-246.

Costantini, Edmond & Craik, Kenneth H. Women as politicians: The social background, personality and political careers of female party leaders. Journal of Social Issues, 1972, 28, 217-236.

Curry, V. Campaign theory and practice—the gender variable. In Githens and Prestage (Eds.), A portrait of marginality. New York: David McKay, 1977.

Darcy, R. & Schramm, Sarah Slavin. When women run against men. Public Opinion Quarterly, 1977, 41, 1-12.

Deaux, Kay. Self-evaluations of male and female managers. Sex Roles, 1979, 5, 571-580.

DeFronzo, James. Differences in the determinants of husbands' and working wives' class and political party identification. Sex Roles, 1981, 7, 355-361.

Diamond, Irene. Why aren't they there?: Women in American state legislatures. Paper presented at the Annual Meeting of the American Political Science Association, Chicago, 1976.

Diamond, Irene. Sex roles in the state house. New Haven: Yale University Press, 1977.

Diamond, Irene & Hartsock, Nancy. Beyond interests in politics: A comment on Virginia Sapiro's when are interests interesting? The problem of political representation of women. American Political Science Review, 1981, 75, 717-721.

Duncan, Beverly, & Duncan, Otis Dudley. Sex typing and social roles: A research report. New York: Academic Press, 1978.

Duverger, Maurice. La Participation des Femmes a la vie Politique. Paris: UNESCO, 1955.

Dweck, C. S. Sex differences in the meaning of negative evaluation in achievement situations: Determinants and consequences. Paper presented at the meeting of the Society for Research and Child Development, 1975.

Easton, David & Dennis, Jack. Children in the political system. New York: McGraw Hill, 1969.

Elshtain, Jean. The public and the private: A critical inquiry. Princeton: Princeton University Press, 1981.

Etaugh, C., Collins, G. & Gerson, A. Reinforcement of sex typed behaviors of two year old children in a nursery school setting. Developmental Psychology, 1975, 11, 255.

Evans, S. Personal politics: The roots of women's liberation in the civil rights movement and the new Left. New York: Vintage Press, 1980.

Fischer, J. L. & Narus, L. R. Sex role development in late adolescence and adulthood. Sex Roles, 1981, 7, 97-106.

Flora, Cornelia B. & Lynn, Naomi B. Women and political socialization: Considerations of the impact of motherhood. In Jane S. Jaquette (Ed.). Women in politics. New York: John Wiley & Sons, 1974.

Fowlkes, Diane, Perkins, Jerry & Rinehart, Sue Tollerson. Gender roles and party roles. American Political Science Review, 1979, 73, 722-780.

Frankovic, Kathleen A. Sex and politics—New alignments, old issues. PS, 1982, 15, 439-448.

Freeman, Jo. The politics of women's liberation. New York: David McKay, 1975.

Frieze, Irene Hanson & Ramsey, Sheila J. Nonverbal maintenance of traditional sex roles. Journal of Social Issues, 1976, 32, 125-132.

Frueh, T. & McGhee, P. E. Traditional sex role development and amount of time spent watching television. Developmental Psychology, 1975, 11, 109.

Fulenwider, Claire Knoche. Feminist ideology and the political attitudes and participation of white and minority women. Paper delivered at meeting of the American Political Science Association. Washington, D.C., 1979.

Gehlen, Frieda. Women members of Congress: A distinctive role. In M. Githens & J. Prestage (Eds.). *A portrait of marginality.* New York: David McKay Co., 1977.

Gelb, Joyce & Palley, Marian Lief. *Women and public policies.* Princeton: Princeton University Press, 1982.

Githens, Marianne & Prestage, Jewel L. (Eds.). *A portrait of marginality: The political behavior of the American woman.* New York: David McKay Co., 1977.

Githens, Marianne & Prestage, Jewel. Women state legislators as marginals. *Policy Studies Journal,* 1978, *7,* 264-270.

Githens, Marianne & Prestage, Jewel. Styles and priorities of marginality: Women state legislators. In Marian Lief Palley & Michael Preston (Eds.). *Race, sex and policy problems.* Lexington: Lexington Books, 1979.

Githens, Marianne & Prestage, Jewel. Education and marginality: Some observations on the behavior of women state legislators. Unpublished manuscript, 1980.

Githens, Marianne & Prestage, Jewel. Women state legislators: A reconsideration of characteristic values and attitudes. Unpublished manuscript, 1981.

Githens, M. & Prestage, J. Who consults them? Women state legislators and pressure groups. Unpublished manuscript, 1982.

Gittell, Marilyn & Shtob, Teresa. Changing women's roles in political volunteerism and reform of the city. *Signs,* 1980, *5,* 67-68.

Greenstein, Fred I. *Children and politics.* New Haven: Yale University Press, 1965.

Gruberg, Martin. *Women in politics: An assessment and source book.* Oshkosh, WI: Academia, 1968.

Gruhl, John & Welch, Susan. Women as policy makers: The case of trial judges. *American Journal of Political Science,* 1981, *25,* 308-322.

Hartley, R. E. Children's concepts of male and female roles. *Merrill-Palmer Quarterly,* 1960, *6,* 83-91.

Hartley, R. E. A developmental view of female sex role definition and identification. *Merrill-Palmer Quarterly,* 1960, *10,* 3-16.

Hershey, Marjorie Random & Sullivan, John L. Sex role attitudes, identities and political ideology. *Sex Roles,* 1977, *3,* 52-57.

Hess, Robert D. & Torney, Judith V. *The development of political attitudes in children.* Chicago: Aldine, 1967.

Horney, Karen. The flight from womanhood: The masculinity complex in women as viewed by men and by women. *Psychoanalytic Review,* 1935, *12,* 241-257.

Hull, J. L. & Frederickson, R. Sex role stereotyping; A function of age and education as measured by a perceptual-trojective device. *Sex Roles,* 1979, *5,* 77-84.

Hyman, Herbert. *Political socialization: A study in the psychology of political behavior.* New York: Free Press, 1959.

Iglitzin, Lynne. The making of the apolitical woman: Feminity and sex stereotyping in girls. In Jane S. Jaquette (Ed.). *Women in politics.* New York: John Wiley & Sons, 1974.

Jaquette, Jane S. (Ed.). *Women in politics.* New York: John Wiley & Sons, 1974.

Jennings, M. Kent. Another look at the life cycle and political participation. *American Journal of Political Science,* 1979, *23,* 755-771.

Jennings, M. Kent & Farah, Barbara. Ideology, gender and political action: A cross-national survey. *British Journal of Political Science,* 1980, *10,* 219-240.

Jennings, M. Kent & Farah, Barbara. Social roles and political resources: An over-time study of men and women in party elites. *American Journal of Political Science,* 1981, *25,* 462-481.

Jennings, M. Kent & Langton, Kenneth. Mothers versus fathers: The formation of political orientations among young Americans. *Journal of Politics*, 1969, *31*, 329-357.

Jennings, M. Kent & Niemi, Richard G. *The political character of adolescence: The influence of families and schools*. Princeton: Princeton University Press, 1974.

Jennings, M. Kent & Niemi, Richard. The persistence of political orientations: An over-time analysis of two generations. *British Journal of Political Science*, 1978, *8*, 333-363.

Jennings, M. Kent & Thomas, Norman. Men and women in party elites: Social roles and political resources. *Midwest Journal of Political Science*, 1968, *12*, 469-492.

Johnson, Marilyn & Stanwick, Kathy. *Women in public office: A biographical directory and statistical analysis*. New York: R.R. Bowker, 1976.

Johnson, Marilyn & Carroll, Susan. *Women in public office: A biographical and statistical analysis* (2nd ed.). Metuchen, N.J.: Scarecrow Press, 1978.

Jones, Mack. A frame of reference for black politics. Paper delivered at the Annual Meeting of the Southern Political Science Association, 1972.

Kagan, J. & Moss, H. A. *Birth to maturity, a study in psychological development*. New York: John Wiley and Sons, 1962.

Keller, Edmond J. The political socialization of adolescents in contemporary Africa. *Comparative Politics*, 1978, *10*, 227-250.

Kelly, Rita Mae & Boutilier, Mary A. Mothers, daughters and the socialization of political women. *Sex Roles*, 1978, *4*, 438-443. (a)

Kelly, Rita Mae & Boutilier, Mary A. *The making of the political woman: A study of socialization and role conflict*. Chicago: Nelson-Hall, 1978. (b)

Kincaid, Diane D. Over his dead body a new perspective and some feminist footnotes on widows in the U.S. Congress. Paper delivered at the American Political Science Association Annual Meeting. Chicago, Ill., 1976.

King, Elizabeth. Women in Iowa legislative politics. In Githens and Prestage (Eds.), *A portrait of marginality*. New York: David McKay, 1977.

Kirkpatrick, Jeane. *Political woman*. New York: Basic Books, 1974.

Kirkpatrick, Jeane. *The new presidential elite: Men and women in national politics*. New York: Basic Books, 1976.

Krauss, Wilma Rule. Political implications of gender role: A review of the literature. *American Political Science Review*, 1974, *68*, 1706-1723.

Lambert, W. E., Yackley, A. & Hein, R. N. Child training values of English Canadian and French Canadian parents. *Canadian Journal of Behavioral Science*, 1971, *3*, 217-236.

Lane, Robert E. *Political life: Why people get involved in politics*. Glencoe: Free Press, 1959.

Lee, Marcia. Toward understanding why so few women hold public office: Factors affecting the participation of women in politics. In M. Githens & J. Prestage (Eds.), *A portrait of marginality*. New York: David McKay, 1977.

Liebert, R. M., McCall, R. B. & Hanratty, N. A. Effects of sex type information on children's toy preferences. *Journal of Genetic Psychology*, 1971, *119*, 133-136.

Maccoby, E. E. & Jacklin, C. N. *The psychology of sex differences*. Stanford: Stanford University Press, 1974.

MacManus, Susan. Determinants of the equitability of female representation of 243 city councils. Paper delivered at meeting of American Political Science Association. Chicago, IL, 1976.

Mardel, Ruth. *In the running: The new woman candidate*. New Haven: Ticknor and Fields, 1981.

Meeker, B. J. and Weitzell-O'Neill, P. A. Sex roles and interpersonal and behavior in task-oriented groups. *American Sociological Review*, 1977, *42*, 91-105.

Merelman, R. *Political socialization and educational climates: A study of two school districts*. New York: Holt, Rinehart and Winston, 1971.

Merritt, Sharyne. Winners and losers: Sex differences in municipal elections. *American Journal of Political Science*, 1977, *21*, 731-743.

Mezey, Susan Gluck. Women politicians and women's issues: The case of Hawaii. Paper delivered at meeting of the American Political Science Association. New York, 1976.

Mezey, Susan Gluck. Local representatives in Connecticut: Sex differences in attitudes toward women's rights policy. Paper delivered at meeting of the American Political Science Association. Chicago, IL, 1977.

Milbrath, L. & Goel, M. L. *Political participation: How and why people get involved in politics* (2nd ed.). Chicago: Rand-McNally, 1977.

Miller, Arthur, Gurin, Patricia, Gurin, Gerald, & Malanchuk, Oksana. Group consciousness. *American Journal of Political Science*, 1981, *25*, 494-511.

Moss, H. A. Sex, age and state as determinants of mother-infant interaction. *Merrill-Palmer Quarterly*, 1967, *13*, 19-36.

Mussen, P. H. Early sex-role development. In D. A. Goslin (Ed.). *Handbook of socialization theory and research*. Chicago: Rand McNally, 1969.

National Women's Education Fund. *Evaluation report: A survey of participants in training seminars conducted by the National Women's Education Fund, 1974-1980*. 1981.

Nie, Norman, Verba, Sidney & Petrocik, John. *The changing American voter*. Cambridge: Harvard University Press, 1976.

Orkin, S. M. *Women in western political thought*. Princeton: Princeton University Press, 1979.

Orum, Anthony M., Cohen, Roberta S., Grasmuck, Sherri, & Orum, Amy W. Sex socialization and politics. In Marianne Githens and Jewel Prestage (Eds.). *A portrait of marginality*. New York: David McKay, 1977.

Parsons, J. E., Frieze, I. H., & Ruble, D. Sex roles: Persistence and change. *Journal of Social Issues*, 1976, *32*, 1-5.

Perkins, Jerry & Fowlkes, Diane. Opinion representation vs. social representation: Or why women can't run as women and win. *American Political Science Review*, 1980, *74*, 92-103.

Perry, D. G. & Perry, L. C. Observational learning in children: Effects of sex of model and subject's sex role behavior. *Journal of Personality and Social Psychology*, 1975, *31*, 1083-1088.

Pierce, John C., Avery, William P. & Carey, Addison Jr. Sex differences in black political beliefs and behavior. *American Journal of Political Science*, 1977, *17*, 422-430.

Pomper, Gerald. *Voter's choice: Varieties of American electoral behavior*. New York: Dodd Mead and Co., 1975.

Rapoport, Ronald B. What they don't know can hurt you. *American Journal of Political Science*, 1979, *23*, 805-815.

Rapoport, Ronald. The sex gap in political persuading: Where the structuring principle works. *American Journal of Political Science*, 1981, *25*, 32-47.

Reid, I. S. Traditional political animals? A loud no. In Githens and Prestage (Eds.), *A portrait of marginality*. New York: David McKay, 1977.

Richardson, Deborah, Vinsel, Anne & Taylor, Stuart. Female aggression as a function of attitudes toward women. *Sex Roles*, 1980, *6*, 265-271.

Rinehart, Sue Tollerson. Amateurism among women political party elites. Paper delivered at the Annual Meeting of the Southern Political Science Association. 1978.

Roback, Thomas H. The role of women and blacks in the Republican party: Attitudinal perspectives of national convention delegates, 1972 and 1976. Paper delivered at meeting of Southern Political Science Association. 1978.

Robinson, J. Interpersonal influence in election campaigns: Two step-flow hypotheses. *Public Opinion Quarterly*, 1976, *40*, 304-319.

Rosenberg, Marie Barovic. Political efficacy and sex role: Case study of congress-women Edith Green and Julia Butler Hansen. Paper delivered at the Annual Meeting of the American Political Science Association, Washington, D.C., 1972.

Ross, Marc Howard & Thadani, Veena. Participation, sex and social class: Some unexpected results from an African city. *Comparative Politics*, 1980, *12*, 323-334.

Rossi, A. *Feminists in politics: A panel analysis of the first national women's conference.* New York: Academic Press, 1982.

Ruble, Diane N. & Higgins, E. Effects of group sex composition on self presentation and sex typing. *Journal of Social Issues*, 1976, *32*, 125-132.

Sapiro, Virginia. Sex and games: On oppression and rationality. *British Journal of Political Science*, 1979, *9*, 385-408.

Sapiro, Virginia. News from the front: Intersex and intergenerational conflict over the status of women. *Western Political Quarterly*, 1980, *33*, 260-277.

Sapiro, Virginia. Research frontier essay: When are interests interesting? The problem of political representation of women. *American Political Science Review*, 1981, *75*, 701-716.

Sapiro, Virginia & Farah, Barbara G. New pride and old prejudice: Political ambition and role orientation among female partisan elites. *Women and Politics*, 1980, *1*, 13-35.

Sapiro, Virginia. *The political integration of women.* Urbana: University of Illinois Press, 1983.

Scott, A. F. *The southern lady.* Chicago: University of Chicago Press, 1970.

Shabad, Goldie & Andersen, Kristi. Candidate evaluation by men and women. *Public Opinion Quarterly*, 1979, *43*, 18-35.

Simmel, Georg. *Philosophische Kulter. Philosophisch Soziologische Bucherei* (Vol. 27). Leipzig: Kronet, 1919.

Soule, John W. & McGrath, Wilma E. A comparative study of male-female political attitudes at citizen and elite levels. In M. Githens & J. Prestage (Eds.). *A portrait of marginality.* New York: David McKay, 1977.

Stewart, Debra W. *The women's movement in community politics in the U.S.: The role of local commissions of the status of women.* New York: Pergamon Press, 1980.

Stone, Pauline Terrlonge. The political ambitions of convention delegates: The relevance of race and sex. Paper delivered at meeting of the American Political Science Association. Washington, D.C., 1979.

Stoper, Emily. Wife and politician: Role strain among women in public office. In M. Githens & J. Prestage (Eds.). *A portrait of marginality.* New York: David McKay, 1977.

Stucker, John. Women as voters: Their maturation as political persons in American society. In M. Githens & J. Prestage (Eds.). *A portrait of marginality.* New York: David McKay, 1977.

Thompson, Martha E. Sex differences: Differential access to power or sex role socialization. *Sex Roles*, 1981, *7*, 413-424.

Verba, Sidney & Nie, Norman H. *Participation in America: Political democracy and social equality.* New York: Harper & Row, 1972.

Verba, Sidney, Nie, Norman H. & Kim Jae-on. *Participation and political equality.* Cambridge: Cambridge University Press, 1978.

Wahlke, John C., Eulau, Heinz, Buchanan, William & Ferguson, Lorna C. *The legis-lative system: Explorations in legislative behavior.* New York: John Wiley & Sons, 1962.

Welch, Susan. Women as political animals? A test of some explanations for male-female political participation differences. *American Journal of Political Science*, 1977, *21*, 711-729.

Welch, Susan. Recruitment of women to public office. *Western Political Quarterly,* 1978, *31,* 372-381.

Werner, Emily. Women in Congress: 1917-1964. *Western Political Quarterly,* 1966, *19,* 16-30.

Werner, E. Women in state legislatures. *Western Political Quarterly,* 1968, *21,* 40-50.

Werner, E. & Bachtold, L. Personality characteristics of women in American politics. In Jane Jaquette (Ed.), *Women in politics.* New York: John Wiley & Sons, 1974.

INTERNATIONAL POLITICS

16

Theory of World Politics:
Structural Realism and Beyond*

Robert O. Keohane

For over 2000 years, what Hans J. Morgenthau dubbed "Political Realism" has constituted the principal tradition for the analysis of international relations in Europe and its offshoots in the New World (Morgenthau, 1966). Writers of the Italian Renaissance, balance of power theorists, and later adherents of the school of *machtpolitik* all fit under a loose version of the Realist rubric. Periodic attacks on Realism have taken place; yet the very focus of these critiques seems only to reconfirm the centrality of Realist thinking in the international political thought of the West.[1]

Realism has been criticized frequently during the last few years, and demands for a "new paradigm" have been made. Joseph S. Nye and I called for a "world politics paradigm" a decade ago, and Richard Mansbach and John A. Vasquez have recently proposed a "new paradigm for global politics." In both these works, the new paradigm that was envisaged entailed adopting additional concepts—for instance, "transnational relations," or "issue phases" (Keohane & Nye, 1972, esp. pp. 379-386; Mansbach & Vasquez, 1981, Chapter 4). Yet for these concepts to be useful as part of a satisfactory general theory of world politics, a theory of state action—which is what Realism purports to provide—is necessary. Understanding the general principles of state action and the practices of governments is a necessary basis for attempts to refine theory or to extend the analysis to non-state actors. Approaches using

*I am grateful to Raymond Hopkins for inviting me to prepare the original version of this paper for the American Political Science Association Annual Meeting in Denver, September, 1982. A number of ideas presented here were developed with the help of discussions in the graduate international relations field seminar at Brandeis University during the spring semester, 1982, which I taught with my colleague, Robert J. Art. I have also received extremely valuable comments from a number of friends and colleagues on an earlier draft of this paper, in particular from Vinod Aggarwal, David Baldwin, Seyom Brown, Ben Dickinson, Alexander George, Robert Gilpin, Ernst Haas, Thomas Ilgen, Robert Jervis, Peter Katzenstein, Stephen Krasner, Timothy McKeown, Helen Milner, Joseph Nye, and Kenneth Waltz.

new concepts may be able to supplement, enrich, or extend a basic theory of state action, but they cannot substitute for it.[2]

The fixation of critics and reformers on the Realist theory of state action reflects the importance of this research tradition. In my view, there is good reason for this. Realism is a necessary component in a coherent analysis of world politics because its focus on power, interests, and rationality is crucial to any understanding of the subject. Thus any approach to international relations has to incorporate, or at least come to grips with, key elements of Realist thinking. Even writers who are concerned principally with international institutions and rules, or analysts in the Marxist tradition, make use of some Realist premises. Since Realism builds on fundamental insights about world politics and state action, progress in the study of international relations requires that we seek to build on this core.

Yet as we shall see, Realism does not provide a satisfactory theory of world politics, if we require of an adequate theory that it provide a set of plausible and testable answers to questions about state behavior under specified conditions. Realism is particularly weak in accounting for change, especially where the sources of that change lie in the world political economy or in the domestic structures of states. Realism, viewed dogmatically as a set of answers, would be worse than useless. As a sophisticated framework of questions and initial hypotheses, however, it is extremely valuable.[3]

Since Realism constitutes the central tradition in the study of world politics, an analysis, like this one, of the current state of the field must evaluate the viability of Realism in the penultimate decade of the twentieth century. Doing this requires constructing a rather elaborate argument of my own, precluding a comprehensive review of the whole literature of international relations. I have therefore selected for discussion a relatively small number of works that fit my theme, ignoring entire areas of research, much of it innovative.[4] Within the sphere of work dealing with Realism and its limitations, I have focused attention on several especially interesting and valuable contributions. My intention is to point out promising lines of research rather than to engage in what Stanley Hoffmann once called a "wrecking operation" (Hoffmann, 1960, p. 171).

Since I have written on the subject of Realism in the past, I owe the reader an explanation of where I think my views have changed, and where I am only restating, in different ways, opinions that I have expressed before. This chapter deals more systematically and more sympathetically with Realism than does my previous work. Yet its fundamental argument is consistent with that of *Power and Interdependence*. In that book Nye and I relied on Realist theory as a basis for our structural models of international regime change (Keohane & Nye, 1977, pp. 42-46). We viewed our structural models as attempts to improve the ability of Realist or neo-Realist analysis to account for international regime change: we saw ourselves as adapting Realism, and attempting to go beyond it, rather than rejecting it.

Admittedly, Chapter 2 of *Power and Interdependence* characterized Realism as a descriptive ideal type rather than a research program in which explanatory theories could be embedded. Realist and Complex Interdependence ideal types were used to help specify the conditions under which overall structure explanations of change would or would not be valid; the term,

"Realist," was used to refer to conditions under which states are the dominant actors, hierarchies of issues exist, and force is usable as an instrument of policy (Keohane & Nye, 1977, pp. 23-29). Taken as a full characterization of the Realist tradition this would have been unfair, and it seems to have led readers concerned with our view of Realism to focus excessively on Chapter 2 and too little on the attempt, which draws on what I here call structural realism, to account for regime change (chapters 3-6).[5]

To provide criteria for the evaluation of theoretical work in international politics—Structural Realism, in particular—I employ the conception of a "scientific research programme" explicated in 1970 by the philosopher of science, Imre Lakatos (1970). Lakatos developed this concept as a tool for the comparative evaluation of scientific theories, and in response to what he regarded as the absence of standards for evaluation in Thomas Kuhn's (1962) notion of a paradigm.[6] Theories are embedded in research programs. These programs contain inviolable assumptions (the "hard core") and initial conditions, defining their scope. For Lakatos, they also include two other very important elements: auxiliary, or observational, hypotheses, and a "positive heuristic," which tells the scientist what sorts of additional hypotheses to entertain and how to go about conducting research. In short, a research program is a set of methodological rules telling us what paths of research to avoid and what paths to follow.

Consider a research program, with a set of observational hypotheses, a "hard core" of irrefutable assumptions, and a set of scope conditions. In the course of research, anomalies are bound to appear sooner or later: predictions of the theory will seem to be falsified. For Lakatos, the reaction of scientists developing the research program is to protect the hard core by constructing auxiliary hypotheses that will explain the anomalies. Yet any research program, good or bad, can invent such auxiliary hypotheses on an *ad hoc* basis. The key test for Lakatos of the value of a research program is whether these auxiliary hypotheses are "progressive," that is, whether their invention leads to the discovery of *new facts* (other than the anomalous facts that they were designed to explain). Progressive research programs display "continuous growth": their auxiliary hypotheses increase our capacity to understand reality (Lakatos, 1970, pp. 116-122, 132-138, 173-180).

Lakatos developed this conception to assess developments in the natural sciences, particularly physics. If we took literally the requirements that he laid down for "progressive" research programs, all actual theories of international politics—and perhaps all conceivable theories—would fail the test. Indeed, it has been argued that much of economics, including oligopoly theory (heavily relied upon by Structural Realists), fails to meet this standard (Latsis, 1976). Nevertheless, Lakatos's conception has the great merit of providing clear and sensible criteria for the evaluation of scientific traditions, and of asking penetrating questions that may help us to see Realism in a revealing light. Lakatos' questions are relevant, even if applying them without modification could lead to premature rejection not only of Realism, but of our whole field, or even the entire discipline of political science![7]

The stringency of Lakatos' standards suggests that we should supplement this test with a "softer," more interpretive one. That is, how much insight does Realism provide into contemporary world politics?

For this line of evaluation we can draw inspiration from Clifford Geertz's discussion of the role of theory in anthropology. Geertz argues that culture "is not a power, something to which social events, behaviors, institutions, or processes can be causally attributed; it is a context—something within which they can be intelligibly—that is, thickly—described" (1973, p. 14). The role of theory, he claims, is "not to codify abstract regularities but to make thick description possible, not to generalize across cases but to generalize within them" (*ibid.*, p. 26). This conception is the virtual antithesis of the standards erected by Lakatos, and could all too easily serve as a rationalization for the proliferation of atheoretical case studies. Nevertheless, culture as discussed by Geertz has something in common with the international system as discussed by students of world politics. It is difficult to generalize across systems. We are continually bedeviled by the paucity of comparable cases, particularly when making systemic statements—for example, about the operation of balances of power. Much of what students of world politics do, and what Classical Realism in particular aspires to, is to make the actions of states understandable (despite obfuscatory statements by their spokesmen): that is, in Geertz's words, to provide "a context within which they can be intelligibly described." For example, Morgenthau's discussion of the concept of interest defined in terms of power, quoted at length below, reflects this objective more than the goal of arriving at testable generalizations.

This essay is divided into four major sections. The first of these seeks to establish the basis for a dual evaluation of Realism: as a source of interpretive insights into the operation of world politics, and as a scientific research program that enables the investigator to discover new facts. I examine the arguments of Thucydides and Morgenthau to extract the key assumptions of Classical Realism. Then I discuss recent work by Kenneth N. Waltz, whom I regard as the most systematic spokesman for contemporary Structural Realism.

Section II addresses the question of interpretation and puzzle-solving within the Realist tradition. How successful are Realist thinkers in making new contributions to our understanding of world politics? In Section III, I consider the shortcomings of Realism when judged by the standards that Lakatos establishes, or even when evaluated by less rigorous criteria, and begin to ask whether a modified version of Structural Realism could correct some of these faults. Section IV carries this theme further by attempting to outline how a multi-dimensional research program, including a modified structural theory, might be devised; what its limitations would be; and how it could be relevant, in particular, to problems of peaceful change.

The conclusion emphasizes the issue of peaceful change as both a theoretical and a practical problem. Realism raises the question of how peaceful change could be achieved, but does not resolve it. Understanding the conditions under which peaceful change would be facilitated remains, in my view, the most urgent task facing students of world politics.

I. STRUCTURAL REALISM AS RESEARCH PROGRAM

To explicate the research program of Realism, I begin with two classic works, one ancient, the other modern: *The Peloponnesian War,* by

Thucydides, and *Politics Among Nations,* by Morgenthau.[8] The three most fundamental Realist assumptions are evident in these books: that the most important actors in world politics are territorially organized entities (city-states or modern states); that state behavior can be explained rationally; and that states seek power and calculate their interests in terms of power, relative to the nature of the international system that they face.

The Peloponnesian War was written in an attempt to explain the causes of the great war of the Fifth Century B.C. between the coalition led by Athens and its adversaries, led by Sparta. Thucydides assumes that to achieve this purpose, he must explain the behavior of the major city-states involved in the conflict. Likewise, Morgenthau assumes that the subject of a science of international politics is the behavior of states. Realism is "state-centric."[9]

Both authors also believed that observers of world politics could understand events by imagining themselves, as rational individuals, in authoritative positions, and reflecting on what they would do if faced with the problems encountered by the actual decision-makers. They both, therefore, employ the method of *rational reconstruction.* Thucydides admits that he does not have transcripts of all the major speeches given during the war, but he is undaunted:

> It was in all cases difficult to carry [the speeches] word for word in one's memory, so my habit has been to make the speakers say what was in my opinion demanded of them by the various occasions, of course adhering as closely as possible to the general sense of what they really said. (Thucydides, Book I, paragraph 23 [Chapter I, Modern Library edition, p. 14])

Morgenthau argues that in trying to understand foreign policy,

> We put ourselves in the position of a statesman who must meet a certain problem of foreign policy under certain circumstances, and we ask ourselves what the rational alternatives are from which a statesman may choose . . . and which of these rational alternatives this particular statesman, acting under these circumstances, is likely to choose. It is the testing of this rational hypothesis against the actual facts and their consequences that gives meaning to the facts of international politics and makes a theory of politics possible. (Morgenthau, 1966, p. 5)

In reconstructing state calculations, Thucydides and Morgenthau both assume that states will act to protect their power positions, perhaps even to the point of seeking to maximize their power. Thucydides seeks to go beneath the surface of events to the power realities that are fundamental to state action:

> The real cause [of the war] I consider to be the one which was formally most kept out of sight. *The growth in the power of Athens, and the alarm which this inspired in Lacedemon, made war inevitable* (Thucydides, Book I, paragraph 24 [Chapter I, Modern Library Edition, p. 15])[10]

Morgenthau is even more blunt: "International politics, like all politics, is a struggle for power" (1966, p. 25; see also Morgenthau, 1946). Political

Realism, he argues, understands international politics through the concept of "interest defined as power":

> We assume that statesmen think and act in terms of interest defined as power, and the evidence of history bears that assumption out. That assumption allows us to retrace and anticipate, as it were, the steps a statesman — past, present, or future — has taken or will take on the political scene. We look over his shoulder when he writes his dispatches; we listen in on his conversation with other statesmen; we read and anticipate his very thoughts. (1966, p. 5)

The three assumptions just reviewed define the hard core of the Classical Realist research program:

(1) The *state-centric assumption:* states are the most important actors in world politics;

(2) The *rationality assumption:* world politics can be analyzed as if states were unitary rational actors, carefully calculating costs of alternative courses of action and seeking to maximize their expected utility, although doing so under conditions of uncertainty and without necessarily having sufficient information about alternatives or resources (time or otherwise) to conduct a full review of all possible courses of action;[11]

(3) The *power assumption:* states seek power (both the ability to influence others and resources that can be used to exercise influence); and they calculate their interests in terms of power, whether as end or as necessary means to a variety of other ends.

More recently, Kenneth N. Waltz (1959) has attempted to reformulate and systematize Realism on the basis of what he called, in *Man, the State and War*, a "third image" perspective. This form of Realism does not rest on the presumed iniquity of the human race — original sin in one form or another — but on the nature of world politics as an anarchic realm:

> Each state pursues its own interests, however defined, in ways it judges best. Force is a means of achieving the external ends of states because there exists no consistent, reliable process of reconciling the conflicts of interests that inevitably arise among similar units in a condition of anarchy. (p. 238)[12]

Even well-intentioned statesmen find that they must use or threaten force to attain their objectives.

Since the actions of states are conceived of as resulting from the nature of international politics, the paramount theoretical task for Realists is to create a *systemic* explanation of international politics. In a systemic theory, as Waltz explains it, the propositions of the theory specify relationships between certain aspects of the system and actor behavior (1979, pp. 67-73). Waltz's third-image Realism, for instance, draws connections between the distribution of power in a system and the actions of states: small countries will behave differently than large ones, and in a balance of power system, alliances can be expected to shift in response to changes in power relationships. Any theory will, of course, take into account the attributes of actors, as well as features of the system itself. But the key distinguishing characteristic of a systemic theory is that *the internal attributes of actors are given by assumption rather than treated as variables.* Changes in actor behavior, and system outcomes, are explained not on the basis of variations in these actor characteristics, but on the basis of changes in the attributes of the system itself. A good example of such a systemic theory is microeconomic theory in its standard form. It posits the existence of business firms, with given utility functions (such as profit maximization), and attempts to explain their behavior on the basis of environmental factors such as the competitiveness of markets. It is systemic because its propositions about variations in behavior depend on variations in characteristics of the system, not of the units (Waltz, 1979, pp. 89-91, 93-95, 98).

To develop a systemic analysis, abstraction is necessary: one has to avoid being distracted by the details and vagaries of domestic politics and other variables at the level of the acting unit. To reconstruct a systemic research program, therefore, Structural Realists must devise a way to explain state behavior on the basis of systemic characteristics, and to account for outcomes in the same manner. This needs to be a coherent explanation, although it need not tell us everything we would like to know about world politics.

Waltz's formulation of Structural Realism as a systemic theory seeks to do this by developing a concept not explicitly used by Morgenthau or Thucydides: the *structure* of the international system. Two elements of international structure are constants: (1) the international system is anarchic rather than hierarchic, and (2) it is characterized by interaction among units with similar functions. These are such enduring background characteristics that they are constitutive of what we mean by "international politics."[14] The third element of structure, the distribution of capabilities across the states in the system, varies from system to system, and over time. Since it is a variable, this element — the distribution of "power" — takes on particular importance in the theory. The most significant capabilities are those of the most powerful actors. Structures "are defined not by all of the actors that flourish within them but by the major ones" (Waltz, 1979, p. 93).

According to Waltz, structure is the principal determinant of outcomes at the systems level: structure encourages certain actions and discourages others. It may also lead to unintended consequences, as the ability of states to obtain their objectives is constrained by the power of others (1979, pp. 104-111).

For Waltz, understanding the structure of an international system allows us to explain patterns of state behavior, since states determine their interests and strategies on the basis of calculations about their own positions in the system. The link between system structure and actor behavior is forged by the rationality assumption, which enables the theorist to predict that leaders will respond to the incentives and constraints imposed by their environments. Taking rationality as a constant permits one to attribute variations in state behavior to variations in characteristics of the international system. Otherwise, state behavior might have to be accounted for by variations in the calculating ability of states; in that case, the systemic focus of Structural Realism (and much of its explanatory power) would be lost. Thus the rationality assumption — as we will see in examining Waltz's balance of power theory — is essential to the theoretical claims of Structural Realism.[15]

The most parsimonious version of a structural theory would hold that any international system has a single structure of power. In such a conceptualization, power resources are homogeneous and fungible: they can be used to achieve results on any of a variety of issues without significant loss of efficacy. Power in politics becomes like money in economics: "in many respects, power and influence play the same role in international politics as money does in a market economy" (Wolfers, 1962, p. 105).

In its strong form, the Structural Realist research program is similar to that of micro-economics. Both use the rationality assumption to permit inferences about actor behavior to be made from system structure. The Realist definition of interests in terms of power and position is like the economist's assumption that firms seek to maximize profits: it provides the utility function of the actor. Through these assumptions, actor characteristics become constant rather than variable, and systemic theory becomes possible.[16] The additional assumption of power fungibility simplifies the theory further: on the basis of a *single* characteristic of the international system (overall power capabilities), *multiple* inferences can be drawn about actor behavior and outcomes. "Foreknowledge"—that aspiration of all theory—is thereby attained (Eckstein, 1975, pp. 88-89). As we will see below, pure Structural Realism provides an insufficient basis for explaining state interests and behavior, even when the rationality assumption is accepted; and the fungibility assumption is highly questionable. Yet the Structural Realist research program is an impressive intellectual achievement: an elegant, parsimonious, deductively rigorous instrument for scientific discovery. The anomalies that it generates are more interesting than its own predictions; but as Lakatos emphasizes, it is the exploration of anomalies that moves science forward.

Richard K. Ashley has recently argued that Structural Realism—which he calls "technical realism"—actually represents a regression from the classical Realism of Herz or Morgenthau.[17] In his view, contemporary Realist thinkers have forgotten the importance of subjective self-reflection, and the dialectic between subjectivity and objectivity, which are so important in the writings of "practical," or "classical" realists such as Thucydides and Morgenthau. Classical Realism for Ashley is interpretive: "a practical tradition of statesmen is the real subject whose language of experience the interpreter tries to make his own" (1981, p. 221). It is self-reflective and non-deterministic. It treats the concept of balance of power as a dialectical relation: not merely as an objective characterization of the international system but also as a collectively recognized orienting scheme for strategic action. Classical Realism encompasses the unity of opposites, and draws interpretive insight from recognizing the dialectical quality of human experience. Thus its proponents understand that the state system is problematic, and that "strategic artistry" is required to keep it in existence (Ashley, 1982, p. 22).

The problem with Classical Realism is that it is difficult to distinguish what Ashley praises as dialectical insight from a refusal to define concepts clearly and consistently, or to develop a systematic set of propositions that could be subjected to empirical tests. Structural Realism seeks to correct these flaws, and thus to construct a more rigorous theoretical framework for the study of world politics, while drawing on the concepts and insights of the older Realism. Structural Realism, as embodied particularly in the work of Waltz, is more systematic and logically more coherent than that of its

Classical Realist precedessors. By its own standards, Structural Realism is, in Ashley's words, "a progressive scientific redemption of classical realism" (Ashley, 1982, p. 25). That is, it sees itself, and Classical Realism, as elements of a continuous research tradition.

Ashley complains that this form of Realism objectifies reality, and that in particular it regards the state as unproblematic. This leads, in his view, to some pernicious implications: that the interests expressed by dominant elites must be viewed as legitimate, that economic rationality is the highest form of thought, and that individuals are not responsible for the production of in-security (1982, pp. 34-41). But Structural Realists need not make any of these claims. It is true that Structural Realism seeks to understand the limits of, and constraints on, human action in world politics. It emphasizes the strength of these constraints, and in that sense could be considered "conservative." But an analysis of constraints, far from implying an acceptance of the *status quo,* should be seen as a precondition to sensible attempts to change the world. To be self-reflective, human action must take place with an understanding of the context within which it occurs. Structural Realists can be criticized, as we will see, for paying insufficient attention to norms, institutions, and change. But this represents less a fault of Structural Realism as such than a failure of some of its advocates to transcend its categories. Structural Realism's focus on systemic constraints does not contradict classical Realism's concern with action and choice. On the contrary, Classical Realism's emphasis on *praxis* helps us to understand the origins of Structural Realism's search for sys-tematic understanding, and — far from negating the importance of this search — makes it seem all the more important.

I have argued thus far that Structural Realism is at the center of contem-porary international relations theory in the United States; that it constitutes an attempt to systematize Classical Realism; and that its degree of success as a theory can be legitimately evaluated in part according to standards such as those laid down by Lakatos, and in part through evaluation of its capacity to generate insightful interpretations of international political behavior. Two distinct tests, each reflecting one aspect of this dualistic evaluative standard, can be devised to evaluate Structural Realism as a research program for inter-national relations:

(1) How "fruitful" is the Realist paradigm for puzzle-solving and inter-pretation of world politics (Toulmin, 1963)? That is, does current work in the Realist tradition make us see issues more clearly, or provide answers to formerly unsolved puzzles? Realism was designed to provide insights into such issues, and if it remains a live tradition, should continue to do so.

(2) Does Realism meet the standards of a scientific research program as enunciated by Lakatos? To answer this question, it is important to remind ourselves that the hard core of a research program is irrefutable within the terms of the paradigm. When anomalies arise that appear to challenge Realist assumptions, the task of Realist analysts is to create auxiliary theories that defend them. These theories permit explanation of anomalies consistent with Realist assumptions. For Lakatos, the key question about a research pro-gram concerns whether the auxiliary hypotheses of Realism are "progressive." That is, do they generate new insights, or predict new facts? If not, they are

merely exercises in "patching up" gaps or errors on an ad hoc basis, and the research program is degenerative.

Realism cannot be judged fairly on the basis of only one set of standards. Section II addresses the question of fruitfulness by examining works in the central area of Realist theory: the study of conflict, bargaining, and war. Section II then judges Realism by the more difficult test of Lakatos, which (as noted above) is better at asking trenchant questions than at defining a set of standards appropriate to social science. We will see that in one sense, Realism survives these tests, since it still appears as a good starting point for analysis. But it does not emerge either as a comprehensive theory or as a progressive research program in the sense employed by Lakatos. Furthermore, it has difficulty interpreting issues, and linkages among issues, outside of the security sphere: it can even be misleading when applied to these issues without sufficient qualification. It also has little to say about the crucially important question of peaceful change. The achievements of Realism, and the prospect that it can be modified further to make it even more useful, should help students of world politics to avoid unnecessary self-deprecation. Yet they certainly do not justify complacency.

II. PROGRESS WITHIN THE REALIST PARADIGM: THREE ACHIEVEMENTS

The fruitfulness of contemporary Realist analysis is best evaluated by considering some of the finest work in the genre. Poor scholarship can derive from even the best research program; only the most insightful work reveals the strengths as well as the limits of a theoretical approach. In this section I will consider three outstanding examples of works that begin, at least, from Realist concerns and assumptions: Waltz's construction of balance of power theory in *Theory of International Politics* (1979); the attempt by Glenn Snyder and Paul Diesing in *Conflict Among Nations* (1977) to apply formal game-theoretic models of bargaining to sixteen case studies of major-power crises during the seventy-five years between Fashoda and the Yom Kippur "alert crisis" of 1973; and Robert Gilpin's fine recent book, *War and Change in World Politics* (1981). These works are chosen to provide us with one systematic attempt to develop structural Realist theory, one study of bargaining in specific cases, and one effort to understand broad patterns of international political change. Other recent works could have been chosen instead, such as three books on international conflict and crisis published in 1980 or 1981 (Brecher, 1980; Bueno de Mesquita, 1981; Lebow, 1981), or the well-known works by Nazli Choucri and Robert C. North (1975) or by Alexander George and Richard Smoke (1974). But there are limits on what can be done in a single chapter of limited size.

Balance of Power Theory: Waltz

Waltz has explicated balance of power theory as a central element in his Structural Realist synthesis: "If there is any distinctively political theory of international politics, balance of power theory is it" (1979, p. 117). The realization that balances of power periodically form in world politics, is an old one, as are attempts to theorize about it. The puzzle that Waltz addresses is how to "cut through such confusion" as has existed about it: that is, in Kuhn's words, how to "achieve the anticipated in a new way" (1962, p. 36).

Waltz attacks this problem by using the concept of structure, which he has carefully developed earlier in the book, and which he also employs to account for the dreary persistence of patterns of international action (1979, pp. 66-72). Balance of power theory applies to "anarchic" realms, which are formally unorganized and in which, therefore, units have to worry about their survival: "Self-help is necessarily the principle of action in an anarchic order" (p. 111). In Waltz's system, states (which are similar to one another in function) are the relevant actors; they use external as well as internal means to achieve their goals. Relative capabilities are (as we saw above) the variable element of structure; as they change, we expect coalitional patterns or patterns of internal effort to be altered as well. From his assumptions, given the condition for the theory's operation (self-help), Waltz deduces "the expected outcome: namely, the formation of balances of power" (p. 118). His solution to the puzzle that he has set for himself is carefully formulated and ingenious.

Nevertheless, Waltz's theory of the balance of power encounters some difficulties. First, it is difficult for him to state precisely the conditions under which coalitions will change. He only forecasts that balances of power will periodically recur. Indeed, his theory is so general that it hardly meets the difficult tests that he himself establishes for theory. In Chapter 1 we are told that to test a theory, one must "devise a number of distinct and demanding tests" (1979, p. 13). But such tests are not proposed for balance of power theory: "Because only a loosely defined and inconstant condition of balance is predicted, it is difficult to say that any given distribution of power falsifies the theory" (p. 124). Thus rather than applying demanding tests, Waltz advises that we "should seek *confirmation* through observation of difficult cases" (p. 125, emphasis added). In other words, he counsels that we should search through history to find examples that conform to the predictions of the theory; he then proclaims that "these examples tend to confirm the theory" (p. 125). Two pages later, Waltz appears to change his view, admitting that "we can almost always find confirming cases if we look hard." We should correct for this by looking "for instances of states conforming to common international practices even though for internal reasons they would prefer not to" (p. 127). But Waltz is again making an error against which he warns us. He is not examining a universe of cases, in all of which states would prefer not to conform to "international practice," and asking how often they nevertheless do conform. Instead, he is looking only at the latter cases, chosen *because* they are consistent with his theory. Building grand theory that meets Popperian standards of scientific practice is inherently difficult; even the best scholars, such as Waltz, have trouble simultaneously saying what they want to say and abiding by their canons of scientific practice.

Waltz's theory is also ambiguous with respect to the status of three assumptions that are necessary to a strong form of Structural Realism. I have already mentioned the difficult problem of whether a structural theory must (implausibly) assume fungibility of power resources. Since this problem is less serious with respect to balance of power theory than in a broader context, I will not pursue it here, but will return to it in Section III. Yet Waltz is also, in his discussion of balances of power, unclear on the questions of rationality and interests.

Waltz argues that his assumptions do not include the rationality postulate: "The theory says simply that if some do relatively well, others will emulate them or fall by the wayside" (p. 118). This evolutionary principle, however, can hold only for systems with many actors, experiencing such severe pressure on resources that many will disappear over time. Waltz undermines this argument by pointing out later (p. 137) that "the death rate for states is remarkably low." Furthermore, he relies explicitly on the rationality principle to show that bipolar balances must be stable. "Internal balancing," he says, "is more reliable and precise than external balancing. States are less likely to misjudge their relative strengths than they are to misjudge the strength and reliability of opposing coalitions" (p. 168). I conclude that Waltz does rely on the rationality argument, despite his earlier statement to the contrary.

The other ambiguity in Waltz's balance of power theory has to do with the interests, or motivations, of states. Waltz recognizes that any theory of state behavior must ascribe (by assumption) some motivations to states, just as microeconomic theory ascribes motivations to firms. It is not reductionist to do so as long as these motivations are not taken as varying from state to state as a result of their internal characteristics. Waltz specifies such motivations: states "at a minimum, seek their own preservation, and at a maximum, drive for universal domination" (p. 118).

For his balance of power theory to work, Waltz needs to assume that states seek self-preservation, since if at least some major states did not do so, there would be no reason to expect that roughly equivalent coalitions (i.e., "balances of power") would regularly form. The desire for self-preservation makes states that are behind in a struggle for power try harder, according to Waltz, and leads states allied to a potential hegemon to switch coalitions in order to construct balances of power. Neither of these processes on which Waltz relies to maintain a balance — intensified effort by the weaker country in a bipolar system and coalition formation against potentially dominant states in a multipolar system — could operate reliably without this motivation.

The other aspect of Waltz's motivational assumption — that states "at a maximum, drive for universal domination," is reminiscent of the implication of Realists such as Morgenthau that states seek to "maximize power." For a third-image Realist theory such as Waltz's, such an assumption is unnecessary. Waltz's defense of it is that the balance of power depends on the possibility that force may be used. But this possibility is an attribute of the self-help international system, for Waltz, rather than a reflection of the actors' characteristics. That some states seek universal domination is not a necessary condition for force to be used.

This ambiguity in Waltz's analysis points toward a broader ambiguity in Realist thinking: *Balance of power theory is inconsistent with the assumption frequently made by Realists that states "maximize power,"* if power is taken to refer to tangible resources that can be used to induce other actors to do what they would not otherwise do, through the threat or infliction of deprivations.[18] States concerned with self-preservation do not seek to maximize their power when they are not in danger. On the contrary, they recognize a trade-off between aggrandizement and self-preservation; they realize that a relentless search for universal domination may jeopardize their own autonomy. Thus they moderate their efforts when their positions are secure. Conversely, they intensify their efforts when danger arises, which assumes that they were not maximizing them under more benign conditions.

One might have thought that Realists would readily recognize this point, yet they seem drawn against their better judgment to the "power maximization" or "universal domination" hypotheses. In part, this may be due to their anxiety to emphasize the significance of force in world politics. Yet there may be theoretical as well as rhetorical reasons for their ambivalence. The assumption of power maximization makes posssible strong inferences about behavior that would be impossible if we assumed only that states "sometimes" or "often" sought to aggrandize themselves. In that case, we would have to ask about competing goals, some of which would be generated by the internal social, political, and economic characteristics of the countries concerned. Taking into account these competing goals relegates Structural Realism to the status of partial, incomplete theory.

Waltz's contribution to the study of world politics is conceptual. He helps us think more clearly about the role of systemic theory, the explanatory power of structural models, and how to account deductively for the recurrent formation of balances of power. He shows that the international system shapes state behavior as well as vice versa. These are major contributions. But Waltz does not point out "new ways of seeing" international relations that point toward major novelties. He reformulates and systematizes Realism, and thus develops what I have called Structural Realism, consistently with the fundamental assumptions of his classical predecessors.

Game Theory, Structure and Bargaining: Snyder and Diesing

Game theory has yielded some insights into issues of negotiations, crises, and limited war, most notably in the early work of Thomas Schelling (1960). Snyder and Diesing's contribution to this line of analysis, as they put it, is to "distinguish and analyze nine different kinds of bargaining situations, each one a unique combination of power and interest relations between the bargainers, each therefore having its own dynamics and problems" (1977, pp. 181-182). They employ their game-theoretic formulations of these nine situations, within an explicit structural context, to analyze sixteen historical cases.

This research design is consistent with the hard core of Realism. Attention is concentrated on the behavior of states. In the initial statement of the problem, the rationality assumption, in suitably modest form, is retained: each actor attempts "to maximize expected value across a given set of consistently ordered objectives, given the information actually available to the actor or which he could reasonably acquire in the time available for decision"

(p. 181). Interests are defined to a considerable extent in terms of power: that is, power factors are built into the game structure. In the game of "Protector," for instance, the more powerful state can afford to "go it alone" without its ally, and thus has an interest in doing so under certain conditions, whereas its weaker partner cannot (pp. 145-147). Faced with the game matrix, states, as rational actors, calculate their interests and act accordingly. The structure of world politics, as Waltz defines it, is reflected in the matrices and becomes the basis for action.

If structural Realism formed a sufficient basis for the understanding of international crises, we could fill in the entries in the matrices solely on the basis of states' positions in the international system, given our knowledge of the fact that they perform "similar functions," including the need to survive as autonomous entities. Interests would indeed be defined in terms of power. This would make game theory a powerful analytic tool, which could even help us predict certain outcomes. Where the game had no unique solution (because of strategic indeterminacy), complete predictability of outcomes could not be achieved, but our expectations about the range of likely action would have been narrowed.

Yet Snyder and Diesing find that even knowledge of the values and goals of top leaders could not permit them to determine the interests of about half the decision-making units in their cases. In the other cases, one needed to understand intragovernmental politics, even when one ignored the impact of wider domestic political factors (pp. 510-511). The "internal-external interaction" is a key to the understanding of crisis bargaining.

As Snyder and Diesing make their analytical framework more complex and move into detailed investigation of their cases, their focus shifts toward concern with cognition and with the effects on policy of ignorance, misperception, and misinformation. In my view, the most creative and insightful of their chapters use ideas developed largely by Robert Jervis (1976) to analyze information processing and decision-making. These chapters shift the focus of attention away from the systemic-level factors reflected in the game-theoretic matrices, toward problems of perception, personal bias, and group decision-making (Snyder & Diesing, 1977, Chapters IV and V).

Thus Snyder and Diesing begin with the hard core of Realism, but their most important contributions depend on their willingness to depart from these assumptions. They are dissatisfied with their initial game-theoretic classificatory scheme. They prefer to explore information processing and decision-making, without a firm deductive theory on which to base their arguments, rather than merely to elucidate neat logical typologies.

Is the work of Snyder and Diesing a triumph of Realism or a defeat? At this point in the argument, perhaps the most that can be said is that it indicates that work in the Realist tradition, analyzing conflict and bargaining with the concepts of interests and power, continues to be fruitful, but it does not give reason for much confidence that adhering strictly to Realist assumptions will lead to important advances in the field.

Cycles of Hegemony and War: Gilpin

In *War and Change in World Politics,* Gilpin uses Realist assumptions to reinterpret the last 2400 years of Western history. Gilpin assumes that states, as the principal actors in world politics, make cost-benefit calculations about alternative courses of action. For instance, states attempt to change the international system as the expected benefits of so doing exceed the costs. Thus, the rationality assumption is applied explicitly, in a strong form, although it is relaxed toward the end of the book (1981, pp. 77, 202). Furthermore, considerations of power, relative to the structure of the international system, are at the core of the calculations made by Gilpin's states: "the distribution of power among states constitutes the principal form of control in every international system" (p. 29). Thus Gilpin accepts the entire hard core of the classical Realist research program as I have defined it.[19]

Gilpin sees world history as an unending series of cycles: "The conclusion of one hegemonic war is the beginning of another cycle of growth, expansion, and eventual decline" (p. 210). As power is redistributed, power relations become inconsistent with the rules governing the system and, in particular, the hierarchy of prestige; war establishes the new hierarchy of prestige and "thereby determines which states will in effect govern the international system" (p. 33).

The view that the rules of a system, and the hierarchy of prestige, must be consistent with underlying power realities is a fundamental proposition of Realism, which follows from its three core assumptions. If states, as the central actors of international relations, calculate their interests in terms of power, they will seek international rules and institutions that are consistent with these interests by maintaining their power. Waltz's conception of structure helps to systematize this argument, but it is essentially static. What Gilpin adds is a proposed solution to the anomalies (for static Realism) that institutions and rules can become inconsistent with power realities over time, and that hegemonic states eventually decline. If, as Realists argue, "the strong do what they can and the weak suffer what they must" (Thucydides, Book V, paragraph 90 [Chapter XVII, Modern Library edition, p. 331]), why should hegemons ever lose their power? We know that rules do not always reinforce the power of the strong and that hegemons do sometimes lose their hold, but static Realist theory cannot explain this.

In his attempt to explain hegemonic decline, Gilpin formulates a "law of uneven growth":

> According to Realism, the fundamental cause of wars among states and changes in international systems is the uneven growth of power among states. Realist writers from Thucydides and MacKinder to present-day scholars have attributed the dynamics of international relations to the fact that the distribution of power in an international system shifts over a period of time; this shift results in profound changes in the relationships among states and eventually changes in the nature of the international system itself. (p. 94)

This law, however, restates the problem without resolving it. In accounting for this pattern, Gilpin relies on three sets of processes. One has to do with increasing, and then diminishing, marginal returns from empire. As empires grew, "the economic surplus had to increase faster than the cost of war" (p. 115). Yet sooner or later, diminishing returns set in: "the law of diminishing returns has universal applicability and causes the growth of every society to describe an S-shaped curve" (p. 159). Secondly, hegemonic states tend increasingly to consume more and invest less; Gilpin follows the lead of Carlo Cipolla in viewing this as a general pattern in history (Cipolla, 1970). Finally, hegemonic states decline because of a process of diffusion of technology to others. In *U.S. Power and the Multinational Corporation* (1975), Gilpin emphasized this process as contributing first to the decline of Britain, then in the 1970s to that of the United States. In *War and Change* he makes the argument more general:

> Through a process of diffusion to other states, the dominant power loses the advantage on which its political, military, or economic success has been based. Thus, by example, and frequently in more direct fashion, the dominant power helps to create challenging powers. (p. 176)

This third argument is systemic, and, therefore, fully consistent with Waltz's Structural Realism. The other two processes, however, reflect the operation of forces within the society, as well as international forces. A hegemonic power may suffer diminishing returns as a result of the expansion of its defense perimeter and the increased military costs that result (Gilpin, 1981, p. 191; Luttwak, 1976). But whether diminishing returns set in also depends on internal factors such as technological inventiveness of members of the society and the institutions that affect incentives for innovation (North, 1981). The tendency of hegemonic states to consume more and invest less is also, in part, a function of their dominant positions in the world system: they can force costs of adjustment to change onto others, at least for some time. But it would be hard to deny that the character of the society affects popular tastes for luxury, and, therefore, the tradeoffs between guns and butter that are made. Eighteenth Century Saxony and Prussia were different in this regard; so are contemporary America and Japan. In Gilpin's argument as in Snyder and Diesing's, the "external-internal interaction" becomes a crucial factor in explaining state action, and change.

Gilpin explicitly acknowledges his debt to Classical Realism: "In honesty, one must inquire whether or not twentieth-century students of international relations know anything that Thucydides and his fifth-century compatriots did not know about the behavior of states" (p. 227). For Gilpin as for Thucydides, changes in power lead to changes in relations among states: the *real* cause of the Peloponnesian War, for Thucydides, was the rise of the power of Athens and the fear this evoked in the Spartans and their allies. Gilpin has generalized the theory put forward by Thucydides to explain the Peloponnesian War, and has applied it to the whole course of world history:

> Disequilibrium replaces equilibrium, and the world moves toward a new round of hegemonic conflict. It has always been thus and always will be, until men either destroy themselves or learn to develop an effective mechanism of peaceful change. (p. 210)

This Thucydides-Gilpin theory is a systemic theory of change only in a limited sense. It explains the *reaction* to change systematically, in a rationalistic, equilibrium model. Yet at a more fundamental level, it does not account fully for the sources of change. As we saw above, although it is insightful about systemic factors leading to hegemonic decline, it also has to rely on internal processes to explain the observed effects. Furthermore, it does not account well for the rise of hegemons in the first place, or for the fact that certain contenders emerge rather than others.[20] Gilpin's systemic theory does not account for the extraordinary bursts of energy that occasionally catapult particular countries into dominant positions on the world scene. Why were the Athenians, in words that Thucydides attributes to Corinthian envoys to Sparta, "addicted to innovation," whereas the Spartans were allegedly characterized by a "total want of invention" (Thucydides, Book I, paragraph 70 [Chapter III, Modern Library edition, p. 40])? Like other structural theories, Gilpin's theory underpredicts outcomes. It contributes to our understanding but (as its author recognizes) does not explain change.

This is particularly true of peaceful change, which Gilpin identifies as a crucial issue: "The fundamental problem of international relations in the contemporary world is the problem of peaceful adjustment to the consequences of the uneven growth of power among states, just as it was in the past" (p. 230).

Gilpin's book, like much contemporary American work on international politics, is informed and propelled by concern with peaceful change under conditions of declining hegemony. Gilpin sympathetically discusses E. H. Carr's "defense of peaceful change as the solution to the problem of hegemonic war," written just before World War II (Gilpin, p. 206; Carr, 1939/1946). Yet peaceful change does not fit easily into Gilpin's analytical framework, since it falls, by and large, into the category of "interactions change," which does not entail alteration in the overall hierarchy of power and prestige in a system, and Gilpin deliberately avoids focusing on interactions change (p. 44). Yet after one puts down *War and Change*, the question of how institutions and rules can be developed *within* a given international system, to reduce the probability of war and promote peaceful change, looms even larger than it did before.

Thus Gilpin's sophisticated adaptation of Classical Realism turns us away from Realism. Classical Realism, with its philosophical roots in a tragic conception of the human condition, directs our attention in the twentieth century to the existential situation of modern humanity, doomed apparently to recurrent conflict in a world with weapons that could destroy life on our planet. But Realism, whether classical or structural, has little to say about how to deal with that situation, since it offers few insights into the international rules and institutions that people invent to reduce risk and uncertainty in world affiars, in the hope of ameliorating the security dilemma.[21] Morgenthau put his hopes in diplomacy (1966, chapter 32). This is a practical art, far removed from the abstractions of structural Realism. But diplomacy takes place within a context of international rules, institutions, and practices, which affect the incentives of the actors (Keohane, 1982). Gilpin realizes this, and his gloomy argument—hardly alleviated by a more optimistic epilogue—helps us to understand their importance, although it does not contribute to an explanation of their creation or demise.

Conclusions

Realism, as developed through a long tradition dating from Thucydides, continues to provide the basis for valuable research in international relations. This point has been made by looking at writers who explicitly draw on the Realist tradition, and it can be reinforced by briefly examining some works of Marxist scholars. If they incorporate elements of Realism despite their general antipathy to its viewpoint, our conclusion that Realism reflects enduring realities of world politics will be reinforced.

For Marxists, the fundamental forces affecting world politics are those of class struggle and uneven development. International history is dynamic and dialectical rather than cyclical. The maneuvers of states, on which Realism focuses, reflect the stages of capitalist development and the contradictions of that development. Nevertheless, in analyzing the surface manifestations of world politics under capitalism, Marxists adopt similar categories to those of Realists. Power is crucial; world systems are periodically dominated by hegemonic powers wielding both economic and military resources.

Lenin defined imperialism differently than do the Realists, but he analyzed its operation in part as a Realist would, arguing that "there can be *no* other conceivable basis under capitalism for the division of spheres of influence, of interests, of colonies, etc. than a calculation of the *strength* of the participants in the division. . ." (Lenin, 1916/1939, p. 119).

Immanuel Wallerstein provides another example of my point. He goes to some effort to stress that modern world history should be seen as the history of capitalism as a world system. Apart from "relatively minor accidents" provided by geography, peculiarities of history, or luck—which give one country an edge over others at crucial historical junctures—"it is the operations of the world-market forces which accentuate the differences, institutionalize them, and make them impossible to surmount over the long run" (1979, p. 21). Nevertheless, when his attention turns to particular epochs, Wallerstein emphasizes hegemony and the role of military force. Dutch economic hegemony in the seventeenth century was destroyed in quintessential Realist fashion, not by the operation of the world-market system, but by the force of British and French arms (Wallerstein, 1980, pp. 38-39).

The insights of Realism are enduring. They cross ideological lines. Its best contemporary exponents use Realism in insightful ways. Waltz has systematized the basic assumptions of Classical Realism in what I have called Structural Realism. Snyder and Diesing have employed this framework for the analysis of bargaining; Gilpin has used the classical arguments of Thucydides to explore problems of international change. For all of these writers, Realism fruitfully focuses attention on fundamental issues of power, interests, and rationality. But as we have seen, many of the most interesting questions raised by these authors cannot be answered within the Realist framework.

III. EXPLANATIONS OF OUTCOMES FROM POWER: HYPOTHESES AND ANOMALIES

A Structural Realist theory of interests could be used both for explanation and for prescription. If we could deduce a state's interests from its position in the system, via the rationality assumption, its behavior could be explained on the basis of systemic analysis. Efforts to define the national interest on an a priori basis, however, or to use the concept for prediction and explanation, have been unsuccessful. We saw above that the inability to define interests independently of observed state behavior robbed Snyder and Diesing's game-theoretical matrices of predictive power. More generally, efforts to show that external considerations of power and position play a dominant role in determining the "national interest" have failed. Even an analyst as sympathetic to Realism as Stephen D. Krasner has concluded, in studying American foreign economic policy, that the United States was "capable of defining its own autonomous goals" in a non-logical manner (1978, p. 333). That is, the systemic constraints emphasized by Structural Realism were not binding on the American government during the first thirty years after the Second World War.

Sophisticated contemporary thinkers in the Realist tradition, such as Gilpin, Krasner, and Waltz, understand that interests cannot be derived, simply on the basis of rational calculation, from the external positions of states, and that this is particularly true for great powers, on which, ironically, Structural Realism focuses its principal attentions (Gilpin, 1975; Waltz, 1967). Realist analysis has to retreat to a "fall-back position": that, *given state interests,* whose origins are not predicted by the theory, patterns of outcomes in world politics will be determined by the overall distribution of power among states. This represents a major concession for systemically-oriented analysts, which it is important not to forget. Sensible Realists are highly cognizant of the role of domestic politics and of actor choices within the constraints and incentives provided by the system. Since systemic theory cannot predict state interests, it cannot support deterministic conclusions (Sprout & Sprout, 1971, pp. 73-77). This limitation makes it both less powerful as a theory, and less dangerous as an ideology.[22] Despite its importance, it cannot stand alone.

When realist theorists say that, given interests, patterns of outcomes will be determined by the overall distribution of power among states, they are using "power" to refer to resources that can be used to induce other actors to do what they would not otherwise do, in accordance with the desires of the power-wielder. "Outcomes" refer principally to two sets of patterns: (1) the results of conflicts, diplomatic or military, that take place between states; and (2) changes in the rules and institutions that regulate relations among governments in world politics. This section focuses on conflicts, since they pose the central puzzles that Realism seeks to explain. Section IV and the Conclusion consider explanations of changes in rules and institutions.

Recent quantitative work seems to confirm that power capabilities (measured not only in terms of economic resources but with political variables added) are rather good predictors of the outcomes of wars. Bueno de Mesquita finds, for example, that countries with what he calls positive "expected utility" (a measure that uses composite capabilities but adjusts them for distance, alliance relationships, and uncertainty) won 179 conflicts while losing only 54 between 1816 and 1974, for a success ratio of over 75% (1981, especially p. 151; Organski & Kugler, 1980, Chapter 2).

The question of the fungibility of power poses a more troublesome issue. As I have noted earlier (see footnote 19), Structural Realism is ambiguous on this point; the desire for parsimonious theory impels Realists toward a unitary notion of power as homogeneous and usable for a variety of purposes, but close examination of the complexities of world politics induces caution about such an approach. In his discussion of system structure, for instance, Waltz holds that "the units of an anarchic system are distinguished primarily by their greater or lesser capabilities for performing similar tasks," and that the distribution of capabilities across a system is the principal characteristic differentiating international-political structures from one another (1979, pp. 97, 99). Thus each international political system has one structure. Yet in emphasizing the continued role of military power, Waltz admits that military power is not perfectly fungible: "Differences in strength do matter, *although not for every conceivable purpose*"; "military power no longer brings political control, but then it never did" (1979, pp. 189, 191, emphasis added). This seems to imply that any given international system is likely to have *several* structures, differing by issue-areas and according to the resources that can be used to affect outcomes. Different sets of capabilities will qualify as "power resources" under different conditions. This leads to a much less parsimonious theory and a much more highly differentiated view of the world, in which what Nye and I called "issue-structure" theories play a major role, and in which military force, although still important, is no longer assumed to be at the top of a hierarchy of power resources (Keohane & Nye, 1977, chs. 3 and 6).

The status in a Structural Realist theory of the fungibility assumption affects both its power and the incidence of anomalies. A strong version of Structural Realism that assumed full fungibility of power across issues would predict that when issues arise between great powers and smaller states, the great powers should prevail. This has the advantage of generating a clear prediction and the liability of being wrong much of the time. Certainly it does not fit the American experience of the last two decades. The United States lost a war in Vietnam and was for more than a year unable to secure the return of its diplomats held hostage in Iran. Small allies such as Israel, heavily dependent on the United States, have displayed considerable freedom of action. In the U.S.-Canadian relationship of the 1950s and 1960s, which was virtually free of threats of force, outcomes of conflicts as often favored the Canadian as the American position, although this was not true for relations between Australia and the United States (Keohane & Nye, 1977, Chapter 7).

In view of power theory in social science, the existence of these anomalies is not surprising. As James G. March observes, "there appears to be general consensus that either potential power is different from actually exerted power or that actually exerted power is variable" (1966, p. 57). That is, what March calls "basic force models," which rely, like Realist theory, on measurable indices of power, are inadequate tools for either prediction or explanation.

They are often valuable in suggesting long-term trends and patterns, but they do not account well for specific outcomes: the more that is demanded of them, the less well they are likely to perform.

Lakatos's discussion of scientific research programs leads us to expect that, when confronted with anomalies, theorists will create auxiliary theories that preserve the credibility of their fundamental assumptions. Thus it is not surprising that Realists committed to the fungibility assumption have devised auxiliary hypotheses to protect its "hard core" against challenge. One of these is what David Baldwin calls the "conversion-process explanation" of un-anticipated outcomes:

> The would-be wielder of power is described as lacking in skill and/or the 'will' to use his power resources effectively: 'The Arabs had the tanks but didn't know how to use them.' 'The Americans had the bombs but lacked the will to use them.' (1979, pp. 163-164)

The conversion-process explanation is a classic auxiliary hypothesis, since it is designed to protect the assumption that power resources are homogeneous and fungible. If we were to accept the conversion-process account, we could continue to believe in a single structure of power, even if outcomes do not favor the "stronger" party. This line of argument encounters serious problems, however, when it tries to account for the discrepancy between anticipated and actual outcomes by the impact of intangible resources (such as intelligence, training, organization, foresight) not recognized until after the fact. The problem with this argument lies in its post hoc quality. It is theoretically degenerate in Lakatos's sense, since it does not add any explanatory power to structural Realist theory, but merely "explains away" uncomfortable facts.

Thus what March says about "force activation models" applies to Structural Realist theories when the conversion-process explanation relies upon sources of power that can be observed only after the events to be explained have taken place:

> If we observe that power exists and is stable and if we observe that sometimes weak people seem to triumph over strong people, we are tempted to rely on an activation hypothesis to explain the discrepancy. But if we then try to use the activation hypothesis to predict the results of social-choice procedures, we discover that the data requirements of 'plausible' activation models are quite substantial. As a result, we retreat to what are essentially degenerate forms of the activation model—retaining some of the form but little of the substance. This puts us back where we started, looking for some device to explain our failures in prediction. (1966, p. 61)

A second auxiliary hypothesis designed to protect the fungibility assumption must be taken more seriously: that discrepancies between power resources and outcomes are explained by an asymmetry of motivation in favor of the objectively weaker party. Following this logic, John Harsanyi has proposed the notion of power "in a schedule sense," describing how various resources can be translated into social power. An actor with intense preferences on an issue may be willing to use more resources to attain a high probability of a favorable result, than an actor with more resources but lower intensity. As a result, outcomes may not accurately reflect underlying power resources (Harsanyi, 1962).

To use this insight progressively rather than in a degenerate way, Realist theory needs to develop indices of intensity of motivation that can be measured independently of the behavior that theorists are trying to explain. Russett, George, and Bueno de Mesquita are among the authors who have attempted, with some success, to do this (Russett, 1963; George *et al.*, 1971; Bueno de Mesquita, 1981). Insofar as motivation is taken simply as a control, allowing us to test the impact of varying power configurations more successfully, Harsanyi's insights can be incorporated into structural Realist theory. If it became a key variable, however, the effect could be to transform a systemic theory into a decision-making one.

An alternative approach to relying on such auxiliary hypotheses is to relax the fungibility assumption itself. Failures of great powers to control smaller ones could be explained on the basis of independent evidence that in the relevant issue-areas, the states that are weaker on an overall basis have more power resources than their stronger partners, and that the use of power derived from one area of activity to affect outcomes in other areas (through "linkages") is difficult. Thus Saudi Arabia can be expected to have more impact on world energy issues than on questions of strategic arms control; Israel more influence over the creation of a Palestinian state than on the reconstruction of the international financial and debt regime.

Emphasizing the problematic nature of power fungibility might help to create more discriminating power models, but it will not resolve the inherent problems of power models, as identified by March and others. Furthermore, at the limit, to deny fungibility entirely risks a complete disintegration of predictive power. Baldwin comes close to this when he argues that what he calls the "policy-contingency framework" of an influence attempt must be specified before power explanations are employed. If we defined each issue as existing within a unique "policy-contingency framework," no generalizations would be possible. Waltz could reply, if he accepted Baldwin's view of power, that all of world politics should be considered a single policy-contingency framework, characterized by anarchy and self-help.[23] According to this argument, the parsimony gained by assuming the fungibility of power would compensate for the marginal mispredictions of such a theory.

This is a crucial theoretical issue, which should be addressed more explicitly by theorists of world politics. In my view, the dispute cannot be resolved a priori. The degree to which power resources have to be disaggregated in a structural theory depends both on the purposes of the theory and on the degree to which behavior on distinct issues is linked together through the exercise of influence by actors. The larger the domain of a theory, the less accuracy of detail we expect. Since balance of power theory seeks to explain large-scale patterns of state action over long periods of time, we could hardly expect the precision from it that we demand from theories whose domains have been narrowed.

This assertion suggests that grand systemic theory can be very useful as a basis for further theoretical development in international relations, even if the theory is lacking in precision, and it therefore comprises part of my defense of the Realist research program as a foundation on which scholars should build. Yet this argument needs immediate qualification.

Even if a large-scale theory can be developed and appropriately tested, its predictions will be rather gross. To achieve a more finely-tuned understanding of how resources affect behavior in particular situations, one needs to specify the policy-contingency framework more precisely. The domain of theory is narrowed to achieve greater precision. Thus the debate between advocates of parsimony and proponents of contextual subtlety resolves itself into a question of *stages,* rather than an either/or choice. We should seek parsimony first, then add complexity while monitoring the adverse effects that this has on the predictive power of our theory: its ability to make significant inferences on the basis of limited information.

To introduce greater complexity into an initially spare theoretical structure, the conception of an issue-area, developed many years ago by Robert A. Dahl (1961) and adapted for use in international relations by James N. Rosenau (1966), is a useful device. Having tentatively selected an area of activity to investigate, the analyst needs to delineate issue-areas at various levels of aggregation. Initial explanations should seek to account for the main features of behavior at a high level of aggregation—such as the international system as a whole—while subsequent hypotheses are designed to apply only to certain issue-areas.

In some cases, more specific issue-areas are "nested" within larger ones (Aggarwal, 1981; Snidal, 1981). For instance, North Atlantic fisheries issues constitute a sub-set of fisheries issues in general, which comprise part of the whole area of oceans policy, or "law of the sea." In other cases, specific issues may belong to two or more broader issues: the question of passage through straits, for example, involves questions of military security as well as the law of the sea.

Definitions of issue-areas depend on the beliefs of participants, as well as on the purposes of the investigator. In general, however, definitions of issue-areas should be made on the basis of empirical judgments about the extent to which governments regard sets of issues as closely interdependent and treat them collectively. Decisions made on one issue must affect others in the issue-area, either through functional links or through regular patterns of bargaining. These relationships of interdependence among issues may change. Some issue-areas, such as international financial relations, have remained fairly closely linked for decades; others, such as oceans, have changed drastically over the past 35 years (Keohane & Nye, 1977, Chapter 4, especially pp. 64-65; Simon, 1969; Haas, 1980).

When a hierarchy of issue-areas has been identified, power-structure models employing more highly aggregated measures of power resources can be compared with models that disaggregate resources by issue-areas. How much accuracy is gained, and how much parsimony lost, by each step in the disaggregation process? In my view, a variegated analysis, which takes some specific "snapshots" by issue-area as well as looking at the broader picture, is superior to either monistic strategy, whether assuming perfect fungibility or none at all.

This approach represents an adaptation of Realism. It preserves the basic emphasis on power resources as a source of outcomes in general, but it unambiguously jettisons the assumption that power is fungible across all of world politics. Disaggregated power models are less parsimonious than more aggregated ones, and they remain open to the objections to power models articulated by March and others. But in one important sense disaggregation is progressive rather than degenerative. Disaggregated models call attention to linkages among issue-areas, and raise the question: under what conditions, and with what effects, will such linkages arise? Current research suggests that understanding linkages systematically, rather than merely describing them on an ad hoc basis, will add significantly to our comprehension of world politics (Oye, 1979, 1983; Stein, 1980; Tollison & Willett, 1979). It would seem worthwhile, in addition, for more empirical work to be done on this subject, since we know so little about when, and how, linkages are made.

Conclusions

Structural Realism is a good starting-point for explaining the outcomes of conflicts, since it directs attention to fundamental questions of interest and power within a logically coherent and parsimonious theoretical framework. Yet the ambitious attempt of Structural Realist theory to deduce national interests from system structure via the rationality postulate has been unsuccessful. Even if interests are taken as given, the attempt to predict outcomes from interests and power leads to ambiguities and incorrect predictions. The auxiliary theory attributing this failure to conversion-processes often entails unfalsifiable tautology rather than genuine explanation. Ambiguity prevails on the question of the fungibility of power: whether there is a single structure of the international system or several. Thus the research program of Realism reveals signs of degeneration. It certainly does not meet Lakatos' tough standards for progressiveness.

More attention to developing independent measures of intensity of motivation, and greater precision about the concept of power and its relationship to the context of action, may help to correct some of these faults. Careful disaggregation of power-resources by issue-area may help to improve the predictive capability of structural models, at the risk of reducing theoretical parsimony. As I argue in the next section, modified structural models, indebted to Realism although perhaps too different to be considered Realist themselves, may be valuable elements in a multi-level framework for understanding world politics.

Yet to some extent the difficulties encountered by Structural Realism reflect the inherent limitations of structural models, which will not be corrected by mere modifications or the relaxation of assumptions. Domestic politics and decision-making, Snyder and Diesing's "internal-external interactions," and the workings of international institutions all play a role, along with international political structure, in affecting state behavior and outcomes. Merely to catalog these factors, however, is not to contribute to theory but rather to compound the descriptive anarchy that already afflicts the field, with too many independent variables, exogenously determined, chasing too few cases. As Waltz emphasizes, the role of unit-level forces can only be properly understood if we comprehend the structure of the international system within which they operate.

IV. BEYOND STRUCTURAL REALISM

Structural Realism helps us to understand world politics as in part a systemic phenomenon, and provides us with a logically coherent theory that establishes the context for state action. This theory, because it is relatively simple and clear, can be modified progressively to attain closer correspondence with reality. Realism's focus on interests and power is central to an understanding of how nations deal with each other. Its adherents have understood that a systemic theory of international relations must account for state behavior by examining the constraints and incentives provided by the system; for this purpose to be accomplished, an assumption of rationality (although not of perfect information) must be made. The rationality assumption allows inferences about state behavior to be drawn solely from knowledge of the structure of the system.

Unfortunately, such predictions are often wrong. The concept of power is difficult to measure validly a priori; interests are underspecified by examining the nature of the international system and the position of various states in it; the view of power resources implied by overall structure theories is overaggregated, exaggerating the extent to which power is like money. The problem that students of international politics face is how to construct theories that draw on Realism's strengths without partaking fully of its weaknesses.

To do this we need a multi-dimensional approach to world politics that incorporates several analytical frameworks or research programs. One of these should be that of Structural Realism, which has the virtues of parsimony and clarity, although the range of phenomena that it encompasses is limited. Another, in my view, should be a modified structural research program, which relaxes some of the assumptions of Structural Realism but retains enough of the hard core to generate a priori predictions on the basis of information about the international environment. Finally, we need better theories of domestic politics, decision-making, and information processing, so that the gap between the external and internal environments can be bridged in a systematic way, rather than by simply adding catalogs of exogenously determined foreign policy facts to theoretically more rigorous structural models. That is, we need more attention to the "internal-external interactions" discussed by Snyder and Diesing.

Too much work in this last category is being done for me to review it in detail here. Mention should be made, however, of some highlights. Peter J. Katzenstein, Peter Gourevitch, and others have done pioneering work on the relationship between domestic political structure and political coalitions, on the one hand, and foreign economic policies, on the other (Katzenstein, 1978; Gourevitch, 1978). This line of analysis, which draws heavily on the work of Alexander Gerschenkron (1962) and Barrington Moore (1966), argues that the different domestic structures characteristic of various advanced in-

dustrialized countries result from different historical patterns of development; in particular, whether development came early or late, and what the
position of the country was in the international political system at the time of
its economic development (Kurth, 1979). Thus it attempts to draw connections both between international and domestic levels of analysis, and across
historical time. This research does not provide deductive explanatory models,
and it does not account systematically for changes in established structures
after the formative developmental period, but its concept of domestic structure brings order into the cacophony of domestic political and economic
variables that could affect foreign policy, and therefore suggests the possibility of eventual integration of theories relying on international structure
with those focusing on domestic structure.

Katzenstein and his associates focus on broad political, economic, and
social patterns within countries, and their relationship to the international
division of labor and the world political structure. Fruitful analysis can also
be done at the more narrowly intragovernmental level, as Snyder and Diesing
show. An emphasis on bureaucratic politics was particularly evident in the
1960s and early 1970s, although Robert J. Art has pointed out in detail a
number of difficulties, weaknesses, and contradictions in this literature
(1973). At the level of the individual decision-maker, insights can be gained
by combining theories of cognitive psychology with a rich knowledge of diplomatic history, as in Jervis's work, as long as the investigator understands the
systemic and domestic-structural context within which decision-makers
operate.[24] This research program has made decided progress, from the
simple-minded notions criticized by Waltz (1959) to the work of Alexander
and Juliette George (1964), Alexander George (1980), Ole Holsti (1976) and
Jervis (1976).[25]

Despite the importance of this work at the levels of domestic structure,
intragovernmental politics, and individual cognition, the rest of my analysis
will continue to focus on the concept of international political structure and
its relevance to the study of world politics. I will argue that progress could be
made by constructing a modified structural research program, retaining some
of the parsimony characteristic of Structural Realism and its emphasis on the
incentives and constraints of the world system, while adapting it to fit contemporary reality better. Like Realism, this research program would be based on
microeconomic theory, particularly oligopoly theory. It would seek to explain
actor behavior by specifying a priori utility functions for actors, using the rationality principle as a "trivial animating law" in Popper's sense (Latsis, 1976,
p. 21), and deducing behavior from the constraints of the system as modeled
in the theory.

Developing such a theory would only be worthwhile if there were something particularly satisfactory both about systemic explanations and about
the structural forms of such explanations. I believe that this is the case, for
two sets of reasons.

First, systemic theory is important because we must understand the context of action before we can understand the action itself. As Waltz (1979) has
emphasized, theories of world politics that fail to incorporate a sophisticated
understanding of the operation of the system—that is, how systemic attributes

affect behavior—are bad theories. Theoretical analysis of the characteristics of an international system is as important for understanding foreign policy as understanding European history is for understanding the history of Germany.

Second, structural theory is important because it provides an irreplaceable *component* for a thorough analysis of action, by states or non-state actors, in world politics. A good structural theory generates testable implications about behavior on an a priori basis, and, therefore, comes closer than interpretive description to meeting the requirements for scientific knowledge of neo-positivist philosophers of science such as Lakatos. This does not mean, of course, that explanation and rich interpretation—Geertz's "thick description" (1973)—are in any way antithetical to one another. A good analysis of a given problem will include both.[26]

The assumptions of a modified structural research program can be compared to Realist assumptions as follows:

(1) The assumption that the principal actors in world politics are states would remain the same, although more emphasis would be placed on non-state actors, intergovernmental organizations, and transnational and transgovernmental relations than is the case in Realist analysis (Keohane & Nye, 1972).

(2) The rationality assumption would be retained, since without it, as we have seen, inferences from structure to behavior become impossible without heroic assumptions about evolutionary processes or other forces that compel actors to adapt their behavior to their environments. It should be kept in mind, however, as is made clear by sophisticated Realists, that the rationality postulate only assumes that actors make calculations "so as to maximize expected value across a given set of consistently ordered objectives" (Snyder & Diesing, 1977, p. 81). It does not assume perfect information, consideration of all possible alternatives, or unchanging actor preferences.

(3) The assumption that states seek power and calculate their interests accordingly, would be qualified severely. Power and influence would still be regarded as important state interests (as ends or necessary means), but the implication that the search for power constitutes an overriding interest in all cases, or that it always takes the same form, would be rejected. Under different systemic conditions states will define their self-interests differently. For instance, where survival is at stake efforts to maintain autonomy may take precedence over all other activities, but where the environment is relatively benign energies will also be directed to fulfilling other goals. Indeed, over the long run, whether an environment is malign or benign can alter the standard operating procedures and sense of identity of the actors themselves.[27]

In addition, this modified structural approach would explicitly modify the assumption of fungibility lurking behind unitary conceptions of "international structure." It would be assumed that the value of power resources for influencing behavior in world politics depends on the goals sought. Power resources that are well-suited to achieve certain purposes are less effective when used for other objectives. Thus power resources are differentially effective across issue-areas, and the usability of a given set of power resources depends on the "policy-contingency frameworks" within which it must be employed.

This research program would pay much more attention to the roles of institutions and rules than does Structural Realism. Indeed, a structural interpretation of the emergence of international rules and procedures, and of obedience to them by states, is one of the rewards that could be expected from this modified structural research program (Krasner, 1982; Keohane, 1982; Stein, 1982).

This research program would contain a valuable positive heuristic—a set of suggestions about what research should be done and what questions should initially be asked—which would include the following pieces of advice:

(1) When trying to explain a set of outcomes in world politics, always consider the hypothesis that the outcomes reflect underlying power resources, without being limited to it;

(2) When considering different patterns of outcomes in different relationships, or issue-areas, entertain the hypothesis that power resources are differently distributed in these issue-areas, and investigate ways in which these differences promote or constrain actor attempts to link issue-areas in order to use power-resources from one area to affect results in another;

(3) When considering how states define their self-interests, explore the effects of international structure on self-interests, as well as the effects of other international factors and of domestic structure.

Such a modified structural research program could begin to help generate theories that are more discriminating, with respect to the sources of power, than is Structural Realism. It would be less oriented toward reaffirming the orthodox verities of world politics and more inclined to explain variations in patterns of rules and institutions. Its concern with international institutions would facilitate insights into processes of peaceful change. This research program would not solve all of the problems of Realist theory, but it would be a valuable basis for interpreting contemporary world politics.

Yet this form of structural theory still has the weaknesses associated with power analysis. The essential problem is that from a purely systemic point of view, situations of strategic interdependence do not have determinate solutions. No matter how carefully power resources are defined, no power model will be able accurately to predict outcomes under such conditions.[28]

One way to alleviate this problem without moving immediately to the domestic level of analysis (and thus sacrificing the advantages of systemic theory), is to recognize that what it is rational for states to do, and what states' interests are, depend on the institutional context of action as well as on the underlying power realities and state position upon which Realist thought concentrates. Structural approaches should be seen as only a basis for further systemic analysis. They vary the power condition in the system, but they are silent on variations in the frequency of mutual interactions in the system or in the level of information.

The importance of these non-power factors is demonstrated by some recent work on cooperation. In particular, Robert Axelrod has shown that cooperation can emerge among egoists under conditions of strategic interdependence as modelled by the game of prisoners' dilemma. Such a result requires, however, that these egoists expect to continue to interact with each other for the indefinite future, and that these expectations of future interactions be given sufficient weight in their calculations (Axelrod, 1981). This argument reinforces the practical wisdom of diplomats and arms controllers, who assume that state strategies, and the degree of eventual cooperation, will depend significantly on expectations about the future. The "double-cross" strategy, for instance, is more attractive when it is expected to lead to a final, winning move, than when a continuing series of actions and reactions is anticipated.

High levels of uncertainty reduce the confidence with which expectations are held, and may therefore lead governments to discount the future heavily. As Axelrod shows, this can inhibit the evolution of cooperation through reciprocity. It can also reduce the ability of actors to make mutually beneficial agreements at any given time, quite apart from their expectations about whether future interactions will occur. That is, it can lead to a form of "political market failure" (Keohane, 1982).

Information that reduces uncertainty is therefore an important factor in world politics. But information is not a systemic constant. Some international systems are rich in institutions and processes that provide information to governments and other actors; in other systems, information is scarce or of low quality. Given a certain distribution of power (Waltz's "international structure"), variations in information may be important in influencing state behavior. If international institutions can evolve that improve the quality of information and reduce uncertainty, they may profoundly affect international political behavior even in the absence of changes either in international structure (defined in terms of the distribution of power) or in the preference functions of actors.

Taking information seriously at the systemic level could stimulate a new look at theories of information-processing within governments, such as those of Axelrod (1976), George (1980), Jervis (1976), and Holsti (1976). It could also help us, however, to understand a dimension of the concept of complex interdependence (Keohane & Nye, 1977) that has been largely ignored. Complex interdependence can be seen as a condition under which it is not only difficult to use conventional power resources for certain purposes, but under which information levels are relatively high due to the existence of multiple channels of contact among states. If we focus exclusively on questions of power, the most important feature of complex interdependence—almost its *only* important feature—is the ineffectiveness of military force and the constraints that this implies on fungibility of power across issue-areas. Sensitizing ourselves to the role of information, and information-provision, at the international level brings another aspect of complex interdependence—the presence of multiple channels of contact among societies—back into the picture. Actors behave differently in information-rich environments than in information-poor ones where uncertainty prevails.

This is not a subject that can be explored in depth here.[29] I raise it, however, to clarify the nature of the multi-dimensional network of theories and research programs that I advocate for the study of world politics. We need both spare, logically tight theories, such as Structural Realism, and rich interpretations, such as those of the historically-oriented students of domestic structure and foreign policy. But we also need something in-between: systemic theories that retain some of the parsimony of Structural Realism, but that are able to deal better with differentiations between issue-areas, with institutions, and with change. Such theories could be developed on the basis of variations in power (as in Structural Realism), but they could also focus on variations in other systemic characteristics, such as levels and quality of information.

CONCLUSION:
WORLD POLITICS AND PEACEFUL CHANGE

As Gilpin points out, the problem of peaceful change is fundamental to world politics. Thermonuclear weapons have made it even more urgent than it was in the past. Realism demonstrates that peaceful change is more difficult to achieve in international politics than within well-ordered domestic societies, but it does not offer a theory of peaceful change.[30] Nor is such a theory available from other research traditions. The question remains for us to grapple with: Under what conditions will adaptations to shifts in power, in available technologies, or in fundamental economic relationships take place without severe economic disruption or warfare?

Recent work on "international regimes" has been addressed to this question, which is part of the broader issue of order in world politics (*International Organization*, Spring, 1982). Structural Realist approaches to understanding the origins and maintenance of international regimes are useful (Krasner, 1982), but since they ignore cognitive issues and questions of information, they comprise only part of the story (Haas, 1982).

Realism, furthermore, is better at telling us why we are in such trouble than how to get out of it. It argues that order can be created from anarchy by the exercise of superordinate power: periods of peace follow establishment of dominance in Gilpin's "hegemonic wars." Realism sometimes seems to imply, pessimistically, that order can *only* be created by hegemony. If the latter conclusion were correct, not only would the world economy soon become chaotic (barring a sudden resurgence of American power), but at some time in the foreseeable future, global nuclear war would ensue.

Complacency in the face of this prospect is morally unacceptable. No serious thinker could, therefore, be satisfied with Realism as the correct theory of world politics, even if the scientific status of the theory were stronger than it is. Our concern for humanity requires us to do what Gilpin does in the epilogue to *War and Change* (1981), where he holds out the hope of a "new and more stable international order" in the final decades of the twentieth century, despite his theory's contention that such a benign outcome is highly unlikely. Although Gilpin could be criticized for inconsistency, this would be beside the point: the conditions of terror under which we live compel us to search for a way out of the trap.

The need to find a way out of the trap means that international relations must be a policy science as well as a theoretical activity.[31] We should be seeking to link theory with practice, bringing insights from Structural Realism, modified structural theories, other systemic approaches, and actor-level analyses to bear on contemporary issues in a sophisticated way. This does not mean that the social scientist should adopt the policy-maker's framework, much less his normative values or blinders about the range of available alternatives. On the contrary, independent observers often do their most valuable work when they reject the normative or analytic framework of those in power, and the best theorists may be those who maintain their distance from those at the center of events. Nevertheless, foreign policy and world politics are too important to be left to bureaucrats, generals, and lawyers—or even to journalists and clergymen.

Realism helps us determine the strength of the trap, but does not give us much assistance in seeking to escape. If we are to promote peaceful change, we need to focus not only on basic long-term forces that determine the shape of world politics independently of the actions of particular decision-makers, but also on variables that to some extent can be manipulated by human action. Since international institutions, rules, and patterns of cooperation can affect calculations of interest, and can also be affected incrementally by contemporary political action, they provide a natural focus for scholarly attention as well as policy concern.[32] Unlike Realism, theories that attempt to explain rules, norms, and institutions help us to understand how to create patterns of cooperation that could be essential to our survival. We need to respond to the questions that Realism poses but fails to answer: How can order be created out of anarchy *without* superordinate power; how can peaceful change occur?

To be reminded of the significance of international relations as policy analysis, and the pressing problem of order, is to recall the tradition of Classical Realism. Classical Realism, as epitomized by the work of John Herz (1981), has recognized that no matter how deterministic our theoretical aspirations may be, there remains a human interest in autonomy and self-reflection. As Ashley puts it, the Realism of a thinker such as Herz is committed to an "emancipatory cognitive interest—an interest in securing freedom from unacknowledged constraints, relations of domination, and conditions of distorted communication and understanding that deny humans the capacity to make their future with full will and consciousness" (1981, p. 227).[33] We think about world politics not because it is aesthetically beautiful, because we believe that it is governed by simple, knowable laws, or because it provides rich, easily accessible data for the testing of empirical hypotheses. Were those concerns paramount, we would look elsewhere. We study world politics because we think it will determine the fate of the earth (Schell, 1982). Realism makes us aware of the odds against us. What we need to do now is to understand peaceful change by combining multi-dimensional scholarly analysis with more visionary ways of seeing the future.

NOTES

1. An unfortunate limitation of this chapter is that its scope is restricted to work published in English, principally in the United States. I recognize that this reflects the Americanocentrism of scholarship in the United States, and I regret it. But I am not sufficiently well-read in works published elsewhere to comment intelligently on them. For recent discussions of the distinctively American stamp that has been placed on the international relations field see Hoffmann (1977) and Lyons (1982).

2. Nye and I, in effect, conceded this in our later work, which was more cautious about the drawbacks of conventional "state-centric" theory. (See Keohane & Nye, 1977.)
3. For a discussion of "theory as a set of questions," see Hoffmann (1960, pp. 1-12).
4. Bruce Russett has written a parallel essay in this volume on "International Interactions and Processes: The Internal vs. External Debate Revisited." Professor Russett discusses the extensive literature on arms control and on dependency, neither of which I consider here.
5. Stanley J. Michalak, Jr. pointed out correctly that our characterization of Realism in *Power and Interdependence* was unfair when taken literally, although he also seems to me to have missed the Realist basis of our structural models. (See Michalak, 1979.)
6. It has often been noted that Kuhn's definition of a paradigm was vague: one sympathetic critic identified 21 distinct meanings of the term in Kuhn's relatively brief book (Masterman, 1970). But Lakatos particularly objected to what he regarded as Kuhn's relativism, which in his view interpreted major changes in science as the result of essentially irrational forces. (See Lakatos, 1970, p. 178.)
7. Lakatos' comments on Marxism and psychology were biting, and a colleague of his reports that he doubted the applicability of the methodology of scientific research programs to the social sciences. (See Latsis, 1976, p. 2.)
8. Robert Jervis and Ann Tickner have both reminded me that Morgenthau and John H. Herz, another major proponent of Realist views in the 1950s, later severely qualified their adherence to what has generally been taken as Realist doctrine. (See Herz, 1981, and Boyle, 1980, p. 218.) I am particularly grateful to Dr. Tickner for obtaining a copy of the relevant pages of the latter article for me.
9. For commentary on this assumption, see Keohane and Nye (1972), and Mansbach, Ferguson, and Lampert (1976). In *Power and Interdependence,* Nye and I were less critical than we had been earlier of the state-centric assumption. In view of the continued importance of governments in world affairs, for many purposes it seems justified on grounds of parsimony. Waltz's rather acerbic critique of our earlier position seems to me essentially correct. (See Waltz, 1979, p. 7.)
10. Emphasis added. Thucydides also follows this "positive heuristic" of looking for underlying power realities in discussions of the Athenian-Corcyrean alliance (Chapter II), the decision of the Lacedemonians to vote that Athens had broken the treaty between them (Chapter III), and Pericles' Funeral Oration (Chapter IV). In the Modern Library edition, the passages in question are on pp. 28, 49-50, and 83.
11. Bruce Bueno de Mesquita (1981, pp. 29-33) has an excellent discussion of the rationality assumption as used in the study of world politics.
12. As Waltz points out, Morgenthau's writings reflect the "first-image" Realist view that the evil inherent in man is at the root of war and conflict.
13. Sustained earlier critiques of the fungibility assumption can be found in Keohane and Nye (1977, pp. 49-52) and in Baldwin (1979).
14. In an illuminating recent review essay, John Gerard Ruggie has criticized Waltz's assumption that the second dimension of structure, referring to the degree of differentiation of units, can be regarded as a constant (undifferentiated units with similar functions) in world politics. Ruggie argues that "when the concept 'differentiation' is properly defined, the second structural level of Waltz's model . . . serves to depict the kind of institutional transformation illustrated by the shift from the medieval to the modern international system." See Ruggie (1983, p. 279).

15. Waltz denies that he relies on the rationality assumption; but I argue in Section II that he requires it for his theory of the balance of power to hold.

16. For a brilliant discussion of this theoretical strategy in micro-economics, see Latsis (1976, especially pp. 16-23).

17. Since the principal purpose of Realist analysis in the hands of Waltz and others is to develop an explanation of international political reality, rather than to offer specific advice to those in power, the label, "technical realism," seems too narrow. It also carries a pejorative intent that I do not share. "Structural Realism" captures the focus on explanation through an examination of the structure of the international system. Capitalization is used to indicate that Realism is a specific school, and that it would be possible to be a realist—in the sense of examining reality as it really is—without subscribing to Realist assumptions. For a good discussion, see Krasner (1982).

18. This is the commonsense view of power, as discussed, for example, by Arnold Wolfers (1962, p. 103). As indicated in Section III, any such definition conceals a large number of conceptual problems.

19. My reading of Gilpin's argument on pp. 29-34 led me originally to believe that he also accepted the notion that power is fungible, since he argues that hegemonic war creates a hierarchy of prestige in an international system, which is based on the hegemon's "demonstrated ability to enforce its will on other states" (p. 34), and which in turn determines governance of the international system (p. 33). This appears to imply that a single structure of power resources exists, usable for a wide variety of issues. But in letters sent to the author commenting on an earlier draft of this paper, both Gilpin and Waltz explicitly disavowed the assumption that power resources are necessarily fungible. In *War and Change*, Gilpin is very careful to disclaim the notion, which he ascribes to Political Realists but which I have not included in the hard core of Realism, that states seek to maximize their power: "Acquisition of power entails an opportunity cost to a society; some other desired good must be abandoned" (p. 51).

20. A similar issue is posed in Chapter 3 of Part II of *Lineages of the Absolutist State* (1974). Its author, Perry Anderson, addresses the puzzle of why it was Prussia, rather than Bavaria or Saxony, that eventually gained predominance in Germany. Despite his inclinations, Anderson has to rely on a variety of conjunctural, if not accidental, factors to account for the observed result.

21. For a lucid discussion of the security dilemma, see Jervis (1978).

22. The fact that sensitive Realists are aware of the limitations of Realism makes me less worried than Ashley about the policy consequences of Realist analysis. (See above, pp. 508-509.

23. Waltz does not accept Baldwin's (and Dahl's) definition of power in terms of causality, arguing that "power is one cause among others, from which it cannot be isolated." But this makes it impossible to falsify any power theory; one can always claim that other factors (not specified a priori) were at work. Waltz's discussion of power (1979, pp. 191-192) does not separate power-as-outcome properly from power-as-resources; it does not distinguish between resources that the observer can assess a priori from those only assessable post hoc; it does not relate probabilistic thinking properly to power theory; and it takes refuge in a notion of power as "affecting others more than they affect him," which would result (if taken literally) in the absurdity of attributing maximum power to the person or government that is least responsive to outside stimuli, regardless of its ability to achieve its purposes.

24. Jervis (1976, Chapter 1) has an excellent discussion of levels of analysis and the relationship between perceptual theories and other theories of international relations. Snyder and Diesing discuss similar issues in Chapter VI on "Crises and In-

ternational Systems" (1977).

25. Waltz commented perceptively in *Man, the State and War* that contributions of behavioral scientists had often been "rendered ineffective by a failure to comprehend the significance of the political framework of international action" (1959, p. 78).

26. Thorough description—what Alexander George has called "process-tracing"—may be necessary to evaluate a structural explanation, since correlations are not reliable where only a small number of comparable cases is involved. (See George, 1979.)

27. I am indebted for this point to a conversation with Hayward Alker.

28. Latsis (1976) discusses the difference between "single-exit" and "multiple-exit" situations in his critique of oligopoly theory. What he calls the research program of "situational determinism"—structural theory, in my terms—works well for single-exit situations, where only one sensible course of action is possible. (The building is burning down and there is only one way out: regardless of my personal characteristics, one can expect that I will leave through that exit.) It does not apply to multiple-exit situations, where more than one plausible choice can be made. (The building is burning, but I have to choose between trying the smoky stairs or jumping into a fireman's net: my choice may depend on deep-seated personal fears.) In foreign policy, the prevalence of multiple-exit situations reinforces the importance of decision-making analysis at the national level.

29. For a more detailed discussion of some aspects of this notion, and for citations to some of the literature in economics on which my thinking is based, see Keohane (1982). Discussions with Vinod Aggarwal have been important in formulating some of the points in the previous two paragraphs.

30. Morgenthau devotes a chapter of *Politics Among Nations* to peaceful change, but after a review of the reasons why legalistic approaches will not succeed, he eschews general statements for descriptions of a number of United Nations actions affecting peace and security. No theory of peaceful change is put forward. In *Politics Among Nations* Morgenthau put whatever faith he had in diplomacy. The chapter on peaceful change is Chapter 26 of the fourth edition (1966).

31. For a suggestive discussion of international relations as policy science, see George and Smoke (1974), Appendix, "Theory for Policy in International Relations," pp. 616-642.

32. Recall Weber's aphorism in "Politics as a Vocation": "Politics is the strong and slow boring of hard boards." Although much of Weber's work analyzed broad historical forces beyond the control of single individuals or groups, he remained acutely aware of "the truth that man would not have attained the possible unless time and again he had reached out for the impossible" (Gerth & Mills, 1958, p. 128). For a visionary, value-laden discourse on future international politics by a scholar "reaching out for the impossible," see North (1976, Chapter 7).

33. Ernst B. Haas, who has studied how political actors learn throughout his distinguished career, makes a similar point in a recent essay, where he espouses a "cognitive-evolutionary view" of change and argues that such a view "cannot settle for a concept of hegemony imposed by the analyst. . . . It makes fewer claims about basic directions, purposes, laws and trends than do other lines of thought. It is agnostic about the finality of social laws" (1982, pp. 242-243). The difference between Haas and me is that he seems to reject structural analysis in favor of an emphasis on cognitive evolution and learning, whereas I believe that modified structural analysis (more modest in its claims than Structural Realism) can provide a context within which analysis of cognition is politically more meaningful.

REFERENCES

Aggarwal, Vinod. *Hanging by a thread: International regime change in the textile apparel system, 1950-1979.* Unpublished doctoral dissertation, Stanford University, 1981.

Anderson, Perry. *Lineages of the absolutist state.* London: New Left Books, 1974.

Art, Robert J. Bureaucratic politics and American foreign policy: A critique. *Policy Sciences,* 1973, *4,* 467-490.

Ashley, Richard K. Political realism and human interests. *International Studies Quarterly,* 1981, *25,* 204-236.

Ashley, Richard K. Realistic dialectics: Toward a critical theory of world politics. Paper presented at the Annual Meeting of the American Political Science Association, Denver, Colorado, September 1982.

Axelrod, Robert (Ed.). *The structure of decision: The cognitive maps of political elites.* Princeton, N.J.: Princeton University Press, 1976.

Axelrod, Robert. The emergence of cooperation among egoists. *American Political Science Review,* 1981, *25,* 306-318.

Baldwin, David A. Power analysis and world politics: New trends versus old tendencies. *World Politics,* 1979, *31,* 161-194.

Boyle, Francis A. The irrelevance of international law: The schism between international law and international politics. *California Western International Law Journal,* 1980, *10.*

Brecher, Michael, with Geist, Benjamin. *Decisions in crisis: Israel 1967-1973.* Berkeley: University of California Press, 1980.

Bueno de Mesquita, Bruce. *The war trap.* New Haven: Yale University Press, 1981.

Carr, E. H. *The twenty years' crisis, 1919-1939* (1st ed.). London: Macmillan, 1946. (Originally published, 1939.)

Choucri, Nazli and North, Robert C. *Nations in conflict: National growth and international violence.* San Francisco: W. H. Freeman & Co., 1975.

Cipolla, Carlo. *The economic decline of empires.* London: Methuen, 1970.

Dahl, Robert A. *Who governs? Democracy and power in an American city.* New Haven: Yale University Press, 1961.

Eckstein, Harry. Case study and theory in political science. In Fred I. Greenstein & Nelson W. Polsby (Eds.), *Handbook of political science* (Vol. 7) *Strategies of inquiry.* Reading, MA: Addison-Wesley, 1975.

Geertz, Clifford. *The interpretation of cultures.* New York: Basic Books, 1973.

George, Alexander L. Case studies and theory development: The method of structured, focused comparison. In Paul Gordon Lauren (Ed.), *Diplomacy: New approaches in history, theory and policy.* New York: Free Press, 1979.

George, Alexander L. *Presidential decisionmaking in foreign policy: The effective use of information and advice.* Boulder: Westview, 1980.

George, Alexander L. & George, Juliette. *Woodrow Wilson and Colonel House.* New York: Dover, 1964.

George, Alexander L., Hall, D. K. & Simons, W. E. *The limits of coercive diplomacy.* Boston: Little, Brown, 1971.

George, Alexander L. & Smoke, Richard. *Deterrence in American foreign policy.* New York: Columbia University Press, 1974.

Gerschenkron, Alexander. *Economic backwardness in historical perspective.* Cambridge: The Belknap Press of Harvard University Press, 1962.

Gerth, H. H., & Mills, C. Wright. *From Max Weber: Essays in Sociology.* New York: Oxford University Press, 1958.

Gilpin, Robert. *U.S. power and the multinational corporation.* New York: Basic Books, 1975.

Gilpin, Robert. *War and change in world politics.* New York: Cambridge University Press, 1981.

Gourevitch, Peter A. The second image reversed: The international sources of domestic politics. *International Organization,* 1978, *32,* 881-913.

Haas, Ernst B. Why collaborate? Issue-linkage and international regimes. *World Politics,* 1980, *32,* 357-405.

Haas, Ernst B. Words can hurt you: Or who said what to whom about regimes. *International Organization,* 1982, *36,* 207-244.

Harsanyi, John. Measurement of social power, opportunity costs, and the theory of two-person bargaining games. *Behavioral Sciences,* 1962, *7,* 67-80.

Herz, John H. Political realism revisited. *International Studies Quarterly,* 1981, *25,* 182-197.

Hoffmann, Stanley. *Contemporary theory in international relations.* Englewood Cliffs, N.J.: Prentice-Hall, 1960.

Hoffmann, Stanley. An American social science: International relations. *Daedalus,* Summer 1977, 41-60.

Holsti, Ole. Foreign policy viewed cognitively. In Robert Axelrod (Ed.), *The structure of decision: The cognitive maps of political elites.* Princeton, N.J.: Princeton University Press, 1976.

International organization, 1982, *36.* Special issue on international regimes edited by Stephen D. Krasner.

Jervis, Robert. *Perception and misperception in international politics.* Princeton, N.J.: Princeton University Press, 1976.

Jervis, Robert. Cooperation under the security dilemma. *World Politics,* 1978, *30,* 167-214.

Katzenstein, Peter J. *Between power and plenty: Foreign economic policies of advanced industrial states.* Madison: University of Wisconsin Press, 1978.

Keohane, Robert O. The demand for international regimes. *International Organization,* 1982, *36,* 325-356.

Keohane, Robert O., & Nye, Joseph (Eds.). *Transnational relations and world politics.* Cambridge, MA: Harvard University Press, 1972.

Keohane, Robert O., & Nye, Joseph. *Power and interdependence: World politics in transition.* Boston: Little, Brown, 1977.

Krasner, Stephen D. *Defending the national interest: Raw materials investments and U.S. foreign policy.* Princeton: Princeton University Press, 1978.

Krasner, Stephen D. Structural causes and regime consequences: Regimes as intervening variables. *International Organization,* 1982, *36,* 185-206.

Kuhn, Thomas S. *The structure of scientific revolutions.* Chicago: University of Chicago Press, 1962.

Kurth, James R. The political consequences of the product cycle: Industrial history and political outcomes. *International Organization,* 1979, *33,* 1-34.

Lakatos, Imre. Falsification and the methodology of scientific research programmes. In Imre Lakatos & Alan Musgrave (Eds.), *Criticism and the growth of knowledge.* Cambridge: Cambridge University Press, 1970.

Latsis, Spiro J. A research programme in economics. In Latsis (Ed.), *Method and appraisal in economics.* Cambridge: Cambridge University Press, 1976.

Lebow, Richard Ned. *Between peace and war: The nature of international crisis.* Baltimore: Johns Hopkins University Press, 1981.

Lenin, V. I. *Imperialism: The highest stage of capitalism.* New York: International Publishers, 1939. (Originally written, 1916.)

Luttwak, Edward. *The grand strategy of the Roman Empire—from the first century A.D. to the third.* Baltimore: Johns Hopkins University Press, 1976.

Lyons, Gene M. Expanding the study of international relations: The French connection. *World Politics,* 1982, *35,* 135-149.

Mansbach, Richard, Ferguson, Yale H. & Lampert, Donald E. *The web of world politics.* Englewood Cliffs, N.J.: Prentice-Hall, 1976.

Mansbach, Richard & Vasquez, John A. *In search of theory: A new paradigm for global politics.* New York: Columbia University Press, 1981.

March, James G. The power of power. In David Easton (Ed.), *Varieties of political theory.* New York: Prentice-Hall, 1966.

Masterman, Margaret. The nature of a paradigm. In Lakatos & Musgrave (Eds.), *Criticism and the growth of knowledge.* Cambridge: Cambridge University Press, 1970.

Michalak, Stanley J., Jr. Theoretical perspectives for understanding international interdependence. *World Politics,* 1979, *32,* 136-150.

Moore, Barrington, Jr. *Social origins of dictatorship and democracy: Lord and peasant in the making of the modern world.* Boston: Beacon Press, 1966.

Morgenthau, Hans J. *Scientific man versus power politics.* Chicago: University of Chicago Press, 1946.

Morgenthau, Hans J. *Politics among nations* (4th ed.). New York: Knopf, 1966. (Originally published, 1948.)

North, Douglass C. *Structure and change in economic history.* New York: W.W. Norton, 1981.

North, Robert C. *The world that could be.* (The Portable Stanford: Stanford Alumni Association.) Palo Alto: Stanford University, 1976.

Organski, A. F. K., & Kugler, Jacek. *The war ledger.* Chicago: University of Chicago Press, 1980.

Oye, Kenneth A. The domain of choice. In Kenneth A. Oye, Donald Rothchild, & Robert J. Lieber (Eds.), *Eagle entangled: U.S. foreign policy in a complex world.* New York: Longman, 1979, pp. 3-33.

Oye, Kenneth A. *Belief systems, bargaining and breakdown: International political economy 1929-1934.* Unpublished doctoral dissertation, Harvard University, 1983.

Rosenau, James N. Pre-theories and theories of foreign policy. In R. Barry Farrell (Ed.), *Approaches to comparative and international politics.* Evanston: Northwestern University Press, 1966.

Ruggie, John Gerard. Continuity and transformation in the world polity: Toward a neo-realist synthesis. *World Politics,* 1983, *35,* 261-285.

Russett, Bruce M. The calculus of deterrence. *Journal of Conflict Resolution,* 1963, *7,* 97-109.

Schell, Jonathan. *The fate of the earth.* New York: Knopf, 1982.

Schelling, Thomas. *The strategy of conflict.* New York: Oxford University Press, 1960.

Simon, Herbert A. The architecture of complexity. In Simon (Ed.), *The sciences of the artificial.* Cambridge: MIT Press, 1969.

Snidal, Duncan. *Interdependence, regimes, and international cooperation.* Unpublished manuscript, University of Chicago, 1981.

Snyder, Glenn H. & Diesing, Paul. *Conflict among nations: Bargaining, decision-making and system structure in international crises.* Princeton, N.J.: Princeton University Press, 1977.

Sprout, Harold & Sprout, Margaret. *Toward a politics of the planet earth.* New York: Van Nostrand Reinhold, 1971.

Stein, Arthur. The politics of linkage. *World Politics,* 1980, *33,* 62-81.

Stein, Arthur. Coordination and collaboration: Regimes in an anarchic world. *International Organization,* 1982, *36,* 299-324.

Thucydides. *The Peloponnesian War* (John H. Finley, Jr., trans.). New York: Modern Library, 1951. (Originally written c. 400 B.C.)

Tollison, Robert D. & Willett, Thomas D. An economic theory of mutually advantageous issue linkage in international negotiations. *International Organization,* 1979, *33,* 425-450.

Toulmin, Stephen. *Foresight and understanding: An enquiry into the aims of science.* New York: Harper Torchbooks, 1963.

Wallerstein, Immanuel. The rise and future demise of the world capitalist system: Concepts for comparative analysis. In Wallerstein, *The capitalist world-economy.* Cambridge: Cambridge University Press, 1979. (This essay was originally printed in *Comparative Studies in Society and History,* 1974, *16.*)

Wallerstein, Immanuel. *The modern world-system II: Mercantilism and the consolidation of the European world-economy, 1600-1750.* New York: Academic Press, 1980.

Waltz, Kenneth N. *Man, the state and war.* New York: Columbia University Press, 1959.

Waltz, Kenneth N. *Foreign policy and democratic politics: The American and British experience.* Boston: Little, Brown, 1967.

Waltz, Kenneth N. *Theory of international politics.* Reading, MA: Addison-Wesley, 1979.

Wolfers, Arnold. *Discord and collaboration: Essays on international politics.* Baltimore: Johns Hopkins University Press, 1962.

17

International Interactions and Processes: The Internal vs. External Debate Revisited*

Bruce Russett

Interactions may be part of a cooperative process, or part of a conflict. International trade and finance are usually characterized as cooperative interactions, involving a mutually beneficial exchange. Dependence theorists, however, emphasize the unequal distribution of many of the benefits of exchange, the existence of elements of exploitation, and asymmetric penetration of poor, weak societies. "Arms races" seem to exemplify conflict, as seen in the vicious spiral of some types of Richardson (1960) processes, though as understood in the prisoners' dilemma they may be held in check by certain kinds of cooperative interactions. Many of the processes central to dependence theory are the result of decisions by non-state actors such as multinational corporations and national or transnational social classes; they reflect less the power of states—though state actors are important—than of these non-state actors; and they usually do not result in interstate war. As such they typically have been ignored in the standard "realist" perspective. Arms race processes, by contrast, are typified by state decisions to arm; they reflect and affect the international distribution of power; and they may result in war. The overt manifestations of arms races (threat, hostility, perhaps war) have long been at the heart of realist concerns. Nevertheless, the internal bureaucratic and organizational processes now widely regarded as central to understanding arms acquisitions have been neglected in realist analyses (Keohane, 1983).

*I am grateful to the National Science Foundation and the German Marshall Fund for their support of much of the research on which this essay is based, and especially to Paul Huth, Jim Lindsay, and Steve Silvia for their excellent research assistance in gathering and evaluating much of the material cited here. I am also grateful to Bruce Bueno de Mesquita, James Caporaso, Raymond Duvall, Alexander George, Robert North, and Dina Zinnes for comments. Of course, no individual or organization is responsible for the opinions I have expressed here.

It is one thing to recognize that subnational and transnational actors contribute essentially to the processes that are part of the phenomena we characterize as dependence or arms races; it is another to regard them as introducing sufficient variation to affect significantly the dependent variable of interest. Their impact may be fairly uniform in most times and places, allowing us to expect universal patterns. Richardson seemed to have imagined that when estimated the coefficients would in fact turn out to be essentially the same in all circumstances. If internal and other processes are reasonably uniform, then we might hope to explain large portions of variance with law-like propositions such as those that appear to operate in many areas of physics.

Most analysts would now conclude that such uniformity does not exist, and that contextual variation, introduced by the effect of additional variables, will be important. The simplest version of this effect would allow us to apply the same model to all states and circumstances by expecting that the same *elements* or variables will always be present but that the *form* of their relationship will vary. The values of the parameters may change, and be of different importance. With this expectation, the strength of bureaucratic inertia may vary substantially in different circumstances, or different regimes may have very different perceptions of threat and hostility ("grievance coefficients" in the classic Richardson formulation). But we would nevertheless be asking the same questions about all states. This view, consistent with a perspective sympathetic to social science, would emphasize the complex multivariate and interactive nature of political phenomena. It would not despair of generalization, but only of the prospect of finding simple, powerful, universally-applicable generalizations.

A more fundamental critique, however, would hold that the models themselves must be different: for example, in capitalist countries depressed demand might stimulate increased military expenditures for the purpose of expanding aggregate economic activity; for socialist countries the economic capacity might be seen rather as a constraint, holding back levels of military spending that would otherwise be desired by the leadership. Not only would we expect a different sign for the "economic" variable, but the specification of the variable would be different. This conclusion still would not necessarily lead to a rejection of science and generalization, but it would complicate still further the investigation, and require careful and detailed model specification.

Similar problems apply to any expectations of making broad generalizations about dependence. Theorists like Cardoso (1977) deplore North American "totalizing" efforts that allegedly neglect contextual factors like the size of a country's domestic market or its particular history of class relations as far back as the colonial era. In its extreme form, this argument asserts that the conditions of each country are so different, and the results of "dependence" so different in each case, that the search not only for uniform coefficients, but even for a uniform model, is doomed. The latter *is* an extreme position, but it is encountered.

Investigation of these relationships has major implications both for arms races and dependence. Early efforts to investigate these topics seemed to assume that the prospects for making strong and simple generalizations were good. They worked with only a few variables, and made little acknowledgment of possible interactions. This is common in the first stages of most investigations, and the failure to uncover strong, simple relationships more usual than not. Later examinations in these central topics of political economy have become much more sophisticated, though they have not necessarily produced clear-cut or widely accepted results. In this chapter we shall look at the experience of these endeavors, and try to draw some conclusions to guide further analyses. Whereas the substantive topics of the two literatures may seem far apart, we shall see that they share many similarities of investigation, difficulty, and promise.

ARMS ACQUISITION MODELS

Models to explain states' military expenditures or weapons acquisitions typically are referred to as arms race models. That label, however, is deceptive, because it assumes what should instead be a question for investigation: the role of international competitive processes in affecting decisions to buy arms. While this is indeed a widely hypothesized phenomenon, often correctly, it should not simply be assumed. Critics of the true "arms race" school maintain rather that arms purchase decisions are determined little if at all by what goes on in the international system, but rather by internal pressures of bureaucratic politics or domestic political processes (e.g., "military-industrial complex" theories). The latter emphasize the virtually "autistic" character of arms purchases. Still other models incorporate both external and internal influences. The relative importance of each should not be pre-judged.

The best-known arms acquisition model is aptly characterized as an arms race model. Its formulation is the most familiar of the Richardson models:

$$\Delta X = kY - aX + g$$
$$\Delta Y = lX - bY + h$$

In this two-nation arms race, the changes (Δ) in the military expenditures (or arms stocks—they are not the same) of the two nations (X and Y) are influenced by three major factors: (1) the military expenditures of the other state (k and l represent coefficients); (2) the economic burden of paying for previous decisions to purchase military goods ($-a$ and $-b$ represent "fatigue" coefficients to indicate the weight of this burden); and (3) the underlying "grievance" held by each state against the other (g and h).

The first efforts to investigate these equations either met with little success or, if initially promising, were found to suffer from crippling methodological flaws. The more prominent ones were reviewed by Busch (1970). At that time, the majority of arms race studies had been theoretical rather than empirical; Busch concluded that these theories were too simple and/or too apolitical (for example, taking models directly from physics without specifying the political processes that might make them applicable). The more precise formulations called for by Busch were appearing by the time of the reviews by Luterbacher (1975) and Rattinger (1976). Luterbacher concentrated on theoretical problems, with a critique of the assumptions of linear relationships and the neglect of cost and resource constraints on arms expenditure. For example, though the "fatigue coefficient" was an integral part of the Richardson model, even to this date it has received only sporadic attention. Rattinger devoted most of his attention to methodological problems of estimation. He highlighted the tradeoff arising between the reality of short time series—requiring models to be as parsimonious as possible—and the demands of complex modelling. The former risks specification error by leaving out essential explanatory variables, and the latter risks having too few degrees of freedom to produce any significant results (see, for example, Hamblin, 1977). He also criticized those specifications that proceeded to complex non-linear relations without first employing linear models.

Despite the familiarity and apparent plausibility of the arms race hypothesis of external determinants, it has not always held up in empirical examinations of the United States-Soviet Union relationship. The reasons for the mixed results appear complex, but they include questions of conceptualization as well as the broader theoretical question as to whether international (action-reaction) explanations are even in principal adequate.

Levels, Changes, and Stocks

One major problem lies in the realm of an adequate conceptualization of precisely what it means to postulate that one country reacts to another's military expenditure. The greatest number of early works assumed that the change in one state's spending depends on the *level* of its rival's spending in the preceding period. (This remained true for many of the studies of the 1970s as well; see, for example, Strauss, 1972, 1978; Gregory, 1974; Ostrom, 1977; Gillespie *et al.*, 1977, 1978.) Some earlier studies assumed that the reaction was to the rival's current spending, but that specification has long been regarded as unrealistic in modern complex governmental organizations. More recently, many studies have shifted to focus on the change in one state's spending as depending on the *change* in its rival's spending during the preceding period (Hollist, 1977a, 1977b; Hollist & Guetzkow, 1978; Cusack & Ward, 1981).[1] This seems to offer some improvement on the first formulation, since a marked increment in a rival's effort may seem threatening even if the level of the rival's effort is low. More plausibly, perhaps, a halt in annual increases, or even more a decrement from the previous year, may constitute a strong signal to call forth comparable restraint from a rival. Unfortunately, neither of these specifications regularly produces convincing results when applied to the action-reaction process of most interest, that between the United States and the Soviet Union. An alternative formulation is the distributed lag model employed by Strauss (1972, 1978), Gillespie, Zinnes, and Rubinson (1978), and most recently by Majeski and Jones (1981). Such a model effectively considers a country's current arms expenditures as affected by its antagonist's expenditures over a long period of previous years, with the earlier years producing progressively smaller effects as one moves back in time.

More plausible are the recent studies that give attention to the existing *stock* of weapons to which any addition may be made. For example, in periods when the United States maintained a stock of strategic weapons far superior to that of the Soviet Union, American leaders could—perhaps mis-takenly—be relaxed about substantial year-to-year increases in Soviet spend-ing so long as the initial stock of Soviet strategic weapons was fairly low; it might take many years of increases and even years of subsequent high spend-ing levels to bring the Soviet weapons stock to "essential equivalence" with that of the United States. Only as the United States' substantial lead over the Soviet Union in stock of weapons—not just the level of spending—diminished would some decision-makers become fully alerted.

Examination of military spending patterns is itself subject to several well-recognized difficulties. The data available are highly aggregated; usually one must deal with total military spending rather than, for example, spending for strategic arms, which might be the most relevant to an arms-race analysis. (Reasonable data on United States strategic weapons spending are now available for most of the period but estimates for the Soviet Union are very crude.) Kugler and Organski (1980) nevertheless have estimated equations for military expenditure on strategic nuclear weapons systems, compiling a measure of strategic weapons and including a parameter to measure depreciation. This is conceptually attractive, but the basis for deriving the measures is very unclear.

The quality of all the data on Soviet military spending is necessarily poor, subject to wide differences in estimation (Holzman, 1980, 1982). Much of the controversy concerns the different estimates of the level of Soviet spend-ing rather than of year-to-year changes; this leads to questions about how American and Soviet spending are to be measured in a common currency. Nevertheless, even some of the data on changes are dubious, with suggestions that estimates of Soviet spending are sometimes made by extrapolating from previous apparent trends—a procedure guaranteed to "support" hypotheses like those of bureaucratic inertia. Although the serial correlation between the major sources, like I.I.S.S. and S.I.P.R.I., is reasonably high, we now know that arms race analyses are very sensitive to any differences, and can produce results strikingly at variance from one data base to another (Cusack & Ward, 1981).

These difficulties are compounded when the theoretical model is con-cerned with stocks of weapons, rather than with spending. Whereas the in-dividual data items are probably more reliable than are those for expen-ditures (but see Ostrich & Green, 1981, and Albrecht *et al.*, 1978, on prob-lems even with I.I.S.S. estimates of strategic forces, and the criticism by Cordesman, 1982, of U.S. Defense Department data), serious validity prob-lems can arise, associated with the familiar controversies about what should be counted. Some use numbers of bombers and/or warheads weighted by yield (e.g., Lambelet, 1973; Luterbacher, 1976), or just missiles (Saris & Mid-dendorf, 1980). Some scholars have experimented with various combinations. Decisions about which measure to use can greatly affect the results, without pointing to any one particular measure as necessarily the "right" one (McGuire, 1977; see also Richelson, 1982).

From a theoretical point of view, however, the case for inclusion of some measure of weapons stocks, not just current or recent acquisitions or spend-ing, is persuasive. A theoretical model incorporating both budgets and stockpiles, and with stockpiles adjusted for depreciation, is presented by Taage-pera (1979/80), though Taagepera despaired of the prospect for measure-ment in any empirical estimation. A more promising approach—but a very complex one requiring some strong assumptions about data quality and the ability to estimate depreciation rates effectively—can be seen in the impor-tant work of Ward (1982). Ward devises an index of the stockpile of strategic and conventional weapons, with their value depreciated over time, and then is able to focus on increments to those stockpiles. Ward's index for the stock of strategic weapons employs the measure of lethality created by Tsipis (1975)—by no means an unchallengeable measure, but arguably the best available.

Reaction To What?

A second kind of theoretical refinement requires a broader specification of what it is that a state may be reacting to. States react not merely to the weapons that other states possess or acquire, but to the level of hostility being generated by other states which includes estimates of what they do with their weapons. For example, arguably the boost in U.S. military spending that began in 1980, and was magnified by the Reagan administration, was at-tributable less to increased Soviet military spending than to Soviet military activities in Africa and Afghanistan. Richardson's grievance coefficient may be seen as an attempt to incorporate this kind of influence, but most empirical arms race models have neglected to specify such a term. Ashley (1980) did in-corporate a term for "intersections," which he usually found to have insignifi-cant effects. But his measure, one for commercial intersections, leaves some-thing to be desired in a model where two (China and the USSR) are not capitalist states. Ward (1982) employed a measure of international tensions taken from Azar's COPBAB data base (Azar, 1980), which seems more valid. Zimmerman and Palmer (1983) find that Soviet military spending reacted to Soviet verbalized evaluations of American behavior.

Incorporating the effects of what is happening in the international en-vironment, of course, involves building in not just international tensions in general, but specifically the effects of any wars a state may actually be fight-ing. Many of the efforts to investigate the post-World War II Soviet-American relationship, for instance, have fallen afoul of the effect of American wars in Korea and Indochina. Part of the initial spurt in American military spending that started in 1950 can plausibly be attributed to a generalized sense of threat from the Soviet Union (stimulating a broad rearmament effort) but a great part of the increment during 1950-1953 was due simply to the costs of fighting the Korean War, as manifested by a drop in spending when the war was over. Even more clearly, American spending increases during the Viet-nam War years were due solely to the costs of fighting that war, not to more general increments in international tension. (Some critics in fact pointed to a neglect in maintaining or modernizing forces in Europe and strategic deter-rent forces in order to divert funds to fight the war.) The work of Nincic and Cusack (1979) represents one effort to incorporate a war-mobilization term; Ward's (1982) use of Department of Defense estimates of the cost of war in-volvement may be more satisfactory.

Finally, any effort to model the international environment adequately must show some recognition of the fact that more than two states are involved. Sometimes this recognition is reflected in models that incorporate alliance partners rather than just the superpowers; for example, the results for aggregated NATO/Warsaw-Pact interactions can be quite different from those for the United States and the Soviet Union alone. More important is the triangular Soviet-American-Chinese relationship. Prior to the early 1970s it probably would have made sense to combine Soviet and Chinese military forces as a single "actor" for purposes of American perceptions (e.g. as reflected in American strategic military plans calling for nuclear "retaliation" against China as well as against the USSR in case of Soviet attack). For the last decade, of course, this is no longer an appropriate assumption. As for Soviet perceptions, surely by the early 1960s Soviet military planning had begun to reflect a perception of China as an enemy rather than an ally; about 20-25 percent of current Soviet military spending is now estimated to be directed toward China. Wallace (1980) seems to find that the United States and the USSR react to changes in each other's spending and to the international political climate, and in addition, that the USSR reacts to Chinese spending. This effect of China on the Soviet Union also shows up in Ashley's (1980) triangular analysis, but not in Cusack and Ward's (1981).

Internal Influences

Of course not all the influences on "arms races" stem from the international (external) environment. Richardson attempted to capture the constraining effects of economic burdens with his fatigue coefficient. That coefficient, though it too has often been neglected in contemporary arms race models, is important because it is, in Richardson's formulation, the only constraint on arms races short of war. That is, without it, international tensions and the mutual stimulation of competitive arms purchases would drive an arms race into an ever-upward spiral. Richardson considered that this fatigue coefficient represented the economic burden of the arms race, and Hollist and Johnson (1982) found evidence for it in the case of American spending. Other efforts to model the contemporary arms race with a simple and stable fatigue coefficient have, however, not had good results. Currently the United States is spending about 6 percent of its GNP for military purposes, and there is talk about the inability of the economy to sustain such exertions for long. But the United States spent about 13 percent of its GNP for military purposes during the Korean War, and over 40 percent at the peak of World War II. States under the direct threat may persuade their citizens to spend even more. Britain and the Soviet Union spent as much as 60 percent of their total product on defense during the worst of World War II; by that standard, the current figure of around 14 percent for the USSR may not seem high. Israel has for quite a few years even in "peacetime" carried a defense burden above 25 percent of its GNP—although a good deal of foreign assistance contributes to its defense budget. Thus it is not clear how effective such constraints may be, particularly if the national sense of threat, or grievance, is high or can be made to appear high.

Nincic and Cusack (1979) tried a different approach to internal influences. Rather than considering domestic economic influences a burden, they developed a model of a "political business cycle," whereby military spending was seen as an anti-cyclical fiscal tool, and *increased* according to political perceptions of the need to stimulate macro-economic activity. This effect is keyed to the political cycle of elections, being strongest in presidential elections when an incumbent president is seeking reelection. Their hypothesis was that presidents would seek or accept higher levels of military spending in those years to encourage popular perceptions of prosperity, and hence popular approval of the incumbent administration. The results supported this hypothesis.

A very different approach to internal determinants is represented by the organizational and bureaucratic politics schools. The inertia of large bureaucratic organizations in maintaining and expanding their scope has been well-recognized in case studies (e.g., for the Department of Defense, Halperin, 1974). Attempts to model these effects stem from the work of Davis, Dempster, and Wildavsky (1966), and have been carried furthest with reference to the Defense Department by Crecine (1971; see also Fischer & Crecine, 1979). These efforts have met with some success.

Other studies have produced some important variations on the original insight. Cusack and Ward (1981), for example, began by testing an arms race (action-reaction) model for the three-nation Soviet-American-Chinese relationship. After finding arms race explanations wanting, they turned to internal models. They began with the Nincic and Cusack model for the United States, and they found it valuable. The "domestic political economy" models they developed for the Soviet Union and China, however, had to be quite different. For those countries, of course, an electoral cycle is hardly appropriate; rather Cusack and Ward keyed their model to the cycle of economic planning. It assumes that arms spending is felt as an economic burden, especially in the beginning and final years of government economic plans; hence they hypothesized that military spending would be least constrained in the middle years of the economic plans. This version of the arms spending as burden hypothesis met with much less success for the Soviet Union, and really none at all for China. Nincic (1983) had more positive results with a subsequent study of the USSR. But the theoretical perspective is attractive and deserves further development, especially if adequate data can be generated.

Internal and External Influences

It should now be apparent that a satisfactory understanding of arms acquisition processes can be derived only by testing for both internal and external influences. Such an effort can be seen in Ostrom's (1978) work, and in more recent works by Lambelet, Luterbacher, and Allan (1980) and Hollist and Johnson (1982). The most sophisticated and potentially satisfying effort to date is almost certainly that of Michael Ward (1982). Ward builds on previous theoretical and empirical works, notably those of Taagepera (1979/80), Luterbacher, Allan, and Imhoff (1979), Lambelet, Luterbacher, and Allan (1979), and the work by Nincic and Cusack. Ward's model includes measures of stockpiles and depreciation as well as spending, variables for the "exogenous" effects of the Korean and Vietnam Wars, and indicators of international tension.[2]

Ward's results are impressive. In what he presents as an arms race model, he finds that the United States and the Soviet Union do react to each other's spending decisions, and that the United States, at least, also reacts positively (i.e., reducing defense spending) to decreases in the level of international tension. His model is the first to produce statistically significant estimates of all the parameters, parameter signs consistent with a priori expectations, and large coefficients of multiple determination *all at the same time.*

Ward seems also to confirm the existence of a budgetary constraint, with a negative coefficient for military expenditures in the previous period. His choice of indicator, however, leaves substantial doubt as to just what he has in fact found. A better indicator for budgetary constraint would be a relative measure of military expenditures as a proportion of the total national budget, or GNP, telling us about the proportion of a society's resources being absorbed by the military. Instead, total expenditures would appear to be a measure of organizational momentum, and have been used as such by other researchers (e.g., Kugler & Organski, 1980; Lucier, 1979; Fischer & Crecine, 1979). If we so reinterpret the indicator, we have not the budgetary constraint of a pure arms race model, but the organizational momentum of a model that *combines* internal and external influences.[3]

This interpretation is puzzling, however, because the sign of the coefficient is negative, indicating that the American government bureaucracy has operated as a force to decrease military spending. This is not the standard bureaucratic-organizational politics interpretation (last year's budget plus a little more). Nevertheless it has some plausibility for the United States during the Eisenhower administration ("more bang for the buck") and later administrations—until Reagan—when for much of the time the perceived need was to find budgetary space to maintain or expand big civilian programs. A recent sophisticated analysis by Fischer and Kamlet (1983) confirms the existence both of a small action-reaction effect of Soviet arms and of a fiscal constraint on American military expenditures. Similar results emerge in work by Domke, Eichenberg, and Kelleher (1983), who find both a reaction to international tension and a fiscal constraint. More work on these and similar models is required.

Even as they stand, these findings fit comfortably with those of other studies emphasizing that internal determinants of arms races are important, and that they may be at least as important for the Soviet Union as for the United States (see Ashley, 1980; Nincic, 1982, 1983; Rattinger, 1975; Luterbacher, Lambelet, & Allan, 1980). This testimony to the importance of internal determinants demands further investigation and specification of the nature of those determinants, especially distinguishing between narrow bureaucratic determinants and broader societal ("military-industrial complex") ones, and between expansionary pressures and constraints.

With our reinterpretation of Ward's expenditure coefficient, his work seems to confirm the facts both of Soviet-American interaction and of organizational-bureaucratic inertia. Most previous efforts had been unable satisfactorily to distinguish the two. Indeed some observers have declared that quantitative arms race models probably never would be able to do so, given the crudeness of the assumptions and the data with which they must inevitably work. For example, it is a serious handicap to have to work with annual expenditure data. Given the phases of decision-making on military budgets—in the United States from requests of individual military services, through the Joint Chiefs and the Department of Defense, through the White House and the OMB, and then through the authorization and appropriation process in Congress—the notion of discrete annual increments, even lagging a year or two behind Soviet actions, seems a gross over-simplification. If we add to that a knowledge of the long leadtimes from the conception of a weapon through its research, development, construction, and deployment phases, and the recognition that weapons may be developed in *anticipation* of the other state's development as well as in response to such development (Allison, 1974), we might well have despaired of finding any interpretable results.[4]

Ward also has some important observations about variations in these processes. He writes that the United States did react to Soviet narrowing of the military capability gap between the two countries, but that budgetary constraints weakened the American response—a finding consistent with studies cited above. The Soviet Union, rather differently, also reacted to the gap, but seems not to have felt a significant budgetary constraint—thus allowing the USSR effectively to close the gap. Furthermore, in a methodologically important new analysis Freeman (1983), reanalyzing Majeski and Jones (1981) data with a sophisticated "Granger causality" procedure, finds, in addition to what may be interpreted as a bureaucratic inertia effect, significant effects of American spending on Soviet spending—although not vice versa. It also is important to note, in several analyses, the reaction of the United States to changes in international tension rather than just to Soviet spending. Together, these studies do confirm the existence of something that can appropriately be termed an arms race. Nevertheless it is not entirely clear who is reacting to whom, or for that matter to what.

This research still leaves many unanswered questions. Reservations must persist about the data base. Ward uses I.I.S.S. estimates of Soviet and American military effort; this is odd since presumably the United States is responding to its perception of Soviet activity, which perhaps is more directly captured by American government (i.e., CIA) estimates. Furthermore, we know, from Ward's earlier work (Cusack & Ward, 1981), that the results of arms race modelling efforts are not very robust across different data sources, yet he uses just the one here. More important, it is impossible, at least from the material presented in Ward's paper, to distinguish the relative importance of domestic vs. international influences. Ward's depreciated weapons stock index is necessarily a construct without an obvious empirical counterpart; from the information available we cannot tell the relative impact of the action-reaction effect.

Finally, it is essential to emphasize a point that Ward himself makes clearly: his results apply to an historical epoch when the United States had a consistent—though steadily declining—military advantage over the Soviet Union. His findings about the relative importance of various influences—

especially about the auto-centric nature of Soviet spending, and the insensitivity of the USSR to changes in either American spending or the level of international tension—cannot readily be transferred from the past to the future. In a period of "essential equivalence" we may well see a significant shift in the importance of various determinants (for example, a greater sensitivity of the United States to any apparent Soviet effort to surpass American military strength, or even a greater Soviet recognition of the nature of international action-reaction processes).

Changing Parameters

The most recent review article is that of Moll and Luebbert (1980), which focuses on some other—and equally serious—complexities in arms race analyses. Many of the earlier empirical analyses were marred by serious methodological problems that have now come to be fully recognized. Small samples and few degrees of freedom meant that several different functional relationships could be fitted to the data. This problem may now be easing, however, as we approach 40 years of experience with the Soviet-American "arms race." Another problem is multi-collinearity among explanatory variables, making it virtually impossible to weight their individual effect. In models that combine organizational inertia and international reaction elements both may give predictions of ever-rising expenditures, which in fact can be observed historically for rather long periods (Ostrom, 1977). This is particularly serious in those models that specify the level of a country's expenditures in one period as dependent on its own level of previous expenditures (bureaucratic-organizational) or on its opponents' previous level (action-reaction).

A major conclusion of the Moll and Luebbert review, moreover, is of central importance: the necessity to recognize, and to build into any model, not only the likelihood that key parameters will be different for different countries, but that they will be different for the same country at different times. Ostrom begins to lay some groundwork for such efforts by his willingness to descend within the "black box" of the state. In his 1977 work, for example, Ostrom used several models (action-reaction, organizational politics, and a "naive" model that the best indicator of this year's expenditure is last year's expenditure). He also devised a reactive linkage model (Ostrom, 1978). Moll and Luebbert (1980) point out—without being able to explain it—that the reactive linkage model is more successful for some years than for others; namely the naive model is more successful for the periods 1955-62 and 1969-73, with the reactive linkage model more successful for the middle years. Moll (1974) himself had found significant changes in parameters in analyzing British naval expenditures prior to World War I, and it is a major component of Choucri and North's (1975) work on all the great powers before World War I. Not only did Choucri and North find different coefficients (at widely varying levels of significance, and even opposite signs) for different countries, but they found the coefficients for individual countries very different in the period 1870-1890 than during 1890-1914. Similar variations in results have been obtained by Bishop and Sorenson (1982), Hollist (1977a, 1977b) and Rattinger (1975), though the first analysis is quite simple and in the last three cases methodological deficiencies (such as autocorrelation, a frequent problem in many such studies) cast doubts on the utility of the findings.

Recent methodologically sophisticated work nevertheless confirms the necessity of investigating the possibility of finding very different coefficients for different countries and/or times. For instance, in applying the basic Choucri-North model to American-Soviet-Chinese interactions in the post-World War II period, Ashley (1980) concluded that the United States partly responded to Soviet spending, but he also found a large measure of inertia sustained by the domestic military establishment and national security bureaucracy. The Soviet Union's patterns, by contrast, seemed dominated by domestic forces, and did not respond in any regular way at all to American military spending. Ashley did, however, find some Soviet response to *Chinese* military spending after the two great communist states broke off relations. This seems to confirm Rattinger's conclusions that action-reaction processes were significantly more discernible in NATO countries' expenditures than in those of Warsaw Pact members. Similarly, in analyzing some pre-World War II data, Lucier (1979) found clear parameter shifts associated with some changes in political administrations within the same country. Gillespie *et al.* (1980) indeed suggest the extreme sensitivity of American and Soviet perceptions of each other's constraints and intentions; slight changes in parameters have the potential to set off an explosive arms race.

It is reasonable, after all, to expect that domestic politics do matter. Certain leaders or administrations may be more tolerant of military spending by the other side, or less willing to divert funds from domestic civilian needs, than are others. We have seen it clearly with the advent of the Reagan administration, which has taken decisions to shift spending from civilian to military purposes to a degree that is unprecedented for the United States (Russett, 1982). This was a deliberate political choice, though observers can disagree as to the degree to which it reflects the change in the administration per se, or the degree to which it reflects a broader shift in domestic political preferences — of which the administration would be only the agent — that in turn may be rooted in the higher level of international political tensions. Some might argue, furthermore, that high international tensions themselves have resulted from the change in the administration. Cause and effect are not readily distinguishable here. Moreover, similar sharp shifts in either Soviet or American military spending are not discernible for previous changes in political administrations of either country. One must beware, therefore, of ad hoc "political" explanations and dig carefully to find the driving components.

We need, therefore, more careful specification of what is meant by domestic or internal influence. Is it basically just a matter of bureaucratic politics or organizational inertia, in effect captured by the autoregressive term in our equations, predicting that this year's budget will be like last year's, only a little more? Despite the apparent plausibility of this explanation for some of the cold war period, it does not hold for all years, especially in the post-Vietnam years of the early and mid-1970s in the United States, when the force of bureaucratic inertia was substantially if temporarily reduced. Nor did the actual drop in American military spending produce comparable restraint by the Soviet Union, as the action-reaction proponents would have us expect. (We would not, however, expect prompt Soviet restraint if weapon stocks were the key variable.) At the beginning of the 1980s, fiscal constraints seemed to be lifted, and a new organizational momentum established. If the auto-regressive expectation is to be modified—damped, as after Vietnam, or perhaps magnified, as under Reagan—how do we explain these political phenomena? Moreover, can we generalize about internal political phenomena as themselves reflecting or responding to regularly changing political or economic conditions?

We can now say, with confidence, that internal processes do matter, and matter a great deal. All levels of analysis (Russett & Starr, 1982) are engaged. This conclusion has important implications not just for academic study, but for political efforts to achieve arms control or disarmament. The most sophisticated negotiations to bring international action-reaction processes under control are doomed if they do not also take into consideration the realities of bureaucratic inertia and wider domestic political processes. Individual actors within governments will change, bringing new motivations and different responses to various stimuli. Individuals may change their motivations. Force planners and political leaders typically develop a sense of strategy. Rather than merely mechanically act and react to their opposite numbers in another state, they will anticipate reactions in ways like those suggested by game theory.[5]

All this requires some retreat from hopes of deriving general and relatively simple propositions about the universal relative importance of internal vs. external influences on arms races. The relatively simple expectations of the early researchers have given way, with the slow accretion of knowledge, to very complex expressions of understanding. The phenomena sometimes called "arms races" are more varied than we might like, and will resist the parsimonious explanations that we would surely like. The implications of this will not necessarily please "realists," and they may be more satisfying to students of comparative foreign policy than to students of international systems.

ECONOMIC AND SOCIAL EFFECTS OF DEPENDENCE

The body of work known as dependency literature[6] has been concerned with the effects of foreign penetration on third world countries. Specifically, proponents of one version or another of this concept contend that economic and cultural penetration of third world countries, incorporating them into the global capitalist system, creates distortions in economic, political, and social conditions. Operating over a substantial historical period, the agents of foreign capital interact with local classes under conditions that vary in different times and in different types of countries. Thus the structure of the world economy, combined with the structure of class relations in third world states, in varying forms and degrees leads to new forms of state organization, intense class conflict, and harsh state repression in those states. External and internal influences are held to interact. Like the arms acquisition literature, the dependency literature is rife with controversy over their relative importance.

The more recent contributions to dependency writing have focused chiefly on the intensification of class conflict and the growth of a state coercive apparatus. Class conflict in dependent societies is seen as resulting from great and frequently growing inequalities within and between classes, that in turn are viewed as a consequence of distorted patterns of economic development. Earlier contributions to the dependency perspective, however, were concerned also with the degree of economic growth. Frank (1972), for example, argued that penetration by foreign capital had the overall effect of depressing economic growth; while it of course might promote growth in certain sectors of the economy, overall it permitted the expropriation of surplus capital and discouraged the formation of local capital in those sectors of the economy that had promise of self-sustained, autonomous growth. This argument was in part supported by economists working with the Economic Commission for Latin America (ECLA) (see Prebisch, 1963) who, though not strictly dependency theorists, contributed to the tradition. They saw the economic stagnation typical of Latin American economies during the late 1950s as a result of excessive concentration on producing primary commodities for which the terms of trade had declined drastically after the Korean War. The solution, according to these observers, was to develop manufacturing industries for local markets, thus encouraging the growth of a dynamic sector by import substitution and some insulation from the interests of foreign capital. Later dependency writers (e.g., Cardoso, 1973) have shifted both the argument and the conclusion. They have argued that the penetration of foreign capital may well promote economic growth per se, in the sense of a more rapid rate of growth in GNP per capita, but nevertheless contributes to distortions in development, inequalities, and the loss of "popular" control over the pattern of that development.

We cannot review all these arguments here, nor consider the body of research that now bears on these questions. Some of the most interesting involve the role of the state and the interaction of insurgency and state coercion under the influence of foreign penetration, a topic on which little conclusive research has yet been done. (But see Duvall et al., 1982; Duvall et al., 1981; Freeman & Duvall, 1983; et al., 1983; and Russett et al., forthcoming.) Instead, we shall focus on two particular questions which probably have been the subject of the largest body of systematic empirical research to date: the effect of penetration by foreign capital on rates of growth in peripheral countries, and the effect of that penetration on patterns of inequality. Both of these questions have been investigated extensively, especially by North American scholars heavily influenced by the "positivist" quantitative research tradition common on this continent.

The attempt to estimate equations for propositions from the positivist perspective, using cross-national data from the last two decades, bears many intellectual resemblances to the arms race modelling tradition we have just reviewed. As we shall see, it also shares many of the same difficulties. It must be recognized that much of the writing in the dependency tradition treats dependence as a contextual condition, rather than as a ready set of propositions for cross-national quantitative analyses (Caporaso, 1978; Duvall, 1978).

Nevertheless it still is fair to treat the dependency perspective as a source of ideas from which testable hypotheses can be generated.

Dependence and Growth

The relationship between foreign penetration and economic growth is not one of the central concerns of dependence theory as it can now be understood, but it has nevertheless been important in the development of that body of literature. Moreover, it is the aspect of that theory on which the largest body of cross-national aggregate-data analysis exists in sociology and political science.

By now there is nearly unanimous agreement that, at least in the short term, penetration by foreign capital is associated with higher rates of overall economic growth as measured by GNP per capita or, occasionally, by per capita energy consumption. A positive relationship between the inflow of foreign capital and economic growth has been found in almost every cross-national investigation of less developed countries (LDCs): Bornschier, 1981b; Bornschier, 1980; Bornschier *et al.*, 1978; Dolan and Tomlin, 1980; Jackman, 1982; Kaufman *et al.*, 1975; Mahler, 1980; Papanek, 1972/73; Ray and Webster, 1978; Stoneman, 1975; Szymanski, 1976. This relationship holds for various measures of financial penetration, though the most common is net foreign investment. The only exceptions seem to be early studies by Stevenson (1972) and Alschuler (1976) limited to Latin American countries only, and a study by Rubinson (1977) which included *all* non-socialist countries in the sample (i.e., developed capitalist industrial economies as well as LDCs). While the latter may provide some useful information, it is inadmissable as a test of conditions in LDCs. Dependence theory clearly is concerned only with the latter—and, indeed, only with capitalist, market economies, not with socialist economies like Cuba or North Korea.

It should be noted, however, that the data themselves merely point to the fact of a positive relationship, not necessarily to a causal relationship. That is, one may contend that the inflow of foreign capital contributes to or makes possible the subsequent economic growth, or that the foreign capital is attracted precisely to those countries that would have grown most rapidly in any case. It is common in these studies to include GNP per capita in the equation as a control variable in order to see whether the effects of foreign penetration are different in poor LDCs than in middle-income countries, but it is very rare to see previous growth rate entered as a control. Nonetheless, there is reasonable theoretical agreement that the short-run effect of an inflow of capital may well be a spurt in growth.

The consensus on the short-term effects of foreign penetration dissolves when we move to the long-term effects. In the arms acquisition literature we found that the relationships that held for flow could be very different from those for stocks. Here too, it is one thing to talk about the flow of capital, another to discuss the effects of an accumulated stock of foreign capital. The majority of studies hold that the long-term effect of capital penetration is to retard economic growth to a rate below that which would apply in the absence of foreign capital. But the situation is theoretically as well as methodologically complex, eluding full agreement.

The argument that a large accumulated stock of foreign capital depresses subsequent growth has been supported most extensively by Volker Bornschier and his colleagues (Bornschier, 1981b; Bornschier, 1980; Bornschier & Ballmer-Cao, 1979; Bornschier *et al.*, 1978; Bornschier, 1975). Their findings are reinforced by similar findings reported by Dolan and Tomlin (1980), and Gobalet and Diamond (1979), as well as earlier and less sophisticated work by Stoneman (1975) and Evans (1972) on Latin America alone.

Bornschier contends that the fundamental mechanism is penetration by multinational corporations (MNCs), attracted by intervention by the state in less developed countries to provide infrastructure, subsidies, protective tariffs, tax exemptions, and so on. This investment will be concentrated in industries where MNCs have already gained an advantage with their advanced technology in developed countries (e.g., manufacturing). But because of the small absolute size of LDC markets and the highly skewed distribution of personal income in those countries, MNCs are unable to create indigenous mass markets for their products. Sometimes foreign investment will move into industries directed toward external sales, often to developed countries—the export platform phenomenon (see, for example, Caporaso, 1981). But if the appropriate conditions, such as a skilled, well-disciplined local labor force and state incentives, do not exist, initial investment in all but the largest LDCs is not likely to spread into other sectors. Overall foreign investment will slacken, MNCs will divert their new investment to other countries, and repatriation of earnings will become substantial. Meanwhile, MNC penetration into what had been the dynamic sectors will have discouraged investment by local capitalists who cannot effectively compete with the advanced technology, ample capital, and vertically integrated markets of the modern MNC, and diverted state capital formation into infrastructure supporting the MNCs' investments. Once MNC investment slackens, relative stagnation results.

At first Bornschier *et al.* (1978) maintained, supported by Dolan and Tomlin, that this effect was stronger in the relatively well-to-do LDCs, a conclusion disputed by Gobalet and Diamond (1979). Reanalysis by Bornschier (1981b), Bornschier (1980) and Bornschier and Chase-Dunn (forthcoming) suggests that the income effect is spurious because of the substantial correlation, among LDCs, of income with market size. Once the smallest—and usually poorest—LDCs are excluded from the analysis, writes Bornschier, the interaction of MNC penetration with wealth on growth rates essentially vanishes. Bornschier also reports that the growth-reducing efforts of an accumulated stock of MNC capital are greatest in countries where that investment has been concentrated in manufacturing and mining, where MNCs' technological advantage is likely to have been greatest.

As we have indicated, these results are not free from controversy. Among those with seemingly contradictory findings, we may dismiss the early studies (such as Papanek, 1972/73) and especially those with samples limited to particular geographical areas (Kaufman *et al.*, 1975; McGowan & Smith, 1978; Ray & Webster, 1978; Szymanski, 1976). All of these suffer from methodological limitations whose details need not concern us here. A more serious challenge appears, however, in Jackman (1982), and in a critique of Bornschier's most recent article by Szymanski (1984). Jackman concludes not only that the flow of investment is positively related to growth, but that among the poorer LDCs even the stock of foreign investment is positively related to growth. He argues that the apparent negative relation of foreign investment stocks to growth washes out when one controls for total population. Population may here be seen as a surrogate for market size (total GNP would have been better) since Jackman argues that the possibility of economies of scale is what promotes growth. He also argues that it is unchecked population growth, not MNC penetration, that restrains per capita growth, and that one must control for birth rates. But as Bornschier (1984) points out, Jackman's results are untrustworthy because his equation is mis-specified. Jackman's dependent variable is per capita income growth 1960-78, yet his data for stock of foreign investment are for 1967 — the latter could hardly be responsible for growth between 1960 and 1967.

Szymanski (1984) contends that by "controlling" for the "spurious effects" of investment in mining and manufacturing, and for the volume of total *domestic* capital formation, Bornschier in fact eliminated the mechanism by which economic growth in most LDCs now is driven — the *reinvestment* of local earnings and the mobilization of local capital. Szymanski nevertheless accepts Bornschier's basic empirical finding while disputing the process which purportedly explains it: Szymanski declares that whereas *among* countries dependent on foreign technology and entrepreneurship those with more MNC investment grow faster; the fastest growing LDC market economies are those with relatively little MNC investment, but with locally funded accumulation and a technologically advanced domestic private sector (e.g., the Asian MICs). Bornschier (1984) nevertheless holds that a significant relationship remains even without the "controls," though it is weaker. It should be noted furthermore that many results (e.g., Bornschier, 1981) that are statistically significant nevertheless seem to have coefficients that are quite small relative to the size of the phenomena in question. That is, the actual "impact" of a variable like MNC penetration may be very small relative to the amount of growth actually occurring.[7]

A further critique (Weede & Tiefenbach, 1981c) maintained that Bornschier's findings virtually washed out with different specifications of the model, notably with inclusion of the relative size of a state's military establishment. Bornschier (1982) nevertheless replied that Weede and Tiefenbach mis-specified the model by using a growth rate initiated before the investment, and by failing to control for the short-term positive effect of a continuing inflow of investment. With these corrections, says Bornschier, his results hold whether or not there is a control for the size of the military. A further reply of Weede and Tiefenbach (1982) seems to me not to be compelling, though it does emphasize the sensitivity of all these results to methodological and theoretical decisions in the analysis.

The controversy doubtless hangs in part on the vagaries of cross-national aggregate data analysis with fairly small and sometimes varying samples. Such statistical analyses are very sensitive to what seems to be minor specification error in the equations, and to the effects of outliers or the exclusion of particular cases. There also is the possibility that analyses will show different results for different periods of time. Recall our earlier conclusion about the arms race studies; here the cause might be, not the change of regime in a single national actor, but fundamental shifts in the mechanisms operating in the world economy. For example, Dos Santos (1970) among many others, identified a period of "new dependence" when the most potent mechanisms of foreign penetration had shifted first from trade to direct private investment, and then from direct investment to the sale of core countries' technology and the accumulation of vast public debt to commercial banks. It would therefore not be surprising if one measure (e.g., direct investment by MNCs) were to show different results at different times. However, that does *not* appear to be the case in any regular way with these studies.

The debate can correctly be seen as one requiring more careful specification of the theoretical model underlying empirical analyses. This is not just a matter of the need for sophisticated measures of concepts or of incorporating appropriate controls into the analysis, but of recognizing the importance of different contexts, and the mediating effects of key variables. Form and structure of explanation will vary. That is, foreign capital affects growth rates not in some mechanical accounting manner, but by provoking, channeling, or stifling state initiative, by stimulating or repressing entrepreneurial and savings decisions by classes within the LDC, and by enriching certain classes and groups at the relative or absolute expense of others. Only if these processes are recognized — allowed for in the model specification, and the empirical results interpreted in light of reasonable interpretations of such processes — can we hope to obtain robust and intellectually compelling findings.

Our own empirical work on this topic illustrates both the need and the difficulty.[8] We did not investigate the short-term effects of capitalist penetration at all, but instead concentrated on the effects of an accumulated stock of capital, as in the Bornschier formulation. Then, instead of relating stock to economic growth in a simple manner, we employed a distributed lag formulation on the principle that dependence theory typically was concerned with the effects of the history of penetration over time, and that the progressively decaying effect captured by the distributed lag most nearly reflected that history. Furthermore, our concern was with capitalist penetration, broadly conceived, from the industrialized countries; hence our measure was a complex one incorporating not just direct foreign investment, but all foreign debt, the stock of imported capital goods, and relative reliance on the stock of "disembodied" foreign capital: licenses, patents, and trademarks (see Jackson, 1979).

Our results were not the same as those of earlier analyses. For example, we found that among most LDCs (all but the most prosperous ones) capitalist penetration seemed to result in higher rates of GNP per capita growth during the period 1970-75. Moreover, this effect was not only a direct one, but part of a process whereby capitalist penetration typically increased the concentration of commodity exports during this period, and the concentration of commodity exports in turn was associated with higher average income levels. This seemed to indicate that capitalist penetration strove to promote greater commodity exports in response to the boom in commodity prices during this period, and that swelled export earnings and thus raised average incomes in these countries. This interpretation seems statistically robust (not subject to distortion by outliers or modest variations in the functional forms of specified relationships), and it is supported by partial results elsewhere in the literature. For example, the direct relationship of capitalist penetration to growth holds for the poorer countries, but not the richer ones, where it is negative in our data base. (But this applies to a group of only seven countries, and we are not inclined to make much of it.) Bornschier *et al.* (1978) and Dolan and Tomlin (1980) found the negative effects of foreign investment significantly stronger in the richer LDCs than in the poor ones, though Bornschier later dismissed that as spurious. We do not feel confident that we have fully understood the processes by which this happened. Clearly resource base, local conditions, and "history" do matter.

Dependence and Inequality

We can turn from the puzzle over the effects of capitalist penetration on growth to a seemingly more consensual set of findings on the effect of that penetration on the distribution of income within LDCs. Save for an early and flawed study (Tyler & Wogart, 1973) that found no significant relationship, until recently there was unanimous agreement that penetration resulted in greater inequality. Most of the relevant studies concerned the effects of financial penetration, i.e. investment (Bornschier & Chase-Dunn, 1984; Bornschier, 1981; Bornschier & Ballmer-Cao, 1979; Bornschier, 1978; Bornschier *et al.*, 1978; Bornschier, 1975; Chase-Dunn, 1975; Evans & Timberlake, 1980; Kaufman *et al.*, 1975; Mahler, 1980; and Rubinson, 1976), but others used as independent variables trade concentration (Galtung, 1971; Dolan & Tomlin, 1980; Jackman, 1975; Ahn, 1981), exports as a percentage of GDP (Stack, 1978), and a measure of position in the global hierarchy (Ward, 1978). No study has found foreign penetration having the effect of reducing inequality.

Recently there has been some challenge to this consensus. Dolan and Tomlin (1980) reported no relationship, and Weede (1980) has reported some reanalyses of others' results with a different specification. All of the more substantial studies have included a linear control for income level when analyzing the effect of penetration on inequality, in consideration of the well-known negative relationship between income level and inequality among poor and not-so-poor LDCs. Weede insists that when this control is properly specified (that is, with a polynomial function, as derived by Ahluwalia, 1976) the control then becomes stronger, and takes up much of the effect otherwise attributed to penetration. He reports (Weede, 1980; Weede & Tiefenbach, 1981b) the positive relationship turns into an insignificant one in Rubinson's work on trade, and in Bornschier's (1981b) work on foreign investment. Bornschier retorts (1981a) that his relationship still holds for LDCs—though not for a sample of countries at all levels of development—and even more clearly when an improved measure of foreign penetration is used. Weede and Tiefenbach (1981b) reply with a caution about changing indicators in midstream, the need for examining multiple indicators, and the need for careful conceptualization before measurement. Bornschier's finding of a positive relationship even with the Weede polynomial specification is supported by Timberlake and Williams (1982) and by recent work on the effects of concentration of export commodity markets (Stack & Zimmerman, 1982).

We also found a positive impact of capitalist penetration on inequality, but the relationship is not a simple one. One route is through the interaction of capitalist penetration with what we call, from the dependence literature, uneven development (differences in wage rates by productive sector). Among the poorest LDCs this interactive term has almost no effect on inequality, but in the richer ones the positive impact on inequality is substantial. This is essentially what we originally hypothesized.

More puzzling, however, is the evidence for a chain of influence that runs through marginalization. Marginalization is defined as "the extent to which groups are incapable of maintaining their economic position in society." By this we mean both the stagnation of living standards over time (measured by real wages) and the creation of a "reserve army of the unemployed," especially the urban unemployed (measured by the share of economic activity accounted for by wages). We found that capitalist penetration, interacting with what we termed economic heterogeneity (differences in output per worker in different economic sectors) usually had the consequence of reducing marginalization. On examining the cases, we inferred that capitalist penetration did this in two ways. When concentrated in the rural areas, especially for industry or extractive enterprises, it had some job-creating effect that slowed the migration of surplus agricultural workers to the cities where they often joined the ranks of urban unemployed in the shantytowns. When concentrated in the urban areas, it did have employment-creating effects in those areas that had already attracted rural migrants—although a fairly modest effect, as is rather typical of capital-intensive invetment. More surprising is a subsequent negative link from marginalization to inequality. This seems counter-intuitive, and certainly is not what most dependence theorists—or we—would expect. It is interpretable, however, especially if we recognize that our measure of inequality is, unlike that of virtually all the studies reviewed above except Ward's (1978), concerned with welfare instead of simply income. It reflects equality in access to sanitation and health care (see Russett et al., 1981). Effectively the relationship captures the fact that marginalized people, driven from rural areas to urban shantytowns, have not necessarily worsened their material conditions broadly defined. Shantytowns, however miserable, are at least part of urban areas where some public health care *may* be available—it may simply be non-existent in the countryside— and where, especially in the last decade or so, many LDC governments have made efforts to provide *some* of the basics for decent existence, such as piped water.

Hence the two negative links may combine to create a complex positive relationship. That is, penetration reduces marginalization, but because marginalization is negatively related to inequality, less marginalization means greater inequality: thus increased penetration increases inequality! This is surprising to us, and we do not want to over-emphasize its importance. It does not rule out the likelihood that the more direct positive relationship usually hypothesized in the dependence literature (capitalist penetration creating a rich bourgeoisie and small labor aristocracy while exploiting masses of poorly- or sporadically-employed workers) also applies. But it does require anyone writing on this topic to reexamine her or his ideas about the processes and class relations underlying these aggregate statistical relationships. It demands that the largely cross-sectional aggregate data analyses be enriched and inter- preted by intensive case studies of changes over time in individual countries. The aggregate data analysis, in its turn, provides some hints for new hypotheses to apply in carrying out those case studies.

CONCLUSIONS

Three conclusions need to be stated. First, in the analysis of situations of dependence the importance of varying conditions within LDCs (size, colonial history, nature and time of foreign penetration, resources, etc.) is apparent; the process is not simply one of external penetration producing reliable regularities everywhere. Clearly this shows the importance of detailed country-specific knowledge, and the country-specialist's familiarity with the details of a particular economy, society, and polity. This is chastening for those of us—international relations specialists or students of the world system —who saw ourselves as striking a blow for the importance of international processes in what had often previously been treated as the largely intra- country analysis of political development. It also emphasizes the role of trans- national actors (particularly MNCs) also traditionally neglected in a "realist" perspective. These complexities are reminiscent of those that emerged in the arms acquisition analyses, where we found "realist" assumptions equally naive.

To be sure, we find patterns of behavior that are complex, interactive, and heavily conditioned; nevertheless they do yield generalizations and regularities. It is *not* the ideographic extreme of "every country so different that no general regularities can be derived." The theoretical and methodological sophistication now built into more than a decade of sys- tematic empirical investigation is beginning to produce some results. As we understand the relationships we can hold the results with greater confidence.

Second, some of the empirical findings reviewed in this chapter, both in the analysis of dependence and that of arms acquisitions, emerge as counter- intuitive. Thus they require a continual re-examination of our hypotheses in a way that is sensitive to these contextual differences. We may still refer to our efforts as hypothesis-testing, but it is not quite a matter of always rigorously deriving our hypotheses from a full deductive system. It is more a matter of working in a tentative, continual "re-modelling" fashion, where we revise our hypotheses to take into account varying contexts. The acceptance or rejection of hypotheses is rarely clear-cut. In one sense the experience reminds me of the caution sounded quite a while ago by Hayward Alker (1966) in countering critics of early mathematical applications to international relations: a good theorist does not expect most relationships to be simple (linear, bivariate, without exception). The world is complex—but the mathematics can handle that complexity if we will allow it to do so. In another sense the experience reminds me of what goes on in most other disciplines, from the practice of a historian to that of a biochemist who must take into account genetics and environment as conditioning factors in the processes (s)he would study. A carcinogen may produce cancer only in a particular patient who has an inherited predisposition and an aggravating environmental influence. Being systematic means expecting complexity.

Finally, the inability of "realist" assumptions to capture reality accurately suggests fundamental consequences. In the realm of theory, it requires us to give more attention to perspectives that can explicate the behavior of thinking, perceiving, choosing actors; actors who can behave strategically, anticipating the choices of other actors. In the realm of norms, it requires us to surmount the determinism often associated with "realism," and provides us with opportunities to specify patterns of behavior that are different from, and alternatives to, those of a global system composed predominately of nation-state actors.

NOTES

1. This review is based on a search of what we judged to be the 14 most relevant journals for the past five years, plus review articles, books, unpublished papers, and other articles known to us. Also helpful was a review article by Intriligator (1982). Our review is perhaps not exhaustive, nor have we cited here everything that we examined. The goal is not to provide a complete set of bibliographical citations, but to cover the major contributions and improvements that have been made to the systematic empirical study of arms races. We concentrate on the Soviet-American arms acquisition process because of its importance and the intense study it has received. Other pairs of states' relations are in some ways simpler, in others (for example, their penetration by super-power influence) more complex.

2. The computing algorithm is also much more sophisticated than those usually employed, and better than ordinary least squares, but in this review I am choosing to concentrate on matters of concept and measure rather than computational technique. The choice of the latter does matter greatly, but involves yet another set of issues.

3. I am grateful to Jim Lindsay for this observation. Stoll (1982) notes that a negative coefficient is likely to occur in cases where one country attempts to maintain some particular percentage ratio over an opponent.

4. One element in Ward's success is his return to the continuous framework of Richardson's differential equations, whereas most other arms race modelers have instead employed the discrete version of difference equations.

5. There have been efforts to derive models based on rational and optimizing assumptions (for example, Simaan & Cruz, 1975, and Schrodt, 1976), but few empirical tests save for Gillespie et al. (1977) where the optimal-control model seems to add little in the Soviet-American case, and Wallace and Wilson (1978) who do not give us the estimated coefficients for their equations.

6. To maintain clarity between the various conceptualizations of this literature, I will distinguish between its main sections by calling one "the dependency perspective (outlook or approach)" and the other "dependence theory." Dependency analysis precedes dependence theory chronologically and includes such authors as Cardoso, Dos Santos, and Gunder Frank. It is written predominantly by Latin Americans and uses a dialectical or "structural-historical" method of analysis. In contrast, dependence theorists use quantitative statistical methods to create rigorous theories

and sub-theories that are derived from the conceptualizations of the dependency perspective. Dependence theorists include Bornschier, Chase-Dunn, Mahler, and Rubinson. When speaking of both sections of this work, I will call it "dependency literature." This chapter focuses on dependence theory.

7. I am grateful to Steve Silvia for this observation.

8. I will here report only briefly on some of the findings emerging from the collective project on which a group of us has been engaged for some years, to be reported in Russett, Duvall, Jackson, Snidal, and Sylvan, forthcoming. It is not possible to report on a complex data analysis sufficiently here, nor would it be appropriate for me to do so, in an essay signed by me alone, on a project that has been so truly collaborative.

REFERENCES

Ahluwalia, M. S. Inequality, poverty and development. *Journal of Development Economics,* 1976, *3,* 307-342.

Ahn, Chung-Si. *Social development and political violence.* Seoul: Seoul National University Press, 1981.

Albrecht, Ulrich, *et al. A short research guide on arms and armed forces.* London: Croom, Helm, 1978.

Alker, Hayward R., Jr. The long road to international relations theory: Problems of statistical nonadditivity. *World Politics,* 1966, *18,* 623-655.

Allison, Graham. What fuels the arms race? In Robert L. Pfaltzgraff (Ed.). *Contrasting approaches to strategic arms control.* Lexington, MA: D.C. Heath, 1974.

Alschuler, L. Satellization and stagnation in Latin America. *International Studies Quarterly,* 1976, *20,* 39-82.

Ashley, R. K. *The political economy of war and peace.* London: Frances Pinter, 1980.

Azar, Edward. The conflict and peace data bank (COPDAB) project. *Journal of Conflict Resolution,* 1980, *24,* 143-152.

Bishop, William J., & Sorenson, David S. Superpower defense expenditures and foreign policy. In Charles W. Kegley, Jr., & Pat McGowan (Eds.). *Foreign policy USA/USSR.* Beverly Hills, CA: Sage, 1982.

Bornschier, V. Abhaengige industrialisierung und einkommensentwicklung. *Schweizeriche Zeitschift fuer Soziologie,* 1975, *1,* 67-105.

Bornschier, V. Multinational corporations and economic growth: A cross-national test of the decapitalization thesis. *Journal of Development Economics,* 1980, *7,* 191-210.

Bornschier, V. Comment. *International Studies Quarterly,* 1981, *25,* 283-288. (a)

Bornschier, V. Dependent industrialization in the world economy. *Journal of Conflict Resolution,* 1981, *25,* 371-400. (b)

Bornschier, V. Dependence on foreign capital and economic growth: A reply to Weede and Tiefenbach's critique. *European Journal of Political Research,* 1982, *10,* 445-450.

Bornschier, V. Reply to Szymanski. *Journal of Conflict Resolution,* 1984, *28.*

Bornschier, V., Chase-Dunn, C. & Rubinson, R. Cross-national evidence of the effects of foreign investment and aid on economic growth and inequality: A survey of findings and a reanalysis. *American Journal of Sociology,* 1978, *84,* 651-683.

Bornschier, V., & Chase-Dunn, C. *Core corporations and underdevelopment.* Forthcoming.

Bornschier, V., & Ballmer-Cao, Th.-H. Income inequality: A cross-national study of the relationships between MNC penetration, dimensions of the power structure and income distribution. *American Sociological Review,* 1979, *44,* 487-506.

Busch, P. Appendix: Mathematical models of arms races. In Bruce Russett. *What price vigilance? The burdens of national defense.* New Haven, CT: Yale University Press, 1970.

Caporaso, James. Dependence, dependency, and power in the global system: A structural and behavioral analysis. *International Organization,* 1978, *32,* 13-43.

Caporaso, James. Industrialization in the periphery: The evolving global division of labor. *International Studies Quarterly,* 1981, *25,* 347-384.

Cardoso, F. H. Associated-dependent development: Theoretical and practical implications. In Alfred Stepan (Ed.). *Authoritarian Brazil.* New Haven: Yale University Press, 1973.

Chase-Dunn, C. The effects of international economic dependence on development and inequality. *American Sociological Review,* 1975, *40,* 720-738.

Choucri, Nazli & North, Robert. *Nations in conflict: National growth and international violence.* San Francisco: W.H. Freeman, 1975.

Cordesman, Anthony H. Measuring the strategic balance: Secretary of Defense Brown as an American oracle. *Comparative Strategy,* 1982, *3,* 187-218.

Crecine, J. P. Defense budgeting: Organizational adaptation to environmental constraints. In R. F. Byrne, *et al.* (Eds.). *Studies in budgeting.* Amsterdam: North Holland Publishing, 1971.

Cusack, T. R. & Ward, M. D. Military spending in the United States, Soviet Union, and the People's Republic of China. *Journal of Conflict Resolution,* 1981, *25,* 429-469.

Davis, O., Dempster, M., & Wildavsky, A. A theory of the budgetary process. *American Political Science Review,* 1966, *60,* 529-547.

Dolan, M. B. & Tomlin, B. W. First world-third world linkages: The effects of external relations upon economic growth, imbalance and inequality in developing countries. *International Organization,* 1980, *34,* 41-63.

Domke, William, Eichenberg, Richard & Kelleher, Catherine. The illusion of choice: Defense and welfare in advanced industrial democracies. *American Political Science Review,* 1983, *77,* 19-35.

Dos Santos, Theotonio. The structure of dependence. *American Economic Review,* 1970, *60,* 231-236.

Duvall, Raymond, Dependence and dependencia theory: Notes toward precision of concept and argument. *International Organization,* 1978, *32,* 51-78.

Duvall, Raymond, Jackson, Steven, Russett, Bruce, Snidal, Duncan, & Sylvan, David. A formal model of 'dependencia' theory: Structure and measurement. In Richard Merritt & Bruce Russett (Eds.). *From national development to global community.* London: Allen and Unwin, 1981.

Duvall, Raymond, Jackson, Steven, Russett, Bruce, Snidal, Duncan & Sylvan, David. From state coercion to insurgency and back in dependent societies. Paper presented to the World Congress of the International Political Science Association, Rio de Janeiro, 1982.

Evans, P. The development effects of direct investment. Paper read at the Annual Meeting of the American Sociological Association, New Orleans, 1972.

Evans, P., & Timberlake, M. Dependence, inequality, and the growth of tertiary: A comparative analysis of less developed countries. *American Sociological Review,* 1980, *45,* 531-552.

Fischer, G. W., & Crecine, J. Patrick. Defense budgets, fiscal policy, domestic spending and arms races. Paper presented to the Annual Meeting of the American Political Science Association, Washington, D.C., 1979.

Fischer, Gregory W., & Kamlet, Mark. Explaining presidential priorities: The competing aspiration levels model of macrobudgetary decision making. *American Political Science Review,* 1983, *77.*

Frank, Andre Gunder. *Lumpenbourgeoisie and lumpendevelopment: Dependence, class, and politics in Latin America.* New York: Monthly Review Press, 1972.

Freeman, John. Granger causality and the time series analysis of political relationships. *American Journal of Political Science,* 1983, *27,* 327-358.

Freeman, John, & Duvall, Raymond. The techno-bureaucratic state and the entrepreneurial state in dependent industrialization. *American Political Science Review,* 1983, *77.*

Galtung, J. A structural theory of imperialism. *Journal of Peace Research,* 1971, *8,* 81-117.

Gillespie, J., Zinnes, D. & Rubinson, M. Accumulation in arms race models: A geometric lag perspective. *Comparative Political Studies,* 1978, *10,* 475-496.

Gillespie, J., Zinnes, D. A., Schrodt, P. A., Tahim, G. S. & Rubinson, R. M. An optimal control model of arms races. *American Political Science Review,* 1977, *71,* 226-244.

Gillespie, John V., Zinnes, Dina, Schrodt, Philip & Tahim, G. S. Sensitivity analysis of an armaments race model. In Pat McGowan & Charles W. Kegley (Eds.). *Threats, weapons, and foreign policy.* Beverly Hills, CA: Sage, 1980.

Gobalet, J. & Diamond, L. Effects of investment dependence on economic growth. *International Studies Quarterly,* 1979, *23,* 412-444.

Gregory, P. Economic growth, U.S. defense expenditures and the Soviet budget. *Soviet Studies,* 1974, *26,* 72-80.

Halperin, Morton H. *Bureaucratic politics and foreign policy.* Washington, D.C.: Brookings Institution, 1974.

Hamblin, R. L., Hout, M., Miller, J. L. L. & Pitcher, B. L. Arms races: A test of two models. *American Sociological Review,* 1977, *42,* 338-354.

Hollist, W. L. Alternative explanations of competitive arms processes: Tests on four pairs of nations. *American Journal of Political Science,* 1977, *21,* 313-340. (a)

Hollist, W. L. An analysis of arms processes in the United States and the Soviet Union. *International Studies Quarterly,* 1977, *21,* 503-528. (b)

Hollist, W. L. & Guetzkow, H. Cumulative research in international relations: Empirical analysis and computer simulation of competitive arms processes. In W. L. Hollist (Ed.). *Exploring competitive arms processes: Applications of mathematical modeling and computer simulation in arms policy analysis.* New York: Marcel Dekker, 1978.

Hollist, W. Ladd, & Johnson, Thomas H. Political-economic competition: Three alternative simulations. In Charles W. Kegley, Jr., & Pat McGowan (Eds.). *Foreign Policy USA/USSR.* Beverly Hills, CA: Sage, 1982.

Holzman, Franklin. Are the Soviets really outspending the U.S. on defense? *International Security,* 1980, *4,* 86-104.

Holzman, Franklin. Soviet military spending: Addressing the numbers game. *International Security,* 1982, *6,* 78-102.

Imhoff, Andre, Luterbacher, Urs & Allan, Pierre. SIMPEST: A simulation model of political, economic, and strategic interaction among major powers. Paper presented at the World Congress of the International Political Science Association, Moscow, 1979.

Intriligator, Michael. Research on conflict theory: Analytic approaches and areas of application. *Journal of Conflict Resolution,* 1982, *26,* 307-327.

Jackman, R. W. Dependence on foreign investment and economic growth in the third world. *World Politics,* 1982, *34,* 175-196.

Jackson, Steven. Capitalist penetration: Concept and measurement. *Journal of Peace Research,* 1978, *16,* 41-55.

Kaufman, R., Geller, D. & Chernotsky, H. A preliminary test of the theory of dependency. *Comparative Politics,* 1975, *7,* 303-330.

Keohane, Robert O. Theory of world politics: Structural realism and beyond. Chapter in this volume, 1983.

Kugler, J., & Organski, A. F. K., with D. J. Fox. Deterrence and the arms race: The impotence of power. *International Security*, 1980, *4*, 105-138.

Lambelet, J. Towards a dynamic two-theater model of the east-west arms race. *Journal of Peace Science*, 1973, 1-37.

Lambelet, J., & Luterbacher, U., with P. Allan. Dynamics of arms races: Mutual stimulation vs. self-stimulation. *Journal of Peace Science*, 1979, *4*, 49-66.

Lucier, C. Changes in the value of arms race parameters. *Journal of Conflict Resolution*, 1979, *23*, 17-39.

Luterbacher, Urs. Arms race models: Where do we stand? *European Journal of Political Research*, 1975, *3*, 199-217.

Luterbacher, Urs. Towards a convergence of behavioral and strategic conceptions of the arms race: The case of American and Soviet ICBM build-up. *Papers of Peace Science Society (International)*, 1976, *26*, 1-21

Mahler, Vincent. *Dependency approaches to international political economy*. New York: Columbia University Press, 1980.

Majeski, S., & Jones, D. Arms race modeling: Causality analysis and model specification. *Journal of Conflict Resolution*, 1981, *25*, 259-288.

McGowan, P. J. & Smith, D. L. Economic dependency in black Africa: An analysis of competing theories. *International Organization*, 1978, *32*, 179-236.

McGuire, M. C. A quantitative study of the strategic arms race in the missile age. *Review of Economics and Statistics*, 1977, *59*, 328-339.

Moll, Kendall. International conflict as a decision system. *Journal of Conflict Resolution*, 1974, *18*, 555-557.

Moll, Kendall, & Luebbert, Gregory. Arms race and military expenditure models: A review. *Journal of Conflict Resolution*, 1980, *24*, 153-185.

Nincic, Miroslav. *The arms race: The political economy of military growth*. New York: Praeger, 1982.

Nincic, Miroslav. Fluctuations in Soviet defense spending: A research note. *Journal of Conflict Resolution*, 1983, *27*.

Nincic, Miroslav, & Cusack, T. R. The political economy of U.S. military spending. *Journal of Peace Research*, 1979, *16*, 101-115.

Ostrich, John T., Jr. & Green, William C. Methodological problems associated with the IISS military balance. *Comparative Strategy*, 1981, *3*, 151-172.

Ostrom, C. Evaluating alternative foreign policy models: An empirical test between an arms model and an organizational politics model. *Journal of Conflict Resolution*, 1977, *21*, 239-265.

Ostrom, C. A reactive linkage model of the U.S. defense expenditure policy making process. *American Political Science Review*, 1978, *22*, 941-957.

Papanek, G. Aid, foreign private investment, savings, and growth in less developed countries. *Journal of Political Economy*, 1978, *81*, 120-130.

Prebisch, Raul. *Towards a dynamic development policy for Latin America*. New York: United Nations, 1963.

Rattinger, H. Armaments, detente, and bureaucracy: The case of the arms race in Europe. *Journal of Conflict Resolution*, 1975, *19*, 571-595.

Rattinger, H. Econometrics and arms races: A critical review and some extensions. *European Journal of Political Research*, 1976, *4*, 421-439.

Ray, J. L., & Webster, T. Dependency and economic growth in Latin America. *International Studies Quarterly*, 1978, *22*, 409-434.

Richardson, L. *Arms and insecurity: A mathematical study of the causes and origins of war*. Chicago: Quadrangle, 1960.

Richelson, Jeffrey. Static indicators and the ranking of strategic forces. *Journal of*

Conflict Resolution, 1982, *26,* 265-282.

Rubinson, R. The world-economy and the distribution of income within states: A cross-national study. *American Sociological Review,* 1976, *41,* 638-659.

Rubinson, R. Dependence, government revenue, and economic growth, 1955-1970. *Studies in Comparative International Development,* 1977, *12,* 3-28.

Russett, Bruce, & Starr, Harvey. *World politics: The menu for choice.* San Francisco: W.H. Freeman, 1981.

Russett, Bruce. Defense expenditures and national well-being. *American Political Science Review,* 1982, *76,* 767-777.

Russett, Bruce, Duvall, Raymond, Jackson, Steven, Snidal, Duncan & Sylvan, David. *Penetration and repression in the global system.* Forthcoming.

Russett, Bruce, Jackson, Steven, Snidal, Duncan & Sylvan, David. Health and population patterns as indicators of income inequality. *Economic Development and Cultural Change,* 1981, *29,* 759-779.

Saris, W., & Middendorf, C. Arms races: External security or domestic pressure? *British Journal of Political Science,* 1980, *10,* 121-128.

Schrodt, Philip. Richardson's model as a Markov process. In Dina Zinnes & John Gillespie (Eds.). *Mathematical models in international relations.* New York: Praeger, 1976.

Simaan, M. & Cruz, J. B. Formulation of Richardson's model of arms race from a differential game viewpoint. *Review of Economic Studies,* 1975, *42,* 67-77.

Stack, Steven. Internal political organization and the world economy of income inequality. *American Sociological Review,* 1978, *43,* 271-272.

Stack, Steven, & Zimmerman, Delore. The effect of world economy on income inequality: A reassessment. *Sociological Quarterly,* 1982, *23,* 345-359.

Stoll, Richard J. Let the researcher beware: The use of Richardson equations to estimate the parameters of a dyadic arms acquisition process. *American Journal of Political Science,* 1982, *26,* 77-89.

Stoneman, C. Foreign capital and economic growth. *World Development,* 1975, *3,* 11-26.

Strauss, R. An adaptive expectations model of east-west arms race. *Peace Research Society (International) Papers,* 1978, *19,* 29-34.

Strauss, R. Interdependent national budgets: A model of U.S.-U.S.S.R. defense expenditures. In W. L. Hollist (Ed.) *Exploring competitive arms processes: Applications of mathematical modeling and computer simulation in arms policy analysis.* New York: Marcel Dekker, 1978.

Szymanski, A. Dependence, exploitation and development. *Journal of Military and Political Sociology,* 1976, *4,* 53-65.

Szymanski, A. Comments on Bornschier. *Journal of Conflict Resolution,* 1984, *28.*

Taagepera, R. Stockpile-budget and ratio interaction models for arms races. *Peace Science Society (International) Papers,* 1979/80, *29,* 67-78.

Timberlake, Michael, & Williams, Kirk. Dependence, inequality, and repression: A cross-national study of political exclusion and government sanctioning. Mimeo, 1982.

Tsipis, Kosta. Physics and calculus of countercity and counterforce nuclear attacks. *Science,* 1975, *187,* 393-397.

Tyler, W. & Wogart, J. Economic dependence and marginalization. *Journal of Inter-American Studies and World Affairs,* 1973, *15,* 36-46.

Wallace, Michael D. Accounting for superpower arms spending. In Pat McGowan & Charles W. Kegley, Jr. (Eds.). *Threats, weapons, and foreign policy.* Beverly Hills, CA: Sage, 1980.

Wallace, Michael D. & Wilson, Judy. Non-linear arms race models. *Journal of Peace Research,* 1978, *15,* 175-192.

Ward, Michael D. *The political economy of distribution.* New York: Elsevier North Holland, Inc., 1978.

Ward, Michael D. Differential paths to parity: A study of the contemporary arms race. Berlin: International Institute for Comparative Social Research, 1982.

Weede, E. Beyond misspecification in sociological analyses of income inequality. *American Sociological Review,* 1980, *45,* 497-501.

Weede, E. & Tiefenbach, H. Rejoinder. *International Studies Quarterly,* 1981, *25,* 289-292. (a)

Weede, E. & Tiefenbach, H. Some recent explanations of income inequality. *International Studies Quarterly,* 1981, *25,* 255-282. (b)

Weede, E. & Tiefenbach, H. Three dependency explanations of economic growth: A critical evaluation. *European Journal of Political Research,* 1981, *9,* 391-406. (c)

Weede, E. & Tiefenbach, H. A reply to Bornschier. *European Journal of Political Research,* 1982, *10,* 451-454.

Zimmerman, William, & Palmer, Glenn. Words and deeds in Soviet foreign policy: The case of Soviet military expenditures. *American Political Science Review,* 1983, *77,* 358-367.

ADDRESSES FROM THE
1982 LASSWELL SYMPOSIUM:
THE USES OF SOCIAL SCIENCE

18

Politics and the Uses of Social Science Research

Donna E. Shalala

When I received this invitation, I knew I could not turn it down, but I have to admit I was terrified. I have been away from my own research for a number of years—something bound to raise the anxiety level of one addressing a gathering of colleagues.

The letter of invitation did not explain: "why me?" I assume it was not my gender because there are very able women who write in this area. No matter. Who could resist the opportunity to join a symposium honoring the author of works like the aptly titled *Politics: Who Gets What, When, How?* Indeed, I assume I was invited as the practitioner and because I am on that short list of political scientists who have survived a tour in Washington—a city dominated by lawyers, economists, and businessmen who prize nothing so much as pragmatism.

I recommend for your amusement Bruce Adams' article in the *Public Administration Review* titled, "The Limitations of Muddling Through: Does Anyone in Washington Really Think Anymore?" In the article Adams suggests that the political decision-making process is characterized by individuals who are "running themselves ragged on a series of marginal, short run issues and problems."[1] And I must confess, "I'm being nibbled to death by ducks" was an all-too-telling decision-maker's refrain.

Indeed, many have argued that Washington is a city where success is measured by long hours and tremendous personal sacrifice. They say the easiest way to identify assistant secretaries at Washington dinner parties is that they start yawning at 10 p.m.

But it was worth every sacrifice, every bit of stress. I am glad I went and even happier I survived. If I have one regret, it is that I was born too late to be an assistant secretary in the Johnson administration or any administration in which budgets and the role of government were expanding, because, quite frankly, I arrived in Jimmy Carter's brave new zero-based world a bit unprepared. No one at the Maxwell School in the late sixties had taught me the politics of scarcity. I honestly did not know how to solve our massive urban problems without spending, or at least leveraging, significant public monies.

And I was not enough of an academic to take much comfort in the fact that no one else did either!

Today, "retrenchment" management is still pretty much a virgin field and, paradoxically, if Reagan's budget slashers have their way with social science research, it will remain one—in theory, if not in practice. It is in the context of this challenge that I want to share some observations on the politics of the uses of social science research.

While some current woes can be pinned on passing political phenomena, many of our difficulties spring from deeper sources. Part of the problem stems from the perception of a vague status and amorphous mission of social science research and social scientists in our society.

In some sense, social science researchers have become the whipping boys (persons) of both the research and political communities. At no time has this been more apparent than in the Reagan administration's recent frontal attack on the budget of the Division of Social and Economic Science of the National Science Foundation. According to the Director of that Division, "1981 may be remembered as the year that social scientists paused from their ancient wars with each other to engage an external threat that became defined as a larger enemy."[2]

This threat triggered a "train of events . . . perhaps unprecedented in the history of the social sciences"[3] that strengthened our view of where and how secure we are on the ". . . wider continuum of scientific and scholarly pursuits."[4]

It has also forced us to rethink the role and nature of federal funding for basic as well as policy research in the social sciences. As one supporter observed: "The slap in the face administered by OMB may contribute more than anything else to social scientists shaping up a compelling case for the value and utility of their field."[5]

THE ATTACK

The official rationale provided by the Office of Management and Budget (OMB) for the recommended 1981 funding reductions was that "the support of these sciences is considered of relatively lesser importance to the economy than the support of the natural sciences."[6]

But Irving Louis Horowitz provided a more honest explanation. Pointing out how Ronald Reagan had made great use of social scientists both as candidate and as President, Horowitz then said that he believed NSF's lack of a clear policy orientation to its research led to its downfall. But in fact, as Horowitz correctly explains, this has always been a conscious policy. The NSF social science group has consistently rebuffed any efforts by Congress and cabinet agencies to make its work more applied. Applied work was left to the cabinet agencies' research budgets.

Then Horowitz addresses a more basic question: Is there really even such a thing as a social science?

The present situation in the social sciences can be described as one of Balkanization, a fragmentation so severe that no unified paradigm prevails. In place of a uniform sense of social science research are a series of belief systems of little concern at the level of presidential decision-making. The inner resolve of social scientists has been sapped not only at the periphery, but at the core. Indeed, a core may no longer exist. Any primary journal within the major social sciences exhibits a range of articles of such diversity and such varied levels of methodological sophistication that it would tax the mind of a schizophrenic to read such a publication from start to finish. This is not to argue that we should determine a priori who is right and who is wrong, or which theoretical framework is inferior or superior, only to assert that the social sciences are being assaulted, not only from the edges inward, but from the innermost core outward.[7]

Prewitt and Sills, acknowledging the lack of support in the past from the leaders of science, add two additional explanations: (1) ". . . social scientists, in comparison with engineers and with physical and life scientists, have been politically naive—not even seeing the need to be a political presence in Washington"; (2) ". . . social scientists have been indifferent toward their own intellectual and practical accomplishments, and correspondingly timid about telling their own story."[8]

There are, of course, additional explanations. OMB clearly perceives this vulnerability. But even more important is the social scientist's apparent lack of political clout. Unlike the so-called "hard" sciences, social science has never enjoyed a broad and active political constituency. No top military brass sings social science research's praises. No tough right-to-life (or choice)-like lobbies work Capitol Hill on our behalf. Indeed, until the recent NSF attack, it was hard to think of a more politically disorganized—and so, politically impotent—group. Small wonder then, that OMB simply regards our research as a nonessential, non-entitlement program. In short, it is easy to cut.

Our political vulnerability is nothing new. Explaining the opposition to social science being included in the National Science Foundation legislation earlier in this century, Roberta Balstad Miller noted ". . . the social science community did not make a strong bid for inclusion with the natural sciences in the Foundation." Again, according to Miller ". . . the opposition of key scientists to NSF support for social science research" was augmented by ". . . conservative fears that social science research would emphasize such potential political problems as racial inequality in the United States; [these fears] undermined Congressional support for the social sciences. . . ."[9]

Thus, although the Reagan Administration is unsupportive, we should keep current attacks in historical perspective. Remembering that while there has been scattered support, no powerful member of Congress has come forward to champion social science research in the last decade. Today's funding cuts are just the culmination of a longstanding federal attitude that can best be termed "benign neglect"—a phrase whose own controversial origin bespeaks the basis of policy makers' not so far-fetched fear that social science research can sometimes become political dynamite because they can't control the results.

Yes, social science research is that favorite political target: the easy mark. The classic example of this is Senator William Proxmire's now somewhat curtailed "Golden Fleece Awards." But I believe it is also something more than that. Indeed, as Roberta Miller's foregoing explanation suggests, such mean-spirited slurs hark back to what I consider social science research's most insidious political problem: not just a lack of well organized support for, but an actual hidden bias against these disciplines.

Much like the rabid Male Chauvinist who dismisses the "Ladies" claim to equality for fear she just may prove superior, the very critics who viciously mock the social sciences' "usefulness" are often those who most secretly dread its untapped power.

THE IMPACT

The implications of the proposed NSF cuts were very serious. Professor Philip Converse told Congress:

> I do not know whether the Subcommittee fully appreciates the enormous impact the social science programs in the National Science Foundation have had on the several social science disciplines in this country in the past twenty or thirty years, despite the tiny fraction of Foundation resources committed in this direction. I am not talking merely about dollars dispensed, although they are obviously important. I am talking more broadly about an interaction between the Foundation and serious social scientists which has progressively drawn the mainstream of social science away from loose speculation and various social advocacies, in the direction of true basic science, by which I mean the confrontation of verifiable theories of social and economic process with hard empirical data collected specifically to illuminate them.[10]

James G. March, a Stanford political scientist, also warned of the serious implications of an NSF cut:

> . . . federal budgets probably do affect the mix of research that is done, the quality of the research, the kinds of research that will come to be valued and the continuity of research and development.
>
> Although the precise effects of the proposed changes cannot be predicted, it is not hard to make some plausible guesses. Reductions in federal support would make social and behavioral sciences somewhat more theoretical, somewhat less empirical, somewhat more case-specific, somewhat less general, somewhat more expressive, somewhat less of a science. In the context of current and future national needs, it is not obvious that such changes are sensible.
>
> These shifts in emphases are important, but they are arguably of less importance than the extent to which the distinctively harsh treatment of social and behavioral science in the current budget has the unintended and more general consequence of weakening those individuals within social science who argue for systematic, empirical testing of social speculation and strengthening those who see social science as essentially social advocacy. Over the past few decades the major national scientific agencies have been allies of serious social scientists in their efforts to improve the capabilities of social science to address fundamental questions of individual, group and institutional behavior in a carefully scientific way.[11]

RALLYING THE TROOPS

There are a number of ways to build political support for the social sciences. The first effective technique used in the NSF case was lobbying and constituency building. This was achieved by identifying the most distinguished social scientists available and bringing them before congressional committees or other public gatherings; by encouraging social scientists throughout the country to write and visit their congressmen; and by soliciting strong support from the scientific community. A most effective coordinating organization, the Consortium of Social Science Associations, led the charge.

Second, the leaders of sciences, represented by the National Academy of Sciences, the American Association for the Advancement of Science, and the National Science Board, all took strong stands in support of basic research. For example, at its April 1981 meeting, the National Academy of Science passed a resolution expressing ". . . its deep concern over the proposed severe reductions in federal support for basic research in the behavioral and social sciences."[12]

More important, the natural sciences community was thoughtful and articulate in defense of its colleagues. Harvard's David Hamburg, the new President of the Carnegie Foundation, wrote:

> It is certainly true that the benefits of social science research may be harder to quantify than in some other fields, nor do social science findings capture the imagination like some of the recent spectacular advances in the physical, biological, and geological sciences. But science is a seamless web to a considerable extent, with many invisible connections between apparently unrelated parts.[13]

Scientists also pointed out that social scientists were being asked to meet a standard that natural scientists were never asked to meet. In calling for support from the scientific community, *Science* publisher William Carey wrote: ". . . the same act of public faith that legitimizes theoretical and applied research in the physical and life sciences has been withheld from the social and economic sciences. . . ."[14] Carey's statement was a significant breakthrough for, as I have noted, traditionally, the natural science community has not been an ally.

Third, supporters carefully identified examples of the utility of social science, and particularly of basic research, which was under challenge. Some of the testimony was extraordinarily perceptive. For example, the economist Lawrence Klein reported on the development of the $100 million information industry associated with econometrics.

> For nearly forty years I have been laboring on development of statistical models of the economy as a whole. Ideas that were developed in research institutes and in academic institutions grew from very modest beginnings, with support from the Rockefeller Foundation, the Carnegie Corporation, the Ford Foundation, and later from the National Science Foundation, to become systems that are now used on a practical basis in private enterprises, banks, international agencies, federal government offices, and state and local government offices. . . . It is still a growth sector of the economy. Fortunately, my associates and I can now

carry on research without support from the National Science Foundation, but such support was instrumental in getting us to this position, in providing the seed money. Ours is a success story of self-financing. . . .

Klein also argued that ". . . some significant part of our productivity slow-down and general loss of competitiveness is due to the disappointing program of federal research support in the 1970s."[15]

Other social scientists also scoured their research for examples of im-mediate utility, sometimes with unintended humor. The American Psycho-logical Association trotted out its hierarchy—president, president-elect, and executive officer—to tell OMB Director David Stockman, "We are Americans first and scientists second." They then proceeded to give examples of basic work which had been applied. One such example linked studies of the psycho-physiological mechanisms underlying taste with the control of coyotes and wolves around the ranches of California.

Ranchers in California are using the conditioning of taste to control predators without harming valuable stock. Coyotes and wolves are fed mutton laced with lithium chloride to produce an unpleasant reaction. As a result the predators are conditioned in one step to cease attacks on sheep, even though sheep have been preyed upon for generations. Estimates of savings in lost stock run in the millions of dollars.

    These conditioning techniques were developed in the basic behavioral research laboratory by researchers who began with no intention of having their results applied in this way. Rather, they were interested in the basic psycho-physiological mechanisms underlying taste. The same techniques now are being modified for application to two additional problems that have both economic and social costs: drug abuse and anorexia.[16]

There are numerous examples of specific defenses. But what is most troublesome is why we have to make the case at all. Why is it that the social sciences—so well accepted and institutionalized in our universities and in the private sector—are so often ridiculed by public officials? Why is their present plight ignored by a private sector that couldn't survive or progress without us? How did we drift into this unenviable position?

Some have suggested that white coats would help and wonder whether it isn't just a style and attitude question, a sad case of "cosmetics is fate." But, of course, as social scientists we have already spotted the common slight implicit in the phrase "just a style and attitude question." And this bias crops up again and again. It is not easy to convince a world overawed by engineers, high-tech experts, and "hard" science that work in games theory and human behavior may ultimately contribute much to our defense and health and safety.

I believe social science research is at a turning point in its history. How it decides to position itself in the next few years may determine its ability to at-tract substantial public and private monies and consequently the nature of the research to be conducted.

PLAYING HARD BALL

I say all of this with some understanding of that sometimes brutal world of public policy-making. Perhaps the most chilling, yet fundamental, truth I learned in government was how incredibly tough it is to keep your integrity, maintain the highest research standards, and continue to be influential. My colleagues and I were in a constant tension-filled struggle to make certain that our research effort dealing with critical public policy issues was absolutely first class, elegant, clear, and useful.

All the classic pressures that Washington could deliver—competition from the parade of fast-pen hired guns and messy policy processes—worked against us. While it is hard to keep your head and play your own game when under fire, never is it more essential. I came to the conclusion that the only way to survive in the sometimes vicious, always tough policy-making politics of Washington is not to compromise on excellence, but instead to strive for a growing sophistication in the initiation, funding, and use of research.

It is just this kind of sophistication and toughness that I believe the social science research community must bring to bear in support of its work. This approach will require a new aggressiveness and, most important, much reflection and perhaps a reorientation of stereotypical ideas of the nature of social science. Indeed, we may be talking about a born-again social science. By that I mean a social science which, after some serious soul-searching, emerges with a clearer sense of its own potential impacts and utility. A born-again social science neither compromises on excellence nor backs away from the necessity or centrality of basic research or the appropriateness and challenges of applied research.

MAKING THE NEW UTILITY CASE

Research for research's sake is not an argument without merit, but it does lack political clout. Indeed, we do well to remember that the value judgments of those who determine social science funding in the private and public sectors have a more utilitarian than idealistic base with "that which is good is that which is useful" as their motto. Harold Lasswell understood this when he wrote:

> It is at once apparent, if it were not obvious before, that the social environment is uninterested in knowledge as an end in itself. The inference is that support for the pursuit of knowledge must be obtained by presenting science and scholarship as means, as base values with which to pursue safety and health, wealth, power, prestige, and similar major outcomes.[17]

In the 1980s we need to make an even bolder point: We need to make the case that, like the natural sciences, this nation—indeed the world—cannot and does not survive without us.

We have had our first experience (in the NSF effort) at making this point. When we reached into our heads to evaluate what contributions to "real world" problems we have made, the lists were impressive. You would think there was not an aspect of American life that had not been improved through social scientists' efforts—to hear us tell it. We have aided American business; we have given politicians vital polls and political analyses; we have informed American journalism and reshaped the judicial process—these just for starters.

THE MISSING LINK: ORGANIZING THE USERS

Social science has never fully come to terms with the utility issue. There are reasons for this. For while it is possible to argue that our work has life or death consequences—as John Kemeny discovered when he wrote that human behavior, not technology, explained the Three Mile Island disaster—such assertions can have a Pandora's box effect. We should be cautious about pushing the utility argument to extremes lest we argue ourselves into that tight spot between Washington's proverbial rock and a hard place. If you convince policy-makers your work is important, all too often their thoughts will run: "If it's important, it must have an impact. And if it has an impact, how then should it be regulated?"

But whatever one's justification, the recent NSF campaign did open our eyes to the need for serious reflection on our aims and justifications. And we have just begun. We need a healthy and productive future, not just in Washington, but with the trustees of our colleges, universities and foundations. To insure that future we must understand our limitations and articulate them.

Ken Prewitt has suggested that we must face up to the fact that "the complexities of the problems for which the social and behavioral sciences might be helpful are always going to be one step ahead of the problem-solving abilities of those sciences."[18] I would put it differently; it is the old "linear answers for a non-linear world" conundrum. But while social science research will never be able to analyze all aspects of a problem or sate supply-siders' seemingly insatiable hunger for easy answers, we have a lot to give to those not hooked on hokey, all-inclusive, "voodoo," quick fixes. I know there is considerable controversy over the effectiveness of policy analysis and analysts. But while I must confess that I went into the government with low expectations for the possibilities of applying social science research to policy issues, I left with considerable enthusiasm for the sheer fun of trying to bring research to bear on massive, real life problems.

If my colleagues and I came to any conclusions it was that there is no model, no single approach to increasing the utility of applied research or justifying funds for basic research. Resisting the reductive bottom line, let me suggest instead a number of semi-conclusions:

- One cannot draw hard lines about the value and applicability of short vs. long term research, basic or applied research. Indeed, we took pains to organize ourselves so that we had significant resources for a variety of syntheses: overnight turn-around, one week to three or four months; or one year to ten years.

- We continually searched for ways to integrate users into the research. This was easiest on evaluations. The $12 million University of Pennsylvania effort to study the Community Development Block Grant program had a local official users' panel as well as a researchers' panel built into the research design from almost the beginning.
- We thought about users before we launched the research—primary users at least. And we defined theorists and methodologists as users.
- We also spent a huge percentage—almost 20% of our discretionary funds—on dissemination and related user activities.
- We continually searched for ways to literally shove the latest research findings into policy-makers ears. From speeches—the only thing a cabinet officer reads more than once—to options papers to press leaks. Getting the attention of busy people takes good humor, imagination, and persistence.
- Sometimes it also required fast, dramatic gear changes. When Patricia Roberts Harris left the Department of Housing and Urban Development to go to the Department of Health and Human Services, former New Orleans Mayor Moon Landrieu arrived to replace her. Mrs. Harris was a "paper person." She loved well written, fancy memos, solid briefing books, and options papers. Secretary Landrieu called me in on his first day to inform me "I don't read." By that startling statement, Secretary Landrieu meant that, like most politicians, he preferred oral briefings. After spending two years building a paper-oriented staff, we reoriented the entire department to a new policy process overnight. I can't say that the quality of discussions changed, but the style was certainly different.

Another Washington experience led me to conclude that it is time that researchers—hungry and as ambitious as we may be—gather the courage to tell members of Congress, cabinet officers, and even assistant secretaries the truth about what research can and cannot do. While we must be flexible, we should not be facile.

One of the things that troubles me about the "utility testimony" is that it plays into the hands of those who think—or pretend—everything is researchable now. Every national problem should not necessarily be subject to scrutiny. There really are some questions that cannot be answered by three-month, or five-year, or even $10 million studies. There are times when we should tell policy-makers, program managers, and other officials that it will take years to answer certain impact questions, and that often our instruments are not sophisticated enough to isolate all causes.

These are just a few insights. I hope we will see a re-energized social science that succumbs neither to the pragmatists nor to the isolationists; a social science that marshals our skills, energy, and enthusiasm for the new battles in Washington; a social science that finds comfortable and powerful allies in the private sector—among the captains of industry, the legal community, and the media; but most important, a social science that remembers that healthy disciplines do not need to be reshaped under utilitarian pressures. Indeed, they cannot, without violating their integrity.

Thank you very much.

NOTES

1. Adams, Bruce. The limitations of muddling through: Does anyone in Washington really think anymore? *Public Administration Review,* November/December 1979.
2. Transcript of remarks by Otto N. Larsen, Director, Division of Social and Economic Science, National Science Foundation, at the Inaugural Celebration of the Cornell Institute for Social and Economic Research (CISER). Cornell University, Ithaca, New York, November 24, 1981, p. 3.
3. Prewitt, Kenneth and Sills, David L. Federal funding for the social sciences: Threats and responses. *Items,* 1981, *35,* p. 33.
4. Adams, Robert McCormick, Smelser, Neil J. and Treiman, Donald J. (Eds.). *Behavioral and social science research: A national resource.* Committee on Basic Research in the Behavioral and Social Sciences, Commission on Behavioral and Social Sciences and Education, National Research Council, National Academy of Sciences. Washington, D.C.: National Academy Press, 1982, p. vi.
5. Holden, Constance. Dark days for social research. *Science,* March 27, 1981, 211, p. 1398.
6. Additional Details on Budget Savings, Executive Office of the President, Office of Management and Budget, April, 1981. Quoted in Prewitt and Sill, p. 33.
7. Horowitz, Irving Louis. Truth in spending. *Society,* Sept./Oct. 1981, *18,* p. 19.
8. Prewitt and Sills, p. 44.
9. Miller, Roberta Balstad. The social sciences and the politics of science: 1940s. Washington, D.C.: Consortium of Social Science Associations, March 22, 1982, p. 11.
10. Statement of Dr. Philip E. Converse, Program Director, Center for Political Studies, University of Michigan, before the Subcommittee on Science, Research and Technology of the Committee on Science and Technology, U.S. House of Representatives, Feb. 23, 1982, p. 4.
11. March, James G. Panel on The Impact of R&D of the Proposed FY 82 Federal Budget, Sixth Annual AAAS Colloquium on R&D Policy, June 26, 1981.
12. Resolution adopted at Annual Meeting of the National Academy of Sciences, April 28, 1981.
13. Hamburg, David A. Letter to Congressman Doug Walgren, March 9, 1981.
14. Carey, William D. Affordable science. *Science,* May 1, 1981, *212.*
15. Klein, Lawrence. Testimony before the Committee on Science and Technology, U.S. House of Representatives, March 12, 1981, p. 4.
16. Conger, John G., President; Bevan, William, President-elect; Pollack, Michael S., Executive Officer; American Psychological Association, letter to David A. Stockman, Director, Office of Management and Budget, Office of the President, Washington, D.C., March 3, 1981, pp. 3-4.
17. Lasswell, Harold D. *A pre-view of policy sciences.* New York: American Elsevier, 1971, p. 5.
18. Prewitt, *Society,* p. 7.

19

Basic Inquiry and Applied Use in the Social Sciences[1]

Donald E. Stokes[2]

It is difficult to probe at all deeply into the relationship of basic to applied research without sensing a remarkable tension between the common understanding of this relationship and the motives that actually underlie these types of research. The dominant view holds that basic and applied research are mutually exclusive categories. But this perceived antithesis is false to the goals that actually drive research in a number of fields.

A CONTRAST OF TWO CAREERS

To suggest the nature of this tension I will begin, concretely, with the way two working investigators perceive the goals that have guided their own research, choosing for this heuristic purpose two of my colleagues in the Woodrow Wilson School, at Princeton. This is a very deanly thing to do, but the contrasting research goals of these two gifted scholars raise questions of much wider significance, as we shall see.

My first case is Frank von Hippel, a physical scientist trained at M.I.T. and Oxford in theoretical particle physics. In the early stages of his subsequent research career he used his theoretical gifts to help push back the frontiers of knowledge in particle physics, pressing especially the insights to be gained by observing the regularities in the interactive behavior of fundamental particles. But later, in the 1960s and 70s, he became increasingly concerned about the societal implications of science. As a result, he substantially refocused his research interests and devoted much of his later work to a series of policy issues with critically important scientific and technological aspects, especially the control of nuclear weapons, the development of energy sources, and the protection of the environment.

This shift did not divorce him from research that required his skills as a physical scientist. On the contrary, he made his greatest contribution by penetrating the scientific structure of policy issues and suggesting options that would have gone unnoticed if the scientific or technological black box had remained closed—and the problem of policy choice was seen purely as optimiz-

581

ing or satisfying across a set of received policy options. As he pursued these policy issues he remained an active research scientist, vigorously employing his scientific insight and technical skills.

But it is also true that he saw this work as far removed from the frontiers of basic research in physical science. He was engaged in a type of applied research that sought to meet important societal needs, rather than to advance what was known of the underlying structures or processes of a scientific field. The satisfactions were enormous in view of the importance of the problems he took on. But von Hippel experienced basic and applied research as mutually exclusive categories. He could do one or he could do the other. But he could not, in the same line of research, do both.

My second, contrasting case is W. Arthur Lewis, an economist trained at the London School of Economics, whose fundamental contributions to the field have been recognized by a Nobel Prize. Arthur Lewis was born on the Island of St. Lucia, in what were then called the British West Indies. As a young man he was awarded a scholarship by St. Lucia's colonial government to study at the L.S.E., where he afterward was invited to stay and teach. He rapidly earned a reputation as a brilliant general economist, although much of his early work was in industrial economics. In 1948 he became Professor of Economics at the University of Manchester.

At Manchester his work was led in a new direction, toward economic development and growth, by a confluence of motives. Important among these was his desire to help with the economic problems that confronted many of the peoples of the earth in a post-colonial era. As a distinguished economist with a keen interest in the Third World his counsel was frequently sought by the governments of the newly independent nations as well as by international agencies attempting to foster economic development. This applied motive was strongly reinforced by his teaching. Students from the new nations of Africa and Asia crowded into his classrooms seeking the intellectual tools that would allow them to better economic conditions in their own countries when they returned home. Arthur Lewis felt almost bound to create and supply to his classes the elements of a new field.

But he was also drawn to his new subject by some of the deepest intellectual puzzles in economics, as he himself would write:

> From my undergraduate days I had sought a solution to the question what determines the relative prices of steel and coffee? The approach through marginal utility made no sense to me. And the Heckscher-Ohlin framework could not be used, since that assumes that trading partners have the same production functions, whereas coffee cannot be grown in most of the steel producing countries.
>
> Another problem that troubled me was historical. Apparently, during the first fifty years of the industrial revolution real wages in Britain remained more or less constant while profits and savings soared. This could not be squared with the neoclassical framework, in which a rise in investment should raise wages and depress the rate of return on capital.
>
> One day in August 1952, walking down the road in Bangkok, it came to me suddenly that both problems have the same solution. Throw away the neoclassical assumption that the quantity of labor is fixed. An "unlimited supply of labor" will keep wages down, producing cheap coffee in the first case and high

profits in the second case. The result is a dual (national or world) economy, where one part is a reservoir of cheap labor for the other.[3]

His resulting two-sector model of economic development was the principal research cited by the Nobel Committee.

Therefore, Arthur Lewis' research career, far from requiring a trade-off between basic and applied goals, strongly fused the motives of basic understanding and applied use. He saw economic growth as a basic *process,* one that challenged understanding on the most fundamental level. But he also saw it as a basic *problem,* one of critical importance for the countries that were trying to raise themselves above the poverty line.

BROADENING THE CANVAS

In view of the clear overlay of research motives in our second example we may wonder how the premise that basic and applied research are mutually exclusive types—rather than just conceptually or analytically distinct—could ever be widely accepted. But this premise is part of the most widely held view of the relationship between these types of research. Indeed, the idea that basic and applied research are exclusive categories continues to influence the organization of the research community and the framing of public policy on the support of research.

It is an idea with a long and interesting history. Plainly it owes a great deal to the outlook of the natural philosophers who made the great scientific discoveries of the eighteenth and nineteenth centuries. This Scientific Revolution was primarily the work of gentlemen who were passionately committed to the goal of advancing knowledge for its own sake.[4] By contrast, the First Industrial Revolution was almost wholly the work of practical men who were intensely interested in the uses to which their inventions could be put.[5] It is no longer so firmly believed that these industrial pioneers had little interest in science and minimal association with the natural philosophers of their day.[6] But from the eighteenth century onward the ideology of science in Western Europe enshrined pure discovery without thought of practical use as the proper motive for scientific research.

This belief did not exclude the possibility that scientific discoveries might later on have worthwhile uses. This companion idea is as old as Bacon, and bore some resemblance to reality, probably for the first time, by the onset of the Second Industrial Revolution toward the end of the nineteenth century.[7] The technological advances that were then achieved in chemical dyes and electric power, for example, clearly depended on prior advances in chemistry and physics. But pure scientific research, on the one hand, and applied research and industrial development, on the other, continued to be seen as radically separate enterprises, carried on by distinct sets of people, who were driven by different goals. The belief that to engage in one was not to engage in the other was as deeply held by the Midlands industrialist who remained in business only until he amassed the wealth that would allow him to become a gentleman scientist, pursuing his experiments without the slightest thought of practical use, as it was by a brilliant applied scientist such as Thomas Edison, who never allowed himself or anyone to whom he paid good money at Menlo Park the slightest leeway to pursue the pure scientific implications of their laboratory findings.

This outlook was heavily reinforced in the nineteenth century by the Germans' success in institutionalizing the separation of basic science from applied science and technology—to the apparent benefit of each. Under the German system, pure science was reserved to the universities and scientific institutes, while applied science and technology were the preserve of industry and the *Technische Hochschulen*.[8] The spectacular German advances in both science and technology made this system widely influential. One consequence, as the German plan of doctoral education spread to this country and large numbers of Americans went to the German universities to be trained in science, was to widen the presence of pure science and its ideology in our own universities, where the earlier "scientific schools" created by Harvard, Yale and other universities, were mainly institutions of applied science and engineering.

The survival of this polarized vision of basic and applied research down to our own time is remarkable. In this country it helped to shape the decisions on public support of science as the federal government became the leading patron of scientific research. It was an inherent part of the conceptual outlook of Vannevar Bush, the director of the Office of Scientific Research and Development during the Second World War, when he wrote the report *Science, the Endless Frontier* that launched the brilliantly successful campaign to commit the federal government to the support of basic research in peacetime.[9] Reading the political situation well, Bush wasted no time arguing the importance of scientific knowledge for its own sake. Rather, he adopted Bacon's premise on the grand scale. By heavily investing in basic scientific knowledge, he said, the nation could reach a variety of its future economic, medical, social, and international goals, just as the basic prewar research in nuclear physics had allowed it to build an atomic bomb and reach its desperately important national security goals during the war. But Bush was equally clear on the radical separation of basic and applied research and the impossibility of applied goals motivating basic inquiry in any direct sense. In the tradition of German science and the natural philosophers he wrote that "basic research is performed without thought of practical ends."[10]

The traditional view is intact today. A simple, two-valued logic—if it's basic it's not applied and if it's applied it's not basic—echoes through congressional hearings on research and development budgets. It helps to sort out responsibilities for the support of R & D by the executive agencies of the government. It partially shapes the organization of the research community itself. It is a staple of media comment on scientific research. It is even equipped with a one-dimensional spatial image that places basic research at one end of a spectrum and applied research at the other. The view of the expounders of the traditional basic/applied distinction is indeed wholly confined by Euclidean one-space, although their spatial imagery in fact typically degenerates still further to a model of only two points.

MODIFYING THE DOMINANT VIEW

Our two heuristic cases would be enough to suggest that the traditional view is incomplete. A different reading of the history of science yields a rich store of scientific advances that were driven by the desire both to extend basic knowledge and to reach applied goals. A clear case is the rise of microbiology toward the end of the nineteenth century. Louis Pasteur and his allies sought a fundamental understanding of the nature of disease. But they also wanted to lessen the ravages of disease in beasts and men. The desire to reach this goal *by the means of* a fundamental extension of knowledge is, in Pasteur's work, almost palpable.

The biological sciences today are equally difficult to bring within the traditional, polarized view. The revolution in molecular biology continues to pose questions, such as how interferon works, that are enormously important both for the advance of fundamental knowledge on recombinant DNA and for major applications—some of which may be immensely profitable. But a similar observation can be made about the non-molecular parts of modern biology. Some of the most fundamental problems in the population dynamics of plants and animals have major applications, which help guide the course of the most innovative research in the field.

Certainly the social sciences offer striking cases of advances that were driven by the desire both to extend basic knowledge and to reach applied goals. A conspicuous example is the unfolding of macroeconomic theory in the hands of John Maynard Keynes and his heirs. Keynes wanted to understand the economy at a fundamental level. But he also wanted to abolish the recurring misery of economic depression. Although the understanding remains unfinished—and sustained growth partially realized—we could not miss the fusion of motives in this distinguished line of social science research.

A further clear example from the social sciences is furnished by demography. Although I will return to the detailed interplay of motives in this field, the importance of both the thrust toward understanding and the concern for social implications is unmistakable. Those who laid the foundations of demography believed that population change could be understood only by the most rigorous scientific work. But they also believed such change was of immense significance for mankind. It was in fact their most sophisticated work on population replacement that revealed a generation ago the staggering potential force of the explosion in the world's population.[11]

But the motives of physical scientists too are more varied than Vannevar Bush led us to believe. There are occasions on which pure physicists and chemists pursue research that is, to some degree, both basic and applied. There is indeed something almost perverse in the claim of the physicists involved in the wartime effort to build the atomic bomb that theirs was only a gigantic exercise in applied science and development. It may be true that the Manhattan Project produced no scientific breakthroughs as fundamental as those of Niels Bohr and others in the prewar decades. But the project reached its goal only by compressing an extraordinary amount of normal science into a brief interval and acquiring a great deal of fundamental knowledge in nuclear physics about such things as the probability of neutrons being captured by very heavy nuclei at various neutron energies.

We will therefore be far more faithful to the actual flow of research in many fields if we free ourselves from the traditional framework. Basic and applied research are indeed conceptually or analytically distinct, but they are not disjoint empirical categories. Whether one or the other or both—or, for that matter, neither—of the basic and applied motives drives particular research is simply an open empirical question.

Having freed ourselves from Euclidean one-space we may indeed find it useful to visualize a two-dimensional image of the relationship of basic and applied research. There is, of course, not the slightest reason why we need think in dichotomous terms, since the presence of the basic and applied motives may be matters of degree. But if we do so it is clear that we have not one dichotomy but two, which now require the cells of a four-fold table where the rows are defined by whether or not the research seeks to extend basic knowledge—the top row yes, the bottom row no—and the columns are defined by whether or not the research seeks to reach some applied goal—the left-hand column yes, the right-hand column no.

Under these definitions the upper right-hand cell of the table is for research that is purely basic in Vannevar Bush's sense, a cell that includes Niels Bohr and the natural philosophers. Let us call this quadrant I. The upper left-hand cell of the table is for research inspired both by basic and applied motives and includes such diverse investigators as Louis Pasteur and Arthur Lewis. Let us call this quadrant II. The lower left-hand cell of the table is for research that is purely applied, work that is undertaken to reach some applied goal and not to extend basic knowledge—although it may of course use the knowledge gained by prior basic research. Let us call this quadrant III. Finally, we have in the lower right-hand corner of the table a cell for research that is *neither* basic *nor* applied. Let us call this quadrant IV. The presence of this only apparently uninteresting category makes the point that we really do have two dimensions and that quadrants I to III are not a slightly more complex version of the familiar one-dimensional basic/applied continuum. Anyone with a taste for the annals of research will, on reflection, know that quite a lot of research is neither basic nor applied and deserves to be assimilated to quadrant IV. Let me offer as an example that is not currently sensitive the very extensive descriptive studies of migration that were mounted from the country's agricultural experiment stations during the Great Depression. This research sought neither to answer questions of general scientific interest about migration nor to clarify any policy issues. Its whole motivation was relief—for the unemployed research personnel it put to work in hard times.[12]

I have worked through this conceptual revision here not for the greater clarity it gives the annals of research, although I believe it does have substantial uses of this kind. We can, for example, gain a far richer insight into the dynamics of research traditions when we are no longer constrained to think of movements across only the traditional model's single threshold between basic and applied research and are instead free to trace the extraordinarily interesting movements in each direction between quadrants I and II and between quadrants II and III.

I would also note as an aside that this conceptual revision helps to clarify issues of science policy and the organization of public support of research. The familiar premise—if it's basic it's not applied and if it's applied it's not basic—has lent too narrow a focus both to the free-standing federal R&D agencies—especially the National Science Foundation—that support basic research, and to the R&D programs of the mission agencies of the government that support applied research. Although the Science Foundation is broadening its outlook, it has traditionally been far more comfortable with Vannevar Bush's quadrant I than it has been with basic research in quadrant II, which is also directly motivated by applied goals. Likewise, the mission agencies of the government have missed a number of opportunities for supporting quadrant II research that is basic as well as applied—and thereby advancing their missions—because they felt their mandate did not extend to basic inquiry—that they were, in effect, limited to quadrant III.[13]

In this symposium on the uses of social science I want to finish my analysis with some observations about institutional and intellectual initiatives that could encourage research that seeks a joint product of basic knowledge and applied use. The experience with such initiatives in other fields raises interesting questions for the social sciences.

STRATEGIES FOR QUADRANT II

Despite the strength of the polarized view of basic and applied research there have been important efforts in a variety of fields to institutionalize quadrant II research. In the biological sciences, the legacy of Pasteur and other pioneers who were partly motivated by applied use is such that a good deal of basic-cum-applied biomedical research enjoys a strong institutional base in the medical schools. Although some biologists, infected by the German tradition, have wanted to draw the distinction between pure and applied biological science in terms of the distinction between biology and medicine, the biomedical portfolio has within it substantial quadrant II and quadrant I research, along with a good deal of quadrant III work, as we would expect. In line with this, the National Institutes of Health have consistently been far more relaxed than the NSF about supporting research in which the basic and applied motives are strongly mixed. Thus local and national institutionalized backing has clearly encouraged biological research that brings together the goals of basic inquiry and applied use.

Institutional encouragement of such work in the physical sciences has followed a different course, in which the rise of the engineering fields has played a critical role. So strong is the hold of the traditional basic/applied distinction on physical science that a number of pure scientists are ready to see all of engineering as a purely applied science. But this would be a misreading of history and research substance.[14] In fact, such fields as chemical and electrical engineering grew in power in an applied sense only as they were able to solve increasingly fundamental research problems and add to more general scientific knowledge. It is indeed fascinating to trace the stages by which research in chemical engineering moved from a low-level concern for engineering problems in particular chemical industries to the more generic "unit operations" of distillation, filtration, absorption, and the like and ultimately to fundamental problems of thermodynamics, material and thermal balances, turbulent flow, and the reaction kinetics of continuous flow systems.[15] But the strongly institutionalized presumption of use allowed applied goals to influence the selection of problems and the interpretation of results at every stage.

The social sciences have not mounted initiatives to institutionalize such research on a scale comparable to the biological and physical sciences. We have, of course, helped to spawn a vast new industry of largely applied research, housed partly on university campuses and partly along the Connecticut Avenues of this and other countries, but this work lies much more in quadrant III than quadrant II. Beyond this, many social scientists who work the quadrant I disciplinary agendas have, with Francis Bacon, an abiding faith that pure research will find practical use, although few who hold this faith have stopped to consider the linking role played by the biomedical and engineering fields in biological and physical science.[16]

But the academic landscape is dotted with forms that could provide an institutional base for social research seeking a joint product of basic knowledge and applied use. Some of the free-standing university research institutes in social science—Michigan's Institute for Social Research and what used to be called at Columbia the Bureau of Applied Social Research (the name was revealing)—are such a form. So are the management schools and schools of public policy. From time to time there are calls for further institutional initiatives, such as the Behavioral and Social Science (BASS) Survey's brief for the creation of schools of applied behavioral science.[17]

I do not want to gloss over the importance of purely institutional factors —and could scarcely do so as the manager of a school of basic-cum-applied social science. But my own view is that the most critical initiatives toward quadrant II research are intellectual rather than institutional. Indeed, the most formative past initiatives have been taken by those who found it intellectually stimulating to define research problems from the standpoint of actors who are required to make decisions.[18] This has happened fairly widely in economics, where a great deal of the intellectual structure of microeconomics is laid out from the perspective of the consumer or firm and a great deal of macroeconomics, as my examples from the work of Keynes and Arthur Lewis suggest, from the perspective of a government or other agency that is required to make decisions of macroeconomic policy. My economics colleagues are not fond of hearing their discipline described as an engineering field, but the fraction of quadrant II research with strongly institutionalized channels of use is almost certainly higher in economics than in any of the other social disciplines.

The nascent research agendas of today include a number of problems of extraordinary intellectual interest that have also a high potential for use in a wide range of applications. Let me cite as one example the systematic study of risk. The essentials of this subject will be laid bare only by the most rigorous intellectual analysis. This analysis will then allow us to cope more effectively with risk across an extraordinary range of problems of which it is an inherent part.[19] A strong ability to define research problems of this kind is our most essential requirement if we are more widely to marry understanding to use in the social sciences.

This is quite a different prescription from the oft-canvassed idea of enhancing our usefulness to the policy world by creating a research paradigm specifically for housing, another for criminal justice, another for health services delivery, and so on. That course seems to me a formula for limiting ourselves to quadrant III research of very modest power that will fail over time to attract creative research talent. This fate very nearly befell chemical engineering in the 1920s, at its very citadel of M.I.T., before it ruthlessly pulled back and dealt with a more fundamental research agenda, one that was in the longer run far more important to the industrial constituency of the field.[20]

We have parallels from the social sciences. There was a point in the early development of demography when its research agendas were under intense pressure from those who wanted studies that would support immediate action programs. At this stage a small core of research demographers consciously pulled back and began to pursue a more fundamental research agenda — but one that would yield knowledge with a high potential for applied use. This research led both to the extremely sophisticated methods of estimating population change where demographic data are desperately incomplete and to the understanding of the sources of fertility differentials that undergirds much of the present effort to control population growth.[21] In broad terms, the parallel with chemical engineering is striking.

CONCLUSION

For reasons that are easily traced, the belief that basic and applied research are not just analytically distinct but are in a logical or empirical sense discrete categories has dominated the view of the relationship between these types of research. The belief that if research is basic it's not applied and if it's applied it's not basic, which owes so much to the outlook of the natural philosophers of the 18th century and the institutionalization of German science in the 19th century, has continued to shape the organization of the research community and the development of science policy in the 20th century.

But a revisionist reading of the history of science yields a rich store of examples from the physical, biological, and social sciences of research that is driven both by the goal of basic inquiry and by the goal of applied use. Indeed, a view of the relationship of basic and applied research that is more faithful to the actual interplay of these motives would see research as driven at times by the desire both to extend knowledge and to meet applied needs, at times by one or the other of these goals but not both, and at times by neither of these goals.

This revisionist view of the relationship between basic and applied research provides a deeper understanding of the development of science and clarifies some important issues of science policy. But my principal focus here has been the influences that encourage significant research that is both basic and applied. What factors yield research that seeks to meet applied goals *by extending* fundamental knowledge?

One group of factors has to do with the institutional base of research that combines these goals. Such a base is often provided in the biological sciences by the biomedical research programs in the medical schools and in the physical sciences by certain of the research programs in the engineering schools. The degree of institutionalization in the social sciences is far less, although a sufficient base exists in the free-standing research institutes and the professional schools to suggest that institutional factors are not of pre-eminent importance.

The most important factors are in my own view intellectual. What has allowed certain of the social research fields to address major problems as they explored fundamental processes are analytic frameworks of high generality that nevertheless yield formal or empirical knowledge of high relevance to social choice. These frameworks cannot be narrowly focused on particular problems. In this respect the experience of the most problem-relevant of the social sciences, such as demography, parallels the experience of the engineering fields: they have enhanced their power in an applied sense by pursuing a research agenda that is more fundamental in a scientific sense—indicating once more that the goals of basic inquiry and applied use should by no means be seen as antithetical.

FOOTNOTES

1. This paper was originally prepared for the Harold D. Lasswell Symposium at the September 1982 meetings of the American Political Science Association. For a programmatic statement of Lasswell's view of the policy sciences, see his "The Policy Orientation." In *The policy sciences.* Daniel Lerner and Harold D. Lasswell (Editors). Stanford: Stanford University Press, 1951, pp. 1-15.
2. It is a pleasure to record my debt to a series of colleagues—Harold A. Feiveson, Gerald L. Geison, W. Arthur Lewis, Michael S. Mahoney, Robert M. May, Robert F. Rich, John W. Servos, and Frank von Hippel—who served as generous tutors to an unlikely pupil.
3. Sir Arthur Lewis. *The Nobel prizes 1979.* Stockholm: Almquist and Wiksell International, 1980, p. 257.
4. A wonderfully concise summary of the interaction of science and technology over recent centuries appears in Kuhn, Thomas S. *The essential tension: Selected studies in scientific tradition and change.* Chicago: The University of Chicago Press, 1977, pp. 141-147.
5. See Multhauf, R. P. The scientist and the 'improver' of technology, *Technology and Culture, 1,* 1959, pp. 38-47.
6. See Musson, A. E. and Robinson, Eric. *Science and technology in the industrial revolution.* Manchester: University of Manchester Press, 1969.
7. See Kuhn, *op. cit.,* pp. 145-146.
8. See Lewis, W. *Das Unterrichtswesen im deutschen Reich.* Berlin: A. Asher, 1904.
9. Bush, Vannevar. *Science, the endless frontier.* Washington, D.C.: National Science Foundation, reprinted 1960.
10. *Ibid.,* p. 18.
11. See Notestein, Frank W. Demography in the United States: A partial view of the development of the field. *Population and Development Review, 8,* December 1982, pp. 651-687.
12. The National Research Council's recent Social Research and Development Study Project documented a number of cases in which the real motive for launching

research on social problems was the sponsors' desire to block the creation of government programs to deal with the problems. See National Research Council. *The federal investment in knowledge of social problems.* Washington, D.C.: National Academy of Sciences, 1978.

13. I have dealt with these questions in greater detail in a paper on "Perceptions of the Nature of Basic and Applied Science in the United States," in *Science policy perspectives: U.S.A./Japan.* Arthur W. Gerstenfeld (Editor). New York: Academic Press, 1982, pp. 1-18.

14. C. P. Snow included in his famous lecture on the "two cultures" this partly autobiographical account of the attitudes of pure scientists toward engineering: "Pure scientists have by and large been dimwitted about engineers. . . . They wouldn't recognize that many of the solutions [in engineering] were as satisfying and beautiful. Their instinct — perhaps sharpened [in Britain] by the passion to find a new snobbism wherever possible, and to invent one if it doesn't exist — was to take it for granted that applied science was an occupation for second-rate minds. . . . We prided ourselves that the science which we were doing could not, in any conceivable circumstances, have any practical use. The more firmly one could make the claim the more superior one felt!" (Snow, C. P. *The two cultures and the scientific revolution.* Cambridge: The University Press, 1959.)

15. See Davies, John T. Chemical engineering: How did it begin and develop? In *History of chemical engineering.* William F. Furter (Editor). Washington, D.C.: American Chemical Society, 1980, pp. 15 43.

16. My emphasis here is on what could be learned from the biomedical and engineering fields about developing research agendas that have a high probability both of extending knowledge and finding practical use. I do not envisage a medical or engineering model for the diffusion or application of social knowledge.

17. See The Behavioral and Social Sciences Survey Committee. *The behavioral and social sciences: Outlook and needs.* Englewood Cliffs, N.J., 1969, pp. 200-210.

18. I do not mean to imply that research problems will have a high potential utility only if they are defined in terms of an individual or unit that will need to act. Nonetheless, this perspective explains why significant applications have more often come from social research that utilizes rational-choice or cybernetic, information-processing models than they have from research that utilizes, for example, models of social structure.

19. The concept of risk, for several centuries the focus of systematic analysis in probability and statistics, is by now also the subject of a vast and spreading literature in economics, psychology, and the other social sciences. For a recent work combining the perspectives of anthropology and political science, see Douglas, Mary and Wildavsky, Aaron. *Risk and culture.* Berkeley: University of California Press, 1982.

20. See Servos, John W. The industrial relations of science: Chemical engineering at M.I.T., 1900-1939. *ISIS, 71,* 1980, pp. 531-549.

21. Notestein, *loc. cit.*

Contributors

CHRISTOPHER H. ACHEN is associate professor of political science at the University of California, Berkeley. He is the author of the forthcoming *Statistical Methods for Quasi-Experiments* (University of California Press).

HERB ASHER is a professor of political science at The Ohio State University. He is the author of *Presidential Elections and American Politics, Causal Modeling,* and a number of articles on political behavior and methodology.

LAWRENCE BAUM teaches political science at Ohio State University. He is author of *The Supreme Court* (1981) and has done research on several aspects of judicial policy making, including implementation of judicial decisions, diffusion of innovative doctrines, and case screening by appellate courts.

DAVID R. BEAM has been a member of the ACIR research staff since 1974. He directed the Commission's studies of *The Federal Role in the Federal System: The Dynamics of Growth* (1981) and *Regulatory Federalism: Policy, Process, Impact and Reform* (1983).

TIMOTHY J. CONLAN received his Ph.D. from Harvard University. He has conducted research on the politics of federal aid reform, regulatory policy, and the politics and theory of governmental growth.

LEON D. EPSTEIN, a past-President of the American Political Science Association (1978-79), is the Hilldale Professor of Political Science at the University of Wisconsin-Madison. He is the author of *Political Parties in Western Democracies* (1967, 1980) and of other books and journal articles chiefly on British and American politics.

ADA W. FINIFTER is professor of political science at Michigan State University. She has published articles relating to political alienation, political deviance, and political efficacy in the *American Political Science Review, American Journal of Political Science, Public Opinion Quarterly,* and other journals, and is the editor of *Alienation and the Social System.*

MARIANNE GITHENS is a professor of political science at Goucher College and past president of the Women's Caucus for Political Science. In addition to coediting *A Portrait of Marginality* with Jewel Prestage, writing extensively on women and politics and developing a number of innovative courses in this area, she has lectured both in the United States and abroad on women's political behavior.

JOHN G. GUNNELL teaches political theory at the State University of New York at Albany and writes in the areas of the philosophy of political inquiry, the history of political theory, and political philosophy.

M. DONALD HANCOCK is a professor of political science and Director of the Center for European Studies at Vanderbilt University. He has written various articles, chapters and books on Swedish and German politics.

SUSAN B. HANSEN is associate professor of political science at the University of Pittsburgh. Her most recent publication is *The Politics of Taxation* (Praeger, 1983).

RONALD INGLEHART is professor of political science and faculty associate in the Institute for Social Research at the University of Michigan. Co-investigator in the Euro-Barometer surveys carried out biannually by the European Community, he has been a visiting professor at several universities in Western Europe and Japan.

ROBERT O. KEOHANE is professor of politics at Brandeis University and co-author with Joseph Nye of *Power and Interdependence: World Politics in Transition*. He is currently writing a book on cooperation and discord in the world political economy.

DONALD R. KINDER is associate professor in the departments of political science and psychology, and associate research scientist in the Center for Political Studies, all at the University of Michigan. He is completing a book on television news and public opinion (with Shanto Iyengar) and in the middle of another on the political consequences of economic predicaments.

NAOMI B. LYNN is professor and head of the political science department at Kansas State University. She has served on the Council of the American Political Science Association and the National Council of the American Society for Public Administration; she is Vice-President and will be the 1984-85 President of ASPA.

JOEL S. MIGDAL is professor and chairman of the International Studies Program in the University of Washington's School of International Studies. His books include *Peasants, Politics, and Revolution* (1974) and *Palestinian Society and Politics* (1980), both published by Princeton University Press.

LEROY N. RIESELBACH is a professor of political science at Indiana University. He is the author of *The Roots of Isolation* (1966), *Congressional Politics* (1973), *Congressional Reform in the Seventies* (1977), and (with

Joseph K. Unekis), *Congressional Committee Politics: Continuity and Change, 1971-1980* (forthcoming).

WILLIAM H. RIKER, University Dean of Graduate Studies and Wilson Professor of Political Science at the University of Rochester, is currently President of the American Political Science Association. His most recent book is *Liberalism Against Populism: A Confrontation Between the Theory of Democracy and the Theory of Social Choice.*

BRUCE RUSSETT is professor of political science at Yale University, Editor of the *Journal of Conflict Resolution,* and President of the International Studies Association. He has published over 100 articles and 16 books, most recently *The Prisoners of Insecurity: Nuclear Deterrence, the Arms Race, and Arms Control.*

DONNA E. SHALALA is professor of political science and President of Hunter College of the City University of New York. From 1977 to 1980 she served as Assistant Secretary for Policy Development and Research at the U.S. Department of Housing and Urban Development.

DONALD E. STOKES is University Professor of Politics and Public Affairs at Princeton University and Dean of its Woodrow Wilson School of Public and International Affairs. His research has sought to analyze both the political and knowledge components of government action in the U.S. and other countries.

DAVID WALKER is Assistant Director of the U.S. Advisory Commission on Intergovernmental Relations. He is the author of *Toward a Functioning Federalism* and has written numerous articles and chapters for books.

Index to
Authors Cited

612

A Note on the Book

This book was copy edited by Mary Curzan and proofread by Colleen Scherkenbach of the American Political Science Association. The cover was designed by Steve Snyder of Graphics. The text was set in Baskerville by TypoGraphics, of Columbia, Maryland. The Banta Company, of Menasha, Wisconsin, printed and bound the book.

UNIVERSITY of WASHINGTON
SEPTEMBER 19, 1983